DAUGHTER OF BOSTON

or something infinitely more disagreable—In a mere
companion—than all most vices—becomes a virtue. If—— ever gets home—which I begin to
doubt—I shall tell him—that I am very glad the
world calls him self conceited—or rather that he is
so self confident—as to draw upon himself the
accusation. Before any experience has sobered our
brains—we measure ourselves by a standard of
our own—and when we come to use that of
the world we fall wonderfully short. By the
by. I met with something in a eulogist of Pope *
which—strikes me—as a good criticism of my own
attempts in a poetical line—I write with too
much hurry and energy to write as smoothly
as the Muses require—And when I succeed in
the latter respect. it is always—by sacrificing
my ideas—

        "I'm like" those wits whose numbers
          glide along—
"So smooth no thought e'er interrupts the song."
    I have always sayd I could write nothing but
"jingle"—and I think that for the future when
I am inclined to think I have done much—I
shall remember how many have done more.
with fewer advantages, and be silent.
Aug 14th 1839. I have been looking over my
Journals for '36—& 7. and certainly if anything
could, make me humble—disgust me with
myself—that would.—Such a mass of frivolous
self-applause—of nonsensical boasting never met
my eyes—such a self satisfied way of talking about myself—and my productions—

Facsimile diary page, August 14, 1839. (Courtesy of Massachusetts Historical Society)

DAUGHTER
OF BOSTON

The

Extraordinary Diary

of a

Nineteenth-Century Woman

CAROLINE HEALEY DALL

EDITED BY HELEN R. DEESE

Beacon Press

BOSTON

BEACON PRESS
25 Beacon Street
Boston, Massachusetts 02108-2892
www.beacon.org

Beacon Press books
are published under the auspices of
the Unitarian Universalist Association of Congregations.

09 08 07 06   8 7 6 5 4 3 2 1

Text design by Patricia Duque Campos
Composition by Wilsted & Taylor Publishing Services

Library of Congress Cataloging-in-Publication Data

Dall, Caroline Wells Healey, 1822–1912.
Daughter of Boston : the extraordinary diary of a nineteenth-century woman /
Caroline Healey Dall ; edited by Helen R. Deese.
p.   cm.
Includes bibliographical references and index.
ISBN 0-8070-5035-0 (pbk. : acid-free paper) 1. Dall, Caroline Wells Healey, 1822–1912—Diaries.
2. Boston (Mass.)—Intellectual life—19th century. 3. Authors, American—19th century—Diaries.
4. Reformers—United States—Diaries. I. Deese, Helen R. II. Title.

PS1499.D83A3 2005
818'.403—dc22   2005011774

For Pat

CONTENTS

———

Introduction

The journal text that makes up this volume has no sensational history. No one found it in a moldy trunk in an attic, nor indeed on an Internet auction Web site. Rather, for about a century, it has been cared for and protected in a major repository; it has even been microfilmed, and the copies offered for sale. Scholars have used it, and dissertations have cited it. But up until now, almost no one has recognized the immense treasure that Caroline Healey Dall's forty-five volumes of journals constitute. In the two decades during which this text has been my life's obsession, I have marveled over and over at its power. It is a remarkable work of contemporary history, certainly, but just as remarkable is its ability to captivate the reader by its eloquence and the compelling story it relates. It is literature as well as history, an engrossing narrative as well as a fund of facts.

The author of these journals was no ordinary person, unselfconsciously keeping a diary in obscurity, little expecting that anyone would read it. Instead she was a woman privileged, educated, and, in her own day, famous—one who, we have every reason to believe, recognized her own diary's significance. "Who will care for these many papers—," she wrote at age twenty, "who will ever read—or at my request, take pains to preserve that I have written?... If I were likely to die wealthy and could pay an institution for taking care of papers so precious to me—I would do it—for to a psychologist, this journal would be worth the pains." By her seventies, Caroline Dall had solved the problem of preserving her papers (in addition to the journals, they include correspondence, notebooks, scrapbooks, drafts of published articles and books, and the like), arranging to give them to the Massachusetts Historical Society. Despite the fact that the papers were not unanimously embraced by the Society—one member objecting to the expense of storing what seemed to him worthless trivia, and quipping that Caroline Dall's name should have been "Caroline Dull"—the Dall Papers have been faithfully cared for. As Caroline Dall must have foreseen, they have proved useful to scores of historians and literary scholars who have mined them for information on major movements and great figures in the nineteenth century; they have become, in fact, one of the Society's most frequently used collections. But I suspect that it has taken much longer than Dall imagined for her journals to be resurrected and valued in their own right, rather than as the source of information on someone or something else. As she reread her old journals when she was in her seventies, she herself was astonished at their power: "My life half forgotten—now reads to me like a Romance," she wrote, and kept on reading compulsively. I myself, who came to Dall's journals in an attempt to ferret out information on the Transcendentalists and their contexts, soon found myself captivated entirely by the journals' compelling narrative, by their near-flawless style, and by the distinctive personality of the author they so vividly project.

This text gives us almost every sort of thing we might anticipate or hope for in a nineteenth-century woman's diary. The journals address a wide range of topics, including family and social rituals and interactions; the routines of "woman's work"; illnesses, both physical and mental, and their treatment; examples of cross-class and cross-race relations; and the larger world of business, politics, literature, reform, war, religion, and science. In these pages, we also find the emotional, intellectual, and spiritual development of the writer. With a mind both informed and acute, and a world-view imbued with a strong gender consciousness, Dall filled her journals with intelligent reflections upon and keen analysis of her world.

Caroline Healey Dall's journal, in its entirety the fullest account of an American woman's life in the nineteenth century, will take its place beside the other great texts of the American Renaissance—Emerson's essays, Thoreau's *Walden,* and Fuller's *Woman in the Nineteenth Century.* It will serve as a counterweight to the skeptical and condescending depiction of woman's rights women in Boston in Henry James's *The Bostonians.* Likewise, it will stand as a complement to *The Education of Henry Adams,* as the story of a *woman* shaped by nineteenth-century Boston culture, told in the first rather than the third person, immediate rather than retrospective, and embodying rather than rejecting the city's moral enthusiasms. Most of all, Dall's journal is a good story. Unlike fiction, however, it is the story of a person as alive as ourselves, told in the continuous present of the diary form as the story itself develops.

The World and Life of the Diarist

The world of this diary is centered in Boston. What Samuel Pepys did for seventeenth-century London or George Templeton Strong for nineteenth-century New York, Dall does for nineteenth-century Boston: the city's celebrations, entertainments, mob scenes, poverty-ridden neighborhoods, rounds of social calls, and lectures, as well as the public academic exhibitions across the Charles River, form much of the stuff of these journals. When the selected journals begin, in early 1838, Boston was the country's fourth-largest city, with a population of some eighty thousand, and was attracting ever increasing waves of immigrants. The rapidly growing city had already (in 1835) become the nation's first rail hub. During Caroline Healey's childhood and adolescence, Boston was also a hub of another sort, a cultural focal point. The lyceum movement flourished, bringing a wide range of lecturers before eager audiences. The movement known as Transcendentalism, a philosophy that held that one should look for truth not from authority figures or sense experience but from one's innate sense of right and good, was in its heyday. Its major figures—Ralph Waldo Emerson, Margaret Fuller, Elizabeth Palmer Peabody, Theodore Parker, Henry David Thoreau, and others—composed a loose circle in which new and often radical ideas thrived. Elizabeth Peabody's new bookshop made available the latest foreign periodicals and fine editions of books. Reform movements of all sorts—dietary, religious, and social—abounded. In particular, as the years progressed, Boston became a center for abolitionist activity and, at times, resistance to that activity. Across the river in Cambridge, Harvard had entered upon its third century, and its Divinity School produced ministers who populated the most liberal pulpits of New England. For intellectual stimulation, especially if, like Caroline Healey, one were upper class and Unitarian, Boston was a prime locale. She might well have boasted, like Henry Thoreau, that she was born in "the most estimable place in all the world, and in the very nick of time, too."

During the years covered by this selected edition, Dall lived elsewhere, too: in the city of Georgetown, in the District of Columbia, for a year; in Baltimore for several months; in Portsmouth, New Hampshire, for a year; in

Needham, twelve miles west of Boston, for nearly three years; in Toronto for three and a half years; in West Newton, just west of Boston, for a year; and in Medford, an even closer suburb, for almost two years. In many ways, all of these places seem tame in comparison to Boston, and returning to Boston always reinvigorated Dall's life, but her journal lends interest to these other locales as well. Her depiction of Toronto is particularly intriguing: when she arrived there she experienced culture shock, finding it a backwater town of some thirty thousand inhabitants, but before she left she was an integral player in its growing intellectual and cultural scene.

Caroline Wells Healey was born in Boston on June 22, 1822. She was the oldest child of Mark Healey—a successful merchant, land speculator, ship-owner, and president of the Merchants Bank when she was a teenager—and of Caroline Foster Healey, originally from Newburyport, Massachusetts. Mark Healey had grown up in a prominent family in Kensington, New Hampshire. His great-grandmother's brother was Meshech Weare, New Hampshire's first post-Revolutionary governor, and his father, Newell Healey, served in the state legislature and state senate. As a young man, Mark Healey had come to Newburyport to live with and work for the merchant Samuel H. Foster, his future father-in-law, apparently becoming almost a family member. After the great Newburyport fire of 1811 destroyed much of the town, both the Fosters and Healey—who had heroically provided for the Foster family during the days of near starvation following the disaster—relocated to Boston. Healey used his inheritance from his maternal grandfather to reestablish Foster in business, and as they came of age he successively set up the Foster sons in business. In 1821 he married the oldest Foster child, Caroline, when she was twenty-one and he thirty.

At least in part because Caroline Foster Healey was ill for many months following her daughter Caroline's birth, a close bond developed between father and daughter. As a child, Caroline, something of a prodigy, became her father's favored companion. Discussing and debating with him questions of religion, philosophy, and politics, she earned her father's respect by developing her own opinions and expressing her own views (a precedent no doubt largely responsible for her outspokenness as an adult). Indeed, Caroline's relationship with her father was to be the single most important one of her life. Unfortunately, his exceptional treatment of her as companion, sparring partner, and intellectual equal was coupled with inordinate demands. The young Caroline wrote several unpublished novels, read four languages, ran the household during her mother's frequent illnesses and confinements, and by the age of thirteen was publishing articles in religious newspapers. Yet her father told her, at age fourteen, that she had disappointed his expectations, and the painful memory of this reproach runs like a refrain throughout her adolescent journals.

Caroline Foster Healey gave birth to seven more children, and apart from the physical consequences of being almost constantly pregnant or recovering from childbirth, she had some sort of mental disorder. Perhaps it was depression associated with the childbearing, but more likely the disorder was manic-depressive psychosis, for it continued to recur throughout her life. Because she was frequently incapacitated, the management of the household often fell to the young Caroline. In later life she remembered having directed eight servants and taken responsibility for up to seven younger siblings, because her father did not wish to expose the family secret of his wife's mental illness to new employees. In retrospect she felt that the granting of such authority to her was a mistake, "a cruel tax upon a child of thirteen," causing misunderstanding among outsiders and resentment among her own siblings. Her relationship with her mother during childhood and adolescence was, like that with her father, problematic. While her father tacitly encouraged her literary endeavors, her mother disparaged them and, when able, was an exacting taskmistress of domestic duty. On the one hand, Caroline believed that her mother did not love her, and on the other, although she knew her father loved her, she found it impossible to please him. The great yearning for love and approval that is palpable in the early journals persists as a continuous theme throughout Caroline Healey Dall's life.

Although Mark Healey's formal education was limited, he valued it for his children, providing them with tutors and excellent private schooling. Caroline attended the highly regarded school of Joseph Hale Abbot until she was fifteen, when her formal tutelage abruptly ended. But her education was hardly limited to what she received through tutors and schools, for she came of age in Boston at a point that was arguably the city's cultural high-water mark, and there could have been no more eager consumer of its aesthetic and intellectual productions. Attending lyceum lectures and viewing art at the Athenaeum were frequent events on her calendar, and the Transcendentalists proved especially significant contributors to her education. By the age of twelve, she was sitting in Ralph Waldo Emerson's lecture audiences and afterwards, by her father's order, writing summaries of what she had heard. At age eighteen she entered the newly opened bookshop of the remarkable Elizabeth Peabody, reveling in the fine editions that she found there, but fascinated even more by the proprietor, a woman with a brilliant intellect and a warm heart. Peabody took Healey under her wing, guiding her reading, advising her on journal keeping, reprimanding her for social gaffes. Healey soaked it all in and never deviated from her appreciation of this mentor, even when, decades later, personal differences left them permanently estranged. Peabody introduced Healey to the larger Transcendentalist circle by urging her to participate in a conversation series led by nineteenth-century America's premier woman intellectual, Margaret Fuller. Here Healey became personally acquainted with, among others, Emerson, Sophia and George Ripley (who were shortly to found the Utopian community of Brook Farm), and of course Fuller herself. Fuller was not warm to Healey, as Peabody had been, but neither was Healey overawed by Fuller: she wrote after the first session, in 1841, "I did not come away as I expected—to do—feeling that it would be impossible for me ever to accomplish as much as Miss Fuller—." Nevertheless, at the time and ever after, Healey looked upon this experience as a landmark in her development, and Fuller became her most important role model. Another Transcendentalist who profoundly affected her was the radical preacher Theodore Parker, whose theology she eventually accepted and whose later political activism she emulated.

When Caroline Healey was nineteen, she fell in love with Samuel Foster Haven, a widower of thirty-five, who headed the American Antiquarian Society in Worcester. From what we can tell from Dall's journal and the surviving correspondence between them, Haven was at least intrigued by this obviously brilliant young woman, whom he introduced to acquaintances as "a lady transcendentalist and loco foco [Democrat]." For some months her relationship with this scholarly yet witty man flourished, giving her, as she wrote in March of 1852, "a joyful confidence in myself." But what might well have been a good match foundered, as financial misfortune befell the Healey family. By 1842, the fallout from the Panic of 1837 had finally toppled Mark Healey's financial world. Caroline, determined to contribute to the family coffers, found a job as a teacher at an exclusive girls' school in Georgetown, D.C., and gradually but surely, for whatever reason, Samuel Haven withdrew. Some months later Caroline became engaged to a young minister whom she met in Washington, Charles Henry Appleton Dall. In 1844 they married, and for several years they led a peripatetic life as Charles Dall went from pulpit to pulpit. They had two children, a son and a daughter. Initially happy, the marriage proved to be a tragic mistake. Although they shared a devotion to serving God and, particularly, to ministering to the poor, Charles's weakness and Caroline's strength did not form a good basis for a long-term partnership. None of Charles's positions paid well or promptly, there were long periods of unemployment, and the family was in nearly constant financial straits. Caroline now turned to writing "for bread." Her father, who rapidly recovered his wealth, at times generously showered gifts on her. But when she needed his help most, he refused, offering it only on the condition that she dissociate herself from the abolitionists.

In the outpost of Toronto, where the Dalls lived and worked in the early 1850s, their marriage began to come apart. Charles had a serious illness that was followed, it seems, by a kind of mental breakdown. Resigning under pressure from this parish too, he returned his family to the Boston area and once again searched for work. Mark Healey let it be known that he would provide financial help to his daughter only if she left Charles and came home. Caroline, however, thought of her husband as she would of a sick child, and apparently never seriously considered divorce, although she was determined no longer to follow him around from one failed ministry to another. For once, Charles took decisive action, making a momentous move: he would leave his wife and his children, aged five and nine, and go to Calcutta to direct a Unitarian mission. Caroline was stunned. Yet she fitted him out for his journey, and for the thirty-one years that he remained in Calcutta—the rest of his life— she publicly supported Charles. He returned home only four times for visits, and Caroline never recovered from her sense of abandonment.

In Charles's absence Caroline was forced to supplement her insufficient allotment from him in various ways, from taking in boarders to writing. Finding herself suddenly, after eleven years, no longer a minister's wife in any real sense, she was also forced to work out a new identity. While Charles's leaving was emotionally wrenching, it gave Caroline a freedom that she would not otherwise have had, a freedom to find a different niche for herself. That niche turned out to be the world of reform, first the abolitionism with which she had already associated herself, and then, more centrally, the women's movement.

She lectured, organized conventions, wrote for and edited a women's journal, circulated petitions, and published books on the subject. The appearance in 1867 of her culminating work, *The College, the Market, and the Court,* was generally reckoned as a major event in the fledgling women's movement of nineteenth-century America. Although Dall's role has been ignored or greatly undervalued in almost all histories of the movement, in the antebellum and immediate postbellum periods, she was recognized as the premier writer on the question.

Shortly after the Civil War's end, Dall's differences with other leaders of the women's movement surfaced: she was more conservative on the marriage question than Elizabeth Cady Stanton; she refused to cooperate, unlike both Stanton and Susan B. Anthony, with alleged racists in order to promote the cause; and she had personality conflicts with her fellow Boston feminists. In the mid 1860s, she began to turn her energies to an organization that she helped found, the American Social Science Association, which attempted to apply scientific methodology to all sorts of social ills. For decades Dall was an officer of this group, working with a largely male power structure to tackle such down-to-earth issues as prison conditions, urban lodging houses for women workers, and the purity of milk.

By 1878 both of Dall's parents had died, her children had left home, she was estranged from her sisters, and she felt betrayed by many of the other leaders of the women's movement in Boston, who had blackballed her from membership in the New England Women's Club. Accordingly, she decided to leave her native city, moving to Washington, where her son was now making his mark as a scientist at the Smithsonian Institution and the Coast Survey. William Healey Dall, still thought of today as the dean of Alaskan explorers, by age twenty-five had published a massive volume entitled *Alaska and Its Resources.* His accomplishments were not only a source of great pride to his mother, but were also in her view a sort of sign that her marriage to Charles Dall, which she had long recognized as a terrible error, was not unblessed by God. Her remaining thirty-four years she lived out in Washington, where she died at age ninety on December 17, 1912.

These are the facts of Dall's eventful life, but her inner life as revealed in the journals is just as compelling. The life of the mind was central to her, and through the record of her journals we follow as she strives to accommodate the new doctrines of Transcendentalism to her religious beliefs, as she comes to terms with the realities of slavery, and as her ideas on the woman question gradually develop. We witness her reactions to lectures and sermons and to her wide reading. She considered all knowledge as her province, and actually published in such diverse areas as literature, politics, education, economics, history, morals, religion, science, and art. Only in the last quarter of the nineteenth century did she begin to experience frustration that she was unable to comprehend all the papers at professional scientific conferences, conferences that she had "covered" as a paid newspaper reporter for years. Through the journals we also witness her moral dilemmas: how to treat unruly servants; whether to accede to her father's demands that she cease associating with abolitionists, in return for financial support; how to deal with falling in love with a man who is not her husband; what to do with a failed marriage.

Most compellingly of all, perhaps, we enter into Dall's emotional life. We follow her through the euphoria of love, and the anguish of its disappointment; the depression following the delivery of a stillborn child; the humiliation of being shouted down by a New York mob; the fulfillment of finding her apparent life's work in the women's movement, and the bitterness of discovering herself eventually excluded from it by other women; the anxiety of having a twenty-year-old son leave home to explore Russian Alaska; the pain of rejection by her sisters, for whom she had sacrificed much. And so the journals spin out the ever-engrossing story of Dall's mind and heart.

Dall's personality was distinctive and unconventional. She was outspoken, frequently dogmatic, more than occasionally abrasive. She repeatedly struck acquaintances as egotistical, a charge that reached her ears numerous times and caused her great distress. She regularly acted out of her sense of duty, even when it was clear that doing so was not in her personal interest. Driven and highly organized, she almost never wasted time, unless occasionally she read a novel that in her view turned out to be worthless. In general, she worked much better with men than with women. She was an exceedingly strong person; despite the self-pity that she frequently gave way to in her journal, she was anything but passive. Her journal is a record of storms braved, obstacles overcome, challenges to her faith wrestled with, and severe blows to her ego parried. The reader of these journals will come away with a real sense of the person Caroline Dall.

Dall was associated with the Unitarian faith throughout her long life, and its influence on her is difficult to exaggerate. The duty of self-culture and a belief in the essential goodness of mankind were bedrock principles for her. Baptized, brought up, and married in the West Church, she found there not only a fulfilling faith but a supportive social circle (especially important to her as an adolescent, when she felt unappreciated in her own family), and many of the relationships developed there were sustained throughout her lifetime. Its ministers Charles Lowell and Cyrus Bartol were father figures to her as long as they lived, and to some extent Elizabeth Howard Bartol, the junior minister's wife and Caroline Healey's former Sunday school teacher, was a surrogate mother. One illustration of the depth of these ties is the fact that in Dall's final years her financial distress was relieved by the daughter of the Bartols, both of whom were long since deceased.

As a young woman, Caroline Healey taught Sunday school classes both at the West Church and in urban missions in Boston. Engaging in the ministry to the poor modeled by Unitarian minister Joseph Tuckerman (1770–1840), she visited the homes of her scholars and other church members in poor neighborhoods, assessing their needs and providing relief in the form of money, clothing, work, medical services, and advice. It was a nascent form of social work and played an enormous role in shaping Caroline Dall's life. To some extent it was what made her an attractive partner to Charles Dall, himself engaged in the same sort of work, and made him an acceptable mate for her. As a minister's wife, she continued to practice these visits—in Toronto, primarily among fugitives from American slavery. These experiences also prepared her for her major role in the formation of the American Social Science Association.

After she had left the West Church, Unitarian ministers Theodore Parker and James Freeman Clarke acted as advisors and confidants to Dall. She was an active Unitarian, serving as Sunday school superintendent in the church pastored by Clarke, for example, and taking a lively part in denominational conferences. Although she was never ordained, Dall herself occasionally preached in Unitarian pulpits in the 1860s and 1870s and was generally well received. But significant as the church was in developing and sustaining Caroline Dall, it failed her in some ways. If she had been a man, there is little doubt that she would have attended Harvard, then the Harvard Divinity School, and then entered the Unitarian pulpit. But when she came of age, in the late 1830s, none of these avenues was open to a woman. During her great search for meaning and identity in the 1850s, occasioned by her husband's departure, she deplored the fact that in her church there was no professional outlet for her talents. Despite the fact that the Unitarian Church provided a more hospitable environment to women than almost any other religious group at the time, it was after all not hospitable enough.

The Diarist and Her Diary

Caroline Dall began keeping a diary when she was "about nine," according to one journal entry, or "about ten," according to another. She considered her diary private, and when she found her father reading it, she destroyed it and did not resume diary keeping until September 4, 1835, when she was thirteen. This second diary, which continued through the end of 1837, survived until Dall was in her seventies, when she destroyed both it and the beginning (January 1–March 17, 1838) of the next one. This destruction was motivated at least in part by her desire to protect her mother, whose mental illness was all too apparent in the journal's pages. Before she destroyed this material, she began composing what she called a "Reconstructed Journal" based on it and, in fact, often quoting long passages from it. The earliest surviving original journal begins with an entry for March 18, 1838, and the last journal ends with an entry for March 4, 1911. This record of seventy-three years is augmented by excerpts from the original journal, preserved in the Reconstructed Journal, that go back two and a half years. Dall's journal thus covers essentially three-quarters of a century and is the longest-running diary of which I am aware.

For most of Dall's life, the diary consists of daily entries of greatly varying length. In the early years, however, entries for every few days are more common, and during a few periods of her life she made entries only weekly. Even when there are separate daily entries, it does not necessarily follow that Dall wrote in her journal every day, for there is considerable evidence in the journals themselves that she often wrote several days' entries at a time. She does not seem to have had a designated time of day or a designated time of the week for journal writing; rather, she wrote whenever and wherever she could make the time. Her consistency in maintaining the diary for over seventy-five years is perhaps the more remarkable in view of the fact that she had no set routine for most of her life, no time inviolably designated for writing her journal.

To what can such remarkable consistency be attributed? How can we explain a person's keeping a journal from age nine to age ninety? Dall's journal served several purposes for her, varying at different points in her life. She described her earliest journal, the one she destroyed, as "a journal of self-exam-ination," and at times her surviving journals also fit this description. On June 22, 1838, she wrote,

> I am sixteen years old today,—! and have these sixteen years been wasted? My conscience trembles—is it not hypocritical, to remember one's sins on anniversaries, to weep in penitence, for wasted opportunities, slighted talents, and ungrateful murmurings, but on my birth-day?... Am I all that my parents wish me to be—do I—or shall I—realize my father's ambitious wishes for me—Alas! two years ago—he told me—that I had not accomplished all which he had a right to expect. Is it so now—am I deficient in industrious exertion...? But again:—ought I not rather to think of my father in Heaven, of him who in exceeding goodness, has given me, my parents upon earth; ought I not to strive, to become a child of God?

This use of the journal to chart and enhance her spiritual development was clearly a conscious one, as Healey acknowledged when she wrote, at age twenty, "I have strengthened my own spiritual nature by the exercise [of journal keeping]—I have purged my heart of whatever is impure on my page." But there is less and less of this sort of probing of her spiritual welfare, reminiscent of Puritan diaries, in Dall's journals as the years go by. On July 1, 1848, she wrote that she kept her journal "chiefly to establish my connections with the outward world—as a sort of link between me, & what I was afraid of forgetting." Here she was thinking of the journal as a recorder of events, a hedge against the ravages of time and the unreliability of memory. At times her journal certainly appears to be a self-conscious act of history writing, as when she recorded the details of such public events as an unruly antislavery meeting, or when she carefully documented her private encounters with public figures, including her conversations with the aging and mentally impaired Emerson. Thus, it seems clear that, at times, she did write with the eye and the intent of a historian.

But much of the journal lies outside this explanation too. Many diary entries include a considerable amount of what an unfriendly critic might call whining. We hardly need look for a clearer motive for "journalizing" (Dall's own term) than the situation the adolescent Caroline Healey found herself in, with a mother who had not the least sympathy with her intellectual and literary interests and a father whose unreasonable expectations she could never fulfill. As a young woman who felt misunderstood in her own family, Caroline Healey needed an outlet for her feelings and thoughts. She wished fervently that Elizabeth Bartol, her minister's wife, could somehow intuit the frustration and anguish that loyalty to her parents prevented her from revealing, writing in her journal in 1840, "I wished a thousand times that there was a window in my heart—that she might open the shutter and look in, but I felt that I could not open it, myself." Earlier in the same year, confessing a fault to her journal, she used the same metaphor in connection with her writing: "would to Heaven—that I had a window in my heart—or that it would sometimes guide my pen so as to <u>write itself out,</u> To be sure I should be obliged to burn up the record—but then it would be such a relief to have the whole once fairly out." Her diary brought her the relief that she imagined from such a disburdening of her soul. In fact, she observed that she rarely wrote in her journal something that she had already had occasion to write elsewhere—in a letter, for example, or in an article intended for publication. She occasionally regretted that she did not preserve certain material in the journal, but her practice did not change. It was as if, having once written something out, she had exhausted the need to say it. The journal was most centrally a place for what, psychologically, she *needed* to say, rather than a place to chronicle events and keep the record straight. Partly in consequence, some of the most compelling journal entries are those written when Dall was at her most miserable, when she had no one in whom she could confide her troubles, and the journal substituted for the missing sympathetic ear of an intimate.

The journal is the vehicle also for a good bit of self-justification. Here Dall took up her failures, the challenges to her sense of selfhood, and worked through them, casting them in a form that she could live with. In one terrible moment in 1870, at the culmination of a series of painful and frustrating events, including being blackballed by the New England Women's Club, she records fellow reformer Thomas Wentworth Higginson telling her, "I can't help it, Mrs Dall, . . . [that] you're such an <u>intensely</u> unpopular person!" This unkind cut clearly staggered Dall (and whom wouldn't it stagger?), but several lines later in the journal she comes back to it and asserts her worth in the face of it: "I do not believe I am an <u>unpopular</u> person. I believe I have had one or two bitter enemies say Towne & Eliz. Peabody—& Mrs Severance, who have done their best to prejudice people against me. I deserved Towne's enmity for my folly & indiscretion. I did <u>not</u> deserve that of Peabody or Severance." Here one sees the extent to which the journal functioned as a kind of self-administered therapy.

Elizabeth Palmer Peabody, her first female intellectual mentor, advised the eighteen-year-old Healey to write a different sort of journal. Healey wrote that Peabody told her that "I needed self culture—and the journal she proposed —was an efficient means of that—Not a journal of emotion . . . a journal of thoughts—stripped of all feeling." Apparently Peabody had not seen Healey's journal, but the remark struck close to home, for Healey recorded, "I thought of my own journal with dismay." But even at eighteen Healey recognized the important function served by the kind of journal she kept, and she did not follow Peabody's advice: "there are some excuses for all these things—which Miss Peabody—does not wot of," she wrote on September 15, 1840. Healey had recognized the cathartic function of the journal when a year earlier she had written, "This Journal is my safety valve—and it is well, that I can thus rid myself of my superfluous steam." Dall wrote her journal, in other words, mostly because she had to *get it out,* whatever *it* was at a given time. That the journal functioned for her successfully in this way is substantiated both by her explicit statements to this effect—"to write out has frequently been with <u>me</u>, to cast <u>off</u>," she declared on August 7, 1842—and even more by the fact that she continued to use it for this purpose for more than seven decades.

While Dall's journal might accurately be termed a journal of self-exploration and self-discovery, there are important differences between it and the typical twentieth-century diary of this sort. The most celebrated woman's diary of the twentieth century, that of Anaïs Nin, is described by its editor as "the log of her journey through the labyrinth of the self, of her effort to find, and to define, the woman Anaïs."[1] Dall's journal is in part the attempt to find not so much the hidden recesses of the self as the self's place in the scheme of things.

For whom was Dall writing? Many of Dall's contemporaries and acquaintances in the Transcendentalist group, all great journal keepers, wrote with a view to sharing their journals with each other. For the most part, Dall did not; for most of her life, so far as we know, she allowed others to read her journal only rarely. Her girlhood friend Anna Renouf was an exception; she "made free with" Healey's journal of 1835–1837, writing comical comments in its margins, and this reminder of a friend who died young long deterred Dall from destroying this journal. Certain kinds of journal entries—mainly, accounts of journeys—she read aloud to family and friends as entertainment. She and her husband seem to have exchanged journals during their engagement and perhaps in the early years of their marriage, but by June of 1853, when the marriage was under strain and Caroline was away from home, she wrote that she was "a good deal annoyed" to learn that Charles had been reading her old journals in her absence. The journals of the preceding year or two would have contained particularly sensitive material, and one can well understand Caroline's dismay. Her friend John Patton apparently considered Charles's action so potentially explosive that, on one occasion when she was away from home, Patton sent Caroline the key to her manuscript chest. But she didn't seem to consider Charles's act a serious violation, and was then annoyed in turn by John's action.

In general, Dall's journal was too private to be passed around from friend to friend. She wrote, to a large extent, to and for herself—but not entirely, and not always. At times she addressed her father, and later her children, imagining their reading the journals after she is gone. One also cannot ignore the fact that she bequeathed the journals to the Massachusetts Historical Society, which suggests that she knew that she was writing for us. Thomas Mallon, author of a book on diaries, argues that "the cheating of death" is an underlying motive in all diary keeping, but for Dall that purpose appears more conscious than it does for many diarists.[2]

If Dall hoped and planned to preserve these writings for posterity, then one might well ask just how self-consciously she wrote and how reliable the resulting journals can be. While it is clear that Dall sometimes composed with future generations in mind, she also seems to have forgotten this audience frequently, writing entries that bare her soul utterly. Dall confirmed, in a sense, this undisguised revelation of her most intimate thoughts when she later read through the journals before giving them to the Massachusetts Historical Society; at that time, she attempted to cancel a number of passages, by writing over them in a looped pattern, and in some instances she cut out pages. Such actions highlight the tension between the private uses that the journal served for Dall—as an outlet for her most protected feelings—and the public audience that she envisioned. Her rule, or at least her practice, seems to have been to write everything she felt and, if necessary, censor later.

As for reliability, I have found no reason to doubt the factuality of anything that Dall reports in her contemporary journal. Nonetheless, every reader must recognize that the diarist filters all facts and events through her own perspective and undoubtedly fashions them to suit her own self-interest. Dall's reader comes to understand and to accommodate for this perspective. In April of 1851, when Caroline Dall's mother was, to use her euphemism for mental illness, "not well," she spoke to her daughter "quite oddly," railing against her journal keeping: "It is absurd to keep one, it is never anything but a tissue of lies!" she asserted. Dall herself reflected astutely afterwards "that a Journal must always be true in one sense. If not true to facts & if the character appears in it gracefully draped, the untruth & the drapery reveal the starkness stalking beneath" (Ms. Journals, April 28, 1851).

Of course we will never know what Dall suppressed, consciously or unconsciously, from her journals. There are places where she deliberately restrained herself and kept out weighty emotional content. Upon rereading her journals, Dall was surprised by what was not there, by what she had left out, and a few times in her late journals she filled in additional information on events that she had written about decades earlier. Despite her excluding certain content, however, Dall was at times willing to depict herself in embarrassing or even humiliating situations; indeed, it seems to have been a major function of the journal to help her cope with such circumstances.

A topic on which the journals are relatively silent is child rearing. The explanation may be in part that Dall always had a servant to care for the young children. But I suspect it has more to do with the fact that Dall was such a veteran of child rearing (through caring for her own siblings) that by the time she had her own children, it came naturally to her. The short shrift given to this subject may further suggest that the journals functioned much more as a space for Dall to work out her own private issues than as a record of achievements or other milestones, even those of her children. This selected edition, in fact, probably gives proportionately more space to Dall's accounts of her children than do the journals in full, simply because the occasions when she did write of them tend to be particularly significant.

The greatest silence of the journals, as is true for almost all nineteenth-century women's journals, relates to her sex life. This silence is broken only by a few rare and oblique references. Dall was less squeamish than most Victorians, however, and although her journals are hardly X-rated, she takes up a number of taboo subjects—birth control, abortion, childbirth, prostitution, and sexual harassment, for example. And the reader will note that the marital bed is the setting for the most dramatic and compelling scene in all of Dall's journals.

What, besides its length, makes this diary an outstanding example of its genre? Dall's journal is extraordinary for many reasons. One major reason is its fortuitously proportionate mixture of the public and the private. Here we find extended portraits and notable vignettes of many of the extraordinary people of the time; a brief and incomplete list would include Margaret Fuller, Elizabeth Peabody, Ralph Waldo Emerson, Henry David Thoreau, Theodore Parker, Bronson and Louisa May Alcott, Dorothea Dix, Harriet Hosmer, William Lloyd Garrison, Wendell Phillips, Frederick Douglass, Daniel Webster, William H. Herndon, Lucretia Mott, Susan B. Anthony, Elizabeth Cady Stanton, Lucy Stone, Anne Whitney, Frances (Mrs. Grover) Cleveland, George Frisbie Hoar, the Alexander Graham Bells, and eminent Canadians such as Paul Kane, the father of Canadian painting, novelist Susanna Moodie, and ethnologist and president of the University of Toronto, Daniel Wilson, who invented the term "prehistory." We also become acquainted with the lives of people whose names have not made it into the history texts—wives and mothers, fugitives, servants, children, starving ministers, single women looking for outlets for their ambitions, and working people of all sorts. Dall reports on the lectures, conversations, and sermons that characterized the circles of Boston's intelligentsia; she describes antislavery meetings and reform conventions of all kinds, including some that turn rowdy. She depicts the mood and activities of Civil War Boston; the split in the abolitionist ranks after the war; Unitarian conventions and politics and the formation of the radical wing of the Unitarians, the Free Religious Association; the social scene in late-century Washington, peopled by senators and Supreme Court justices and their wives; the scientific community in Washington centered around the Smithsonian; a major cholera epidemic; and the beginnings of an intellectual and artistic elite in the Toronto of the 1850s.

At the same time that she reports on high-profile people and public events, Dall comments on the routines and annoyances of daily life: on plumbing problems, for example—her comment "Came home & found the plumber had upset the whole house & gone away as plumbers will" strikes a resonant note; on sewing—it is staggering to contemplate the amount of Dall's time, especially during the first half of her life, that she spent sewing; on illnesses and their treatment—plasters, blisters, blue pills, and leeches, for some ailments, and high-tech electric shock treatments for a strange malady in her hands (in the last decade of her life, when she suffered severely from arthritis, she noted with great hope the advent of a new miracle drug: aspirin); on her frustrations with servants—she must have run through hundreds in her lifetime. One January morning in 1851, she arose to face almost all these frustrations at once: not only were she and both children sick, requiring "two mustard plasters on the children, last night, one on myself this morning, before I could speak a loud word," but she "found the water & drain pipes frozen when I got up," and to crown the occasion, her servant "informed me this morning that she would rather I would get another girl, for she would like to live with a pleasanter-<u>look-ing</u> lady—at which," Dall further commented, "I did not wonder" (Ms. Journals, January 23, 1856).

The chief topic of this diary, however, is Caroline Dall herself, her mind and heart. Dall gives us accounts of actual happenings, and these accounts include facts and details, but the true subject of the journals is not so much these events and facts as her response to them. Events are filtered through *her* consciousness, judged by *her* light, "spun" according to *her* agenda. It is, above everything, the sense of Dall herself that the journals cumulatively convey.

Dall's diary, then, is part chronicle, part an exploration of the self, part emotional catharsis, and part artistic creation. Although Dall was probably largely unconscious of the last of these while she was writing, I believe that when she reread her journals late in life, she recognized what she had created. In the 1890s, when she was in her seventies, almost every day for weeks she was engaged in the same intense and engrossing activity that for a long time I have been engaged in—reading her account of events that took place generations ago. In her current journal, she wrote her reactions to her earlier journal, reactions that often paralleled my own; she recorded, for example, how painful she found it to read over the events of a certain period. In comparing her journals to "a Romance," Dall suggested not that her journal was a love story, but that it seemed to have the elements of a fictional narrative: plot, dialogue, recurring themes, character revelation, and the growth and development of a heroine.

In what sense, though, can a diary have a story, a plot? From the perspective of its author, she cannot know where her diary is going, only what has happened or what she has thought on a given day that she finds worthy of recording. Although it could hardly have been consciously conceived, the story told by this diary is one of its most fascinating features. Having read all of Dall's journals, I enjoy a kind of Godlike perspective: I know the end of the story, yet I see the protagonist struggling against personality flaws that I know she will never be able to overcome; I see her driven in her old age by the same needs that drove her as an adolescent: the need for approval and especially for love. Because the moments when either of these needs was satisfied were rare, we might well consider Dall's life story tragic. But in many ways, Dall's journal depicts a successful life, successful both in terms of influence and in terms of her devotion to a high moral imperative. The notion of "success," however, did not matter to Dall: having imbibed from her youth the Unitarian-Transcendentalist ideal of self-culture, Dall saw the goal of life not as happiness but as development—and for development, in her view, unhappiness and failure were often more useful than success. So she strove constantly to make sense of her troubles and failures, to learn the lessons they were sent to teach. It is part of the great appeal of the journals that this learning, this making sense of her life, this attempt to identify the themes and second-guess the plot, was never easy, and Dall's emotionally vivid representations of these cruxes draw us irresistibly into her struggles.

It is not just *what* this diary contains, of course, but *how* it is written that sets it apart. Although we might still take an interest in Dall's accounts of public persons and events had she expressed them poorly, that would hardly be the case when she writes of purely personal matters. Dall is a truly expert and fluent writer. As a result, the journal is stylistically polished, pithy and acute, sprinkled with searing judgments of friend and foe, and written practically without revision. Furthermore, these qualities characterize even the very earliest journals. In fact, after reading the journals of Dall's maturity and then returning to the earliest surviving volumes, I was struck by the fact that Dall was essentially as articulate a writer at age fifteen or sixteen as she ever became. Indeed, Dall herself, rereading her early journals in her mid-seventies, recognized the same phenomenon: "Nothing puzzles me more in this early writing than the style. Except that I have learned to condense, I cannot see that I write any better than I did at 16," she wrote in her Reconstructed Journal. Surely Caroline Healey was not born with a fully developed prose style. But by age sixteen, she was a voracious reader and already quite a veteran writer, with six or more years of diary keeping behind her, several unpublished novels completed, and a number of articles published, not to mention the compositions that she would have written at school. Her apprenticeship as a prose stylist was essentially complete by the time the earliest surviving journal begins.

Though readers will come to Dall's journals for many reasons, I believe that the ultimate interest and appeal of this text will derive from its subjectivity. It presents the fascinating human story of a woman both ordinary in her needs and flaws, frustrations and failures, and extraordinary in her intelligence, vision, and commitment to her ideals. The journals constitute a great text because Caroline Healey Dall was a great subject and because she was remarkably articulate in presenting her story.

Dall once struggled in her journals to understand why God who, "having gifted me so strangely," had not yet made clear to her her vocation. She could not quite see that her greatest legacy was not to be what she would have called her "work." It was to be instead her life story itself—this romance-like story, preserved in the journals that both resulted from and helped shape her life.

The Diarist and the Editor

"No editor can be trusted not to spoil a diary." So wrote Sir Arthur Ponsonby, reader and scholar of diaries.[3] The text of this selected edition of Caroline Healey Dall's journals represents a collaboration between Dall herself and me, the editor. I find myself a somewhat unwilling editor because I am responsible for determining which parts of the text readers will not see. I am acutely aware that readers are nearly completely at my mercy. Unless they go to the trouble of reading the entire text on microfilm, they can't judge how fairly I have presented Dall's text. On the other hand, I am responsible for presenting some text that Dall herself would not have published, those passages that she attempted to cancel and that I have deciphered. I have overridden her wishes in those cases because these parts of her story deserve a telling too. If she wished that they never be read, she could have removed the pages entirely, as in some cases she did.

The Editorial Note (see page xxx) explains my selection policy, but there is a real sense in which I have selected those parts of the text that I couldn't bear to leave out. I have included segments that look forward to other passages down the road; I have chosen passages from early in Caroline Healey's life, for example, that illuminate her relationship with her father, because I know how significant that relationship proved for her whole life. Thus I have countered some of the randomness that one would find in the complete text of the diary. Something is lost as well as gained by this practice. Yet the length of Dall's complete journals means that only a handful of scholars will ever read them in their entirety. Surely the solution to reducing their bulk is not to choose entries randomly or to include *x* number of pages per month or year.

It seems to me that Dall's journals demonstrate definitively that women's diaries can be viewed as serious literature. I have thought of them as an artistic creation. Dall had an aesthetic sense that led her to construct many entries as composed artistic units. I hope that my selection policy has enhanced rather than nullified that aesthetic tendency for the edition as a whole. I have tried hard to heed Sir Arthur's warning.

Editorial Note

*O*nly a small proportion of the text of the entire journals of Caroline Healey Dall has been included in this edition. The entire journal, as well as correspondence and other Dall papers at the Massachusetts Historical Society, is available in a microfilm edition, *The Caroline Dall Papers*. The entries presented here are chosen from the first twenty-seven years of the surviving original journals. They depict Caroline Healey (later Dall), from the age of fifteen, when the basic personality traits that will persist throughout her life are already becoming apparent—as well as some of the factors that help explain these traits—until age forty-three, the prime of her life, when she is fully engaged with reform issues, still full of vitality, and devoted to living out her principles and doing her part to improve the world.

The overriding principle of selection has been to preserve the thread of Caroline Healey Dall's life story. I have taken care to ensure that the selected entries be not simply a series of vignettes of Dall's encounters with the great and famous, but that they reflect as accurately as possible the fabric of her life and as fairly as possible the complexity of her personality. While I have included a good proportion of Dall's accounts of encounters with persons well known to history and events of a public nature, I have also included passages that reflect more routine occurrences and her interactions with historically obscure acquaintances. Nevertheless, the final selection, I believe, is somewhat skewed, not just toward famous people, but toward private affairs of an extraordinary rather than a routine nature. In other words, the selected journals are proportionately more *eventful* than the complete journals. I hope that no careful reader will get the sense that Dall was constantly going from one incident of great moment to another; anyone in danger of thinking this should note the great gaps in dates between selected entries. I have had no conscious agenda of presenting Dall in a favorable or unfavorable light, but have attempted to represent all aspects of her character and life as they appear in the complete text of the journals.

I have doubtlessly included some passages for their intrinsic literary power, whatever their subject matter, and for this additional principle of selection, I offer no apology.

Transcription Policy

My transcription practice has been in general to present a clear text version of what Caroline Healey Dall wrote. Thus I have produced only the final form of the text after insertions, deletions, or other revision. In the interest of readability, I have regularized Dall's apostrophe usage, corrected her rare misspellings, and spelled out her abbreviations. In the occasional cases in which the author's punctuation might lead to misreading, I have supplied other punctuation. I have regularized her punctuation only by supplying missing second sets of quotation marks and by ending sentences with periods, when end punctuation is missing altogether or when the mark at the end of what is clearly a sentence appears to be a comma in the manuscript. I have also silently deleted quotation marks in passages where Dall, to mark a quotation of several lines, used quotation marks at the beginning of each line of text. These have been reduced to the current convention of quotation marks at the beginning and end of the quoted passage. Superscript letters have been brought down to the baseline. In a few rare cases when Dall has omitted an obvious word, I have inserted that word in brackets. A forthcoming scholarly edition of the Dall journals, produced by this editor and published by the Massachusetts Historical Society, preserves Dall's revisions, deletions, insertions, abbreviations, and misspellings intact.

Dall, like many nineteenth-century diarists, often wrote pages without clearly rendered punctuation. Frequently she used a multipurpose mark, most closely resembling what we would call a dash, to terminate a sentence, separate a series, or simply indicate a hesitation. In this printed version of the text, Dall's dashes appear as single em dashes, their length regularized: one dash at any given site represents a single or multiple dashes in the manuscript. I have attempted to be consistent in my determination of what constitutes a dash, a period, a comma, or a stray mark, but as any editor knows, the ambiguity of such marks on the handwritten page makes a completely systematic process impossible.

I have attempted to follow Dall's paragraphing practices, although often her intentions are not entirely clear. She sometimes used indentation of a new line to indicate a new paragraph, but sometimes (perhaps to save space) simply skipped a larger than usual space between the end of one sentence and the beginning of the next. Occasionally it is difficult to discern whether such a space is a deliberate paragraph marker or simply accidental, and in such cases I have simply used my best judgment. This edition signals all new paragraphs, after the first paragraph of a new diary entry, by the indentation of the first line.

This is a selected edition. Ellipses (. . .) mark omissions from within entries. The reader should take note, by observing the dates of entries included, that large portions of the text are often also omitted between selected entries.

Dall undertook to censor some of her journal entries, occasionally cutting out a leaf, part of a leaf, or several leaves. When such an excision occurs within an entry included here, I have reported it in the notes. Dall also sometimes attempted to obliterate certain passages by heavily canceling them in a looped pattern in different ink from the original. When such cancellations occur within entries selected for this edition, I have attempted to recover the original text and have indicated Dall's attempt at cancellation in the notes. Words that I have been unable to recover are indicated in brackets as [illegible word] or [illegible words]. A bracketed question mark following a word indicates that a reading is conjectural or questionable; because Dall's handwriting is extremely legible, such cases occur almost entirely in connection with Dall's later attempts at cancellation.

Annotation

My annotations identify, whenever possible, persons, published material, and events that Dall mentions. I have attempted to ascertain birth and death dates and other relevant identifying information for all persons mentioned, although this information is by no means complete. I have referred the reader to other documents in the Dall Papers relevant to the text at hand—for example, letters that Dall mentions receiving. In general I have not annotated instances when I could not identify a person or when a document mentioned is not in the Dall Papers. Exceptions to this general policy are those instances when Dall makes a point of saying that a particular document will be found among her papers, but in fact it is not there; in these cases, I have noted the discrepancy. Occasionally an explanatory note will supply information from the unselected text of the journals or other documents in the Dall Papers that illuminates the selected text. This edition uses both footnotes and endnotes. Footnotes are used to identify persons, places, things, or events that are necessary to understanding the text. Endnotes provide information supplementary in nature, useful but not necessary to the general reader's understanding of the text.

Because of the great gaps between journal entries, I have occasionally used transitional sentences between entries, to prepare the reader to understand the context of the following entry or simply to supply important details in Caroline Dall's story that the selected text has not provided. Each chapter introduction also partially fulfills this purpose.

CHAPTER ONE

Aspiring to Something Noble

March 19, 1838–April 27, 1840

$\mathscr{T}$he Caroline Healey who emerges from the diary entries of 1838–1840 was intelligent, well read, intellectually curious, pious, ambitious, emotionally needy, and, most of all, remarkably articulate. At the beginning of these selections, the family of this fifteen-year-old diarist included her father, Mark Healey (1791–1876), a prosperous merchant and land speculator, business associate of Daniel Webster, and recent president of the Merchants Bank; her mother, Caroline Foster Healey (1800–1871), who suffered from a mental illness of some sort and was in her final pregnancy; and six younger siblings. They lived at 6 Hancock Street on Beacon Hill and attended the nearby (Unitarian) West Church. Caroline had previously been taught by private tutors and most recently at the private school of Joseph Hale Abbot, but a few months earlier her father had, much to her dismay, ended her formal education.

By far the most important figure for Caroline during these years, and indeed during her entire life, was her father. From her childhood she had been his intellectual companion, a sparring partner on questions of politics and religion. He was probably chiefly responsible for the fact that she had an amazing confidence in her abilities, having fostered in her the belief that "if a man believes that he has the power to do any-thing—he can do it." But his unreasonable expectations had a deleterious effect too. The need for his approval was a dominant theme during these years, as was her unfulfilled need for love, particularly the love of her mother.

Caroline's spiritual life was earnest and profound, and like her Puritan forebears, she sometimes used her journal for religious self-examination, measuring her spiritual progress and upbraiding herself for her shortcomings. She was no pietistic hermit, however; organized religion played an important part in her life, both spiritual and social. She actively participated in the life of the West Church and worked in two Sabbath schools. Besides serving as a teacher, she made regular charitable "visits" to the homes of her largely poor pupils, acting as a sort of social worker, to identify problems and help provide necessities. The Unitarian Church provided Caroline with the acceptance that was often lacking in her own family.

Although her church work increasingly commanded more of Healey's time, she still managed to fulfill her household duties, find time for reading (although no longer in school, she seemed intent on keeping up her studies), attend lectures, exchange social calls, and write. Writing, in fact, must have taken up a significant portion of her time, for she kept detailed records of her charitable activities, composed articles for publication, wrote novels and then critiqued them, and composed often lengthy entries in her journal.

During this period, Caroline Healey was already becoming conscious of the gender issues that would limit her current and future choices. Her mother was interested largely in developing her daughter's housewifely skills, regularly denigrating her literary endeavors. Although Caroline's schooling had ended at fifteen, she observed that many a man's has "just begun" at twenty-five. Still, she had not quite worked out woman's place in the scheme of things. While she resisted the idea of entering "the market of matrimony" and initially opposed the idea of a coming-out party for herself, she clearly enjoyed the attention it brought.

Her interactions with the opposite sex, in fact, were curious. Spurning the social convention that a young lady should refrain from directly criticizing young men of her acquaintance, Healey said what she thought. Already, this lifelong disposition to express herself forthrightly was drawing critical attention, particularly in regard to her relations with the young men in her circle. She dismissed such criticism, thinking of herself as "a sort of <u>universal sister</u>" to her male contemporaries, assuming thereby her freedom not to participate in the usual diplomatic games of flirtation. Yet she clearly had more than a platonic interest in some of the young men she met. She was more comfortable, however, interacting with them in intellectual or religious arenas than in strictly social ones.

Among Healey's personality traits revealed in the journals of these years, the most remarkable is her early sense of her potential greatness. Read as egotism by many, her perception that she was meant to do some great work was not simply an adolescent fantasy, but a lifelong conviction. At seventeen she wondered whether succeeding generations would search out her birthplace, as she did that of Benjamin Franklin. (As I have sought for images of the house at 6 Green Street, long since destroyed, I have felt myself confirming her expectations.) Would children of the future, she asked, read her journals to discover what she was like as a child? Whatever her faults—and she was aware of some of them—she felt certain of making her mark, for, she observed, she had "always aspired to something noble." This self-analysis may seem self-serving, but it is essentially true, and as true in her old age as in her youth.

MARCH 19TH. 1838.

I believe I comply with Mrs Farrar's requisition, that "every lady should be an hour at her toilette," although my dress is exceedingly plain.* I rose this morning, at half past six, and did not go down till full half past seven! Luckily the people overslept themselves, as it was still unpleasant weather, and we did not break-fast till 8. Immediately after breakfast, I made my bed, and cleared away my room, and having yielded to lazyness for five minutes or so, read five chapters in "Silvio Pellico," and three in "Cartas Marruecas."[1] Wrote Journal, and read Chateaubriand translation of "Gaul."[2] Macpherson's Ossian[3] used to be a great favorite of mine, but I am tired of it now. Wrote in "Grace Lethbridge"† for about two hours, dined and attempted to mend some French embroidery. Had a slight attack of dyspepsia, and mother advised Exercise. Did not like to leave her alone, but went down to Mrs Wild's.[4] Talked very comfortably for an hour; Caty was out. Called at Mrs Littlehale's, and asked Ednah to go out with me.[5] She consented, and asked if I had seen Anna[6] today.

---

*Eliza Rotch Farrar (1791–1870), author, prominent Cambridge intellectual, and wife of Harvard professor John Farrar, gave this advice in her popular manners manual and domestic advice book, *The Young Lady's Friend* (Boston: American Stationers' Co., 1836).

†One of several novels composed by Healey as a teenager; all remain unpublished. A number of them, including "Grace Lethbridge," are in the Dall Papers, Schlesinger Library (Radcliffe Institute for Advanced Study, Harvard University).

Told her "no, but that I called on her Saturday." She said Anna was too sick to be at school this morning. I felt alarmed for I thought Anna quite imprudent Saturday. We went down to see her directly. Found Anna quite sick, though she would not acknowledge it. Sat with her till near dark, walked round the Common with Ednah, just as the sun was setting. Came home, to finish mending my collar; Mr Haughton[7] came in, during the evening—promised to obtain me, a ticket of admission to the Exhibition of Italian paintings,[8] which I am very desirous to see. I withdrew at 9 o'clock, and got to bed, at ten.

APRIL 17TH 1838.

I shall never make an elegant seamstress, I am sure, for my sewing never suits mother. She was vexed with me, the other day because I did not take sufficiently short stitches in some, I did for her. "Well!" said she at last, "I would learn to be a beautiful seamstress, if I never knew any thing else, Caroline!" My colour rose, and I said somewhat hastily, that "I considered myself born for a better purpose." Ellen* repeated this to father. I was very much to blame, but he was not angry, with me, as Ellen expected—

"This is all very well," said he, "but let her <u>fulfil</u> the purpose of her existence!"

My dear father! for your sake, let Heaven prosper my efforts!

JUNE 22ND. 1838.

...I am sixteen years old today,—! and have these sixteen years been wasted? My conscience trembles—is it not hypocritical, to remember one's sins on anniversaries, to weep in penitence, for wasted opportunities, slighted talents, and ungrateful murmurings, but on my birth-day?

Oh, let me avoid such pharasaical doings—and exclaim with the publican—"God be merciful to me a sinner—"[9] The first thought, which disturbs my brain is the enquiry—"Am I all that my parents wish me to be—do I—or shall I—realize my father's ambitious wishes, for me— Alas! two years ago— he told me—that I had not accomplished all which he had a right to expect— Is it so now—am I deficient in industrious exertion, do I aggravate my own diseases, by selfish indulgence? God of Mercy take pity on my distress! had my father once guessed the agony, these words would cause me; he had never uttered them. I have disappointed him,—he who would do any-thing rather

---

*Caroline's nearest sibling, Ellen Wells Healey (1825-1876), three years her junior.

than disappoint me!— But again:—ought I not rather to think of my father in Heaven, of him who in exceeding goodness, has given me, my parents upon earth; ought I not to strive, to become a child of God? Death will come—and after Death Judgement;—of what avail will the laurel wreath, and the myrtle, for which I am so anxiously striving be to me then? will <u>their</u> scanty foliage cover the multitude of my sins, or hide the nakedness of my soul? No! in those days, I shall call upon the rocks, and the mountains to fall upon me—and better "would it have been, had I never been born!"[10]

JUNE 25TH. 1838—

Was obliged to leave my desk—again, to make blanc-mange for M.A.* I wish I was a man, in that case I might hope to make something of myself;—but being a woman I never can. Got a long lesson on Tytler—[11] I congratulate myself upon my method of studying history—it is very effectual— Having read a chapter. I go back to the head of it, and running my eye over the list of topics give in my own words, & with my book shut—a brief abstract of what it contains. Speaking of women—Artemisa's counsel might have saved Xerxes, so they are worth something![12]

JULY 24TH. 1838.

My situation increases in trials, mother's complaints grow upon her, and our anxiety is undiminished;—a heavy burden is mine. Two days ago, I resolved to complain no longer, and yet—God forgive me—I have bitter cause for complaint.

Mother thinks that I hardly fulfil my duties, and father upon her motion, talked long, and in a severely critical manner, to his poor child this evening. I could not have borne it, save through pity to him—among many faults for which he reproved me, he condemned my want of perseverance— "In this," said he, "Ellen has greatly the advantage of you—!" Ellen! a child without a care—unless—her sash be of the wrong color—or her hair out of curl—! I burst into tears,— "Alas! my father," I exclaimed, "no painful thoughts press upon her brain, no distracting cares are hers," I would have said more—for I felt that it would be indelicate,—he was silent, but kind and considerate as ever— God of Mercy—! Omnipotent and Omniscient, Thou, who seest alike, through my temptations, and my errors, am I to blame or is my conscience cold?

*Perhaps Healey's sister Marianne Wells Healey (1827–1890).

On July 31 Caroline's mother gave birth to her eighth and last child, Emily Wells Healey (1838–1916).

AUG 23D. 1838.

My exertions are discouraged on every side— I paused a few moments at my mother's bedside, this morning—with some blank books in my hand— She enquired what they were— I told her, and mentioned the price— "All that you will ever write in them, will not be worth the money." was her reply— "Perhaps not." was my cool rejoinder—but the hot tears which chased each other down my cheeks—belied my calmness. Yes! every-one discourages me, but thou Oh my Father! when the frail vessel is disturbed by opposing currents, or deserted by her proper officers, thy gentle hand is on the helm, and quietly and steadily, she moves her, on her way— But thou! thou art gone!—and thy child is alone—! But once, did I hear words of reproach drop from thy lips,— and never, Oh never! can I forget their import— I have not fulfilled thy expectations, I have hidden my talent in a napkin— Oh! my God! teach this proud heart submission—may he never know the anguish I endure—

Teach me, Oh! Merciful Father! to know myself—cast me not off from thee, but—in great kindness support thy suppliant child. Oh! if vanity or conceit or the flatteries of this world, have tainted the purity of my soul—have created a false consciousness of talent, within my bosom, Oh! by severest chastening punish, and by great Mercy pardon the voice, the still, small voice,—which speaks within me—yet—for I cannot relinquish every hope—yet if in thy Love Thou hast granted to thy unworthy—servant the boon she so ardently prays for, support her mind in the arduous undertaking and punish—her presumption with success!—....

SEPT. 2ND. 1838.—

I have been wondering what it is that raises my spirits, and encourages me in the task which I have undertaken? Certainly neither father nor mother, brother nor sister, have ever expressed any interest in what I have written, or ever desired to read anything I have published,— It is strange, I think I should take pride, & pleasure in the virtuous endeavors of a child of mine—and this apathy, this indifference breeds coldness—on my side, and there is no sympathy between me, and my parents. My mother oftentimes expresses harsh disapproval of my love of study, and her daily life seems to express but one wish—that I were as fond of housewifery as my sister Ellen. She knows not the

depth of the wound she probes, and the unbidden tears, which often spring
to my eyes, are imputed to childish weakness— Why then should I persevere,
if those whom I wish to honor, seem insensible to my truly filial feeling? Because, in my father's anxiety to procure me every literary advantage, in his kind
smile, and gentle voice, I find at least one assurance that <u>he</u> will joy in his
child's success, and grieve for her disappointment. People talk of <u>literary
struggles</u>, and of the trials which a man who chooses this department of life,
has to endure. These do not spring from the nature of literature, but from the
interference of friends, the obstacles raised by the envious, and the discour-
agements, the cold indifference, with which his labors are regarded by the very
ones who should be the first to support and aid him. Nothing is easier, than
this, if he be a man of talent, he forgets in the inspiration of his genius, the disagreeable manual labor, to which his inclination subjects him. This is a pleasure & not a task.

NOV. 3D. 1838.

A trifling altercation between my sister and myself—called my father's attention to us, and words of bitter disappointment dropt from his lips—words
which will rankle in my bosom—long after all memory of many things is dead
—words which have filled my cup of misery to the brim— . . . .

 Yes! rather than be the source of my father's sorrow—would I this moment
lay down my head in the dust and die—sure am I that this family will never be
united, while I live—my mother would love me better were I like Ellen—fond
of housework and my needle—and though she is very, very, dear to me, never
have I sat at her feet and poured out as I should love to do—the full affection
of my soul, never has she spoken the one word which like oil upon the waves,
calms the troubled soul—never has she encouraged me in my literary labors,
never expressed the slightest desire to see what I have written—and such neglect touches the sore spot— Oh—if God ever grants to me, a child, carefully
and fondly will I nurture it, never shall it be as I have been all—all alone! The
children of course, seeing that mother has no sympathy with my pursuits,
ridicule and despise them too, and this is very, very wrong—and I am very, very
wrong, for I am hasty & impatient under the lash— My father, who is nearer
to me, than aught else in this world—cannot feel with me, for he is not a
woman—and so—but now Oh! God! that I have poured forth my complaints,
give me strength to recapitulate my blessings— there is no temporal advantage
that is not mine—it is the soul's necessities which are forgotten—my slight-

est wish is gratified before expressed—and my mother is ever my advocate—when a new hat, or a new dress is to be purchased, and my father seems to take pleasure in giving me every thing which may adorn my person—the greatest care has been taken to form my manners,—to render them graceful and dignified, and Affection has seemed to invent ways to satisfy the eye, to gratify the ear or the taste, grateful am I for all—but does this satisfy the craving within me?

NOV. 20TH. 1838.—

Would to Heaven every body cared as little for dress, and entertainments as my quiet self. My mother is very desirous that a party commemorating my progress in years, my ignorance and indolence, should be given,—when she first mentioned the subject, I burst into tears, but by earnest argument she has convinced me however unwillingly, that I had better be "brought out." The next question which arises, is this, can I muster, an <u>exclusive</u> party—which seems to be the necessary thing, and I have no hesitation in answering in the negative. Mamma is not so easily convinced, and has already begun to canvass the next subject—my dress!— I have already decided that book muslin, with no ornament save a plain white satin fold, shall make me look as well, as perfect simplicity can, but my hair which I have always parted on my forehead, and gathered in braids behind—"à la Grecque—" must be tortured to please her, into some more becoming knot. I have borne all this as well as I can, but I do most sincerely hope that something may chance—to prevent this long looked for event. My interest, my affections, my all, are in my home—loving rather than loved, self-condemned, rather than self conceited, I seek no intercourse with the vain and the frivolous. God—knowing the yearnings of every human being, for the sympathy of a single soul, has instituted the holy ordinance of marriage, but the duties of a wife and mother I will never take upon me; physical weakness, and an innate jealousy, counter-balancing in my mind, every more valuable qualification, why then a slave to custom, should I enter the market of matrimony? my delicacy revolts at the idea, and some of my sentiments would find decided expression, were it not for the unsympathizing crowd by whom I am surrounded.

By this time Healey was contributing occasional articles to the Christian Register, *a weekly unofficial organ of the American Unitarian Association. The following entry mentions one such article.*

My communication was published in the Register today,* and I was gratified, of course, but I am not <u>satisfied</u>. I wish to do something for myself—my subjects must be chosen to suit the character of the paper— I had rather be free—; I cannot, for never will I take a step, upon which so much of my future lot depends, without the advice of some <u>literary</u> friend—who shall inspect and criticize my manuscripts—but such a friend, I neither have nor am likely to have. With such considerations come others of a more discouraging kind— I have perhaps overrated my own abilities,—my friends—If I have any may be laughing at my self-conceit and as it is, but too evident that my father is dissatisfied with my progress, had I not better throw down my pen forever—? I will seek my closet, and if the influence of prayer cannot frighten away, these demoniac thoughts, as the name of Jehovah sunk the magic boat in Arabian Nights—then I am wretched indeed!

...I wonder if it is right & Christian, for any one to lay by Dante, and spend six or eight hours, in making baby clothes for a little sister? It is strange that when I make these sacrifices—I am never rewarded by an approving conscience. Is the dissatisfied feeling, I have, the result of conscientious remorse, or the voice of a criminal & selfish Ambition?[13]

In the following entry, Healey describes the coming-out party that her mother had proposed on November 20, 1838, and that she had then opposed.

...As to outward appearances, my party was the most successful—of the season—. It is a common saying that many a thing is pleasant to the palate, which is painful to the stomach—but—it is just the opposite, in the present— case—my morsel was bitter to the taste, but easy & pleasant of digestion — Marianne was not so dangerously hurt as I expected, George† was well enough to sit up till eleven, and although I regretted, that neither _____ nor

---

*Healey's untitled article, signed "C" and headed by a quotation from *The Faerie Queene,* is a defense of courtesy. The author argues that true courtesy is not to be confused with the hypocritical paying of insincere compliments (*Christian Register,* December 15, 1838, p. 197).

†Marianne Healey and George Wells Healey (1834–1887), Caroline's sister and brother.

E.S.* had accepted my invitations, my spirits rose gradually, as guest after guest, assured me—that he or she, had not enjoyed himself or herself—so much at any previous party. The supper table looked splendidly, and the flowers with which it was tastefully ornamented were far too frail & fair, to stand the heated atmosphere of the room.[14] "I will say what I do not often say," said ____† as he departed, "that this affair has been exquisitely managed, that I have had a delightful time,—and that you are entitled to the sincere gratitude of your friends, for your unremitting exertions in their behalf." "And I—" said another—"have enjoyed myself to the utmost, you were exceedingly happy in your managers, Miss Healey, they have fulfilled their duties—with graceful aptitude."

I received every attention, that any one, could wish—several bouquets, were sent me, but I gave the preference, to a lovely collection of exotics, sent me, by my first manager—among which the white camelia, held a conspicuous station.—

An amusing incident, occurred during the evening, which I have urgent reasons for commemorating _____ _____[15]—a collegian, and a near neighbor, was dancing the Virginia reel, I stood near, watching the easy motions of the dancers— "I was quite surprised, when I heard that you intended giving a ball" said he—as he turned his partner— "I thought you had conscientious scruples upon the subject!—" I replied in the negative very coolly, saying that I did not wish it to be understood that I disapproved of a harmless amusement, because I took no—interest in it myself— I reminded him that I had danced with him at his own party—just two years—since—that it was the last time, and that it was not reasonable to suppose—that I should be contented to dance with every man—after having enjoyed such an honour!—" adding in the words of Chesterfield,[16] that "I had gone to dancing school, to learn to sit still gracefully—" He swallowed the sugared morsel—without tasting the physic it contained with a low bow, and begging my pardon, said that he had always supposed that I did not know how to dance—![17]

The fellow seemed perfectly insensible to the rudeness of his remarks,

---

*Probably Joseph Coolidge Shaw (1821–1851) and Elizabeth Willard Shaw (1823–1850), Healey's two earliest and closest childhood friends. They were neighbors and the children of Robert Gould Shaw (1776–1853) and Elizabeth W. Parkman Shaw. See Mary Caroline Crawford, *Famous Families of Massachusetts* (Boston: Little, Brown and Company, 1930), 1:243–248, and *NEHGR* 39:225–226.

†Healey uses the blank line to avoid identifying this guest.

which explained many circumstances, which had till now, worn an air of mystery— I bowed coldly & crossed the rooms to speak to a friend—....

We broke up before 1, some time, & I sought my pillow with delight,— Our music was very fine—the softest & sweetest I ever heard, the principal performer—an Englishman named Fitzmantle upon the harp.

APRIL 14TH. 1839.

It still rains—hails, and snows, by turns with insatiable fury— I went to Sabbath School this morning, in a driving storm, but had not a single scholar— Took a class of four, whose teacher was absent. Mr Walker[18] preached for us all day—.... In the afternoon from Mark—9.27.—on self confidence. He advocated a doctrine which father broached long ago—that if a man believes that he has the power to do any-thing—he can do it.— This is good news for me— for I am sometimes so confident—I cannot call it, as many would—so conceited,—that I am ready to think like Archimedes, that if I only had a lever long enough—I could move the world! Alas! my own experience would teach me the immortality of the soul—without the aid of revelation. I cannot realize the existence of this material world—and tremble wonderingly, as I gaze upon the plodding, sensual beings—who inhabit it— What are ye thinking of? restless—dissatisfied ones—yet a little while and the rank grass—groweth over your graves—and your names have passed from the memory of man.

JULY 7TH. 1839.

... I do feel deeply interested in the young Graduates—at Harvard—and I find that I am fast losing all personal feeling, in my devotion, to our public & national advancement. Still, I wish that women might enjoy—the advantages— of college education, of the severe and studious training, which is lavished upon our young men,—ah! wherefore—are they so often regardless of their— blessings—? At fifteen—a woman's education—in common parlance—is finished—at twenty-five—a man's—but just begun!—Heigho!—

AUG 14TH. 1839.

I have been looking over—my Journals for '36—& 7—and certainly if anything could, make me humble—disgust me with myself—that would—such a mass of frivolous self-applause—of nonsensical boasting never met my eyes—such a self satisfied way of talking about myself—and my productions—that certainly I would rather take a dose of Tartar Emetic than read them again. I was half-inclined to burn them up—but I remembered how sorry I had been for a similar act, and reflected that exposed as I am—to flattery and folly—it would be well to preserve them—as a powerful antidote— It was a sore trial of temper—however—to be obliged to own—such trash— I think my bitterest foe —could wish me no greater misfortune than the publication of those papers— and yet—they might be useful—to another generation— Suppose—for instance—I should ever attain—all that I wish to attain—and all that I am—as I begin to believe—perfectly incapable of attaining—the first inquiry of a child would be—upon hearing—that I had done such & such a thing—"I wonder what sort of a little girl Miss Healey was—" I would no matter how much it might pain myself—I would hand her that Journal—and—she would hardly ask the question a second time—she would see for herself—that after all— "Miss Healey was more foolish—than the generality of children—and that she had no excuse for her many extravagancies—but this—that she had always <u>aspired</u> to something <u>noble</u>—" ....

NOV. 12TH. 1839.

... This Journal is my safety valve—and it is well, that I can thus rid myself of my superfluous steam. . . . I trust posterity will remember this, should it ever be gratified by a glimpse at these pages. My Journal shall not share the fate of Lord Byron's[19]—while silver and gold—have any influence over the human heart.

Healey's ambivalent assessment of the learned Hypatia, whom she perceives as having stepped outside her proper sphere to become what she calls "the first lecturess," foreshadows her own later lecturing career.

DEC 27TH 1839.

Went to Mr Gray's[20] lecture this evening and to Sarah D.'s party—afterwards, notwithstanding a terrible storm. Mr Gray really <u>treated</u> us—after the very disagreeable and unskilful attempts of Prof. Adam.[21] His subject was "Lectures—" and by considering Heraclitus—Socrates Plato and Aristotle, with their masters and pupils—as the first lecturers—he made what most people would imagine a dry subject—very interesting. He concluded his address —with the story of Hypatia, who was murdered, by the monkish rebels—in Alexandria in 415.[22] She was the first lecturess—her beauty her virtue, her exceeding erudition, and her modesty were—alike remarkable—but the author who has so graphically delineated her character concludes a recital of her sufferings with the following words—"And from her story—let females of all ages take warning—in eloquent language it tells—us, that although a woman be the envy of her own sex—and the admiration of ours, yet that—if she oversteps the modesty of nature, she can derive true happiness from neither— If she leave the circle of her own duties and, share the labors—of man—she loses—in his reverence and affection far more than she can gain in his esteem." I never felt the truth of this—so deeply as now—it is as true of the female who braves the censure of the press, as of her, who walked in the Academical Groves of Alexandria. Peace be with the manes[23] of Hypatia,—but—how strange that when once a woman's earnest convictions are given to the world, the world seem to doubt her humanity. At the very moment perhaps, when her pen, is giving evidence of her deep sympathy with her sex and with her kind, men stand aloof from her as if she could not feel for, or sympathize with, them,— those whom she best loves,—look coldly on her—regard her as a being of another sphere—incapable of familiar converse—or free intercourse with them —and this too, when she is natural and unaffected— Oh God! that I could write my heart's history here—it would however be but—to write wild words —on dust—with a hand trembling from its own eagerness. Enough—the Omniscient Spirit, which has written on my soul—the characters of life—and truth & beauty—can reveal—at his pleasure—its inmost workings—man could not understand them, though in plain language—they should fall from my lips. . . .

FEB. 14TH. 1840.

Have just heard that the Franklin House is in the process of demolition—and went down to see it. It is a small, three story building—upon the corner of Union and Hanover streets, and although—142 years old—bears no remarkable indications of antiquity— A large wooden ball—hangs from a projecting iron bar—into the middle of the Square—bearing date in gold letters—1698. The tears started to my eyes—as I gazed upon the walls of the very room in which Benjamin—Franklin was born—in 1706— Grateful were the throbs, which agitated my breast, and yet—while I thought of him—so dear to every American heart—the Prometheus of our age—the first in the scientific remembrance of our city, and were it not for Washington I should say—first in my own heart—thoughts of self intruded, and I could not help wondering as

Caroline Healey, age nineteen. Sketch by Alvan Clark.
(Courtesy of Massachusetts Historical Society)

I retraced my steps—if any would ever visit with such devotion—the scene of my birth—my early—joyous life—. There are many—I dare say, who will assert—that none but a conceited fool—could harbor the thought—but what man has done, man may do—and all things are possible with God—if life and health—are spared me—I may reap in the love of ages yet to come—that which my own has denied me. Dryden said of Shadwell—that the most poetical thing about him, was his longing for immortality[24]—perhaps the great progenitor of English composition—might say the same of me—were he now living. And yet—God knows—I do—not seek it, for myself—and gladly would I shelter myself under the first protecting arm—which offered—were it not for—one—.*...

APRIL 27TH. 1840.

... It has always been my custom—to speak what was uppermost—to those whom it most concerned—. Brought up in <u>comparative</u> retirement, I associ-

---

*Healey has later written over "one—" with "my father."

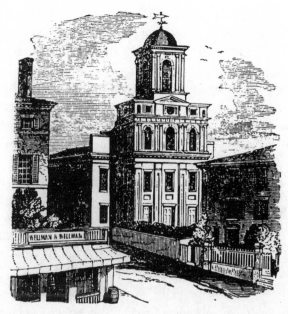

The West Church, Boston, circa 1840, where Caroline Healey was baptized and married.
(Courtesy of Old West Church and the First Methodist Religious Society of Boston)

ated at a very early age with gentlemen far advanced in life,—to whom I spoke
with perfect freedom—and who of course could not in any way—mistake my
motives. As soon as I entered society, the same manner—or rather the same
want of manner—was preserved in my intercourse with younger & less experienced men. I scorned the dissolute—reproved the idle—and cherished the
well meaning <u>stupid</u>; and it is with this that Caroline[25] finds fault, she thinks
it indelicate and forward in a lady—to dictate to, a gentleman—to counsel—to
advise—or shield him. A couple of instances—will suffice—some months ago
—a gentleman—a cousin of Caroline remarked in my presence that he had
gone to church to see the Eldredge girls[26]—who are some fashionable neighbors of Mrs Choate. I had never spoken to this same cousin but once, yet I
turned immediately and said with playful severity—"I am ashamed of you—if
you go to church with no better motive than that—you owe it, to human nature—to present us with a more honorable—"— Yesterday—in returning from
church—I said in Caroline's presence—to a friend[27]—who I was afraid—was
in a fair way to make himself ridiculous—and liable to censure—by rendering
himself rather too conspicuous—"Do not lead—let your companions do so—

and then—if all does not suit them—they will have nothing to complain of."
Both these individuals were young, unmarried men— Caroline would not—
she said—have spoken thus to anyone but a brother— I—would speak—thus
to the <u>whole world</u>— Perhaps as I have no brother*—I have been inclined
—to make myself—a sort of <u>universal sister</u> and am I to believe that I have been
doing wrong? The idea would never have entered my head if it had not been
put there, and now it will only embarrass the utterance of sentiments which
have hitherto been perfectly natural, and disinterested. Embarrass their utterance I say—for I am sure that I shall not be able to keep them to myself. Utterance is characteristic of me—and the world would stare—if Caroline Healey
should hold her tongue—and as to the friend alluded to—he would put on his
spectacles—to see—if, in his near sightedness he had not made a mistake—in
the person—with whom he was walking talking—or arguing—did he not find
himself at the end of every five minutes to all intents and purpose—<u>used up</u> by
a Scotch Blessing! I cannot <u>stop now</u>— I had better never have got into the
scrape—to be sure—but it would [be] as out of character—as the square cap—
of our most honorable—president Quincy[28]—upon the head of an old fash-
ioned jester. . . .

*That is, no brother near her own age; Healey had two younger brothers, aged five and three.

CHAPTER TWO

The Transcendentalist Circle

August 7, 1840–November 4, 1841

*A*s fate would have it, Caroline Healey came of age in Boston at exactly the right moment to reap the intellectual fruits of the Transcendentalist movement. In the fall of 1840, at the age of eighteen, she entered the newly opened West Street bookshop of the remarkable Elizabeth Palmer Peabody. Peabody, an educator, writer, and businesswoman, carried foreign books and periodicals in her store, and her shop accordingly became a gathering place for Boston intellectuals, particularly the Transcendentalists, who devoured English, French, and German literature, philosophy, and theology. That same fall Healey heard lectures by Frederic Henry Hedge, minister and scholar, a central figure in the Transcendental Club (begun in 1836 as an informal gathering of Transcendentalist thinkers), which was sometimes referred to as the Hedge Club.

In the spring of 1841, at Peabody's suggestion, Healey attended a conversation group led by Margaret Fuller, thus sitting at the feet, as it were, of America's foremost woman intellectual. This experience served to acquaint her personally with members of the larger Transcendentalist circle, including Hedge, Ralph Waldo Emerson (whose lectures she had first attended at age twelve), George and Sophia Ripley (on the verge of founding the Utopian community of Brook Farm), Transcendentalist editor and preacher James Freeman Clarke, and several others. Also in 1841, she heard the preaching and later the lectures of Theodore Parker, the Unitarian minister whose liberal views were causing a sensation in Boston and which, she wrote, "startled me . . . into admiration and dread." Parker had a crucial effect on Healey's thinking almost from the beginning, precipitating a struggle within her between the more traditional views espoused by her West Church ministers and the more shocking, iconoclastic religion preached by Parker. Clearly Healey was becoming a Parkerite, though hardly an uncritical one, following him in theology as she would later do in his commitment to reform.

She continued to partake of the immense intellectual banquet that presented itself to her in Boston by reading Emerson's *Essays,* hot off the press in the spring of 1841. At every turn, she found herself confronted by—indeed, she deliberately sought out—Transcendentalist thought (often called "the Newness"). Although Transcendentalists held diverse views, the common denominator was the notion that man could grasp intuitively the highest order of truths, which opposed the Lockean view that the mind developed strictly through sense experiences. Transcendentalist thought was most controversial in its ramifications for understanding the locus of religious authority, in effect placing that locus within the individual rather than in a religious organization or sacred text.

The Transcendentalists served as more than an intellectual stimulus for Caroline Healey. In Elizabeth Peabody, twice her own age at thirty-six, she found a mentor. Peabody was learned, brilliant, enthusiastic, and wonderfully sympathetic to all lost persons and lost causes. For a young woman whose own mother disparaged her every literary endeavor, Peabody was a godsend. She lent Healey her own articles and journal, taught her the basics of Transcendentalism, introduced her to the works of Coleridge and Goethe, read and critiqued Healey's own writing, and advised her on the sort of journal she should keep. She gave Healey serious attention, and Healey responded with gratitude and affection. Margaret Fuller, on the other hand, kept her distance from Healey. Nevertheless, Healey recognized her as a great intellect, and Fuller became her most significant role model. Theodore Parker treated Healey as an equal, thus helping her confirm her sense of the validity of her own thought.

But Healey was not a blind disciple of these charismatic Transcendentalists. She expressed her criticisms of Peabody's untidiness, of Fuller's "want of logic," of Parker's shock tactics, and of Emerson's "unsafe" views. She admired these individuals, but she was hardly overawed by them. When Peabody urged her to make her journal one of thought rather than of feeling, she was dismayed by the criticism, but didn't change her practice of using her journal as an instrument of emotional catharsis. When Peabody chided her for her inappropriate behavior at Fuller's conversations—her boldness, as a young outsider, in participating so freely—Healey refused to concede the point. Even the formidable Fuller, who intimidated almost everyone, did not intimidate Healey.

Although Healey did not have to learn self-confidence from the Transcendentalists—her father had fostered this in her by having her develop and defend her own views—they served in various other ways to mark her growth into the woman she became. Attempting to sort out her place in the world, the adolescent Caroline Healey pondered her options. Just what was the nature of her genius, she wondered in her journal—was it literary, or was it philanthropic? The forces of the larger intellectual world represented by the Transcendentalists, combined with the influences of family, friends, and church, enabled her to attain, eventually, a sense of self.

———————

AUG. 7TH. 1840.

*W*alked to the United States Hotel.[1] I think the gentleman's dining room, here the finest hall I ever entered— The washing apparatus—including cisterns & reservoirs, is very complete. As I returned—went into Elizabeth—Peabody's Book Room[2]— Saw a magnificent illustrated edition of the new translation of the Arabian Nights.[3] My heart felt sick—when I came away,—I longed for once—to have money at my own command—those splendid English Editions of the Classics—how my eyes longed to read them! and Dante Petrarca—& Ariosto[4]—in the finest of Paris print & paper.

AUG. 17. 1840.

Went into Miss Peabody's Book Room—and possessed myself of Plato—Sympathy was never so grateful to me—as to-day and the kindness which offered to lend me—her articles upon the "Spirit of the Hebrew Scriptures,"[5] was duly appreciated I love to hear her talk—to see her smile—although I return from both—amazingly humbled in my own conception— So deep learning—so youthful joyousness so great experience & perfect simplicity I never saw united in one character. She told me much of her early life—of her opportunities—of her progress—& the unfolding of truth—& religion to her view. It repaid me for a great deal to know—that she was willing to teach me. . . .

AUG. 19TH. 1840.

... Read—E. Peabody's Spirit of the Hebrew Scriptures—it is very beautiful—
& satisfies perfectly—many a doubt—which has disturbed my faith. A most
beautiful inference she draws from the story of the intoxicated father & his
sons.[6] I am afraid that I have not felt it my duty—to shelter the faults—my parents have exposed—but I have learnt from those beautiful essays—a well deserved lesson— Oh! how I envy the meteoric genius—which flashes with such
brilliant haste—that my eye—scarce follows in its wake—how I envy—the
knowledge of men & books—which enabled their author to compose them
fourteen years since.

SEPT. 15TH. 1840.

... Saw Miss Peabody yesterday afternoon. She was very kind—spoke highly
of the style in which my articles were written but—the matter was evidently
too sublunary for her.[7] She wished me to keep a journal she said— My homilies were excellent for others—but not severe discipline enough for myself. I
needed self culture—and the journal she proposed—was an efficient means of
that—Not a journal of emotion all—thought—in woman—blushes into feeling—and that she did not wish to cherish—a journal of thoughts—stripped
of all feeling. I am sure I thought of my own journal with dismay—while she
spoke—but there are some excuses for all these things—which Miss Peabody
—does not wot of.

FRIDAY OCT 2. 1840.

Dropped in upon Miss Peabody who is full of the new Dial.* She would dearly
love to make a transcendentalist[8] of me—if she could—but I think she cannot
succeed—common sense—I have—and that is apt to—look upon the specula-
tions of so styled wiser heads as <u>uncommon nonsense</u>.

WEDNESDAY. JAN 27. 1841.

... I will say little <u>here</u> of Mr Hedge's lecture[9]—as an affair of literary merit—.
I only know—that it made me weep—that it stirred up my innermost being
—and urged me anew to action— It is better to wear out than to rust out—
I fully believe—and when I heard him tell of the uncomplaining—nay grateful poverty of Jean Paul Richter—of Schonner who inherited nothing as

---

*The Transcendentalist journal *The Dial* began publication in July 1840, with Margaret Fuller as editor.

he said but his ugly—person—and beautiful wit—of—Fielding—Burns—and Spenser—[10] I hung my head—in shame—that my little trials—ever find a place on my pen—.[11] Yet mine—all those which while they would be nought to man—sever the last chord of harmony in woman's heart—. A loveless life—it seems—to me—that if I had a mother—I could spare all else—! A mother! and have I not one—who nursed my infancy—who loved my early prattle—well! well! let these atone for later deeds—and may God—forgive her—as fully—more fully—if it may be—than I— He said much of following out one's genius—whether for high literary attainment—or practical beneficence—I wish I could define my genius— I think I may write homilies to the end of my life—and yet be mistaken. A third of my time during the last two years has been spent in the abodes of poverty,* and here arises a question of duty, I find it most difficult to answer. I know—that if my sense of responsibility—to God—did not lead me out—into the world—I might become at least a highly cultivated woman—as familiar certainly as others are with the classics of my own country—but I cannot do even this while I aim at so great a degree of practical benevolence—each occupation in its turn—creates a disgust for the other & I am ready to declare—now—that I will be a Howard†—and—anon—a Hannah More—‡Duty lies between—alas! that 18 years have passed without my finding her. . . .

MONDAY. FEB. 15. 1841.

. . . _____ § has taken it into her head, that it is a sin, for me to seclude myself from society, and reproves accordingly. It seems to me that it is perfectly natural and—proper—that I should not like to go, where I am not —appreciated. I am perfectly aware of my own deficiencies, and I yet think that had I craved admiration in my earlier years—I might have been—not only brilliant—but—confessedly so—in a very brilliant circle—.—but I have always been too busy in watching others—in fashionable society, to think much of the effect which I am myself to produce—the noble—blood—which flows in my veins forbids me to pander—to anybody's wishes—. I cannot fawn—I cannot flatter—I cannot—will not—be fawned upon nor flattered, and this severity

---

*Dall's charitable visits among the poor were mostly connected with her Sunday school work.

†John Howard (1726–1790) was an English philanthropist noted as a prison reformer.

‡English author Hannah More (1745–1833) wrote poetry and drama early in her career, then largely turned to religious writing.

§An unidentified friend of Healey's.

leaves me to my own resources—. I think I could be witty without being sarcastic—but I do not like to try— I would rather talk sense—even when I am
conscious that others—are acting like fools on purpose to draw me out. And
who ever knew a gentleman who liked to hear a lady talk sense—? And better
reason still, for my antipathy—I am always—disappointing father, in society—
I think—he would like to have his daughter—something more than sensible
—and a kind of consciousness—of this—makes me more than naturally awkward— Do not imagine thou patient sheet—that—I am—humpbacked—or
cloven footed—no! nature has made me a very decent person—but I want
manner—a something I fancy I shall never acquire in my closet. There are few
large circles—in which I do not find myself out of place—. . . .

*At Elizabeth Peabody's suggestion, Healey became a member of a "conversation"
series on mythology conducted by Margaret Fuller (1810–1850), Transcendentalist editor and future critic, women's rights advocate, and supporter of the
1848 Italian revolution. The discussions took place at the George Ripley home,
Bedford Place, Boston, and later at Elizabeth Peabody's bookstore. This series
was atypical in that it was the only one Fuller conducted that included men.
Among the prominent participants in this series of conversations were the hosts,
George Ripley (1803–1882), minister of the Purchase Street Church (Unitarian), Boston, and member of the Transcendental Club, and his wife, Sophia
Dana Ripley (1803–1861), a partner with her husband in the planning and im-
plementation of the Brook Farm Utopian experiment; former minister and now
author and lecturer Ralph Waldo Emerson (1803–1880); the brilliant Elizabeth
Sherman Hoar (1814–1878) of Concord, engaged to Emerson's brother Charles
before his death in 1836; James Freeman Clarke (1810–1888), Unitarian minister, member of the Transcendental Club, and later a prominent social activist
and literary man as well as religious leader; William Wetmore Story (1819–
1895), who would become a famous sculptor; Transcendentalist minister Frederic Henry Hedge; Elizabeth Peabody; and her sister Sophia Peabody (1809–
1871), engaged to Nathaniel Hawthorne. Healey memorialized her attendance
at these conversations in her published work* Margaret and Her Friends *(1895).*

MAR 1. 1841.

I met with Miss Fuller's class this evening at Mr Ripley's and although I suppose this to be below the average specimen of advance I was delighted. I think

Margaret Fuller was one of the nineteenth century's most brilliant intellectuals and a role model for Caroline Healey, who attended Fuller's conversations when she was eighteen. (Courtesy of Concord Free Public Library)

I never enjoyed an evening so much— Mrs Ripley pleases me more than any woman I ever met—she has not forgotten her body in cultivating her mind[12]— of Miss Fuller—I have not yet made up my mind. She talked exquisitely but more like a woman than I anticipated. There was a want of logic in her conversation—and a want of <u>grammar</u> which last—is a great trial to my ear— I did not come away as I expected—to do—feeling that it would be impossible for me ever to accomplish as much as Miss Fuller— I found [her][13] more agreeable—<u>modest</u>—than I anticipated.

MAR 8. 1841.

I enjoyed my evening at Mr Ripley's again very much—. Miss Fuller is lively and sarcastic in general conversation—of an under size—delicately framed— with rather sharp features, and light hair—. Her head is small—but thrown almost wholly in front of the ears—. Her forehead of a good height, her nose inclining to the Roman and her mouth, thin—and ungraceful—. Her eye is small and gray, but its flash is very vivid, and her laugh is almost child-like. Her manners are reserved but those of one who has seen good society—

We found it very difficult—to appreciate Greek beauty in a Greek way— sufficient proof Miss Fuller thought that no Greek genius could be in the present age—suppose a man—ever so gigantic, she said and he would stand upon a pedestal of Boston instead of Athens—and seems a pigmy in comparison.

MAR. 19. 1841. . . .

Miss Fuller was out of the vein tonight, and although we had Mr Hedge— we had a less pleasant talk than usual. I was very unwell—and as my poor abstract* will probably testify when it is written. Mr Emerson's book is out,[14]—I long to read it, and judge for myself, of its mysticism. . . . .

Healey's mentor Elizabeth Peabody was capable not only of great kindness to those whose interest she took to heart, but also of stinging criticisms of them. The note that Healey reports receiving in this entry was the first of several such letters she would receive from Peabody through the decades, each of them causing her significant emotional trauma.

*Healey kept a record separate from her journal of "abstracts"—that is, summaries—of these conversations. She published them as *Margaret and Her Friends.*

TUESDAY MAR. 23. 1841.

I had a singular note from Miss Peabody this morning, in which she advises me not to speak at Mrs Ripley's—the bulk of those I meet being strangers to me—and the meetings not being intended for conversation so free, as those held in the day—and subjoining an opinion, that I had best refrain from joining in a tête à tête unless particularly requested to do so. The last remark—I forgave her at once—however unfounded the inference to be drawn from it .... And now to the important charge—in the first place she acknowledges that what I said at the last meeting was as good in itself, and as well delivered—as anything—said, there—save by Ralph Emerson, as sufficient proof that she is a little mazed—for can I be expected to converse as well as—Henry Hedge—James—Clarke[15]—Mr Wheeler[16]—William Story[17] or Mr Ripley, and Eliz. Hoare—? In the next place, she says the circle is composed of intimate friends —among whom I am the only stranger—and—that it is not intended for conversation Whatever it is intended—to be—my abstracts bear witness that it is—conversation, and as to my being a stranger there are not half a dozen persons—in the class whom I have not met—before—and who do not know me —far better than Miss Peabody—. My abstracts will witness that I have frequently refrained from speaking when I felt inclined—and that on the 1st evening I did not speak at all. on the second—I spoke twice—and on the third asked two questions as modestly as I knew how.

I wonder that my patience is not threadbare—and that I do not throw these notes & messages back into people's faces—with a bold determination not to heed them. And I suppose that it is the admiration with which I look upon my own philosophy—which reconciles me to the mortification they convey.... If I felt inclined, I might retort upon Miss Peabody in regard to her own dress and manners—which the world admit to be very outré—but my love & admiration for her character is greater than I can express—and—I will forgive even untidy dress—a thing I never could forgive myself....

SUNDAY APRIL 4. 1841....

This afternoon—I felt that I needed a walk very much—and I went to Purchase st. to hear Theodore Parker.[18] His sermon startled me waked me up—into admiration and dread. I felt that talents like his might do what they pleased with me—and yet that upon a common mind, his views would have the worst effect....

The radical Unitarian preacher Theodore Parker. "His sermon
startled me waked me up—into admiration and dread." (Courtesy
of Andover-Harvard Theological Library, Harvard Divinity School)

THURSDAY. APRIL 22. 1841.

On some accounts our meeting tonight* was pleasant. I saw Sophia Peabody's copy of Mr Allston's Lorenzo—& Jessica[19]—also—a pencil sketch of Crawford's Orpheus—.[20] The former Howard has been cleaning, and it looks exceedingly well— The latter I mean to borrow to copy.

Mr Emerson sent Sophia a splendid present of engravings today.[21] They crazed me completely. By the way, at our last meeting—Mrs Farrar[22] was present—a portly lady—looking like a lady bountiful. I have often been laughed at for not allowing a gentleman to arrange my cloak— Martha† says it is very prudish and that if Mrs Farrar had not forbidden it in her Young Ladies Friend —I should never have dreamt of its being improper— Of course that had nothing to do with it—but when I heard Mr Wheeler ask Mrs Farrar if he should not assist her to put on her cloak—I was a little curious to know how she would get off. She threw her head up with considerable dignity saying as she did so— "Thank you—! but I have been so long accustomed to wait upon myself that I find it much the more pleasant way."

FRIDAY APRIL 23. 1841.

As I am too stupid today—to do any thing more important here is a description of my holy of holies.[23] Opposite my low French bed—is my mantel piece —over which hang three pieces from my own pencil—a Psyche—a St Cecilia and a Thalia[24]—beneath these some porcelain bijouterie a few shells—and a pair of gilt candelabras—mounted in white marble. beneath the mantel a small stove juts out—a copy of Domenichino's Sibyl is my fileboard[25]—and the grate itself is filled with mosses, before the Sibyl reposes a cast of fidelity and behind it are some five Chrystals of Sulphur & Quartz, & a few Indian curiosities. On either side the mantel hangs—a Chinese landscape—prized only for the beauty in its coloring. In the recess—beneath the right hand—picture stands my Cabinet of Shells—with a few specimens—conspicuous—beneath that on the left is a neat mahogany bureau—and on that my walnut desk inlaid with ivory. My windows command a fine view of the Harbor—the blind Asylum—the public Square the State House—and the East End of the Common.

---

*Margaret Fuller's conversation group.

†Martha Hubbard Choate (1820–1910), daughter of the widowed Sarah Gardner Fairfield (Mrs. John) Choate, was Caroline Healey's closest friend at this time. See E. O. Jameson, *The Choates in America, 1643–1896* (Boston: A. Mudge & Son, 1896), 213, 321.

They are draperied with white muslin and contain a few pots of plants. Between them is a dressing table—upon which is my Chinese workbox—and over this hangs a mirror—supporting a portrait of Marco Bozzaris—drawn by myself.[26] Opposite the bureau—& between the bed & the window is my wash-stand. Opposite the dressing table—hangs my book case—a low chair is by the side of my bed, and that as well as the other furniture is of clouded maple. A large closet is within my chamber—where I keep my manuscripts my clothes—and all the usual appurtenances of the dressing-room.

    I believe I had a mania for writing this description—but I have also a mania for knowing all things about those of whom I read—which must excuse it. My chamber is a sort of Elysium (to me?)

THURSDAY. MAY 6. 1841.

Succeeded in finding a tolerable bouquet for Miss Fuller—but was not satisfied that there was no—heliotrope—her favorite flower.[27] Got half a dozen little bits—but they were not—what I wanted. I could have wept—easily when we parted—never have I enjoyed any society so much as that of these "reunions"—* I dare not hope—that I may live to see another winter— I dare not hope—that with her Orpheus—I may not ever exclaim—

"Already done is all that he would do."[28]

but away—have I not said that all this shall not be.

THURSDAY JUNE. 3. 1841.

I scribbled all the morning and read Mr Emerson's Essays in the afternoon. That on Compensation is the finest thing upon the subject—which I ever read, ditto to that upon History—but the views advanced in that upon self reliance—are extravagant and unsafe. When I read the Essay upon Friendship, I was moved to find a man—who had gone through the world—feeling—like a girl—under the first development of her passions—for there is a time when friendship is a passion. Martha[29] who listened while I read aloud —thought it very fine— The first sentence of that upon Love—which I have not read—is peculiar— "Each soul is a celestial Venus to every other soul."

---

*This was the tenth and final conversation of the series.

Austin* declares that if Mr Emerson had ever seen his soul—he would not have—written that. But it is essentially the same statement as that of William Story, "that beauty dwells on every brow." . . .

FRIDAY JUNE 11. 1841.

Found Mrs Fairfield[30] and everyone else—in a great state of excitement occasioned by Mr Parker's sermon—.† Defended him wherever I could— and was an infidel for my pains. Gave Elizabeth Peabody to understand that I would rather take no active part—in the discussion but think I shall write an Essay tomorrow—which will bear upon the subject. Mr Parker is so afraid that he shall not be independent enough—that he foolishly says—more than he means—and abstract truths as other people state them—are taking the likeness of the rankest infidelity in his pages. But this alarm is nonsensical—it cannot last. . . .

Healey often attended public exercises at Harvard, commencements and class days. She was personally acquainted with many of the young men who participated, as well as with Harvard professors and their families. Although as a woman she was excluded from a Harvard education, she clearly found no little satisfaction in critiquing the public presentations of her male contemporaries. Her account of this particular commencement exposes a graduate's embarrassing performance and details the social activities "on the green" following the ceremony.

THURSDAY—JULY. 15. 1841.

. . . It is useless to criticize Orne's‡ performance—so disgraceful a failure never occurred in Cambridge. It had neither point nor pretension—the address to woman—was an insult to her name—the speech—concerning the Classics a reproach to the faculty, and the moral tone of the whole oration—

---

*Austin Kuhn (1824–1844), son of George H. and Martha Frost Kuhn, a Harvard student in whom Caroline Healey took a great, and probably romantic, interest (*NEHGR* 51:445–446).

†Theodore Parker's controversial sermon, *A Discourse on the Transient and Permanent in Christianity* (known also as his South Boston sermon), preached on May 19, 1841, at the ordination of Charles C. Shackford at the Hawes Place Church in South Boston.

‡William Henry Orne (d. 1842), member of the graduating class at Harvard, from Concordia Parish, Louisiana.

disgusting hypocrisy. Orne's father arrived last night to hear his son's oration —just as he was borne home—senseless from a drunken revel—. A pleasant greeting to a parent truly—. Judge Orne sat up with him all night bathing his head & applying restoratives—and this was the result—. He drank in the course of his oration a pitcher of water which it would have given me real delight to have broken—. He could not remember of course—and in attempting to read—invariably lost his place—which error—he corrected—by the indelicacy of drinking in the presence of the audience. Worse & worse was the order of every sentence and the Class listened in silent agony. The Faculty and Dr Walker[31]—among them—were convulsed with laughter. . . . We found a large collection on the green—Sarah Johnson—danced without her hat—and if observed—seemed quite comfortable—. The Feltons[32]—Reeds[33]—and—Whitneys[34] I saw as also Prof. Bowen[35] & Jones Very,[36] to both of whom I wished to speak but had not opportunity. Orne—too much excited to dance with composure—was lolling round in every set. His mother fronted him once— and I really pitied her— . . . The pleasantest item, in the afternoon's experience was an introduction to Dr Walker—with whom I had a few moments chat—doing myself—of course great injustice—by making an effort. If I revere a man on the face of the earth, I revere him—to Austin he is a sort of guiding star. Dr Wyman[37]—seemed to enjoy the dancing and to be amused at the flirtation—which was going on—quite as much as the rest of us—. Mr Babcock[38] who was chaplain of the Class—asked me to dance but I was not well enough. His face is very beautiful at times—once this afternoon it glowed with surpassing radiance—. . . . After the dance the procession formed—and when the buildings had been cheered as usual—the dance round the tree to the tune of Yankee Doodle—had—revived every body's sinking spirits, the Professors— & tutors had been cheered—Wheeler excepted—there was a loud hurrah for the expelled students and for the bravo—who would not betray his class.— . . .

SATURDAY SEPT. 11. 1841.

. . . I do not wish—to be known as a Sabbath School Teacher—so much as a literary woman—not that I do not appreciate the privilege—but that I would rather draw attention towards myself by my own merits as well as by those of my cause. . . .

Healey was deeply attached to the ministers at the West Church, Charles Lowell and his junior colleague Cyrus Bartol, as well as Bartol's wife, Elizabeth

*Howard Bartol, and numerous other friends. Increasingly, though, she found
herself pulled between these old loyalties and the radical ideas of Theodore
Parker, whose series of five public lectures on religion (published in 1842 as Dis-*
course of Matters Pertaining to Religion) *she was attending. Parker's position
on the authority of the Bible made him the subject of increasing public debate.
Healey found Parker's views persuasive, yet she resisted cutting herself off from
her West Church family.*

WEDNESDAY OCT 27. 1841.

I went this afternoon to the sewing circle where Dr Lowell and Mr Bartol[39]
—both met us. I talked with Charlotte[40] about Mr Parker's lectures—and
thought he could say nothing with which I should not perfectly agree. I told
her how these thoughts had been in me from my infancy and had never found
the expression they wanted. This evening I have attended another lecture—it
was upon the Bible— In as far—as he spoke concerning the old Testament,
I perfectly sympathized in every word he said—but when he came to the New
—and I found that I must reject the miracles in toto—I rather shrank—Not
while—he spoke—for the richness of his voice—as he pursued his arguments
—did not so much persuade—me—as the likeness to my own thoughts ever
presented— I believed him then—notwithstanding James Fisher's[41] earnestness—and Mr Mosely's whisper every now and then— "then beginning at
Moses and the prophets he expounded unto them."[42]—but when I came
home—and sat down to talk—with them—, with Henry Hudson[43] and Miss
Taylor—and saw how much it involved—my reason nearly gave way under the
struggle— I knew that God must see my—earnestness— I felt with Theodore
Parker—that this view—did not—detract from the beauty of Christ's character—that on the contrary it involved more in him—than—the wisest Divines
had ever drawn out of him—that the Bible would not pass away in his day or
mine—and I did not know—how to discriminate fairly between the transient
and the permanent. I had seen Mr Parker making a great effort to speak what
he believed to be the truth the perspiration starting to his forehead—and his
limbs trembling as he said that he spoke—"well knowing what it meant—"
what would close the door of every pulpit in our land—against him—rob
him of his brother's heart—put his hand against every man's and every man's
hand against him— I had loved him for his independence—and I wondered
if I too—could do this— I saw—that from—Martha—the Bartols, Horatia[44]
—<u>Austin</u>—this new faith must separate me forever—could I bear the <u>last</u>? I

feared not—and when I went to sleep—I prayed earnestly—for truth faith and power. The same prayer was in Sarah's[45] heart—and we spoke it together. I felt—that fifty years hence—Mr Parker's might be among Unitarians the only recognized view of Scripture and Christianity—<u>he</u> had said so—he said that we might put it off until tomorrow—but the offence must come—and woe! unto the man by whom—.[46]

THURSDAY NOV. 4. 1841.

Heard Mr Parker's last lecture—last night—and have been stronger abler ever —since. I think that if I lived in the atmosphere of such a life as his—I should be always right, why may I not live in Jesus' life— I resolved as he showed me how false and degrading our position as he appealed more and more strongly to the consciousness—within that I would live the divine life—that the energy of God should be in me—and carry me through—but with this morning's early rising came a sinking—it shall not be—however—from—this day—I will strive to renounce the weaknesses—and answer the cries of my heart. The poverty of life—I felt—while he spoke most deeply—and I wondered why I had consented, but a few hours before—to waste a day at least in preparing for a ball—.

CHAPTER THREE

From Heiress Apparent
to Independent Woman

November 10, 1841–September 8, 1842

$\mathcal{I}$n November 1841 Caroline Healey, who had experienced various teenage crushes, began to fall in love with a man who might well have been the sort of husband she needed. Samuel F. Haven was the librarian, in effect the executive director, of the American Antiquarian Society in Worcester, Massachusetts. Healey met him there while visiting family and friends. A scholar and a former practicing lawyer, Haven had been widowed five years earlier and had a ten-year-old son. When he and Healey met, she was nineteen and he thirty-five, intelligent, witty, debonair, and well established in his position, which he continued to hold until his death forty years later. Caroline Healey seems to have been something of a sensation in Worcester; her host joked that, when she went about town, he desired her to "inform the town that I came from their house, as they wished all possible credit," and Haven himself introduced her to a friend as "a natural curiosity a lady transcendentalist and loco foco." Haven commanded Healey's respect in a way that the young men with whom she associated in Boston and Cambridge, and whom she tended to "mother," did not. He was a Whig and she a Democrat, he apparently a conservative Unitarian and she a Parkerite Transcendentalist. With good humor they sparred over many issues. She befriended his son, Haven visited her in Boston, and for months they corresponded steadily.

But two tragedies interrupted what was beginning to look like a courtship headed toward marriage. The sudden death of Caroline's five-year-old brother, Charlie, from complications of scarlet fever, for a time commanded all of Healey's emotional energies. Charlie's death served also to help illuminate family dynamics. It was Caroline who took charge after the death, notified relatives, planned the funeral, tended to her mother, and tried to keep painful reminders of Charlie out of sight of her father. And, to her surprise, the tragedy produced, if ever so fleetingly, a sign of affection from her mother: "for the first time that I can remember—beside my dead brother's body, my mother pressed my cheek in love—."

After Charlie's death, life gradually returned to a more ordinary routine in the Healey household. Caroline had a sketch done of herself; she attended Emerson's lectures and initiated a long correspondence and friendship with Theodore Parker. Bravely, she declared herself to a West Church Bible class as a follower of Parker, fully expecting that the action would alienate her from her friends and pastors there. But she had much underestimated the tolerance of pastors Lowell and Bartol, who remained father figures for her as long as they lived.

In the spring of 1842, Caroline began to notice strange behavior on her father's part. To her puzzlement he suddenly began refusing her requests for money for the most minor purchases. The truth, which she soon learned, was that Mark Healey's financial world was collapsing. Like many other businessmen, in the wake of the Panic of 1837, he had managed to stay solvent for only a short time. By June of 1842 he faced bankruptcy. Once Caroline understood the situation, she immediately devised a plan of action: she would find work, perhaps as a teacher, and contribute her earnings to the family coffers. She energetically wrote letters, made calls, used all her connections in order to find a job. These efforts mortified her nearest sister, Ellen, who threatened that if Caroline were indeed to become a schoolteacher she would hire herself out as a chambermaid. But Mark Healey had no such class-conscious objection to his daughter's taking a paying job, and Caroline continued her search. Eventually she was successful, securing a position at a highly regarded school for young ladies in Georgetown, at the time an independent city in the District of Columbia. When she learned that her father intended to remove his other children from school, Caroline objected strongly, successfully arguing that if she worked to earn money, it was to be used to educate her siblings.

Samuel Haven's reaction to the news of her father's failure did not please Caroline. He at first minimized the seriousness of the situation, and preached that adversity was good for the soul. In any case, he couldn't see that the situation required action on her part. The tone of his letters shifted from slightly flirtatious to paternalistic. The change was not lost on her.

But the financial crisis and Healey's response to it had another and more favorable result: expressions of love and sympathy from her mother. Unable to believe even then that her mother had actually loved her in the past, Caroline wrote, "I am glad that now when I am like to need it, she is beginning to love me."

On September 8, 1842, Caroline Healey took leave of her family and friends and left for Georgetown, going by rail as far as Albany. She was saddened when Samuel Haven did not appear at the stopover in Worcester. And thus she continued her journey as "that loneliest of lonely things, an independent woman," comforting herself that "He who knows all—knew best."

In November of 1841, Healey was visiting relatives and friends in Worcester, some forty miles west of Boston. There she was fascinated by the American Antiquarian Society, incorporated in 1812 as an organization to collect and preserve American antiquities, and by its librarian, Samuel Foster Haven.

WEDNESDAY. NOV. 10. 1841. [WORCESTER, MASS.] . . .
*M*aria* had sent word to Mr Haven[1] that she would like him to go to the Hospital[2] with us in the afternoon and at two o'clock he came—, I like him very much—full of life and spirit—yet of disinterested kindness—. . .

As we came home—I was lured into the Antiquarian rooms[3]—having a discussion with Mr Haven on faith—. I could hardly say what interested me—most—here—there were many things—perhaps, the old pictures and engravings the Library and—the <u>Librarian</u>. There were Cotton Mather's desk[4]—the old looking glass and the picture of the Antiquary[5]—there were—but why catalogue what will not interest my readers—and what I have scarcely yet seen? This evening we spent at home— Mr Haven came in—and—I knitted—my purse as busily as possible—.

THURSDAY NOV. 11. 1841.
This morning I believe—I practised,[6] wrote letters—and withal started early for the Antiquarian Rooms—. I spent my morning here—Mr Haven's kind-

*Maria Foster (1807–1856) was Caroline's aunt, her mother's half-sister. See Frederick Clifton Pierce, *Foster Genealogy* (Chicago: F. C. Pierce, 1899), 284.

*Samuel F. Haven, librarian, American Antiquarian Society,
and an early suitor to Caroline Healey. (Courtesy of Stephen D. Pratt)*

ness exceeding every reasonable expectation—.... when we returned we went for a moment to Miss Prescott's and then to the Antiquarian Hall—where Maria wished to show me some—letters of Lucretia Bancroft—and Mrs Jo' Willard.[7] Mr Haven provided us with two large volumes of autographs—they were part of the Library Wm Lincoln has—given—to the Society—and were left him by Mr Baldwin.[8] I saw letters from every body under the sun—and got very much interested in them. Lucretia Bancroft's were best worth reading— but she uses—bold language—not shrinking from naming his Satanic majesty as often as I could wish— Mr Haven was copying my abstracts[9]—which I loaned him the other night. He looked for an autograph of John Quincy Adams[10]—which he did not find for me—and promised—to call for us to go to the Union Church to hear the first Lyceum lecture. We heard in the beginning a stupid preamble from Mr Kinnicutt[11] about the resources of the institution—and then an equally stupid lecture it seemed to me—from some one —whom—Mr Kinnicutt introduced as the <u>Hon</u> Richard H. Dana[12]—whereat the <u>Honorable</u>—laughed in his face. It lasted two hours—was upon the influence of literature on mind—and the converse—. Diffuse—illogical—and unnecessarily spun—out if that means—more than diffuse—it was. It told me nothing I did not know—before—and dilated upon truisms as if they were newly started problems—. Mr Haven & I agreed about it— Maria gave it extravagant praise—. I saw John Davis—and Lucretia Bancroft[13] after the lecture—and they seemed to feel as I did—. Mr H. introduced me to the latter—as a natural curiosity a lady transcendentalist and loco foco[14]—the former I disclaimed but she said she had no doubt there was some truth in the remark. . . .

Having returned to Boston, Healey wrote a long letter to Theodore Parker, expressing her general agreement with his positions, but criticizing what she considered his shock tactics in presenting them. Parker responded in such a way as to cement their relationship for life, taking her seriously and treating her as an equal.

SUNDAY DEC. 5. 1841. . . .

I had today the kindest of letters from Theodore Parker[15]—how nobly he writes—of himself—how humbly he submits to my arrogant rebuke—and as if I were in every respect as well fitted to judge as he: tells me frankly the motive for his conduct—and deigns to defend it— Let no one tell me of his self conceit— I love him better than ever—more truly and dearly than I ever loved any one of whom I knew so little. In regard to the argumentative part of his letter, I am no—better satisfied than I was before—he seems—to rest as I do—confident of two things which seem to oppose each other—.

WEDNESDAY DEC. 8. 1841.

I wrote pretty steadily through the morning—but Charlie* was taken very sick, in the night, and I felt anxious about him. I had engaged to go to Mrs Choate's to tea,—to meet Mr Farnsworth[16]—but begged mother to let me stay at home— She would not consent, and after going to Anna's[17] and carrying Mr Parker's letter to Elizabeth Peabody to read, I went over—Elizabeth had told me, that Mr Haven was in—for a bundle—in the morning and had returned to Worcester this afternoon—so feeling secure that he would not come

---

*Charles Wells Healey (1836–1841), Caroline's five-year-old brother.

—I neglected the pasteboard which I had thought of—for Foster's* flowers—
and began to read my letter to Martha— I was hardly seated—before Anna &
Georgy†—came to say that Mr Haven was at our house—.... Martha remonstrated—but I was deaf to all that— I went as quickly as anybody could—and
was richly repaid—for doing so. He staid to tea—and until nine—.... He said
when he left me—that I should hear from him— "I will write—" he said in a
low voice when I asked him how soon he would come again and he added in
the "face of the congregation—" that I must not be surprised if I received some
poetry from Worcester—. I told him calmly that I hoped it would be poetry
and not rhyme—and wondered at myself for saying so—after I turned away.
At nine,—I went over to Martha's and apologized to Mr Farnsworth—
for running away—but I left—Charlie so ill—that I took little comfort— I
should scarcely have enjoyed so highly Mr Haven's visit had I known—of it—
before—.

THURSDAY DEC. 9. 1841.

Charlie is much worse. His is the most violent case which Dr Warren[18] has
had this season—. He has been raving all day, a physician four times— Mr Parker came to see me—this evening— I was so distressed by other thoughts that
I hardly—remember a syllable he said—and am sure—that my conversation
could not do me justice. I went in the evening to Mr Emerson's lecture—[19] I
would have staid at home, but father said go— I enjoyed and remembered
—little—. It was upon Conservatism and Reform—....

FRIDAY. DEC. 10. 1841.

Little rest for any of us, Charlie's screams—filled the whole house, last
night—, the Doctor who came early spoke anxiously—....

SATURDAY DEC. 11. 1841.

Last night, Dr Warren came in late and ordered nine new applications for
Charlie—. I found that fatigued as she was—mother gained new wakefulness
—in prospect of this increase of labor. She seemed to think it impossible that
he should die when she was doing so much for him—.... the Doctor came in

*Samuel Foster Haven (1831–1862), known as Foster, was the ten-year-old son of Samuel Foster Haven.
He graduated from Harvard in 1852 and from the Boston Medical College in 1855. As a physician in the
Union army, he died of wounds suffered at Fredericksburg (*NEHGR* 17:176).

†Caroline's sister Anna Wells Healey (1832–1897) and her brother George.

Ralph Waldo Emerson, 1857, from a drawing by Samuel K. Rowse.
(Courtesy of Andover-Harvard Theological Library, Harvard Divinity School)

at ten—he said that his orders thus far were well executed,—I did not ask any questions— I knew that no physician ever gave so many orders—unless confident that none would be of much avail— Of one thing I felt sure—Charlie had been blind all day—his little hand frequently strove to brush the cloud from before his eyes—and I thought them distorted— Dr Warren ordered his hair cut close and tincture of flies to be applied—. I did not see that he feared water on the brain. During his illness Charlie had seemed much changed— I should not have known—him out of my own house— I left him in great distress at eleven and tried to rest, father too—went up stairs, and worn out with watching and anxiety—threw himself upon the bed. I was so fatigued—that in spite of myself, I sank to sleep—at a few minutes before one—mother called me—father had gone for the Doctor—and Aunt Anne[20] thought there was a great change— I put on my wrapper—and went down—. It was indeed—a change—my blessed brother lay in perfect quiet—no longer throwing himself violently from one side to the other—his breath—came short and distinct at regular intervals— His eyes and mouth were open—he looked more like Charlie—but I knew the approach of death—. By degrees—there were longer intervals between the pulses—at ten minutes past one—I screamed in agony —"Oh—mother—they will be too late—." at a quarter past—his next and last breath was drawn—. I heard father's step upon the stairs—mother said—"He is gone!—" I folded him in my arms as he entered. "Oh! father! this will be hard for you and I to bear—!" "We must bear it patiently my child—" was his reply and I felt a hot tear upon my cheek which was not mine—. He threw himself upon the bed—and tried to recall his child's life— The Doctor's step—now made itself heard upon the stairs— I met him in the entry— "It is too late— sir—" he started and I returned with him to the bedside—. He gave his verdict "water on the brain—" and praising the child's loveliness departed—. I assisted Aunt Anne and Mrs Tucker—in laying out his little body— I wanted socks for his feet—mother burst into tears—and went to get them. She brought me one—fitting size for father. I moved—to change it—but she saw her mistake and brought a pair—father lifted Charlie's little mattress in his arms—and carried it to the upper room. Mrs Tucker lay beside the body. I left father & mother alone—and lay down—but my eyes would not close— All love— all life—went from me with him my cherished one—. I recalled his beauty— my own anticipations—all the bright thoughts connected with him—but tears would not flow— At five o'clock I rose and dressing by candle-light—wrote a

few lines to Worcester, desiring grandmother's[21] immediate presence—....
At about six—I heard the wail—which rose from the nursery—as mother
communicated the sad news— "The inward feeling of tears" swelled my heart
— I hurried to the chamber where Charlie lay—removed the weights from
his soft eyes—and lingered by all that remained of what I had so loved—. After breakfast mother was taken very ill—... Mother soon went to bed—and I
nursed her as carefully as possible— Martha soon came in—and after a sad
conference took my orders—. Friends poured in—our affliction had already
one use—it revealed to us a multitude of kind hearts of which we had known
nothing. Charlie was a public loss—all mourned with us—. I retired to my
room—to write family letters—so different from those I had so lately written.
Mother continued very ill throughout the day. I gave the orders for Charlie's
robe—, and when at night—the coffin came—I went up—with Mrs Tucker
while she arranged it—and combed the golden curl over his forehead— I bore
it all—ay! even the low laugh of the undertaker—at some misfit—in the coffin
screw—. I wrote to the ministers—prepared the inscription for the plate—and
thanked God that he gave me strength. We laid Charlie in his coffin—and I
gathered the robe about his little feet while father untied the bandage about
the head— A slight souvenir—of him—was now to be perceived—and my eye
caught the little scar—distinct in death—of the wound which I had so often
dressed.... I have borne twenty or thirty calls today—and the sight at every
step of something that he loved— First in the morning—the bust of Louis
Philippe which I brought him from the Joinville Ball—,[22] struck my eye—and
then came his teacher with the book and slate—his little hands had pressed on
Tuesday— It seemed more—hard—to bear—with every passing moment—
and I put them where father's eye might not see them.

MONDAY DEC. 13. 1841.

The stern fixedness—again today—would to God—that I had wept last night
—... The bell has done nothing but ring since we got up—it is hard to sit
like a statue—while successively—indifferent people pass by—and try to feel
for you—.

THURSDAY. DEC. 30. 1841.

...I heard—Ralph Emerson—tonight—on "Manners"[23] and was a little better pleased than on last Thursday—. I liked his idea of courtesy—and fash-

ion—but think he loses the fruit of his teaching from his want of system—. What a noble Ideal one could make from fragments of Messrs Emerson & Haven—well cemented—with Liberality.

FRIDAY. DEC. 31.ST. 1841.

... The unuttered prayers of sixteen years—have accumulated within me —and now—I cry out—for love—"give me back what I have been giving to thee—" is my demand upon the Universe—of course unanswered. ... As I look back and see to how many diverse oddities I have been inclined—I thank God, who has spared me from any meanness or manoeuvre— I thanked him—when for the first time that I can remember—beside my dead brother's body, my mother pressed my cheek in love—. That kiss to me—was worth all the agony of his death—at least it would have been—if it had presaged a lasting result—but it is all over. Mother is as she was—not chastened—not loving.

MONDAY. FEB. 7. 1842.

I laid awake a long time last night, in the hope that pleasant remembrances might so fill my brain—that I should sleep quietly, but it was not so. I dreamt of once more laying out dead bodies—of once more arranging a funeral—and in one connected story—my grief seemed to fill the whole night. It was not one darling, petted brother but three sisters—who now claimed from me the last care— For each of these, as for him, I seemed to be the only mourner. I woke to pleasanter thoughts of S.* but these were broken in upon by a letter from Theodore Parker which brought me back to Charlie. ...

When Caroline's father bought her a ticket to her first lecture series, when she was twelve, he required that she write a summary or "abstract" of each lecture. She continued the practice, and made careful summaries of Dr. James Walker's lectures on Natural Religion. To accompany a package of these abstracts sent to Samuel Haven and other friends in Worcester, Healey composed a playful poem, complete with German accent (a nod to the German origins of some aspects of American Transcendentalism), in which she cited the respected Walker as a defender of the doctrine of innate ideas.

*Probably Samuel Haven.

MONDAY. FEB. 14. 1842.

Sat thinking that my <u>last</u> package of Abstracts would go to Worcester this week,[24] and produced the following original on the occasion.

To the people who wont believe in anything they don't see—and who cherish "good old definite Mr Locke—"[25] beyond their own souls.

————————"————————

I hopes you is conwinced folks
That "good old Mr Locke"
Is not the visest shepherd
That ever led a flock—

I hopes you is conwinced, folks,
That there is "innate idears"
And 'gin to trust yer "inner lights"
Without perwoking fears—

I hopes you is conwinced folks
The Doctor's vise as I,
That <u>he</u> trusts intuitions, too,
Nor calls his soul a lie—

I hopes you is conwinced folks
And vill bother us no more
Vith logic that <u>ve</u> can't digest
And metaphysik lore—.

I hopes you is conwinced folks,
How tedious 'll be the time,
Ven days roll on—unLeonarded—
Vith packages of mine.

I hopes you doesn't think folks—
That this is meant for rhyme
I never—made that veak mistake
But once in auld lang syne—

> But I guess my vords, will jingle folks
> As well upon the whole—
> As the spirit of these verses—fits—
> My really saddened soul—
>
> I never enwies "Straws" folks
> Ven I judge his lot—by mine
> And think that all his jesting
> Is but a <u>dreamy</u> sign—
>
> And Dreams—goes by contraries folks—
> As Rory, used to say—
> So ven you vake—to rosy clouds—
> Expect a stormy day—.

MONDAY, APRIL 11. 1842.

I wonder if any body in town would believe me, if I were to say, that I have been waiting for a fortnight for paper—upon which to write—and have not yet got any. I asked father for some money for the third time today, and got the usual answer, that he had only enough to get his dinner—that he could not afford to buy anything but necessaries.[26] I wonder if the two boxes of oranges—the boxes of lemons and—raisins sent home last week, were necessaries—! My father must be insane, I cannot otherwise excuse what he does of late,— I will not dwell on the past, but I have to struggle now—for paper pens and ink—...

SUNDAY APRIL 17. 1842.

... At the Bible Class—tonight I struck my own death blow— God forgive me the suicide—at all events—I feel happier now that I have candidly confessed my faith—candidly owned that I am—a humanitarian—a disciple of Theodore Parker's in part—a more venturesome—thinker in part. I gave my own view of Christ's character mission & death— I considered his miracles—as the manifestation of the power of spirit over matter which was natural to highly pure spirits—a power enhanced in proportion as Christ—came near the purity of God. Any man—equally faithful—and this I thought possible—might work miracles.— I did not believe in the story of his birth, I considered him the child of Joseph & Mary. Of course, I met, with no sympathy except from Charlotte[27]—and my dear Judith[28] and very unexpectedly from Miss Robinson. I suppose that some of the elderly ladies to whom it was all—alpha & omega—will report me to Dr Lowell—& Mr Bartol—and then,—Thank God, I <u>fear</u> no result—if I have not told them all—I have never concealed any thing from them. I would not force upon them, a state of mind which might give them pain. . . . I spoke long—but I was not aware how earnestly until, as I came out—I heard—the class confessing on all sides, that it had been struck dumb—by my <u>eloquence</u>! I prayed eloquently when I got home for strength to Justify the Truth I had confessed. I prayed that all thought of earthly joy, might be laid aside and that my faith might henceforth see the silver lining on the cloud—that Horatia[29] might no more reproach God's truth with the errors of my wilfulness. There is one, who has lived truly—if I have not.

Healey and Elizabeth Peabody had in common an interest in Samuel Haven's son Foster, whom the Peabodys had cared for during and following his mother's fatal illness. In the following entry, Elizabeth entertains Healey with an account of her sister Sophia, who would marry Nathaniel Hawthorne within a few months. The Hawthornes were preparing to rent the Old Manse in Concord as their first home. Elizabeth and her other sister, Mary Tyler Peabody (1806– 1887), marveled at Sophia's sense of sumptuousness in what were actually very modest circumstances.

THURSDAY MAY 19. 1842.

. . . I went in to see Elizabeth Peabody—she promised again to show me Foster's* picture—and then went into raptures about Sophia and Nat. Hawthorne. "All things are relative," said she "as I and Mary remarked afterward. Sophia had been to Concord and seen all her rooms and came home to calculate the expense of furnishing them— She thought she could do it, simply, and prettily for $300.—there was a little room, with a fine light, which she thought, she could fit up for a painting room—and in the excess of her delight at this she exclaimed—"Oh! how—sumptuously I am fitted out." Mary and I laughed at this expression and Mary said that she thought it expressed the greatest wealth—of nature, which possibly could be under the circum-

---

*Foster Haven. Peabody and her family were friends of Samuel Haven's late wife, Lydia Sears Haven (1811?–1836), and had cared for Foster for a time after her death.

stances." I enjoyed Elizabeth's anecdote, and grieved that there was so little "wealth of nature" or the appreciation of it, in my own family. It brought me, as I walked home to my own destiny, and its probable working, I asked—myself anew—whether I could be—conceited, crazed, lovesick, or visionary— could it be true that I had no reason to believe my affection returned—? That the question arose—expresses that there was a little doubt in my own mind, but farther than the mere questions I could not get— I had as firm faith in my cousin's* affection as I had in my own existence; I could not say how I came by it—he has certainly spoken no word—of direct meaning—, but a thousand things come to me as proof—which,—cannot be spoken—scarcely thought for the second time without losing their beauty; I could not blame him, were I never to hear his voice nor see his hand again—and yet this were the last thing I could expect.

. . . I went this afternoon to Alvan Clark[30]—to engage him to sketch my face—being determined to have it done, before I was more ill. I think I should scarcely have felt so decided about it, had it not occurred to me—that <u>he</u> might sometime value it. . . .

TUESDAY MAY 24. 1842. . . .

Father took the revelation of Mr Clarke's sketch, quite calmly— It has been presented to several persons oddly enough, among these Dr Lowell—the Cunninghams and Parkers[31] all of whom knew it directly. Horatia Weare to whom I carried it—was perfectly delighted. "It looks like a high calm soul—" said she—"such as you were—not ruffled as you have been of late— Such a head and face would take my fancy anywhere, if I knew nothing of their original—" Elizabeth Peabody says, "the air is very like yours—but the mouth not so good"— This is the common complaint—my upper lip—curls—considerably, it has the Greek shortness; in this sketch it is "long drawn out" which father thinks a great mistake.

I am curious now to know what Mr Haven will think of it. I should not wonder if he were more critical than anybody, for he has a good deal of taste for drawing—I do not mean for execution—for of that I know nothing—but his most common remarks on a landscape or a person—indicate that he carries the "right line" in his eye.

*Samuel Haven.

I have been reading Madame d'Arblay's Journal,[32] and am exceedingly interested in it. Although a great part of it is written to friends—an occasional folly
reconciles me to mine. I almost despise her—for remaining in the presence
of all the flattery she received, and yet with what simple naivete she escapes
from it. I hate Dr Johnson[33] worse than ever, the great literary bear—thank
Heaven—left no cubs. I think I should enjoy Miss Burney's Diary more if
no one had seen it, during her life time—it is not so emotive—as this silly
thing—. God spare the world such another. Why do we hanker after Diaries?
But enough—I am going to write to Mr Haven about this book one of these
days. . . .

An hour after I should have been asleep last night, I crept down stairs and
found father's lamp still burning—. This morning he looked miserably, I felt
more disturbed than I can express, when we met at the breakfast table. Father
came to church which he had said he should not do—this morning . . . When
I returned from Sabbath School in the afternoon—I found Mr Howland[34]
with father—and the earnestness with which he wrung my hand—told me all.
There is bankruptcy in prospect of that I am certain—. He did not go until
six o'clock—and then father began to walk the room—with heavy and rapid
strides— He walked until my nerves were shattered by the echo of his step—
and then I rose—and throwing my arms about him walked by his side until
fairly <u>spent</u>. He took no notice—he did not pass his arm about me, I felt that I
was an incubus—, and could have wept bitterly. He shivered, as at the touch
of ice, and unable to master his emotion—farther—finally left the house— . . .

. . . I did my few errands and hurried home—staying longest at Elizabeth
Peabody's, to look at Sophia's furniture.[35] She showed it to me herself—explaining the beautiful designs upon her chairs taken from the life of Pene-
lope[36]—the return of Aneas[37] & so on— Her toilet table—is ornamented with
a Venus—attired by the Graces—& Persuasion—. On one part of her wash-
stand—was Neptune—on the other the effect of purification—Venus—rising
from the waves. On her bedstead—was Guido's Night—and his day break
—Aurora—lighting up the East with her torch the morning star—above—

and Apollo with his courses—and retinue.[38] . . . Thank God that[39] Mr Haven wrote me a line—to tell me how much he was surprised, at this sudden move —it saved me from delirium, I believe to see his "truly thine"—close the sheet.[40] . . .

TUESDAY. JUNE 14. 1842.

. . . Chs. G. Loring[41] was here all last evening. Nothing will be known till next week—father wishes to settle all outstanding bills this [week]. My own plans are already laid. I have talked with mother— Sitting down at my desk this morning—I grew so sad for father's sake, that I went away to pray, perfectly calm—I soon became—& mother opened the door, She was full of errands— said that father said he had found his property depreciated $150,000 the past year—& thought it best to settle now. I said "my dear mother you must not let me see you so sad— I am able to support myself and partly to support you— Wealth I have never abused— God knows I never willingly wasted a moment or a copper— I have been faithful to my friends—and if I am surrounded by the false it is time I knew—it— Nothing will bring tears to my eyes but see-ing them in yours— I must give up playing the invalid—and go to work." Mother wept bitterly—but I consoled her— I told her that I had been told fre-quently that I was an heiress—but I never thought it true, and had no "expec-tations—" to conquer. . . . I shall not be able to send Emily Whitney a cap for her baby[42]—nor Sophia Peabody a bunch of flowers, in season for her wed-ding— I cannot relieve Mrs Freeman—[43] nor have as much stationery as I want. This last is a cut—. . . .

WEDNESDAY. JUNE 15. 1842.

Uncle Charles[44] came, early, this morning, but father was quite worn out with expectation—, he slept little last night—and I could bear the sight of his anx-ious face no longer—so when I had poured out Charles's coffee—I ran up stairs, and wrote him a letter[45]— I finished & copied it before their confab ended—and threw it into his hat. My hand trembled so, that it was with dif-ficulty I could command it—. About half an hour afterward—mother came upstairs—in great distress. "Where did your father get that paper—?" said she— "What paper?" "That which he is reading—he is crying over it like a child?" "I suspect it is a letter of mine—" I replied— "I was afraid some one had brought him bad news—" she returned, & hurried away. Father did not allude to it to me, Mr Howland came to dinner. In the afternoon, I went after some of the small bills, which I find the tradespeople very unwilling to send in. I did not forget the poor. I went beside to Mannie Smith,[46] and inquired into a teacher's salary,—and asked her, to ask Mrs Sears[47]—and Mrs Ritchie[48]—if either of them would be glad of a private teacher or if they knew of any one who would. I spoke of myself as of another person—without suspicion—. I did think that I was capable of earning $500, but found after talking with Mannie, that I must reduce my pretensions to $300.— I do not expect to get a situation of any sort until September—and shall not feel very much distressed although disappointed—if I do not ere January. . . .

SATURDAY. JUNE 18. 1842.

Father told me this morning that he did not come last night, to that conclusion with his creditors which he desired, and upon my asking who they were—handed me a list of his debts. I <u>was</u> surprised by the names of his creditors —they were not, those of our first merchants, but generally those of mediocre —importers. The claims against him amounted in all, to $655,140.00. My father says that he does not wish to go into bankruptcy—because he knows that he has more than property enough to pay his debts—if he be allowed to manage it, himself—still we were liable to a visit from an officer, at any time after breakfast—to attach our furniture, and he would send up from the bank—for—the silver. John E. Thayer is the refractory creditor,[49] and I would rather be my father than him. There was no attachment—. . .

SUNDAY. JUNE 19. 1842. . . .

[At Sabbath School] Martha said when she came in, "I think you are a wonder to be here this morning—" Horatia turned quickly saying—"But I always expect Caroline Healey to be great in emergencies" Shall I always have greatness enough in me, to repay such noble faith. Augustus[50] was very much surprised. Martha seemed quite troubled, until others dispersed—and then said —"Just tell me one thing—Do you consider Mr Haven—as anything <u>more</u> than a common friend?" "Yes!" replied I, "a very uncommon one. I hope you do not misunderstand me—" I added as I saw her eye brighten—"I have no claim upon him—we are very dear cousins to each other—and that is all—we are very intimate." "I am very glad of it," said she— "I wish you might be more so. The admission takes quite a load off, of my mind." At that moment, we were forced to separate— I was struck at first by Martha's magnanimity. She has always been just jealous enough to dread my marrying, but she cannot look forward to a life of labor for me, and is glad that there is a gleam of hope that I may be relieved—the next moment—by the impropriety of even this admission.

Mr Coolidge[51] came in, to see father after church, father handed him a list of debts—and a schedule of the property—which I had not before seen. Every kind of stock was entered on the schedule, at the lowest possible rate—every needed allowance for depreciation—made, and $18,000. worth of factory stock—thrown aside entirely and yet there was a preponderance on father's side of 6 or 8 thousand— There is no doubt then but at all events he will pay his creditors. . . . After I read the Bible—Ellen[52] pained me very much—by saying that she thought my desire to take a school, arose from love of show— and was not necessary. I had no right she added—to insult her so much—& if I did—she would hire herself out as a chambermaid. I determined to know what father thought—so sounded him when we were alone. He would be glad, he said—if I could get a situation as governess in David Sears's family.

TUESDAY JUNE 21. 1842.

. . . after tea—Father gave me a letter from Mr Haven—.[53] Nothing has moved me so painfully—perhaps, if he live a thousand years—he may admit—that I have some experience, that I have seen some suffering—. Why is it, that I do not yield to this grief—if not because I have known greater? The tears would stream upon the paper—on which I tried to write an answer of a few lines, which summoning Mary to my aid—I carried down to Mr Gould's.[54] I had an intense headache, and felt that I was growing rapidly ill. Came up stairs as soon as I returned.

THURSDAY JUNE 23. 1842.

. . . [received] a note with a birthday remembrance from _____* The remembrance was a pretty sketch of Aurora and Apollo, by Sophia Peabody which he interpreted, yet <u>more</u> prettily—but there was a tone in the note, which brought the tears to my eyes—and when I had read thus far—"I thought you inclined to exaggerate your calamity—and I think so still—", I laid it down and wept bitterly—[55] It may be very foolish, but I do feel as if it would be

---

*Samuel F. Haven. The letter of June 22, 1842, is in the Dall Papers, MHS.

a greater satisfaction to me to know that _____, understood me—knew my strength;—than to have the unqualified admiration of all the world beside. I have been seeking work all the afternoon, Mr Gannett[56] promises me something to do—in the shape of translation and Mr Waterston[57] looked very kind. . . .

MONDAY JUNE 27. 1842. . .

After I came home, I had a most sad talk with father— It was his birthday, and 31 years since he first came to Boston—and he was very dull—said, he had not a friend in the world, did not know anybody, who would give him a dollar, to keep his family from starving and so on— I could not bear it all—without a burst of tears—but seized the occasion to remind him, of the one unfailing friend.

If any body desires to know how useful I can make myself at home behold—I worked from five o'clock till nine this morning with broom and duster, to satisfy, mother, and then because she could pass a linen cambric handkerchief over a marble slab in the parlor, and find its color slightly changed she said she should dust it all over!

TUESDAY JUNE 28. 1842.

. . . I read [Isaiah 55:10–13[58]] to my father at the breakfast—table and he seemed a little moved for he spoke to me afterward with tenderness—and seemed not to know how, yet to desire to thank me. This afternoon, I called on James Clarke and was received with the utmost interest and kindness. My eyes filled with tears, when I told him that last Saturday night, I was so tired of the sight of strange faces,* that I felt sick for one familiar smile— And yet —said he—I dare say you have found strangers less strange than you thought— I acknowledged their kindness, I am only sick when I can find none, in father or mother, brother or sister— Have I either? I sometimes ask myself—and I fear to wake as from a dream, and find myself the child of nothing. It is hard in an emergency like this with a heart willing to love the meanest thing—claimed of nobody, without the slightest look of interest—without attention when I would speak, to force my way through difficulties of all sorts—that loneliest of lonely things, an independent woman. Dr Shattuck[59] told me the other day to

---

*Healey had been calling on people with whom she was not well acquainted, in her quest for work.

tell my parents what he said for they were my best counsellors—and I honestly meant to. I opened the matter by telling father that he had sent his compliments, to <u>him</u>. "What good will that do?" asked he— I then began to repeat what he had said about myself, but mother interrupted me suddenly by asking the most irrelevant question— My courage failed. I paused, answered her, and as nobody asked me to go on—came up stairs with a swelling heart. There was a meeting at Mrs Bartol's I went—for wherefore should I stay at home? At <u>home</u>, the bitterest mockery I ever spoke.

TUESDAY. JULY 19. 1842....

They had heard from Sophia Peabody.* She is still weak and ill but seems infinitely happy She says that she and Hawthorne have done nothing as yet, but enjoy each other— I thought I knew him she writes, but hitherto we have been too much in a hurry—we have met only to part— Now we have eternity before us, and are calm!

It was very ridiculous in Elizabeth to repeat this—but she did. I believe it is really true that she wishes to join the Baptist Church and for no better reason that I can find, than that William Green[60] has joined it. "Ever since I saw him baptized" she says "I have wished to join the church—" Father in Heaven, when shall I cease to blush for my sex?

THURSDAY. JULY 21. 1842....

Had the kindest letter from Theodore Parker— I do not like the flattery which he writes, but suppose it must grow out of naturally deficient delicacy.[61] If the universal love which greets me, were the harvest of my own good deeds—I must have been wiser than Solomon—and purer than light—it makes me humble indeed to feel that it is all of God. The orthodox Dr _____[62] parted from me this afternoon, earnestly entreating me, to let him be of service to me—and here—the spiritualist of Roxbury asks the same as a favor....

FRIDAY JULY 29. 1842....

My evening was one of entire discomfort, father sad <u>desperate</u>—mother irritable and self willed. Well might my father say, that 'change† on the day of his

---

*"They" apparently refers to the Peabody family, although Healey neglects to mention where she is when she hears this news. Sophia Peabody and Nathaniel Hawthorne were married on July 9.

†Probably the Exchange, where commodities were traded.

failure was more tolerable to him than his home. Oh my dearest, and best friend, could you but know the truth—how would you grieve for your cousin Carrie, how would you soothe the sadness—you now dare but reprove. Bless him—oh God—as thy child is not worthy to bless, and spare him every pain— even that of knowing that her grief is no chimera.

SATURDAY AUG 6. 1842. . . .

There seems to be a strange interest in me awakening in my mother—she has called me Carrie twice today—and once when Marianne* was insolent she reproved her rudeness. God knows that I would bear much more than I have yet done—to but win this love, to which the world <u>can see</u> I have a right.

SUNDAY AUG 7. 1842. . . .

I have been arranging and writing a list of my Mss. and other private papers. As I have glanced over my Journal, I have felt mortification and reproach. If the weak tears of which this index of my life bears record—have not yet washed out every impress of truth—they soon must—

Who will care for these many papers—who will ever read—or at my request, take pains to preserve that I have written? No one— Shall I then regret so to have spent my time? Oh no—. I have strengthened my own spiritual nature by the exercise— I have purged my heart of whatever is impure on my page—to write out has frequently been with <u>me</u>, to cast <u>off</u>. If I were likely to die wealthy and could pay an institution for taking care of papers so precious to me—I would do it—for to a psychologist, this journal would be worth the pains—but as it <u>is</u>, as it is <u>like to be</u>, I must trust the common chance.

THURSDAY AUG 18. 1842.

Father has reproached me today, anew with my want of success,—saying somewhat scornfully that I saw now the result of "living for others." He had been urging me to take a school, upon my own responsibility, which for prudential reasons, shall be only my last resource. I begged him to wait patiently until the last of October—but he seemed in a great hurry—. . . . [He said] bitterly that "it was very strange, that I† sought only to teach & help others— but refused teaching and aid, myself. . . . as much influence as I had—as many

---

*Her sister Marianne, five years her junior.

†The "I"s here refer to Caroline.

friends—I could not now find one to offer me pupils— I should find that my faith was all nothing— I should be obliged to act from selfish principles." It is difficult for me to remember what is ungenerous or unkind, I have in regard to it only a confused sense of pain, He talked a long while in this strain, and I said nothing for I felt I could say nothing in the gentlest spirit that would not be unfilial—but as he concluded—the tears started—and I said quietly— "Dear father I have not lost my faith. I have never served God for money—for help of any earthly sort—and though I have not a friend and gain not an iota from the past—but such moral strength as I have already received, I shall not be sorry to have lived for others— Father, I have known men labor selfishly for thirty years and lose all at last." He was evidently displeased. I had a letter from Mr Hill with an offer which had it not come from Worcester, I should have accepted—but, I will not <u>lead myself</u> into temptation. . . .[63]

For the first time, Healey attends Harvard commencement exercises not as a rich man's daughter but as a young woman who is reduced to using her every connection to find a job. She is surprised at how she is received by these acquaintances of more prosperous times.

WEDNESDAY AUG. 24. 1842.
[CAMBRIDGE, AT HARVARD COMMENCEMENT EXERCISES]
. . . Mrs Parker[64] took pains to bow—and put my arm within hers to lead me to Henry's room— The whole Gurney house[65] was open—there were chambers and a withdrawing room for the ladies & a general reception room, communicating with the dining parlor.

The entertainment was elegant everybody was there—from little I—up to —or <u>down</u> to—the ridiculous Harrison Gray.[66] I had quite as much attention as my head could stand for one day,— Mrs Judge Shaw introduced herself and husband[67] to me. Mrs Abbott Lawrence shook hands very kindly. Her husband was there looking as if he were proud of the settled treaty.[68] . . . I never enjoyed a day so much—on the whole—for I felt how wholly disinterested— must be every attention paid me—and wished my father there to count them. With them no insulting condescension mingled. . . .

. . . I watched the procession as it entered today with more emotion than ever in my life So many who were or should have been in it whom I had known grieved wrinkled sick or dead—since the last year. My own change of fortune was very remarkable—I think it was last year that the richness of my dress elicited so much undesired remark—and this year its scrupulous plainness— told the story of my reverse—of my heart grief, grief which should have kept me, at home—. . . .

The attentions I have received today are an everlasting proof that something beside money is valued in the world.

TUESDAY AUG. 30. 1842.

Last night after I had retired came a note from Mrs Abbot Lawrence—which I could scarcely read—begging me to see this morning—Miss English of Georgetown—D.C.[69] on the subject of teaching. I did as she desired—was delighted with the lady, but a little dissatisfied with the idea of going so far from home—for what seemed an inadequate compensation. Still, the interview was pleasant in its results, and I came home hoping we might arrange together. . . .

WEDNESDAY. AUG. 31. 1842.

Mrs Choate[70] told me last night that it was a source of great astonishment to every one that father should be willing to allow me to teach—and still retain his house. I was indignant at this— I bade her—at once—tell every one how the matter stood, and that my father would move as soon as possible. They are but half friends after all, that will not speak for one's family as well as one's self. I went early to see Miss English—she made me an offer—which involved no risk—for me—and amounted to about the same in a pecuniary point of view, as that of Vinson.* There was in addition the disadvantage of distance—the advantage of change of scene—knowledge of the world—a residence in an established institution of high repute—and a prospect before me, of something better. I left it to my father to decide— As Miss English took me as a supernumerary, the offer was exceedingly liberal—she showed great anxiety to have me accept—said she had done as much as, in these times she properly could—and would have done so much for no other, but I had interested her, &c &c. My father said at once—if the pecuniary gain be no greater—stay in Dorchester— I went to Miss English with this, who said would an increase of pecuniary gain, induce you to go—? I said I left that to my father . . . . My father enumerated

---

*Cornelius M. Vinson (1817–1893) kept a school in Dorchester and had offered to hire Healey as an assistant at a salary of $300 per year (*NEHGR* 141:148; Dall Journals, August 30, 1842, MHS).

advantages, which I could not hear—for I thought, to my shame I confess it, only of the agony of being so far from _____.* At his wish I promised to accept, Miss English's offer—but said, that he must arrange affairs with Mr Vinson. This he promised to do— I passed the afternoon in visiting such of my poor, as I could—...

... My mother told me this morning, that it was [father's] intention to take the children from school. I contended the point with him this evening. I told him that if I left family and friends, for Georgetown—and gave not only my time but my money to the cause, I thought I had a right to require that they should be well educated. He began to talk of <u>his</u> education, and of its being time for them to be able to instruct each other; I asked him, if he thought any of the family more able to teach than I— I told him that I was going to earn the means of having them taught, because I did not feel sufficient weight of authority to teach—them. This point I would not yield.

MONDAY. SEPT. 5. 1842.

... Grandfather[71] had come down from Worcester, and brought me several letters, I bore them as philosophically as I could—but the tears flowed freely until dinner time.† ...

A strange thing happened to me, today, While I was weeping mother wept too, and mistaking the cause of my emotion—came and sat by me. "I have a word to say to you, Caroline," she said "which I never should have spoken, had you not been going away The other Sunday when talking with your father about our future plans, you said I did not love you, as I did the other children— Do you not—know, that if anything you must be dearer to me, than they?" I pleaded guilty to not knowing, and speaking gently—told her my whole tale of sorrow—yet my pride would not allow me to complain,— She said she felt me very near to her, and I felt happier to hear it, but her overhearing my remark explains her new tenderness, that change in her manners which I have remarked—. Have I been doing her injustice for years—? I cannot think it— but I am glad that now when I am like to need it, she is beginning to love me....

---

*Samuel Haven, no doubt.

†The letter that caused Healey such pain was undoubtedly one from Samuel Haven. In a letter dated September 4, he implicitly severed his romantic ties with her. He wished her happiness in the South; noted that he was in no danger of having a wife; depicted his advice to her as "fatherly," the sort given by "ancient gentlemen and antiquarians"; and refused to promise to write to her. On the back of the letter in Healey's hand is written: "Even so—good night" (Dall Papers, MHS).

Healey leaves Boston to begin a new life in Georgetown, going by rail as far as Albany, with a stopover in Worcester. She is disappointed that Samuel Haven does not appear when she stops in Worcester.

THURSDAY. SEPT. 8. 1842.

I rose early, still very ill—everything seemed to be in the process of going — Father looked very sad—....I went through an hundred agonies—before I was finally seated in the cars—....Our journey was quiet—the "no-welcome" at Worcester rather saddened me—but I felt that He who knows all—knew best....

CHAPTER FOUR

To the South and Back

September 10, 1842–April 10, 1844

$\mathscr{I}$n Georgetown, a homesick Caroline Healey found herself in a new and strange world. "At the South" the flora was different, the food abundant, the manners courteous; more significantly, in this new environment she was forced to confront the institution of slavery, and she unexpectedly found that the Unitarianism that was a mark of many of the elite in Boston was suspect in Washington. Daughters of members of Congress were among the students at Miss Lydia English's highly regarded school, and slaves were among the workers. Healey immediately befriended the latter, but initially she seems to have had no strong feelings about the institution of slavery. In fact, she counseled Christie, a young enslaved woman whom she was teaching to read, to reconcile herself to her situation, as her people were not yet ready for freedom. But she felt a bond with Christie, who, upon Healey's confession that she was herself "a slave to my own heart," commiserated with her that "It is a hard thing to live." The love woes of Mary Smith, another of Miss English's enslaved workers, also touched a chord with Healey, reminding her of her own heartache. When Healey took the lead in an effort to start a "free colored— Sunday and sewing school" at the Unitarian Church in Washington, she came up squarely against the reality of Southern prejudice: a wealthy and powerful church member warned her off this project. In addition to the effect of her continuing daily interaction with human beings in a state of bondage, Healey's thinking on slavery was affected by a recently published volume by Henry Wadsworth Longfellow, *Poems on Slavery*. In the Boston Unitarian paper the *Christian Register*, she published a poem of appreciation addressed to Longfellow, adding an account of the sad love story of Mary Smith.

Healey's Unitarianism was an unforeseen source of conflict with Lydia English, who worried that employing a teacher reputed to be so radical would be bad for business. There was no Unitarian Church in Georgetown, and English was anxious that Healey not go into Washington to attend the congregation there, at least not until she was well established. For a short time Healey complied, attending Episcopalian services in Georgetown, but her religion was too much a part of her identity for her to abandon it. She rejoined to Lydia English, "I trust . . . that having kept so celebrated a seminary as this, for eleven years that Miss English's reputation does not depend upon my Uni- or Anti-Unitarianism." She ultimately chose to walk the two miles into Washington every weekend, Miss English notwithstanding.

And there she found new friends. Healey had arrived in Georgetown with a letter of introduction to William Cranch, chief justice of the U.S. Circuit Court in the District of Columbia, a New Englander by birth, the first cousin of John Quincy Adams (their mothers were sisters). Judge Cranch and his family lived on Capitol Hill and attended the Unitarian Church in Washington. The family virtually adopted Healey—she was a frequent overnight guest, and their daughter Margie became her confidante.

These new friends and others, mostly transplanted New Englanders whom she met at church, made Healey's life happier. Still she had to cope with bad news from home—the loss of one of her father's ships, his final succumbing to bankruptcy—and no news from Samuel Haven. What caused her relationship with Haven to collapse (and it is clear that it was collapsing before Healey left Boston) remains something of a mystery. The most obvious explanation is Healey's loss of wealth and status. But Healey, in Georgetown, analyzed the situation and came to the conclusion that she had deceived herself as to his interest in her. Our understanding of the situation is hampered by Healey's later attempts to obliterate her journal passages on this subject, usually by canceling them, and occasionally by actually cutting out the passage. But having read the surviving correspondence between the two, I find it difficult to agree with Healey's assessment. On the other hand, it is notable that the two remained friends as long as Haven lived, without any apparent embarrassment on his part. Yet, nearly forty years later, Dall wrote in her journal of meeting an unnamed former suitor "whose wife I should have been doubtless, if my father had not lost his property." "It was a lucky thing for me," she reflected, "that the misfortune brought out the true character of his attachment, for I had believed him disinterested & in his courting days, his attentions gave me great pleasure from their great delicacy. He is 20 yrs older than I am and looks a hundred."[1] But in Georgetown in 1842–1843, it was apparently less painful for Healey to believe that it was her self-deception, not Haven's designs on her fortune, that was at the root of the problem.

At the end of 1842, after four months in Georgetown, Healey reviewed the drastic alteration in her status over the past year. Instead of an heiress she was now "a poor—schoolmistress." "But do I repine?" she asked rhetorically. She did not. She believed that "the great points of my duty—[have] been clearly seen and promptly met." The great weakness of the past year, which still beset her dreams, had been believing Samuel Haven's attentions to be serious. But she speculated that if hope and love had perished in the old year, they might rise "phoenix like from the rekindling ashes" in the new one.

And so indeed it proved. During the Christmas season of 1842, a young minister to the poor in Baltimore came to Washington to fill for a brief time the Unitarian pulpit there. Charles Henry Appleton Dall, with the help of Healey among others, took it upon himself to visit the poor, particularly poor blacks, in order to assess their needs. Caroline Healey and Margie Cranch found him somewhat comical, socially awkward, overly polite, and lacking in what Healey called "manliness." But he was hard-working and sincere. Hardly had he returned to Baltimore than he wrote Healey what was essentially a proposal. Stunned, her first instinct was to say no outright, but she thought of his goodness, and then began to hope "that he might in time induce me to forget what it was worse than folly to remember," that is, Samuel Haven. She wrote him, confident that he "would not care for the second freshness of the heart." When Charles replied, she wrote in her journal that she "never felt such calm despair," for he was undeterred by her confession of unrequited love for another, and she felt that her "destiny was fixed," that she was somehow obligated to accept him. And so the engagement was soon agreed to, an engagement between two persons who had spent only a few days in each other's company and had corresponded a mere few weeks. Healey resigned from Miss English's school, effective at the end of the school year, and went to Baltimore with Charles to meet his family. Her reception there was not altogether pleasant, apparently, but his Aunt Sarah and Uncle William in Boston, who had largely reared him, embraced her fully. Caroline loved them as her own family for the rest of their lives.

In Boston Caroline moved back in with her family and opened a private school in her home. Charles returned to his work in Baltimore, but spent extended periods in Boston. Though Caroline grew to love Charles, they had enough time together to demonstrate clearly that their personalities were unsuited to each other. She was organized, precise, punctual, resolute; he was indecisive and unpredictable. He frequently missed or was late for appointments, keeping her on the rack for expected letters or visits. Mark Healey recognized that Charles was often making his daughter miserable, and Caroline herself was not blind to these problems. But she seems never to have considered ending the engagement. And so the wedding date was set, and the course of two lives altered forever.

SATURDAY. SEPT 10. 1842. . . .

In leaving Baltimore, I first began to understand that I was going South— The weeds by the road side, sometimes differed a little from those at the North —there was a richness in the foliage an occasional slave village—a salaam from a white turbaned black at the road side, and sometimes a pretty glen or corn field—that did not look natural—. The prettiest spot was at the junction of the Ohio and the Washington Railroad— There, was a sweet view of an arched bridge of stone over which the cars afterwards pass, embosomed in green— and from a pretty little farmhouse—by the road side, half covered with vines, tripped a white turbaned black—bearing a tray filled with fine melons— peaches—grapes and other fruit. I felt the presence of the fiend at that moment. . . . We drew into Washington about an hour before dark—, but I closed my eyes, upon the Capitol, and the White House, determined to see them for the first time feeling brighter than then. It took me sometime to settle my accounts with Mr Bulfinch*—and be off. It seemed as if Georgetown were two hundred, rather than two miles—distant for as I entered it, only one thought pressed on me—there is a year between me and home, and I never before knew

---

*Stephen Greenleaf Bulfinch (1809–1870) had escorted Healey on the journey from Boston to Washington. The son of Boston architect Charles Bulfinch, he was minister to the Unitarian Church in Washington, 1838–1844 (*General Catalogue of the Divinity School; Heralds* 3:49–50).

what it was to pass a month without the <u>hope</u> of seeing him.[2] Miss English met me with a sisterly kiss, she herself laid cushions beneath my head, and begged me to lie still—until supper could be prepared. The housekeeper was out, but a servant was sent for her—and after a few moments, some pie bread, butter, milk and meat, were provided. I saw at once that I was not likely to starve. I retired directly, with her own hands, Miss English made provision for the necessities of my sickness and after providing me with every needful thing uttered a musical good night.

GEORGETOWN. SEPT. 11. 1842.

I rose this morning to not a little hard labor in the shape of arrangement—. My room—which in pursuance of the wish I expressed by letter—Miss English has been so kind as to allow me to occupy alone, is also my class room. . . . My supper was on quite as liberal a scale as ever—cake—bread & butter, I ate lightly and took a volume of De Wette[3] to read upon the piazza. The scholars had been singing sweetly—I had listened to their music with great pleasure, but curiosity about me, broke through it all—. . . . "I expect we shall see a great lady when she comes out," reached my ears once or twice, and when I went out, I found all eyes upon me—. . . . Willing to gratify them I seated myself, so that they could see their new teacher as they promenaded. Suddenly, there was a pause and they began to sing "I would not live alway." I could not withstand my own desire for a better acquaintance any longer—so I went out, and asked, if I had not heard voices singing the Messenger Bird.[4] One of them said yes —and sang it, at my request sweetly— I staid with them one of the girls bringing me a chair, and all of them calling me m'aam until I saw Miss English at the other end of the piazza— I went to sit down by her, and was introduced to a certain Miss Allen—[5] . . . After she went into the study with the girls— I had a nice talk with old Aunt Abbie,[6] and—a young slave named Christie. I went down for some water, and Christie sat trying to get a lesson, upon the stairs—. I asked her if I should not help her and she came to my room where I spent half an hour in teaching her to read—and learning what I could of her history. She did not know how old she was—but seemed about seventeen in appearance and eight or ten in mind. She was good natured—said she had been with Miss English four years—her old master was dead—by his will he left all his slaves free, but his heirs broke up the will and now she was afraid she should never be free. "Do you wish to be free Christie?" "Oh yes—for I should not have so hard a time." "What does it mean to be free—" "To be like the whites—and do as I please." "The whites must be servants of God Christie —and you are very happy now." "Yes, but if anything happens to Miss English— It is well enough, while they treat me kindly but it may not be always so—if I am not free—I must bear everything, and that is bad." She went away to get her lesson which she afterward said—she could not learn to save her life— "Christie" said I "do you know any reason why we cannot free the blacks at once—?" "They say we should be poorer—" she murmured. "I did not mean that, it is because few of you are wise enough, and good enough to be trusted with liberty— Now if you want to be free, you will want to know how to read." "Yes—but the whites have to behave theirselves as well as we— If I am ever free—I may be lonesome—& shall want to read the Bible to cheer my heart up." "You can read a little in the Bible can you not? If you are free, your duties will be different, fulfil that you have before you, faithfully, and trust to God for the end. You think I am free—but in many ways I am the slave of my own heart." "It is a hard thing to live" said Christie. "Yes even Jesus was obliged to bear." "Well, the Jews treated him pretty much—as the whites treat us—there are good whites to be sure." "I will read to you a little—" I said— after a long repetition of her wish for freedom—and while the poor girl knelt —by my side, I read from Philippians, concerning the duties of masters & servants and from another epistle concerning him who took upon himself the form of a servant.[7] "I like to hear reading if I cannot read" she said sighing, and asked if she might come to me, tomorrow. I told her yes— As she went out Miss English called me to walk with her upon the upper piazza, where a hanging Madeira vine filled the air with fragrance, and the music of the catydid—half deafened us. Our talk was upon religious subjects, and I left her so sad and sick, that it was well my letters home, were already written and sent. She is not willing I should attend at Mr Bulfinch's*—had she forbidden I could have resisted—but she says it is better for my sake and hers—and pleads liberally. She told me a great deal about a certain Miss Wright whom she dearly loves, whose father was a Unitarian, but who never went to church after he came to Georgetown and was esteemed an infidel in consequence. "If you have peculiar sentiments, I would rather you were known—before you publish them, believe me, it is better for your cause itself—make it lovely in your

---

*That is, the Unitarian Church in Washington, whose minister was Stephen Greenleaf Bulfinch.

own person, and believe me that is the best way to show us that it may be lovely in itself."

Oh God! I thank thee, that there is not a year between <u>me</u> and <u>thee</u>,—thou canst feel my heart throb—and dost not chide— Duty where shall I find thee?

GEORGETOWN D.C. SEPT. 26. 1842.

A visit from Miss English, was the forerunner of evil— I had made up my mind—to let matters take their course—without making any fuss, and I hoped I should hear nothing more from her of a religious nature. I cannot repeat a conversation which agitated me so much. She renewed the expression of her desire that I should attend the churches in town for some time yet,—she left me free with perfect delicacy & good breeding—yet much as I respect her—I could not but feel that she knew my weakness to lie in my magnanimity—and wished to move me through [it].[8] She had been made uneasy in the first place, by a remark made in the Abercrombie[9] class—upon total depravity— It was repeated, to some body else, by Katie[10]—and the third person, asked Miss English, whether I were a Unitarian. She replied that she did not know. I told Miss English—that my sin was one of ignorance, for I had supposed the doctrine of <u>total</u> depravity entirely given up—that much as I conscientiously desired to avoid the expression of a thought upon such matters, in the presence of a pupil,—yet it was here, included in the lesson—& that I dwelt upon it, before I thought detected myself—hesitated—& so drew the attention of the class upon me;—I had bitterly repented of this unintentional violation of trust —& confessed it yesterday to Mr Bulfinch. She said that added to this—she had visited several friends in the city—yesterday—that there was a general enquiry about me—& my Unitarianism, that one lady [was] a Unitarian herself, and highly valued as a friend. She said that she had heard Miss Healey was a Unitarian, that she had said—that she "should come to Washington to church, come what would"—and she added you know that I shall think more highly of her—for that, but it will be a great injury to your Seminary! "I trust" was my calm reply, "that having kept so celebrated a seminary as this, for eleven years that Miss English's reputation does not depend upon my Uni- or Anti-Unitarianism—the absurdity of the remark equals its unkindness. Of course I need not deny the speech attributed to me. The lady who said it—could have been no friend of mine,—but must have judged Episcopalian hearts by her own,— I assure you, Miss English I have found little of the illiberality for which you prepared me—." She continued to say—that she was told in

Boston, that Dr Lowell[11] was not a Unitarian—that when asked about her
arrangements in New York her friends expressed an anxiety in regard to
her arrangement with me—which they afterward—allayed by asking if she
could not induce me to attend church in Georgetown where there was no Unitarian Church. I interrupted her to say—that that question was never asked
me—had it been, so I should not have hesitated to decline coming to the South
— She said that she was glad that Miss Hale[12] was an Episcopalian, I told her
I was glad of that (feeling that one Unitarian was as much as she could manage) . . . . Well a great deal she insinuated in regard to my connection with the
Cranches[13] but it is better to leave the subject— I threw myself in tears upon
my knees—when she left the room, and though saddened—too much to fulfil
my duties, as I ought, I did not lose my faith. I had intended to give up, every
hope of comfort when I came hither, but not that—the reality. . . .

*Although Healey struggled to forget her feelings for Samuel Haven, berating
herself for bringing to Georgetown a book he had given her as a "mnemonic,"
her troubled emotions surfaced in her dreams.*

MONDAY—GEORGETOWN D.C. OCT. 3. 1842.
I threw myself upon the bed last night with a heart sickness that I fancy few
could have understood— Forgive me—oh my God—if I cannot so soon forget
—scenes living on my heart once more seized upon my memory and imagination, the book which I have passed with palsied emotion ever since I arrived,
made me shiver from head to foot as I looked at it—fool that I was—to bring
here—where all other mnemonics—are banished—this,—consecrated by his
own expressed wish—but I must school myself—to bear it.[14] Well, I had a talk
last night with Mr. Abbott[15]—about Unitarianism—and he assured me that
the objection had never been made to his school. On the contrary, Mrs Stringfellow the wife of the Episcopalian minister[16] had sent her children to him, because she understood that he did give direct religious instruction. After I came
home, I felt as if I had been too much disturbed by the matter, and as if Miss
English might well reproach me, with unjustly accusing her. My mingled dis-
tresses produced the most horrid dreams—. I thought I was in the room at
_____,* that it was as still as the grave, that I asked where he was—and they
said that I had killed him—and then the arch foe—she who has curst me—

*Probably the American Antiquarian Society, where Samuel Haven was librarian.

The Tarquin, *one of the ships built and owned by Mark Healey, engaged
in the China trade. Healey believed it to be "the largest merchant ship owned
in the United States" when built. (Courtesy of Peabody Essex Museum)*

while I blest her*—stood hissing between us—the Demon of Revenge—;
at times her face changed to Miss English's—and I awoke so filled with horror—that it seemed to me as if I never should dare sleep again. Alone—how
the word—chilled me—and yet not so—the warm throb of my heart replied,
for still with God. I went through with the usual operations, but dinner time
brought me letters from home— Mother had returned—father's Tarquin was
in—the New Orleans lost†—and <u>the</u> Miss Phelps of Quincy,[17] engaged to Mr
Bulfinch— I was so distressed by the news in regard to the New Orleans, that
I hastily dismissed my last class—and prepared to walk to town. . . . I found Mr

*Probably Healey's aunt Maria Foster, whose interference had caused problems in her relationship
with Haven.

†The *Tarquin* and the *New Orleans* were ships owned by Mark Healey.

Elliot[18] at home and reading from a Boston paper—but that & those of New York although both of the right date, were searched in vain for news—of the ship. Mr Eliot promised to enquire at the reading room—.... I wonder whether father thinks I play all the time that he advises me not to send home letters, until I can finish them in literary style. He grieves over his dull evenings —and says he is so glad that I am so much better off than any of the rest— I too am glad & grateful to God—glad that he does not know how much I suffer— I trust he will not make me anxious—by repeating these moanings, which I am too far from home to relieve. I have been to Miss English & requested her to keep my letters from me, until after the mail hour—until my duties for the day are closed— I cannot attend to my classes—while still so recently agitated—& until I am better, I am afraid I could not leave the seal long unbroken.

On Christmas Day at the Unitarian Church in Washington, Healey, who was spending the Christmas holidays with the Cranches, heard the preaching of Charles Henry Appleton Dall. Dall served a ministry to the poor in Baltimore and was filling the Washington pulpit in the absence of the regular minister, Stephen G. Bulfinch. Dall remained in Washington for more than a week and undertook to recruit Sabbath scholars among the poor in that city. Healey, herself experienced in the same sort of work in Boston, accompanied him.

WASHINGTON D.C. DEC 26. 1842.

This morning I devoted to visiting among the poor, with Mr Dall[19]—and Mrs Brown—[20] As I have no other holiday—I would have liked to spare it—but I knew that the only way to restore my own cheerfulness—was to lighten some fellow sufferer's heart, so I went cheerfully. We were successful, we seemed to be gladly received—and found beside, a few, who were willing to send their children to the Unitarian Church—about twenty children whom we might gather in to a free colored—Sunday and sewing school. Mr Dall, and myself had some discussion about the probability of our being able to succeed if we attempted this—and Mrs Brown promised to enquire of Mr Purdy,[21] a member of our church—whether he would be able to furnish us with a room.... As I returned home, I went with Mrs—Brown to see Mr & Mrs. French.[22] A strange man is Mr French—the chief clerk of the House. He and the Browns— have harsh Yankee voices—they are full of energy and intelligence and though I must laugh at—yet I like them. They have such exquisite self complacency

Charles Henry Appleton Dall, a Unitarian minister-at-large and future husband of Caroline Healey. (Courtesy of Massachusetts Historical Society)

—never are they out of place—never are they subdued or conscious. Mr French—is the king of pure drawling good nature—large and fat—and his wife—oh she is tall and thin and withered looking—tight laced withal—so that her faded breasts are thrust up above her low necked dress—and boast more fulness, than one had otherwise suspected upon her whole body. He is still "green," and often does submit to do the drudgery of distinguished men as if it were a favor. He kindly offered to carry me home this afternoon, to which I consented. . . .

THURSDAY. DEC. 29. 1842.

This morning I walked home* in a violent snow storm, which Mr Abbot was too fastidious to allow me to brave alone. We talked by the way of slavery and Mr Longfellow†—which put me in mind of a strange incident which occurred the other night.

It was on a Tuesday, my face was very painful—and I was going for a moment to the teachers' room—before I retired, when there was a knock at the door, and Mary[23] presented herself—. "I want you to do a favor for me missy" said she "but if you are going out—I will come some other time—" "What is it?" "I want you—to write a letter" said she—with some embarrassment— "it is a secret it is to a young gentleman." Mary is about two thirds negro blood—about eighteen well formed and capable.

I took out a sheet of paper—expecting her to dictate—but she wished me to write her thoughts, without her taking the trouble to express them; so I bade her tell me the whole story—

"I am a slave" she began—"and it is for some time that this young man has been a visitor of mine, and though I like him, I must give him up—for my owners don't." "What is the difficulty?" I inquired. The tears started to her eyes she clasped her hands and said earnestly "I did think everything of him—and please tell him that I will not forget him—" she went on—;— "He belongs to an estate Miss—and nobody can tell who his owner will be. My friends do not like me to marry a slave—I like him very much only I don't want to marry him at least not now—but when I told him so—he wasn't satisfied, he wanted me to write to him—. I never wrote such a letter and don't know—what to say, write it as you think best Miss Healey—say no—but don't say it unkind— I want it to be interesting, what you would call an <u>affectionate</u> letter." I saw the woman's struggle, and reflected for a moment. It was likely that Mary's owners would soon set her free— I spoke—"Mary, would you wish your children to be slaves?" A shudder passed over her—"That's it missy," was her confused reply—. Considering my own sadness, there was too much mischief in my next query. "Mary—" said I—"do you wish him to forget you?" "Yes Miss" was her reply, "but he said he wouldn't though!" "I mean to understand," said I—

*That is, from Washington back to Georgetown.

†Poet Henry Wadsworth Longfellow (1807–1882) had recently published *Poems on Slavery* (Cambridge, Massachusetts: John Owen, 1842), which Healey had seen at the Abbots' home.

smiling in spite of myself—"whether you refuse him utterly—or whether you wish me to put him off." "I would rather you would put him off—tell him I sha'n't forget him—something may happen—" her lip faltered—. Poor thing—I remembered how often I too had said—,—"something may happen—"—I could well enough have written for myself—just then—but how should I write out—her plain common sense—wish— I would do my best by her at all events— "I know you know how to write" said she— "How do you know that" thought I—but I only took up my paper and wrote

To Mr James Everinboro'

Georgetown Dec. 27. 1842.

Dear sir—

I hardly know how to thank you, for the honor which you have done me, without saying more than I wish. I am willing to love you and receive you as a friend, but I do not feel as if I could marry you. At least not now— I have a high respect for your character—I thank you for the many kindnesses which you have done me, but I would beg you for your own sake to forget me— I shall not forget you. I will often think of the pleasant hours we have passed together, but, I owe a certain respect to the opinion of my friends—and they are not willing, that I should marry one situated as you are. I hope that you will not think hard of me, that you will not blame me very much. I wish to do that which is right and have not resolved upon this, without a struggle. If I were to do an imprudent thing which might bring suffering upon us both —I never should forgive myself—and it would be right for my friends to forsake me.

Once more, I beg you to forget me and

remain your friend

Mary Smith.

I read this to her and asked if it would do—if she wished me to add anything— "it is beautiful" said she—looking as if she did not know which she loved best, the letter—or him to whom—it was written— "Can you think of anything else—missey—he said something about a longer conversation—and would it be worth while—"— I sighed—and said out of the experience of my own heart—"Nay, Mary—you must not encourage him, too far—nor put yourself in his power—wait and see whether he answers this—." "Well" said she brightening, as her woman's nature took the hint—"that would be the best way." and so she left me.

Healey again spends a few days with the Cranches in Washington.

SUNDAY. JANY. 1ST 1843.

WASHINGTON D.C.

For the first time in my life, I sat the Old Year out—and the new year in— I felt as I looked the future in the face, that I could make no new resolves—all sorts of unheard of plans for getting a livelihood came into my head, and sick and dizzy grew my brain. As I looked back—feeling that I had made little literary advancement—I was also sure that, for the last—six months—the great points of my duty—had been clearly seen and promptly met. On one side only—did I see weakness and error, and while I looked at the afternoon of the last New —Year—and remembered how in the hour of grief and loneliness, I deceived myself into the belief that God had sent me a new loving support—when I re-membered that on that very account—I was now willing, tired as I felt—to go late in the afternoon, on an errand for my mother, with my previous let-ter in my pocket unread—that I never owned to anyone how happy he had made me—and how I went on deceiving myself throughout the year—my spirit fainted.

Deceiving myself, I say—for never has <u>he</u> in word or deed sought to influ-ence me beyond a friendly limit— I deceived myself— At first—I said—I shall be happy forever to have seen him and loved [*leaf cut out*]²⁴

... I was tearfully sad—tonight—but I sat up late—endeavoring to scold Margie out of "a hoot"—which she had taken, because Mr Dall—had taken a seat opposite to me—and asked Mrs Cranch—if he should cut some bread when there was enough cut—adding—"Service is my motto." Now, Mr Dall is not awkward—only singularly polite and elegant in his manners—and though I would not own it—this "hooted" <u>me</u> quite as much. I miss <u>manliness</u> in him, nobody is more energetic, and yet—he is not strong. I know not why.

But again how many changes have come since the old year—began—. Death—loss of fortune—and various anxieties to my family— Love—and new responsibility to me. At that time we were one— I was an heiress, somewhat a blue*—flattered and caressed and with few anxieties save—for the characters of my brothers and sisters, the sufferings of the poor—and a heavy care of my own reputation. And now—? I watch with interest the spiritual progress of

---

*That is, a bluestocking.

my father and mother, I fear for my own health and strength— I am responsible for debts. I am worn—out with illy repressed longing for that I find not —, a poor—schoolmistress. And do I repine? God knows I do not—what shall the next year bring forth—? In this Hope and Love have perished—in another may they not rise—phoenix like from the rekindling ashes? I ask it not—I ask but to be willing—to be content with God.

WASHINGTON, D.C. MONDAY. JAN 2. 1843.

. . . Soon afterward—Col Brent's[25] carriage—came for us—to go to the levée at the White House—. I would have walked that I might go also to Mr Webster's and Mr Adams's,* but my lameness would not permit—and Col. Brent did not seem to have a thought beyond the White House. . . . I never saw a greater crowd. It was almost impossible to move, but a few feet cleared about the President [John Tyler]—gave him room—to take my hand in both his as he repeated my name. I saw that he looked noble—that he was worn and tired—that Mrs Tyler—although once an actress—dressed in the plainest mourning, that Robert was altogether too plain,[26] and then I was hurried by—crowds of gayly dressed people, to make room for two little beggar children, who came with worn out clothes to ask a blessing.

. . . Mr Cushing[27] uplifted himself near the Centre of the East Room. He was smiling proudly—a lady whose face I could not see, was whispering to him—"How can you ask me that?" said he—"when I am standing face to face with you?" I hope she enquired if he ever saw so many ugly women together for surely, I never did—and for honesty's sake—that her face was better than the rest. I had no patience with Bodisco[28] and his purchased honors, yet could not find out, which was the greater curiosity—his overladen coat—or his overhanging wife. Just like a little child is she—, and in spite of etiquette always at his side—;—the more respectable—Miss English says. At the door, we met Mr Dall—who became an attaché and was extremely doubtful whether to offer me the whole of his arm in exchange for the half which I held of Col Brent's. He went with William[29] to Mr Adams's and thought it was not at all republican in me, to ride home. Would he have thought it very Christian to stop as we did— at fat, good natured Jane Sweeney's[30] for a glass of her New Year's Egg-nogg—

---

*That is, Daniel Webster (1782–1852) and John Quincy Adams, senator and representative from Healey's home state.

I raised the brandied liquor to my lips and laid it aside again—but Mrs Brent having asked Jane, "if she thought it would upset her," drank two glasses to the dregs. Good easy soul—she loved it—she acknowledged, but she did not have it at her own house—because there were boys growing up. . . .

At a meeting of Sunday school teachers in Washington, Healey learned the limits of Southern sympathy for blacks, even among some Unitarian Christians.

WASHINGTON D.C. JAN. 21. 1843. . . .
It was an unsatisfactory teachers' meeting nothing suited anybody. I advocated Mr Dall's plan—and every body seemed to advocate it beside, until the meeting was over, when Mr Purdie advanced—saying—"Good night Miss Healey, but give up your plan of a colored free school—" and threatened to leave the congregation if I did not. It was necessary to drag Mr Bulfinch off into a corner, and put him in possession of this. . . .

GEO'TOWN D.C. JAN. 30. 1843.
I was thinking this morning how many things, I should have to write home, about Mr Gwin,[31] Mr Calhoun,[32] and some others when as I rose from dinner—Miss Jane handed me a letter from Baltimore— I opened it carelessly, but found enough in it, to keep me troubled and confused all day. I do not know to this moment, whether I have understood it rightly, whether as I believe— Charles Dall—asks permission to address—me. I would that it had never been written—;—I would that I could judge my own heart—that I could say at once and decidedly—no—to his inquiry. Are you free to be addressed upon this subject. At first, I wished to do so—but as I remembered the purity of his own character,—the loftiness of his devotion to the cause of Jesus—I half hoped that he might in time induce me to forget what it was worse than folly to remember. I meditated for two or three hours upon the matter, growing every moment more distressed. That I was enabled to keep my composure through the recitation I humbly thank God— These over, it was gone, I sat down and wrote such a letter to my father as I thought I ought—but I scarce know what I said. I nerved myself to make the one humiliating confession and thought of nothing else. I carried my letter to the Office myself—and then returned to write to Mr Dall. I wished my letter to be calm; and I copied and recopied—

read and reread—but, as a last resource—gave up the contest.[33] I knelt and asked God's blessing—and then went smoothly on. I felt when I had written all, that I had much to be ashamed of and my woman's blood—mounted to my forehead, but I knew that I was right—and tried to strengthen myself with that. I felt sure that Mr Dall—would not care for the second freshness of the heart, and I made up my mind—that it was now a settled matter.

GEO'TOWN D.C. JAN. 31. 1843.

I spent a most uncomfortable night, and was far more inclined to burn my letter than send it to the mail. Then came a "weak" letter from Mr Gwin, which I made no trifling effort to answer—and a list of troubles from father. He has applied for the advantage of the bankrupt law, his affairs are in a worse state than when he left—and I—I must go write to his solicitor and learn the rest.

GEO'TOWN D.C. FEB. 2. 1843. . . .

I must come to it—at last—that noble letter from Mr Dall— I saw as I opened it, that my expectations had not been answered— It was too long a letter for one who had given up all hope. I glanced through it—to be sure that he was not angry—and then, bending my head upon my hand I allowed the free tears to start. Perhaps I have never felt such calm despair— I knew—or it seemed to me that I knew—that my destiny was fixed—for after a term of months or years—how could I disappoint the patient waiter? I, at last gained courage to read the letter—through—and then, if my heart warmed towards the writer, for his generous confidence in me—it sank within itself—as I remembered, how very little I could give him back— It cannot cannot be—and yet—. God knows how far I have done wrong.

FRIDAY MAY 26. 1843. . . .

I had a letter from father today—which gave me a good deal of pain— Instead of urging me to remain, and strengthening me to do so, mother entreats me to come home before the 17th of June. Father speaks as if he had not known till now that my engagement was a settled thing, and very much as, if he would like to wake up and find it all a dream. I wept over the few lines he wrote. Have I been too hasty—have I been indiscreet?— Alas! where on <u>earth</u> shall I look for guidance? When I first asked the aid of my Heavenly Father in considering this subject—I felt as if his voice spoke clearly to my heart. God knows that so far as marriage is concerned—it would be the last responsibility, I should desire to assume, and sometimes when I think of the conflict it will bring about, between my taste and my duty, I can scarcely keep the balance of my mind— I feel as if I were sacrificing much to think of it—yet as if—the right to love and be loved—without offending, would pay me,—for it all. If my father could but love me with that confidence, that I desire, I might find it easy to forget— any other love—forget even the sad past. He has felt that I was a burden in the days of his wealth;—will he not feel it now? Oh my father! would to God that you could see the heart, which has throbbed thus long only for you—you do not know it—you do not trust it, as you should. And Thou—Infinite and Almighty Father—give me strength should need be to draw back my foot—as readily as I have advanced it—show me the right path & grant—that happiness may come with the future, or at least—such happiness as is found in faithful grateful submission to thy—will. May I be willing to give up <u>all</u> and come and follow thee, may I have strength to bear the frequent reproach—"her affections are none of them very strong—" the bitterest to those who feel as I do—, Father may I rest on thee, I ask no more— Do for me, as thou wilt— I know not what is good for my distempered soul—yet forget not to bless him, who labors for thy Glory—who seeks in me—only one who may help him with his work.[34]

Having resigned her position and finished out the school year, on July 29, 1843, Healey left Georgetown, accompanied by Charles Dall, and went to meet his family at their home, Spring Vale, outside Baltimore. Charles then accompanied her home to Boston, met her family, and introduced her to his Boston relatives, Uncle William and Aunt Sarah, who had largely reared him. He remained in Boston for several weeks before returning to Baltimore.

WEDNESDAY. AUG 16. 1843.

... Charles sat with me a little while; It was an hour of weakness with him—he had little faith in his own purposes, & I saw more clearly than ever, how much he needed aim—& unswerving determination. I wondered tonight if the time would ever come when he would lay my head on his shoulder with the same feeling that I now rested his on mine. When Margie first teazed me in Washington, I used to say, "No! I will never marry Mr Dall. He has not strength enough. I wish to <u>lean</u> upon my husband." God knows I have long enough re-lied upon myself. Ever since my engagement I have felt that Charles was strong enough, but I too proud. I fear to trouble him with trifles, I cannot complain to him, I am only willing to lay my lips to his, and rest.

On September 18 Healey opened a school in her home with three pupils—her sisters Fannie and Anna, and one paying student. When she closed it on July 2, 1844, in anticipation of her wedding, she had five students. As both Caroline and her friend Sarah Balch looked forward to marriage, they discussed family planning issues.

TUESDAY. OCT. 10 1843.

... After Sarah[35] came we had a strange but earnest talk in regard to the law of increase, Mrs _____ is nursing and yet in the family way. This brought us to the subject as connected with the poor—. Certainly it does not seem fit that the marriage relation should be a matter of bargain, all the beauty of conception is destroyed, if it be any thing other than the spontaneous result of a mutual love. One cannot demand of the poor who have so few pleasures that they should deny themselves that of sexual intercourse yet the number of mothers who have children faster than they can educate them, is certainly a curse. There is a natural law somewhere, which the common people—by reason of ill health—excess—or want of intellectual balance—are continually infringing. ...

SUNDAY. DEC. 31ST. 1843. ...

As the close of the most eventful year of my life, I may well pause over this 31st. of December. "Greater gladness hath God poured into my heart, than in the days when the corn and the wine increased."[36] Charles's love—my richest earthly good—has come to me, since the last first of January—. Much pain mingles with the thought of him it is true, but how much more would I gladly bear—for his sake. That first letter to his mother,* my reception at Spring Vale,—Henrietta's† want of consideration—the thousand things felt, never

---

*Two months after her engagement, Healey wrote a letter introducing herself to Charles Dall's mother. Henrietta Austin Dall (1788–1866), in whom Charles had not fully confided concerning the engagement, apparently found it in poor taste.

†Henrietta Dall Whitridge (1814–1866), Charles's sister.

to be described—press on me now—yet the love of the family here,* his own most precious heart, outweigh it in the balance. I suppose I should scarce allude to these as trials, if my mind had not for a long time dwelt upon the hope of knowing—some time a mother's tenderness. Beside I have needed this rebuke. Considered as I have been here, it never occurred to me that I could enter any family without receiving as glad a greeting as I gave. Even in Washington, after my engagement was suspected, it was often said, "Well—if Miss Healey would only fancy a son of mine!" I went to Spring Vale, full of fear—and trembling—yet I did not know why— I little guessed with how much reason—. The short comings of the year have been bitterly lamented—for its mercies I have never thanks enough—but most of all I thank thee, oh God! for the crowning gift of the year, the means afforded to "my own"†— Wilt thou graciously bless to us the opening season, wilt thou of thine own wise will crown us with loving kindness and tender mercy. We leave all things with thee. Grant that our hearts may be thine.

MONDAY MAR. 4. 1844.

Last night, it was exceedingly clear, but today broke in the midst of a tremendous snow-storm. I was glad, for this, as it kept my scholars at home, and gave me two or three hours in Charles's arms—which I needed for I slept little last night. In the course of our talk—it seemed very clear, that so far as it might be apparent, in this delusive world—the last of Sept. or the first of Oct. was the fittest season for our wedding. Our wedding! how much it means! Best of all—that oneness of presence—for which my heart longs so much! However—at about twelve, Charles went to the Fishers who had asked for him, and to his Aunt Sarah's. I saw nothing of him again until night. I was reading Bullock[37] to father, when he came in, and from the easy mode of living in Mexico found an easy transition to our future life in Baltimore: Father had been previously prepared for this talk, but he made it very hard to Charles, whom I pitied exceedingly. Perhaps it was hardest to father, after all—for I know well, that his ambition had figured to itself, years back—a different sort of wedding for me,

*That is, those members of Charles's family living in Boston, particularly his aunt and uncle (siblings of his father), Sarah Keen Dall (1798–1878) and William Dall (1794–1875), whom Healey felt had fully accepted her, as opposed to the Baltimore Dalls.

†The Boston Dalls had conveyed to Charles a house in Boston with rental income, thus increasing his income to at least $300 per year.

from that which is likely to be.— No matter:—as we sow, we reap—and after father was gone—we sat with our arms about each other, and talked over the future. Charles said, that Uncle William had been putting very unfilial notions into his head. Had suggested that his father ought to furnish his house &c— &c— Charles seemed to think it could hardly be so. This caused me, some painful thoughts of our entire dependence for comfort—upon those, who may not love me altogether. Oh Charlie!—thy children—shall at least be taught the mutual dependence of men.

WEDNESDAY. APRIL 10. 1844.

... At noon father gave me $50.00[38]—saying "As fast as you want it I will give you back what you paid to Mrs L."* The tears almost choked me—though they did not fall. It seemed to me, as if I hardly loved Charles well enough to go from him [that is, her father], to Baltimore. ...

---

*Caroline Healey's earnings for teaching at Miss English's school went to pay for the education of her sisters at the school run by Anna Cabot Jackson Lowell (1811–1874).

CHAPTER FIVE

The Minister's Wife

September 24, 1844–March 15, 1847

𝒞harles and Caroline Dall began married life in Baltimore telling each other "at least 20 times a day" that no one was ever so happy as they. They had financial difficulties almost from the start, and within a few months they realized that Caroline was pregnant. Before a year was out, more complications developed: Charles's health was not good, he felt that the trustees of his ministry were not sufficiently supportive, and both Dalls began to look longingly toward Boston. Charles explored the possibility of getting a position working among the poor of Boston—unsuccessfully as it turned out, but by then they were committed to the move. In June 1845 they took up residence with Caroline's family. Charles supplied pulpits in the area—preaching in vacant pulpits or filling in for ministers who were temporarily absent—and searched for a permanent job.

The Dalls had returned to Boston just as the Theodore Parker controversy was reaching a climax. Parker's radicalism alienated the mainstream clergy to the point that almost none of them would exchange pulpits with him, and one who did—John T. Sargent, a minister to the poor—lost his job as a consequence. Mark Healey was one of five Boston businessmen who guaranteed Parker's salary if he would preach for a new society in Boston, organized for the express purpose of giving him a pulpit. Parker accepted and regularly addressed audiences of thousands in first the Melodeon, then the Music Hall. Charles Dall's Uncle William was treasurer of this congregation, known as the Twenty-eighth Congregational Society. Charles and Caroline felt that the controversy surrounding Parker and the high profile of their relatives in his Boston congregation complicated Charles's chances of obtaining a Unitarian pulpit.

By now the Dalls were parents of a son and had moved to a boardinghouse in Roxbury. Caroline discouraged Charles from taking on yet another ministry to the poor—an insecure post in Portsmouth, New Hampshire. But having few choices, and eager to escape Boston, where he feared having to reveal himself as pro- or anti-Parker, Charles accepted it. They moved to Portsmouth in April 1846, and by September he had lost the position. Caroline stayed on for several months in the house they had rented there, while Charles traveled about, supplying pulpits and seeking another permanent job. At last he was offered the Unitarian pulpit in Needham, west of Boston, his first position in a regular parish, and there the family moved in March 1847.

Besides worrying about the family's financial solvency and the success or failure of Charles's career, Caroline had other things on her mind. Above all there was her son, Willie, whose future accomplishments she speculated might be the reason for her existence. As a wife and mother, she found her own literary activities severely curtailed. Yet she read extensively and thought seriously on two major questions: slavery and the role of women. Before she left Baltimore she had published an antislavery article in a Unitarian publication. In this article she observed that a Northerner who went South was much less likely to be drawn into the slave-holding culture than to be revolted by it, because of the presence of the human beings who were its victims. We can only guess at the reaction of her Baltimore in-laws, who held household slaves, but her own father was extremely displeased. Yet if she were silent on this issue, she mused, "would not stones cry out?" In Portsmouth she was active in a women's antislavery society, and through those connections attended an "Abolition party" in Boston. There she met William Lloyd Garrison, who dispelled her prejudices against him immediately; she found him "really very lofty and noble, and well-mannered, notwithstanding the vituperations of his pen."

From shortly after her marriage, Caroline Dall puzzled over "that mixture in woman's duties which has troubled me so much." At a time when domestic duties seemed to overwhelm the possibilities of using what she considered her considerable literary talents or somehow serving the public good, she wrote to her friend Theodore Parker concerning this question. Was it true, she wondered, as a visiting clergyman had suggested, that women could learn "the Science of Universals" while cooking fish? Parker expressed skepticism of this theory ("Set ten women to cooking fish all their lives & nine of them will know nothing but how to <u>fry, stew, boil broil</u> & <u>bake</u>."), but refused to spell out for her woman's duty; that, he thought, only women could decide. Dall even considered communitarian solutions to the problem; she found herself agreeing with many of the ideas of French socialist Fourier, some of which were being incorporated into the Utopian Brook Farm community. She recognized in Fourier's writings what she called "the root of all truth" about marriage, that there could be no significant improvement in the relationship until woman's lack of power, particularly economic power, was rectified. She found appealing the communitarian idea of sharing domestic chores and childcare responsibilities, yet she could hardly imagine turning her own baby over to someone else: "No one can even bathe it for me!!"

Intertwined with this question, for Dall, were reproductive issues. At the time the Dalls moved to Needham, after two and a half years of marriage, she had had one full-term pregnancy and one miscarriage, or possibly two. When she believed herself pregnant in the last of these instances, her response was, "Oh that I could have been spared a little longer!" She wished "no exception from the common lot, except as far as may keep me, from losing my reason, as I increase my family." She and a friend discussed the "abuses of 'married life,' . . . when strength went—even faster than children came." She saw the solution as self-control on the husband's part, but when her friend rejoined that the husband would likely be "driven to bad courses," Dall could only sigh. These matters remained a great mystery to her.

Dall was also considering the plight of prostitutes and of women in marriages without love, a situation she called "legalized vice." And she was privy to a classic case of sexual harassment of the powerless by the powerful: As she prepared to leave Portsmouth, her servant Lucy Walsh was left alone with her new employer in the empty house that the Dalls had just vacated; this man— a naval lieutenant, married man, and father—made inappropriate advances toward her. A traumatized Lucy came weeping to Dall, who could only counsel her to resign her new position immediately. In such experiences it is not difficult to trace the making of Caroline Dall, future woman's rights woman.

TUESDAY. SEPT. 24TH. 1844. BOSTON.

*E*arly on the morning of this, my wedding day, I wrote the above paragraph in my Journal—.* Later, I helped Charles to pack, and occupied myself in various ways—to drown the thought of leaving home. Most distressing was it to us all. Catie, and Martha[1] came to dress me, and by twelve o'clock I was ready to go with Charles to the church. I wore a high necked dress of rich light silk, and a plain silk Brussels veil. I was very cold and faint—and father's loving hand brought me a few drops of wine, which contrary to my usual practice I swallowed. I saw no one but Dr Lowell in the church—although they say, it was crowded. Every thing was admirably managed through Seth's[2] kind care. Every thing went smoothly. We were first at home—and father with his tearful eyes, the first to embrace us as one. Mother wept—freely—our friends crowded round us during the levee, and the nearest of them lingered yet longer about what was truly, an elegant table. Its chief ornament was Charles's beautiful pyramid of Dahlias. After the repast—we had more time than we desired but it could not be helped. We left at three—for the Western cars—where Uncle William met us. . . .

We arrived at Springfield at about ½ past 8—and found thanks to Mrs John Parker's[3] recommendation—excellent quarters at Day's Railroad House.— . . .

The Dalls settled into married life in Baltimore, Charles continuing his work with the ministry-at-large and Caroline keeping house and helping him.

FRIDAY. NOV. 1ST. 1844.

This the first day that I have been left alone; the first that I have had only <u>one</u> servant—& been my own "hewer of wood & drawer of water." I succeeded so well, that although suffering from a good deal of nausea I read about 60 pages of Xenophon.[4] A sort of despair of ever writing again came over me, and gave me a species of blue fit, until Charles's kiss drove the fog away. At least 20 times a day, we say to each other—Surely no two people ever began life so rationally, none were ever so happy, or so bound in <u>one</u>—so of course—we bear those pecuniary anxieties which have already heavily beset us, with becoming patience. . . .

*That is, the last paragraph of the previous section, dated September 23, 1844, not included here.

BALTIMORE—TUESDAY. DEC. 10. 1844.

This saddest of all days—save one;—the anniversary of my sweet Charlie's death, has been made to glow with a lively hope to me—. For the first time the conviction presses itself upon me—that I am myself a mother. It is received with a holy fear—and yet for my husband's sake with a very precious thankfulness— Would that the laws of physiology were made clear to me that I might in no point offend against the will of God—that I might in this matter be entirely subject to most absolute right—but it is difficult to walk confidently in the dark—and all the books I can consult—give me little light— Father in Heaven thou who art able and willing to unfold thy truth—fill my soul with the holiest emotion—strengthen me to know and do thy will in the spirit of Christ.—

On January 25, 1845, an article by Dall (signed C. W. H.) appeared in the Christian World, *a newspaper founded in 1843 by James Freeman Clarke and some of his parishioners. Dall's article sympathetically recounted the stories of free blacks, former slaves, whom she knew in Baltimore and Boston.*

BALTIMORE MD. WEDNESDAY. FEB. 5. 1845.

...A letter from father full of remonstrance about my anti slavery article. Would to God, his eyes could be opened, no one is more opposed to the stand taken by the Abolition party* than I, but were I to stop—writing—would not stones cry out? ...

The Dalls moved to Boston in late June 1845 and lived with Caroline's family. Charles supplied area pulpits and looked for a permanent position.

SATURDAY. AUG. 16. 1845.

I wrote several letters this morning, and was then so tired, that I believe I slept for an hour or two— In the mean-time, Mrs Cunningham[5] came in, and said in speaking of my size, that if she were I, she would not go out any more. Mother said that I went against her wishes—leading to the inference that she thought it improper for me to go,—and was then foolish enough to tell me of the conversation— I felt it a good deal—it made me rather unhappy— I could have forgiven it in a young person who did not know the importance of

---

*Probably Dall refers to the abolitionists' call for an immediate end to slavery.

exercise, the tediousness of the last few weeks of pregnancy, and the effort necessary to a walk—in the healthiest persons under such circumstances—but here were persons who had had large families—candidly admitting that they thought it my duty to let my health & that of my child suffer, rather than offend against common prejudice. Charles had gone to Lynn to meet Mr. Sargent[6] at a pic-nic. This conversation was still dwelling, on my mind, when he returned somewhat earlier than I had expected him. Feeling sure that he would sympathize with me, and help me to sustain my moral courage—against such foolish talk—I repeated Mrs C.'s remark to him— What was my surprise to hear him reply, "I have been thinking for some time that you had better walk after dark—you are constantly attracting observation as it is." and he went on, to give some instances. When I remembered how I had struggled with my false shame—again & again, for the sake of <u>his</u> child—; how I had often walked alone, rather than ask, any one who might have these foolish notions to walk with me—it seemed to me very hard, and I burst into tears. I am ashamed to say that I wept an hour steadily—but so it was—. Oh my husband, if you had but understood a woman's nature—you would have soothed & cheered me— in my way of duty, and kept from me, every thing like the unpleasantness—of my situation. Oh my child; God grant, should you ever be in your mother's situation, that you may have wiser friends about you, than she has had the last two months. I have chosen for my evening walk the hour between six & seven. . . . My supper—(the family hour—is 7.) relishes better after my walk than before it—and this walk is my sole privilege—my sole luxury—how barbarous then to strive for the fiftieth time to deprive me of all comfort in taking it. I am never conscious of impertinent observation, and now I must walk alone in future, for I will not run the risk of detecting it in my husband's eyes. When will the law of God—govern men and women against the law of folly—when will my own sex learn—that the child within their bosoms—is as precious & pure in his sight as that they lead by the hand? I have seldom been more unhappy than I am tonight, and that not so much on account of my husband's weakness or Mrs C's—as on account of my own. That weakness which makes it hard, for me to be satisfied with doing what God's law requires—unless it coincide with the requisitions of man's folly—that weakness, which keeps me from taking my usual walk tonight—because I could not go out, without feeling my own eyes full of tears—& those of "all the world"—as full of rude curiosity!![7]

The Dalls' first child, William Cranch Healey Dall (1845–1927), was born on August 21.

SUNDAY. SEPT. 14. 1845.

Mr Dall left me early yesterday morning, to preach at Hubbardston—where perhaps he may supply during the winter. The supply came—at a moment when our hearts were a little cast down—by the strange want of sympathy— among other clergymen—and what seemed likely to prove the impossibility of cheap board in Boston. This is a long rainy Sabbath— My beautiful boy, who grows bigger & bigger,—& perfectly astonishes me by his appetite—I have named William Cranch—for my dear, old, friend the Judge. He is not four weeks old until next Thursday—and I am so—well! though rather weak. Certainly I have had most skilful attendance. The day after my confinement Miss Alexander[8]—enquired whether I felt any lameness—or strain in performing— my natural function—and when I answered—no—she said, "well—I must give you great credit for being an extremely well made woman—and myself some little, for not hurrying you—with so large a child—there was every danger of a rupture." Much as I liked her, I cannot help feeling that the wiser course, would have been to have left nature to herself, after the birth of my child. If the placenta had not been torn away—I believe my pains would have returned and expelled it as soon as I was strong enough to bear the flooding that must ensue.

I am not strong enough to write—how grateful to God I am—for my precious child....

SUNDAY. SEPT. 28. 1845.

So quiet a life as I lead now—scarce requires a daily Journal—and yet as my strength increases—I shall resume it. Willie has been brighter—& stronger the past week— I also—have gained— ... I have been busied with dress-making, and my reading has gone no farther than the 4th vol. of the exploring Expedition[9] and an admirable review of the Question put to the Boston Association by Theodore Parker.[10] When I am more used to my maternity I shall be a better reader— Now—I am often obliged to stop in order to admire my sleeping Willie.... For our own plans—nothing seems yet determined. Mr. Dall preaches again today at Hubbardston—and as for me—I ask for nothing but a home. The face of my own home—has changed to me very much, since my marriage—father seems a good deal depressed—nothing reanimates him, not even Willie's sweetness—upon which I had built much hope. Austin Dall[11] who came to see me tonight, said to father, who was tending Willie—"You have had a good deal of that business to do Mr. Healey." I laughed—& said "yes he <u>was</u> a very good nurse, and it would not take long—to get his hand in again." Father answered in a cold bitter tone, "I have no desire to get my hand in again." I swallowed a good deal of pain, and disappointed feeling—& said "Many people take more comfort in grandchildren than children." "That is only in their <u>second</u> childhood" answered my father. Perhaps I have needed this sort of chastening—for I have been so very happy since I have been married—& had so little to trouble me. I was wondering this morning whether with so quiet a conscience—so serene a spirit—I could be in a healthy religious state. But for Willie's sake—I could meet—the last hour calmly—. God bless the husband who shedding the light of his own spirit—on my life and death—has made both so glad and beautiful to me. Him I shall <u>never</u> leave—. Wherever he is—there I must be. . . .

In October the Dalls moved into a boardinghouse in Roxbury, a Boston suburb.

ROXBURY SUNDAY. DEC 21. 1845.

This has been another week of severe pain.—when I consider how greatly my strength and power of usefulness has been reduced, by my confinement—I can only find consolation in the thought that Willie's life may be worth more than mine—and that to be useful to him—to have even brought him into the world, may for aught I know—have been the best service I have ever rendered to humanity. . . .

. . . In the evening [of Friday] Mr. Dall left me for Templeton via Boston. Why should I say again—that I pray daily that this life of separation may have an end. . . .

ROXBURY. SATURDAY [JANUARY] 31ST.

I got cold on Wednesday—and have been [doing] miserably ever since. Today has been one of summer heat and drizzling rain—and no success to Mr. Dall— who has endeavored to get a supply for—tomorrow. Mother was speaking to him of Mr. Waterston's[12] indifference to our interests—. I can say with truth that I never knew what it was to lose friends—to feel the coldness and neglect of those who had been kind—until the clergy of Boston taught me. To be sure —I can see that in this instance and many others, it is owing to the interest my

own father, and my uncle by marriage, have taken in Theodore Parker.[13] I care
not half so much for the personal suffering I endure on account of it—as for
the mean opinion which it forces me—to have of them.

ROXBURY. THURSDAY. FEB 19. '46.

...A long talk with Charles about going to P.* I try to discourage him, because
I fear that the situation cannot be permanent and for his reputation's sake
I would not have him begin and leave another work. I can see clearly that
his strongest desire is to escape the Parker controversy. "If I stay here,"—he
says "I must take sides—and if I take sides it will be with Mr. Parker. They are
grievously unjust towards him. It was only today that I argued against six of
them at Mr. Briggs's[14] who said he was a <u>dishonest</u> man." Heaven grant he <u>may</u>
escape this.

ROXBURY FRIDAY MAR 27. 1846.

...I staid a few moments to talk with Mary,[15] who was full of the abuses of
"married life." She did not know what was to be done—when strength went—
even faster than children came. I told her what I thought—that a husband's
passions were to be controlled— "And—be—driven to bad courses," was the
reply— I could only sigh— ... I threw myself into an Omnibus entirely worn
out at six o'clock. As I came home, two of the most wretched beings imitations
of Dickens's Nancy† were in the Omnibus—in company with one of the coars-
est of men— One of them wept—I thought from jealousy, but God knows best.
If I am to live in this world oh father! teach me to help this miserable class of
fellow—beings— I cannot look upon this sin with any calmness. Such meetings are growing common, I believe the miserables come out here to consult a
physician—.

The Dalls have recently moved to Portsmouth, New Hampshire.

PORTSMOUTH N.H.
WEDNESDAY. APRIL 29. 1846

...Had a pleasant call from Louisa Simes[16] who talked with me, about "legalized vice" i.e. marriage, until we were both tired....

---

*Portsmouth, New Hampshire, where Charles Dall was considering a position with the ministry-at-large.

†Nancy is a street girl in Dickens's *Oliver Twist*.

PORTSMOUTH N.H.

SUNDAY. JULY 12. 1846.

... In the afternoon, heard Mr. Dall—* Mr. Moore of Duxbury, came to tea with us. He is a fine man—talked nobly—and felt nobly—especially about that mixture in woman's duties which has troubled me so much. Still he is in several theories mistaken—and I would like to yoke him in, to our harness for a short time that he might see it.[17]

PORTSMOUTH N.H.

SATURDAY. AUG. 1. 1846.

... I met at Mrs Kittredge's, Mrs Lyman, and Mrs Dr. Parker.[18] The latter is a very agreeable woman—but is said to be very insincere, a terrible fault I should think for a minister's wife—but after all perhaps not half so bad as "obtrusive-ness." † After tea a letter arrived from the Committee, stating that for want of funds, the Mission must close by the first of September. Mr. Dall in his letter had asked them for what sum, they would be responsible, if not for $600. They distinctly reply—for no sum—showing thereby their wish that his ministry should be ended, since they could if they pleased promise the same sum, as that already gathered, or could call the Association together, and state the matter to them—enquiring which of them would double their subscriptions, and who would not. Our hearts are at peace in spite of many a bitter disappointment.

PORTSMOUTH. N.H.

SATURDAY, AUG. 8. 1846.

Reading Fourier, through Parke Godwin[19] all the morning— Was much reminded of Swedenborg,[20] and the author of the Vestiges of Creation.[21] How many minds are now to be found upon the same mysterious track, and although I am neither reader nor former of dreamy philosophies, yet I found in Fourier few thoughts that were new but only such—as in consequence of his greater ingenuity he had reduced to system. He makes his "Fancies" out of whole cloth. I should never have courage to write down such dreamings, lest I might delude men, and yet I can see—that this very philosophy vague as it is, is full of valuable suggestions to the men of NOW. Courage, oh woman

---

*That is, she heard her husband preach.

†John Lord, one of the Dalls' critics in Portsmouth, had accused Caroline of this fault.

everywhere learn to value thine own influence thine own words—thine own thoughts. In his thoughts on Marriage I see the root of all truth—which I have myself spoken to the world in many forms, viz: that until woman be rescued from her present pecuniary dependence, until all matters of marriage are regulated by her approval, the—world will move on, somewhat as it does now.

In his thoughts on the formation of a township I sympathize entirely, and yet I have not moral greatness enough to <u>begin</u> this township. If I had money, I would give any amount of it, to see his thought realized but what were that, without clear-headed people? I should hardly be willing to sacrifice myself to coming ages, so entirely—for a life in a Phalanstery,* could never be agreeable till the third or fourth generation. In respect to Economy of Labor—I have always seen that a dinner could be prepared for three families as easily as for one, and that the children of a whole street could be well taken care of, by the amount of devotion—expended on those in the first house. I have longed for some mode of solving this problem—and setting woman free from domestic cares.— So do I still. And yet who should take any charge of my child, but me? No one can even bathe it for me!! . . .

PORTSMOUTH N.H.

FRIDAY SEPT. 18. 1846.

Read aloud to Sarah[22] from papers—on Literature and Art by S. M. Fuller,[23] which I think are written with a great deal of discrimination and strength. What she says of Madame de Stael[24] is true of herself—she can discourse, but she cannot converse. At least I think she does the first better. To <u>converse</u>, a person—must appreciate the minds of others must draw them out and make use of them & so send them back to their solitude proud and happy. I do not think Margaret has an uncommon tact at doing this, but I <u>have</u> seen her do it, in the <u>best</u> way. Her flow of language and power of association is very great. . . .

Dall went to Boston for a visit of a few weeks.

BOSTON. MASS.

FRIDAY. NOV. 20. 1846.

. . . After we left Horatia [Ware] we went to a Miss Southwick's[25] in High St. where Miss Haliburton[26] boards, to an Abolition party. The only two persons,

*The dwelling house of a Fourierist community.

who interested me much—were Mr. Garrison*—really very lofty and noble, and well-mannered, notwithstanding the vituperations of his pen—and Ambrose Wellington an intelligent young man, who has taken charge of the much abused public school for colored children in Belknap St.[27]

TUESDAY. JAN. 19. 1847.

Rose feeling miserably. Have a presentiment that I am in the family—way, which has depressed me, in spite of [illegible word] philosophy and religion. Have risen every morning for 10 days with a distressing headache and slight nausea, Oh that I could have been spared a little longer! I am not yet certain of my condition—but the pain which I suffer, undoubtedly proceeds from an excitement in the region of the uterus, though of what nature I cannot tell— I desire no exception from the common lot, except as far as may keep me, from losing my reason, as I increase my family, and I feel every excitement connected with maternity—through my brain.[28]

WEDNESDAY. JAN 27. 1847.

My low spirits do not leave me, and yet I would be in harmony with the purposes of God. It does seem very hard to go among strangers—†suffering from nausea, and in hourly expectation of a confinement. . . .

WEDNESDAY. MAR. 3. 1847.

Packed books for two or three hours this morning, with the help of Margaret Harris and Harriet Stevens. At—eleven o'clock A.M. began to flow. Felt disheartened but sat down quietly. In the afternoon that I might not be tempted to work went down to Mrs Shores's[29] to the meeting of the Missionary Society. Came home somewhat worse. Slept soundly through the night, but the flow was immense and on

---

*William Lloyd Garrison (1805–1879), leading Boston abolitionist, founder and editor of the abolitionist paper *The Liberator,* became in 1832 a founder of the New England Anti-Slavery Society and in 1833 of the American Anti-Slavery Society. He supported the public participation of women as speakers and officers in the movement, thus causing a break in 1840 with more conservative factions. By this time Garrison had suffered mobbing and imprisonment for his views *(DAB).*

†Dall is thinking of her impending move to Needham, where Charles has accepted a ministry.

THURSDAY. MAR. 4. 1847.

became so copious and exhausting a stream, that I sent for Dr. Cheever.[30] He presupposed, a miscarriage, ordered me flat upon my back—forbade my attempting to go to housekeeping until some time after my arrival in Needham— &c &c. . . .

Just as she was leaving Portsmouth, Dall was confronted by a case of sexual harassment in which her servant was the victim and a naval officer the perpetrator.

PORTSMOUTH N.H.

MONDAY. MAR 15. 1847.

Went after prayers, at Mr Peabody's to the house in Austin St. where I superintended the cleaning.* . . . Every body very kind, and pressing in their invitations for the future. Just as I rose from the dinner table, Lucy† sent for me up stairs. Alone in the deserted house, Lieut. White,‡ had grossly insulted her— And full of tears, and distress, she came for advice. Nothing could be said but "break off your engagement with the family instantly," but I felt very sorry to be obliged to say it, as I had this very morning recommended her highly to her new mistress. . . .

---

*Andrew Preston Peabody (1811–1893) was minister of the Unitarian South Parish in Portsmouth. Dall was temporarily staying with the Peabodys after having moved out of the rented house on Austin Street.

†Lucy Ann Walsh, the Dalls' servant, who was staying in Portsmouth rather than move with the Dalls. She was hired by the Whites (see below).

‡George McAllister White (1813–1882), a Georgia native and a lieutenant in the U.S. Navy, stationed at Portsmouth. His wife was Henrietta Nichols White (b. 1819). The White family was moving into the house the Dalls were vacating (1850 U.S. Census; *Ancestry.com*, accessed October 7, 2004).

CHAPTER SIX

The Needham Years

June 3, 1847–December 30, 1849

$\mathcal{T}$he Dalls took up residence in the rural town of Needham in the spring of 1847. Although it was only twelve miles southwest of Boston, travel from Needham into the city was inconvenient, requiring a journey first by road some five miles to Dedham to reach the railroad. The Dalls were thus effectively beyond the reach of Boston's social and cultural offerings; their world was largely that of small-town agricultural life, domestic duty, and church activities. Caroline wrestled with servant problems, finding it difficult to keep "girls" in Needham's relative remoteness. In the less than three years of their residence in the town she gave birth twice. Still, she managed to maintain an intellectual life: she taught a French class in her home, free to neighboring girls and women; she continued to read widely; she published her first book, *Essays and Sketches;* and she wrote significant articles on the Mexican War, slavery, and women's rights. And she thought earnestly on other social, moral, and religious questions, using her journals as a sounding board to explore such issues as class (she agonized over her relationship with servants, and was appalled at the plight of emigrants), sex, reproduction, and marriage in general, as well as the meaning of suffering.

At about the time the Dalls moved to Needham, it became apparent that Mark Healey, Caroline's father, had regained his fortune, and then some. He dispensed gifts generously, took Caroline on a trip to Niagara Falls, underwrote the publication of her book, purchased a fine estate in Lynn, on Boston's North Shore, and entertained Daniel Webster. But his newly restored prosperity was dependent on a stable business environment (he had business interests in Mississippi), and he was acutely conscious of the potential for serious disruption posed by the widening gap over slavery, a gap constantly exacerbated by the abolitionists. Although Mark Healey had paid for the publication of his daughter's book, he did not, it turned out, approve of its mildly reformist agenda. He exploded in fury upon learning that his family had attended an antislavery lecture, and he threatened Caroline that her continuation of such activities would "risk . . . losing his affection forever." Caroline, who had dedicated her book "To my Father, who first nurtured in me the love of truth and of God," now grieved to think that she had dedicated it "to my father as he was." This "schism" between them, as she called it, would only grow deeper over the next dozen years.

During this period (and after her father's explosion), Dall attended her first full-fledged antislavery convention in Boston. She was transported by the speaking, particularly by the eloquent oratory of Frederick Douglass, who "seemed to me while he spoke, greater than any man to whom I had ever listened." When she went to the stage to thank him, she could not help wondering, "What would father have said, had he seen me then?" But the threat of her father's displeasure was no match for Caroline Dall's sense of duty. And thus, although her first publication in *The Liberator* was a plea not to judge harshly the motives of Southern slaveholders who had sent aid to the Irish, she gradually aligned herself with the Garrisonians.

And she put in print, for the first time, the results of her thinking on the woman question. In *Essays and Sketches,* published at the close of 1848, she had deliberately dissociated herself from women's rights; by April 1849 she was composing an article that would put her in the forefront of the fledgling movement. She felt strongly the weight of responsibility, knowing that "No one can write as earnestly as I do, without influencing some few"; and thus, although she "might have written the article out at the first sitting," she instead wrote slowly and deliberately, "lest I should mistake my own vagaries for the suggestions of the spirit." The article, appearing in *The Liberator* in June, set forth the plea that she would spend the next two decades of her women's rights career simply elaborating.

In the journal entries that follow, Dall recounts in surprising and spellbinding detail the two childbirth events of these years. The first of these passages, tracing a tragic experience, is a small literary masterpiece, in which the reader's sense of horror is enhanced by the diarist's dispassionate listing of the child's unspeakable deformities. Dall's record of the unintended cruelty of friends who told her she was somehow to blame, and of her husband's failure to heed her "earnest entreaties" that he not publicize the details of the deformity, further engages the reader's sympathy. For once, in this extremity, her father rose to the occasion; he held her as she wept on his shoulder, and she observed, "Long as I may live it will be impossible for me ever to forget his tender fatherly pressure." When, only ten months after this experience, Dall recognized that she was again pregnant, she acquiesced to her fate in the thought that "Willie needs a companion and I ought to be willing to give him one." But she could not help fearing the birth of another deformed child. The birth of her daughter Sarah, however, had a happy outcome, and Dall's relief and maternal feelings overflowed in her description of the baby, "so cherub-like—so full of waving dimpling health," with "Not an awkward line—not an excrescence of any sort" on "her well developed head and frame!"

Charles Dall's pastorate at Needham ended unhappily; with his salary undependable and key members of his congregation displeased with him, it was clear that it was time to move on. He tried but failed to get a position as chaplain at the almshouse and reformatory in Boston. Caroline tried to see "in every discipline of Providence . . . the lesson God would teach." Yet at times, through all the perplexities of these years, she admitted, "I have been puzzled quite. It has been hard to keep my faith in God." But after all, she did. She continued to listen to the "voice—which I hear so plainly" and to wait "until I also receive—as I am sure I one day shall—some distinct call to some special work."

E. NEEDHAM MASS.

THURSDAY. JUNE 3D. 1847.

𝒲ent into town, to see father, and was well repaid for devoting my day to him, by seeing him, stronger, and in far better health than usual. He certainly seems to be gaining in temporal affairs also, for he was prodigal of presents today. He was preparing to give Ellen a gold watch, but thought it would not answer, to give his <u>second</u> daughter one first, so I was included in his bounty. I came home loaded with gifts. The watch, and a pongee* dress from him, a bottle of

*A soft, thin fabric woven from raw silk.

wine, and one of mead from mother—a dress for Willie and trimming from Ellen. It does my heart good to see him in such good spirits. He said that he bought a ticket to the opera—last night, thinking I should come in, and should like to go, but as I did not, was obliged to go himself. How thankful I am that Providence protected me, and that yielding to the desires of the children, I did not go into town. It seems to me, very important to decide, whether the clergy —or all good men, should support the drama or not. While I doubt, I do not consider it safe to go, but it would have been a severe trial to have disappointed so kind a father as mine. . . .

E. NEEDHAM, MASS.
SATURDAY, JUNE 5. 1847.

A busy morning. . . . In the afternoon, my class* assembled, 6 in all. My mind greatly exercised about my cook. She is restive, self willed, and by no means prompt to obey. Asking her where the water-pail was—she told me indifferently "some-where about." Frank Stedman[1] was waiting for a drink of water, and I obliged her to get it at once. Query: Was I right or wrong? As service now stands,—ought I not, for her own good, to oblige her, to be constantly respectful—? Yet is it always worth while, to break love—for the sake of doing it.— How can she see the difference between wilfulness and perseverance on my part—and why should the former be more becoming to my character than hers? God grant me light for these problems are in this country, as important as those of slavery or war. It is extremely difficult to manage Irish servants without maintaining the strictest subordination. With Americans, I always proceed easily, by flattering their self-respect.

E. NEEDHAM.
SUNDAY. JUNE 13. 1847.

Was hardly through with my arrangements for dinner, before father and mother arrived. I had on the whole a delightful visit from them, though their departure left me, somewhat depressed. Mother was in high spirits, for father has recently bought a fine place at Lynn,—where he moves his whole family on the 15th of July. . . . Just at the close of his visit, father told me, that he was going to Chicago, on the 25th instant, and mother was going with him as far as

*The French class that she taught free to neighboring girls and women.

Niagara. If I were willing to leave Willie, he would pay the expenses of my journey. This gave me much exercise of mind, so I dressed and walked down to the church to the 3d. meeting ....

Dall accepted her father's offer to take her to Niagara Falls.

BUFFALO. N.Y.

SUNDAY. JUNE 27. 1847.

... Averse as we all are to travelling on Sunday, we found ourselves obliged to leave Buffalo at 8 o'clock this morning—for Niagara—.... When we left the cars, we walked directly to the Cataract House—passing the pleasant residence of Miss Elizabeth Porter.[2] In the meantime Mr. Warren and his wife[3] had been persuading me, to ask father to let me return by way of the Canadas with them. I inclined to this—because I should in that way be much sooner at home, and in fact see more of the country, but I did not like to tell father— so, lest I should wound his feelings—always so tender— ... We then went down to the American fall—where standing on a projected platform, fastened to the rock by bolts and the weight of several tons of broken stone, we got what I consider the <u>finest</u> view of the fall—. No subsequent experience changed my opinion. ...

Dinner is an important matter at the Cataract.* The table is very good, and dressed beautifully with fresh flowers. On week days the waiters evolve to music but on Sunday, the band is dismissed; They enter however two by two and so scrupulously observe the directions of the head waiter, that every man keeps time with his neighbor. In placing the dessert—a procession of four— moves round each table—and at one instant is dropped a plate—knife fork & spoon—from those who have the charge of them.

The confectionary is beautiful & elaborate. The water is very fine to the taste and probably safer than any seen, since we left Albany.

... We were let down the bank about 300 ft—, in a curious little car—that looked like a wheelbarrow with shelves in it, and was moved by a wheel turned by water to the ferry landing—. A pleasant little row boat carried us as far up into the mist as it dared—and then drew up on the opposite shore. The first view of the falls from the Canada side is almost overwhelming, yet, I do not prefer it, nor should I like to stay at the Clifton House—where the wearisome

---

*The Cataract House, a Niagara Falls hotel.

ongoing of the waters would be ever in sight. . . . From Table Rock—we gazed with intense and ever growing wonder on the fall. On this side—we are impressed with its grandeur—as before with its beauty. Thousands of rainbows encircled it, and as the wind parted the spray, it was beautiful to see them fade & form, and fade again—. . . . After our return to the drawing-room we had a short conversation with the Warrens, in which it was decided that mother and I should accompany them to Canada, provided Mr. Warren would pledge himself to avoid the ship-fever—and upon looking at our watches, were surprised to find it 12 o'clock.

OGDENSBURG. N.Y.

FRIDAY JULY 2. 1847.

We arrived at Ogdensburg at 12 (PM). last night. . . . After breakfast—we came along side of the British Empire, a larger and better boat, crowded however like the Lady of the Lake, with emigrants. A child had died on board, during the night and they went on shore to bury it. Five or six children with their parents, were washing themselves at the side of the boat, and wiped upon one towel, as coarse as any floor cloth I ever saw. Many were sick and the common suffering had made them very harsh toward one another. A mother had lost her bonnet overboard, and struck her children when they ventured to condole with her—for the rest, she evidently expected no sympathy—from those who were best able to afford, her help. Mr. Warren is not very quick to seize an opportunity—and we were obliged on account of a movement in the Empire to press through the crowd of sick emigrants in order to reach her. A man on either side, held a stick—and cried "back back—!" as if they were a pack of animals, and they stared at us, as if we were of another species, as we passed. I wrote to Charles just after we reached the Empire— I did not tell him how homesick I felt—but at the moment I felt that no increase of knowledge or experience could compensate for a longer absence from home. There were several sick emigrants still on board, and we were meeting more ghastly forms at every landing. . . .

MONTREAL. CANADA,

SATURDAY JULY 3D. 1847.

. . . . Our boat was the Burlington, which Capt. Sherman—has left within the year. It was without exception delightfully clean, the boards were polished and if any-thing like a tobacco spot were observed, a wet mop immediately removed it from the deck. The dinner on board this boat, was served with elegance and precision, the cloth was taken off, and the dessert regularly laid. It is now in the hands of Capt. Anderson— Spit boxes—were placed in all directions, but they did not offend the eye, for they were green painted pots, filled with fresh and growing turf.... Our boat was crowded with Emigrants, who while we were at dinner desired to press aft for more air— All through the dinner hour—we heard the heavy tramp of the guard, and the words often repeated—"back—back!" The evening was beautiful—the Warrens enjoyed it on the upper deck—but I was tired of the moans of these poor prisoners, and weary of the sight of their parched lips and glazed eyes, so I sat alone in the stern of the vessel—meditating on their fate, and praying the great father that he, would give me, knowledge of how to serve them....

Having returned home, Caroline accompanied Charles to a preaching engagement in Lexington, Massachusetts; from there they went, via Boston, to her family's new home in Lynn.

LEXINGTON BOSTON—LYNN—MS.
MONDAY AUG 2. 1847.

... Thence we went down to father's office and thence to Lynn, where he has indeed a princely house & garden. I was surprised at the beauty of the place, at the wideness of father's plans, at the richness of the furniture he has ordered &c. but I was grieved at the selfishness and want of appreciation of all this, in the children. Two of the best years of my life, I sacrificed to them, and much of my health—it is hard to feel that they entirely despise all that I struggled for. It is hard to feel that father no longer thinks education the important matter he once did. The tears came, into my eyes when I found that George had not applied for admission to the Latin School—and I had to reenter the quiet of my Needham home, before I felt happy after this visit. In the cars had a pleasant talk with Mr. Wait of Gloucester[4] & read my own article on War[*]—fewer misprints than usual— ...

E. NEEDHAM MS.
SATURDAY AUG. 7. 1847.

It began to rain early this morning and has continued to pour all day. Fortunately, we got our oil-cask early this morning—and every vessel we could find

---

[*]It is likely that Dall is the author of an article in the Boston *Daily Chronotype* (July 22, 1847, p. 1) entitled "The War" and signed "Domino." The article presents a scathing critique of the Mexican War.

Ashton, the Healey family home in West Lynn, Massachusetts: "indeed a princely
house and garden." (Courtesy of Lynn Museum and Historical Society)

is full of water. I have written an article for the Liberator, too strong to be inserted I fear.[5] I read Carlyle's German Romance.[6] I looked forward all day with
anxiety— I have settled it in my own mind that I am in the family way
—and the <u>moving</u>,* the changes and so on, which must come, if not before—
perhaps at the very period of my confinement fill me with alarm. God be merciful to me, and send me greater health and strength—.

"Letter from Mrs. C. W. H. Dall" appeared in The Liberator *for August 27,
1847. In it Dall took exception to the objections expressed by American abolitionist Henry C. Wright (1797–1870) and Dublin merchant and abolitionist James
Haughton (1795–1873) regarding contributions taken up in the American South
for the destitute in Ireland. She asked for moderation in judging the motives of
these slaveholders, arguing that many of them were ignorant and well meaning,
that they should not be condemned for the good work of helping the starving Irish,
and that those more enlightened than they should attempt to educate them out of
their ignorance rather than question their philanthropic motives. The article
was accompanied by a rejoinder by Edmund Quincy (1808–1877), reformer and
author, a frequent editor of* The Liberator *in Garrison's absence.*

---

*The Dalls were to move to a parsonage being built by the church.

CAMBRIDGE. MASS.

THURSDAY AUG. 26. 1847....

We stopped at the post as we returned, and took out the Liberator. There was my letter at last—well cut up by a most one-sided article of Edmund Quincy's. I think however I might safely trust to the common sense of any one, who should read the two articles.

His review of it is very blind. He does not at all touch my point, which is—that the motives of men—only <u>God</u>, can or ought to judge.

E. NEEDHAM MASS.

SUNDAY. AUG. 29. 1847....

...To my great amusement Wm Ritchie[7] thought Mr Quincy had <u>entirely used me</u> up. My eyes are still open however. He said to me at parting—that there were a plenty of people ready and willing to speak for the slave holder. I told him I did not think so—<u>to do justice</u> to an obnoxious person—required in these days—no small amount of moral courage— In my case, it pleased neither one party nor the other. I knew this when I wrote the article—but my object was, <u>not</u> to please—but to do my duty, therefore I did not hesitate.

Mr. Pike* dined with me— I went to bed—as soon as he had gone—and did not rise till dusk—when in spite of much suffering, I walked three miles to console Mrs Hersey,[8] who was very much afflicted that on this the first Sunday after her bereavement Mr. Dall should exchange.

SATURDAY OCT. 16. 1847.

...I wrote several letters, and had a long painful talk, with my husband—in which I proposed to him—, that I should either remain silent at our evening meetings, or should cease to go to them. I made this proposal with many tears, and feeling that it was a great sacrifice, but it was accepted, for my husband feels as I do, that my earnest enthusiastic nature, is in great danger of being misunderstood—by these plain country people.

E. NEEDHAM MASS.

FRIDAY. DEC. 31. 1847.

...I have had many trying thoughts in connexion with the close of the year. My heart is not so light as it was last year—at this time. I have committed one

---

*Richard Pike (1813–1863), Unitarian minister at Dorchester. He had exchanged pulpits with Charles Dall for the day (*Heralds* 3:265).

great fault, I have required too entire an appreciation of my own character by my husband—while in my turn, I have not shown that indulgence toward him, which <u>he</u> especially needs. I have had many wretched hours— May God forgive me, and spare me such in the coming year.

E. NEEDHAM MASS.
SUNDAY, FEB. 6. 1848.

I woke up in the night and heard it snowing hard, and when we rose—the storm still continued. We must go to church three miles in an open sleigh, and I should not have thought of venturing, had it not been, that it was Communion Day, and I knew my husband had as usual two new sermons. I would not have lost the glory of the day, however for a great deal. A stiff northwester blew the snow in my face, like thousands of little knives, but the snow was on all sides at least eighteen inches deep—on top of many of the pines large snow banks had collected the forest was bowed in oriental prostration—birches, alders, and other yielding trees—swept the earth with their foreheads —or had planted their very tops as if with the intention of a new growth—in the bosom of an immense snow bank. My heart was full, I was so glad that I longed to dash through the drifts like some frightened horses that we saw on our road. . . .

TUESDAY MAR 14. 1848.

. . . occupied myself with Mr Parker's sermon on the death of John Q. Adams.[9] This event,—so much greater than any sermon that has been written on it,—occurred while I was in the hurry of my moving. Mr Parker's sermon possesses one merit over any other I have seen. It does not hide his faults. It might have added one to the catalogue—in his ambition to be a poet—for which he was no better fitted by Nature than myself. We have both of us written much that "rhymes well—" and it is on account of the difficulty which we met in our first attempts, that we are proud of it. Our power over language—makes "rhyme" at last come easy—but poor Poetry blushes when we call on her. It is well that we have faith in God—for it certainly seems as if the nation, never could more ill afford the loss of such a man—. But all is for the best. He died with a great No! upon his lips.*

*That is, his staunch opposition to slavery and the Mexican War.

FRIDAY. APRIL 21. 1848.

It is five weeks tomorrow since my confinement; and I take up my pen—with a heavy heart, and retrace my painful steps.

On Saturday morning March. 18. 1848. I was seized with pains slight at first but rapidly becoming more severe, at the breakfast table. I washed up my silver, however & made some blancmange,[10] and prepared my basket— while Mr. Dall went for Mrs Parker, and to ask Dr Noyes[11] to remain at home through the day. I was just on the point of preparing my bed, when I felt a sudden relief—from the breaking of the water. I undressed & threw myself hastily on the bed, from which I was not destined to rise again, till all was over. Meanwhile my girl ran for the Doctor and Mrs Revere[12] my nearest neighbor. They staid with me—until my husband returned which was at half past nine A.M. At one P.M. we had dinner—and as my husband left the room, he stopped and held me, through my first severe pain. Our Irish cook came up to stay with me —while they ate— Two pains rending—spitting—tearing me asunder—with inconceivable rapidity, followed quick upon the first, and while my girl went to the head of the stairs, to call Mrs P. I fell back exhausted by agony and my child was born. My child! why should I call it so—! but after one has borne a second life about with her, for eight months—it is impossible not to love it, though it should prove an abortion. The babe was a boy—& had a hare lip— Its hands & feet were bent in, and enlarged at the wrists & ankles. It had no thumb on the right hand—but instead five fingers—the fifth growing out of the first. The smaller intestines were formed on the outside and the scrotum was deficient. It had been dead at least a fortnight the cuticle slipping at the touch. On Friday March. 3d. I was attacked with ague fits and nausea—and it was probably at that time the child died. Its feebleness will be readily understood, when I say that I felt as much motion on the 17th of March, as I have ever done.

My mother—and attendants referred all my trials, to previous mental impressions—but I could not yield to this— I still believed in the benevolence of God. I was thankful to him in His Infinite Mercy—for prompting the ride to Boston—which by accelerating my confinement probably saved my life. During the first week—Aunt Sarah took care of me, God bless her for her faithful love. Mother came to see me, and sent me out several things which made my condition more comfortable. Mrs. Rowe[13] came as soon as she could be spared from the side of her sick mother. I was spotted almost as if with putrid fever for several weeks. I did not gain very fast—for Charles in his love of truth—after having buried his little one, with his own trembling hands—was altogether too communicative* to those who enquired, and the consequence was that the town rung with the peculiarities of the case—and constant aggravations of them, coming from the neighbors to my bedside, worried me. My husband would not understand my earnest entreaties, that I might—be spared this bitter trial—and his want of sympathy, finished my misery. I was already bent beneath the hand of God—quite low enough—but the hours have past —and may the Father of Mercies grant—never to return. A very sore mouth bore evidence of my weakness—and, dyspepsia followed every mouthful I ate. Charles remonstrated with one of the gossips who troubled me most—and this piece of indiscretion raising her ire—she has been teeming with malice & mischief ever since. I have suffered a little from her—, ignorant & designing as she is. As I did not gain, as was desired—on Wednesday April 12 I left my husband my child—and my home to stay in Lynn—a few days— After innumerable delays & fatigues—I reached Lynn—at 7 o'clock on that evening, perfectly worn out. I led a very lazy life, reading, riding &c for several days and gained perceptibly. . . .

★The extent of Charles's statement was that "the intestines were on the outside": thus accounting for its death. This & more I had previously told him to state by letter to my family at Lynn & his in Baltimore. [This note at the bottom of the page is in Charles Dall's hand.]

LYNN MASS. SATURDAY APRIL 15. 1848. [WRITTEN APRIL 21]
My nurse had left me and returned to Boston. We were just at breakfast when father returned from the West— I caught his first embrace in the entry, and the Question "where is your baby?" brought the ready tears to my eyes. He held me—with a father's pressure—to his bosom as I sobbed—forth my reply. I laid my head upon his shoulder and wept there—for our mutual suffering brought back the hour of Charlie's death. Long as I may live it will be impossible for me ever to forget his tender fatherly pressure. . . .

BOSTON, TUESDAY, APRIL 18. 1848. [WRITTEN APRIL 21]
Father kindly gave me 50 dollars this morning, after enquiring what furniture I wanted for my new house. I told him I desired only to pay, for the few necessaries that I had! God will reward him for thinking of me so constantly. . . . I

went to see Dr. Warren[14] at half past twelve o'clock. After a long interview he told me to dismiss the subject of my confinement entirely from my mind, that I was in no wise responsible for its results—that he did not believe in the effect of mental impressions on the child—that children deformed like mine were the common result of a great weakness—either in the mother or the child. . . .

E. NEEDHAM MASS.

TUESDAY. JUNE 6. 1848.

Charles came home late to dinner today, after a long meeting with the Parish Committee, discussing various affairs. They have raised our rent five dollars, to which my husband did very wrong to submit considering our circumstances. They insist that the salary cannot be raised punctually, and Mr Stedman[15] volunteered to find us provision dealers in town, who would <u>wait our convenience</u> for pay. This impudent interference in our affairs is more than I can tolerate. I sometimes think that we are sent upon a mission of punctuality—and that we must go from place to place—teaching people the need of it. God's will be done, but I beseech Him, that there be no delays in Heaven. One thing is certain—we must leave this place, provided a greater punctuality be not speedily found.

I wrote for the Liberty Bell this morning,[16] and this afternoon, I finished Schiller's Life.[17] Carlyle has never written anything more pure, more just and affectionate than this. I was forcibly reminded of myself—by what he says of Schiller's censurable habit of working by night. He loves Schiller better for this fault, better because "if it were an error, so to waste his strength, it was one of those which increase rather than diminish our respect, originating as it did in generous ardor for what is best and grandest." Because the "toil-worn, but devoted soul, alone under the silent starry canopy of Night, offering up the troubled moments of existence on the altar of Eternity," was "a sight to warm a heart of stone." Something of such a consideration as this, I feel that I often times deserve when I receive, only even from my husband or my friends, cold censure. I spend my body—and my soul, they say, & I <u>might</u> help it—when shall I be repaid? I demand too much of people, I tell them the truth too plainly—I persist in an activity which destroys them and myself. Good God! can they not recognize thy voice—which I hear so plainly? See they not the love of thy Justice which urges me on? Alas! through what a troubled and unworthy medium, must the clear rays of these pass if no man perceive them.

E. NEEDHAM MASS.

SATURDAY JULY 1ST. 1848

Ill & weary but gathered strength enough to seat two pairs of pants. While I was working, Miss Spalding read to me from Victor Hugo's Rhine.[18] Could not attend it for my mind was on Channing.*

I have read in the 3d vol. the account of the progress of his mind on the subject of slavery with great interest. I have read it too, without feeling rebuked, for it is the history of my own progress. My opinions were not as important to the world as his—but they were equally important to me—with the same conscientiousness and thoroughness were they decided. My tears flowed freely, over the pages of the Memoir—for his doubts and difficulties recalled to me my own—and yet I doubt whether I have any where recorded my own. My Journal—I have kept chiefly to establish my connections with the outward world—as a sort of link between me, & what I was afraid of forgetting—I never forget that on which I have deeply thought nor have I ever had the time, even had I possessed the inclination to do justice to my struggles. Nor have I ever had the inclination for it wearies me to dwell—on what—in the experience of it—has so utterly exhausted my mind. Thank Heaven! that true progress of soul does not depend upon the annotations of the pen. It is helped by them nevertheless. Those who are interested in me—would be diverted to know how little I have read on the subjects which have chiefly occupied my mind and pen. It always puzzles me to read reasonings & opinions—I like to express them—after I have worked my way to them—but I cannot take them from another. From my youth up—passionately fond of reading of logic—metaphysics, mathematics—I yet never could bear controversy, about primary ideas of religion and morality. Instinctively—I avoided it— I could not listen to such sermons—hardly indeed to any, for my mind would go about better business. I had written Essays for publication for two years—when I accidentally read one or two numbers of the Rambler, & found that Johnson[19] had written on the same subjects & in the same way long before me. I could not however, but think, that I had the advantage of him in earnestness, and still later—I found my own lucubrations nearly word for word in Knox's Winter evenings.[20]

---

*Dall had been reading the three-volume *Memoir of William Ellery Channing,* edited by William H. Channing (Boston: William Crosby and H.P. Nichols, 1848). William Ellery Channing (1780–1842), Unitarian clergyman and author, for nearly forty years minister of the Federal Street Church in Boston, was the leading figure in the early development of American Unitarianism.

On the matter of slavery I meditated for years—though in my extreme youth I was singularly indifferent to it—that is, considering I was interested in correlative reforms and realized that they were all united in the spirit of Christianity, and must advance <u>together</u>, to advance surely. I was about twelve, I think—when at the lectures before the American Institute of Education,[21] Mrs Chapman* became interested in me and urged me to come and see her. I knew nothing of her, I lived among pro-slavery people—I should say, among people who were indifferent to the matter—for I heard nothing on either side—not even of Mrs Chapman—but I had heard my father say, that "we had no right to interfere in the matter— The South must act for itself." I went to Mrs Chapman's. She was very kind to me & showed me pictures. Among them was a strange caricature—upon slave institutions. It pained me—I think it would pain me quite as much now. I turned it over quickly. "Do you not like it," she asked— "No" said I. "I think we have no right to meddle with the subject." I remember now, the expression of deep grief, which passed over her then beautiful countenance. Ann Chapman[22] was in the room. There was a pause. I felt that I had said something which disturbed the harmony between us. It was interrupted by an exchange of glances between the two. Why they said nothing more, I cannot guess, perhaps they were moved by a vague feeling that it was not honorable to attempt to influence a child without its parents' knowledge. They should rather have remembered that I was a human being, and had a right to every influence for good.

I went home and told my father quietly what had happened. He exchanged a glance with my mother and said, "I do not think she will ask you to come and see her again." It dwelt on my mind—months passed— I heard no more of Mrs C. and I finally asked my father the reason. "I thought you knew—" said he "she is an abolitionist and you have offended her." "She is not very candid" said I—"to give up a child as hopeless in that way." and then I forgot all about her. I thought but little on the subject still— I believe I never saw a[n] Anti Slavery paper—until after my first article in the Liberty Bell was published. I have never to this day read an Anti Slavery Work—not even Channing—. I never heard an anti-slavery argument but once—and that was in Greenfield.[23] I never attended an Anti Slavery Convention until this last May. Without any

*Maria Weston Chapman (1806–1885), prominent Boston abolitionist, was a founder, in 1834, of the Boston Female Anti-Slavery Society. She was editor of *The Liberty Bell* and author of the annual report (1836–1844) *Right and Wrong in Boston.*

help of this kind, it was not to be expected that my progress would be very rapid. It was not until I went to the South—that my mind was made up determinately— I had always been interested in the free colored poor, of Boston— and when I went among the poor both white & colored in the District, I could not help seeing that more demoralizing influences were brought to bear upon them—than upon the Northern poor, & I inquired into it. When I became thoroughly, interested in the subject—I was still at a loss—as to what I should do. I owed a duty to the slave but what was it? I weighed the question well, but I decided differently from Dr. C. Three years—I longed to write & speak upon the subject—but feared to hurt—rather than help the truth. At last, I saw that if I hoped to make any impression upon those whose harshness I did not approve—I must show a willingness to bear their cross, and with gentle remonstrances I placed myself at the side of Garrison—where I hope to be able to stand. It is beautiful to see so great a man as Dr C. so conscientious, but when once assured of his duty, why could he not press the matter more? In commenting upon his first visit to an Anti slavery Convention, he spoke of the almost universal talent for public speaking in this country. Mr Hincks of England, also directed my attention to this. May it not arise in part from that habit of independence and self reliance—which our institutions foster? Why should not the man speak—who feels himself <u>free</u>?

BOSTON MASS.

WEDNESDAY. JULY 5. 1848.

Went this morning to see the Greek Slave.* All else that I have done today, sinks into insignificance beside the sight of, Powers' beautiful work of art. I have seen only casts of the Venus & Apollo[24]—but this I am convinced exceeds them in beauty and purity as much as Christianity excels the Roman mythology in its tone & spirit. The right hand of the slave rests on a pile of clothing at her side 2 richly embroidered shawls—her cross & rosary—surmounted by her greek cap. Her hands are chained together. Her head is turned aside as if to escape the consciousness of her degradation. Her throat swells—

---

*Perhaps the most celebrated single statue of the day, the *Greek Slave* was sculpted by the American artist Hiram Powers (1805–1873), who lived from 1837 in Florence. The statue was at Horticultural Hall in Boston at the beginning of a multicity exhibition tour. Powers did several marble versions of the work; the version that Dall saw is now in the Newark Museum. See *DAB* and Richard P. Wunder, *Hiram Powers: Vermont Sculptor, 1805–1873* (Newark, New Jersey: University of Delaware Press, 1989–1991), 2:164.

wounded reserve dwells on her beautiful but trembling lip, I know not what
the people mean who speak of the want of sadness in the face— I can fancy I
see the eloquent blood mounting there. How glad I am I have lived to see this
work of Art—so spiritual—so impossible to have been produced in the Past.
It is sad to remember how the artist studied the forms of the degraded,—before he could have conceived this beauty, but God send us—speedily a state of
feeling which shall give Nature to the artist without degradation, and without
shame. The block of marble itself is so pure that it is worth going miles to see.
It is from a new quarry which promises us a great deal of Art in the future, by
its vastness.

LYNN. MASS.

MONDAY JULY 31ST. 1848.

I took a carriage this morning, and after finding my way to my baggage at the
Worcester dépôt, went to Lynn as fast as possible. I came down with the intention of going to the Anti Slavery Convention tomorrow—but finding that
father was very angry about it, and insisted that no one should go from his
house, I resolved to stay at home.

I did not know what to do—for I feared to sacrifice principle.— Still I remembered that my name was publicly pledged to the cause, and that all I had
hoped from the pic-nic was the pleasure of hearing Lucy Stone*speak. I therefore resolved to do what was most difficult to myself— It could not be a right
feeling I thought which prompted me to offend my father—in his old age, and
borne down as he already is with many trials. . . .

W. LYNN MASS.

MONDAY. AUG 28. 1848. . . .

Read today the greater part of the second vol of Mrs Fry's Life.† Impressed as
before—with parallel passages to many in my own life. I think I have the faculty

---

*Lucy Stone (1818–1893), the first Massachusetts woman to hold a college degree (from Oberlin Col-
lege, 1847), became in 1848 a lecturer for the American Anti-Slavery Society. She soon began speaking
out on women's rights as well and helped found the American Woman Suffrage Association. She and her
husband, Henry B. Blackwell (whose name she did not assume), edited the *Woman's Journal* beginning in
1872 *(NAW)*.

†Elizabeth Fry (1780–1845) was an English prison reformer and Quaker preacher. A two-volume
American edition of *Memoir of the Life of Elizabeth Fry, with Extracts from Her Journal and Letters,* edited by two of her daughters, appeared in 1847–1848.

she had, of making up my mind rightly and quickly, without being able to explain the process to others. I have also throughout my life been the staff of many older than I. In seeing how much she accomplished in the care of prisons—I feel myself so moved that I have hardly patience to wait, until I also receive—as I am sure I one day shall—some distinct call to some special work. . . .

TUESDAY. SEPT 19. 1848.

. . . I kept myself busy with my needle for a time, then commenced an article for publication and wrote till dinner, took care of Willie for an hour. . . . We had letters from Lynn & Boston speaking of mother's departure—which led Charles to say that the last time he saw her, she and Ellen were praising the neatness and order of my housekeeping. I was only afraid lest she might have found something to find fault with. I desire to be a perfect housekeeper—but am always afraid lest in a higher love of better things, I should omit some necessary trifle. I would not add to the reproaches cast upon literary women—and truly believe—that I often work or scrub—when I might read because I so fear the being led astray by my inclination.

E NEEDHAM MASS.

WEDNESDAY. SEPT 27. 1848.

. . . Reached Lynn—at half past five and found them all in great commotion, dressing the house with flowers and so forth—in honor of Mr Webster's expected arrival.* Mrs. Hawes[25] came in the same train from Boston as myself. I liked her very much. Mr Webster did not come to tea, but a note from him, saying that he would be here to breakfast. The house was full of Committee men, all the evening, and I had a great deal of interesting conversation with Allen Dodge, formerly a New York lawyer, now a farmer in Hamilton who has sent 1270 lbs of butter to market this summer.[26] Went to bed at 10—well tired.

W. LYNN. MASS.

THURSDAY. SEPT. 28. 1848.

Rose this morning very early and made some rye bread for breakfast. Mr Webster came at about eight, suffering dreadfully from catarrhal influenza which

---

*Daniel Webster was coming to Lynn to speak at the Annual Exhibition of the Essex Agricultural Society, at which he was described as the "greatest attraction" (*Lynn News,* October 6, 1848, p. 2).

attacks him annually on the 22nd of August—departing about the first of October. At about ten o'clock the Committee waited upon him with Mr Fay's[27] barouche and took him to the Cattle show & ploughing match. He brought down Mr Charles March with him, brother to Susan March of Portsmouth— a dissipated man I fear.[28] I was very much interested in the ploughing match. More than sixty teams were entered for the competition and some of the work was beautifully done. After this there was a trial of the strength of working oxen on Tower Hill. Then we went to the Horticultural exhibition, one of the finest county shows I ever saw.

At dinner time, Mr Webster was escorted from the house with a band of music. I left the table soon after, in order to hear such speaking as might be done in the church— Mr Webster however was not able to remain, and in the course of an hour returned in his carriage to Boston.

He was suffering from both bodily and mental indisposition. He often threw himself back in his chair and groaned—oh so heavily! When I came in, from walking, he said "I meditated a very sentimental kind of intercourse with you, but this very young woman, your mother, stepped up before you, I was about to ask you for a handkerchief." Some idea of his catarrh may be had, from the fact—that in the few hours he was with us—he used nine handkerchiefs, five of which he borrowed of my mother.

He was in a state of great depression owing doubtless to both political and domestic disappointments.* I never saw a man more changed in one year than he. It seemed to me that God's hand was upon him; and I could not even judge him as severely as is my wont. Once I said accidentally that although I did not like to impute such apparent injustice to God—yet there were times when—I could hardly help believing that men were born with different degrees of conscientiousness— "No doubt of it" "no doubt of it—" he repeated with emphasis, and from some cause or other seemed to derive satisfaction from the thought. He talked with me a good deal—but if he had been well—there were things on my mind which I meant to have said as it was—he suffered quite enough—. He explained to me the difference between the English and American mode of ploughing, alluded to by Mr Dodge last night— The English do

---

*Webster had lost the Whig nomination for president to Zachary Taylor, and two of his adult children, Edward Webster (1820–1848) and Julia Webster Appleton (1818–1848), had died during the course of the year. See Charles M. Wiltse and Harold D. Moser, eds., *The Papers of Daniel Webster: Correspondence* (Hanover, New Hampshire: University Press of New England, 1974–1989), 6:272–273, 284.

not turn their sods wholly over, but incline them at an angle of 45 degrees—
Mr Dodge thought it was to drain their heavier soil better. Mr Webster explained that it was to admit the air more fully.

In the evening, I went with Ellen to the levee, as an act of condescension[29]
to the Lynn people—who had allowed us to monopolize Mr Webster all day.
Mr Rufus Choate Mr King[30] and others were expected but I presume Mr
Choate detained them too late at Salem—listening to his address—in behalf of
General Taylor.* I went late to bed, very weary. . . .

WEDNESDAY NOV. 29. 1848.

Mr Revere[31] offered to take me in to Boston. Rode away from the door with a
heavy heart. Saw Simpkins, and he promised to manage the publishing of the
book,† provided I could get anybody to furnish the funds—viz: $130.—he hav-
ing at this time none to spare.

Went down to Lynn just after dinner, talked the matter over with father, who is very willing, and offers all I need. They were extravagantly glad
to see me—

W. LYNN. MASS.

FRIDAY. DEC 29. 1848.

. . . Received some copies of my book [*Essays and Sketches*]—and distributed
[them]. I was in hopes he [Dall's father] would be pleased by the Dedica-
tion‡—but he was not— He read it steadily through, and then said that the article on the Sabbath had better have been left out. That on Reforms would do
me no credit—nor that on War—nobody would buy the book but abolitionists— I could not expect it would sell. This was hard to bear—but I swallowed
my disappointment. Oh God—have mercy on him—show him the right way—
and grant at least, this prayer of thy servant—that she may never blush for one
word that volume contains. Successful it may not be—profitable it may not

---

*Zachary Taylor (1784–1850), the Whig nominee, and soon to become the successful candidate, for
president.

†Samuel Grant Simpkins (1802–1889) was a Boston bookseller and publisher. See Peter Thacher,
Samuel Grant Simpkins: A Memorial (Boston, 1890). Dall was negotiating the publication of her first book,
to be entitled *Essays and Sketches*.

‡The dedication for Dall's first book-length publication, *Essays and Sketches,* read: "To my Father,
who first nurtured in me the love of truth and of God, this volume is affectionately dedicated. / 'We never
see the stars, / Till we can see naught but them. So with Truth.' "

be—but if it be not thy truth, let her be led through disappointment and chastisement to a clearer sight.

We spent the evening pleasantly with the Shackfords.[32] I was weary—and sad at heart.

W. LYNN MASS.

SUNDAY DEC 31. 1848.

Mr Higginson from Newburyport preached.[33] In the morning the text was— "Be not weary of well doing."[34] In the afternoon—""Silver & gold have I none &c".[35] Both very fine.

In the evening he took tea with us, and delivered a very fine lecture on American Slavery at Lyceum Hall. Five of us—Mother, Ellen, Fannie, Anna* and myself went to this lecture, supposing that father permitted us to do so. We were wrong. A terrible explosion followed our return. We came home very happy and though I write this on the 3d of Jan. I cannot to this hour imagine how father could have found the heart to make us all so miserable.

He was very angry and told me that if I continued my anti slavery efforts I should do it at the risk of losing his affection forever.

I told him—that I had borne the comparative poverty that would result from that before, and could bear it again. It would be hard God knew—to lose his affection—but harder still to lose the Love of God.

I took the whole blame of the affair on myself—and told him that I could not believe, he was so different now from what he had been—&c—but enough the subject makes me sick— It was a sad close to 1848 and 1849 had dawned before I could close my eyes—

At mother's intercession—dear kind mother—father allowed me to kiss <u>him</u> before I went to bed.

JAN. 1ST BOSTON MASS. 1849. . . .

I have thought a good deal of father—I feel so grieved that this schism should have appeared just now as if to give the lie to the spirit of my dedication. It is so sad to feel as if I had dedicated my book to my father <u>as he was</u>. He did not find out that the book was dedicated to him, until yesterday after noon—when

---

*Three of Dall's five sisters, including the previously unidentified Frances Wells ("Fannie") Healey (1829–1902).

we were all at church. Little Emily was the only person with him, when he made the discovery—and she thought he was highly pleased. He said nothing to me or mother about it—and he easily might for I am sure our discussion in the evening, must have reminded him of the words—

—"We never see the stars—

Till we can see naught but them; So with Truth."

E NEEDHAM MASS.

THURSDAY. JAN. 4. 1849....

As I sat reading—Mr D[all] was busy looking over his past year's Journal, from which he read in a tone of amusement the following—entry. "Today Carrie made a choice pudding—from crackers too old to eat." "What in the world did you enter that for?" said I laughing. "Because," said he "when I am gone, I want people to know—that writer and reader that you are, you are also a good mother and a good housekeeper." Many persons would have laughed at this, but on the contrary, my eyes filled with tears, for I know how very anxious he constantly is that I should be rightly understood.

In January 1849 Dall realized that she was pregnant again.

E. NEEDHAM. MASS.

SATURDAY. JAN. 20. 1849.

... At times I feel quite anxious in looking forward to another confinement, but Willie needs a companion and I ought to be willing to give him one. Yet at times the thought will come over me that I may bring into the world a deformed child. And if I should? May not mercy mingle with this judgment? May not such a trial be the very thing I need to teach me humility and patience? God knoweth.

E NEEDHAM MASS.

FEB. 27. 1849. TUESDAY.

Another week of suffering—suffering almost too severe to bear. Suffering of body and suffering of mind— In every discipline of Providence, I have hitherto striven to look it in the face and meekly learn the lesson God would teach—but of late I have been puzzled quite. It has been hard to keep my faith in God. I sometimes feel as if he were trying to teach me that there is no such thing as peace on earth—no true support—no source of sympathy to be trusted. But do I need this lesson? Have I not looked forward earnestly enough to a better life? Have I not pressed towards it? Have I not been almost sternly and severely dutiful thus far? Teach me oh my father! teach me—am I not willing to learn? And for the anguish of the body, that is hard to see through— If I were to give up to my devouring pain & live absorbed in utter selfishness, I should do no more than many of the excellent have done. But I am a mother, mistress, wife, and the duties of these press on and torture me— I cannot give up— May God grant me at the last a healthy well-formed child.

How sad is one's condition when one finds comfort for it, only in remembering the greater miseries of others! I have at least two great blessings—in my darling Willie and in my faithful Sarah.* I could not contend with servants— in my present state.

I was weeping bitterly this morning, when Willie who was chattering over Hitchcock's Geology,[36] came and put his arms round my neck. "Dear mother," said he, "why do you cry, when I am reading to you so nicely." I could not answer. "I know," said he, at last "I read nice, but they are bad stories. Do not cry dear mamma," and he went back and tried again. Dear Willie—I will not even look forward for thee, but I will thank God—for this hour of thy love. . . .

E. NEEDHAM MASS.

SUNDAY. MAR 18. 1849. . . .

This day was the anniversary of my terrible trial of last year. I am afraid I have not blessed it to myself as I ought. I have gazed wistfully at the grave of my little one, under the white pine, and grieved over him whom I never held in my arms—but whether I have learnt from it what God intended is still a matter of doubt to me. I feel as if I should have received from it, a revelation of physical as well as spiritual law—but in what am I really the wiser?

How little we know of God! and shall we ever know him wholly. I sometimes fancy that when the veil of matter is withdrawn and men look upon the Unknown for the first time, the disappointment to many will be very great. It seems an easier matter to me, to understand his spiritual relation to our souls— than his imminence in Creation—his will with regard to our own bodies. The

---

*Sarah was the Dalls' current servant.

subject of Marriage is a continual puzzle to me—and so important do I think it and yet so difficult to treat, that if I could begin Life with the knowledge I now have—I would devote myself to physiology—and kindred science and unblushingly in a prayerful spirit—preach everywhere reform in this matter.

E. NEEDHAM MASS.

MONDAY. APRIL 2. 1849.

I have been reading Grote's 3d vol. containing an interesting account of Solon —and sketches of the Assyrians, Phoenicians and Egyptians.[37] I have also accomplished vast quantities of sewing. Yesterday detained from church by a cough which would [have] disturbed others, I—continued an article begun a week ago on the Rights of the women of the Present.* I feel strongly on this subject, and might have written the article out at the first sitting, but I have written slowly—lest I should mistake my own vagaries for the suggestions of the spirit & lest I should some time, repent of what I might say—as God grant I may—if I be still misled.

No one can write as earnestly as I do, without influencing some few—; how deep is my sense of responsibility when I consider this! This last week has been full of other anxieties and I am afraid, I have born them with an impatient spirit....

The Dalls were in Boston for the annual meetings (known as the "Anniversaries") of various religious and reform groups.

BOSTON. MASS.

WEDNESDAY. MAY 30. 1849.

I went with Charles this morning to the Prayer meeting at Mr Clarke's[38] Chapel.... I had intended to make several calls, but on coming out, I found it raining heavily, and under the shelter of Aunt Ann's umbrella I went down to

---

*"Woman in the Present" appeared in the *Liberator,* June 1, 1849, p. 88. Admitting at the outset that "It is not so long since we felt, that no modern reform had so little interest for us, as that in behalf of the civil rights of women," Dall went on to develop a long and closely reasoned argument for women's rights. She observed that at present men "kneel with hollow offerings of compliment at [woman's] shrine, while [they] themselves withhold from her the substance of recognised human rights." She pressed for equality in three spheres: the educational, the social, and the civil. Dall thus articulated a number of the fundamental positions of her lectures and writings over the next two decades.

the meeting of the Anti Slavery Society where I staid all the morning, through the heavy storm. I was glad I went, for I heard fine speaking from Wendell Phillips—Foster & his wife, Frederick Douglass, and Remond.[39] In this speaking, there was nothing fanatical, nothing severe— It was creditable to the Christianity of the speakers. Douglass in eloquence—argument, and <u>force of will</u>, a much neglected but very important part of public speaking far surpassed them all. . . .

BOSTON MASS.
THURSDAY, MAY 31. 1849.

I sewed and taught Willie until it was time to attend the Anti Slavery meeting. It was intensely exciting and chiefly because after Stephen Foster had made one of his most disagreeable and repulsive speeches, Douglass rose, and vindicated his own Christianity, and that of true reform, in one of the finest that ever fell from the lips of man. God bless Frederick Douglass! God bless him— and his cause, so prayed I while he spoke so pray I now. During the violent address of Foster, too weak in soul & body, to rise myself—I was inwardly praying that God would raise up an apostle to speak against such folly. He was followed by Charles Burleigh[40] in a noble speech—but one of those quite likely to be misinterpreted. I prayed again with a broken spirit—for I felt that this was not what was needed but after Douglass had risen I sang—and my song was an anthem of praise. I could not restrain my enthusiasm, he seemed to me while he spoke, greater than any man to whom I had ever listened, and the moment the meeting had closed, I went upon the stage and thanked him in person. What would father have said, had he seen me then? No matter—. God knows I was in the way of my duty, and with an undivided heart, I asked no questions then. May I never in the future. . . .

ASHTON* W. LYNN MASS.
THURSDAY. JUNE 7. 1849.

. . . After dinner arrived the artist George P. A. Healy,[41] to see about taking father's portrait. Father drove him over to Mr Fay's,[42] and he returned to take tea with us, leaving for Boston in the 7 o'clock train. We found him quite agreeable— Not altogether <u>polished</u> in his manners, and somewhat <u>over</u> polite. He tells stories in a pleasant manner, but I think I should grow weary

---

*The name of Mark and Caroline Healey's estate at Lynn.

Caroline's father, Mark Healey, age fifty-seven. Caroline's mother, Caroline Foster Healey,
age forty-eight. Portraits by G. P. A. Healy. (Courtesy of Massachusetts Historical Society)

of his excessive—obtrusive courtesy. He took up my sister's watch chain &
played with the seals in quite an ill bred manner. He has a sort of forced ease
of manner....

ASHTON. W. LYNN MASS.
SUNDAY. JUNE 10. 1849.

... In the afternoon I staid at home with Willie and read Thoreau's "Week on
the Concord & Merrimac."[43] The descriptions of Nature are very beautiful
and the excursions into spirit land, such as seem blasphemous to me. Pity that
such a short limbed fellow should limp after one tall as Emerson!

ASHTON. W. LYNN MASS.
SATURDAY. JUNE 16. 1849.

Was detained by sewing, until so late that all the reading and writing, I intended to do, were prevented by Aunt Sarah's arrival. I sat with her, hemming
handkerchiefs for mother until Mr Healy came to paint [her portrait]....

He told us a good deal about General Jackson—with whom he staid by order of Louis Philippe during the last three weeks of his life.[44]

When he was too weak to receive visitors he was too gallant a man, ever to refuse a lady. One day a card was sent in to him—with the inscription—"A lady from old Ireland wishes to see General Jackson for two minutes." "Let her come—" was the immediate reply. It seems that some of Gen. J's political opponents had declared that he was not born in this country, and could not be legally its president. A close investigation resulted in proving that he was born immediately after the arrival of his parents. Upon this question, Gen. J. continued very excitable, and when the unfortunate gentleman, who accompanied the Irish lady, stumbled on the query, "How old were you, sir, when you first came to this country?" he thundered out in answer, "In the name of God, sir, can't you read?" Mr Healy said this reply gave him an impression of concentrated passion such as he had never received before.

ASHTON W. LYNN MASS.
SUNDAY JUNE 17. 1849.

. . . I did not go to church this morning, for father was expecting company and it was thought best some one should be at home to receive them. I read Blanco White,[45] enjoying it fully. At noon—the young men came—two cousins— Charles and William Orne.[46] Unfortunately W. O. is the son of the gentleman whose kind attentions saved my father's life, in his severe sickness at Pontotoc.[47] I wish to show him how grateful we felt—but he is a slave-holder, at the age of twenty three. To my sorrow the conversation turned on slavery. Unkind & unjust things were said of the abolitionists. I listened quietly as long as I could without betraying my trust—

When I spoke, I spoke "as one having authority," but I kept not only my temper but my good humor, which means far more. How sorry I am to oppose my father & his friend in this house! . . . I invited Charles Orne to come and stay with us at Needham whenever he chose. In the evening I—& M.* read Macaulay[48] to father.

ASHTON, W. LYNN. MASS.
MONDAY. JUNE 18. 1849.

. . . After dinner, I watched the progress of Mr Healy's picture. It is a young and handsome likeness of mother—but very excellent, representing her as she was in her best health ten years ago. . . .

*Probably Dall's sister Marianne.

E. NEEDHAM MASS.

OCT. 16. 1849. MONDAY MORNING.

Mr. Dall has had no time to make up my journal for me, and so after an interval of three or four weeks, I return to it again.

The time has not passed heavily, for it has been marked by the richest mercies of God; neither has it been without its trials, for we have pecuniary troubles, troubles in the parish and domestic disarrangements to discompose us. After changing my cook several times I procured an American woman from Charlestown, capable and trusty who came on the morning of the 24th of Sept. to stay three weeks— By that time I hoped to look on the face of a living child, and I regarded my being able to get her assistance in the mean time as a great blessing. I was quite ill—it seemed to me with actual labor pains —through the 24th and 25th. On the 26th—occurred the first cattle show at Dedham. Mr. Dall had interested himself a good deal in the formation of the County Agricultural Society and I wished him very much to go—but when I rose in the morning there were unequivocal signs that I should be confined within twenty-four hours— I had no pain, & as I had heard that Mrs Dr. Noyes[49] had set her heart on going to Dedham, I felt very unwilling to call on the Doctor for nothing. Mr. Dall went up to him before breakfast, and asked him whether he would prefer to stay at home, or whether we should call in another physician. He was very anxious to go to Dedham and there was no other physician within five miles. I hope it was not foolishness alone, that made my eyes fill with tears, when Mr D's return, showed me how wholly indifferent the Doctor was to my protracted suffering. Little as I have found in Needham to satisfy my highest social aspirations, there lives not a person in the town whom I could have left for the sake of a cattle show, at such an hour. It was not safe for me to be left alone, and as I was acquainted with Dr. Teulon,[50] the Universalist minister and physician, at Newton Upper Falls, Mr Dall went to his parishioners, the Mortons[51] to see if one of them would go for him and ask him to come up for the day. I shall never forget how kind the Mortons were to me, on this day. I had no claim on their kindness except that of having taught Mary, French gratuitously for the last year. Dr. T. came, but had patients in Boston, so ill he did not like to leave them. He said he would go back to the Falls and get a midwife, a Mrs Gardiner in whom he had perfect confidence. If she could not come to me, he would return himself.

Mrs. Gardiner came, I had no pain through the day, but went to bed at 9. with a severe nervous headache. I slept quietly till a little after eleven when I

woke with pains so severe that they drove me out of bed like a rocket. I bore
them quietly as I could till ten minutes of twelve when I hurried Mr Dall to
wake Mrs Rowe* and Mrs Gardiner. There was no interval between my pains,
they overlapped, and my agony was almost too great for human nature. Thank
Heaven, they did not last long. At twenty minutes before one—the first low cry
of a daughter rung upon my ear, and I shall never forget the voice in which her
father audibly thanked God—for the precious gift.† I was so much exhausted
by my pains that the afterbirth did not come away till ten minutes past two, an
hour and a half. I could not have borne the slow tedious suffering 10 minutes
longer. With the exception of an attack of confluent nettle rash which kept me
wakeful for the first three nights after delivery, & was cured by a decoction of
the common nettle, I have got up rapidly. Charles went to Boston the day after I was sick to purchase stores. Instead of congratulations, I had <u>thanks</u> from
Parker and Garrison[52] for a new reformer born into the world. . . .

My baby weighed 10 pounds and a half—never was a father happier than
Charles—every moment that he could spend in my chamber was a jubilee to
me. And God knows I needed at this hour that his love should pour itself out
afresh. . . .

On Sunday afternoon, feeling it quite important for me to have the fresh
air every pleasant day, before Mrs. Rowe's departure, Mr Dall got a horse and
took me to ride. By his request we went to see Deacon Lyon,[53] he not having
been at church for two or three Sundays and Mr Dall fearing that he might be
sick. I did not get out of the carriage, but Mr D. found him more cross than
sick. He was hardly willing to speak to Mr. Dall, but had only two things to
complain of. He said Mr Dall was partial—for he was one day standing in the
entry after Church with Thomas Kingsbury,[54] and Mr. D. came up to Mr. K.
and taking his hand inquired after a sick child he had at home, without taking
any notice of him!!! Those who know the countless enquiries to be made after the close of a country service, will I think be able to pardon this momen-
tary inattention to the oldest Deacon of the Church. The other charge was that
Mr Dall took too much interest in the children. A man had no right to <u>ne-
glect his studies</u> for the sake of the Sabbath School. He had no business to
preach about it—that was not what he was hired for!! I recognized Mr.

---

*Mary Rowe, whom Dall had hired as nurse.

†The baby born at this time was first called "Lily" by the family but was eventually named Sarah Keen
Dall, after Charles Dall's Aunt Sarah. Her later nickname was "Sadie." She lived until 1926 (Family Genealogy, Dall-Healey Family Papers, MHS).

E. K. W.'s[55] handiwork in these last speeches, and if my heart was heavy with the weight of unappreciated labors, as I came home, who shall blame me? Thank Heaven, no judicial throne has been promised to the town of Needham at the last Day. We shall be judged by a Merciful God. My French Class have been quite devoted to me, since my illness commenced. I ought to be very grateful for that.

As I glance over Charles's memoranda for this month, I find that he thinks that he tried to persuade me not to get a new carpet for our little dining room which I felt to be very essential to my comfort. I was not aware of it. He asked me one morning—if I thought we could afford it. I replied that notwithstanding our diminished means, I had been so economical that I thought we might do so, but if the worst came to the worst, I would apply to father for help, & there our conversation stopt. The cost of the carpet was $17.63—& since I have known that our expenses for repairs amounted to so much—I have felt very sorry it was bought.

THURSDAY. OCT. 18. 1849.

Charles went to Boston to have a tooth filled. I was left alone with my baby, yesterday morning. I felt stronger through the morning than I expected but went to bed with a most shocking headache—and feeling as if I could not endure the care for another day. The baby cried for nearly two hours with colic, and my head throbbed for every cry. Charles came home full of the plan of going to South Boston to take the post of Chaplain to the House of Industry.* The talking with him about it agitated me a good deal. As he has never been willing to think of leaving Needham, I thought the desire he manifested to pursue the inquiries already begun, had better be satisfied. It is a noble field of work, especially when it is considered that the moral direction of the House of Reformation for Juvenile Offenders will come into his hands. I welcome such an opening chiefly as affording Charles an opportunity to discharge the debt of self-culture which God requires of every man.

SUNDAY. NOV. 11. 1849.

My sweet little babe! how it grows in beauty! It is a perfect model of infantile loveliness. It is so cherub-like—so full of waving dimpling health. Not an awk-

---

*The House of Industry was the almshouse, erected in South Boston in 1822. See Justin Winsor, *Memorial History of Boston* (Boston: J.R. Osgood and Co., 1881), 4:648–649.

ward line—not an excrescence of any sort, marks her well developed head and frame! how thankful I ought to be to God for this great mercy! My heart opens toward her so, that I wonder how I have lived without a baby so long. I never thought I could love another child better than Willie but I believe I do. God be thanked for this fresh image of his divine Life. . . .

E. NEEDHAM. MASS.

SUNDAY. NOV. 18. 1849.

On Tuesday, the Parish Committee held a meeting, with Mr. Dall, stating to him that it would be impossible to raise more than two hundred dollars towards his salary for the coming year. Mr. Dall told them that he should immediately ask a dismission, and desiring to do it without haste, they appointed a fortnight from next Monday to receive his communication— Mr Dall begged them to report to him any rumors of dissatisfaction that they might have heard, as the means of future growth. They mentioned his great interest in the Sunday School, and preaching to the young—his being an Anti-Slavery man—his having used the arrangement of Carpenter's Harmony[56] in reading the Scriptures, and his being too much of a politician! Dear Charles, his heart was sore, I know when he came home. I asked him no questions that night but pressed him to my heart & soothed him to rest, as a mother does a sick child. On the next morning, he told me, we must soon leave our pleasant home.

God's will be done.

On Tuesday afternoon, I went with Miss Harris and carried the poor little Prentiss baby some clothing, and on Wednesday, the weather being uncommonly pleasant, we took a carriage and made farewell calls; on the Misses Parker, Mrs. Baury Wm. Shimmin, Sarah Sawyer, Dr Teulon, and Mary Shannon. After returning Mr Dall walked over to the Harrises to a Society meeting and by the news of our approaching departure grieved both them and Betsy Kingsbury.[57]

The poor and the young will grieve for us I know.

On Thursday, Charles walked with me as far as Mrs Macintosh's[58] to stop our butter and get our bill. The air was delightful, Willie was with us and in spite of our troubles, we could not but be happy. . . .

On Saturday . . . When Sarah* returned, she was quite excited. She had been at Mr Mills'.[59] They had declared that everybody liked Mr Dall—but no-

---

*The Dalls' servant.

body liked me. I wrote Mr Dall's sermons, put him up to every thing, & had all my own way. She was very indignant, and denied all these foolish assertions. They talked about Mrs Noyes as my declared foe. When I remembered how generously I had treated Mrs Noyes—in order that she might not think I was offended with the Dr. for leaving me the day I was confined, sending her rare flowers &c &c—she being no member of our church, the tears would flow, I was too weak to resist them. I feel that I have needed this lesson, may God give me grace to improve it. Poor Sarah! I went early to bed. This week I have only read the report of the Boston School Committee[60] & Browning's Dramatic Lyrics,[61] with many of which I have been delighted.

I hope no one will ever tell Mr Dall, what Sarah has told me— It would grieve him to his heart. I have heard Mr Stone[62] all day. Without knowing any thing of our leaving, he preached sermons very pertinent to the state of things. Many persons greeted me warmly. I lost all control of myself and burst into tears, when I tried to speak to my French Class. I still feel the effect of Friday's illness. I heard some say in the Porch, that they would never again engage a minister for more than a year.

Charles Dall failed to get the position at the House of Industry. He returned to Needham with the shocking news of one of the most sensational murders in Boston of the century: the charred remains of the missing physician George Parkman (1790–1849) were found near the laboratory of Harvard professor John White Webster (1793–1850), who owed money to Parkman. Both victim and suspect were respected members of the establishment.

E. NEEDHAM. MASS.

SUNDAY. DEC. 2. 1849. . . .

. . . Mr. Dall went into Boston to look for a boarding place, and hear the end of the South Boston matter. On Saturday I went on packing. It was a very stormy day, Mr D. returned. At the house of Reformation there were 5 votes for Mr Dagan[63] and <u>four</u> for him. Lost of course. He had found a nice boarding place, which I am to look at on Monday, at a reasonable rate. It is in Roxbury. He was full of excitement about the murder of Dr Parkman, and the imprisonment of Dr. Webster. I had heard nothing of it, but received a violent shock from the news. I could not sleep for thinking of the poor Dabneys![64] The details are too horrid and too uncertain, I will not record them. I nursed the baby as I listened, and felt the milk grow cold in my breast. . . .

E. NEEDHAM. MASS.

SUNDAY. DEC. 9. 1849.

On Monday, I went into Boston, and had my tooth filled. The whole city was full of excitement about the Webster and Parkman case. My own suspicions fixed on Littlefield* from the beginning and I was glad to hear from Uncle W. before I left that he was arrested. I would not believe Dr W. guilty, if he should confess it himself, thinking it more likely that he should be frightened or crazed into such a confession, than that he should commit the deed.[65] It stormed heavily, but I went out to Roxbury and engaged my board at Mrs Fairbanks's.[66] We are to furnish our room, washing materials &c—and—have a cot for Sarah in the attic, and pay $12.00 per week. The two children Charles & myself—must occupy one room, but we can afford no better arrangement, $2 are to be deducted for every week Charles is absent. Tuesday & Wednesday, I spent chiefly in packing, and Thursday after Charles had gone to Boston to his club,[67] I was surprised by Miss Tucker[68] who came to do my dressmaking. I sewed with her all day, and got very weary. Sat up late— . . . I have been reading Ruskin's Seven Lamps,[69] and find it a most delicious and refreshing book. . . .

The year ended with a lavish family Christmas at the Healey home in Lynn, yet more evidence of Mark Healey's growing prosperity.

ASHTON. W. LYNN. MASS.

SUNDAY. DEC. 30. 1849. . . .

Never was such a Santa Claus seen, as visited Ashton this year. Everybody's stocking was full. Willie had several beautiful toys—and in the bag, mother hung under my stocking was a fine silk dress, a Copy of Longfellow's seaside,[70] a transparency of a mountain torrent crossed by a maiden & child, a copy of Irving's Book of the Hudson,[71] and a fine purse—crocheted by Marianne. . . .

---

*Ephraim Littlefield (b. 1809?) was the janitor at Harvard who discovered Parkman's remains (1850 U.S. Census). The rumor of his arrest was false.

CHAPTER SEVEN

A City Simmers

March 24, 1850–April 28, 1851

*W*hen the Dalls left Needham in early 1850, Charles was unemployed. The entire family was reduced to living in one room in a boardinghouse in the Boston suburb of Roxbury, with a cot for their servant in the attic. The children and Caroline were ill throughout the winter. Persuaded that their close quarters were unhealthy, she found another boarding place in Roxbury, this one with two rooms. She considered moving to Lynn, close to her family, but perceived that they would find it embarrassing for her to be nearby in such straitened circumstances. She found herself writing an article for a religious journal "for bread." "Never in my life wrote for that object before," she lamented, "wept as I read it over." Charles was away from home during much of this period, supplying vacant pulpits, and Caroline sometimes felt "as if God had left me alone on the earth."

Her life improved significantly when, in September 1850, she moved to rented quarters in Boston. Here she was able to attend lectures, conversations, and antislavery meetings, and to interact once again with many Transcendentalists. She became involved with Delia Bacon, a brilliant but eccentric woman who came to Boston to deliver historical lectures. Dall helped make her arrangements, publicized the series among her friends, and gave moral support. Bacon was a demanding woman who nearly wore out Dall's goodwill; she once appeared unannounced at the foot of Dall's bed to press her concerns, and she refused a request by Dall to announce a lecture by another woman.

Other intellectual feasts attracted Dall. The most significant of these, in the winter of 1851, was a series of conversations directed by Transcendentalist educator and philosopher A. Bronson Alcott. Whereas the earliest conversation series that Dall attended, directed by Margaret Fuller, had focused on ancient mythology, Alcott's topic was seven contemporary New Englanders, one of whom was Fuller herself, recently deceased. In these sessions Dall associated with a number of prominent figures, including Ralph Waldo Emerson (also the subject of one of the talks) and his wife, Lidian. In her journal Dall reconstructed these conversations from memory, sometimes days later, and the resulting accounts provide an informative glimpse into both the dynamics of the conversation form and assessments of Webster, Garrison, Parker, Fuller, Emerson (with a note on Thoreau), William Ellery Channing, and William H. Channing (the latter two passages not included here) by their contemporaries. Dall's own acute appraisal of Fuller—"there is no American woman that stands near her"—delivered a mere six months after Fuller's death, is itself worthy of note.

Dall's move into Boston coincided almost exactly with the signing into law of the Fugitive Slave Act, and Boston was immediately in ferment. At a meeting in Faneuil Hall, Dall joined with a crowd of six thousand who determined "to trample the law under foot." But this feeling was not unanimous in Boston, and an organized mob prevented the English abolitionist George Thompson from speaking publicly. Dall followed with keen sympathy the cases of the first two Boston fugitives arrested after the law's passage: Shadrach Minkins, who was dramatically rescued by a band of African-Americans and sent to freedom in Canada, and Thomas Sims, whom the authorities successfully sent back to his master. The issue was brought even closer to home with the warning that the slave-catchers were after Charles Williams, a fugitive who worked for the Healey family. Dall acted as intermediary in negotiations between him and his owner in Georgetown. She also mentions in her journal the excitement generated by attempts to capture the fugitive couple William and Ellen Craft; what she does not reveal until decades later, perhaps for reasons of security, is that Ellen was hidden for a time in her father's house.

Indeed, Dall's own profile in reform circles was rising. She was a public well-wisher of the first national women's rights convention in nearby Worcester; though she could not attend, she published in *The Liberator* a congratulatory letter to its president, Paulina Wright Davis, and restated her own position on the woman question. Remarks attributed to her about slavery and Daniel Webster, reported in *The Liberator,* caused a critic to refer to her in print as "a hurricane of a woman." One suspects that that characterization did not offend her.

The city of Boston during these months seethed with tension and excitement. Dall, finding herself in this hub of activity, associated with leading activists and thinkers, at the center of momentous events, and playing no inconsequential role in them herself, was profoundly invigorated. But by early 1851 Charles Dall, who had been supplying a pulpit for some time in Toronto, was seriously considering accepting a regular position there. Caroline contemplated this possibility with "strange thoughts & feelings": "I have been thinking today," she reflected, "how much society I should lose—how many distinguished people I should miss far off in the West." And though she told herself that distinguished people were no more dear to God than humbler souls, her reluctance to leave this cauldron of political and intellectual activity is obvious—and understandable.

HIGHLANDS ROXBURY. MASS.

SUNDAY. MAR. 24. 1850.

*A*fter a month's silence I resume my pen. For the first time in my life I have dropt it for a whole month. Dropt it not because I have had no leisure moments, but because I have been too weary and ill to hold it. We have had no health since we first came to Roxbury—partly I suspect because we have been pent up in one room. First Willie had the croup—then before he had begun to rally the baby, was seized with it. She was hardly better before—a few days after my last entry here—Willie was seized with a bronchial fever, resulting in Inflammation of the Lungs, and the raising of some blood. His illness was longer and more serious on account of our close quarters. In the midst of it the baby had an attack of strangury, most distressing from the violent pain it occasioned. I was also seized with Influenza, and a violent earache, Mrs Wells and Martha[1] came in, one afternoon, and found me crying with pain, and so deaf that I could not attend to the children's wants. As soon as I dared to leave Willie I procured a girl to be with him, and trusting to his father's care went home,* to get fresh air and rest. I had blisters blue pills and warm baths in plenty but nothing really did me any good till I tried leeches. During all this

---

*That is, to her family's home in Lynn.

time I had very inefficient help. A gathering in my head— discharged into the throat 3 times, and I began to get well. I came back to Roxbury—on Tuesday Mar 19th and found Willie looking very wretchedly. The baby however had gained a pound in our absence of five days. I have done little but sew during the last month, but have read at odd moments or when too ill to sit up—the following books Layard's Nineveh—The Caxtons—The Wilmingtons—Pugin's Christian Architecture—Valpy's National Gallery—Winckelman's Hist. of Ancient Art Vol. 2nd. Hawthorne's Scarlet Letter, &c &c—[2] The Scarlet Letter is a fine story and has a needed and touching moral. If the sketches in the Preface are from Life, I feel sorry that so great a writer should have taken such small revenge.*

My American girl lived with me a fortnight and went away because her sister had found a place in Boston for her, Willie was at the sickest when she left— Her place was supplied by a green Irish girl—who could do nothing without my direction and who if she was kind to the baby during my stay at Lynn, was so dirty that I could not keep her after my return. A few days since I procured an Irish girl, neat and well educated, who has lived in Philadelphia, for a year and a half with Geo S. Appleton the publisher.[3] She seems likely to answer my purpose.

Since Willie has been ill, it has been very apparent, that we could not healthfully continue in our present quarters. I could not help seeing while at Lynn that the family did not wish me to come down there. I knew that they felt that it would not be pleasant to them, to have me living so economically as I should be obliged to, in their neighborhood. I shed a good many tears—about it, foolish as it showed them, for I felt that if our situations could be reversed, I would willingly endure any mortification for the sake of the aid and comfort I could give. I returned to Roxbury however, and after much searching and painful experience, engaged board at Mrs Champney's[4] for six months. In doing so, I considered the health of the children more than any-thing else. There is a large garden, and I have two airy rooms. Mrs Champney is a <u>lady</u>, a widow, with four single and one married daughter at home and takes no other boarders. I trust we may be tolerably happy.

---

*In the introductory chapter, "The Custom-House," Hawthorne included uncomplimentary portraits of the men who had worked at the Salem Custom House during his three-year tenure as surveyor of the port (1846–1849).

ROXBURY. MASS.

MONDAY. JULY 1ST. 1850.

. . . I went to the Post, took out the Liberator, with an extract in it from the Boston Bee, calling me a "hurricane of a woman," proof, my remarks on the Boston Anniversaries.* As the Author—had either never read—or deliberately falsified the remarks he criticised, I did not think it worth while to become a tempest on his account. . . .

WEDNESDAY. JULY 3D. 1850. ROXBURY.

Wrote an article for Huntington†—wrote it for bread— Never in my life wrote for that object before, wept as I read it over— It has no glaring faults and little ability. It is a foundling and no real child of mine. God send it success. In the afternoon it rained heavily and I went with Charles and engaged board in Hancock St for next winter. He grieved me by not keeping the appointment as promptly as I expected.

ASHTON. W. LYNN.

TUESDAY. JULY 23. 1850.

I spent this morning sadly in a long talk with Ellen [Healey, Dall's sister], in which she told me what she thought of my faults—of my bluntness etc. etc. and in which she undertook to tell me that father was on the eve of disinheriting me, on account of my reform notions. A great deal that she said, she misconceived. I answered very little—but wept freely— I despair of ever being understood rightly in my own family. I believe I bore it well—but I did not

---

*The *Boston Bee* article, reprinted in *The Liberator* of June 28, 1850, p. 101, described a "group of assailants of Mr. [Daniel] Webster who figure in [*The Liberator's*] columns," including among others William Lloyd Garrison, Horace Mann, Wendell Phillips, and "a woman rejoicing in the protracted name of Caroline H.W. [*sic*] Dall, a hurricane of a woman, doubtless. Each seemingly emulous to hit Mr. Webster the hardest blow, in which the woman of the protracted name seems to have been the most successful." Dall pasted this article in her journal. The so-called "Anniversary" meetings in Boston were annual gatherings, over several days in late May, of religious and reform societies. Dall had published an article, "The Anniversary Week," in *The Liberator,* June 14, 1850, p. 95, that actually counseled moderation in the abolitionists' attacks on slaveholders and the clergy; she mentioned Webster only in passing.

†"How to Make Children Happy," a moralistic story in which charity is shown to poor Irish children by allowing them to work, appeared in the *Monthly Religious Magazine,* n.s., 7 (1850): 398–406. This Unitarian periodical was edited by Frederic Dan Huntington (1819–1904), who also preached at South Congregational Church in Boston. In 1855 he became Plummer Professor of Christian Morals at Harvard. Later he converted to the Episcopal Church and in 1869 was made Bishop of Central New York.

contend against the verdict. I am not blunt in trifles; I well know, I am blunt with regard to right or wrong action—or abstract questions in reference to them. I know and God knows how I have struggled against the indulgence of my peremptoriness. He knows The Loving Father—that in this struggle I have conquered. It was hard to hear her say, that she had heard that I had trouble in Needham with regard to my habit of using my glass—to look round people's rooms when I entered, and of criticising the dirt in them, afterward. When I heard my own sister quote this as if she believed it—I felt as if I should be quite willing to go out to the Valley of the Mississippi, or anywhere, where I might begin life freshly— I had no comfort that afternoon—save in resting my aching head & eyes on my husband's bosom—as I wept. I began to read "Jane Eyre"[5] over—for comfort.

In mid-September the Dalls moved to rented quarters on Hancock Street, Boston. The Fugitive Slave Act was signed into law by President Fillmore on September 18, requiring citizens in the North to cooperate in the capture and return of fugitive slaves to their owners.

BOSTON MASS.

SUNDAY. OCT. 20. 1850.

.... I could not resist going to the meeting at Faneuil Hall in the evening.[*] It was a grand meeting. There was but one feeling among the 6,000 persons assembled there, and that was to trample the law under foot. There was no bluster in the matter but may God bless Douglass, Phillips, & Parker for the noble words they spoke that night.

... All the week I have been very sad and low spirited—longing for Charles[†]—grieved at some differences of opinion—which we had before we parted—and feeling on the whole as if God had left me alone on the earth. Every spare moment I have given to Miss Bacon's[‡] interests and I think better

---

[*]This meeting on October 14 was called "to consider the condition of the Fugitive Slaves and other colored persons of this city, under the new Fugitive Slave Law" (*Liberator*, October 18, 1850, p. 167).

[†]Charles's supply preaching often took him away from home for days at a time.

[‡]Delia Salter Bacon (1811–1859), author and historical lecturer, who had recently come to Boston from New Haven. Dall was helping her to arrange and publicize a series of historical lectures. Bacon later achieved notoriety as an early proponent of the theory of non-Shakespearean authorship of Shakespeare's plays; thirty-five years later, Dall included a brief chapter on Bacon in her *What We Really Know about Shakespeare* (Boston: Roberts Brothers, 1885).

of her every hour. She has now been in town about a fortnight. I had this afternoon a very interesting conversation with her—about her own affairs—I am glad to have seen her. . . .

BOSTON. MASS.

SUNDAY. OCT. 27. 1850.

The week has been so little marked, save by my husband's precious letters, and the hope that another would bring him home, that I have small material for journalizing. . . . I have been a good deal excited by interest in the Woman's Rights' Convention—and by the agitation consequent on the attempt to arrest Ellen and William Crafts.* I went this morning with Miss Bacon to hear Theodore Parker. He preached nobly on Woman's position.[6] This evening I took tea with him to talk over the Slave matter. Had a very pleasant time. . . .

BOSTON. MASS.

SUNDAY. NOV. 3. 1850.

I have spent two evenings away—this week—at Mrs Daniel P. Parker's and Mrs Wadsworth[7] and Monday with mother at Lynn— The remainder of the time has been devoted to advising Miss Bacon, sewing, and writing an article for Garrison, a letter for Mrs Davis† about the Condition of Woman.‡ . . . This

---

*The Woman's Rights Convention took place in Worcester on October 23 and 24, presided over by Paulina Wright Davis; see John F. McClymer, *This High and Holy Moment: The First National Woman's Rights Convention, Worcester, 1850* (San Diego: Harcourt Brace College, 1999). In Boston two "slave-hunters" from Georgia were attempting to arrest the fugitives William (c. 1826–1900) and Ellen (1828–c. 1897) Craft but were meeting with harassment on every hand. The city was greatly excited, as reports in contemporary newspapers make clear. See *Transcript,* October 26, 28, 1850, p. 2; and Walter M. Merrill and Louis Ruchames, eds., *Letters of William Lloyd Garrison,* 6 vols. (Cambridge, Massachusetts: Belknap Press, 1971–1981), 5:283).

†Wealthy and cultured, Paulina Wright Davis (1813–1876) of Providence, Rhode Island, was an activist first for health reform, lecturing in the East and Midwest to female audiences on anatomy and physiology. She was now beginning her activities in the cause of women's rights and had presided over the recent first national Women's Rights Convention in Worcester. In 1853 she would begin publication of *The Una,* a paper devoted to the interests of women, and to which Dall would become a major contributor and coeditor (*NAW*).

‡The article for Garrison was Dall's long "Letter to Mrs. Paulina W. Davis," appearing in the *Liberator* of November 8, 1850, p. 3. It congratulated Davis on the "able, graceful and prudent address" that she delivered to the recent Woman's Rights Convention in Worcester, then went on to present Dall's own thoughts on woman's education, the need for equal wages for women and men, and the causes of prostitution.

evening. I went to the Masonic Temple to hear Wm. H. Channing[8] on The Fugitive Slave Bill. If I must ever take a leader, I think I will take him. It would be sacrilege to attempt an abstract of his address. He took the boldest position in a peaceful attitude. The building was thronged, and throughout the service, one might have heard a pin drop. God bless him,—faithful champion of the truth that he is.

BOSTON. MASS.

FRIDAY. NOV. 15. 1850

I went to bed early last night sick and weary. . . . I had hardly closed my eyes —when I was roused by a strange voice, and saw Miss Bacon, standing at the foot of my bed. "In the name of common sense what are you here for?" I exclaimed. "I am miserable and I have come to talk to you." Of course this waked me thoroughly. I found that she wanted me to write some notices for tomorrow's paper, and send—round tickets to all the people I could think of, for the first two lectures, for she too had begun to suspect that it would be a failure. She said she had done wrong to forbid reporters, that some claptrap must be used—that the papers must notice it. That she would not fail now —cost what it would. As I saw the undisciplined ambition struggling with her indecision and womanly passionate nature I sighed and wished she had a husband and two children. I counselled patience and faith. Diminishing expenses starting in a more quiet way—attempting but one course—&c &c —all of which I had of course said before, but all in vain. "If I should go to the room" said she "and find only a few people there I could not go on—I must go home." In vain I urged her to be content to bide her time—. It all ended in my writing a note to Wm. Channing,[9] in bed, and asking him to write a notice— in my positively refusing to put any more gratuitous lectures within reach of my friends, and in my privately determining—to see her man of action Mr. Clapp[10] this morning, and put affairs into a business like train for this evening. She declared there were but 16 tickets sold, and I declared that proved nothing—. After she went away I lay awake a long time, wishing that people, who have unsuitable organizations, should not bring themselves into public life —and wondering why Delia had not rather written a book on History. Her genius is undeniable, but her physique very insufficient, and her sensibility altogether too great.

This morning I fulfilled all my intentions with regard to her, and saw Mrs

Parker[11] hoping to hear some pleasant news that I might send Miss B. to cheer her in preparation. I bade Delia shut herself up in her room—study all day, see nobody and hear nothing, which she promised.

I lay on the sofa all day, and this evening went with Wm. H. Channing and Anna Parsons—Mr & Mrs Wm. F. Channing and the Blackwells[12] to Faneuil Hall.* We went very early but the galleries were nearly filled. The meeting was opened, and after a few words from Francis Jackson[13]—the officers were appointed. Mr Garrison then rose to read a welcome to Mr Thompson.— He was listened to with unanimous enthusiasm. Even when he said the Boston of 1835 was not the Boston of 1850, the building rang with the cry of no! no! The Hall was crowded from the beginning of the evening and suddenly my attention was withdrawn from Garrison by a bustle near the door. Looking back I saw a stream of men 5 or 6 abreast—of a character & aspect differing entirely from that of the gentlemen who occupied the floor. They were just entering the left hand door—no disturbance being perceptible anywhere else, and pressed steadily on to the front of the platform. As they advanced it became impossible to hear Garrison who did not seem aware of the reason—but attributed it to the impatience of his previous auditory, which was not the fact. I watched this stream press in for 10 min. by the clock. When the uproar subsided sufficiently I heard at intervals a sound like that of a bass drum—and tin—kettles from without the Hall. Mr Garrison having left the stand, W. Phillips came forward. We in the galleries could not hear his voice. In the mean time, the crowd from without appeared to have all entered the Hall dislodging its previous occupants & pushing them into corners— They formed in a wedge—the point of which pressed steadily toward the platform. It was half past seven when these men entered the Hall by the new clock—and all had gone on in perfect quiet for three quarters of an

---

*The Massachusetts Anti-Slavery Society was sponsoring "a gathering of the friends of Reform, International Amity, and Universal Emancipation" to welcome George Thompson (1804–1878), English abolitionist, to the country. The galleries at Faneuil Hall were reserved for ladies (*Liberator,* November 15, 1850, p. 182). On a previous visit to Boston in 1835, Thompson had aroused so much resentment that a mob broke in on a meeting of the Boston Female Anti-Slavery Society where he was to speak; Garrison was pulled through the streets of Boston with a rope around his body until he was rescued by the authorities and put in jail for his own safety; Thompson himself was forced to flee the city in an open boat to New Brunswick. On the present occasion, as will be seen, he is treated little better. On his third visit to America, during the Civil War, a public reception was given Thompson in the House of Representatives *(DNB).*

hour. Suddenly the friends in front of the platform—perceived the onward movement—their ranks thickened, the wedge was thrust back and broken. It systematically formed in two smaller wedges—and attempted to approach the platform, on the sides. This was prevented, and the wedges again broken up scattered through the crowd. Personal fights between two, now became frequent, and an empty space was cleared in the middle of the Hall, by a ring where various antics were performed. All this was done with an accompaniment of riotous yells and confusion which seemed to preclude all concerted action. But I was not able to doubt the evidence of my senses— This body had organized outside the Hall. They aimed at the platform—and wished not only to silence the meeting, but to force Mr. Thompson to leave it. I observed that a peculiar whistle which now & then made egress through the din, was always followed by a concerted rush, & that after being broken & repulsed, three cheers for Daniel Webster, gave them cover under which to rally. The majority of the meeting was not represented by these rioters. Turning to the stage I found that Wendell Phillips, had left the stage for Mr. Thompson —who not being able to make himself heard—took a chair and sat down— facing with sad and solemn resolution the angry mass. After this—the noise became so intense that great excitement prevailed in the gallery & I could not always see the platform. At one time I saw Wm. Henry Channing—at another Theodore Parker—trying in vain to get a hearing. At last, I saw Frederick Douglass gesticulating in a manner otherwise so unsuited to the occasion, that I felt sure he was put forward for a purpose. Looking back, I missed Garrison & Thompson—and saw through the whole— Very soon the gas was lowered, and at about ten minutes before nine—Mr Quincy came up—and feeling weary I went home with him and his wife.[14] We stopped in Court St. for an ice. In reply to a question from his wife Mr Quincy said that he did not call on the police—for they could not do any good. That I think was wrong. The civil power should have been tested. I was surprised to find that Mr.— Q. knew nothing of the entrance of a body of persons just before the close of Garrison's reading. I wonder if all the people on the platform were equally ignorant.

May God forgive the men who urge the rowdies of a city to violate law and order in this sort, and enact the fugitive slave law—and carry it into effect out of pretended reverence therefor. . . .

BOSTON. MASS.

MONDAY. JAN. 6. 1851.

Reading Richard Edney*—a fine thing—maugre [i.e., in spite of] the consciousness. Otherwise nursing Lillie† who is miserable of course. As Mr Alcott began his conversations this evening—I left her to attend the first on
Daniel Webster.‡ His sketch was very fine of D. W. as he is, not true of the
man—I believe God meant him to be. He said he was built from the brow
downward—not from the brow upward. Nature—gave enormous breadth—
to the hind head—but she forgot the crown. No very distinguished persons
spoke....

BOSTON. SATURDAY.

JAN 11. 1851. ...

I have strange thoughts & feelings about Toronto.§ I have been thinking
today, how much society I should lose—how many distinguished people I
should miss far off in the West, and then again came the thought that all souls—
were dear to God, and I ought practically to learn the worth of humbler minds.
Some one asked Marianne [Healey, Dall's sister] today, "which of her sisters read the Mécanique Celeste** as an amusement?" In speaking of this to a
friend and wondering who could be so malicious or so ignorant as to tell such
a story—she told me that she had heard it said that I could read LaPlace & play
backgammon at once! The word backgammon seemed to touch some familiar string—and after a little thought I remembered very well the remark of mine
made when I was not twelve years old, out of which all this nonsense had
grown. Some one was ridiculing Judge Shaw[15] for saying that he went through

---

Richard Edney (Boston, 1850), a novel by Sylvester Judd (1813–1853), Unitarian minister of Augusta,
Maine. See *Biographical Dictionary of Transcendentalism*, ed. Wesley T. Mott (Westport, Connecticut,
1996).

†The baby Sarah Keen Dall was for some time called "Lily" or "Lillie."

‡A. Bronson Alcott (1799–1888), Transcendentalist educator, writer, and philosopher, was leading a
series of seven conversations (although they were advertised in the *Liberator* as "lectures") on "certain individuals whom he takes to be peculiarly the representation of New England character and genius." Daniel
Webster represented "Order" (*Liberator*, January 17, 1851, p. 11).

§Charles Dall had been preaching in Toronto for several weeks and was apparently about to accept a
permanent position there.

**A work by the French mathematician and astronomer Pierre Simon, Marquis de LaPlace (1749–
1827). A translation with commentary by Bostonian Nathaniel Bowditch had appeared in four volumes
from 1829 to 1839.

A. Bronson Alcott, educator, philosopher, and leader of a conversation
series that Dall attended. (Courtesy of Concord Free Public Library)

with a difficult Theorem in Geometry daily as a recreation. I said I could understand that, for a problem in Euclid gave me more pleasure than a game of backgammon. Backgammon—gives me so little that I should never have remembered the remark but for the cruel constructions put upon it at the time.

MONDAY. JAN 13 1851.

I am almost disheartened waiting for letters from Charles. It seems so sad to be prevented from hearing as well as seeing, the only one whose life is identical with mine. Oh God! what <u>could</u> I do, without him!

This morning I heard Miss Bacon's lecture which was uncommonly fine, but she grieved me so much at the recess, that I could not enjoy it at all. I was asked by the Officers of the Ladies' Physiological Institute[16] to request her to give notice to the class—that Mrs [Paulina Wright] Davis would lecture before the Institute on Wednesday P.M. I did so, writing a notice myself, which I had not the slightest doubt she would read. To my surprise, she utterly refused—refused after I pleaded with her earnestly, assuring her that the Ladies who made this small request were those to whom she was most indebted for the getting up of her class—and a popular movement in her favor; refused & her only excuse was, that it would injure her character to be associated in the public mind with the Defenders of Women's Rights. I contended that Mrs. Davis was as refined as retiring—as thoroughly prepared as herself—in her peculiar line, & I wondered at her want of sympathy— But nothing—would avail. The "character" which needs such tender nursing must be a somewhat infirm affair, I think We none of us asked, what effect our defence of Miss Bacon would have on <u>our</u> characters, but I for one, would never have undertaken it, had I supposed her capable of a littleness like this. I made light of it to the Officers of the Institute, but they looked petrified. I would have given the notice myself, but I thought it might not seem respectful to Miss Bacon—so I forbore. I have spent a good deal of time in forwarding her interests, and this is the first request I ever made her. Good Heavens! what are people made of! I know nothing of this Institute, a somewhat obscure affair, I fancy—but I wished its officers to be treated with common civility.

In the evening I went to Mr Alcott's conversation on Garrison as the exponent of "Progress." Mr Lothrop—George B. Emerson[17]—Sarah Adams,[18] Parker Pillsbury[19]—the Littlehales,[20] the Whipples,[21] Charles Hovey,[22] Anna Parsons, Frederick Cabot[23] and others were there. It was a fine conversation, but Parker Pillsbury—threw poison into it. He was hardly in place, but was perhaps needed, where all sorts of people were represented. I came home with Mr Gould.[24] Pillsbury by his rudeness drew from Mr Alcott a very beautiful piece of autobiography, which I would not on any account have missed. Prejudiced as I was against Mr A. before I went to these conversations, I really love him now. The pure noble lofty way in which he speaks of men and things makes his presence a benediction to the City. It ought to pay his Expenses for the mere benefit of his living— I joined naturally in the Conversation tonight, but in spite of many compliments do not think I helped it. Mr Alcott came to me after the meeting and said that he wished I had spoken sooner. "I think," said he, "that our two conversations have owed a great deal to you, and I hope you will continue to be interested." This from the pure Idealist! Mr P. congratulated Mr Alcott on the firmness with which he had refused to pay his taxes. With an abashed look which I shall never forget Mr A. replied, "I take no credit to myself for that Mr Pillsbury. It was a little piece of divinity that I could not help." Mr Lothrop had kept quite sober until now, but at this he went off into a laugh which I thought would never end.

BOSTON MASS.

MONDAY. JAN. 20. 1851.

... After tea, Mrs Parker[25] went with me, to Mr. List's,[26] where Mr Alcott converses. Ralph Emerson was there, and gave in a cool [way a] beautiful tribute to Mr. Parker* as the man of action. The finest thing was a tribute of admiration, <u>hardly</u> appreciation from Mr Lothrop. In an artistic sense, this conversation was not so fine as either of the preceding two. No fine full portrait, scarcely a profile, of my noble friend, was drawn. I had it on my lips to say—because I felt as if his sarcasm—severity and force would be objected to—"Every word falling from Mr Parker's lip is a battle axe—it cleaves a skull— It is not all temperaments that can stand his tremendous trepanning, but the intention is to remove an unnatural pressure—and if the light which is let in, does any mischief, it shows how weak the brain is." but there was no—chance. This "momentum" in him was not alluded to. The reason was that a Mr. Fernald[27] and Mr List—presented an entirely novel issue, which we were obliged to combat. They accused him of cunning conservatism, of meanly buying the ear of the people &c &c—by sacrifices of absolute truth; of inconsistencies &c &c.

This started me, and according to Mrs Parker I "flared up finely." I only know that I spoke the truth about this great good man. After the lecture Mrs R.W. Emerson[28] to whom I was introduced, said she was much obliged to the lady—who repelled the charge of cunning, which she thought entirely undeserved. She had no idea I was the person—but on being informed by a lady who stood near, paid me a gentle compliment. Mr Alcott's own sketching was not so fine tonight as usual— He spoke of him as a formidable man—mainly, a true Anglo-Saxon with a cross of the old Roman in him— But he dwelt on the

---

*Theodore Parker, the subject of this discussion.

word formidable, and returned to the idea. He thought Mr P. had added nothing to permanent literature, but all that he wrote was immediately serviceable. Ednah[29]—spoke a few words—fitly—in reference to the strength of his love and faith. . . .

BOSTON. MASS.

MONDAY. FEB. 3. 1851. . . .

In the evening I went to Mr Alcott's with quite a large party. As a discussion of "Margaret Fuller" or of "Woman" it was entirely a failure but it was a fine talk. Mr. Higginson[30] of Newburyport, Ralph Emerson, and Miss Hunt[31] were there in addition to the usual company. There were some facts stated about the severity of her early training, the wonderful character of her mind. Mr. Alcott said she was no New England woman—she might as well have been born in Greece or Rome. Greece & Rome were wherever she was. He spoke of the great ability of the letters to the Tribune.* Anna Parsons spoke of the great power of love in her, to which Mr List objected the cutting severity of remark to which those who attended her conversations were exposed. He attributed this to her self-love.

I objected to this expression. I did not think it right to assume a reason for it. I had heard her speak to others when the tears came to my eyes, and my throat swelled at the bitterness of her words. But she had been long an invalid, suffered intensely, and it seemed to me that half of her irritation was physical whenever it occurred. Mr Alcott thought there was no doubt she was born under Scorpio, but she knew it, and strove to conquer it— She had confessed to having been a very unamiable child. Ednah said that she had attended her last three winters' conversations, that in them all, but one instance of such severity, and for that she immediately and amply apologized. I said I felt that she would become capable of that, but she was not when I knew her. General conversation occurred on the subject of woman. Higginson spoke of Margaret's great intellectual activity. I spoke of her want of serenity, said what I had hoped from the influence of marriage and motherhood on her— Mr Alcott believed that she became nobler after it. The news of her marriage was a surprise to

---

*Beginning in 1844 Fuller contributed pieces to the New York *Tribune,* including criticism of literature and art, articles introducing German culture to America, and (from 1846) on-site reports of the European scene.

her friends but they were soon resigned to it. She was always more feminine than he had expected to find her. At moments—she was the ideal woman. Mr Emerson had with him a daguerreotype taken from a picture, made after her marriage,[32] which answered all my questions. The love and serenity in it were—beautiful. It is an admirable likeness & yet I have never seen her look so. . . .

I wish Mr Emerson had said what he thought of Margaret. I want to <u>know</u> that she had warmth and geniality. Perhaps however he thought our (frivolous conversation) filagree hardly fit to set a jewel in. The gentle men seemed unwilling to talk about Margaret.

Mrs Alcott[33] came and thanked me for the help I had given Mr. A. He had felt it deeply— I had done what no one but Margaret Fuller had ever before done. My eyes filled with tears—for in truth Margaret's death was a private grief to me, & there is no American woman that stands near her. Others followed Mrs Alcott's example after the conversation was over. Mr Alcott said that Margaret could carry a title well. It belonged to her, she was born a queen —Victoria wherever she went.

The failure of this conversation was owing in part to the fact, that gentlemen seemed unwilling to criticize a woman—and women could not do her justice alone.

BOSTON MASS.

MONDAY. FEB. 10. 1851.

. . . went this evening in a warm rain, falling on a glaze of ice to hear Mr Alcott.

This evening—Mr Alcott spoke of Mr Emerson as the exponent of literature.— He began by speaking of Genius itself—which he seemed to consider as transparency— Genius permits Divine light to pass through it— We seldom find it true and universal for most men have obstacles and biases within, which reflect—refract or color the light. The end of all true culture is of course to develope the individual, not that part of a man which was before him, and will be after him—but that which is for the first time in him. Emerson though eminently individual is also eminently universal. We know of no man who reminds us of so many of the great names of the past; of Plato & Socrates—finer than Montaigne,[34] often reminding us of Goëthe[35] and though not to be compared to Shakespeare yet worthy to be named in that fine company. If we were to drop the quotation marks, the ornament with which he is fond of loading his pages, is so nearly texture that few would separate it from his own words—and yet on all these his genius leaves a certain if a slight impress. There is not enough of the Hebrew in him. We would rather have had a more devout sweetness in him—there is a want of that entire surrender in him, which makes the enthusiast and invites us to him— He can never half put himself into any of his works or words. We never any where meet the whole man, he is not one but two—the <u>deuce</u> is in him. He is a very circumspect person—very discreet—he does not commit himself, is never mortified or embarrassed in the presence of another— We sometimes wish he were. He is always capable of that which he himself proposes. This person's manners are scientific. He knows very well what he is about. The fatality in which he believes, is oft-times harsh and offends our faith. Yet this person has been a college to New England—enforcing a richer culture than Harvard. Find anywhere in town or country, the lovers and readers of Emerson, and you shall find fine minds. You will perhaps wish that they took a more active interest in reforms, but you shall find fine minds. What would New England be if we were to subtract Emerson from the last twenty years? No other mind would she miss so much— How much of the riches of the past, has he made familiar from Hermes through Pythagoras[36]— to Christ. If Boston knew what she needed, she would demand of this man what he is capable of giving her. I know no man who more delights to write a lecture and deliver it to a fine company—no man who dislikes more to speak to a multitude or be reported in the newspapers. He lives in a constant reverence for the soul. Finer things are done through him than he knows. He is fitful. His sentences are gathered for his diary and in his published works—we ofttimes find 1820 side by side with 1850. We should prefer the Diary itself. His sentences are biographical. I know the original of many of these fine portraits— Some one sat for each. It was thus Plutarch wrote his Miracles (query: morals?)[37] Multitudes are mastered by him and will not own him—but his pupils are increasing day by day. We need a new Dial* where the Times shall be daguerreotyped—and master and pupil stand side by side. There is a vast deal of brave true life in the world, which does not get chronicled at all. Mr Emerson is no New Englander— We marvel how he came to be born here. Yet no Greek, or if a Greek a Greek Yankee.

We have one American—Thorough†—a man who owes much to Emerson, but not so much as many believe, a man whom E. would reverently and grate-

---

*That is, a new journal like the defunct Transcendentalist journal *The Dial* (1840–1844).

†The reference is to Henry David Thoreau. Dall's spelling captures the contemporary pronunciation.

fully receive into himself but cannot. He is a true Aesop. In his Walden Water, are finer fish than were ever caught. Fond of the woods, of water, of animals with whom he can talk. Yet something of a savage—the city cannot hold him long. "I was never solitary but once," he says, "and then I discovered that to be solitary is to be insane." What a depth of truth in these few words! Emerson has rather too much reverence for city and citizen for civilization He is— shall I say it?— Yes I will—he is a little too conservative,—conservative of institutions. He has a prodigious memory—not Egyptian and mythological like Miss Fuller's, but classic—Greek. His influence on fine women—is a tribute to him. He has also a wonderful knowledge of affairs—though his funds are in no bank. He is the millionaire of Cosmos.* This idealist who makes us familiar with Hermes and Plato, understands also the price of cotton and the rise of stocks. Hence the merchants respect him—and wonder at him.

This is a very imperfect sketch but I came home, to watch the baby through the night, and fight off the croup. Hence it is the best I can give—

BOSTON MASS.

SATURDAY. FEB 15. 1851....

I have been much delighted today by the manly rescue of a fugitive slave by about 100 colored people.† Seizing a favorable hour, they broke into the court room, where the slave was confined, and with no weapons but their fists, and in a perfectly good humored way—bore him off, without opposition....

BOSTON MASS.

SATURDAY. FEB. 22. 1851....

Last night I had a strange dream. I thought I was taken up for aiding not Shadrach but "Meshech and Abednego" ‡ and carried to the Court House. I

---

*Dall later inserted here in pencil the following sentence: "He does his business not in the Exchange or in State St but up on the plain of the intellect."

†In a celebrated rescue, Shadrach Minkins (d. 1875), a fugitive from Virginia who had been living in Boston for several years before he was arrested, was taken from the courthouse in Boston by a group of black men. He then made his way to Montreal, where he lived for the rest of his life. See Gary Collison, *Shadrach Minkins: From Fugitive Slave to Citizen* (Cambridge, Massachusetts: Harvard University Press, 1997), especially 125–126. Collison's carefully researched account estimates the number of rescuers at twenty, far fewer than the rumored one hundred of whom Dall heard.

‡The Old Testament characters Shadrach, Meshach, and Abednego were Jewish exiles in Babylon who refused to worship the golden image as decreed by King Nebuchadnezzar. They were cast into a fiery furnace but were unharmed and released (Daniel, Chapter 3). Shadrach Minkins was the fugitive slave who had been rescued a week earlier.

declined all counsel and after a great deal of ridiculous cross-questioning, I was told that I might make my own defence. I rose with my Bible in my hand and beginning at the sermon on the mount, read all the pertinent passages on Christian duty, until I came to the words of Peter & John "whether it be right in the sight of God, to hearken unto you, rather than unto God, judge ye" I spoke these words in the most solemn manner, looking sternly at Commissioner Lunt[38] as I did so. I thought he trembled as his eye met mine, and all of a sudden the forms of the prosecutors melted shrinkingly away, and I found myself alone, under the open sky. . . .

BOSTON. MASS.

WEDNESDAY. APRIL 2ND. 1851.

I finished my calls this morning. I had a very pleasant call on Miss Finch. I read to Mr Alcott my sketch of his talk about Emerson. He said it was the most life-like sketch he had ever read of anything he had done. It had a fine color—. He thought on the whole, it must be better than the talk itself, because I left out all irrelevancies. I said, I had not written many abstracts this winter for want of time. "That is not right," said he "It is clearly demanded of you; to write abstracts." He made me promise to copy the fragments I had and send them to him, & I parted from him sorrowfully really glad to have given him so much pleasure. . . .

. . . Mr Dall went with Mr Bartol to Miss Bacon's lecture, which turned out an entire failure . . . .

BOSTON. MASS.

SATURDAY. APRIL 5TH. 1851. . . .

I have found it hard today to think of any thing but the chains about the Court House, and the miserable Sims.* People have—laughed a good deal at Judge Shaw's being obliged to lower his head as he passed in†—but they need not. Is it not impossible to forge chains for others without wearing them ourselves?

---

*Thomas Sims, a seventeen-year-old fugitive who had escaped from Georgia two months earlier, had been arrested in Boston. After several unsuccessful attempts by the Boston Vigilance Committee to free him, he was escorted to a ship in Boston Harbor by three hundred soldiers and returned to slavery. See Merrill and Ruchames, eds., *Letters of William Lloyd Garrison* 4:700; C. Peter Ripley, ed., *The Black Abolitionist Papers,* 5 vols. (Chapel Hill, North Carolina: University of North Carolina Press, 1985–1992), 2:146.

†The courthouse, surrounded by soldiers and federal deputies in anticipation of an attempt to rescue Sims, was also fortified by heavy chains ringing the building. Like everyone else, Judge Lemuel Shaw was forced to stoop to get under them and enter the building *(ANB)*.

W. LYNN. MASS.

TUESDAY. APRIL 22ND. 1851.

... Father saw Mr [Daniel] Webster at the Revere* today, and says he never saw him look so ill—he seems to be failing rapidly. The change in his <u>moral</u> features might have convinced men of that one would think. He spoke to the people from the balcony of the Revere today at eleven and the whole square was densely crowded with men.

Another piece of news father brought home with this, an appropriate pendant in truth— The slave hunters are after Charles Williams. John Torrey[39] came to father today, and told him that the slave who had lived with him [i.e., with Dall's father], concerning whom negotiations had been going on of late, had better look out for himself. Father told him quite gleefully that he was safe. I believe I have never said much in my journal about the letters I have been lately writing on this subject, & I will synopsize the whole matter.

Williams has lived with us in all five or six years. He was a fine servant but no more truthful than slaves in general. Soon after the passage of the new law,—he went to Montreal, but was persuaded to return, as nobody thought him in danger. A second time he ran off, and as he left behind him an old mother, and a wife and child, who suffered for his aid, my father thought I had better write to Mr Ridgely of Georgetown D.C.[40] and see if I could not obtain his free papers. I was very unwilling as I thought it might give the Ridgelys a clue not only to him, but to others of their slaves now in this neighborhood.

After purposely forgetting it and making a great many shifts, I was induced to write to Mr. Butler,[41] the Episcopal clergyman in Washington D.C., and as he had once been settled in G.[eorgetown] I asked him to sound Mr R. & see what might be done. I wrote to him that if the facts stated by the slave were true there were so many mortifying considerations connected with his name, that I thought any application would be worse than unavailing. In the first place, Williams's mother, had been defrauded of the liberty left her by will, for more than 20 years, & had obtained it at last only by a vexatious and mortifying suit. In the second—Williams had paid for himself to within a small sum, and going one night to his master to make the last payment was informed that it was useless for that for a slight misdemeanor, he would be sent the next day to a New Orleans Market. He found means to escape that very night. I told Mr But-

*The Revere House, Boston hotel at Bowdoin Square.

ler that I did not wholly believe this story which sounded rather boastful, but that if it were mainly true, I could not help thinking negotiation in the case useless. I received a reply from Mr Butler immediately expressing his willingness to proceed, giving the highest estimate of his friend & former parishioner Mr Ridgely. A few days later came another letter.[42] He had had an interview with Mr Ridgely—& was afraid that he should disappoint me by stating the result. Mr Ridgely had told him the whole history of his management of his slaves, and it had been, as he had known from his character, it must have been, generous & kind. There had been an agreement among the heirs, not a promise to the slaves themselves, that on coming of age, they should receive their freedom, but the experiment had not worked well. Mr R. was convinced that he ought not to have given liberty to any, except on the condition that they should go to Liberia. No one could change this decision, He would give Williams his free papers—pay his passage, and add a hundred dollars on his arrival, if he would consent to this. If not he would grant them only, after a sum of money, (not yet decided, in the absence of two of the heirs) should be paid, that this money Mr R would not receive for his own benefit, or that of the other heirs—but would devote it to some charity—of which he would furnish proof after its reception. He denied the truth of all the slave's story, but said that at the time he ran away, Williams was approaching the age at which he should have freed him. My father was then in Ohio; not having my letter book at hand, I cannot give the dates of my letters but without consulting with any one, I replied as follows.

I was not disappointed,—Williams would not go to Liberia. Mr Ridgely if he were to be separated from his family would probably prefer Canada to Liberia and he could not blame his slave for doing the same. It only remained to let us know for what price he would sell him. Not that we should be disposed to give a very large sum for him, no rather than do that, we should contribute to send the wife mother & child whose existence Mr R ignored to him in Canada. I did not deign to allude to the matter of charity; it was all I could do, to suppress my scorn, of the man, who would bribe the Most High with the price of a brother man. I refrained from alluding to a willingness the slave had expressed to pay for himself, but added that if it were not impertinent, I would be glad to know why he had run away, just as the moment for receiving his freedom approached.

Just before my father's departure for Ohio, he had placed in my hands a letter from Ira Gould Esq. of Montreal.[43] It expressed a willingness on Williams part, who was then acting as his servant, to pay $200 for himself. After writing Mr Butler, I wrote to Mr Gould. My letter contained a synopsis of what I had done, and I spoke to Mr Gould of W.'s want of veracity, and added that if he desired to buy himself his promise to do so ought to be secured in some legal manner, to impress him with its importance. I urged also the necessity of great forbearance in all letters just now written to the States. Mr Gould's reply was brief—he & Williams both approved of the judicious course I was pursuing. Williams would rather be hanged, than go to Liberia, but was willing to pay $200 for himself.

In his last letter Mr Butler used this expression, "Williams will be <u>liable</u> to be apprehended unless" &c—but I confess I did not seriously anticipate Mr R's acting on this threat—but today behold the news—from a gentleman a stranger to all our proceedings—that if in Boston, his liberty was in danger! So much for the vital Christianity of the Episcopal slaveholder—! He does not believe W. is in Montreal. Now for my next step.

Mr Gould said that he might write to Mr Ridgely himself, and that if he did, he would send a copy of his letter to father. That would convince Mr R. & I shall take the responsibility upon myself of advising it.[44]

W. LYNN. MASS.

MONDAY. APRIL 28. 1851.

Mother is not well today & spoke to me, quite oddly about my Journal. It is absurd to keep one, it is never anything but a tissue of lies! After the painful talk was over, I could not help thinking that a Journal must always be true in one sense. If not true to facts & if the character appears in it gracefully draped, the untruth & the drapery reveal the starkness stalking beneath. I sent a message to Edwd ____* tonight through one of the Committee of Safety, for I dared no longer delay—bidding him go to Canada as soon as possible—for he was watched.

---

*Obviously a fugitive slave, but unidentified further.

CHAPTER EIGHT

A Yankee in Canada

May 8, 1851–Sept. 2, 1853

$\mathcal{T}$he Dalls' sojourn in Canada did not begin auspiciously. Toronto, with only thirty thousand inhabitants, contrasted starkly with the liveliness of Boston, and Caroline experienced an immediate culture shock. The Dalls' first night was spent in the home of church members, a "darker, dingier,—worse kept house" than she had ever entered, and Caroline described herself as being "at this moment as wretched as I was ever in my life." Things soon got worse. In financial distress from the beginning—the congregation in Toronto was no more prompt with Charles's salary than the one in Needham—the Dalls were forced to appeal to Caroline's father for help. But he flatly refused, that is, unless she were willing to promise what she would not promise: to have nothing "directly or indirectly" to do with the abolitionists. Her mother, sympathetic to Caroline, tried to make peace between her and her father. Caroline came to live for her mother's letters and to fear that her father would prevent her writing. Homesick, pressed by serious financial concerns, and heartsick at the estrangement from her father, she was plunged into a severe depression.

Nevertheless, Caroline eventually began to make a new life for herself in Toronto. She taught a history class in her home, entertained church members at weekly gatherings, provided aid, some of it sent from Boston abolitionists, to fugitives from the United States, and met the marvelously garrulous Susanna Moodie, successful Canadian novelist. Most importantly, she came to know, and began to fall in love with, John Patton, the church treasurer and one of its trustees, some five years younger than she. An emigrant from Northern Ireland, Patton was a china and crockery importer, an intellectual, and a bibliophile. He must have been in awe of this brilliant, well-read woman from

Boston, whose "natural element," she herself judged, was conversation. Caroline was equally attracted to John, appreciating his near-worship of her, and feeling a heavy weight of responsibility for the influence she exercised over him. He soon became a boarder in the Dall household, notwithstanding Caroline's wariness of the "mischief" that might come of the arrangement and her recognition that the "chains of husband and children" must be "sacredly respected." The children called him "Uncle John," and he called her "Mamma." On November 24, 1851, something happened between them that for years afterward she observed as an anniversary. At some point she removed the entry for that date from her journal.

It is not surprising that in such circumstances the Dalls' marriage began to show signs of stress. The fault line that had existed from the beginning of the marriage was exposed: Despite his goodness, Charles was too weak to command Caroline's respect, and she was perhaps too strong to allow him to respect himself. She began to admit to herself the shortcomings of her marriage.

In the early spring of 1852, Caroline read the newly published *Memoirs of Margaret Fuller Ossoli* and was profoundly moved. The coincidence of this reading with the unsettling events in her own life precipitated her writing, on March 20, 1852, by far the longest and the most revealing journal entry that she ever composed. Point by point she compared her own life with Fuller's, disclosing along the way childhood traumas, including her apparent sexual abuse or attempted abuse by a governess. She saw herself and Fuller as extraordinary "steadfast natures" who must take their own paths aside from the mainstream. Though she recognized Fuller's intellect as greater than her own, when she considered her own "quickness of apprehension," the faculty that allowed her to pull together the threads of fact and thought, she concluded, "I never encountered its equal not even in Margaret Fuller." Their marriages too, she believed, were similar: "we both in a period of sorrow and isolation learned to lean upon the heart, that we intellectually knew to be unsuited to us." Though Margaret had died "before the mist dissolved," Dall now realized that "The true union must be not only a union of heart and flesh—but of mind," and she bleakly foresaw that for the remainder of this life her "heart must ache, through long long years."

This painful recognition tormented her as she wondered later, "Is it indeed best, that life should go on as it is when every act of it is a profanation to the soul? Must every woman large hearted and broad brained like George Sand, commit actual sin, or be tied forever to one narrow insufficient being?"

At times she thought that even a flawed marriage was necessary to develop her "womanhood"; but in another frame of mind, she thought that if she could marry again, she "would not submit to the loss of power." And she found that her idea of "virtue" had changed: She used to congratulate herself for repelling the advances of men whom she actually despised, but she now knew that "if I held my heart tight in both hands when it was struggling to get free, there would be some virtue in that—no otherwise." Clearly thinking of herself and Charles, she wondered why "two individuals, each of them capable of leading the noblest lives, should really endanger each other's way."

Caroline had also to deal with a serious accident to six-year-old Willie, who lost part of three fingers on his left hand. The accident occurred when she and he were in the Boston area, and Caroline's actions in response are telling. She immediately sent word to John Patton, whose support she needed, and she delayed writing to Charles, to whom she felt responsible. But even more striking is her reaction to her father's gift of ten dollars after the accident: she saw it as "the symbol of a change for which I fear I should willingly spare my Willie's fingers." Nowhere in the journals is the overriding significance of her relationship to her father more distinctly revealed than in this terrible confession.

Out of the crucible of pain through which she passed during these years, Caroline Dall ultimately came to a kind of peace with her situation, and a new sense of selfhood. She remained Charles's wife, and she did not, I believe, become John's lover. She accepted that the reason her marriage had turned out as it had "is truly a question with which I have nothing to do." She found resonance in Goethe's recognition that "the individual can only be joyous and happy when he has the courage to feel himself in the whole." Thus she achieved something beyond simply a personal peace, what she called a "deeper knowledge of life," a "more earnest acquaintance with the human heart" that also made her "more gentle in judging, more patient with human lapses than I was once." What survived through all of her trials was "a consoling faith in God and goodness." Reflecting upon the contrast between her life and that of her sisters, she rhetorically asked, "But with which of [them] would I change places?" Her own trials, failures, and hard-won victories seemed preferable to their rich and apparently carefree existence.

The following entry opens with Caroline recalling their journey to Toronto.

TORONTO CANADA—
THURSDAY. MAY 8. 1851.

I wish I were not so weary and heartsick, that I might do justice to all we have enjoyed today. My arms are still so very lame, that I cannot lift Lily, and I have sat on the open deck almost all day. . . .

. . . We had a delightful sail on the Lake—from Queenstown to Toronto, dining in some state on board, where things were very neatly served. We reached the wharf at about half past five. William Burgess* was looking for us, and we drove up to the House. His father and mother had driven out, and I was glad they had, for I would not have had them see the discomfiture, the prospect of spending the night there produced. Such a hurly burly as the house was! no fire any where, and no prospect of any in any of the chambers. I sustained myself as well as I could & resolved to get into my house on Saturday night dirty as it might be. The children had their suppers, and by and by the host & hostess appeared. Smart cordial people both of them, and truly kind, but prim as if they had just stepped out of Thread Needle st.[1] A bed was put up in the parlor for the baby & us, where I had already procured a fire— I bore up until every body had left us & when we were really alone, I had a good cry. A darker, dingier,—worse kept house, than this I had never entered. I felt how much Charles must have endured to have imagined that his family could pass a night in it. I felt afraid we should displease our host, who was evidently the very soul of generosity. Altogether I was at this moment as wretched as I was ever in my life.

The Dalls moved into a house on Church Street near the corner of Queen, where they would remain as long as they were in Toronto.

TORONTO. CANADA.
THURSDAY. JUNE 5. 1851.

Among my letters from Boston, was one from father, the longest I think I ever had from him. It refused me the hundred dollars I asked for, unless I would pledge myself neither directly nor indirectly to give my sympathy to the "en-

---

*The Dalls spent the first few nights in Toronto with the Burgesses, William and his parents, Thomas (1807?–1886) and Jane (b. 1814?), members of the congregation.

Toronto, Canada West. From the Top of the Jail. Ontario 1854. *The city as
it appeared when the Dalls lived there. Lithograph by Edwin Whitefield.
(Courtesy of Library and Archives Canada/C-016467)*

emies of my country" viz. Channing—Garrison & Parker. I can do without the
money—but I cannot do without my father—without the integrity & liberality that I have honored in him. Charles & I were bitterly tried by this letter. I
should not have been so much surprised had it happened in the States, but it
was at this moment wholly unforeseen. We did not sleep last night and this
morning my eyes were swollen out of my head with tears. I wrote to my father,
weeping all the while refusing to take one cent upon conditions. When I remember my life at Georgetown, I can hardly believe his cruel letter has been
written. . . .

Mark Healey Esq.*
Boston Mass.
Toronto Canada. July 10. 1851.

My dear father,

I have just received a letter from mother, dated Hampton July 3d. It is so
affectionate that it has in some measure comforted me, for all I have gone
through of late. She says, I have had an hour's conversation with your father
since his last letter was sent. "He does not wish you to give up a single friend
you have—, nor your own opinions;—only to abstain from writing or aid-

*Dall included this copy of a letter to her father in her journal.

ing those whom he considers traitors." . . . If I had not known your feelings, I should been far more active in this cause. This knowledge did not make me a hypocrite but it made me cautious. It made me determine never to do anything in opposition to your wishes, which I could not justify to myself in the sight of God. I stand alone, & with no party. Only the ignorant connect me with one. When I saw to what the contest was coming, I knew that it would be impossible for me to live in the States. I felt that I must do there many things, which would pain you more, than in your declining years—& with mother's delicate health, I could bear to do. I knew that I could serve the cause of Human Rights in Canada, & I urged Charles to come here. It seems to me that you ought to be satisfied with this proof of my affection. . . . If you ask me to promise, never to write another word on the subject, I cannot do it. In the first place, you have no right to demand it. In the second, I have no right to promise it. I cannot tell what my duty will be. It costs me a great deal to write a word that you do not approve, I do not do it lightly. Mother, says, "it would not be a great sacrifice to give up writing altogether." No it would be nothing, if I were sure that I could keep my promise—but when a power not my own, seizes my pen, & guides it, & a voice not human, says "Write," then it is no longer in my power to resist, & the promise that was at first only cowardly & weak, would become wicked. . . . Give my love to mother & tell her I thank her for her kind words, without them I could not have written this letter.

God forever bless you my father, so prays

yr affectionate Carrie.

I had hardly sealed the above letter before Charles received one from father, in return for one he had written to him beseeching comfort for me. All my previous suffering seemed nothing as I read the cool—almost vindictive words. I was thankful my letter was finished before I saw it— I could have written nothing conciliatory with that before me. And now oh God! for strength to bear in silence—all my grief! Too many words have passed, but the daughter must be satisfied, in spite of maxims & worldly prudence.

TORONTO. CANADA.

JULY 11. 1851.

I am tired of waiting for the payment of Charles's salary. We have written to Charles's father for help—help which we need not have asked, if they would only be punctual. . . .

TORONTO. CANADA.

SATURDAY. JULY 19. 1851.

It has been raining I think ever since Wednesday, and I have been sick quite sick. Yesterday I was not off the bed. It was one of my usual ill turns— made much worse by my complete nervous prostration. No one who knew me in Boston could recognize me now. All my firmness & energy are gone. From Thursday morning till Saturday night of every week I watch nervously for mother's letter. None has come this week. I keep fearing that father will prevent her writing and sometimes this fear comes so darkly over me —that it shuts out the sight of God. I should like to go away into the woods & scream.— It seems as if violent bodily anguish might relieve my burning brain. . . .

TORONTO CANADA

THURSDAY. OCT. 16. 1851.

Sewing through the morning, and after dinner called on Mrs Latham[2] & Mrs Copland.[3] I was going up to see Mr Hunter[4] but hearing from Mary, as I returned that Mr Patton[5] had called, I sent him an invitation to tea, and staid at home. He came directly up, and glad enough we were to see him, and a long pleasant talk of home, followed.* He remembered everybody and every-thing and as he got up to go away, he said with genuine kindness, "Ever since I left Toronto for Boston, I have been anticipating the hour when I should return and tell you this." He told me he had brought plenty of new books—and as he named over the books, he had purchased, I found with emotion that there was not one, that I had not spoken of lately, as desiring to read. May God bless his kind heart. . . .

TORONTO. CANADA.

FRIDAY. OCT. 24. 1851.

A heavy headache, but tried to study. A visit from a poor colored woman in distress about her rent. In the afternoon I walked as far as the Coplands, but returned feeling quite ill. The Burgesses & Mr Patton came to tea. I like Mr P. better every time I see him, something was said tonight which may result in his coming every day to dine & take tea, instead of going to a hotel. I wish I

---

*Patton had just returned from a buying trip to Boston.

could see the end of such an arrangement. I do not care to gain an inmate at the expense of a friend. It makes my heart flutter to think of all the mischief that might grow out of it—but I think I can trust him.

Within a few days John Patton had moved in with the Dalls, becoming their boarder.

TORONTO. CANADA.

SUNDAY. NOV. 9. 1851.

... I had a long talk with ___* about his own affairs. It kept me awake long into the night,—and roused me before day—but I did not regret it. When I reflect upon it—and consider how necessary, I have suddenly found myself to be, to some of those whom I have loved best on earth—how a few words of mine have seemed to decide the destiny of more than one fellow creature, I feel almost terrified at the weight of responsibility I find myself compelled to bear. A few words—uttered at a moment that I remember only too well, at the time Mr Hosmer[6] was with us, seem to have bound ___† to me—by one of these mysterious chains, and how it has been gradually strengthened—I hardly know. At all events I feel sure that not only his happiness, but his manliness will in a great measure, depend upon my conduct at this hour. If it were hard to use such an influence rightly, before I married,—it is doubly hard now—when the chains of husband and children must be sacredly respected. I would gladly have pillowed his head on my heart, & stilled its throbbings tonight—& the few words of affection and hope I felt it right to utter, seemed to fall with too little significance for the emergency. God sees us both may he give to him the comfort & peace it is not mine to bestow. The fullness of his confidence in me, has grown out of those two or three words used in conversation with another—"the end of Human Life, is not success, but development."

TORONTO. CANADA.

SATURDAY. DEC 13. 1851.

... my History Class ... was again very full— After it was over I drew the great temple of Persepolis for Mr Patton & sent him early away. Leaning over

---

*Dall later filled the blank line with the letter *N*. She no doubt refers to John Patton.

†Again, Dall later filled in with the letter *N*.

Mourier's[?] pictures of Persepolitan remains tonight in the History Class,
_____* suddenly turned round & caught a kiss from my lips, with such vio-
lence that it frightened me. I thought of Fourier's words—"Absolute liberty is
possible only with absolute self-control."[7] If I had apprehended any emergency—I should have been adequate to it, as it was I neither spoke nor moved,
but felt my heart turning to stone. Now I reproach myself for it.

TORONTO. CANADA.

MONDAY. FEB. 2. 1852.

A letter from Samuel May jr proposing to make us the dispensers of about
$100 for the relief of fugitives—[8] Luckily Lizzie Thompson came down with
some yeast; so I had some one to stay with the children while I went out and
made investigations. It took nearly the whole day—to do this, and answer the
letter. An interview with Mr. Henning—with Mrs H.[9] and with a fugitive up in
Agnes st—&c— I advise them not to send on money at present.

TORONTO SATURDAY MAR 20. 1852. . . .

In Margaret Fuller's Autobiography[†] I see my own life renewed. The same
dreams, especially that of following my mother to the grave, appear to have
haunted us both.[10] Neither of us appears to have had natural childhood. Her
father & mine were alike impatient, and we were both injured, by the imperative demand for clearness & precision in our statements, before it was possible that we should have clearness & precision in our thoughts. If I did not read
Latin at the age of six—I read metaphysics at 8—and knew more of Geometry
and Cartesian vortices at 10 than of my dolls or silkworms of which I then had
a good many. Once in very early childhood I had with much labor finished a
long well written letter to my grandmother. A relative was waiting to take it to
the country. I sealed it in a hurry, and when my father saw that it was with a
wafer,[11] and that a little too moist, I was not allowed to send it— From my earliest years however, I respected this accuracy, and should have found the greatest pleasure, "in doing" as he often commanded, "what I did—well—" had he

---

*Dall has filled in the blank line with the letter "C." Both this letter and the insertion "in the History
Class" are probably attempts to disguise the identity of the person who kissed her, in all likelihood John
Patton.

†That is, *Memoirs of Margaret Fuller Ossoli,* edited by Ralph Waldo Emerson, James Freeman Clarke,
and William H. Channing (Boston: Phillips, Sampson and Co., 1852).

but shown the least tenderness toward me. I had no loving mother, at that age—like Margaret— He was my all—and my heart—froze—and broke—under his coldness—a coldness which covered as I now know, the very tenderest affection. Earnestly like Margaret, I <u>prayed for a sign</u> (Vol 1. p 21.) but it was not a sign of Roman vigor that I needed, but a sign of God's life, that I then doubted. I needed but could not find the Infinite. Life was bitter. Like her—I only lived in my books, and with out them, life would have been insupportable. I loved nature, the bees in the wall—the ants and aphidae in the old peach tree—the rats that thronged after the crumbs I daily scattered for them, the big—dragon flies that half frightened me with their noisy burr—but none of these so well as the sun-rise over the harbor, which I watched every morning while I braided my long hair—or the golden evening clouds that hung over the blue hills of Milton. How God spoke to me—out of these. I can seem to hear the terrible distinctness of that voice now! . . . The classics of all lands in the originals & translations were my earliest and to <u>this hour</u>, my best friends. Like Margaret, I might say that they did me—good—but also harm & were it not, that my experience of life has convinced me, that no such minds as ours were, can be developed by proper childish life, I too should wish that I had read no books till later. Some children like some flowers will not expand in the sun —like Margaret's Yuca Filamentosa,[12] they wait for the full of the moon—of such were we. My first friendship—it was for my teacher Caroline Wilby[13]— and long before I loved any girl of my own age—was much like Margaret's. Grace,—and perfect external refinement, won me also—and I was a perfect slave to her Sapphic head, & firm brown ringlets—but I was less fortunate than Margaret[14]—this vision did not float softly away into the blue heaven— leaving me no bitterer legacy than a superficial letter now & then. No—when my unreasoning affection had persuaded my father, to appoint this person my governess—and she came with her brilliant talent—to share my chamber and my bed—then I found that this grace and delicacy was like the caution of the spy, who is more patriotic than patriots, only because he fears to be found out— It was because her imagination was not pure enough to be trusted, because the possibilities of evil were within her, that she never allowed anything that looked like them to be seen without. She knew Lucifer when she saw him, and challenged at the gates, her auld acquaintance. In her chamber, she no longer showed delicate self respect—suitable reserve—or unselfish regard— I had opened my heart to her, too far—but I drew back into my shell—and for three months I shared child as I was—her bed & chamber, without ever speaking to her a single word. What a lovely spring day it was when she left us! What a relief it seemed—never was the sky so blue before—I scrubbed all the furniture in my chamber, to purify it from her presence—as Southey's aunt aired her cushion after an unwelcome guest[15]— I danced out into the garden —and thanked God—under the clear sun—which scorched my cheeks, like my human love, as I looked up to it. My sisters were little to me. Owing to my mother's illness, I had a heavy amount of care. They were my children, and I was more dogmatic & less affectionate I fear, than their proper mother would have been— They felt towards me, as Margaret's brother felt towards her,[16] and still farther, in their early years, they felt that it was quite a misfortune to have a sister whose uncommon acquirements made their father expect most unreasonable proficiency from them! Like Margaret I took nothing on trust —very early my father amused himself, with offering me, the most heretical notions in metaphysics and political economy, and listening to my violent rejections, and when reasons failed, my persistent assertions of faith in God and man— He would pretend to doubt me, when I planted myself—on my "je pense donc je suis"[17] but I could not be shaken—and much of whatever faith he has—he owes to me. . . .

Margaret felt as I did, her own want of external grace. It always puzzled me that she should not have a sweeter voice. I never could see why a cultured nature, should not give volume, depth and intonation to that. I felt the power in myself, and the wonders of expression, I could pour into my tones, partly atoned to me, for other defects. For this reason, I shut myself into my room, and read much aloud, for this reason, I often declaimed in the open air, and astonished all the passers by,—by talking to the roots of the great elms, under which I loved to sit on the Beacon St. Mall. But I knew—I was awkward, plain, and intractable, and I wondered why God did not give beauty to one who loved it so passionately. If I had had it I should not have been vain of it, I should only have felt myself in harmony with it. I was very conscious—had in my most spontaneous moments power to arrest myself—and I would not trust my inspiration. In really fine moments—on the brink of a great action, I often drew—back—for my keen love of artistic completeness, made me fear, that my plainness or my awkwardness, would spoil the whole—. Of course, I could do nothing beautiful or simple in that state, but I should never have recovered from it, but for a strange accident. Talking a few years after with SF.H.* who

*Samuel F. Haven.

had the dangerous power of moving my deepest nature, I became excited and warm, when he left me, I turned towards the window, and approaching the pier, where a fine mirror extended from floor to ceiling, the honest words that sprang to my lips were, "who is that beautiful girl?" When in an instant after, I recognized my own dress, a blush of mortification, burning even now in my cheeks, seemed to suffuse my whole being—. But the vision did me good, a joyful confidence in myself, succeeded my wholesome mortification, and I felt that I might at times have the power to please. To have faith in this power is essential to happiness. Never afterwards did my consciousness disturb me to the same degree, and as I grew older I learned to forget my own personal deficiencies, in the force of thought and feeling.

When my husband first knew me, he used to say that I reminded him, of two passages of Scripture, "for judgment—am I come"—and "he shall judge the quick and dead—"[18] so trenchant were my decisions, and so absolute my convictions. This demanding of others, the best that they can do, so often stated of Margaret, was from the beginning true of me— I spared nobody, and myself least of all, so that a young friend who saw me refuse a sofa in an hour of extreme pain, and continue bolt upright in my chair, said bitterly, "To make yourself comfortable, is to you the unpardonable sin." Not consciously, but I thought so little of rest, that I hardly knew what would conduce to it. Margaret's conditions of friendship were like mine. To many a sufferer have I given peace—from Judith with her young sad eyes to Mrs Hedge[19] who hails even now her "spiritual deliverer," from how many have I not drawn their life secret, but who has as yet grasped mine? No, there is not on earth, the shoulder upon which it would strengthen me to lean, I win hearts as Margaret did. We had both had wide experiences—and when feeling passed into experience, we valued it as personal no longer. Thus in speaking out of our experiences we spoke with life and truth— Those who were addressed knew that we had <u>felt</u>, and answered often as they thought to our whole life—always in truth to but a part of it. I was always more willing to take the world for my confidant than the individual. I could trust the race, more truly than the man, to answer to my thought, and I have not been wrong, for from every part of the States, words of comfort and sympathy have come to me in acknowledgments of the influence I have exercised for good, over single souls. Soon after his return from Boston, ___* said to me—"It is very strange what an influence you have over

*John Patton.

me, ever since the second evening I met you, when you said in speaking of Napheygi[20]—that he must be an impostor, for no man of honor could speak lightly of a woman he had once loved—I have felt my soul bound to yours. It was not the words merely which riveted me, it was the tone in which you spoke." After these words were spoken I no longer felt alone in Toronto, I saw there was at least one person here, to whom I could be, what I had been to so many before—and of being such a friend, I never tire.

A few words have often great power, and many which I have spoken, and wholly forgotten, have been afterwards brought up to me—by others often older than myself—as pivots upon which their whole life turned. One would be foolish not to prize such moments, when "The Gods speak through"—us and when the bliss of serving, takes the sting from suffering. . . .

Margaret says "the lasting evil was to learn to distrust my own heart."[21] I could never do that. Instant is the decision of my nature in a given case, and I have never once had occasion to revoke or distrust it. Neither has my "yes or no been conventional."[22] I am not wild enough to think Margaret's conversational powers were ever approached on this continent, but I know what she means when she says "Conversation is my natural element, and I never think alone, without imagining some companion."[23] To me also, "thoughts have ever been things." These two volumes, are full of statements in which I deeply sympathize. "I feel quite lost" she says "to see so many acquaintances, to talk so many words & never tell my mind completely to one."[24] Here I seem to see that need of quiet and communion with self which I have always felt. A great deal of "hard work" have I had to do for myself—and I must have daily rest from the tide of life about me. I would always have my chamber to myself—and do not believe I have led so calm and true a life since I have not. Have not we a right to be exacting, who never forget those we love? But why does God bring into the world, these few steadfast natures? Is it only to show the world the divineness of persistency? . . . Like Margaret "I must take my own path"[25] —and I am grieved that others cannot help me more substantially than they do—but I think out all their problems first or last. "A man's ambition & a woman's heart is indeed an evil lot."[26] In my early youth however I was so conscious of both, that a rich cloud-land encompassed my daily life, and I shared Margaret's idea, that she was the child of other than her parents. Very sacred I kept that thought but I was certainly <u>sixteen</u>, before I ceased expecting that my parents would one day make me a revelation to that effect. I thought that if it had been otherwise I should have seen myself in them more clearly. No more painful feeling have I ever had, than that which often comes over me in conversation—that I really have a great deal to say which I think valuable, that others would not have patience to hear. I can never tell half that is in my mind, nor give myself leave to utter half my wealth of illustration—for fear of obtruding of taking too much time. I have often felt this when suffering much, when "pain like a girdle" braced me to clear emphatic thought—and to be arrested in the expression of it—was to be brought suddenly back to earth, from a better day....

... Margaret tore up her youthful journal. She could not have hated hers more bitterly than I hate what survives of mine.... Whenever I look at it, I am tempted to burn it up—for it is in no sense pleasant—not sweetly childish, but officious—the "mountainous me,"[27] swelling up through all its depressions. What has prevented my doing so, thus far, has been the thought that it might sustain my children, through their faults and follies to know that the mother whom they loved was once weaker than they—and also a strong unwillingness to destroy the traces of Anna Renouf's loving and graceful spirit. If it were but a real child's journal how I should love it—but it is so full of assumption! I only wonder that anybody had patience with me in those days!... Margaret says "Spontaneously I appropriate all the material of other people, and turn it to my own use. By prompt intuition I seem to be superior to those who have reflected far longer and know a great deal more."[28] I have often felt this, and sometimes when others have applauded the spirit and tone of what I have said under such circumstances I have felt so ashamed that I have longed to go and tell them how it was that I seemed to know so much—and I have only been restrained from doing it by the reflection that they would not understand my honesty. It is undeniable that a mind may be stored with facts & reflections, which do not live, because their owner does not perceive the threads which bind them, and when I compare my own quickness of apprehension with that of others—, I can truly say, that I never encountered its equal not even in Margaret Fuller. She was so much greater intellectually that she must have known a great deal by experience that I only apprehend. It may be objected to all this however, that in comparing mental states—I must bring my apprehension into play—and am in danger of slipping the whole circle, through that first dropped stitch. In her credo, Margaret says "I have no objection to the miracles, except where they do not happen to please one's feelings."[29] I do not like these words—true to her temperament & mine they may be, but they look like unworthy evasion. One has no right to <u>feel</u>—a matter of fact, instead of judging it. "She bound her body to the mast," says her biographer, "while sailing past the Sirens."[30] How near each other lie the most profound truths, and the most profound falsehoods—of life! I feel that these words are true of me, but I do not know how to find any virtue in this self imposed restraint. It seems a necessity of my nature. If I had been differently situated I must have done the same thing, I feel thankful that God has saved me by creating this necessity, but what in that case becomes of human responsibility, of sacred duty? Honestly I do not know, but I believe, nevertheless, "I return to my native bias, and feel as if there was plenty of room in the universe for my faults, and as if I could not spend time in thinking of them, when so many things interest me more."[31] These words are true to my frequent feeling. Last night I had been entertaining some strangers, and talking with several persons—not accustomed to meet, and equally strangers to me, I was obliged to keep the thread of general conversation in my own hands, to prevent their minor threads from tangling. It was on great subjects religion and politics—the relation of man to God—and of man in God to his fellow men. Charles could do nothing with them—he left all the burden on me, and soon left the room. When I went to bed, serious yet elate, I would have kept quiet & followed the thoughts I had started, but he said to me—"I cannot help wishing that when you lead conversation as you did tonight, you had the rare tact not to <u>seem to lead</u>." Tears choked my utterance— I was in the seventh heaven—must I be brought down to that?[32] "Take me as I am," was the longing prayer of my heart—"take me as I am, accept what is fine in me, and be sure the ages will bury the rest." It seemed incomprehensible to me that such lofty thoughts should have been spoken before him and he had when we were alone, no words of sympathy and encouragement for me—and admiration of others—only a regret—, and of this regret, I do not in this instance perceive the justice. And of what use was it— can one give tact to one who has it not—& failing in that—who would be cruel enough to destroy another's unconsciousness! So hardly have I gained it!

I wept over the sweet note from her mother[33]—one such note would have been happiness enough for a lifetime but it was not permitted to me. "—resigned I could do well but happy I could do excellently"[34] Therefore is it that happiness is the gate of our Heaven—our well doing.

I was delighted to find that Margaret had an interest in that wretched class of women—who have been so earnest a subject of thought with me for years.

I thought her too deeply absorbed in intellectual growth—to think much upon this subject—nor do I suppose that she had ever had much intercourse with the wretched creatures in their habitual position, before she went to Sing Sing.[35] These pages have been written out of my full heart—there remains to be spoken of, Margaret's romantic marriage. The parallel between our lives—follows even here. We both met our husbands—first in a church—we both refused the first offer—and we both in a period of sorrow and isolation learned to lean upon the heart, that we intellectually knew to be unsuited to us. What is said of Ossoli—well suits my husband.[36] He is capable of the sacred love—the love passing that of woman. He cannot speculate about love—or anything. The spirit and the affections are his domain, and he cannot feel an interest in intellectual gymnastics. His appreciation of his wife is the best proof to those who know her, and not him, that he is worthy to possess her. But I feel that Margaret was happy to die, before the mist dissolved. The true union must be not only a union of heart and flesh—but of mind. We must think together until we have outgrown the rude discipline of earth, until we are great enough to spare each other the subservience of perpetual sympathy. We are not yet. Those who have tried the experiment know well that it is so, and the agony of a married life which does not answer its purpose is a thousand times worse than the loneliness of maidenhood. While we have hope to sustain us, we can endure anything, but when we felt that the matter is settled for this life, and that whatever may open to us in another, the heart must ache, through long long years, the spring of life is broken—and we need an infinite faith in the Love of God to live. And yet, if we could be married only thus, neither Margaret nor I would have it otherwise, for marriage is needed by both to develop our womanhood—and give us wide charity for others—true cognizance of our duty towards them. In her own words—"I neither rejoice nor grieve—I acted out my character,"[37] but what a testimony are they to the emptiness of a relation which should make the whole heart to "sing for joy."

I used to think that my life would end like hers in storm and sorrow—but I do not think so now—weak suffering as I am, I shall lead for many years a hard life—and die with some little thing achieved.

TORONTO. CANADA.
WEDNESDAY. MAY 5. 1852.
... Many things have troubled me today. Often have I been on the point of saying—"The iron has entered into my soul."[38] Nothing prevents my giving way

to despair except the feeling that I must not waste time. How strangely am I constituted! In the midst of the deepest grief comes the feeling that God will call me to account for the use I make of the hour—that I must not grieve if I can work. And yet before I know it, I find myself leaning on my hand, and my thoughts in far off forbidden regions. Oh God forgive me— If I am sometimes unreasonable exacting and unhappy—may it not also be said of me—that I "loved much."[39] Why do we so question fate? . . .

TORONTO CANADA.

WEDNESDAY. MAY 19. 1852. . . .

Read the North British. Found a great deal of pleasure in the article on Milton.[40] If a mind like his, could be so unsettled by an unsuitable marriage, weaker people need not be astonished to find their own in the same plight. Oh when will God's will be clear to us in this matter. Is it indeed best, that life should go on as it is when every act of it is a profanation to the soul? Must every woman large hearted and broad brained like George Sand,[41] commit actual sin, or be tied forever to one narrow insufficient being? . . .

Dall and her son Willie went to the Boston area in July 1852 for a visit of several weeks.

W. LYNN. MASS.

FRIDAY JULY 23D. 1852.

I am sorry I was not well enough to go to Cambridge[42] yesterday—but there it is. This morning I drove over to Mrs John K. Mills's fine house, and spent nearly three hours with Mrs Colman.[43] I talked over with her, all the <u>external</u> experience of my married life, and felt confirmed in my own views of life—and my own peculiar duty—by the story she told me of her own life. Nearly 70 years old she feels it hard—after years of bitter toil—to be dependent on her children. "If you would not get into debt—keep the purse-strings in your own hands." This was the burden of her song—& she added—"no clergyman unless he is hatefully avaricious, can know how to save— It is also better that his wife should bear the odium of necessary parsimony."

"All the romance of life is gone, after marriage— It is impossible for men & women to judge whether they are fit to live always together, while under the excitement of passion." I felt it very sad to hear these words fall from her lips— superior in mind & advanced in years as she is, but are they not true, and do they not pathetically shadow out all that is amiss in life & society. I have often felt that if it were possible for me to marry again, I would not submit to the loss of power, to help my husband. It seems sad that we cannot in this matter learn from each others' experience. If I could give what I have gained, to my little Lily, when she needs it, I should be content with my sorrow—, but—can I? It really seems sometimes as if those who engage themselves coolly, without feeling much love, are more likely to be happy than others. But does that look like obedience to the Divine Law? Who can resist Love, when the way is open in the sight of God—who can compel it—when it no longer exists? Yet short sighted that we are, we promise to love till death. We may well promise to cherish—that is our duty—but it seems to me, that many marriages I know—if they continue to exist as marriages, are only legal prostitutions, and for a wife to bring children into the world, after she has ceased to love their father, has as bad an effect on society, as the grossest licentiousness. . . .

W. LYNN. MASS.

SATURDAY. JULY 24.TH. 1852. . . .

. . . I spent the evening in reading Hawthorne's Blithedale romance.* He has played his usual pranks with individuals in the strangest way. Zenobia is a compound of Mrs Ripley, Margaret, and Mrs Parks.[44] I like the book however and it reminds me every where of my talk with Mrs Colman. In Heaven, we shall have other work to do I trust—but we cannot be all nuns? What will become of our thirst for love.[45]

Dall visited the Harris family, Eliza and her daughter Hattie, old friends in Needham.

E. NEEDHAM AUG 6. 1852 . . .

I went to the Parsonage this afternoon. House & land have been bought by Galen Orr[46]—for $1500. The house alone cost much more. He is an honest man, but I wish I could feel sure that he would not cut down my trees. The old oak and the elms looked splendidly. The larches & silver maples are doing well. I gathered two pears off of Charles's pear-trees for him, Then I went &

---

*The setting of *The Blithedale Romance,* published in 1852, was a fictionalized version of Brook Farm, where Hawthorne lived for less than a year.

stood above my poor baby's grave. Here more than anywhere else, I seem to realize what Life is. Here love, and power & fame seem undesirable and futile. As I recalled in bitter anguish all my sad experience of hard hearts and bitter tempers—as I brought back the terrible hour of bodily suffering, when at the birth of that child, I was left alone with God, and the weeks of still more utter loneliness that followed—it seemed as if it could scarce have been I, that so endured. God was merciful, for he did not let my poor little deformed one live. If I had ever seen the breath quivering through those little blue lips, I do not think I could have borne it— But with which of my sisters would I change places? With purple sails all spread, their pleasure laden barks have floated down the breeze. Strong canvass have I spread, and many a rent—made by the overbold wind, have my own hands repaired. God grant that they be not "made worse" by the patching.

BOSTON. MASS.

THURSDAY. AUG 12. 1852.

I got a long letter from Charles today, giving the pleasantest accounts from home.

I received one from Beloeil* which gladdened my heart—. God bless him who wrote it, if he had but come to his senses a little before—however, it would have saved me somewhat. Directly after breakfast, we went over to South Boston, & examined the Houses of Industry, Correction & Reformation the insane & Blind Asylums.[47] As none of these were new to me, I experienced the same intense consciousness of the sweetness & calmness of nature without, and the contrasting wretchedness within as on previous visits. If I lived here, I would go often to visit these wretched women—in the house of Correction. Many of them have been brought near to Hate by excess of Love. The only new thing about the visit was that I was called upon to make an address to the Boylston school[48] which I did with pleasure. This is the first time I have spoken in public for many years, I had not three seconds to prepare. It was well I was not asked yesterday or the day before, my spirits were too low, my thoughts too far off, but today I was lighthearted again. With those two letters in my pocket, I could do anything. The woman is always stronger in me

* "Beautiful Eye." Clearly Dall refers to John Patton. This is the only instance in which she disguises his identity in this way. On other occasions she uses a blank line (_____).

than the Artist. The teachers looked somewhat astonished at my presumption. Louisa[49] & Uncle W. thought I suppose that I made a very plain speech, but I knew in my soul, that it was better than that— It had a beginning middle & end. Like Margaret's conversation at Jamaica Plain every prefatory paragraph had an artistical relation to the close & contributed to heighten its effect.[50] If every word had been written as I spoke it it would have done me no discredit. . . . Got up to see Mrs Park & to prepare Willie to go out of town with Lizzie March.[51] If not homesick, he is to stay till next week. He has his father's sweetness of spirit, and added to his strength of will—, it ought to accomplish much.

BOSTON. MASS.

MONDAY. AUG. 16. 1852.

. . . I went up to Garrison's to make a call. In the midst of it Aunt Sarah white as a sheet, hurried up to me—Willie was hurt* and they wanted me in Newton. Mr Shannon[52] came in soon after dinner, but as there was nothing for me to do, would not have me sent for. Writing now after the lapse of several days, I remember little of my half distracted walk home. I knew I was not told all, & I dared not ask any questions, Mary Willard who had seen him, could only say that it was done with a hay-cutter which he had promised not to touch & that the tips of three fingers were gone. He had borne it like a hero, had not winced, & all his anguish was for his poor father & mother. "Oh, if I only had minded." burst again & again from his little heart. After the operation, he begged to have the story of the Crucifixion, read to him, and said that he would learn patience from what Jesus suffered. He waited in anguish the arrival of every hourly, and when at last my carriage stopped, he begged to be allowed to run down to meet me, because "I should feel better." Failing this he said—"I will get out of your lap, Aunt Mary or else mamma will think I am sick." In the mean time—Aunt Sarah packed my valise, and while she did it, I wrote a few hurried lines to dear Uncle John.[53] I know not what, I was too distressed to think. Once in the cars—by the light of a flaming western sky, at 7 o'clock I tried to read his letter just received. I saw that he wished to go to the Saguenay,[54] & I thought I would never believe in Voices of the Soul again, if the wild cry—of my despair, did not reach him this night & induce him to turn back. I found a sort of carryall

*Six-year-old Willie lost parts of three fingers in an accident with a hay-cutter.

going up to the Centre—, when I stopped Mr Shannon came out & relieved me of my baggage— Mary & Lizzie[55] passed each an arm about me, & led me up to the House, not a word was spoken. Even in this agony, I felt the silent sympathy of these two children inexpressibly affecting. I went up to the chamber, in an instant my poor little mutilated boy was in my arms, & weeping on my shoulder. "Oh Willie," I said "mamma will not mind the loss of your fingers, if you can but save your soul. What would your whole hand be, without a conviction of the sacredness of a promise." In a few moments, he was undressed & in bed, the poor little hand supported on a pillow. Into his evening prayer—I inserted the words, "Teach us to do & <u>bear</u> all thy will—," but he sobbed so violently I was afraid to proceed. I kissed his cheek & in about two minutes fast holding my hand he dropped to sleep. Mary chose to watch with him tonight as it[56] was supposed to suffer great pain. I consented, for I knew I had enough to do to struggle with my own heart and the angel. First, however I sent for the surgeon, & tried to learn from him, what the probabilities were, with regard to Willie's travelling—the treatment and so forth. The fingers I found were severed just <u>below</u> not just <u>above</u> the first joint.

Mary brought in a waiter with the face of a sorrowing angel, but I could only think of my husband—nothing passed my lips this night.

BOSTON. MASS.

THURSDAY. AUG. 19. 1852. . . .

. . . I was going to write to Charles, which I had delayed until the examination was over, in order that I might tell him the exact truth. I foresaw, I should never be happy till it was done, but it was best to wait. Oh if I could only be beside him, when he gets the letter! Poor, poor Charles! . . . Willie never was lovelier. It rested my eyes to look at his pale sweet face, as he bent over a comic book ' Mrs Cabot[57] had sent him.—

Directly after dinner, I began to write in earnest, I was interrupted by Theodore Parker. We had a long talk— I went to the door with him alone, & to my surprise he stooped down—put his arm round me, & kissed me, saying, "You will always send to me, when you are in trouble will you not? Mary[58] wrote me word how beautifully you bore it. I have not yet answered her letter but when I do—I shall tell her that I knew you would." Beautifully! God knows.

When he had gone, I went back to my bitter task. . . . I was preparing to go

[to] bed, when a thundering rap brought me a telegraph notice. My heart rose to my mouth, was anything the matter at home?, no, it was from Mr Patton, he will be here tomorrow. They were glad words—but I dread to meet him—almost as much as I should Charles. He dearly loves the child, and will suffer for us both.

John Patton escorted Caroline and Willie back to Toronto.

BOSTON & NORTHFIELD VT.

TUESDAY. AUG 31. 1852.

This morning dawned clear enough to encourage our starting. Mother Fannie & Emily came up to see me—also Lizzie March, and I think some others. Mother brought kind words and $10 from father. I cannot tell how grateful I felt to him for both the $10—as the symbol of a change for which I fear I should willingly spare my Willie's fingers. How little I realized last summer, that it was at such a cost I should purchase reconciliation. Then, I felt that nothing was too dear. . . .

TORONTO. CANADA.

WEDNESDAY. SEPT 29. 1852.

This has been a marked day for me, for I had a long visit from Mrs Moodie.* However good her books may be, they are dull and stupid things compared to her talk. She talked steadily all the time she was with me, a full brilliant flow with a hearty winning charm of its own. She began by making many enquiries about Willie, by comforting me—for his accident and adding that she did not think it strange that he should have thought his fingers might grow out again, for she had seen a hen's grow to nearly the usual length—but "nature is not so bountiful to man" she continued "in him mind must supply all deficiencies." I then spoke of Hawthorne's "Wonder Book"[59] and the pleasure Willie had derived from reading it. "She was almost sorry" she said, "children should know anything about those old myths—or see the brute passions deified." I

---

*Susanna Strickland Moodie (1803–1885) belonged to an English literary family in which five of the six daughters made significant careers for themselves after their father's loss of fortune and his death. In 1831 she married John Wedderburn Dunbar Moodie (1797–1869), and they emigrated to Canada a year later. Their arduous pioneer experiences are chronicled by Susanna in the Canadian classic *Roughing It in the Bush* (London, 1852), which Dall had just read, and in later works. The Moodies lived in Belleville; Susanna was visiting a married daughter in Toronto (*DCB* 12).

Susanna Strickland Moodie, famous Canadian author and friend of Caroline Dall:
"However good her books may be, they are dull and stupid things compared to her talk."
(Courtesy of Library and Archives Canada/C-007043)

tried to give her a glimpse of later light on this subject. She diverged to Willie's cleverness, and said it seemed to her as if all clever children died, and she spoke of her darling Johnnie, saved from the burning house only to be drowned.[60] Her tears flowed with violence while she spoke of him. . . .

. . . Willie came in, eager curiosity in every line of his face. "Here I am," said she "the very person you wanted to see so much—nothing but an old woman! I am glad your hand is better." . . .

. . . "Once Willie I went to see a farmer's wife at Bellville—her husband was one of Sheriff Moodie's sureties. We were shown into a handsome parlor—at last she came in, and laying her hands on her knees she said—

"So you are Mrs Moodie?"

"Yes."

"The woman that writes?"

"Yes—"

"Well if I had on my Sunday gown & my new cap, I'd look as braw. You're but a wee bodie after a'— How old are ye—?"

I told her my age— "You look ten years older nor that at the least— So you're the woman that writes."

"A young Irishman was with me, who loved me very much, & always called me "mamma," he was shocked at her way of speaking and I could hardly help laughing at his indignant interruptions. I disliked this woman very much. I was afterwards in a sick room with her where I think she frightened the patient out of several hours of life, by her unfeeling harshness."

I expressed my horror of this.

"Yes, but it is very common, my mother—had an old servant, who married somewhat imprudently, and was an invalid. She sent him out to my brother, who promised him a small grant of land. When he was dying of consumption, I went to read to him, and tried to talk cheerfully— "What's the use of talking so," said his wife, "he smells of death already." The poor man turned pale, turned his face to the wall—and never spoke again. He died that night, & in 3 months, she married again."

... She then said, she had read my book[61] last evening & liked it very much!— "It is a young book" I said, "I hoped to do better." "I am sure you will" she answered "and this boy better still." ... I had been setting the table while she sat—& now declaring for the third time that she should spoil our dinner she hurried away.

We all sighed when the door closed & wished she were to live near— This visit in Canada, was a real treat. . . .

SUNDAY. OCT. 24. 1852.

A pleasant morning & a fuller church. Sick and depressed all day. Reading The Vindication of the Rights of Women.* Am delighted with it. I feel that she

---

*This work, first published in 1792, is a fundamental statement of women's rights by English feminist Mary Wollstonecraft (1759–1797).

must have been a great a <u>virtuous</u> woman, say what the world will. Her coming in time, decided her preeminence, for there is nothing in the book I have, which my own articles[62] have not suggested, save that I have dwelt more at length on the questions of prostitution than she in the first vol.[63] . . .

TORONTO. CW.*

TUESDAY. NOV. 2. 1852. & WEDNESDAY NOV 3.

The same wet depressing weather occurs— I have been writing up letters, mending for the week and doing my shopping.

I have written to mother today about Daniel Webster. Very sad his death seems to me[64] . . . . Magnificently endowed in mind and soul—how sadly was his life wanting in encouragement & strength for the weaker! I never felt his strength in personal intercourse, perhaps it was because I never knew him[65] till all moral force had departed. The nation surely felt it—for the renown he has is not founded on nothing, and it surely is not founded on his <u>deeds</u>. His magnetism controlled men. It seems to me that his downward course began in 1842. When he found the state indignant because he had not sustained the tariff—and saw that wise men deemed the dollar of more importance than the soul—he was disappointed & having miscalculated for the first time—had no courage to work for liberty as he afterwards worked for slavery. "Out of the heart are the issues of life."[66] Out of its hope and elasticity and spring—men work when they work at all successfully. Within it are also the issues of death— as his sad history has proved. I have worn sackcloth for him since the 7th. of Mar. 1850.†

TORONTO. CW.

FRIDAY NOV. 12. 1852.

This day we received from Boston a copy of Thomas Higginson's sermon on Webster.[67] I prefer it to Theodore Parker's[68] because it directly attacks the weak point of the man—his personal sin.‡ How much more deeply I feel every year that no public good can be advocated with stained hands! How my ideas of virtue alter also! I can recollect that years ago I thought I was virtuous, because once before my marriage and once, after—I kept off the unworthy ad-

---

*Canada West.

†On March 7, 1850, Webster spoke in the Senate in favor of the compromise that included the Fugitive Slave Bill.

‡Dall probably refers to Webster's reputation as a philanderer. See Robert V. Remini, *Daniel Webster: The Man and His Times* (New York: W. W. Norton & Co., 1997), 307–308, 533.

vances of men who had been fascinated by my intellectual gifts. Virtuous! did I not despise both those men with all my strength, and was there ever for me, in my loneliest and poorest days, any thing desirable in money & luxury! I have learnt better than that—and I know now, that if I held my heart tight in both hands when it was struggling to get free, there would be some virtue in that—no otherwise. And this deeper knowledge of life, this more earnest acquaintance with the human heart—makes me more gentle in judging, more patient with human lapses than I was once. But Mr Webster's were not lapses. His was the systematic pursuit of sin. God forgive him, and warn us through him.

TORONTO. C.W.

NOV. 23. 1852.

... This night I kept with my own heart & God—an anniversary which properly falls upon tomorrow night.* One of the crises of my own life, it will always represent to me, very precious in the memory and possession.

THURSDAY. DEC. 2. 1852. . . .

As I sat over my work this morning I could not help wondering, if it were right to take hours precious for higher purposes—for this slow earning of half a dollar by my needle.[69] Thousands & thousands of times since I came to Toronto, have I thought over all my past life, and very mysterious do some of the recent dispensations of Providence seem to me. Oh God! give me peace—and some day when I have suffered enough, show me that this suffering has done me good & not evil all the days of my life. If it does not end in want of faith in Thee, I can bear all things—my own struggles & unbelief and the scorn—& coldness of others, but that I cannot bear—I will not think of.

Caroline and her daughter Sarah visited her in-laws, the Dalls, in Baltimore.

SPRING VALE SUNDAY.

BALTIMORE MD. JUNE 26. 1853.

Rose early, but felt sick and faint. Wrote letters home, A good deal annoyed by finding that Charles had been reading my old Journals. I have no desire to con-

---

*The anniversary of November 24, 1851 (the account of which Dall has torn out of the journal), a date significant to her relationship with John Patton.

ceal from him the truth. On the contrary, I earnestly wish that he could see the whole truth with regard to me, exactly as it is. But that is impossible in this world. The reading of my Journal will deceive him—what is past and gone, will seem present to him—for I have not dared to record in it, all the changes that have taken place in me, in their full force. . . .

After dinner I tried to sleep for I felt ill. after putting Sarah to bed, I went over to Henrietta's* to tea. Had a long three hours discussion, with Austin and Mr Whitridge[70] about slavery. They both got very warm, but I did not raise my voice nor lose my temper once—though sorely tempted many times— I thanked God for the whole matter was inexpressibly painful to me.

SPRING VALE.

BALT MD. THURSDAY. JUNE 30. 1853.

. . . After I had finished my sewing, I read Goëthe,[71] Every day the sense of this man's wonderful knowledge grows upon me. Was he not near and dear to God in spite of his dissipations that He blessed him with such fulness of light? It is a great delight to me, becoming fully acquainted with Goëthe so late in life, to feel that I have worked out most of the grand problems of life, unassisted and decided them; as he the master thinker has. He nowhere surprises me, and I sometimes wonder why it is that I feel his nature so much greater than my own. In the passage, dear John quoted in his last letter concluding with the words that "only mankind together is the true man, and the individual can only be joyous and happy when he has the courage to feel himself in the whole." I recognise what has been my own comfort for many years,—the substratum of my philosophy of life. Yet man never wrote a profounder thing. How often have I consoled myself when compelled to drop a clue that I had firmly grasped—with the thought, "if it is worth doing it will be done— God does not depend on me alone." trampling my personal ambition under foot, and caring only for the great interests of the whole. I have been nearer to God at these moments I feel sure, than at any other—and it was this consciousness—perhaps for a humility founded on it, which made Jesus—, so careless about recording his own words— Those good seed of his—Could he not trust

---

*Henrietta Dall Whitridge, Charles Dall's sister. Her husband, mentioned in the next sentence, was Thomas Whitridge (1802–1883), a shipping merchant whose Baltimore clippers ran to Rio de Janeiro for the coffee trade. At his death he left an estate of four and a half million dollars (*American Biographical Index* 1734:190–197). "Austin" was Austin Dall, Charles's brother.

them to the air? Did he not know that there was one who would guide them to deep soil, and water them by inevitable necessity until they bore a hundred fold?...

SPRING VALE.

BALT. MD. SATURDAY JULY 2. 1853.

... Mother and Louise[72] went to town, and left me in more pain than I could bear without moaning. I tried to watch the house while they were gone, but it proved nearly impossible, and Susan* got to Miss Louisa's cologne and after using what she wanted filled it up with water!! She is a perfect Topsy,† only I believe there is not so much <u>good</u> in her— If I owned her I should whip her I know, and living in the house with such a torment makes me feel more than ever before the horribleness of such a responsibility...

W. LYNN.

SATURDAY. JULY 16. 1853.

... I mentioned to father that next year I intended to bring Willie on to go to school. I did not mention it complainingly, but father took it up, and urged that it was Charles's duty to earn a livelihood for his family, that he ought to leave Toronto. &c &c— I bore it all patiently and without recrimination, but quivering in every fibre; a state of things I could ill bear after all I had endured. At last Ellen sprang up and burst into tears, exclaiming that she would not go to Europe, if I could not be made comfortable. She would not spend $1500 on her own gratification, if I had to pause before I could buy a chest of tea or a barrel of sugar. I had to follow her to her room and remonstrate and soothe her.... In this greater annoyance—I had really forgotten that I got in an envelope tonight the key of my chest of Mss. I cannot think what John was dreaming of to send it. I got no letter from Charles and was altogether worn out with worry tonight.

W. LYNN MASS.

MONDAY JULY 18. 1853....

"I believe that it would be as impossible for you to do anything not noble or magnanimous, as for the sun to emit darkness instead of light." These words

---

*Apparently a slave in the household of Dall's in-laws.

†Topsy was an undisciplined young slave in Harriet Beecher Stowe's *Uncle Tom's Cabin,* first published in book form in 1852.

came in a generous letter from my husband this evening I wish I could engrave them on a locket and wear them always about me— I think they would help me to be as true as he thinks I am. I have sometime wondered why, two individuals, each of them capable of leading the noblest lives, should really endanger each other's way. But this is truly a question with which I have nothing to do. . . .

W. LYNN MASS.

WEDNESDAY. JULY 20. 1853.

. . . Father brought me home a letter from ____* enclosing one from Lizzie Hedge.[73] There was much to rejoice over in Lizzie's letter and I shall enclose it to Mr Dall next time I write. With ___'s letter I was a good deal pained. There was not consideration enough in it for Mr Dall—there was a want of strict conscientiousness in it. But alas! how can I tell him that? May I not be myself, more to blame than he is for it, and could he comprehend—my censure if I uttered it. For the future at least, I will secure the right to speak the truth, by living faithful to my sense of right. He offers me a present, to assist in the expenses of my journey, but I cannot accept such a gift from him. I hope he will forgive me for declining it.

. . . A dreary kind of evening with painful disturbed thoughts but underneath them a consoling faith in God and goodness.

Caroline and Sarah Dall returned to Toronto.

TORONTO C.W.

FRIDAY SEPT. 2ND. 1853. . . .

. . . We first came along side the "Maple Leaf" and John, who had been watching the boat sometime, found his way on board. He had hardly reached us however, before we put off, & though I soon saw Mr Dall and Willie on the wharf,—it was sometime before they were able to come on board. How deeply glad & joyous was the meeting of the children! They were all glad but John was as happy as a little child and followed me round like a pet kitten. I could hardly help laughing to see him.

*John Patton.

CHAPTER NINE

Tribulations

October 10, 1853–October 17, 1854

$\mathscr{D}$uring her final year and a half in Toronto, Caroline Dall found a way, though expatriated, to participate in the American women's rights movement. She contributed regularly to *The Una,* a monthly paper "Devoted to the Elevation of Woman" and published in Providence, Rhode Island, the first such American periodical. Dall researched and wrote articles that were among the earliest examples of women's studies in America: studies of women of the past whom history had neglected or maligned, whose lives she now interpreted in a positive light. Her contributions, which began with the journal's first issue in February 1853, continued until *The Una's* demise in October 1855.

The year covered by these entries was also marked by Dall's entertainment in Toronto of two distinguished American women: Dorothea Dix, who had come to inspect the city's insane asylum, and Dall's old mentor Elizabeth Peabody, who was promoting a chart for teaching history. And her group of acquaintances grew to include a remarkable circle of the Canadian intelligentsia: besides Susanna Moodie, to whom she paid an extended visit in Belleville, she was friends with Paul Kane and Daniel Wilson. Kane, generally thought of as the father of Canadian art, had traveled earlier to the Canadian Pacific coast and the American Northwest in order to sketch the Indian cultures of those areas. Dall was frequently treated, along with her guests, to evenings of viewing these sketches and the oil paintings that Kane was producing from them. She recognized the significance and artistic merit of these works, and seems to have considered these "showings" as the best entertainment Toronto had to offer. It was likely Dall who made the connection between Kane and Daniel

Wilson, newly arrived from Edinburgh to become chair of history and English literature at University College of the University of Toronto. Wilson had already produced an archeological work on Scotland that helped establish prehistory (a word that he coined) as a science. During his distinguished career in Toronto (capped by his becoming president of the University of Toronto), he and Paul Kane were among the founders of the Canadian Institute, and Kane's work was important to Wilson's study of North American Indians, culminating in his *Prehistoric Man*. Wilson arrived in Canada without his family; Dall helped in the preparations for the arrival of his wife and daughters, and the relationship thus established lasted as long as the Wilsons lived. Their home was a haven for Dall during the worst of her distress in her final months in Toronto.

Caroline's distress was associated with a double crisis: division within the Toronto church, and the serious illness of Charles Dall. The church troubles revolved around the financing of a proposed new church building and pitted the Dalls, leading Americans in the congregation, and John Patton against the strong-minded Dr. Joseph Workman and his allies. Workman, a physician who became Canada's most prominent nineteenth-century psychiatrist, headed the insane asylum. Caroline felt, in hindsight, that he was turned against her and Charles because of the inspection visit by Dorothea Dix, whom they hosted. In any case, the church split, and although a vote of the congregation approved Charles's "piety and general conduct" in the matter, the minority began meeting on its own. Simultaneously with these troubles, Charles was taken ill with what Caroline called a "brain fever." He was delirious for days and unable to keep down food or medicine. In one of the journal's most affecting scenes, John Patton fed Charles crumbs soaked in brandy and Charles, too weak to speak, "fold[ed] his arms round John's neck, . . . drew him down and kissed him." When he was able, Charles went South in order to recuperate; unsure of his physical and mental health, Caroline sewed his name and destination into his clothes. When she received reports from George W. Hosmer, Unitarian minister in Buffalo, and Dorothea Dix as to Charles's mental incompetence, Caroline shifted from trying to defend him to attempting to persuade him to resign his position. His mental condition seemed to her "like a horrid dream"; she wrote his family of her fears, and his brothers showed the letters to Charles himself, enraging him and giving him, she feared, "cause for life-long dissatisfaction with me." He now became hostile to her, turning his family—including Aunt Sarah and Uncle William, so beloved of Caroline—against her; he told other ministers that she was the reason he had had trouble at Needham, and he vehemently protested his mental competence. Charles returned briefly to Toronto, and in the barrage of his irrational accusations against her, Caroline could only pray that God "have mercy on us both, but restore his peace, and yield back the old look to his eyes." Though she effected a tenuous reconciliation with Charles, she had "no confidence, his faith would last five minutes under opposing circumstances." In despair she turned to her family for support, asking them to come to her. Although she expected them several times, they never came. At last she traveled to Lynn to lay her case before them; although they were sympathetic, her father made it clear that he would not help her unless she left Charles. If she ever seriously considered doing so, she did not reveal it in her journal; rather, she maintained that Charles was "sick not criminal." These days were the darkest of Caroline's entire life, and at one point she wished she were "dead and laid with my children in the grave."

As despondent as she often was in the midst of this crisis, however, Caroline showed a remarkable resilience. Her favorite walk in a beautiful cemetery could reassure her of God's presence. Toronto suffered through a serious cholera epidemic in 1854, and Dall, herself untouched by the disease, was a bastion of moral support and practical help in the serious illnesses and deaths of friends and acquaintances. Her description of that grim time bears comparison with Pepys's account of London's plague. And during the worst of her troubles she was able largely to forget them as she took two extended trips. The first of these was a visit to Susanna Moodie at Belleville, during which she recognized from the first moment that "all my journalizing here, will be the jotting down of anecdote which flows from Mrs M's lips in one unceasing stream." Dall gives us an incomparable picture of Moodie, seated on the floor, shelling peas, telling tales of her adventures as a young woman in the London art scene. Dall herself was something of a sensation in Belleville, as she "sat up till late playing at 'blue stocking.' It is some years since I have tried it before." Dall's second trip was more extended and took her northwest to Lake Huron, up to Sault Ste. Marie, down to Detroit, and back across southern Canada. Her friends gave her this trip in appreciation for her services rendered during the cholera epidemic. She traveled with American George Beatty, a railroad executive, and his Canadian wife, Eliza, who had supported her through the worst of the crisis with Charles. The trip was eye-opening, giving her "an impression of vastness that I never had before." She bore with good humor the inconveniences of travel with sometimes the most rudimentary accommodations, and was able to laugh when Mr. Beatty came bearing her unmentionables (left to dry overnight before the fire) up to their common attic chamber. As they came back home across southern Ontario, Dall came to appreciate "this splendid country" where " 'Canadians' may be born, for here is a land capable of exciting patriotic feeling!"

Now that she had come fully to appreciate the land, to have found her own place in Toronto's intellectual life, and to have made friends so devoted that they would last a lifetime, she had to leave it all and join Charles in an uncertain future near Boston. Most painfully, she was leaving John Patton, whose support and devotion had sustained her through the worst times of her life. He accompanied her and Sarah to Niagara Falls, and then they parted. Her journal captures the exquisite moment when four-year-old Sarah "looked up, and with eyes swimming in tears took my hand—& said with extreme pathos— 'Aren't you sorry for parting from him?' Dear child, then my own tears overflowed."

TORONTO. CW.

MONDAY OCT. 10. 1853.

*H*ave been tormented all the morning between fugitives beggars, and dressmakers. Almost wished I were a pauper, that it might be my duty to think only of myself. Felt crazy to write my article for the Liberty Bell[1]—calmed my impatience with the thought—that there was no use in writing what the world did not need; that if the world did need it, God would no doubt open the way, through what seemed to make it impossible.

And then I have had ample time to think of Goëthe's words, where he tells, us so plainly that the thread we drop will be resumed by some one else, if indeed it is strong enough to avail— God does not trust his truth to any single creature, and when we fail there are always better and stronger to be found.

TORONTO CW.

THURSDAY. NOV. 16 [*actually* 17]. 1853.

<u>Miss Dix</u> *

I feel as if this week had been privileged among the weeks of my life. On Monday, I was very busy all the morning with my needle. In the afternoon, I went to see dear Mrs Copland, who has lost her mother. Returning from thence I sat half an hour with Mrs Brown[2] who has been quite ill. When I went home, I found a lady sitting in the parlor, in her bonnet & mufflers— She had a serene pleasant motherly face, with a familiar look yet I could not call her by name. She rose as I entered and said "I have taken possession of your house, Mrs Dall, without any obvious excuse. Do you know me?" and she seized me, by both my hands.... "Have you forgotten Miss Dix?" "Miss Dix—so fat! and teasing me so," I rejoined, and yet as I remembered that I had not seen her for 11 years, and only twice in twenty one—not so much disheartened by my failure. "I had no claims that you should remember me," she said, and went on to say, how she had driven to Dr. Workman's[†] how he had been surprised to see her, flustered—embarrassed, and would not go to the Asylum that night. How she feared the place would be prepared for her coming— how she wished to talk with Mr. Dall and myself and so came to us, instead of a Hotel. How proud and happy I felt in preparing her room for her—! God bless her....

All this evening [November 14] she talked with Dr. Workman, and showed him her beautiful plan for the Nova Scotia Hospital. He told her, two or three times, that she would never build it for the proposed sum $100,000. She answered gently, but when he reiterated in a manner that was almost insulting, she replied decidedly "Having built three or four for the same sum,—I suppose I may be allowed to know." In her two or three minutes interview with him, she had taken up the idea, that he was not fit for his place....

---

*Dorothea Dix (1802–1887), reformer, advocate of humane conditions for the insane and prisoners. Dall's later note in pencil in the margin reads: "This visit by irritating Dr Workman broke up our Toronto home—"

†Joseph Workman (1805–1894) was a political activist, physician, and leader in the Toronto Unitarian Church. In 1853 he was appointed temporary (and the next year, permanent) medical superintendent of the Provincial Lunatic Asylum in Toronto. This institution, which opened in 1850, was racked with problems and scandals, but during Workman's twenty-one years as its head it became known as a model institution (*DCB* 12:1122–1127).

TUESDAY NOV. 15. 1853 [*written Nov. 17*]. . . .

At 10. AM. Dr. Workman came and we went up to the Asylum, where we remained till one P.M. It is of no use—to speak of the wretched condition of the whole affair— Yet it was evident that Dr. Workman was making important changes. It was hard for me to restrain myself and say only what would do good. I think also it was hard for her [i.e., Dix]—nothing could be worse than what may be called the housekeeping, and her face several times, grew very red, but she spoke beautifully to the nurses, and always courteous, made her true object understood. I rode round through the University Ground to rest her, for she seemed very much exhausted. We then went to the Normal School, and Model Schools, where she was greatly entertained, and refreshed. Then we went to the Jail, where as it was the hour for serving out the mush and milk it was not easy to go through, but we found things very clean, and agreed that we should rather eat, sleep, and live at the Jail than the Asylum. . . . Then came Dr Wilson* at tea-time with his book of Archaeology[3] for me, Full of life because he had unopened letters from home[4]—bright & beautiful—. When he went out—Miss Dix said emphatically, "I like that." In the evening Dr Workman and Mr. Whittemore[5] one of the Trustees, came, and she had a long talk with them. It is evident Dr W. and she lost no love between them. . . .

God bless her, pray we all tonight.

The Unitarian Church in Toronto was planning a new building, toward which each of the five trustees had pledged a contribution of £100. But the trustees subsequently withdrew their offer and agreed to borrow the money from Dr. Joseph Workman, securing the loan with a mortgage on the building. The Dalls were not initially informed of this agreement, and when Caroline learned of it from her friend John Patton, who was also one of the trustees, she determined to avoid putting the church in Workman's power at all costs. She had the letter of agreement retrieved before Workman received it and pledged herself to raise most of the money (including three hundred dollars that she had set aside for Willie's schooling). She kept her own hand in the matter secret, even from her husband.

*Daniel Wilson (1816–1892), artist, author, ethnologist, university professor and administrator (he was later president of the University of Toronto), and member of Toronto's intellectual elite, was to become a lifelong friend of Dall's. A native of Scotland, Wilson had arrived in Toronto in late September and had just assumed his appointment as chair of history and English literature at University College, Toronto. Wilson was knighted in 1888 *(DCB).*

Daniel Wilson, eminent ethnographer, soon after his arrival in Canada in 1853.
Caroline Dall helped him and his family get settled in Toronto, and they remained lifelong friends.
(Courtesy of The Thomas Fisher Rare Book Library, University of Toronto)

When Charles learned of the trustees' withdrawal, he too opposed the Workman loan. One of the concerns of the Dalls was that, in response to their personal appeals, the Unitarian Church in Portsmouth (and possibly others) had previously committed money for the building, on the express condition that the Toronto church not go into debt to build it. Thus the Dalls felt that their honor was staked, and they held that any money so raised would have to be returned.

TORONTO—C.W.[6]

SATURDAY. NOV. 19. 1853....

Mr Dall came in while I was writing. He had heard from Mr Burgess that the Trustees had withdrawn, and without consulting the congregation had accepted this loan from Dr W. Overcome, he hastened to Mr Patton's office, to see if there were no escape from this dishonor. John informed him that he last night dispatched a note to Dr W. informing him that he could raise the $2,000 at 6 pr. ct. which had of course virtually set aside the first plan. All day long, Mr Dall was thinking what course he had better pursue, and finally decided that it was his duty to go to the five Trustees, and endeavor to persuade them to resume their first responsibility. As he was preparing for Sunday, I wrote out a circular letter for him to take with him, and John & Mr Brown promised to furnish him with letters on their own part—pledging the sums required.

Mr Dall approved my circular and copied it. I did not let him know that I had offered the $2,000—because I knew he could not conceal it from the Trustees, and I wished no one to perceive the true ground of my opposition to the Workman loan—viz: my want of confidence in the man. I should not have dared to take the risk of raising the money, had I not been frightened at the thought of falling into his power....*

One of the eminent Canadians who became friends with the Dalls was Paul Kane (1810–1871), now often thought of as the father of Canadian art. Kane was at this time on the verge of recognition as a major artist documenting the Cana-

---

*At this point in the journal, Dall includes a copy of the "circular letter" to the trustees, written by her and signed by Charles Dall, imploring the trustees to give as much as they could and not incur the debt to one individual, a situation that would require returning money raised in the East on the condition that the society not go into debt.

Dall later added a note in the margin of this entry that reads: "Every fear I had was justified, & it was his resentment at Miss Dix's visit, which made Dr W. hunt us out of Toronto.—1861."

dian West. The Dalls probably came to know him through John Patton, whose business, like Kane's studio, was in the Wellington Buildings on King Street East. His wife of less than three months, who also became close to Caroline, was Harriet Peek Clench (1823–1892), from Cobourg. In the 1840s Paul Kane made two sketching tours west from Toronto: the first in 1845 to the region of Lakes Huron and Michigan, and the second, lasting two and a half years (1846–1848), with the Hudson Bay Company through the Canadian West and the American Northwest to the Pacific. His purpose on both tours was to capture in art the Indian culture and wildlife of the region, as George Catlin (whom Kane had met in London) had done in the United States. He made extensive sketches on the trip, and was at this time executing oil paintings of many of them. Today the sketches are often considered more valuable than the paintings. Many of the sketches survive at the Royal Ontario Museum in Toronto (DCB).

TORONTO C.W.

THURSDAY. DEC 1. 1853.

A wretched day. Walked up to Paul Kane's to tea with John & Mary Patton.* Had a very delightful evening, looking at a vol. of Italian costumes,[7] and a series of Paul's own sketches. I have never seen any as good as the latter. It is a refreshment to look at many of them. Mrs Kane has no girl and is certainly not strong enough to do many days without. She said I looked better and so I do— It is one of the mercies of Providence that time will have its effects even while the heaviest sorrows are in immediate store.

TORONTO C.W.

THURSDAY DEC. 8. 1853.

I sat up very late this night till John came home from the meeting. I was sadly disappointed in the result. True, the majority of the very full meeting went clearly for Mr Dall. True there were only—five in the opposition viz: Workman Bentley, Henderson Manning and OMalley, of whom only two were respectable—but Walton[8] offered a resolution which he wished to have passed —to the effect, that the congregation do approve of the conduct of their pastor in this affair. It was of John's preparing. The opposition would not hear of this, but Bentley prepared a resolution, not pertinent to the case, which Workman seconded. It commended Mr Dall's piety & general conduct! As if <u>they</u>

*Mary Patton (1837–1915) was John's sister.

Self-portrait of Paul Kane, the father of Canadian art and a friend of Caroline Dall. (Courtesy of Stark Museum of Art, Orange, Texas)

were fit judges of it! John was obliged to convict the Dr of false statements, several times, and they got very angry with each other—but I cannot write about this affair, it makes me too sick.

At the height of the church crisis, Dall, with the help of John Patton, produced a wonderfully celebratory Christmas for her family and friends.

TORONTO CW.[9]

SATURDAY. DEC 24. 1853.

The ten days that have passed have been full of anxiety for me, I have sewed somewhat— I have written an article on Kingsley['s] Hypatia,* out of the fullness of my indignation &c &c— In the meantime Mr Dall had without my

---

*The novel *Hypatia,* by English clergyman, novelist, and Christian Socialist Charles Kingsley (1819–1875), appeared in 1853. Dall was disturbed at Kingsley's fictionalized treatment of the historical figure Hypatia. Her review of the book appeared in *The Una* 2 (February 1854): 220–221, and was reprinted in her *Historical Pictures Retouched.*

knowledge, and in suddenly conceived distrust of my judgment held an interview with Mr Bentley and exchanged letters with Dr Workman.[10] On Monday last, I received an answer from Dr W—and opening it, was first informed of the correspondence. I confess I felt—indignant, and most so, when I read Mr D's letter any thing but suited to the occasion. It was a weak letter—injures Mr Dall's cause and leaves the matter in a worse condition than before. Mr D. acknowledged this when he came to ask my advice at the last. It has worried Mr. P.—& myself very much. As soon as I could divert my thoughts I began to prepare a Christmas tree, for my own children & as far as possible those of the parish. All the expense was John's—all the labor mine. Yesterday morning—I went out into the woods to get a tree—one that was brought in not suiting. It was snowing fast, when I went out—and I never saw a greater or more beautiful variety of winter clouds, than drifted over the sky.

This morning after breakfast—I spread down a sheet—and set a stone jar or open pot in the midst. Then John brought in a white pine, about eight feet high, and placed it in it—and I proceeded to decorate it—with candles. My Angel with white gold spotted wings proved too heavy so she was placed amid the hemlock over the mantel. One tall candle was placed at the top of the tree, a few scattered through it, and the rest in five concentric rings at different points on the trunk. The jar was set round with candles—as close as they would burn. I then hung the tree with brilliants—crystallised bonbons—lace —bags—of sugar plums—prisms &c—and last of all the presents of which there were a good many. John had Grays Elegy illustrated[11] a pair of horsehair mits and a pin-cushion. Charles Neander[12] from John—Thackeray's Humorists[13] from me—and a sermon cover from Mrs Brown. Willie had a globe, Sinbad the sailor—a china inkstand &c &c— Sarah—a boy doll—Goody Two Shoes—A Jenny Lind Doll—some tin pans—cups & saucers from Mrs Beatty* —a squirrel & song book from John. Mary Patton had the bust of Sir Robt Peel[14]—. John gave me the bust of Jenny Lind on a beautiful gutta percha brackett.

While I was arranging these Mrs Rowe[15] came to help me, cut gold paper—and dear Mrs Beatty to read Ellen's letters.[16] I was quite busy till long after dinner, and as usual when I am much fatigued at about 4 o'clock a diar-

---

*Eliza Ansley Beatty (1806?–1880), whose husband, Dr. George Beatty (1803?–1888), was secretary-treasurer of the Ontario, Simcoe and Huron Railway (*Canada Directory* 1857–1858; *Municipality of Toronto* 1:474; DFN; *Ancestry.com,* accessed May 1, 2003). The Beattys were close friends of Dall.

rhoea set in. Mary Patton came to tea which we had in the kitchen. The company were invited at ½ past 6—but they were all late, but the Goodenoughs[17] who came an hour before. Mary Fitzgibbon[18] came all alone. The tree looked handsomer when it was lighted than any I ever saw. I wore, for the first time since I was married a white japonica in my hair—with real lace in the neck & sleeves of my black silk. The children sat under the tree, and the grown persons a little back between 40 & 50 in all. I told them of the first Christmas gift— of the tree and the angel—and then distributed the toys. It was pleasant to see their faces— When I gave Sarah her squirrel—she said of her own accord, that pretty little piece from the book Miss Dix gave her—

> Oh there's the squirrel perched aloft
> That active little rover,
> See how he whisks his bushy tail
> Which shadows him all over!

She said it promptly & so as to be heard all over the room. After the tree was stripped the children went up to my room and played till nine—Mr Dall leading them. Every child (there were about 20,) had one present, and most of them, more.

Mr & Mrs Beatty, and Mr & Mrs Kane—staid till quite late.

THURSDAY. DEC 29. 1853.

Mr Dall's letter[19] produced no effect, and advised by his friends to such a step—he went down to Dr Workman's house and saw him, with out waiting for his consent. The conversation was disagreeable in the extreme, Dr W. saying every thing that an Unchristian man with a talent for sarcasm, might be expected to. He said he would have answered Mr Dall otherwise than by words, if his cloth had not protected him!!

Mrs Beatty sent me a beautiful present—a white crape shawl. I went in there & received it, in the very height of my trouble about the Dr. so I could not help bursting in tears, when with her usual delicacy she gave it to me.

TORONTO CW.
TUESDAY. FEB 7. 1854.

Every thing went wrong this morning, so that for the first time in my life I think I was 15 minutes late at an engagement. It was a quarter past ten, when Mrs

Beatty, Mrs Fitzgibbon[20] and myself entered Paul's room.[21] I wish he had more ambition. How many able men—live and die unknown, because they want it. I think his painting, of the wounded buffalo, one of the very finest in existence. I do not believe Wouverman[22] ever did any thing better....

TORONTO CW.

THURSDAY. FEB. 9. 1854....

... after writing a long grieved letter, which I afterward burnt up, I went to bed and wept half the night. It seems that the dissatisfied meet in Dr. Workman's lecture room, to preach and teach their Sunday School.

TORONTO. C.W.

FRIDAY. FEB. 10. 1854.

Was very ill, after a night of bitter suffering. Laid flat upon my back and read rapidly Mrs Mowatt's Autobiography.* Only one thing I envy her—her loving trusting father, who said to her, "My brave girl!" when she was taking a step which he knew all his own friends must disapprove. Oh! my dear father, why have you never said one word of commendation to the child who has loved you so well. When I went to Georgetown—when I returned, when I was married you were silent. It is true I know you loved me—but if I could only look back and remember one word like that "brave girl!" God knows I have deserved it.— ...

TORONTO C.W.

SATURDAY. FEB. 11. 1854.

Mr Burgess is carrying round a paper for people to sign, pledging them not to enter the church while Mr Dall remains the minister. He told Mr. Major[23] that 16 had so pledged themselves. Mr Dall has this morning written out a few thoughts to be communicated by his friends, Messrs Sisson[24] & Henderson, to Mr. Burgess....

Mr Dall has grown rapidly worse today and we called in the Dr. He seemed to be troubled at the idea of giving up the Sunday School tomorrow, so I suppose I must keep it open. At dusk tonight, his pain became so violent that he

---

*Anna Cora Ogden Mowatt (1819–1870), American writer and actress, began giving public readings and then acting on stage after her husband's financial failure. In 1854 she published *Autobiography of an Actress; or, Eight Years on the Stage (DAB; NAW)*.

began to sing and shout, & became in fact delirious. Mr Briggs[25] came in and tried to magnetise him, and seemed quite alarmed at his condition. I was called down from his room at 9 o'clock to receive a visitor—Mr Hosmer from Buffalo.[26] I found him chilled by a cold and most fatiguing journey, and made him some hot ginger tea. Staid up till nearly twelve, giving him information about the state of affairs.

TORONTO C.W.

SUNDAY. FEB. 12. 1854.

Mr Dall had a dreadful night vomiting all night. As Mr Hosmer was to preach and I had to hold a Sunday School, I don't think I realized how ill he was. Did my utmost but could not spend many hours with him. Felt very ill & exhausted myself. Just before morning service, he dressed and came down to my room, although he had promised me, he would not. Mr Hosmer then went up to see him, and to use his expression, he seemed "quite lost." He was so weak that I soon got him back to bed.

TORONTO C.W.

FEB. 13. 1854. MONDAY.

A heavy rainy day. Mr. Hosmer went out directly after breakfast and spent the whole day, in seeing the disaffected. I suppose they filled his mind with all sorts of stories but he is a candid generous soul and we may trust him.[27] I sent Willie to sit with his father while I washed up the breakfast things, and when I went up, I found them both weeping together. I saw immediately that there was no time to be lost—and that whatever was the consequence to children still delicate with scarlet fever, the rooms must be changed. In less than an hour, I had him safely in bed below stairs. He seemed refreshed by the well ventilated pleasant room. "It ought to cure me," he said; the bad symptoms are the excitable brain, the excessive nausea—and the impossibility of keeping any medicine down. Friends are all very kind. Many of them evidently alarmed. Tonight there was a meeting of Trustees and others, to meet Mr Hosmer. Mr Hosmer told me, Dr Workman had complained to him of the mischievous influence of the sewing circle!!

At 10 tonight—gave Mr D—20 gms of Dover's powder[28] but it would not stay down. Three doses of morphine also had no effect. Neither of us got any rest.[29]

TUESDAY FEB. 14. 1854.

TORONTO CW.

Mr Hosmer left. Had breakfast for him at ½ past 6 o'clock. Sent for Mrs Copland to sit with Mr Dall through the day. Was suffering too much with prolapsus* to stand myself. Mr Dall very low—nausea continuing. At 7 this evening —the Dr having been in 3 times & no medicine availing we began to give him brandy once in 15 min. John held some crumbs of bread to his lips soaked in brandy. He could not speak but folding his arms round John's neck, he drew him down and kissed him. By nine, he was so much raised, that I thought I might lie down in my clothes—Mrs Briggs having come to watch. I went down to the dining room for that purpose, well wearied out.

TORONTO C.W. MONDAY.

FEB. 20. 1854.

Spent the day in watching Mr Dall and the children and in assorting my notes for the life of the Countess Matilda.† I ought to have $100 for this article, and I suppose I shall not get $5. I believe it will be the best article ever written on this subject—that is the most complete and reliable. It has cost me a vast deal of study.

TORONTO C.W.

SATURDAY. MAR. 11. 1854.

This week has been a sad one, every way— First the passage of the Nebraska Bill, through the Senate,‡ cast a damp over my spirits, from which I have striven in vain to recover. I was utterly disappointed by it—I did not think such a thing could be done. Not even Mrs Stowe's beautiful appeal to the women of this country comforted me.§ Then Charles does not gain. He has evidently failed in health—in memory in spirits, and while I own this a thousand dark anxieties crowd upon me. Then little Annie Simpson,[30] grows weaker and

---

*The slipping forward or down of the uterus.

†Matilda, Countess of Tuscany (1046–1115), controlled the most powerful state in central Italy. She supported Pope Gregory VII in his conflict with the Holy Roman emperors. Dall's article "The Countess Matilda" appeared in two parts in *The Una*: 2 (May 1854): 258–259, and 2 (June 1854): 284–285; it was reprinted in her *Historical Pictures Retouched*.

‡The Kansas-Nebraska Bill was opposed by abolitionists because it left to the decision of the inhabitants the question of whether the territories would allow slavery, thus negating the Missouri Compromise of 1820. The Senate passed the bill on March 3, and it was signed into law on May 25.

§Harriet Beecher Stowe (1811–1896), author of *Uncle Tom's Cabin*, published in the *Independent* 6 (February 23, 1854): 57 and in *The Liberator* 24 (March 3, 1854): 33, "An Appeal to the Women of the Free States

weaker. Three days from seven A.M. till ten P.M. and one night of this week, I have watched beside her, leaving my own home to the care of servants. It seems as if each hour drawn out by spasm after spasm must be her last, but still she lives. Today Mrs Kane has been down and taken my advice about her pregnancy. I like her very much. Have worked a little at my Index Rerum,* but fatigue head ache & so on, have made the work amount to little.

TUESDAY MAR 14. 1854

Little Annie died last night. Mrs Kane & I went together to the "Grange" for flowers—

When I came home I found Emily a handsome yellow girl waiter to Mrs Dr Whitridge in Baltimore[31] waiting to see me— She escaped—last October, with only the clothes she wore, walking out of town Sunday afternoon just as people went to church—

The Dr had sold her brother and another servant to New Orleans—for slight offences, and she felt as if it might be her turn next. She three times asked him to allow her to buy herself and he refused— She had been his slave for eleven years. She expects her lover, who is a cooper to get away this spring.

On March 20 Charles Dall went to Baltimore for rest and recuperation.

TORONTO C.W.

SUNDAY. APRIL 9. 1854....

We† walked out to Mrs Brown's to tea, both of us feeling very unhappy, At all events I did—and never have I come nearer to the "Valley of the Shadow of Death" than this evening since my return....

TORONTO C.W.

MONDAY APRIL 10. 1854....

After tea Mr Hall[32] came in, after talking of some of the disagreeable parish matters at which he had hinted yesterday, he begged a private interview, and proceeded to ask my advice about marrying the slave girl Emily now in

---

of America...." In the article she set forth the cruelty of slavery and urged women to respond by informing themselves, circulating petitions, employing lecturers, distributing speeches, and, above all, by praying.

*An alphabetized notebook for the systematic preservation of items, quotations, and the like.

†She and John Patton.

my family. I must confess I was struck dumb, but I told him as gently as I could that she was engaged and expected her lover to follow her in a month or two. He talked at some length about her, and on the whole very well. It never seemed to have occurred to him that she could refuse him! He really seemed much disappointed. . . . He said on leaving that he was glad he had asked my advice so early, as it was very painful for him to give such a matter up after he had once <u>set his heart on it</u>!!

Hearing from friends who had seen Charles since he left, and were seriously concerned about his health and competence for his position, Caroline decided to abandon the "false position" of defending him. A few weeks later she wrote Charles, attempting to persuade him to resign.

TORONTO SUNDAY APR. 13. 1854—[33]

Went to Paul Kane's to tea to meet Dr Wilson[34] and the Beattys— When John joined us he brought a letter from Dr Hosmer[35] that went through me like a sword— It repeated all his assurances of Charles's unfitness for labor, and besought me to leave Toronto at once;—all this in the kindest manner. I ought not to have opened it— My evident distress spoiled the evening for all. Paul showed his sketches & talked about them well. I went through my sharpest struggle long ago—& when the constraint is removed life will be easier. To sustain a false position has always been foreign to my nature. . . .

Had letters from Miss Dix and Horatia Ware— Miss Dix is much disturbed about Charles—wishes we could all take six months rest. She thinks his friends are not in the least aware of his condition—do not think him ill or in any special need of rest.[36] To know this, & keep up appearances & supply his deficiencies hoping health might return has been the severest trial connected with the gradual change which I have so long seen going on— I wrote from Paul Kane's tonight to Mr Hosmer, Miss Dix—Mr Channing.[37] It will be hardest to make Charles's friends understand the truth— Some, not realizing that it is no surprise to me, will say—"Strange, it has not altered Mrs Dall much." Others will say—"It is all her own imagination—there is nothing the matter." I shall not wonder at this last remark much— There are times when it looks very improbable to me, and I wonder any one can believe it—when it seems like a horrid dream to me.

Poor John suffered silently with me, all the evening.

TORONTO. C.W.

TUESDAY. MAY. 2. 1854.

At my sewing all the morning. . . . Outwardly I am calm enough—and there are some who wonder I seem to care so little. But within! Oh God send me some peace— Why do I not hear from Charles—whether he is better or not—?[38] Is Miss Dix away, that I have no answer to my three letters?[39] And my father? can he not tell me now as well as a month hence, whether he will save me from starvation or not?

TORONTO. C.W.

THURSDAY. MAY 4. 1854.

Yesterday & today I have given mostly to preparations for the Wilsons.* This morning, I carried out some bread, and then thinking it was too late for the Cape Vincent Boat, I wandered away to the Cemetery— It was a lovely morning— The May Flower the Anemone and the Hepatica were wide awake — The heavy rain of yesterday had given to mosses and lichens their fullest green. Birds, butterflies, grasshoppers, & bees were singing. Scarlet funguses looked out of thick beds of moss. Never saw I, the woods so lovely—never felt I God's presence nearer. In the afternoon, I was writing to Katie Moodie,[40] when Dr Wilson came to the door— To get into the cab with him, and go up to Yorkville to resign the keys[41] and pour out the tea, was only the work of a few moments. I had from Mrs W. and the children, a cordially affectionate greeting and many thanks. I walked down with the Dr. after tea—and purchased iron, woodens and china ware— The Kanes came down in the evening but I was too weary to talk to them.

Dall enjoyed a brief respite from her Toronto troubles, traveling with her friends Mrs. Beatty and John Patton to Buffalo to see Anna Mowatt on the stage. When she arrived home, she discovered that Charles's brother Austin, to whom she had written her concerns about Charles's mental competence, had shown the letter to Charles himself.

---

*That is, for the arrival of Dr. Wilson's wife and two daughters from Edinburgh, Margaret Mackay Wilson (1816–1885), ten-year-old Jessie Eleanor (1843–1877), and eight-year-old Jane Sybil (1846–1917). See Elizabeth Hulse, " 'A Long and Happy Life': Daniel Wilson with Family and Friends," in Marinell Ash and Elizabeth Hulse, eds., *Thinking with Both Hands: Sir Daniel Wilson in the Old World and the New* (Toronto: University of Toronto Press, 1999), xvi, 268, 278, 281, 285.

BUFFALO & TORONTO.

SATURDAY. MAY 12 [*actually* 13]. 1854.

This day was occupied by going home—and suffering.— I did not lift my head after we left Buffalo—and when we reached home, a pile of letters were poured into my hand— From Uncle Wm Charles Austin[42]— I thank God that all the misery did not come at once— Austin's letter was an insult of which I dare not trust myself to speak— Greater insult to himself than to me however, for no gentleman could have written it, though a lady might be so unfortunate as to receive it. May 4th—I wrote to Charles requesting him to ask a dismission— Mr Brown's resignation[43] and other things made this necessary. It was done after consultation with his nearest friends. As my letters from Miss Dix, keep me very anxious about him, and I had no certainty that he would be able to bear so severe a shock as this would be—I was therefore very cautious—I am sorry that I am not strong enough to keep copies of all my letters now— I wrote gently & affectionately to him, begging him to trust in my judgment and assuring him that the step was necessary— I enclosed the letter to Austin— telling him for the first time, that I was anxious about Charles's mental condition, and begging him to communicate my letter gently. This I enclosed to Miss Dix, because I preferred that she should communicate with Charles if possible— Miss Dix not being in Washington, the enclosure was forwarded to Austin and here we have his reply which I shall be too wise to burn as I did his last rude letter. . . .

An hour after I had read these letters, as I lay spasmodically suffering from their perusal, another from Mr Dall was handed me.* It was written after seeing the letter I had written to Austin, and cut me to the heart. Could I have thought, Austin would have betrayed my confidence in such a way? If I were mistaken, did I not deserve to be respected? Did he right when he thus gave my husband cause for life-long dissatisfaction with me—and deprived my husband of his best chance of cure, namely—unconsciousness of his position? Oh God forgive him, and help me. I suffer as I write and the pages should have been shorter, but that sometime my children may wish to know what their mother thought and felt.

*In this letter of May 10, Charles Dall declared his annoyance at Caroline's expression of doubts about his mental competence: "One more such letter from you [as the one written to Austin] will call me back to Toronto, to provide for your health." He objected to her attempts to "manage" his affairs, assured her that he had no intention of leaving his position in Toronto, and expressed his belief in "the strong probability . . . that three weeks will bring me home to you, strong and well" (Dall Papers, Bryn Mawr).

TORONTO. CW.

THURSDAY. MAY 17 [*actually* 18]. 1854

This morning when I was struggling to write a few lines of Journal, Mrs Brown came in. She talked long with me, and was kind. She thought I had done right every way, and said no true friend would wish me to yield to my father's conditions. She said that Mr. Brown had proposed my receiving all the money earned by the sewing society, and she approved of it.

We dined early, because I was to take a large party to see Mr Kane's pictures. Mr & Mrs & Miss Sisson,[44] Mr & Mrs Beatty Mrs Wilson—Mrs Sisley[45] Donald Moodie[46] Mr & Mrs Simpson Mr Patton and the Misses Hincks.[47] They all enjoyed it. Sarah & Willie went too for myself—I lay under the brooding of coming evil.

I came home and was in great fatigue laying the table when Elizabeth Peabody from Boston was announced. She came to interest the Normal School—in Genl Bem's Chart.[48] She met at tea Prof. & Mrs Wilson & Mr & Mrs Beatty.

TORONTO. CW.

FRIDAY. MAY 18 [*actually* 19]. 1854—

I went early this morning to Dr. Ryerson[49] with Miss Peabody. She engaged to give a lecture at 2 o'clock. We then went to Paul's room,[50] where in spite of his fatigue of yesterday, he was so kind as to show her three or four pictures. After dinner I went again to the Normal School with Elizabeth, and liked her lecture very much.

We came home, & were to have gone to the Wilsons to tea, but a heavy rain came up. We had a long and pleasant talk about Margaret Fuller—Raritan Bay[51]—John King,[52] the Hawthornes and others.

TORONTO C.W.

TUESDAY. MAY. 23. 1854.

. . . Mr Dall has written one of those mortifying letters to Mrs Simpson.[53] He is perfectly well & coming back &c—. Annie said nothing but—

"He is coming back to trouble poor man."

TORONTO. C.W.

FRIDAY. MAY. 26. 1854.

The day of the Eclipse of the Sun. It was not dark enough to be very satisfactory. Not so dark as in my own soul—. After doing some business was com-

pelled to go with John to Mrs Briggs's to tea. We left early, John had a kind letter from father begging him to comfort me, which pleased us both very much.*

It is strange, they none of them understand this matter at all.

TORONTO C.W.

SATURDAY. MAY. 27. 1854.

... In the afternoon, I took Mrs Patton & her daughters[54] out to the Cemetery.
We did not have as pleasant a time as we ought for Mary was out of humor. But
I shed the ill humor out from my soul, and drew in the holy influences of the
blue sky and genial sunshine. "God is love!" In spite of all bitter conflict and
sorrow, I believe it, when I am thus face to face with nature.

TORONTO C.W.

MONDAY. MAY 29. 1854.

I tried to calm myself by sewing. In the midst of my work, I got a telegraph from
Charles, saying that the letter of resignation is on the way. This gave me a feeling of relief—and I sat down, and wrote a note to Aunt S. but the buoyancy
evaporated with the effort, and I felt an unaccountable depression. In the evening came a pleasant little note from Charles, at Trenton,[55] where he had gone
to prove to Miss Dix that he was not insane! My poor husband! He seemed to
be anxious however, at my having sent Austin's letter to my father. It was however all that I could do....

FRIDAY JUNE 2. 1854.

Filing letters—making up accounts &c all the morning. Quite unhappy about
Charles—whom I have telegraphed to remain where he is, and—restless at the
thought of meeting father.

Poor father. He thinks it hard when he speaks of the hypocrisy and falsehood of the Abolitionists to be referred to his daughter— He forgets that when

---

*Although this letter has not survived, John Patton's reply to it (dated May 26, 1854) has. He wrote
that he "always [has] done, and will do all in my power to comfort Mrs. Dall. I could not do more for mother
or sister than I am willing to do for her, but no one can relieve her distress in mind but Mr. Dall, and he only
by sending in his resignation at once" so that he might be saved from "a discourteous dismissal." He defended Caroline's actions with regard to both Charles and church affairs, and added, "I would not allow
Mrs. Dall to suffer for want of pecuniary aid, but it would undoubtedly, be more pleasant to her to receive
it from her father" (Dall Papers, Bryn Mawr).

I speak of the Webster Whigs, which I do too gently I fear—I am told to look at my father.

Oh my father! I can help you, but in one way, by proving to you, that I act from a principle which will enable me to bear much suffering. You shall never be a slaveholder if I can help it, which you will be, the moment I close my lips, at your request, for my daily bread.

After dinner—I waited impatiently for my father, but he did not come. Minute after minute passed—and at last, I went down to the Office. Mr Patton brought me a letter from mother. Charles was in Boston, well, happy, and pleasant. They thought as his resignation was sent in, and he seemed well enough to return to Toronto, they had better defer their visit, till I had seen him, and "settled affairs with him." Alas! what have I to settle with Charles? The letter threw me into despair, I wrote immediately to beg they would try to keep Charles in Boston. Mrs Beatty came in, and was indignant at the coolness with which they took the matter. I was weeping bitterly, and as John was going in to Dr. Simpson's[56] to a meeting, at which he purposed to resign his Trusteeship—she begged me to go down to the Hotel with her, which after posting my letter, I did—It was late before John came in, and then he had nothing satisfactory to tell me.

On June 6, Caroline Dall traveled to Buffalo to consult with George W. Hosmer, the Unitarian minister there, concerning Charles and the Toronto church crisis. Hosmer approved of her urging Charles to resign. But a week later, Charles, now in Buffalo, apparently persuaded Hosmer that certain of Caroline's actions were unjustified and that he was mentally competent.

TORONTO C.W.

TUESDAY JUNE 13. 1854—

I had a calmer day. Mrs Beatty said this afternoon, "you look a little better." The words pierced me like a knife, & an hour or two afterwards, John brought me a letter from Mr Hosmer, blaming me very severely, both with regard to the loan last winter and the letter of resignation also assuring me, that my affection exaggerated the causes of anxiety with regard to Mr. Dall.

My heart sunk very low—for I know that unless I am willing to do the church a great injury, I must bear all sorts of unmerited blame with regard to the loan. Ought I to be sorry that I thought I could trust Mr Dall's brothers to keep a secret? I conjured Joseph* to show my letter to no one, and he went away and showed it to Thos. Whitridge and Austin! As to the letter of resignation I had nothing to do with that except to decide whether I would write it myself or get some other friend to do it. And Charles's health! God knows how much I wish that he were well, but he could never write to me as he does, if he were well. I decided to go at once to Buffalo, and in Mr. Hosmer's presence, tell Charles—how unfairly he was acting to complain of me to Mr Hosmer and Dr. Gannett,[57] before he had ever had an opportunity to ask me a question concerning the matter of which he complained. John was very indignant and sat down at once, to write a letter taking the whole responsibility of the resignation &c. For my part, I went weeping to show Mrs Beatty my letter.

In the following entry, Caroline leaves Toronto intending to confront Charles in Buffalo, in Hosmer's presence.

TORONTO CW.

WEDNESDAY. JUNE 14. 1854.

I started on foot for the boat with John—and feeling wretchedly ill, lay down as soon as I got on board. I passed quietly out of the boat, and seated myself in the first coach for the Falls.[58] Just as I fell back exhausted in my seat—I heard a voice saying—"Carrie, are you here?" I looked up and saw what I thought was Charles's wraith standing beside me. So pale, so ill, he looked! He was as he afterwards acknowledged dreadfully shocked at the sight of me. Ill and altered I knew I was, but I did not think it would produce such an effect on him. I had told him I was ill, and I thought, he believed me, and was prepared.

I said, "I am going to Buffalo. Come with me." "No," he replied. "Dr Hosmer has gone to Meadville for three weeks." Of course I got out of the Coach— and went back with him to the Boat. I felt as I looked at him that he was far more ill than I had imagined. I wondered how any one who loved him, could say, he was well and bright as usual. He soon began to talk and with such an utter absence of reason that I knew not what to do. At first I tried to answer, but at last sat still, silently weeping. "What faith could he put in me," he said,

*Joseph Edward Dall (1823–1889), Charles's brother. See John William Linzee, *History of Peter Parker and Sarah Ruggles* (Boston: S. Usher, 1913), 133.

"when I [i.e., Caroline] asserted that he <u>never took</u> Quinine,* that this that and the other happened, which he knew did not happen— Could he not remember as well as I what took place while he was sick?" "I said "no—you were not yourself you could not remember. Would it do any good" I said, "if you were to see those who watched with you, and if you were persuaded that you were mistaken in some things might you not allow yourself unable to remember all?" "I am willing to see them but not in your presence, they would not speak the truth, with you to <u>overawe</u> them." I said, "I was willing he should see them alone only I thought it hardly fair, as they might not take the full import of his questions."

When we reached Toronto, I told him I wished he would take a cab, and go for the children, so that they might be with him as long as possible. In the mean time, I went up to Mrs Beatty, told her how dreadfully shocked I was, at the condition in which I found him, and begged her to come up to tea. "There can nevermore be peace between us," I said "unless some one takes my part roundly— Oh be to me the mother and sister that I need, make him ashamed of these unworthy suspicions." She readily promised through her tears, and I went home.

After dinner, Charles and John had a talk, just a repetition of what we had had on board the Boat. Two things on which he harped especially distressed me, one was, my total want of veracity—the other was the admission that neither he nor his friends believed I was ill, when Mrs Beatty wrote for mother to come on. It was what is vulgarly called a "fetch." Rather strange I think, that I should urge my friends to come on, and find that I had been deceiving them! Still farther, how could he, how could he, if he were still what he once was, give to Dr Gannett and Dr Hosmer a distorted impression of a matter, which I had begged him almost on my knees to <u>keep secret</u>. I was positively terrified at the state he was in. Mr Patton was distressed to tears, yet very angry—and once or twice had hard work to refrain from saying to him, "That's a lie!"

He accused me, how falsely, God knows, and it is no matter whether man does or not;—of being the whole cause of his leaving Toronto. Unwilling that he should spread such a report, Mr Patton tried to persuade him by relating

---

*Charles had taken quinine during his "brain fever," and he was blaming it for whatever confusion he might have suffered. On April 10 he wrote to Caroline from Baltimore, "By the occasional ringing in my ears &c I am persuaded that my only difficulty lies in having been over-dosed with Quinine— Dr Buckler says my case is a common one & will <u>work itself off</u> soon" (Dall Papers, Bryn Mawr).

facts, that he had never been thought <u>able</u> enough for his post, by his best pecuniary supporters— He [Charles] said the Circular proved the contrary of that. I said "Charles the circular was never seen by one of the trustees but Mr Patton, before it was printed. Mr Brown was out of town & Mr Patton signed his name to it in his absence." "There" he exclaimed in a tone of triumph, more resembling the ravings of a madman, than anything I ever heard from him, "There—how can I ever believe a woman who talks so—<u>that</u> is not true." I hope my children will believe that it is the simple fact. He now broke off and went out, partly at my suggestion, to see Mrs Walton, and ask her, what she thought of his situation, and partly to see Mrs Delaporte, who wanted him to see about baptising her baby.[59] In the meantime I went into Annie's[60] and asked her, if she would be willing to tell Mr. Dall that she had heard him wander.[61] She begged so earnestly to be excused that I said very little. She said that he had just been in to see her, and looked & <u>acted</u> very unwell. I replied "Yes—he is worse than ever," and went home. At home, I found John and Mrs Beatty, talking earnestly. She took tea with us, and Mr. Dall grew still more excited, accusing me over and over again. I shall thank Mrs Beatty all my life, for the nobleness with which she stood by me, and the calmness and justice she showed. Again he accused me, in a frantic manner, of falsehood about the circular. I stopped my tears and said decidedly, "Charles, that is the second time you have said that today— I have told you the simple truth—I will bear that charge no longer. Prove your charge, by telling me of at least one person, who saw that Circular."

I did him the honor to believe that he thought he knew of one who had, when I asked this question—but he answered in an excited tone—"Hundreds —hundreds have seen it." "I only ask for one name Charles—" "I have none to give you—I will prove it sometime."

I turned mutely to Mrs Beatty, "That is not right Mr Dall" she said & so went on— He then spoke of my health—&c. & I could bear no more, I went out of the room to weep—and when I returned, she had her hand on his shoulder pleading with him, they were still on the same subject, I heard her say— "Mr Dall—if your wife had given up—had yielded, your children would ere this have been motherless."

She soon left us, as she passed me in the entry, she said— "Do not talk to him—it is of no earthly use, nothing makes any impression."

Mr Dall went home with her, and I laid down to weep. Since we met at

Lewiston, without one affectionate word, he had not approached me, After an absence of three months—he had neither taken my hand nor kissed me. Could cold and cruel relations change him so, in so short a time! Oh God spare me such another day, does my sin deserve it? Oh have mercy on us both, but restore his peace, and yield back the old look to his eyes.

TORONTO C.W.

THURSDAY. JUNE 15. 1854.

Such a night as last night—Oh Father, grant it may never be repeated. Charles did not come in till late, & after waiting as long as I could, I went to bed. I placed a basin of water at the side, and laid a wet sponge on my forehead. By and by Charles came up— I could not refrain from asking, "Did you see Mrs Walton?" "Yes." "Did she say what I expected?" "No—she said I was excited, but perfectly coherent." I felt that this could not be so, for she is a woman of entire sincerity, and I said to myself, God forbid that all these troubles should resolve themselves into a mere question of veracity between us two! He undressed and came to bed. He lay down on the farthest part of it, without speaking, but I knew he did not go to sleep. We lay thus about two hours I should think—and I rose once or twice to cool the water, with which I was bathing my head.

I did not dare to speak to him. At last I heard him sob—and in a short time he was perfectly convulsed with weeping. I thought that this would calm him, and as I could not judge in what state he was—kept silence. At last, I felt him lift my hand, and press it to his lips, sobbing out a few words I could not understand. I threw aside my sponge, and leaning towards him, passed my hand under his neck—and drew him towards me—"Charles," I said "what is the matter?" He could not answer, but repeated the same inarticulate cry—I listened in vain, "Have patience with me" I said "I cannot hear you—" At last, I heard these words—"I have been so cruel to you." "I have been so cruel to you." My tears began to flow—but I answered him—"Charles" I said "I have never blamed you, but those who pretending to be your friends have prejudiced you against the mother of your children." We then had a long talk—he weeping on my bosom— He first said—"Oh why is there nobody I can trust in the world but you; I thought I could trust Aunt Sarah—" and there came a fresh fit of weeping. I said—"Charles, God is good, if he gives us one friend whom we can wholly trust. I never expected to have more than one. Remember that just now you were doubting me."

We talked on—it grieved me very much to hear him say, that he had allowed Dr Gannett to blame me, and to say, that he [i.e., Dr. Gannett] knew it was not him [Charles] whom the people of Needham were dissatisfied with without answer. If my husband be indeed himself, how he has altered! how dishonorable I must think him, did I believe him to be responsible. In the course of the night, he said "I believe Mrs Walton—told me, all she told you, I think she agreed with you—in opinion— I am sure she is a very sincere woman."

Our talk lasted till morning, when Willie waked and coming to me, said as he tenderly took my hand—"Dear mama, do not talk any more on these disagreeable subjects. If you do not forget them, you can never get well."[62]

His father raised himself and looked at me— He sighed two or three times, and said as he stroked my face—"That poor hollow cheek!"

... I went to Mrs Beatty's to thank her for her kindness last night. She told me that Mr Dall went home, with her and sat two hours—and that she did her utmost to influence [him]. He reminded her of a child continually. Raved about the Quinine until she told him never to mention it to her again. She told him also, not to mention Austin—when he attempted to defend that letter. She made him own that his family did not like me, and added "I can tell you why they do not—she is far superior to any of them." Charles said—"Ah you love Mrs Dall—but nobody loves me." "Yes," she replied, "I do love you—as well as Mrs Dall, and it is because I love you, that I beg you not to yield to those who would injure your wife."

He said how much shocked he was at my appearance— "Mrs Dall is looking much better than she did," replied Mrs Beatty—"at one time, I thought she would hardly rally." Did she look worse—he asked Yes, she answered—"she failed steadily till she got that letter from your Aunt Sarah, that was so unjust that it roused her." He asked if I was not much distressed to hear of the unkind letter, I might expect from my father. "No" said Mrs Beatty, "she was too glad to get one kind word [from] you, to care much for that."

This seemed to touch him. I went home, and found him writing to Aunt Sarah. He did it generously—but not so explicitly as I wished. I had no heart to suggest a change—he certainly could not blame her much, for repeating censures which he had originated.

After dinner I tried to sleep, but could not. John's face expressed such an agony of feeling for me, and my own heart had fallen so, that I could not. It is very strange that he[63] does not caress me, now his heart is touched, or that if he does—his touch is cold and stiff— His kiss showed a greater change than all the rest. Once today he took my hand that is all.

At half past four—I took a cab to Mrs Copland's where I met him and took him to bid farewell to Mrs Brown. Everybody is shocked at his appearance and thinks him looking worse than when he left us—. Mr Patton's father,[64] who knew <u>nothing</u>, urged him not to preach again for a twelvemonth. I saw that Mrs Brown was shocked though he was much calmer today than yesterday. We went to the Wilson's to tea. To the enquiry— "How do you do, Mr Dall?" Mrs Wilson received the emphatic answer—"Very well indeed, never better in my life." which caused a significant exchange of glances—and the moment I reached the bedroom Mrs W—said "I see we must not ask him that question." I looked over the rest of the Calotypes and at a vol. of Billings' Baronial & Ecclesiastical Monuments of Scotland[65]—to excuse myself from talking. We came home early.

TORONTO U.C.

FRIDAY JUNE 16. 1854. . . .

Mr Dall wrote letters to Dr Gannett and Dr Hosmer, this morning, doing his best to counteract the unfortunate impressions he had given them—but alas! he can never unsay what he said. And now my children, if you should ever read these lines—and doubt the justice of your mother's fears, heed these two facts. After writing with his own hand a letter to Dr Gannett of less than a page in length—he fell back against his chair exhausted.

"I cannot write any more," he said, and he looked very weary. I did not dare to offer to write for him, after what he had said about the draft which I sent to Baltimore and the indignation with which he had denied <u>wishing</u> me to write in the winter. At last he murmured—"Must it be done today?" I said "Charles would it tire you to copy it—altering it to suit yourself as you went along—if I <u>thought</u> it out for you?" "Oh no!" he said brightening. I took the pen & wrote in about five minutes all that was necessary—while he lay on the sofa. He then copied it, altering the phraseology in one or two places—especially changing the words I <u>know</u> to I <u>believe</u>. He looked very weary— He sealed the letters but put them aside to mail from Buffalo. . . . The weeping on Wednesday night has done him good— He professes now to believe all I could wish, but I have no confidence, his faith would last five minutes under opposing circumstances. God be gracious to us both.

After dinner, I tried to go to sleep—and he went out to call on Dr Adams[66] and others. At six, I went to Mr Patton's[67] to tea, I was too ill and exhausted to enjoy much. The Kanes were there and a young student. Mr D. took the advice I gave him, and made his conversation less emphatic—he appeared well to me all the evening but Mr Patton Senior & Mrs Kane, felt very anxious and thought him looking far worse than ever before. We came home early. I wrote a few kind lines, which I told him, I wanted him to carry in his pocket and read whenever he felt troubled. I was grieved that he did not ask for my miniature nor seek to carry it away—but dared not ask him if he did not want it. He said several times tonight, "I am too easily influenced." "Yes, Charles—I know that & it is as well to be influenced by your wife, as by other less conscientious persons." "I wish I could remember it" said he, and went on mending dear Sadie's toys. I would not allow him to talk after he came to bed, for I saw that—he was positively ill with fatigue—but he told me these two things— That he had seen Dr Aikon,[68] who told him that Quinine had nothing to do with the state of his brain, and that he had written so to Uncle William. Also that he had seen Dr. Adams who had told him that he observed the failure in his services, before he was taken ill, also, the incoherency in his conversation. I hope these things will increase his faith in me. If Uncle William were as candid with me, as I have been with him, he would have written to me, that Dr Aikin had said this. As for myself I have never seen him since he left tending Charles, in February.

On June 17 Charles, accompanied by Willie, left Toronto for good and went to Boston.

TORONTO CW.

MONDAY. JUNE 19. 1854.

No letters—no arrival*—my heart sinks. All this morning I sewed or wrote. I wrote a letter for the Register, with regard to the present position of the Church Building and sent it to Chs. for his approval.[69] _____† says "I would never write another line for him— If you were my sister I would take care of you, and you should never be allowed to help him again—" Alas! why will they all forget that he is sick not criminal, and that I cannot refuse to help him so long as he is near me. . . .

*Dall was expecting the arrival of her mother.
†Clearly John Patton.

TORONTO C.W.

THURSDAY JUNE 22. 1854.

I woke with the sorrowful birthday feeling much deepened by the peculiar circumstances under which it dawns this year. Wrote my usual lines to father.* ...

I thought I should have no gift in honor of it—but in the afternoon, Mrs Beatty came into the Hall [where an antislavery bazaar was in progress], & bought two or three pretty things among others—a beautiful travelling bag, towards which I had been much attracted and which she gave to me. At noon John brought me a beautiful gold locket—containing. the children's hair on one side, and on the other, a likeness of himself. God bless his thoughtful heart. There came, more than all, a kind letter from Charles—also one to Mrs Beatty —thanking her for standing by me.

Dall was traveling to Belleville to visit Susanna Moodie and her family. Her traveling companion for part of the journey was Harriet Kane, on her way to visit her family at Cobourg. This journal entry takes the form of a letter home to John Patton.

COBOURG. C.W.

TUESDAY AM. JUNE 27. 1854.

Dear John, I suppose Paul[70] will want to know something of the package he sent by the "Magnet" yesterday noon, so I write a few words with a very short pen—...

We reached Cobourg at a quarter before seven.... Harriet's brothers met her at the boat, and we went up in a cab.[71] I received a warm welcome. You who always are so glad to see me appreciated would have been pleased and proud to see how warm— They tried to induce me to stay a day here and go to Rice Lake but I resisted. As I leave for Belleville at 8 AM. in the stage, I must stop and close my trunks— Kiss my babies for me and believe me your affectionate

Mamma—.

BELLEVILLE C.W.

TUESDAY JUNE 27. 1854.

I left Cobourg after writing to John, at 8 AM....

... Found Aggie† and Mrs M. watching at the gate of a stone cottage on a

---

*That is, the verses that she always wrote for his birthday, which followed hers by five days.

†Agnes Moodie Fitzgibbon, Susanna Moodie's daughter, visiting her from Toronto.

hill overlooking the town. Grounds badly kept. Katie in bed, with severe Erysipelas. . . . I foresee that all my journalizing here, will be the jotting down of anecdote which flows from Mrs M's lips in one unceasing stream. . . .

BELLEVILLE CW.

WEDNESDAY JUNE. 28. 1854. . . .

Looked over many fine old Autographs, while Mrs Moodie sat on the floor shelling peas. She showed me a water color drawing of Cheeseman the artist,[72] done by himself in the style which he made famous. It looks like Mrs Fitzgibbon and has the calm noble Strickland face— His mother was a Strickland and he was very fond of Susanna— He had a splendid house in London, where after his mother's death he lived on as little as possible, that he might help starving brother artists— He had a noble heart, but the House was a miracle of dirt. When you walked over the rich drawing room carpet, you left tracks as if you walked through the dust of the streets. . . . His dining room was hung over with splendid pictures dark with dirt. One day in a freak Susanna said to the housekeeper—give me some milk and water and a sponge and let me wash the pictures. "You'd better not" said the old woman—but Susanna did not mind. She mounted the side board—the first picture that she uncovered, was a magnificent Venus, but wholly naked. A little startled, she still thought she should have better luck next time, so she tried a second. It proved a Perseus & Andromeda, as large as life and wholly naked— Still a third— It was Perseus holding the head of Medusa— He held it so that the spectator could not see the lovely features, but they were reflected from the placid fountain at his feet. Discouraged at so much bare skin, she gave up the task hoping Cheeseman would not discover the luminous pictures. But alas! his first words were, when he sat down to dinner "What a magnificent Venus! I have not seen it for these 20 years." . . .

After dinner Mr Moodie played on the flute—and then drove us a little way toward Smithville. We returned and dressed for tea— Mrs James Fitzgibbon,[73] Mrs & the two Misses Murney[74] and Wm Breckenridge came; although really ill I sat up till late playing at "blue stocking." It is some years since I have tried it before.

Dall returned home a few days later.

TORONTO CW.
TUESDAY JULY 11. 1854.

A letter from father this morning which almost took away my breath. Day after day, I have been watching for him; so many times put off, so often disappointed and now Charles has overthrown as it were my last hope—they are not coming, my mother is worried and anxious, father says I am driving her to her grave or the mad-house. Dear Mrs Sisley was here, when this trouble came upon me— She saw I could not bear it, and went for Mrs Beatty, who comforted me with kind words—but could not take the sting <u>out</u> of my heart. There is but one human being on earth, who <u>can</u> aid me, and he will not come—my father! oh my father! may God forgive you this cruelty. His letter will speak for itself.[75] Oh my children, when years hence, you read it, forgive your mother, if through any imprudence of hers, she has injured your future prospects. Forgive her, for she loved you only too well, she sought above all things to leave you an honorable name.

But there is no comfort for me— If they do not come to me, I must go to them. Dear John is better to-day but much worried by business. In spite of all my trouble—I have been this afternoon to look at some rooms which his father wishes to take for him, when I go away.

Oh my husband! my husband! It is hard that such a stroke as this should come from your hand. Would to God—that I were dead—and laid with my children in the grave.

Dall was on her way to Lynn to explain her situation to her family.

JULY 15 1854—

. . . I took the cars at Niagara, on the new road which seems well built. Got out at the Suspension Bridge and walked across, carrying my small bag. I was so ill, that I had to stop several times, but I shall never forget the beauty of that river from the spot. It was a cool lovely morning. Took the cars to Boston on the other side. Went to the Stanwix House—because it was so late, when I arrived.[76] Had a good deal of difficulty in getting a room, but proving obstinate was at last superbly accommodated. Wrote a letter home, instead of sleeping. At 5 o'clock started on the Eastern Road for Boston. . . . Reached Boston at two. Felt too ill to take a carriage, and tried to walk but had to give up. Reached Lynn at the usual hour, stopped the carriage, a little before it got to the house so as not to alarm any one, and went to the kitchen door. The new dog barked and George came out to stop him. My heart beat so, I went quietly upstairs, and into mother's chamber. She looked sick and anxious—our meeting cannot be described. Very, very glad I was for her sake that I had gone home. Fannie and Marian came and spoke to me, that was all. I asked mother about this, and was told that her suffering proceeded not from my troubles, but from the impossibility of getting any sympathy concerning them. Fannie & Marian had taken a great prejudice against me in the beginning. Charles had talked with and persuaded them, many dishonorable things had been done.

Tired as I was, I began to read my letters to father and mother. It was a comfort to feel that I had their entire sympathy although father began by saying that Charles was as well as he ever had been.

I did not go down stairs to tea, but took a warm bath and some valerian and went early to bed.

W. LYNN MASS.

SUNDAY JULY 16. 1854.

Rose early after an anxious restless night. Talked with father and George all the morning. Dear George, I am glad I have a brother. Marian has not spoken to me, but mother discovered her listening while I talked to father. I told father not to send her away for I had no fear of being overheard. I shall say little about the painful interviews of this day. I felt Fannie's insults very deeply. At dinner F. said she wished she knew whether Grace Greenwood had directed Mr Lippincott's studies ever since he was a boy.[77] I said, I should not be surprised he looked so very young beside her. Marian said he looked as all women's rights' women's husbands—looked beside them— I turned to Mary Hurlburt, and said "I suppose you know Mary, that I am a woman's rights' woman, and that is a hit at me." "Oh," she replied, "I did not understand." Under all the painful circumstances of the case there was a coarseness in this, that I could not easily forgive. Mother came to my room tonight and talked with me till late. It is evident her heart is right, and <u>as</u> evident that father thinks I have no right to call on him for advice unless I am ready to separate from my husband. It is <u>as</u> evident that he will make no further pecuniary provision than to pay the expenses of this journey. When I told Fannie that George was going home with me—she said "she did not see what that was for, they had had mortification enough about it—and it was no business of his."

Dall returned to Toronto, her brother George accompanying her as a kind of witness to reports of Charles's behavior.

TORONTO. C.W.
MONDAY. JULY 24. 1854.

At eight o'clock this morning we went to see Dr Aikin, whose testimony—concerning Mr Dall's medicine, and illness was emphatic. He said he considered Mr D—to have a monomania about Quinine, that his friends had behaved strangely, that he would not have answered Uncle Wm's letter—but out of consideration to me. Was willing to state the same on oath before a jury. . . .

TORONTO. C.W.
TUESDAY. JULY 25. 1854.

Went early to see Mr Briggs. We found him ill in bed—thence to see Mrs Simpson[78]— Testimony of both strong and clear. A letter from Charles about buying a house in Cambridge—made me very anxious. At 3. PM—I went with George and the Misses Patton[79] to see Paul's[80] pictures—thought of Mrs Sisley and her pleasure at seeing them, the last time. Did a little shopping with Mrs Kane, who was over weary, and insisted on her and Paul going back to tea with me. While we were at tea, Mrs Beatty came and urged me to go with her to see Mrs Sisley—who had been seized with cholera in the shop this morning. I told her I had company, but if she would go tonight, I would go in the morning. She took a cup of tea and went away, In a few moments she returned, just as I was receiving the new minister Mr Murray[81]— Convulsed with grief, she said, "My dear Mrs Dall, we have no Mrs Sisley—" She had died at three o'clock, while we were looking at Paul's pictures. I sent Mr Murray away—and listened to the particulars. Constipated, she had applied to Dr. Primrose[82] for medicine without telling him that she was in the family way. The medicine over acted and after an exhausting night, she walked at 7—this morning, one of the hottest I have ever known to the store. The Dr. saw her there at 10 AM. and gave her medicine to check the action of the first—. She was seized with vomiting and purging soon after he left her—and finally cramps in her limbs —and died at a little after 3 having lain two hours unconscious.* She never

*Dall describes here classic symptoms of cholera and its rapid progress, often resulting in death within a few hours of the onset of symptoms. See Geoffrey Bilson, *A Darkened House: Cholera in Nineteenth-Century Canada* (Toronto: University of Toronto Press, 1980), 3–4.

spoke of danger but looked a little alarmed at the cramps. We were all terribly
shocked. The Kanes went home— Geo. went down with Mrs Beatty to get
some cigars. I begged John to go up to Mr Sisley's with me. Mr S. told Mrs B.
that no one but himself and the two physicians were with her, and that she was
to be buried tonight—therefore I went by the store where the body lay, that
if anything were the matter I need not lose my walk. The door was open,
and two candles shone from the head of the stairway—and a hearse with one
carriage stood before it. Not a soul—but a rude undertaker's man—appeared
in the Hall— There was no clergyman. I asked for Mr. Sisley—no one knew
where he was. The shop door was open—it was pitch dark. I moved a little towards it—and the light of the candles fell on my face. "My God! Mrs Dall—"
exclaimed a voice— "I could not leave you alone Mr Sisley, on such a dreadful night," "Oh! I must bless you," he exclaimed, and pressed my hands to his
heart. After a most trying scene I left him—and passed in going out, the black
shell, which contained the mortal remains of my friend. Dear lovely, living
creature, I shall never realize my bereavement. It seemed she was too full of
holiest life, to pass away thus.

*Toronto was in the midst of a major cholera epidemic, and Dall vividly rendered
this frightful time.*

TORONTO C.W.

TUESDAY AUG 1. 1854—

Went to visit my round of patients, and sewed quietly afterward. I do not feel
well this week. So sick and exhausted that I wholly forgot it was the first of
Aug. till I saw the colored men, parading.* Still I have no fear. There were 219
deaths last week—but the vital power seems strong in me—and the dear children keep uncommonly well. Nothing speaks such volumes of misery to my
mind as the draggled white plumes of the hearse. Heavy with dust and drip-
pled with rain, they look as if they had been used for centuries. . . .

*The epidemic continuing, Dall's entry a week later, with its crowding in and
piling up of crisis upon crisis, conveys the frenzied spirit of the time.*

---

*This parading was in celebration of the emancipation of slaves in the British West Indies on August
1, 1834.

TORONTO C.W.

WEDNESDAY. AUG 9. 1854—

A journal of one day in these dreadful times, may answer for many— Truly, I never felt the terrors of death so hem me in on every side— First, there is the hospital cart, which sadder to look at than the hearse, goes creeping about the town to garner in its victim. Then there is the hearse with white feathers, and the hearse with black—and the hospital hearse which has no feathers at all— Thus every morning is ushered in, and so it was today, while I sat as long as possible at my needle. I felt as if I must give up at noon—and I lay down upon the sofa Index Rerum in hand. As I lay, Annie[83] came in to tell me how ill they were at Mr Brown's. Champion and both the servants are down with fever and ague, Ida[84] was so ill with it all last night that they feared hydrocephalous, and old Mrs Simpson[85] has had a paralytic stroke. Poor Maria with an infant not five weeks old,[86] is the only person well enough to wait on all these sick ones. Of course, I felt that I must go out—but not till I had seen if I could not put off an expected visit of the Sisley children[87] tomorrow so as to give Maria the whole day. I went directly after dinner to Mrs Walton, to see about the baby for whom I have been prescribing for a day or two. To my surprise I found Mrs W. very ill with cholera— I was alarmed at the symptoms. When I left her, I went to Sisley's to tell him the children had better not come over. He met me, with the intelligence that the baby was very ill, and as I listened, Lucy—came running down to say, that if the Dr. did not soon come, the nurse would be afraid to stay with it alone. Of course, I went back with her— I gave the child camphor and ipecac as soon as I got inside the door, which revived it wonderfully. I staid till after Dr Primrose came, put warm flannels to its feet, and cold linen to its head, and gave it a dose of oil, much against my homeopathic[88] will. But for the Browns, I could not have left them tonight. I went down to the store, & told S. how they were, & that he ought to go home. As soon as I had taken a hurried cup of tea, I hastened to the Browns, John went with me. It was a deplorable sight— I promised to give them the whole of Friday—and after a short pleasant call for refreshment at the Wilsons—hurried into town—and to bed. Mrs Brown told me that some accident had happened to the Doctor's[89] child, severe enough to prevent his going out to them today— I must go there in the morning.

MONDAY. AUG. 28. 1854—

Went this morning to the Sisleys, where Mr S. gave me a cedar jewel box, in the memory of his wife. Came home to a long morning of hard work. In the afternoon I went as usual to see the sick. In the evening I lay upon the sofa, and finished Gan Eden a noble generous book and read Ruskin.[90] I tire of Thoreau.* Parts of his book are ingenious and striking but there is little that is practical. I doubt whether the world will be the better for the book. I have been ill all day—oppressed by a bitter suffering that I did not care to analyze—

Dall's friends George and Eliza Beatty took Dall with them on a trip by rail, wagon, and steamboat northwest to Lake Huron and Sault Ste. Marie, south to Detroit, and back home across southern Ontario. The trip, she wrote later at the head of this entry, "was given to me by my friends who thought me worn out by my efforts during the cholera."

PENETANGUISHENE.[91]

SIMCOE, CO. L. HURON.

FRIDAY. SEPT. 8. 1854.

We left Toronto, this morning at 7 o'clock. I never saw a more magnificent sunrise than that I waked John up to see. But it was cloudy before we reached the cars....

... When we reached Barrie, it looked portentously cloudy. We heard that the steamer Kaloolah on her last trip had taken fire, and in repairing had delayed so long that we should have to wait for her some hours. Kempenfeldt Bay looked very lovely, through fringes of trees as we turned into the woods from the town. We drove in an open van, with straight board seats, and a kind of rack letting down behind. It was too <u>long</u> to upset, that was the only comfort. We went through unbroken primeval forest, on a narrow corduroy road made by Govt— A vehicle could hardly have passed us— Once in about 7 miles, there was a cluster of houses at one of which we watered our horses. The grass was sprinkled with small purple or yellow asters—not named for John Jacob[92]— reader though they were pure golden—but because they are "bright,"

"stars that in earth's firmament do shine."[93]

---

*That is, of *Walden*, published in Boston less than three weeks earlier.

The <u>woody</u> funguses, bright crimson yellow, & maroon color—astonished us with their beauty, and the driver promised to gather some for us, as he returns tomorrow.

The clouds grew darker & darker—we had not expected an open wagon, & were obliged to put up our umbrella, and cover ourselves with shawls & cloaks very soon. A kind young man who sat behind me, kept the Buffalo round me, at great inconvenience to himself I am sure. A girl who sat beside him was sick with the ague, & had neither cloak nor umbrella. Question: Was it a duty to give her ours, when we knew we should be sick in consequence. We got to the Half Way House—kept by an old pensioner, of the 79th named Hamilton, without being wet through! It was a long low cottage built of squared logs—neatly fitted. The wooden floors—walls & ceiling were beautifully clean. . . . We got just such a dinner as I expected. Fried eggs & salt bacon—fine potatoes, butter & cheese, with poor bread. I made my dinner on potatoes just bursting from their jackets—and a few eggs, I was wise enough to ask to have boiled. It rained very heavily when we started again—and at my request, the driver drove nails through the stiff offensive buffalo which covered our other wrappings, & into the back of the seat, In spite of this, I found myself every now & then kindly shaken up by my friend behind, in such a manner, that I reached my destination, in some doubt whether I was the amiable Mrs Smallweed[94] or not. Rain, rain, dark dark—we got on only about four miles an hour—but at last Penetanguishene appeared—that is its lights glimmered in the distance. Penetanguishene is an Indian word, which means "banks of rolling sand." The Hotel is shocking—kept by ignorant & strange to say, <u>dirty</u> Fr. Canadians—, so Mr Beatty went just beyond it to a <u>private</u> log house, owned by a Mrs[95] Jeffrey an English woman from Brighton, who lived first at Niagara & came round here 21 yrs ago, in his own schooner. They kindly took us in—at first things looked very discouraging. They had been preserving fruit all day, in maple sugar, the kitchen & stove were sticky & dirty, and they were just going tired to bed. They made us a warm fire, and gave the Beattys good tea. My <u>cold water</u> was warm & they had no milk. I thought both bread & butter poor, and confined myself to eating some warm crabs & pears, preserved in maple sugar. I found the drippings of the umbrella had penetrated to my skin— I was the first to penetrate to my chamber, & was rather amused to find we had all to sleep in <u>one</u> whitewashed attic!! The beds looked delightfully clean. There was a convenient chimney in the middle of the room

& I nailed a quilt from that to the window with the help of one of the girls, & made a nook where Mr Beatty might retire. When I undressed, I found all my clothes in the region of the 'bustle' so wet through that I was obliged to send them down to the kitchen to dry, during the night. I got into the clean bed with a feeling of deep thankfulness that John had not been exposed to such weather as I had, all day.

PENETANGUISHENE—& STURGEON BAY.

SIMCOE CO. LAKE HURON.

SATURDAY SEPT 9. 1854.

I had requested the young lady of the house, to bring up my unmentionables before I rose this morning. for I hoped to dress before Mr Beatty woke. But she failed me! Mr B. woke—soon enough, but was lazy about getting up, and chose to have a long talk about Indian mounds, before he got up, from behind the Quilt. When Mr Beatty disappeared behind the sheet, which formed a temporary door to our attic, in the imminent danger of getting down stairs quicker than he meant to—I called out, "please send up the girl with my clothes, Mr Beatty." To my great amazement, he soon returned, holding up my unlucky garments, & composedly asking if that were all!!!? After dressing I wrote a letter to John—& journalized. . . . We walked up the road, where we found plenty of pleasant haws, the fruit of the white thorn, lying as if they had been dropt from a basket. The Bay of Penetanguishene was lying in loveliness before us, the town stands admirably, and a century hence, when buildings of brick and stone, look down from the benches, upon the water, it will be most charming. At the shop loitered many Indians—one with his cheeks painted with vermillion. They call Indians as distinguished from white men—nichin-aubak— Mr Smith brought us a nice lunch from a garden opposite consisting of Canada plums blue plums, egg plums, & sugar plums, with russet apples & pears, and small chicken grapes. He laid these in a plate and decorated them with roses and marvel of Peru. At dinner Mrs Jeffrey offered us a tart of ground plums— They are sometimes called Indian figs, and are more like figs when cooked than any other fruit. After dinner we went out for a little, the boat not being in sight. We bought a birchen box of maple sugar for Sarah, and met Mr Smith who [had] been so kind as to get some fine ripe sugar plums for us to take on our journey. While we were talking to the Indians, Mr Beatty came up, and I suggested to him that if we were to take a ride to the fort we might perhaps "bring the boat." We started at once, having coaxed the stage driver, good natured fellow to take us in his lofty coach & four. We had a most rapid ride, and enjoyed it highly, looking down from an elevated plateau—through the richest slopes & surging forests to the lovely lake. The whole scenery gave me an impression of vastness that I never had before—and the road was embowered like an English lane. It is three miles to the military station (for there is no proper fort,) & log houses all along the way— Just beyond the Eng. Ch. we saw our steamer coming and wheeled rapidly round. We raced through the woods, got our baggage & reached the boat just as she neared the wharf. Now how shall I give any idea of the scenery of Georgian bay. Its deep waters of an inky blue, its rounded knolls projecting into the bay, and flattened at the top as if for <u>use</u>—foliaged with almost tropical luxuriance. I watched all with delight, while we ran down to Sturgeon Bay. Soon after we went on the boat— we found some Iroquois women on board, and they sang to us with sweet voices some of their Catholic chants and read in their native tongue to us. They were shy & sensitive as fawns, and wore a semi-civilized dress decorated with much taste. I then watched the sunset— I never saw any thing so intense & magnificent as the hues. When I came out from tea, a heavy bank of castellated cloud was tinged with pink upon a sea of creamy gold—this gold deepened into lemon color—thrown out more vividly by a few smoky flecks—and that again into a faint green—shaded off to a rose amethyst. Oh John, if you could but have seen this cloudless glory—. . . .

I saw this afternoon a lovely little canoe of birch bark, fresh & new ornamented with quills. In many positions it looked like a nautilus shell on the water.

STURGEON BAY—& OWENS SOUND.

SUNDAY. SEPT 10. 1854.

. . . I lay long awake looking at the stars and the delicious moon, and thinking of home, and the week I had voluntarily sacrificed to this trip. I had a painful half waking dream, and woke from it in tears.

This morning I rose early, and made such a toilette as I could with the assistance of the wretched accommodations of the Lady's Cabin. Such a sunrise! It was intensely cold and clear, & for the sake of warmth, Mr. Beatty & I walked up the road to Coldwater, five miles off. A few rods on, a rude Irishman joined us, and said "If ye be going to the village, I'd like to go along wid ye." We said no, we were not going, for we did not like his appearance—& turned back wondering at his anxiety for company. A little farther down the hill, we observed him returning behind us, and at the same moment a man came out of the log hut & called to us saying, "It is not safe for you to walk, there is a team coming that will take you over the Hill. It is but a day or two since a man was nearly torn in pieces by a bear—a mile up—" "Nonsense," said I, "what do you do with bears here?" "Indeed ma'am," replied the man, "there were three of them about a mile up a few days since." By this time, our first friend had got up with us, and said quite bravely, "I was in hopes they were walking to the town, & I offered myself to them for company." It was quite late near nine before we left for Penetanguishene, for although it was Sunday, there was a good deal of freight to put on. I read in my dear Willie's Testament, and enjoyed the Heavenly Sunshine. After we left Penetanguishene and went out among the Christian Islands, the scenery seemed bold and fine—rather than beautiful. It gave me the idea of vast natural resources, and finally overpowered me with it. We entered Matchadash Bay[96] where the Islands are, and finally crossed the Nottawasaga.[97] The day has been uneventful—except in spiritual life. "God talked with them in the garden—"[98] He has talked with me on these broad waters, and how nearly only one beside myself will ever know. . . .

TUESDAY SEPT 12. 1854
SAULT STE. MARIE—STEAMER ILLINOIS.

. . . We soon came in sight of the Sault— It gives one the impression of boundless space, The river I should think at least a mile & a half wide here, and the rapids—peaceful looking rapids enough, extend about a mile. On the English side, the only very good, house, is Mr Thompson's[99] own—and on the American, quite a tidy little town has sprung up. A great many Indians & half breeds loitering about, and here as every where, a number of fugitives. Capt Scammon, who fancied he had met me before, was very attentive, and rowed us across in his boat—to the corner of the Am. fort. We determined to do nothing till we had seen Lake Superior so we walked right through the town, till we came upon two large steam-boats, the Milwaukee & the Sam Ward loaded with native copper. We looked forth over the tossed greenish waters, from the deck—& then busied ourselves in collecting specimens of the ore. I got a very good one of mixed silver & copper, from a mass marked 4666 lbs—and Mr Beatty a beautiful specimen of copper—much larger. I got a specimen of iron—

also. I was sorry to see that when I paid the man for breaking off the ore, he only looked upon it as a little drink money & yet he seemed a fine intelligent fellow. Coming back we carefully examined the Canal, & its enormous locks, & I took specimens of the red & yellow shale through which they are cutting it. They use the hardest of the shale to make a rubble wall on both sides. The director of the work Mr Brooks[100] is called here the Napoleon of railroads— from what I <u>saw</u>, I should think he deserved the name. To keep 15 or 1600 men employed on such a work requires some genius—and it was beautiful to see the workmen file off with their wheelbarrow—along narrow planks running up the sides. The locks of this Canal are said to be the largest in the world— 350 ft long, 100 ft wide at the top & 76 at the bottom and the fall 12½ ft. each. There are but two locks— The canal is [*blank space*] ft deep. It is said the gates & wickets will be magnificent. The stone of which the locks are built comes from Drummonds Island[101] and is Bath Stone. The walls are immensely thick. The Co. bought an American Island, Lime Island,[102] hoping to use the stone, but it came out in too thin slabs.

I was greatly delighted with all I saw here. As we returned, we went on board the Illinois, and it looked so tempting to Mr Beatty that he decided to go down by Detroit. He took the ferry boat, and went over to the Kaloolah for our things, while we took tea at the Saginaw House. There was nothing on this table fit to eat however, and there were in the parlor, some as vulgar specimens of western girls, as ever I should wish to see.

We went on board the Illinois and saw a lovely sunset over the Sault as soon as Mr Beatty returned.

ILLINOIS—

AND DETROIT.

THURSDAY. SEPT. 14. 1854.— . . . .

We entered Lake St. Clair, 36 miles long, and where the channel is very narrow, a schooner was aground—and a propeller with four cables was trying to tug her off. It was impossible to get by. In the attempt we grounded, & when the propeller at last tugged us off—the stern of the schooner carried away two buckets from our wheel. The Detroit River, in spite of the heavy rain, had many charms for me, and reminded me of the Niagara. . . . Detroit looks well from the river—better than Toronto, but much the same—. It is so flat! but filled with fine brick warehouses—and signs of growth. . . . I had a warm welcome from the Mumfords.[103] . . . After tea, he went out with me—to show me the town. It is well built, I went in to the Biddell House to see the Beattys. Was surprised to see a beautiful Parian[104] statuette upon the mantel of Christ blessing little children. At the little Inn at the Sault—there were good enamel pictures which is a great advance on the red & yellow pictures in the Canada Inns. After I returned from this walk, I read aloud to the Mumfords many things relating to Margaret Fuller.

Dall and the Beattys left Detroit and traveled back across southern Canada by rail.

TORONTO C.W.

FRIDAY PM. SEPT 15. 1854.

. . . After we started we went at the rate of 30 miles an hour. The road seems strong and well built—for the first hour we could see the muddy waters of Lake St Clair, with the schooner still aground. We passed many fugitives' houses— and the country was low and marshy. It improved toward London—and from thence to Hamilton through Dundas—the road—sank & rose—and swelled —through the loveliest country. Forests of elm & ash, gave way to knolls covered with hickory and walnut & oak & beech. At one spot above Dundas— we could get a glimpse of Burlington Bay—with Hamilton seated on it—and lovely rolling valley land between that, & the beautiful thriving town of Dundas. I am glad I came this road, & saw this splendid country— Here "Canadians" may be born, for here is a land capable of exciting patriotic feeling! Then the road swept along Burlington Bay—a beautiful bay, with wooded heights rising on all sides, and the town quite hidden in a hollow at the foot of the mountain which does not rise so abruptly as I expected. Coming down in the Queen City we touched on the North shore of Ontario at Bronte—Oakville & Pt. Credit—pretty—romantic looking towns— The sunset was clear and glowing, & I sat in the cool air looking at the burning belt in the West as long as I could see. When I got home, I found John & Susan* at Annie Simpson's taking tea. I found also that dear Sadie had been ill with dysentery, and was soon immersed in home anxieties.

---

*An old friend of Dall's, Susan Austin (1808–1885) from Cambridge, widow of Richard Thomas Austin (1809–1847) and aunt of Austin Kuhn, had kept house in her absence. See Norman Seaver Frost, *Frost Genealogy in Five Families* (West Newton, Massachusetts: Frost Family Association of America, 1926), 126.

In preparation for her leaving Toronto, Dall's furniture was auctioned on October 11; she spent the night with the Wilsons.

TORONTO C.W.

THURSDAY OCT. 12. 1854.

A very refreshing night I passed, sleeping alone & quietly as an infant on Mrs Wilson's great feather-bed. I woke to find a heavy rain, and to feel a little anxious about Sarah. I should have passed this day & another night at Yorkville, but thought it not safe to bring or to leave her. After our comfortable breakfast, the pleasant family worship—came—and the Dr. went in search of a cab to take me into town— Meanwhile John gave me a great fright about Sarah by appearing at the door in a cab. Nothing was amiss, however, only with his customary devotion, he knew I should wish to come down, & feared I might not be able to find a cab. Mrs Wilson told him—she would not shake hands with any one who came to take me away—dear little Jess gave me a meat she had made for me, and I rattled away. Can it be—that I have entered this house for the last time? . . .

. . . At 3 o'clock Closson came once more to take me up to the Kanes for the last time. I spent the afternoon & evening in tending the baby—and feeling worried—for she looks sick. The last hour Paul devoted to showing us his sketches. It was a sad farewell.

TORONTO CW.

OCT. 13. 1854—FRIDAY.

John seems sad today, and weary too. After breakfast, as I had let Lizzie* go home for the day, he staid with Sarah while I ran down to see if I could get Mr Copland's brooch marked, and to ask Mrs Beatty to come up for an hour or two. Came back to clean my room, write up Journal, & make preparations for packing.

Copy—

Dear Mr Copland,

When I looked at the money, that you enclosed to me, the other day, it seemed to me, that the shadow of your gray hairs rested upon it, and that the light of Mrs Copland's tender love, beamed forth from it. It seemed to me,

---

*Her servant.

more sacred than common money, and I thought, "if I put this into an article of household furniture or personal clothing, it will 'perish with the using,' and what will remain to tell my children how tenderly these dear friends loved me to the last, and how they blest my future when I was leaving them with tangible good wishes?" I felt that it ought not to be so appropriated, so I have put it into the shape of a solid gold brooch, marked with your name, which will live after I am gone, and tell how we loved one another. I wish I had time to come & show it to you—but I have not. If we never meet again in this world, we surely shall in that which is to come, and meanwhile my brooch will symbolise to me, the 'anchor' of both our hopes,

In sincere affection,
Caroline H. Dall—

... Then came my account from Wakefield,* a very cheering one, for everything sold for more than I gave, and the total was $100 more than I expected.... I then went down & showed my last presents to the family,[105] and dear John & I were left alone— How unspeakably sad, our last evening in this pleasant room has been, only God will ever know. I am going out, from[?] under the shelter which has been a safe & sure[?] protection for my [illegible word].[106]

TORONTO &
CATARACT HOUSE. NIAGARA FALLS.
SATURDAY. OCT. 14. 1854.

I went to John's room before day, and asked him if we had better go in the heavy rain. He was awake, thinking of me, and said no—but something within me, urged me on— ... Mr Sisson came [to the boat] to bid me farewell, and Margaret[107] to take leave of Sarah— The rain kept all my other friends away, I do not think they thought I would leave, in it, Sarah being so unwell. Mr Sisson took me aside to make me a present. I said, "It is not necessary Mr Sisson" "Not necessary to your feelings" he replied "but entirely so to my own," so I wear his opal ring upon my finger. "Let me advise you," he added in parting "never to go into another parish with your husband the white-headed old man, has come down here through the rain to tell you this."

---

*William Wakefield, auctioneer and commission merchant, who had charge of selling the Dalls' household goods (*Toronto Directory* 1856).

God grant poverty may not drive me to it. . . . [At Niagara Falls] John and I went a short walk and read Tennyson in the parlor, after which we took tea and went early to bed.

W. LYNN. MASS.

TUESDAY. OCT. 17. 1854.

A sad morning. John—saw us safely over the river—gave me the checks of my baggage and went in a heavy rain down to New York. After we left Albany— the woods were so lighted up by Autumn splendor that I never missed the sun. . . .

After we parted from dear John—Sarah sat very quiet for an hour. At last she looked up, and with eyes swimming in tears took my hand—& said with extreme pathos—"Aren't you sorry for parting from him?" Dear child, then my own tears overflowed. In Boston, we got a carriage without finding Mr Dall, but I saw him, as we sat waiting for the baggage & called him to us. He seemed to have a severe cold, and told me, that mother father and Anna, had gone to N. York, to meet Ellen, and would be gone several days. Fannie was in town spending a week with Louisa Hall, and only Marion and Emily were at home. This was sad news & made my heart sink. We were much delayed at the Lynn depot—as well as the Boston and reached home wet & tired at 8 PM. instead of ½ past six as we should.

Marion had a Miss Lander with her, & complained of not feeling well. She received us civilly at the door,—but left the servant to pour out our tea—that is—my milk— Emily—and the excellent waiting maid did all they could to supply mother's place.

CHAPTER TEN

In Search of a New Identity

October 22, 1854–November 25, 1857

$\mathscr{B}$ack home in the Boston area, Caroline Dall faced an uncertain future. Her father remained intransigent on the subject of her abolitionist activities, raving that "the worst sin I could commit, was trivial" in comparison to them. Although Charles secured the family a house in West Newton, where Caroline had friends and there was an excellent school for Willie, his supply preaching appointments were irregular and sometimes unremunerated. After preaching several weeks in Bedford, he was unexpectedly terminated, just as Caroline "had begun to feel, that with our severest sacrifices, we could hardly get through the next six months!" She faced constant financial worries, and it was becoming increasingly clear that she could not rely on Charles to support the family. In the troubling circumstances of her new life, it is no wonder that, for some time, whenever she used the term "at home," she referred to their old home in Toronto.

Charles's mental condition, Caroline believed, was still unstable, and when he came home one day speaking of going "out West or to Madras," she seems to have dismissed the idea as yet another evidence of his instability. But a few weeks later, on February 17, 1855, the entire entry in her journal reads: "Mr. Dall came home it is decided he is to go to Calcutta." Caroline seems to have been almost in a state of shock until he left, a mere ten days later, although she worked hard to outfit him for the journey. Charles was going as a missionary of the American Unitarian Association; Caroline herself, as she wrote, "did not sympathize in the least in the step he was taking, and could only respect his own interest in it." From Charles's point of view, his decision was actually rather brilliant, if also desperate: It gave him the opportunity to salvage his wrecked career and to escape his failed marriage, doing both with the sanction of church and society. What he engineered might be termed a "Boston divorce" (as opposed to the term "Boston marriage"), for it preserved respectability while achieving the end of putting half a world between him and his wife.

Charles's actions, however, looked very different from Caroline's perspective. To her it seemed that Charles was abandoning not only her but their children, ages five and nine. She pitied him, feeling "such tenderness as we do for a sick child," but she never really forgave him for leaving. The scene of their parting is poignant, Caroline feeling "a common sense certainty" that she would never see him again. Although several members of her family helped to see Charles off at the wharf, her father did not. When he soon thereafter appeared with apologies, Caroline clutched at what straws she could: "If it was sad he could forget what was of so much importance to me, it was pleasant to hear him speak in a tone of real feeling for the first time since my return."

Charles provided some financial support for the family, but it was not enough. Caroline immediately took in a boarder, and soon agreed to teaching duties in exchange for Sadie's free schooling. She appealed for advice to male friends who had had literary success; one of them suggested that she translate the novel *Spiridion,* by French novelist George Sand, and she bent herself to the task. But bitter disappointment was the result; even with the help of her friends, she could not find a publisher. She continued writing for *The Una,* and, if nothing else, these tasks helped her "to compose myself, to get off the rut of sorrow, so deeply sunk."

Dall's depression is palpable in the journal entries of these months. Her transparent face made her sadness obvious to all, and she easily broke into tears, even in public. She analyzed the failure of her marriage, remembering that when she had stood at the West Church altar, she had felt "impregnable" in "my double strength." She mused that if she and Charles had disappointed each other, she could "at least look back on those first few years with a clear conscience, and can Thank God—that we both, seeking to love him & serve him, have borne with some patience what was so unexpected in itself." She prayed, "Oh Father, strengthen me, against my own despair, make me willing to live." When she was at her most desperate, she relied on the belief that God "will sustain me, I feel sure, till all I need to do for my little ones is done."

The Una, which might conceivably have been a source of both financial

reward and fulfillment for Dall, proved instead to be chiefly a source of be-
wilderment and frustration. Agreeing to become its coeditor, she was soon
embroiled in a triangle of misunderstanding, incompetence, and perhaps deliberate mismanagement, involving Paulina Davis and the paper's publisher—
and now its proprietor—S. Crosby Hewitt. Davis was in Providence, Dall and
Hewitt in the Boston area (Dall moved into the city after a year in West Newton). It appears that Hewitt misrepresented Dall and Davis to each other, and
was at least partially responsible for their estrangement. The periodical's financial affairs were in a hopeless muddle by the time Dall was named as coeditor, and it abruptly ceased publication with the October 1855 issue. Dall
was mortified that the paper had ended in the middle of the serial publication
of her *Spiridion* translation, since she had secured many subscriptions because of it.

So Dall continued to ponder how to best use her talents. At times it seemed
"as if unused powers would drive me mad." Believing that God had "gifted me
so strangely," she tried to trust him when she found "yet no work on earth
for me to do." But as it happened, an outlet for her talents was indeed beginning to emerge: Along with Paulina Davis and others, she organized Boston's
first women's rights convention in 1855, for which they managed to secure
Emerson as a speaker. As vice president Dall herself presided during one session, and during another delivered her report on the legal status of women in
the New England states. She was greatly pleased with the success of the convention and in truth with her own reception. She tested the waters of public
speaking a little further, delivering a lyceum lecture in Needham, speaking at
the public meeting of the Ladies' Physiological Association during the Boston
Anniversaries, and participating by invitation in a debate on woman's rights
at the Mercantile Library Association. (Of this last invitation she wrote ex-
ultantly, "The world moves—!") Although her family opposed such activities, she believed that she could appeal to a public that more radical partisans
might alienate. And just as importantly, she was beginning to see such work as
a useful outlet for her energies and the answer to her crisis of vocation.

John Patton continued to be a significant presence in Dall's life. He and
she corresponded regularly, he visited occasionally, and his crucially timed
Christmas gift allowed her to pay Willie's school bill. Still, much of the time,
Dall felt herself "utterly alone." She was willing to "pour out love, love love &
never ask for any" except in the case of "one soul alone." John Patton, how-

ever, had his own problems, including major financial reverses within the first year of the Dalls' leaving Toronto, not to mention his tenuous position as the intimate friend of a married woman who, despite being in love with him, and despite her husband's virtual abandonment of her and their children, clearly intended to stay married.

By the end of 1857, Dall was emerging from the depression into which Charles's leaving had plunged her. She seemed on the verge of forging a new identity out of the unsought-for freedom that his absence had made possible. But her relationship with her father deteriorated further, he telling her in a moment of irritation, "It is entirely impossible that any thing—you should do, should be satisfactory to me." "God forgive him—and me, for remembering that he said it," she prayed. Her yearning for love remained unassuaged, and it is no wonder that she found herself wishing to claim "only one human heart . . . a heart which belongs to me which is mine—& yet I cannot hold."

The Dalls spent their first few days back in New England in Lynn, with the Healey family.

W. LYNN. MASS—
SUNDAY. OCT. 22. 1854. . . .

. . . Father walked into the room, and began a most painful conversation. It was a reiteration of my first Toronto letters from him, and it is kindest to say of it only that it was utterly unreasonable. I spoke kindly but plainly to him, and we parted, he heaping anathemas upon my, head, and saying that he would never aid me in any way, while I remained an ingrate (i.e. an Abolitionist) that the worst sin I could commit, was trivial, compared to writing such articles as I wrote. &c &c.— On my part—I kept a tearful dignity & truthfulness assuring him that I should never change, but would always think rather of the eternity we must some time spend together, than of the few years of Earthly Time.

It was this evening, I think, that father told the children they had spent too much money the past year in dress—$1500 in the last six months— Marianne spoke up and said—she did not think that was much—father must remember that mother gave a great deal to Carrie and her children! For a moment I was speechless with shame, that a sister of mine could under present circumstances, make so mean a remark, but the next, I rallied indignantly and told father, that all I had had during the six months alluded to, had not amounted to eight dollars—. Alas! Alas!

In late October, the Dalls moved into a house that Charles rented for his family in West Newton, west of Boston.

W. NEWTON MASS.

SATURDAY. DEC 9. 1854.

... My thoughts have been at home all day, I have grieved over the past—have despaired for the future. When I came home yesterday found the wood bill and Willie's school bill,—not a cent to meet either.

Dall was caught between her need to earn money and the restrictions of society— and in particular her own family—as to what sort of work was appropriate to a woman of her social status.

W. NEWTON. DEC 20. 1854

WEDNESDAY.

I spent all the morning in putting away clothes—and sewing. I could not translate well,* Ellen being here. We had but little conversation about my own affairs. She said if she were married, whatever troubles she might have, she should keep them to herself. I ought not to expect sympathy from my father. Many men beside, considered a daughter lost to them when she married and went away—would not help her, unless she were starving.

Afterwards—she denied my right to speak in public, or get money for my family, in any way, displeasing to my family.

Strange logic! In the afternoon Louisa Hall[1] came out to spend the night— and in the evening Mr and Mrs Ayres called.[2] We should have had a pleasant evening. but I was sad. A little while ago, I sent W's school bill to mother at her request. She returned it yesterday, begging that I would take it in—to father myself. I shall not do so—if I am poor— I need not humiliate myself forever— I will beg of strangers who will not insult me, but not of him.

---

*Dall was translating George Sand's novel *Spiridion*.

W. NEWTON. MASS.

SATURDAY. DEC. 23. 1854—

... I found on getting home last night a precious letter from John, enclosing a Christmas gift—which will enable me to pay Willie's school bill. The letter was worth more than the money. I sat all the morning trying to answer this letter, to prepare the children for Christmas, &c &c—but my worried brain & heart could accomplish little. . . .

W. NEWTON. SUNDAY.

DEC. 31. 1854.

... I shall not think tonight as I usually do on the 31st. of Dec. of the past year. There is no need to make a record here of all that I have suffered, my children will see enough of it, as they grow up, I can trust them to judge. God knows all that I have endured—if I have done wrong, he will forgive me, because I have loved much—if not he will sustain me, I feel sure, till all I need to do for my little ones is done. . . .

The unexpected termination of Charles Dall's preaching in Bedford was one failure that could hardly be blamed on Caroline, for she had never entered the church. In the same entry, Dall records hearing the most famous and successful preacher of the time, Henry Ward Beecher.

THURSDAY. JAN 11. 1855.

We had a very pleasant time at the Savages'[3] last night, and when we returned home found Charles arrived with the evil news that his engagement at Bedford was ended. And this, just as I had begun to feel, that with our severest sacrifices, we could hardly get through the next six months! It must be a severe disappointment to Charles, so I said little. He had been so confident, poor fellow! of holding this as long as he wished. Do the best I could, however, the news kept me awake most of the night. I was little fitted to go into town this morning. On my way to the Depot, I stopt at the Office, and took out a letter from my dear absent child [i.e., John Patton]. The news it contained was so utterly unexpected, that it froze the very blood in my heart.* . . .

... I was glad to hear Henry Ward Beecher for the first time, and to see the

*Patton was apparently suffering business reverses.

radiant joy in his father's face, while he spoke.[4] I was astonished to find how long he took to warm up, and how much dramatic power he used. His people do not need to go to the Theatre. . . .

W. NEWTON.
FRIDAY. MASS.
JAN. 12 1855.

This morning, Charles brought me, from the office, a note from Mr Hewitt, requesting me to take the Editorship of the Una—[5] After a good deal of consultation it was decided that I should go in and see this person. Did so, but could not find him, and left a note with Bela Marsh.[6] Came out disappointed, and worrying a good deal, about John.[7] . . .

W. NEWTON. SATURDAY.
JANY 13. 1855.

Spent this morning in reading Dr. Lowell's sermons, and preparing to review them.[8] Just as I got fairly under way, having first written a long letter to John, Mr Hewitt came out. He did not impress me as having much energy, but I agreed to sell him my name for a certain sum,* and he is to decide by letter. . . .

W. NEWTON. MASS.
TUESDAY. JAN 16. 1855—

Gave all this day, to finishing and copying my tribute to Dr Lowell— I was very, very weary, when I finished at nightfall—but dressed and went in a heavy snow-storm as far as Captain Savage's, to get him to take my article, to town. As I went through the blinding storm, I had many sad thoughts about John and the Wilsons.[9] Dear John, and his unforeseen business trials! I cannot guess why the Wilsons have not written, but they certainly would if they had had any idea of my great need of cheering words. . . .

W. NEWTON. MASS.
SATURDAY. JAN. 20. 1855.

. . . Charles came home unexpectedly—preaches for nothing at Needham to-morrow— Is talking about going out West or to Madras! . . .

---

*That is, her name would appear on *The Una* as coeditor. Dall was to receive a one-time payment of twenty-five dollars and the subscription money collected from her Canadian friends. Hewitt was now the owner as well as publisher, Paulina Davis having given it to him in order to save it. But Davis seems to have thought of herself as still wielding the editorial power.

W. NEWTON MASS.

SUNDAY. JAN. 28. 1854 [*actually* 1855].

... Wrote many letters and in the evening—my Editorial for the Una.[10] I did all this to compose myself, to get off the rut of sorrow, so deeply sunk.

During my last hour, I read what I usually read on Sunday night in Toronto*— The well known precious words comforted me, and I went up, stairs to sleep.

W. NEWTON. MASS.

SUNDAY. FEB. 4. 1855

... To my great surprise, Mr Dall came home from Watertown. He seemed fuller than ever of the Madras scheme. I cannot express the longing that I have to see some one, to whom I may pour out my whole heart—. Oh that John or the Beattys were here. Mr Dall cannot comprehend my feelings and I dare not speak to him, of half the matters concerning which I greatly need counsel.

I could not talk much about Madras, and when that subject was disposed of, I began my Biographical work for March.†

W. NEWTON MASS.

SATURDAY FEB. 17. 1855.

Mr. Dall came home it is decided he is to go to Calcutta.

BOSTON MASS.

WEDNESDAY. FEB 28. 1855. ....

We went early to bed, and Charles prayed with me. It is singular that in this prayer which was on many accounts the most memorable of our lives, he failed in eloquence and power, more than I ever knew him to do. I was sorry that I could not join him from my whole heart and soul—but I could not— I did not sympathize in the least in the step he was taking, and could only respect his own interest in it.

This morning[11] we rose early. Everything was packed before breakfast. After breakfast Charles wrote a few words to the Children. He has felt his separation from them much less than I expected. We then took leave of all—and went down to the Tremont.‡ All were engaged at breakfast and unprepared to

---

*She and John Patton often read Elizabeth Barrett Browning's poetry on Sunday nights.

†Her article "Maria Gaetna Agnesi" appeared in the March 1855 issue of *The Una* (3:43–45). Agnesi (1718–1799) was an eminent mathematician and professor at the University of Bologna.

‡The Tremont House, the hotel where Caroline Dall's family was staying for the winter.

see us. Ellen gave Charles a little pocket book memorandum—and Marion dressed herself and went down to the Wharf with us. Many persons came down to see him off. . . . At last, the time came for us to go ashore, Charles went with us, and staid on the wharf, as long as he could. Then came the farewell. Under the shelter of the buildings we watched them detach themselves from the wharf and get ready for the steam tug. It was ½ past eleven and the steamer that was to have left at 10 had not yet come. My teeth were chattering and Uncle William and Marion seemed too cold to stay. I thought if they got ill on my account they would not like it, so I waved a last farewell and walked up Milk St. I had no prophetic intimation that I should never see Charles again, as I had in Dr Russell's* case, but I had a common sense certainty, of it, so as soon as they left me, I took George's arm and walked down to [the] Wharf again. I hoped to reach it so that Charles would know I came, but as I went on to the Wharf, I saw the Napoleon with her sails set crossing the head of it, and soon had evidence that—the steamer was hold of her, for when I reached my old post, she was out in the stream. I waved my handkerchief, but I know C. did not see me. Where could father be,? when I once more reached the Tremont, and sat dejectedly by the fire, he came in, and exclaimed with real feeling, "Well, Carrie, I entirely forgot to see Charles off!" If it was sad he could forget what was of so much importance to me, it was pleasant to hear him speak in a tone of real feeling for the first time since my return. I wept a little as I went up to Wendell Phillips's with the will. . . . Home to lie down— Lizzie Bartol brought me, the Rose and the Ring,[12]—to amuse myself with, but my thoughts were far away—

W. NEWTON. MASS.
SATURDAY. JUNE. 23. 1855.

An inexpressibly sad day to me, I looked again for letters but finding none, went with a depressed spirit in search of strawberries. . . . While I read Ernest the Seeker,[13] I could not help thinking, what a mistake it is in the Protestant Church that it does not provide for its broken hearted members. How much happier for me, if when Mr Dall left, I could have gone into some retreat, approved by my own friends, where I could have been useful to others, & not separated from my children, have educated them in the best manner, without

*Dr. Gavin Russell, a member of the Dalls' church in Toronto, who left Toronto for California.

pecuniary anxiety. But our church is no mother to her desolate children and I have not a friend on earth whom I dare ask to share the whole burden of my soul.

Dall, vacationing with her daughter Sadie in North Conway, New Hampshire, was confided in by an unusual woman.

N. CONWAY & FRYEBURGE.

THURSDAY. AUG. 2. 1855.

...I found Mrs Champney,[14] with whom I had had a pleasant talk about books just before dinner, talking sadly with Miss Dresser.[15] Her husband who is a strikingly attractive man, had gone away to fish with his brother. She came forward with her eyes filling, then seizing my hand she burst into tears. "It is too bad" she said, "you are going, you, the only person to whom I had taken a fancy, & I meant you should go with us to Jackson Falls tomorrow. After our talk this morning—I said to my husband, that he must find out who you were, for I was sure of you—" & she tried in vain to check her sobs, saying "You will think I am only a silly baby!" I drew her into my chamber to comfort her, & she told me a singular history— Beside her deafness, she is unwell, & morbidly sensitive.... She has been married eight years & has never had a child— simply because she has what she calls, <u>no physical courage</u>, and is afraid to bring a child into the world! How can they have helped it? Young, loving—devoted as they seem, married & rich what strange self-control must not both have exercised! She seems, too, very fond of children.[16] And he?—if he has really kept himself pure, & lived thus for her sake? It is no less than a miracle! Here no one forbids—save a foolish fear—and how many there are longing hearts—between whom Fate has thrown an impossible but adamantine barrier! I promised to go and see her at Woburn....

While John Patton and Eliza Beatty were in town, Boston's first women's rights convention, organized by Paulina Wright Davis, Dall, and others, took place.

W. NEWTON MASS. <u>BOSTON—CONVENTION—</u>

WEDNESDAY SEPT. 19 1855.

Of the unexpected successes of this day—it belongs to me to say little. In pages which may never meet, any other eyes, than those of my children, I shall

Paulina Wright Davis, founder and editor of The Una, *which Dall
later coedited, and co-organizer (with Dall) of Boston's first women's
rights convention in 1855. (Courtesy of Library of Congress)*

be forgiven for recording a few personal remarks. We went into town, after all manner of trials at half past eight. Mrs Beatty met Fanny—John went to his sale*—I to the Convention—and late as it was—I was the earliest there. There was far too little time for consultation—before we began. Miss Hunt welcomed the people, Mrs Davis read her address, & then I followed with my report—which had a most unmerited success.†

E. P. Whipple said it was the ablest thing done in the Convention, some <u>stupid</u> person that it would have done Dan. Webster credit!—!! Lucy Stone & Mr. Higginson‡ followed me, and then I had a brilliant little brush with that brute of a John C. Cluer,[17] about the Legislature, which I hope the phonographic reporters will preserve. As I left the stand at the moment of adjournment, Louise[18] rushed, up with her eyes full, & said "I must kiss you—" I did not go off the platform—for I did not wish to force any conservative friends,

*John Patton was the houseguest of Dall at West Newton; Mrs. Beatty was staying in a hotel in Boston. "Fanny" is probably Dall's sister Frances Healey.

†Harriot K. Hunt and Paulina Wright Davis; Dall's report was a survey of the laws of Massachusetts regarding married women, noting their objectionable features.

‡Thomas Wentworth Higginson.

either to speak to me, or to cut me—but they sought me out, several of them, and spoke with warmth—strangers came to be introduced and several persons, intimated a wish to call. Higginson said, "You have silenced Cluer but don't try it again—" Elizabeth Peabody said—"you don't know, how much better you did than I thought you would." Several pressed my hand silently— or said "I am glad you belong to Boston—" Miss Hunt said "How brave & beautiful you've been—" Mrs Severance,* with her clear true face—"Noble words!" I dined at a Mrs Toppan's[19]—who threw her house open, but could not eat, & asked for a glass of wine. In the afternoon, I felt that the whole thing rather dragged— I had to coax Lucy Stone, out of a pet— She was annoyed at having to speak, but came round at last. She said she had been announced, without being prepared. I was obliged to answer Mr Sennott—who in trying to help us, talked rare nonsense.[20] I know what I wished to say, but my head reeled with pain, and I do not know, what I did say when I got up. I went to tea with John at H. K. Hunt's. Here I saw Miss Grimke, Sally Holley, a Miss Putnam from Catteraugus.[21] Miss Grimke wished to know me better. Sallie Holley with tears in her eyes, said, "I love to hear you speak, I wish it were every day."[22] Miss Putnam said, "I am glad you realize all the anticipations I had formed, & that is saying all I can—" Harriet Carleton, was full of delight saying often, "Oh Mrs Dall, you were splendid!"

We went back and had a very full house for the evening— I was in the chair and introduced Lucy Stone. She & Wendell[23] were the only speakers— I went home with Mrs Beatty†—excessively tired. John also staid in town.[24]

BOSTON CONVENTION.
REVERE HOUSE, THURSDAY. SEPT 20. 1855.

Rose early— . . . Again, every body late at the preliminary meeting— Mr Phillips did not come, as he had half promised he would. This morning, I was able to win Sallie Holley to open the Convention with prayer. She did it beautifully. I urged Garrison, Parker, Wasson, Hodges, and Johnson all in vain—[25]

---

*Caroline Severance (1820–1914), reformer, and a new friend of Dall's, had until recently lived in Cleveland, Ohio, where she had been lecturing, writing, and organizing in behalf of women's rights. Along with her husband, Theodoric C. Severance (1814–1892), she moved in 1855 to Boston, where she was also active in reform causes. In 1868 she became the first president of the New England Women's Club (*NAW; Ancestry.com,* accessed November 7, 2004).

†That is, she stayed in Boston with Mrs. Beatty at the Revere House.

Antoinette Brown[26] & Wendell Phillips & myself filled the morning. In the afternoon, we had Miss Anthony[27] Mrs Fagan[28] and Garrison— I followed Garrison in defense of the first resolution, breaking a lance with him, in a speech that was considered my great effort—* "It was very noble—" said several people & if applause meant anything, the audience were pleased. As I went off the stage Elizabeth Peabody came & said, "Oh Caroline, you are the soul of the Convention, and the best of it is, every body thinks so. You speak so well—in such good taste— Oh you have not a single thing to regret!" Any one could see that she was thoroughly in earnest. John, Mrs B,[29] & I went up to Aunt Sarah's to tea— John & I dined at Copland's and then I went to Mrs Toppan's[30] and lay down, I felt hardly able to stand up— After the PM. session closed—I closetted myself with Garrison & Mrs Severance, until we got the 1st resolution, so that it would pass without discussion.[31] At the opening of the evening session, I had to move the resolutions— I was glad to have a very full house. I had told Garrison before—to cut his bear's claws—namely Hovey's[32] and there was no trouble. Emerson followed with his finished poem†—but I confess my heart failed when I saw Mrs Oakes Smith,[33] in opera costume—walk upon the stage and deliver a Poem—

Garrison & H. K. Hunt said afterward, that the greatest fun of the whole Convention was the watching the various expressions of regret, disgust, & annoyance—as they flitted over my face in listening. I told G. I would wear a black veil the next time I went— John, Mrs B & I, went out before she closed, and awkwardly enough, for the door keeper had locked the door that led from the Committee room and we had to return and pass through the hall— Uncle Wm. took Mrs Beatty to the Revere, and John & I came home. John said he was proud of me—and the words were a good deal sweeter than the more exaggerated praise I left behind in the Hall.

---

*Garrison, himself a nonvoter, objected to the first resolution (urging suffrage for women as the only way for women to advance) as equivocal. Dall defended the resolution (*Liberator,* September 28, 1855, p. 156).

†That is, the lecture published as "Woman," in the *Miscellanies* volume of *The Complete Works of Ralph Waldo Emerson,* edited by Edward Waldo Emerson (Boston: Houghton, Mifflin and Company, 1903–1904), 11:403–426, and as "Address at the Woman's Rights Convention, 20 September 1855" in *The Later Lectures of Ralph Waldo Emerson,* edited by Ronald A. Bosco and Joel Myerson (Athens, Georgia: University of Georgia Press, 2001), 2:15–29.

W. NEWTON MASS.

SUNDAY. SEPT. 23D 1855. . . .

Wendell[34] asked me in a few moments intercourse, if I was not satisfied with the Convention— I told him yes, with all but the Poem—* "Parker told me that was miserable" replied he— "It whittled the Convention down to a point, and was a striking example of all the faults we had succeeded in avoiding," I returned. He praised Emerson— "Yes," I said "he seemed to lure the Conservatives on over his flowers, till all of a sudden their feet were pierced with the thorns of reform." . . .

W. NEWTON MASS.

MONDAY. SEPT 24. 1855.

. . . I felt very weary and lay down with the eleventh no. of George Sand† in my hand— Just as I had made up my mind that I was too tired to eat, and had ordered a bowl of cocoa, Elizabeth Peabody appeared. I had a very pleasant evening with her, and we talked of many things— Elizabeth told me that the first time she ever saw me, she set out to mortify me, because she thought I had too good an opinion of myself—but when she saw how magnanimously I bore it, she forgave me. She said very strongly that Margaret was wanting in that— was a heathen in fact—while I had the <u>advantage of the christian religion</u>—!!

W. NEWTON MASS.

TUESDAY. SEPT. 25. 1855

Just after breakfast, Elizabeth went into the kitchen with me, where I busied myself in preserving barberries. . . .

Miss Peabody talked a great deal about the sister of Kossuth,[35] just divorced from her husband— Jas. F. Clarke has offered her a home for five years at Brooke Farm—& I must try to go and see her. Elizabeth is interested that I should lecture and write. Mrs Davis[36] has written to me, today, to come to Providence and lecture, & I shall accept. I had also a beautiful letter from Louisa Hall—[37] Nothing from my mother—can she be still too ill—it is too hard to wait. Elizabeth left me at 4 P.M. She had heard all manner of good things about me, but one surprised me—

---

*The poem delivered by Elizabeth Oakes Smith.
†Dall was reading *Histoire de ma vie,* the autobiography of George Sand.

From Dorchester some ladies had gone in, who had heard my name mentioned as vice-president— "What!" they said "that Mrs Dall who makes so much trouble for her husband every where—we don't want to hear her." "What about that Mrs Dall?" said Elizabeth, and heard a general opinion that I was a very troublesome individual. She said nothing, however, the day wore away— They went home delighted with that Mrs Dall—. They even found out I was beautiful—looked first like Wendell Phillips and then like Margaret Fuller—but at all events they could listen to me all day. "Do you think," said Elizabeth, "that is the Mrs Dall who makes trouble for her husband?" They were entirely conquered. Poor Lizzie she could not see, that I have made trouble for my husband simply by being stronger than he. That is to reverse the natural order and only very strong souls—can acquiesce in that. How I could have loved him if he had been magnanimous enough for the test—and now I feel such tenderness as we do for a sick child,—a state of things, which bereaves both. . . .

Some in the audience of the women's rights convention questioned whether Emerson's speech there could actually be seen as an endorsement of the movement. Dall argued that it was; in her letter thanking Emerson for speaking, she acknowledged some differences from his position, but concluded, "That [women] are fully capable of becoming 'innocent citizens' was all we needed you should admit."38

W. NEWTON MASS.

THURSDAY. SEPT 27. 1855.

. . . Made a short call—on Sarah Beck. She said James thought Mr Emerson did not intend to encourage the movement but to throw cold water on the whole thing. He must be stupid. The facts are these, Mr Emerson gave Mrs Davis to understand through Mr Alcott, that he was ready to speak in our behalf. Unwilling to lose the benefit of his sympathy, which would aid us abroad, our meeting was held last May, and Mrs D. empowered to hold a correspondence on the subject, which resulted in this convention— We had no other excuse for holding a Convention, at this precise moment. Went up to Aunt Sarah's where I heard some one said I had been depreciating Florence Nightingale.39 . . .

Took tea at Ellen Tarr's, with William O'Connor.40 Last night, the doorbell rang and I went to the door and there stood a little fellow about ten.

"Please Mrs D" "have you any woman's rights' tracts?" "What in the world do you want of them?" said I, much amused. "Oh there's going to be a debate at our Lyceum (Mr Allen's School Lyceum)[41] and I want to take that side!" I gave him what I could, & promised to get more today, so when I came home, tonight, I found him waiting like a guide post for more.

Here, Dall learns for the first time that The Una *is on the verge of collapse.*

W. NEWTON & BOSTON
SATURDAY SEPT 29. 1855.

I was sitting this morning busily making up my phonographic report when I received a letter from Mrs Davis, saying that she hoped I would put the legal reports into this paper* as Hewitt was unable to sustain it and we might not have another. I was extremely startled—it seemed so dishonorable to stop the paper before the end of the year, and what were we to do with the subscribers to whom Spiridion was promised.† Without changing my dress, I hurried into town, but before I arrived there, I had made up my mind, to print Spiridion through even if I had to borrow the money to do it. I did not find H. I left a note for him saying, I would be at H. K. Hunt's till half past one—and if he did not call would come to the office again on my way out of town. I talked with Sarah Grimke about affairs, and then returned. Providence helped me for I met H. at the turn of Bromfield st. Went back & made close inquiry into his affairs. Mrs H. was with him. She is worth a dozen of him— He does not intend to give up before January. Showed me his books—out of 1,000 of Mrs Davis's subscribers 600 have not pd. In Chicago out of 53—50 have not pd— I could not blame him—but told him to take the most energetic measures— and then dashed about town in search of the Reports of N.H. & Vt.[42] No one knew any thing of them. . . .

W. NEWTON MASS.
SUNDAY SEPT. 30. 1855.

. . . Mrs. Ayres[43] stopped me after church to say, that all her Dorchester friends thought I was the life of the Convention, the very best of the <u>lady</u> speakers—

---

*That is, Paulina Wright Davis was suggesting that Dall's "Reports on the Laws of New England" presented at the convention on September 19 and 20 be printed in the next issue of *The Una*.

†Dall's translation of George Sand's novel *Spiridion* was being published serially in *The Una*; up to this point, four segments had appeared in the July through October 1855 issues (3:97–101, 113–115, 129–133, 155–160).

including Lucy & Antoinette.[44] Poor soul! she need not have laid so much emphasis on the word <u>lady</u> as if there were any danger of my fancying myself the equal of Higginson or Phillips. She half apologized for telling me, but said her friends made her promise she would— She added also that Caroline Thayer of Boston[45] made her promise that she would tell me, how satisfied every body was,—and how grateful they felt that I had imparted so much dignity to the Convention &c &c— I asked if she had heard from Theo. Parker. She said Mr A. had seen him, and she thought he must have been satisfied, because he said, what a pity Mrs O. S*—should have whittled the whole thing down to a point, when we had gone on so nobly for two days....

W. NEWTON MASS.

MONDAY OCT. 1. 1855.

Letters from John, Mrs Davis,[46] and dear mother. The last two perplexing— compelled to answer at once, and dated both wrong the 2nd. Perhaps it is well—that mother should tell me so plainly, that none of them approve my course— I might otherwise be inflated by all this undeserved praise. Yet she is so tender & loving.

WEST NEWTON. MASS.

MONDAY. OCT. 22. 1855.

Spent this day in and around Boston, seeking houses in vain.... Went to see father about houses—he was not as cordial as when he spoke of my moving before, but I wept two or three long hours over his words. He thought the rent of the house in Roxbury too high, and was not willing to give me any security as to paying it. I said then, I will give it up at once, for I wish to do what will be satisfactory to you. He said, "It is entirely impossible that any thing—<u>you</u> should do, should be satisfactory to me." God forgive him—and me, for remembering that he said it....

In early November Dall moved her family into a rented house at 49 Bradford Street in the South End of Boston.

---

*Elizabeth Oakes Smith. The reference is to the poem she recited at the women's rights convention on September 20.

BOSTON. MASS.
MONDAY. NOV. 12. 1855....

... I went down to Marsh's[47] to look up some Una's & to Hewitt's to see if I could get any satisfaction. Every trace of the Una office, is swept away, and he is evidently wholly absorbed in his new paper. I hardly know what I said to him, for I was confused & worried by fatigue & anxiety to the last degree. He met me at every point with the assertion that he & Mrs Davis understood each other—alas! if it be true, for her and him. I came home very sad, and after writing several necessary letters read George Sand with an aching head.

BOSTON TUESDAY.
NOV. 13. 1855.

I had an uneasy night dreaming all night of Hewitt and the Una—and awoke to wonder whether I had done him an unintentional injustice. I had no trouble with Mrs Davis, until he came in the way—can it be that she is to blame for what seems his fault now— I should like to keep my respect for her, but how is it possible, after such a letter as her last.[48] Last night, I wrote her to know, whether she has any information to give me, and this morning my first duty was to file all the Convention & Una papers, and restore those that belonged to her. It was a sad duty....

FRIDAY NOV. 23D 1855

... I worked nearly all the morning & then was about to rest, when Elizabeth Peabody came full of a new plan. She believes she has persuaded Mrs Davis to print the two remaining nos of the Una—& wishes me to take charge of it next year. God knows I will not, unless he sends a fresh North wind to blow away clouds. We held a Committee meeting after, and considered all this. Dr Channing had taken the trouble to go to Providence, & see Mrs Davis. He pleaded well for her, and I was content it should be so—for it seemed to me that a person in so bad a condition needed all the help that anybody could honestly give them. He probably does not care so much for me, but he paid me the compliment of thinking that I was able to take care of myself.

I let many false statements pass, that I would not had Mrs D. made them herself. But absent it was only proper that she should have the benefit of my silence.

I knew she would not come to the meeting. She knew I had the proofs in my own hands. Elizabeth P. came home with me, and corrected in this little room the little proofs of Mad. Meszlenyi's memoir.[49] We had much interesting talk. I was worn out, and wept a little over my disappointments.

When Dall became acquainted with Walt Whitman's "powerful" Leaves of Grass, her response was predictably Victorian.

BOSTON MASS.
WEDNESDAY. NOV. 28. 1855
. . . Miss Clapp[50] showed me "leaves of grass"[51] a strange book—but powerful. He has led a sensual life that poet, and cannot but show the slime the serpent has left. There could not be a greater contrast, than the description of a conception by him, and Alfred Tennyson at the close of In Memoriam—when the latter speaks of a star as "striking its being into bounds."[52] If a man ever truly loved, he would feel the acts of generation in their noblest sense & relation, only—he could not descend to details, revolting except as inspired by the creating God in Man, & most acceptable when looked at through the inspiration.

Dall here records her brief association with Mary Webb, a little-remembered mulatto performer whose dramatic readings were popular.

BOSTON THURSDAY—
DEC. 6. 1855.
. . . I went over to Mrs Brooks's[53] early & we went down to hear Mrs Webb read the dramatised Uncle Tom—[54] She was tastefully, yet too much dressed. In black silk & a black Malta veil—with a silver coronet of singular beauty. She read well—but only one thing was remarkable—the exquisite manner in which she sung, when personating Evangeline.[55] The house was crowded & brilliant.

BOSTON MASS.
THURSDAY. DEC. 20. 1855.
Mrs Severance—came in at about 10 this morning and I went with her to the Fair,* where I had a pleasant interview with Mrs Child, Mrs Follen—Mrs Loring, Mrs Dwight Dr & Mrs Channing, Jeannie Tarr[56]— Mrs Dwight made me

---

*The Anti-Slavery Fair.

do a very silly thing, by joking me about looking sad. As I playfully defended myself I found my face convulsed & the tears running down. As poor Bridget[57] says, I find my tears very <u>near</u>. I wish my face, were not so transparent for it speaks so plainly that I am often driven to justify its expression, in words, an indelicacy that grates on my own heart & costs me many hours of weeping when I am alone. Ah well—! did I think when I stood to be married before the West Church altar—that I should ever be left thus <u>alone</u>— How impregnable seemed my double strength. God knows how & why I married— If I have not been to my husband what he needed, if he has not been to me the provider & comforter I expected—I can at least look back on those first few years with a clear conscience, and can Thank God—that we both, seeking to love him & serve him, have borne with some patience what was so unexpected in itself. [Approximately 20 illegible words] it is better to have the disappointment on both sides if on either.[58] I went on studying today—& did not even go to the anti-slavery lecture. Dr Channing told me, he had settled his accounts with Hewitt, I am sorry I did not know it before I wrote Mrs Davis.

"Oh world—how hard thou art!"

JANUARY 1ST. TUESDAY. BOSTON MASS.
May God give me grace to accept all his will, to learn how unimportant and unwise I am—to take to heart sufficiently the disappointments of this last year, to trust him to the end, when I find, that having gifted me so strangely, there is yet no work on earth for me to do—

Oh Father, strengthen me, against my own despair, make me willing to live— . . .

BOSTON MASS.
WEDNESDAY. JAN 23. 1856. . . .
My girl informed me this morning that she would rather I would get another girl, for she would like to live with a pleasanter-<u>looking</u> lady—at which I did not wonder. Two mustard plasters on the children, last night, one on myself this morning, before I could speak a loud word. Found the water & drain pipes frozen when I got up— I was not cross, but I know I looked very much depressed. Not one loving word to cheer me—not one kind heart against which I might lean! Only the stranger kindness of dear Miss Willey,[59] who seems to have been providentially sent to me— Laid down in the afternoon, and enjoyed having Carrie Dresser to talk to.

BOSTON MASS.

SATURDAY. FEB. 23. 1856.

A memorable day, because one of the Standing Committee of the Mercantile Library Association [came] to get some information about the Woman's Rights Question—& to invite me to their discussion of this subject, next Tuesday evening hoping that I would come prepared to speak. The world moves—! I shall go—

...I went with Mrs Dudley to Mr Parker's Saturday afternoon conversation.[60] It was a fine talk for the kind on moral training— Mr Parker always provokes me, when he speaks—by his mannish views of women. At this time, he has annoyed me, by his opinion of Georges Sand—! He really believes that she has led for years a licentious life— It is not in her— Oh man! why must you always take the lowest view of people—& motives. How innocent—how inspiring do I often find the pages which reek with corruption for others. . . .

BOSTON MASS.

TUESDAY. FEB. 26. 1856.

Reading most of the morning— Calls from Hatty Stevens,[61] Dr Channing[62] & mother— Mr & Mrs Severance & Miss Willey[63] came to tea, and we went down to the M[ercantile] L[ibrary] Rooms together at 7 o'clock. I felt very timid about going. Dr Channing had said in the morning, that I must regard myself as the special instrument of Providence. I felt that a person strong enough to appear properly—before so conservative an audience might be so— but I am not strong—yet I think my speaking is modest, perhaps impressive and, those who had never heard a woman speak, had better hear me, than one who would offend good taste.

Three or four very good speeches on behalf of woman's rights—a faltering utterance against them, and I rose—taking shelter under the invitation to strangers to participate in the debate. I never could imagine a greater change in an audience than there was in this—from the moment I rose. The most, intense attention—you could have heard a pin fall— There was a sort of atmosphere that said, it would not be respectful to clap—but they forgot it twice —when I spoke of C. F. Hovey's[64] willingness to take a woman into partnership—& of the need of womanly conscientiousness in legislation.

I was followed by one or two feeble utterances—in the negative, but some very noble ones in the affirmative. A young Irishman a stranger spoke nobly in the affirmative as did a man named Griffin from Georgia. I should like to meet the latter in private.

Mr & Mrs Severance left at ½ past 9—& in the midst of a feeble wail for man, we soon after left.

It was singular that the reform <u>expression</u> was so strong—for I have no doubt the <u>vote</u> will be against us. Many of the debaters were like myself strangers—.

If I have not done the best possible—I have at least done no ill tonight.

BOSTON. MASS—
SUNDAY. MAR 9. 1856. . . .

I spent some time in burning John's letters— It went to my heart to do it, those free noble affectionate letters, I would rather lose any I possess—but they are necessarily full of personalities, and liable as I am to be taken away suddenly, I dare not run the risk of their accumulation—and yet I could wish that my children might know, as only such letters can show them, what he has been to me— . . .

BOSTON MASS.
FRIDAY. APRIL 11. 1856.

. . . Father brought Sadie home yesterday—he told me that they had had a dis-agreeable day—a contest between M. & F.* about going to New York with him & that probably he should take neither. He seemed to come up for comfort & took more interest in me & my affairs than usual—in fact, I may say it was the first fatherly visit, I have had from him since I was married— . . .

Dall was attending a short conversation series conducted by Bronson Alcott, the first session of which had taken place two weeks earlier at Dall's house. The topic of at least some of these conversations was marriage. At a previous meeting, Dall noted that a Miss Hinckley who was present had seemed to "paralyze" Alcott.

BOSTON MASS.
TUESDAY. MAY 6. 1856.

. . . We had a fine conversation at Mr Alcott's— I arranged the people so that Miss Hinckley[65] could not possibly sit down right before him. She came late,

*Marianne and Fannie Healey, Dall's sisters.

& wanted my seat—but I passed her in behind me, and sat down resolutely in front. Christ's complexion being under discussion, <u>she</u> said she always thought he was <u>mouse</u> colored! Fortunately for our risibles, she did not offer her reason— As it was Dr Channing & I came near expiring!

Mr Scherb[66]—defended human freedom—nobly.

We were sorry it was the last.

As usual, Dall attended the annual meetings of reform societies in Boston known as the "Anniversaries."

BOSTON MASS.

WEDNESDAY. MAY. 28. 1856.

I am so late in writing my Journal that I can hardly tell, but I believe it was this morning that the discussion began in the Anti Slavery Convention between Phillips & Foster.[67] It followed an appeal from Mr Nute[68] for help for Kansas. Mr Foster criticized the resolutions of the Society, fearing that the popular admiration of Sumner* would destroy the absolutely consistent Abolitionist party. Mr Phillips rose grandly in reply as well as Garrison but Mr Foster's invective left our hearts strained & sore, at so pathetic a moment. After dinner I delivered my own lecture before the Physiological Institute.† A very large & most attentive audience. Many persons from the West Church. Mr Cordner[69] & Mr Nute, came to speak to me, after it was over. We went back to the A.S. Convention—and heard a magnificent eulogy on Mr. Sumner from Mr. Parker[70]— Surely no man ever had so fine things said of him before his death —and Mr Parker never made a finer effort.... I never spoke under so many disadvantages as today. My personal interest for Mr—Sumner—my public feeling for Kansas—my struggling faith in God—all reached a crisis just before I went into the Hall. These brought on as usual a diarrhoea and that, a nervous paralysis, which had nearly proved fatal to my voice. Three times in the course of the lecture, I spoke a word and it did not come—but I rallied so soon that I heard no one remark upon—it. At the close of Mr Parker's speech—a

---

*Charles Sumner (1811–1874), U.S. Senator from Massachusetts, 1851–1874. On May 22, Sumner, a strong abolitionist, was severely beaten in his Senate seat by South Carolina representative Preston Brooks with a heavy cane. Sumner was a leader of the Radical Republicans during Reconstruction *(DAB)*.

†The Ladies' Physiological Institute; Dall lectured on "The Body as the Temple of God" (Register of Public Addresses, Dall Papers, Bryn Mawr).

gentleman from Baltimore came & thanked me for my lecture. He said somewhat indignantly, "There are not more than <u>six</u> women in the United States." I laughed and told him, I hoped I was one! . . . Had a word-fight in the Omnibus with L. G. Pray,[71] who thinks it is wicked to send rifles to Kansas—and that no human freedom is involved in the struggle <u>there,</u> only the Presidential Election.

BOSTON MASS.

SUNDAY. JAN. 11. 1857.

A severe lameness made it impossible for me to go out—today—otherwise it was bad for me to have E.P.P.* here—for I ought to have written all day—& when she is here, I always put everything aside, and listen, for her conversation is a great treat, which I cannot expect to have often renewed. She told me the details of Dr Solger's[72] life, & confided a plan she has for the establishment of an independent professorship in Boston. She told me how shabbily Goodrich[73] had really treated Hawthorne in the days of their early connection, and threatened to expose him—if he claimed too much in his book. She suggested to me that I had better write a volume of Italian biographies, illustrating the poems of Robt Browning. She thought such a book could not but sell. I will think of that suggestion. She read some of Una's† letters—about her music in which she excels—& Julian‡ of whom she is very proud. She told how since they had left London, he had (at nine yrs old!) put off his shyness, become quite gay, gone into society everywhere—& grown quite a dandy, spending more time than papa over his toilet. Una's mind is very pure, she is 12 yrs old—has never read a novel, & has no conception of the horrors of American slavery, which poor child, she could not have escaped had she lived in Boston. . . .

BOSTON MASS.

THURSDAY. FEB. 5. 1857.

Began to write a story which has been in my head for some time. Hope God will forgive me if I am wasting time— Know that I ought to be hard at work among musty Mss. but circumstances forbid— I don't believe this story

---

*Elizabeth Peabody had spent the preceding night with Dall and was full of talk and schemes.

†Peabody's niece Una Hawthorne (1844–1877), oldest child of Nathaniel and Sophia Hawthorne.

‡Julian Hawthorne (1846–1934), second of the Hawthornes' three children.

(of S.B.*) will ever sell—but if it does not the disappointment will never be so hard to bear, as it was in regard to Spiridion, and the writing it will keep fancy at least employed. It seems at times as if unused powers would drive me mad— and yet my hands are always busy— God knows all— May He comfort me—, for no earthly power can. . . .

BOSTON MASS.

SATURDAY. MAR. 7. 1857.

Spent the morning in hearing the French lesson and seeking a girl. My head ached in consequence so that I was glad to lie down most of the afternoon. In the evening got two letters from Charles. He wants Willie to come to India for a year!! and for the first time expresses some compunction for leaving me alone.

Dall has been invited to speak at the lyceum in East Needham. Her subject is "Power and Dignity of Woman."

BOSTON MASS.

MONDAY. MAR. 23. 1857.

Sewed and sat with my children until 12 o'clock when I went out to Needham. Wm. Harris met me at the cars and took me to his mother where I dined and took tea.[74] Just before it was necessary to start, a smart hail storm came up, and I felt afraid my audience would be thinned. It was not so— I was warned that I should probably be disturbed by noise and the coming in late. When I got there, the house was nearly full, and after I rose to speak, I do not think that a single person entered—& you might have heard a pin drop— Three ladies fainted & some windows were opened. Old Brave walked across the Hall, & insisted on lying down at my feet. Otherwise all went well. A few moments before the lecture closed, there was an alarm, of fire given. I was requested to pause for a moment—which I did saying that as I was within six lines of the close of the lecture it would not be worth while to renew it. However—the alarm proved false and they crowded round the desk to hear the last words. Mr Winch[75] restored order, and I was surprised to see that the Hall was as full as before— All the seats were filled & apparently the same number standing.

*Perhaps her late friend Sarah Balch Beck. Other journal entries indicate that Dall was contemplating writing a novel, perhaps to be entitled *Sidney Bartlett*. In any event, the work was apparently never finished.

I read the remainder of the lecture—& received the compliments of the assembly— One lady said to another—"I don't see that woman's rights are anything more than they ought to have." Mary Eaton* said in a dejected tone —"Oh Mrs Dall, it is all true, but how long it will be before people believe it!" I told her we could afford to wait God's time, if we did not wait idly. Mrs Gardner my old midwife,[76] came up to me, and asked me, if I would go to Milford and speak, if she could get me a hearing—which I promised to do. I heard after I left the Hall, that B.G.K†—had expected to continue the discussion of the Woman's Rights Question after the lecture—from the last meeting, but the lecture had completely conquered him, and he was the first to move an adjournment. Rude as he is, he felt instinctively that it would be too discourteous to involve me in such a discussion. He behaved more like a gentleman than I ever saw him— ...

John Patton visited from Montreal, where he now lived. Bronson Alcott called, reporting on apparent sexual licentiousness in New York.

BOSTON MASS.

THURSDAY. MAR. 26. 1857.

We were sitting quietly this morning for John felt weary, with yesterday's exertions when Mr Alcott was announced— He staid more than an hour to give me an account of his recent visit to New York— I cannot write down what he said, for it makes me thrill to my fingers' ends, and I am sick and ashamed of life— The whole City is corrupt—marriage has no longer any sanctity, its holy uses—are scoffed at—the love of two is counted an absurdity, and one can hardly comprehend why people unite in families at all. No where are you safe — Mr A. talked with Stephen Pearl Andrews[77]—with that vulgar untamed brute Walt Whitman—the author of Leaves of Grass—the only man, he says, he ever met who was a fit mate physically for Fannie Kemble[78] a very low creature one must think—if one may judge from that side of his experiences which he chooses to remember. He had a conversation at Lucy Stone's and among the ladies whom she invited to meet him was a Mrs DeGrove at whose house the next conversation was appointed. He went to see this lady—and if I understood aright was as cordially invited to her bed, as if it had been her par-

*Mary J. Eaton (b. 1829), Needham teacher (1860, 1880 U.S. Census).
†Unidentified.

lor—. At all events—she assured him it was open to whoever pleased her, and set forth her doctrine with so much intellectual acumen, so much power and seductive grace, that he was almost bewildered. The second meeting was held at Mrs DeGrove's house—but Providence preserved him—he did not hear of it, and they waited for him in vain. He told her—"Madam, I do not think I am good enough to hear these things you are saying—" She apologised for the freedom of her remarks and said her practice and her theory were different— Afterward Mr Alcott ascertained from reliable sources that her practice and her theory sustained each other. He went to Dr Wellington's,[79] a water cure establishment, and this man—once, God shield us, a clergyman—now says —I am a whole pharmacopeia in myself—and treats his patients by conjugal embraces instead of physic— In his hospital were women who seemed respectable, who quietly told Mr Alcott that they fulfilled the same office toward the men. At the door was a carriage—the Dr sent for by a lady! He was wasted to a shadow—human nature could not stand it long—of course— Oh God! to what abyss of social degradation are we coming when these things are so. Andrews—said to Mr Alcott that two thirds of the women, and one third of the men are exclusive but it is the result of habit & education! Oh God! sank ever Athens lower—! What wonder that slavery reigns in a land so tenanted. . . .

BOSTON MASS.

TUESDAY. MAY 5. 1857—

A busy day. At night went very tired to Dr Channing's to an Alcott conversation on Life as a Pursuit. There was assembled an unusually brilliant company, Mrs Howe—Mr. Alcott—Mr—Scherb—Emerson—Brown Mr Whipple— Sewall—Gould—Ednah Cheney—and Dr Channing.[80] I had a little tiff with Mrs Howe—& Mr Scherb—about Mrs Kemble, whom they insisted on attacking because of her masculineness, and because she read out the Falstaffs & Trinculos & Nick Bottoms[81] of her plays. I could not take the great gifts of her genius & repay them by such revilings! God forbid—& I was vexed at Mrs Howe's inconsistency and want of self knowledge— I had been fighting the same battle for her "World's Own"* all the morning. "What!" say the critics,

---

*Julia Ward Howe's play, *Leonora, or The World's Own* (1857), the story of a young woman who, unable to kill the lover who has abandoned her, commits suicide. It was condemned by reviewers as indecent and closed after one week *(NAW)*.

"a delicate woman write such a play—describe that scene of riotous wassail it is impossible!"

It is a woman—doubtless & about the delicate, we shall see.

At the close of the talk Mr Alcott threw the ball into my hands, that I might speak of Life as a pursuit—to women— I did it—too earnestly for the esthetic atmosphere in which I was—too earnestly for Emerson, perhaps for Alcott. Alas!...

The manner in which Emerson speaks of the deity &—of Christ seems to me very artful—I wonder if it is so.

BOSTON MASS
SUNDAY—MAY 17. 1857.

A noble sermon from Mr Wasson[82]—on Love— It was a fit sermon for me for it taught that one must pour out, love, love love—& never ask for any—finding all in the love within— I am willing to have it so, one soul alone excepted, but if I constantly hold him between myself & Heaven—asking God—to save him rather than myself—if either must be lost—is it not natural nay, is it not right indeed,—that I should ask of him a little love?

John Patton was visiting once again.

BOSTON MASS.
TUESDAY. SEPT. 15. 1857.

John left in the early train— It was a sorrowful parting to me; as my health & strength decline, I feel my loneliness more & more, & home is only home, while he is here. The children need him also—he is next best to their father— & they are never sad while uncle Don—is by....

BOSTON. WEDNESDAY. NOV 25. 1857.

The most precious anniversary of my whole life,*—to be kept utterly alone — I thought when I got a delayed letter from ____† today it would at least show some consciousness of the season—so near which it would reach me — Six years ago—what a gleam of sunlight flashed athwart my sky—nay! not

---

*The anniversary of November 24, 1851, a date significant to her relationship with John Patton.
†John Patton.

flashed, but shone steadily for two perhaps for three years and in that, was all I am ever to know of love & life—[83] Alone all alone—forgive me God that I am not patient under it, that I cannot bear it well— "The meek shall inherit the earth"— alas! I do not want the earth—only one human heart—within it—a heart which belongs to me which is mine—& yet I cannot hold.

CHAPTER ELEVEN

Woman's Rights Woman

January 6, 1858–February 19, 1861

$\mathscr{D}$uring the years from 1858 to early 1861, Caroline Dall found her vocation at last, establishing herself as a professional lecturer and writer on behalf of women's rights. Dall developed and executed a long-range plan, in which she prepared a series of three new lectures for each of four seasons, on various aspects of the woman question. She delivered the full series each year in Boston, then repeated the series or individual lectures from it in surrounding areas, and as far away as Bangor, Maine. Perhaps most gratifying to her were the lectures she delivered to appreciative audiences in Worcester, where her old beau Samuel Haven was among the auditors, and the one she gave in Concord, where her audience included the Emerson, Alcott, and Thoreau families. Along with Caroline Severance, Dall organized and ran women's rights meetings in Boston in 1859 and 1860. She also spoke, or attempted to speak, at a New York City meeting in 1859, a traumatic but almost comical episode in which she was shouted down. And, entering the political process directly, she addressed a committee of the Massachusetts legislature, advocating for the franchise for women.

Dall did not rely solely on the spoken word, however, to disseminate her views. She put one of her lecture series into print as the pamphlet *"Woman's Right to Labor."* She collected her *Una* essays and other pieces into a book called *Historical Pictures Retouched,* the title accurately suggesting her new readings of the lives of historical women. In addition, she published a significant article on Margaret Fuller in the *North American Review* and edited an autobiographical work by Marie Zakrzewska, a contemporary woman physician.

Dall's financial rewards from all of this activity were minimal. On one occasion, balancing her expenditures for a lecture against her expenses, she figured that she had earned a mere five dollars. After delivering the entire series in Boston one season, she barely broke even. Engagements outside of Boston, where she did not have to pay for the hall, were more profitable. But these activities did succeed in establishing Dall as a leading women's rights woman; she was flattered that the new periodical *The Dial* suggested that the mantle of Margaret Fuller had fallen to her. But even this sort of success was beside the point to her; she was disappointed to learn that her minister and friend James Freeman Clarke had complimented one of her lectures by describing it to a mutual friend as "quite equal to any of the Mercantile Library lectures." "This remark took the life out of the pleasant words he said to me on Sunday," Dall complained, going on, "As if I had no higher aim than that!" She believed in the value of her vocation and felt that it had "a suitable dignity." When the census taker came to her home in 1860, Dall (rather proudly, one assumes) had her occupation listed as "Lecturer," an anomaly among the typical listings for women of "At home," "Keeping house," or "No occupation"—if the line were filled in at all.

Dall's commitment to her work enabled her to overcome many obstacles. One of these was poor health during much of this time, as she battled one after another of the painful carbuncles on her face, neck and shoulders, caused we now know by a staphylococcal infection. The temporary near deafness caused by one of these abscesses was at least partially responsible for her failure at the New York meeting. Another hindrance was the opposition of her own family, especially her sisters. But her father and brother George attended some of her lectures, and she was pleasantly surprised that her father was sometimes pleased by them. When she was asked to deliver a Parker Fraternity lecture to perhaps the largest audience of her career, her father brought a family brooch for her to wear. By putting herself in the public eye, of course, Dall invited criticism, and some of the most scathing came from her old mentor Elizabeth Peabody, who declared that she "would not go to hear your lectures with a gentleman by my side," and from an ally in the reform arena, T. W. Higginson. She offended some of her auditors by the supposed vulgarity of her lectures, especially her plain speaking on such topics as prostitution. "Such a charge against me," she expostulated, "who may safely challenge the world to produce the first profane or vulgar word I ever spoke." She was criticized on the one hand for her egotism, and on another because her dress was by general consensus "too short." Perhaps most disturbingly, she was attacked in print by one Parsons Cooke, an Orthodox clergyman who publicized her irregular marriage and suggested that her admiration for Mary Wollstonecraft spoke volumes about her own sexual morality. This attack on her respectability she felt keenly, for Caroline Dall was nothing, in her own view, if not what her society called a *lady*. As a result of this attack, before she could deliver her next scheduled lecture, she was requested to submit "a late letter of Mr Dall's to prove we had never been separated—a volume of Channing to show that somebody beside myself thought well of Mary Wollstonecraft—my lecture to read to the Committee & show that I had not been advocating free-love."

Dall's sense of fulfillment in her work did not, however, lessen her feeling of loneliness. Something was amiss in her relationship with John Patton; we cannot be sure what it was, but in any case, he was pressed by heavy cares of his own. From Calcutta, Charles wrote that when he returned home he wished to room with Willie, having developed a new " 'monkish' determination." This declaration was more a relief to Caroline than otherwise, saving her from "the mere chance—of repelling him—for children I would never give to one of whose mental soundness I am not sure." "And yet," she continued, "when I look back and think what life might have been in the sunshine—the perfect fullness of life and love—it seems to be more than I can bear." On one occasion she "felt deserted of God, even." But she came to believe that she understood why her life was so solitary: only so could she devote herself fully to her work. Still she wondered, "may there not yet come an hour—when I shall be no longer alone—if earth is lost—may not Heaven be saved?"

The life of a professional lecturer often involved many discomforts, as Dall's experience in Bangor, Maine, in the following entry demonstrates.

WEDNESDAY JAN 6. 1858— <u>BOSTON & BANGOR</u>
I had ordered my carriage last night, but it did not come— It was driving a violent storm of rain & sleet & Ann[1] went round to the stable, but it was not open. She asked if there was any other she could go to, but I told her no, & rushing at the last moment into the dark street caught an Omnibus, & asked it to drive fast, which as I was the only passenger proved easy. I had a heavy valise & got quite wet— Gov. Anderson[2]—a former Gov. of Maine had called

last night & invited me to take charge of his little motherless niece,[3] who was to go 17 miles beyond Bangor. I was sorry as I had taken very little baggage, in order to avoid fatigue, but I consented & so they met me at the cars. We had hardly time to get tickets. She was a bright little thing— I had a few crackers & the storm raged so, that we did not leave the cars all day, & were too late to dine at Portland as the passengers, generally do— It was 8 P.M. when we got to Bangor, & I had to look after Miss Anderson's luggage, with the thermometer 12° below zero— When I finally got into the carriage to take her to the Bangor House the driver said— "What may I call you?" "Mrs Dall" I answered— "Law ma'am" said he—"Mr Strange[4] has been a looking everywhere for you." As I had not the least idea who Mr Strange was, I was not so much rejoiced as he expected. . . .

Meanwhile Mr Strange appeared. He proved to be the president of the Mechanics Association which had invited me—& looked with absolute adoration on a woman who could speak which—perhaps accounted for his appearing perpetually in low spirits! I found I was to go to my old friend the Hon. Franklin Muzzy[5]— I was soon on my way & found Mrs M—waiting for me, before a blazing wood-fire. I was soon divested of my wrappers, & Mr Strange had to stay, till he had chosen his lecture & wished me well. When he went out—he said he would call for me tomorrow evening in a carriage & as Mrs M—shut the door, she said—"I thought he never would go." I was then led to some hot tea & rice fritters, but I felt too weary, & begged to be permitted to refuse all, & seek my pillow. I also said distinctly it was very doubtful whether I could get up to breakfast, at which—they all laughed remembering my sunrise expeditions two summers ago. The gas was lighted & a fire burning in the pleasant chamber but I think water would have frozen on the hearth— After I had thrown myself into a great down bed I heard Lizzie Muzzey[6] exclaiming "I should like to see that Mr. Strange, turning that refined, lady-like woman round, as if she were a piece of furniture! He may keep his carriage to himself— I guess I've got a father & I guess he can take her down to Norombega Hall himself." Thereupon I fell asleep.

BANGOR MAINE.

THURSDAY. JAN 7. 1858.

I got down to breakfast after dressing on the hearth, at about a quarter to nine. I found to my mortification that all had waited. It was snowing hard—& I spent the morning in looking over my lecture,* & taking up the stitches two years had dropt in my acquaintance with the young people. After dinner (we were freezing all this while) Mr Muzzy took me, in his sleigh to examine the Hall, which is the largest in Maine—frescoed & named after an old Indian tribe—Norombega—[7] I am sorry I forgot to ask how many it would hold—but it seemed once & a half as long as Faneuil Hall—but narrower—& with narrower galleries. I got the desk right & then went home. Mr Muzzy was nearly an hour, getting the feeling back into his fingers though the distance was quite short. I said nothing, but knew very well, I had reason to be thankful for double flannels, & to wish the evening well over. . . . I was wrapped & rewrapped & finally put under a buffalo—& reached the Hall comfortably—but I could not long remain so. It would have been impossible to heat that Hall for such a night in less than two days & they had taken four hours. It was the largest audience out this winter—some rowdies went down from the gallery, as soon as they decided it would not do to hiss me, & left a door open. I never suffered so much from cold feet—in my life, as in the hour which followed. The speaking seemed like a kind of night mare. Fortunately I forgot Mr Godfrey[8] was present, if I had remembered it I should have done worse. He is a rich lawyer, to whom I had letters last summer, & has a fine place—three miles out of town. He thought it too cold to ride so he & his wife & wife's sister—walked in & back! As his remarks were all I heard about the lecture, I will give them to you. He said my elocution was the finest he ever heard from man or woman—& that though I did not seem to raise my voice above a conversational tone, he had no doubt the remotest person heard. This may be true, I hope it was, but it was the largest Hall I ever spoke in & every word was a pain to utter—so I felt entirely used up. Many persons came up to thank me—& I tried to be civil—was paid, bundled up, & carried home, where Mr Muzzy laid me on a sofa & I did not speak for half an hour, when "Mrs" Muzzy, "careful soul," brought me some hot cocoa—& with words of warm sympathy from Mr Muzzy, I went to bed.

While Dall's brother-in-law was near death in Springfield, Caroline was scheduled to deliver at the Meionaon in Boston the first of her series of three lec-

---

*Dall was lecturing on "The Power & Dignity of Woman" (Register of Public Addresses, Dall Papers, Bryn Mawr).

tures on the topic "Two Phases of Womanhood"; the first was entitled "Mad. de Chevreuse, or the Political Intriguer." Marie de Rohan Montbazon, Duchesse de Chevreuse (1600–1679), was a major player in the plots and intrigues of seventeenth-century France.

BOSTON. MASS.

MONDAY. FEB. 1. 1857 [*actually* 1858].

After many days passed without leisure or calmness to write I resume my Journal at this point to try to trace, the outline of the last week. It seems hardly possible to do it with interest.

On this day George[9] came to me—saying that the news from Mr. Childe[10] was a little better—still he thought I ought to give up my lecture, which of course, I felt entirely unable to do. It was hard enough to speak under the pressure of such anxiety—but to know that I did it, with my brother's disapprobation was harder still. I told him that if worse news came in the course—of the day, I did not want him to let me know. I never was so nervous & ill, as today— I could not write plain, even, & I was unfortunately left alone all day. I had expected Miss Payson[11] in the morning and Mrs Severance to dinner— Kate did not come till the middle of the afternoon, & Mrs Severance until tea-time. I was excited when I went down— I had an audience of about two hundred—smaller than I had reason to expect. Father & George were both there. The Hall was cold & not well lighted, I thought. I was told I read the lecture well, but I know nothing about it— Had I been stopped at any point & asked where I was, I could not have told. Near the end occurred a point at which I was obliged to extemporise. By some blind instinct, I found it out—& spoke I think with more animation than while I read. After all was over—father—Mrs J. A. Andrew[12]— Mr & Mrs Whipple[13] & others came to the dressing room. I took more than enough to pay the expenses. Mr Whipple said "You got through it nobly, the discrimination was very fine—"—father seemed happy & attentive. As I came out—I saw James F Clarke,[14] and he said—"That Episode near the close was better." I could not help smiling at the qualified interest! Two gentlemen, lawyers, who had left before the close of the lecture, stopt & apologized to the Doorkeeper—& just as I was leaving an engraved card was handed me

Wm. de Rohan[15]—

And underneath was written in pencil, a descendant of Marie de Chevreuse.

The incident was so interesting as to keep me from sinking utterly.

On February 12, 1858, Dall and Thomas Wentworth Higginson appeared in the hall of the Massachusetts House of Representatives before the Committee on the Qualification of Voters in order to plead for the right of suffrage for women.

BOSTON MASS.

FRIDAY. FEB. 12. 1858.

Went down this morning at ½ past 9, but the pleading did not begin till 10 AM—all the Committee loitering in.* Mr Higginson was there in good time & the Hall was well filled. I spoke first—was listened to with great attention & repeatedly questioned, which I considered a good sign. After the speaking— most of the Committee desired to be introduced—and had something complimentary to say. Mr. Earle, of Worcester,[16] asked me, to come & visit his family. Mr. Chase of Salem,[17] said "Is thy father Mark Healey?" & when I answered that he was, he replied by saying that he had known him, many years, and some complimentary words about his daughter. A Mr Foster of Monson,[18] a showy man—with a good deal of self-esteem, desired to be introduced, and said— "I do not consider myself converted Mrs Dall, but I have been very happy to hear your speech, & should like to hear you again—" & then some compliments. I said "we ought to be fighting on the same side, for I believe we have the same blood in our veins—" He said "I am descended from Miles Standish?"[19] somewhat enquiringly—"so am I—" I answered "& from John Rogers too!" Then Mr Usher,[20] the Chairman had a good deal to say— He had not felt the least interest in the matter when the hearing was granted, but felt himself now—really enlisted. He is chairman of the Lecture Committee at Medford—& asked me, if I would lecture there next week. Though perfectly worn out & very unfit to consent, I yielded a reluctant yes— for I thought it, my duty to follow up the favorable impression I had made upon him.

Coming out of the Hall, a Spiritual medium desired to be introduced to

---

*The *Boston Daily Advertiser* (February 13, 1858) and the *Liberator* (February 19, 1858, p. 30) reported on the occasion, and the latter paper later (March 5, 1858, p. 40) printed Dall's speech in full. In it she asked rhetorically, "Why should I stand here, and plead for a right conferred upon me by God, at my birth?" In addition to claiming the franchise for women, she demanded for them "the human right to choose our own vocation"; she observed that there should be "no taxation without representation—a maxim of which it seems impertinent to remind you, so many years after the Declaration of Independence"; she argued for the right of women to sit on juries; and she spoke of "the need which <u>women</u> have, of a noble and sustaining occupation of mind and heart, such as a practical devotion to the interests of their country would afford."

me, & wished me to call on her, saying that she was <u>impressed</u> to offer me a communication!

On the whole, we made a very fine impression on the Committee—better I am sure than ever before— I was much exhausted, & lay down for the rest of the day.

The Transcript, had a very weak & unworthy notice of our proceedings—forestalling judgment—in a very unhandsome way.[21]

Mr Sennott says members told him that I put the <u>Extinguisher</u> on the Rev. T. W. H—completely! This may be understood I suppose in more ways than one![22]

Three days later Dall delivered at the Meionaon the final lecture of her series on the general topic "Two Phases of Womanhood," entitled "Woman's Claims."

BOSTON MASS.

MONDAY. FEB. 15. 1858. . . .

Two things troubled me tonight, the gas was not turned on when the hour arrived for the lecture—& I was obliged to send some one to see to it—and a terrible noise in the cellar—which seemed to be made on purpose, disturbed the first five or ten minutes. I stopt & asked some gentleman to attend to it—

With these two exceptions & the great one that the gatherings in my two ears & the three headed carbuncle on the back on my neck, made every muscular movement painful, the lecture was what I call a perfect success. I had a good audience in numbers, when my expectations are considered & the best as to quality— It included the Sewalls,[23] Dr & Mrs Howe,[24] & Theodore Parker—Mr & Mrs Bartol & many others of like distinction. I began with giving Mr Scherb's notice & went on, "May I not be permitted before an audience, hardly larger than I might gather in a drawing room, to thank the kind friend, who has twice decorated my desk with flowers, beautiful symbols of the resurrection & the life, they have soothed & sustained me, as nothing else could." This little speech, I write down as nearly as I can remember, because it pleased my father, & it is so seldom alas! that I do anything to please him.

I then paid a little tribute to Margaret Fuller & Mary Patten, to the first—as the only woman having the intellectual right to urge Woman's Claim upon the people of Boston & to Mary Patton as having the practical right—[25] This was extemporaneous—& I carried my audience—I went on—then, to my Mss

—making only two or three short episodes—on the fact that no woman had ever been judged by her peers,—on the <u>value</u> of the right of suffrage—& on the antiquity of the right as exercised by women—reading from some old chronicles by the way. I never saw a more thoroughly interested audience, & when I closed they broke into gentle, & continuous applause. As I passed down carrying my beautiful bouquet, Mr Kuhn, Mr Fisher Mr Whipple, Miss Littlehale Dr Channing,[26] pressed forward to congratulate me, & I saw my father's eyes glisten with proud tears. But best of all I loved the praises of grey-haired men, & of the Sewalls who had brought me as I found all my flowers. How precious they seemed now! Mrs Severance turned & kissed me—noble woman that she is. "I am proud of you" was all she said. My old teacher Joseph Hale Abbot[27]—looking sick & weak had been to the last two lectures. He thanked me for the pleasure they had given adding,—"I could not but feel some pride in remembering, that a great many years ago I had something to do with forming that style!" The "great many years ago"—was thrown in with a sort of diffidence that made my tears start.... I came home separated my flowers, and counted my gains, when all expenses are paid—I shall have about five dollars left! No matter—if any good seed has been sown, or real pleasure given—& of the latter I feel quite sure.— It was eleven when I went to bed & two before I was asleep.

BOSTON MASS.

SUNDAY. MAR. 14. 1858.

...An accident affected me painfully yesterday. Sadie broke my Naomi pitcher—[28] I could not help crying bitterly and she cried with me for she knew I prize it as ___'s* gift—and that I am superstitious about the destruction of any of the frail memorials of that happy time. Her mind however, could not keep pace with mine. ____ had it & it was broken, & with the playful assurance of one who is loved, I took it away—& said I would mend it for he did not deserve it. I can see his smile, the place he stood etc—& the broken pieces—this minute. When I afterward restored it whole he refused to keep it—and it became very dear I was going to say to us both—but I had better say to me. It was associated with one of the most precious [illegible word] I ever [illegible word] It makes my heart ache bitterly—to recall these things [illegible words].[29]

*John Patton's.

FRIDAY MAR. 26. 1858.

... I see as I look up the page that I did not record that on Monday—as I came in town I met Mrs Holman[30] who told me that the Medford ladies had put off the lectures till Oct. and advised me to leave out the incident about the Duchess de Chevreuse on horseback—& asked if I had ever said in public that I once came very near losing my own virtue—& that was the reason I felt a deep sympathy for fallen women!!! Good God, give me patience—if women will stupidly choose to see the vulgar side whenever it is possible am I to blame—? Well might E. E. Hale[31] tell me, that I could not imagine how low the average human intellect was,—it is true I did not think of a swine's brain—fed on garbage—

No—I will not leave out these things—I will dwell on them—draw attention to them & have them understood hereafter—but when I write new lectures—I will remember, that angels have not yet descended. Mrs Champney[32] wants me to come to Woburn, was here this afternoon.

Mr. Sewall[33] told me tonight that the Committee on the Right of Suffrage have reported more favorably than ever before—but his account did not satisfy me, & I must go to see Mr Usher[34] as soon as I am able— Oh weary weary heart & head! Is there no end to this aching but the grave?

BOSTON SUNDAY APRIL 11. 1858.

I should be a little ashamed to tell any one how I have spent this week—Cleaning house, & oh so busy & so weary—! You have no right to work so! said my German girl the other night, & I believe it, yet why should I rest—? For what delight, what pleasant thought is reserved for my quiet hour? None alas! nothing remains for me—but a deep unsatisfied yearning the only fruit of a strange mystical experience. There have been two breaks in the strange monotony of the week. Every night, weary as I might be, I went down to mother's, for George[35] was in an unsettled & unhappy state. Wednesday night, I felt that I must go to hear Mr Emerson,* yet was so weary that I hardly dared. I took a cup of coffee & went. I never enjoyed an hour so much it was <u>full</u>, full to the brim of thought.

So grand a subject—! Self-possession in <u>his</u> sense! Coming out—I said

---

*Emerson was lecturing at Freeman Place Chapel on "Self-Possession" (*Transcript*, March 17, 1858, p. 3).

"Mr Emerson, you must let me thank if not praise—you"— "Thank you Mrs Dall" he answered—"and I suppose I am obliged to you also, for the argument you delivered at the State House, the other day— I read it & took heed to it— you have a great cause & a sure one!" . . .

TUESDAY APRIL 27. 1858.
Went down to finish my shopping—in a storm of sleet. As Mr James Dall[36] is so low, I have decided to make no change in my dress this year. Indeed why should I ever? There is not a person living who takes the slightest interest in my dress—and my plain black is neat & lady like, and saves, a world of speculation & thought.

Hearing a lecture on women's rights by George William Curtis, Dall felt less like a freak or a pariah herself: the women's rights cause seemed respectable, her vocation endowed with dignity.

BOSTON WEDNESDAY.
MAY 5. 1858. . . .
Mr Curtis's lecture* was as fine as any thing, I ever heard. Everybody who had a true interest was enthusiastic and I could not refrain from going down to thank him. . . . I lay awake this night—but not to weep—for in my eyes, my vocation had a suitable dignity, and my heart's necessities might for a little be put aside. For a very little alas! Why was I made so weak—for made I was, education has not fostered but repressed the need.

Dall and her reform companions were traveling to New York to attend anti-slavery gatherings associated with the "Anniversary" meetings of reform groups. Additionally, Dall herself had been invited by Lucy Stone, now living in the New York area, to speak at a women's rights convention there on May 14 and 15. The convention was to pay her expenses.[37]

---

*George William Curtis (1824–1892), who had lived at Brook Farm in the 1840s and was greatly influenced by Emerson, was a highly regarded writer, editor, and orator. In 1853 he became associate editor of *Putnam's Monthly Magazine* and began writing the popular "Editor's Easy Chair" column for *Harper's New Monthly*. He later became a leading Republican *(DAB)*. On this occasion, Curtis delivered at the Lowell Institute what the *Liberator* of May 14, 1858 (page 79) called "a most eloquent and radical lecture on Woman's Rights."

BOSTON & NEW YORK.

MONDAY MAY. 10. 1858.

Went on with Garrison, May, Wright, Jackson—Nell & Remond to New York.[38] Mrs Chase of Salem[39] joined at Worcester. . . . I was much fatigued on reaching New York—, delivered first a parcel to Mrs Severance who was not at home, and then drove to the place where the Committee had written me I could find board. A more dirty, disorderly place I never saw—[40] I was obliged to go to the tea-table without going to my room—& though I reached the house at about half past five it was nearly nine before I was shown to the dirtiest apartment I ever attempted to occupy. Dust an inch thick on everything—no curtains—washstand & crockery filthy—bed alive the moment I laid down on it. Alone & in New York what could I have done had I been well? As it was—agitation & fatigue brought on a sharp attack of angina pectoris, severer than any I have had for four years. As I felt the grasp of the demon tightening—I knocked on the walls—& finding there was no bell—crawled into the entry & cried for help— My already half suffocated voice—raised no one— I got to the Dr's office, but the gas was out—& I returned to endure alone till death or morning released me— I was alarmed—more than ever— I kept my light burning to keep off the vermin—& to put on the wet bandages—the only medicine within my reach. As the paroxysm subsided & I felt chiefly weakness & nervous dread, I found that the head of my bed was placed against a door, on the other side of which was a person dying in consumption—the coughing, raising, turning, & quick breathing—all seemed to wear on my own organism.

NEW YORK.

TUESDAY. MAY 11. 1858.

At 6 this morning I arose & without taking a mouthful at this disgusting lodging place—I walked up to Aunt Louisa's.[41] Fortunately, it did not rain though it had stormed all night—& having taken no medicine, I had more strength than I could have thought possible— I got up with the intention of taking the boat this PM for Boston, but I thought I must see Aunt Louisa & Mrs Felt[42] first. I found Aunt Louisa just going to breakfast in her elegant house, & could not help smiling as I contrasted it with the place in which I had passed the night. Some of her coffee did me temporary good & then I went after two hours rest to call Maria[43] from the neat little house in 24th St—where she is going to housekeeping. She went with me to the Harlem cars, & in a pouring storm, I soon reached Mrs Felt's. Thank God for this interview—the curtain

was lifted between us. She told me that the evening Mr Dall spent with her—
he was very wild & that Aunt Louisa remarked it at her own house.

It was not all in my imagination then—

After lunch I rode back to see the Committee & excuse myself from any attempt to speak. No one was reasonable, but Wendell Phillips who said decidedly that I ought not to remain. All the rest pleaded—that just once couldn't
hurt me. Even Carrie Severance, who knew what open wounds what bitter
pain I had borne all winter without shrinking— Well!...

TUESDAY. JUNE 22. 1858

My thirty sixth birthday—as young as weak as childish in heart as when I was
sixteen, and yet how disappointed! A little wilfulness when I was too young to
understand myself or others—set my whole life awry. It is too late to save myself—but will my children learn the lesson from me, I wonder or must they
learn it through suffering also? They too will remain young for many years—
& feel old. God help them— I took no birthday license except to omit the
Dante I generally read....

*Dall was vacationing in western Massachusetts, where John Patton joined her
for some days.*

W. WHATELY MASS
THURSDAY. JULY 8. 1858.

Tired with yesterday's pleasure busy all the morning—weeding all the egotism out of my new lectures. There is more egotism in the weeding out than
the putting in—but when I begin to look with other people's eyes it is aston-
ishing how much I find. If I were to write them over fifty times, it would be all
the same. Worked two hours at my embroidery, and then went up to take tea
with Mary Hedge.[44] Had peas stewed in cream, and some fresh cherries. Then
we went out beyond the quince bushes & watched the haying. It was a lovely
night, the men were in the valley below, and all the labor was clothed in beauty.

SOUTH DEERFIELD MASS.
MONDAY. JULY 26. 1858....

...John lay down, while I read to him my last lecture, and although I was tired
to death, I found it hard work to drive him home. *No wonder, when he lay lis-

---

*At this point, and for the remainder of the entry, the handwriting changes to John Patton's.

tening to my lectures! At last he went off to "Bloody-Brook House", and I was very glad to get to sleep. He was very dull and stupid during the day; perhaps he was overcome by the brilliant conversation of Miss Rowe,[45] Mary Hedge and myself. He listened so tenderly to the words of one of the party as to suggest the idea of a probable softening of the brain. I hope it is not the case.

Back home, Dall contemplated, on her wedding anniversary, what the "error" was that had led her into an unsuitable marriage.

BOSTON MASS.

FRIDAY. SEPT 24. 1858.

Just fourteen years ago, I took the misstep which has been at the bottom of much sorrow—took it in good faith, meaning to do right, loving very tenderly him I married and earnest to serve God & man— I have often wondered where the error began— I think it must have been in the lack of humility. May God spare my Sadie, the life I have led; and surely if any painful experience I have had, makes me a fitter guardian—I ought not to mourn as one without hope— but God and Father who knowest all, may there not yet come an hour—when I shall be no longer alone—if earth is lost—may not Heaven be saved?

I went down to make arrangements for my Hall & tickets. Wiser than I was last year, I got Mr Hovey[46] to go to the Mercantile Library Rooms with me, and received more attention in consequence. Mr Butts[47] to whom I went about my tickets was very kind, and the auspices seem favorable. The rain hurried me home....

BOSTON MASS

SUNDAY. OCT. 24. 1858.

Had a very sad morning. Willie was moved to tell me of many things, that had been said at Lynn, about my extravagance! the folly of my trying to earn money —& my lecturing. Among other things Fannie[48] told him that Mr Winkley[49] who defended my course more than any one else, had said that he should not like it, if I were his wife or sister. It led to a full explanation with Willie, which I would gladly have put off for years longer. I told him that only last week I asked my father to pay my tax-bill that he expressed unwillingness—until I told him that in November, I should lecture, and that then, I should have some money probably and that if so, I would pay him immediately, then he put it aside and said he would attend to it, when he attended to his own. When I first began to lecture I hoped to get a little money to buy books, to help myself in the path I long ago laid out. Not one cent has yet gone for that purpose— I cannot show a luxury nor a comfort bought with my own earnings. All has gone for necessaries. Perhaps it will always be so, I do not expect to make $50 the amount of my tax-bill, from my next week's lectures—but I shall make a little, & instead of buying a book—I shall pay it all to my father & shall feel that I am out of his debt—[50] At Georgetown, I gave <u>him</u> all— It is not well to write of these things, but I must now & then— . . .

BOSTON MASS.

MONDAY. OCT. 25. 1858.

This morning Mrs Tolman[51] called to get tickets for tomorrow evening. She said in expressing an earnest hope that my lectures would succeed, that a gentleman had lately said to her, that he wondered [if] Mr Healey was not ashamed to permit so gifted a daughter to languish in <u>obscurity</u> while he and his other children lived in so much style, "but," said she, "I defended your father by telling him that you were altogether too independent a spirit to receive any assistance." "Where M'Gregor sits is the head of the table,"[52] flashed through my mind, but I saw that she wished to know the truth—& self respect required me to say, "You were mistaken in my character, there is nothing in me, which under the pressure of ill-health, would forbid me to receive assistance from my own father—" She looked astonished & said "Let me be frank, so long as we have touched the subject. Before Marian went to Europe, she came to see me—my mother was staying with me. We did not speak of you, but she forced the subject upon us— She said you had no need to lecture that your father was willing to support you, that all their accounts were as open to you as to them, and that you could get what you pleased at any of the stores."

I was so appalled at this tremendous falsehood that I hardly knew how to answer—coming as it did, on top of what Willie had brought up from Lynn— I however rallied and told the simple truth—how my mother had given me wearing apparel, & shoes and that even that I always felt it painful to accept, in such a spirit was it given— I stated the facts in regard to the tax bill & the wine—the latter, the Dr ordered a year ago—and supposed me to be taking daily, but I could not buy it, & though my father knew of it—he did not provide it. It was the first time I ever spoke to a stranger on the subject & I said as little as possible. Mrs T. said that M. gave as her excuse for speaking on the subject that they had had a letter from New York concerning my affairs—which had very much pained them. I wonder who from?

After Mrs T. had gone—I felt much distressed. I have known for the past 4 yrs that I was living under a cloud of inconsistencies, but I did not suppose it quite so thick. I determined now to know how far this misunderstanding, which steals the bread from my table, prevailed, & after a good deal of thought, I went down to see the Rev. Mr. Winckley.

In a private conversation with him, I found that he shared it. He actually supposed that if I wanted any supply of any kind, I had only to get it—& send the bill to my father who would always pay it!! I put the facts into his possession & came home feeling more disgraced & saddened than ever in my life. If my friends have generally believed this, I don't see why I was not provided with a straitjacket long ago. Mr Winckley asked me, if my father should be willing to support me wholly, whether I would give up lecturing. I told him no—I had followed it long enough to know it was a power given of God, and that I could not possibly know how valuable it might become to me or to the world.

BOSTON MASS.

THURSDAY. NOV. 11. 1858.

Was at home sewing all the morning. Was obliged to go down town with my advertisements this PM. Whenever I lecture I engage my hall and porter and distribute my advertisements myself. Not because I have not many friends who would be glad to do it for me, but because I conceive it my duty to do what little I can to make all business thoroughfares comfortable for women. I am not likely to be treated with disrespect, their offices must have many female visitors and yet it is only at the office of the Daily Advertiser that I am treated exactly as I should be. I always go there first to get courage for my other visits. When I came home, I found Sally Holley & Miss Putnam[53] here— They had been waiting three hours. Miss Holley said that Sam May told her she must not miss my next lecture, that he had been "amazed" by my last. She said that he was very enthusiastic and said I was "honored" by my audience, for so many distinguished people were rarely seen together. I know this is true—& thank God for it. Would that my father and mother might take the comfort they could naturally find in it. . . .

On November 15, 1858, Dall delivered her third and final lecture in the series
"Woman's Claim to Education." The topic was described in an advertisement
as "Individuals whose lives modify Public Opinion, and Exhibit the Spirit
of the Age. Mary Wollstonecraft, Sidney Morgan, Anna Jamieson, Charlotte
Bronte, and Margaret Fuller."[54] *Dall's interest in this public appearance was*
checked by letters she had recently received from John Patton that were somehow
disturbing (they do not survive), including a "short cold note" that arrived a
week earlier.[55]

BOSTON. MASS.

MONDAY. NOV. 15. 1858.

A long call this morning from Olivia Dabney. I was glad of it for it helped to
break the day. Mrs Livingstone[56] and Aunt S. came in to enquire about a bad
headache, which seemed to threaten my utter defeat for the evening. Louisa
Simes[57] came in the middle of the afternoon, and expressed a little anxiety, for
a fine snow was falling which threatened to become rain & might interfere with
my audience. I half dressed & was waiting for Mrs Severance to complete my
toilette, when Mr S.[58] came in, and said that neither he nor Carrie could be
present tonight. Mrs Stanton[59] has returned no replies to the letters or
telegraphs, and it is decided that Mrs Severance is to lecture tomorrow night—
and she needs all the time for rest & preparation.[60]

None of these things troubled me. A fortnight ago they would have added
greatly to the burden of the night—but I had missed a sympathy dearer than
theirs. I felt utterly alone at the best, and found it difficult to feel even a proper
care for the result. The reception of this night's lecture was almost an ovation.
My desk was crowned by the most beautiful flowers on either side. I spoke an
hour & a half. My unhappiness made me reckless—and so imparted a greater
freedom to my delivery, which was perhaps an advantage. At all events, I had
a splendid audience who did not move—during the whole time. They said I
had never given so good a lecture, nor delivered one so well—Louise[61]—Mr
Garrison—Arthur Fuller[62] with his eyes full of tears, Mr Dudley[63] and others
came to congratulate me—but I only knew that the long strife was over—that
my heart might bleed now in peace, and I thanked God for the release. Sadie
& Willie had taken tea with Aunt S. and gone to [the] lecture with her. Ann
the servant also went—& the children came home before me with her. When
I got home, I found them in high glee over the "splendid success" which Willie

declared I had had. Sadie said that a strange gentleman took her on his knee in the cars, and his wife kissed her, and told her to kiss her mother for <u>her</u> and tell her that she <u>loved her dearly</u>, and "mother" added Willie, "the car was all in a buzz with "splendid lecture" "great abilities" "noble woman.""

Dear children! may this be all that they will ever know of what it costs to give such a lecture! Father was there and came to the dressing-room, greatly distressed at the length of the time. I could not even be glad at his presence for my heart was in Montreal.[64] . . .

BOSTON MASS.

FRIDAY. NOV. 19. 1858. . . .

Last evening Mrs Severance showed me a note from Elizabeth Peabody— from which I took the following extract. I saved it as her first testimony to my lecturing four years ago, was lost—in some mysterious way & I never even read it.

"Mrs Dall's last lecture was the best thing she ever did. Every body says so, I would not have missed it on any account, weary as I was. Taking off the first paragraph & a few at the close it was quite perfect. Nothing so exquisite has ever been said about Margaret Fuller."

This is a high compliment & a sincere one. I can't think how she dared write it to Mrs Severance. The "first paragraph—" was the introductory retrospect and did not belong to the lecture.

WOBURN & BOSTON—

SATURDAY. NOV. 27. 1858.

. . . Louise Hall told me yesterday, with an exultation which showed she thought it a great thing, that Mr Clarke[65] had spoken very highly of my lecture, thought it quite equal to any of the Mercantile Library lectures. I suppose I should be thought rather mulish, if it were known how this remark took the life out of the pleasant words he said to me on Sunday. As if I had no higher aim than that! What! some one will say, don't they have the best lectures in the country? Yes—but—there are better lectures than that.

BOSTON. MASS.

TUESDAY NOV. 30. 1858

. . . Had a pleasant interview with Mr Browne,[66] and a talk with him about Margaret Fuller. He said some one said of her that she was an inspired Bac-

*Elizabeth Palmer Peabody, late 1850s. "I love to hear her talk—to see her smile . . .
So deep learning—so youthful joyousness so great experience & perfect simplicity
I never saw united in one character." (Courtesy of Concord Free Public Library)*

cante and that it was in that style that she sought influence—therefore Emerson retired and so forth.

Browne so out Emersons, Emerson, that I could not ask him if he meant her influence was sexual—yet surely that is the English of that phrase? It is unjust—it is unworthy—certainly her vigor lay partly in the hot current of her blood—but so does that of all women to a degree seldom understood by men —& well it is so—for that remark shows it would be understood to be misunderstood.

I shall enquire about this. . . .

Dall delivered her series of three lectures on "Woman's Claims to Education" in Worcester. The first, given on February 15, 1859, was entitled "The Ideal Standard of Female Education, depressed by Public opinion, but developed by the Spirit of the Age. Female Education in Egypt and Algiers."[67]

BOSTON & WORCESTER MASS.

TUESDAY FEB 15. 1859.

Was sorry to find it snowing hard when I got up. Went over to market and bade 834[*] good bye. Then prepared my valise & made the skirt to Sadie's dress. At ½ past one, I went down to the cars, and at the Worcester depot was received by Sallie Holley & Mrs Firth[68] a most lovely looking woman. We drove to Mrs W. Brown's[69] who made me as happy and comfortable as heart could desire. Here I met Mr & Mrs Theo. Brown[70] & Sallie Holley at tea, and also had a pleasant call from Mr Haven—[71] Nothing could be sweeter and more cordial than my reception. I liked every body. The lecture was well received. Mr Higginson[72] & Dr Martin[73] went home with me, and Higginson seemed a little annoyed that I had one thing in my lecture that he did not know. He said I had made a monopoly of it—that is of Alice Holliday's Egyptian service.[74]

Sallie told me confidentially, that he was annoyed—that the lectures could be got up without him, and was surprised at the aristocratic character of the audience I drew out. Every body wanted to know what had interested Mr Haven in the lectures so much. It seems he had really done a great deal for me, and interested others largely.

WORCESTER & DORCHESTER MASS. WEDNESDAY FEB 16 '59

I rose in time to breakfast at 8—with my kind & pleasant friends. Mr Haven made me a call & confessed that he liked the lecture better than he expected. He said that his friends the Misses Burnside[75] wholly liked the literary character of the lecture and thought the rest "novel." Sallie[76] came soon, and we went to the dépôt together, Mr Wm. Brown, kindly carrying my valise. I had a quiet ride down—encountering only Katie Wild's aunt Mrs Park. I went from the Boston dépôt to the Meeting House Hill Omnibus and got to Eliza

*That is, William and Sarah Dall, at 834 Washington Street.

Clapp's* in time for dinner. We talked about all sorts of things till tea-time when I went to Mrs Hall's[77] where I met Miss Bithia Hincks—and a Mr Coffin[78] at tea. The walking was so very bad, that I was not surprised to find my audience smaller than it was last week—[79] As soon as I had concluded, however, I found dear Mrs Hall and Miss Clapp were not happy in the lecture.

Dall was distressed to find that the Dorchester friends who were responsible for bringing her there to speak were shocked by her last lecture. Sarah Hall was appalled by its frankness about prostitution, and Eliza Clapp objected to its negative depiction of men and found it "unwomanly."

DORCHESTER & BOSTON—
THURSDAY. FEB. 17. 1859.

I rose early and after breakfast, Mrs Hall came in, and perfect frankness on my part, led to the same on theirs, and we had a talk of simple truthfulness, which I took very calmly at the time, but which has made me ill, by its nervous reaction. Dear Mrs Hall, no wonder that she cannot understand the need of such a lecture as that on public opinion—nor that Eliza Clapp—should believe in the necessity of stating always the affirmative side. I rode into town with Mr Hall, and we had a long serious talk, with him, and I think he fully appreciated all I had said after it. He knew, he said, my facts were facts, the only question was, as to the expediency of <u>my</u> stating them. He especially thanked me, he said for the testimony which I bore in the last lecture to the unwritten history of Harvard (i.e. its licentiousness) he told me that he himself had talked with Dr Walker[80] about it, and that Dr W. acknowledged it, but said it was impossible to help it— "How can I expect purity of young men," he said, "when I do not find it in their fathers?" As we approached the house I live in, I pointed to the four houses opposite my door. "There" said I "Mr Hall are four houses of ill fame—for four years I have lived opposite to them—have seen <u>young</u> girls enter them to their death—and the "solid men" of Boston visiting them openly by daylight—do you wonder that I find strength to speak?"

He seemed greatly shocked, but answered with much emotion, "Indeed I do not—but may God give you strength to succeed." "If I do not," I answered "it will be because I am not worthy." and my eyes filled and overran— Oh how

---

*In Dorchester, where she was to lecture this night.

I wish I were as pure as Uriel, when I see what work there is before me—work which no one else seems to perceive—far less undertake. And if I should fail—because I am not good enough—! Oh Father—help me and make me worthy of the duty!...

I went out to try and throw off the nervous pain resulting from my morning's talk, but I was not strong enough— I was made so ill by it that I had to lie down directly. A precious letter of encouragement from Montreal.*...

Despite the painful and disfiguring carbuncles that Dall was enduring, she traveled to Worcester to deliver the second lecture in her "Woman's Claims to Education" series. It was entitled "Public opinion, as it is derived from the study of the classics and history, general literature, customs, and newspapers."[81]

BOSTON. MONDAY.

FEB. 21. 1859.

Rose with such a very distorted face—that it seemed impossible to lecture—had Miss Daly[82] here too, for more than an hour trying to get some leeches to apply but they would not. In despair, I kept up the hot water, while Aunt Sarah packed my valise.... At ½ past one I was on my way to Worcester... In the evening, we went to a new and larger Hall, called the Warren. I had a good audience. The cream of Worcester aristocracy I was told. I gave the lecture, on Public opinion Prefaced by an apology—for the discourtesy of appearing with my swelled face, explaining that I would have refrained had it been possible to notify them.

I believe the lecture may be considered a very complete success. Mr Pickering Dodge,[83] Lucy Chase[84]—& Mr Haven congratulated me. Dr Martin said it was the best thing he ever heard from a woman, & Antoinette Brown, who had apparently remained to hear it echoed the cry. Some of the women kissed me in spite of my cheek! I got home as soon as possible, but very faint & exhausted. Had leeches on and turned into bed.

While still in Worcester, Dall took advantage of the opportunity to hear another lecturer who found in Worcester an appreciative audience, Henry David Thoreau.

*That is, from John Patton.

BOSTON TUESDAY.

FEB. 22ND 1859....

Had calls from Lucy Chase who came to take me to ride—Mrs Gordon & some others. At ½ past 7 went to Mr Harry Blake's to hear Thoreau—read a paper on "Autumnal tints"[85] It was as dear Miss Putnam[86] said, a very charming report, but I did not carry away a very high idea of Thoreau himself....

Dall went again to Dorchester to deliver the third lecture of her series "Woman's Claim to Education."

DORCHESTER MASS.

WEDNESDAY. FEB. 23D. 1859.

... I went directly from the cars to the omnibus and reached the Hinckses[87] at about one P.M. I left my valise and went up to Mrs Hall's[88] first, where I found her quite recovered from the effects of the last lecture, cordial and sweet as one could possibly be. She said she thought Eliza was altogether morbid to feel it as she did. I stopped at Mr Clapp's,[89] to see her for a moment. She looked ill, and I fancy this has made her so, though she did not own it. She was kind but the pained look had not passed away. I hoped the impression tonight might reward her in part for what she had undergone.

I dined sumptuously with my young friends and then took a book and kept quiet till the lecture hour. I got to the Hall before Mr May[90] had opened it, and had an excellent audience. It was more select I believe than any night, and so far as I can judge I gave general satisfaction. Eliza—did not speak to me, after it was over and that saddened me—but she brought me the purse before the lecture, which contained more than double what they had promised. I drew her to me & kissed her—telling her—that I was grieved that she who had done so much should not have entire and perfect satisfaction in the lecture—but said I, do not give me the grief of knowing that it has so chilled your enthusiasm—that you could not do as much at some future time for another.

She said it should not—but the assurance left me the heart ache.

Several grey haired persons were present who seemed to enjoy it. Dr Jarvis,[91] the old physician, enjoyed the lecture, and said he was sorry he had missed the other two. So was Mrs E. V. A. Smith[92] and Mrs Julia B. Quincy[93] and several others who came and spoke to me. The whole seemed quite a success. Mr Hall was enthusiastic in his quiet way, and said there certainly was not a word in this lecture which any one could object to.

I went home & to bed—not immediately to sleep for cramp.

Dall's lectures inflamed Elizabeth Peabody against her.

BOSTON MASS.

FRIDAY. FEB. 25. 1859.

Early I went up to Edwd Hale's to speak to him, about the article on Mad. de Chevreuse. Got a letter from Eliz. Peabody on the way—written after being fully magnetised by Miss Clapp's condition— It is the only letter written <u>against</u> myself that I ever destroyed, but it shall be burned.* It is absolutely mad—full of misstatements, and yet evidently written from a sense of duty. God was kind to me—I went right down to Dr Wesselhoeft's[94] where I found her, and had a long talk. I showed her her mistakes—how much trouble I had taken to ascertain the exact truth in regard to Antioch, &c— I found that Miss Clapp was so much disturbed that she kept her bed two days after the lecture, <u>said</u> she would not go to the last, and reproached E.P.P. with not having told her—saying

"You did not tell me there was anything <u>unwomanly?</u> in Mrs Dall's lectures!"

The account E. gave of her—relieved my pain about it, because it showed how very morbid she was.

One great suffering I had to bear—the knowledge that Mrs Severance had been careless or untrue.

---

*Dall did not destroy Peabody's excoriating letter dated February 21, 1859, which is in the Dall Papers, MHS, and is printed in Bruce A. Ronda, ed., *Letters of Elizabeth Palmer Peabody, American Renaissance Woman* (Middletown, Connecticut: Wesleyan University Press, 1984), pp. 295-298. Peabody was livid that Dall had, in one of her Dorchester lectures, attacked her brother-in-law Horace Mann for not allowing female students at Antioch College, where he was the president, to "read their parts." Peabody denied Dall's charge and fiercely defended Mann's position on the woman question. But further, she said that she was glad that Dall had separated herself from Mann, since "I thought the lecture in which you spoke of him in so bad taste that it would be an argument against woman's education." She objected to Dall's "want of womanly delicacy"; having heard that Dall's next course of lectures, on labor, would make "<u>painful statements</u>" (apparently about prostitution), she added, "I do not think I am squeamish—but I would not go to hear your lectures with a gentleman by my side.— . . . I would go to a Magdalene Refuge to <u>work in the reform of the inmates</u>—but I would not talk to men about prostitution—in a public assembly." Peabody felt constrained to say these things, she said, because she heard that Dall spoke of her as "an intimate friend and counsellor," and she was now acting in those capacities.

I begged her to converse with Miss Peabody, both before & after the delivery of the lectures, & ascertain if she had any objections to make to my statements about Horace Mann— Mrs S. assured me that E. expressed no disapprobation—& <u>could not</u> (these were the words) since she knew it to be true.

On the contrary, E.P.P. told me this morning—that she commissioned C.M.S.[95] to tell me that she wholly disapproved of it—& that one part of the statement was wholly untrue.

Ambitious people who love popularity like C.M.S. can never be straightforward. That is the great pity— God help me to trust to none but him. . . .

After working busily several hours, I went down to see Sallie Hollie, who of course <u>exploded</u> all Elizabeth's nonsense.

Perhaps I ought to keep two specimens of E's letter. She renews—that absurd charge of last winter—& says—"I do not think that in the whole range of classical literature, there is a single passage so indelicate as your broad allusion last winter to Mad. de Chevreuse's '<u>menses</u>.' "[96]

Good Heavens! how can I believe, that women judge women thus!

Such a charge against me, who may safely challenge the world to produce the first profane or vulgar word I ever spoke.

When I told her how the lectures were received in Worcester, she said— "Well—if Sam Haven liked them, it is certainly a point in your favor. He has a great regard for you—he is a scholar & a very fastidious man."

I received tonight a beautiful notice in the Worcester Spy of this very lecture, & was half shocked to hear my preaching had got into the Christian Inquirer.[97] I ought to have expected it but I did not.

Dall lectured again in Worcester on March 7 and remained there a few days with the Firth family.

WORCESTER MASS.
WEDNESDAY MAR 9. 1859.

I began this morning to work on Frank's[98] Autographs, and to train Mrs Firth's ivy, but was interrupted by a short call from Mr. Haven,[99] & then Lucy Chase called to take us to Mrs Foster's[100]—where after a lovely ride, we were cordially welcomed. The rain had coated all the trees which looked like branching gems. The grass sparkled like an asparagus bed in early morning.

The Fosters have a pleasant house among the hills, kept in the nicest order. It made me sad to see Alla the child—whose spine complaint seems to me fixed.[101]

Nothing could exceed the solemnity and depth of Abby's welcome for me— With heart & soul & mind & strength she blessed my coming. The party was unexpectedly large so large as to deprive us, of much of our anticipated— enjoyment. There was myself & Mrs Firth & May,[102] Lucy & Sarah Chase[103] —Anne Earle Southwick[104] and a Miss Clapp matron of the Worcester Water Cure,[105] and Miss Eleanor Buffum,[106] & Dr Rogers little girl[107]— I believe that was all—but there were too many strains of talking.

The morning was filled with sewing—Abby's preparations for dinner—& Stephen's scolding of Mrs Firth—for not being a different sort of Abolitionist.

We sat down to a very ample dinner—chicken pie & potatoes—preserves & cream—custards & punkin pie—nuts & apples; all good and well prepared — After dinner I read Mrs Foster—what I had said about the Brownings in my lecture at her request, and then Stephen began to attack the Bible, & I asserted its power & we got into a long tiresome argument which [made] my head ache & then it was time to go home. I was so exhausted that I had to lie down— Calls from Dr Hill—& Mr. Higginson & Mr & Mrs Harry Blake.[108]

In the evening I rallied to go to hear Mrs Macready recite the Mid Summer's Night's Dream.[109] With my memory of Mrs Kemble, it was too severe a trial— Not a particle of sense or feeling—not even the proper external training & Nature has done everything for her! She was handsome & well dressed voila tout. Theo Brown & I made fun mercilessly all the evening. I came home & took a warm bath & to bed.

BOSTON MASS—
MONDAY. MAR. 14. 1859.

. . . I see in glancing back that I have said nothing about two letters from Misses Clapp & Peabody,[110] that I received on Saturday night & which made me go to bed, sick at heart. They are on the old subject & simply demand that I should be no longer myself but somebody else. I wrote to Miss Clapp & Mr Hall,[111] yesterday in reply, but had not time to copy the letters into my notebook—nor indeed inclination for I am weary of hearing my own egotism discussed.[112] If they could live with me a few weeks, and see that I never get time to think of myself, except when attacked—or in writing a few lines of Journal once a day, how ashamed they would be.

When I look back over the last four years & remember their bitter griefs &

agonies, which I have never asked <u>one</u>—not even him who should be nearest to share, then I see how little I deserve this charge. I know what errors in my own past—laid the foundation for it, and I try to bear the penalty with meekness since I cannot <u>undo</u> the errors. I can only smile, when I think how many people might do far worse things, and no one dream of fault-finding!

Father! keep me meek—keep me willing—if these reproaches avail, send them thick as rain—but if not—and there is in thy universe, one soul that can comprehend me—and still love me—comprehend me, well enough to know—that I shall not forget thy law—though all the world should hold its peace,—then permit it to strengthen & console me. . . .

After nightfall came a second note from E.P.P. in which she says Miss Clapp does not wish to enter into controversy, and thinks I am not a person to <u>bear advice</u>—&c—but E.P. Peabody truly says—I have <u>borne so much</u> from her, that she feels bound to act as if I love the truth better than <u>myself</u>. She adds that I may be transfigured on the mount of my <u>self-love</u>—if I will only—conquer it!*

Will—<u>only</u>! No words would be of use between us two—if understanding had been possible, as Emerson says, then would not misunderstanding have come!

BOSTON MASS.
THURSDAY MAR. 17. 1859.

This morning when I had made Willie comfortable upon the couch—I went down town to do innumerable errands. Beside others—I went to see Dr Gannett, Mr Waterston, & Mr Winkley,[113] in reference to my plan, of getting <u>one</u> alcove of the City Library devoted to reports upon all matters relating to Societary Reform, Government—Reports &c—and organising it in such a manner—as should be available for all persons interested in Pauperism—Vice or Employment as a Social Question.

Mr. Waterston was cooler than I had hoped.

I came home & wrote out my idea and determined to apply to the Trustees. Willie was still quite sick, some beautiful letters from the Halls, denying Miss Peabody's imputation which I answered directly.[114]

---

*This letter justifying Peabody's recent frank and harsh attacks on Dall compared Dall's egotism with that of "great Margaret" Fuller, whose "<u>Me</u>," Peabody asserted, was "<u>mountainous</u>" (undated letter, located at end of correspondence for 1859, Dall Papers, MHS; printed in Ronda, *Letters of Elizabeth Palmer Peabody*, p. 302).

BOSTON. MASS.

THURSDAY. MAR. 24. 1859.

Willie quite ill, devoted myself to him. Carrie Severance came in, in the morning with a letter from Miss Anthony,[115] desiring me to speak in N. York in May. Under the new regulations of an <u>Anniversary</u>, celebration in place of a Convention, I am very glad to do it.

Mrs Severance looked sick. I read her the letters from the Halls,[116] but I dared not ask what <u>ailed</u> her. In the afternoon I went down to the Athenaeum, and met Mr Emerson, with whom I had a pleasanter talk than ever before in my life. I told him I wanted to say "Thank you" last night[117] but could not get near enough— "Ah!" said he, "did you honor us—then—"? After a few words about his own lecture, he said "I have been too far away, to hear any of your expositions this winter, but they were well worth it, no doubt, for Miss Peabody is a good judge & <u>she</u> was very enthusiastic, and she especially wished me to hear that in which you spoke of Margaret."

"I am accustomed" I answered "to have my thoughts <u>under</u>valued—but I dread far more, such praise as hers. Miss Peabody is too warm to be a valuable critic, & nothing but disappointment could follow on her representations."

"Perhaps you remember" he said "that fine saying of Mr Alcott about the ebb which follows on the <u>flow</u> of praise?"

"No," I replied "but I have always felt it," & then I told him how I had proceeded with my lectures, and how clear I had tried to keep of common humbug.

He looked really pleased— "That is architecture—" said he—"that is building on a basis, all <u>should</u> prosper so. I always like private courses especially for their independence."

A strange report of Miss Peabody after her late letters!

BOSTON WEDNESDAY APRIL 6. 1859.

...Miss Holley & Miss Putnam, came—in a very merry state. I had a letter from Mr Dall—the first for a long while. It was a letter of so private & peculiar a nature that I felt obliged to burn it immediately—but I wished much to keep it— The time <u>may</u> come, when it will be almost necessary to my justification. He says he never wishes to increase the number of his children—and should prefer to room with Willie when he returns. He begs me not to <u>reproach</u> him for this "monkish" determination which he says his Indian life has led him to form—and which he regards as safest and best for himself—<u>probably</u> for his health of body & brain. "Reproach" Oh God—what strange words people come to use in this life— I thank my husband for saving me—the mere chance—of repelling him—for children I would never give to one of whose mental soundness I am not sure.

And yet, when I look back and think what life might have been in the sunshine—the perfect fullness of life and love—it seems to be more than I can bear. Oh Father! is my thirsty heart never to be filled—!

My poor, <u>poor</u> children,—but this will not do. I wrote to John—from whom I got a sad skeptical letter that made my very heart ache. In the evening I left work and went with my friends to hear Mr Emerson. The subject was clubs[118]—many fine things were said but I could not keep my thoughts from wandering . . . .

At the invitation of Susan B. Anthony, Dall traveled to New York to speak at a women's rights meeting associated with the annual Anniversary meetings.

N.Y. <u>THURSDAY</u>. MAY 12. 1859.

<u>Woman's Rights Meeting.</u>

I shall try to write the account of this meeting, so far as I am concerned, truly & fully, for my children's sake. It will be difficult—for if one were to believe the three newspapers—Times, Tribune, & Herald—my appearance was not only a complete failure, but disagreeable to the audience, and I was unamiable in my deportment & expression.[119]

Hoping there would be some preparatory meeting, I went to Mozart Hall, about an hour before the time— No one came—even Miss Anthony was late. She took the chair when she came, as if she had a right to it, and no organization of the meeting was attempted—wholly wrong—that thing.

The Tribune called me Secretary, but I was not. I had promised to prepare some resolutions, bearing on the Sickles case[120]—which I did,—& had them in my hand. As there was evidently not the slightest preparation for this meeting by the officers, and as I felt heartily ashamed that there was a man present, I did what I could to save it. What success it had I may say without vanity was owing to the bias I gave it. Mrs Gay[121] was there—& made a pleasant little speech. My first words were an appeal to the women—to prepare for the anniversary properly— I spoke once or twice in reply to others— I made a speech

of 10 minutes on labor—and another of the same length—sustaining the resolutions I offered, which were finally passed. I liked several of the women—
whom I do not know— Howland of Worcester[122] took rather captious notice
of the resolutions— When the meeting adjourned—after putting me on the
Committee to memorialise the several States, a great many persons desired to
be introduced to me, but as I was so deaf[123] that every sound became confusion, I do not know who they were. One Philadelphia lady—a lady in every
sense of the word—came up & said—

"I must thank you for what you have said this afternoon, It has done me
good. It was so fresh and new, so brilliant— It has fed me— I can employ myself with your thoughts for the whole year"

This is what ought to be said to every woman who speaks, well & it comforted me—for I needed comfort. I was in great pain—half helpless from deafness—& however pleasantly I might impress my audience—I knew that I was
not doing—what with even tolerable health I might. As I turned from her I met
the eyes of Lucretia Mott[124] looking kindly at me. "I am glad to see thee so
earnest and eloquent" she said, "it does me good, now I feel myself worn out"
& so on— As I was very much exhausted & we had hardly two hours before
the evening session—I hurried away. Mrs Severance—Antoinette* and myself—went to the Smithsonian[125] & took supper—& changed our dresses.
Miss Anthony promised to come but did not, and on this promise, we relied
so far as to order her supper—& to trust to it for the evening arrangements.
The swelling in my ear, had increased so much during the day, that I was
obliged to resort to mechanical means to make it even partially safe to attempt
to speak. I bent a bit of watch-spring & inserted it in such a way as to secure
an orifice— The only objection to this was, that fearing that it would become
imbedded, I had to change its position now & then & the change was painful.

In such a condition—dear children you will see that there was great presumption in attempting to address a public—audience—but I had spoken very
successfully to my lecture audience under such circumstances, & did not re-
alise the difference. I did not willfully deceive myself or pain my friends.

At 7 o'clock finding Miss Anthony did not come, I insisted on going to the
Hall, where we were advertised to open at ½ past. People were already throng-
ing in. Mrs Rose[126] came at 25 min past 7—Susan Anthony at 25 min. of 8—

*Antoinette Brown Blackwell.

and we did not go upon the platform, until after that time. You who know my promptness will guess how much I suffered— No preparation was possible— Lucretia Mott did not appear,—the truth was, that coming late, she became entangled in the immense crowd—& could not reach the platform— I never saw a more confused & excited audience— Many hundred persons must have been standing, & were of course restless. So far as I could judge the 2000 persons for whom we received fees—were mostly desirous to hear, but in the gallery were noisy rioters either hired or malicious, who taking advantage of their memory of Mr Pearl Andrews[127] & H.C. Wright[128] last year, were disappointed by the propriety which reigned & proportionately indignant—

Miss Anthony insisted on my opening the meeting—. I was a stranger— never spoke in Mozart Hall—knew nothing of my audience—& I began to see & feel that no written address—least of all that which Miss Anthony's arrangements had forced upon me, would answer the purpose. I appealed to each of the three N.Y. women on the platform—asking them to precede me. They refused & too proud to beg, too honest to shirk—I went forward. The sentence with which—I introduced myself, I shall write down here—because while nothing is more silly than to make excuses to an audience, there are occasionally circumstances which justify a <u>statement</u>— In my eyes—those of this evening were such— I felt that there were friends near that platform who ought to be reminded why in such a condition I ventured upon it—& with the thought of death very near me, I said—.

"Gentlemen & Ladies, I come before you this evening—in a condition of bodily exhaustion, which would be without excuse—if it were not, that I wished to compensate my friends, for the disappointment I occasioned them last year,—and that I desired—once at least, in an invalid life, to bear witness <u>publicly</u> in this cause."

This I dare say may have been very silly—but I wished to say it.

Soon after I commenced, in fact before one sentence was uttered—I was interrupted by cries of "louder—louder"— I should have gone through my duty, in a dignified & proper manner but Miss Anthony came forward & explained—that I was speaking as loud as I could & the audience were requested to be quiet. &c &c—

This annoyed me, but the second time she spoke, I added—"If the audience is quiet—every person in this hall can hear me, If I raise my voice above its natural tone, you <u>will</u> not.—"

The applause which followed this, may have been ironical but I do not believe it. As I went on the disturbance continued, but I should have thrown aside my notes, & mastered even this turbulent crowd—I fully believe, if it had not been for Miss Anthony, who plucked at my sleeve, continually—saying— "Do stop the biography" That is too tame—they won't bear that—& so on— Lucretia Mott adding—"If thee would only speak as thee did this afternoon." These interruptions—which every speaker, knows the folly of—prevented me not only from getting possession of my audience, but from getting possession of myself—. I dared not lay down the Ms. but my children will believe me when I say, that I <u>was not</u> out of temper— Indeed bodily pain would have quelled anger had I felt it. At last Miss Anthony came & said you had better stop—I said I did not intend to give Margaret Fuller, but one page (of common paper) would finish what I had to say of Mary*—& I thought I had better give it— She objected & I stated to the audience that as she had decided that I could not be heard—I would retire—

I think this was bad policy, not so much for me—as for the Convention, for as the mob had their way with the first speaker—they grew more arrogant.

That I sat down before I finished was apparent—because I was giving the history of a life—but so did every other speaker if I except Mr Phillips. Mrs Mott spoke 8 minutes, Antoinette 20, Mrs Rose 18—[129] After I sat down, I gave my attention to the character of the crowd—the tone of the voices, &c. <u>not</u> to what was said.

The abominable folly of the women, in not providing police—in not being on the platform in season, I cannot forgive. The audience also, were in fault, it would have been easy to insist upon their rights, and it seems to me, any male friend present ought to have had sense enough to have called in an officer.

I heard no voices in that Hall better calculated to fill it than my own—the disturbance was uniform throughout not greater for me than another— Antoinette's speech—astonished me—by its power & breadth— I said while Mrs Rose was speaking that I should like to hear "my own voice beside hers, to know which could be heard the farthest"— Mrs Mott replied "You ought to be content with what you did this afternoon."

"You do not understand me" I replied— "I express no mortification only a desire for self knowledge."

---

*The subjects of Dall's talk were Margaret Fuller and Mary Wollstonecraft.

One thing mortified me much— There was constant talking on the platform— Women might be civil to each other.

I think Sallie Holley was right when she said Miss Anthony & I, should never understand each other.

In the Ante-room I found Wendell Phillips, who had not eaten—a mouthful—for 48 hours, and was as unfit as I to be there— I said "If you had come to the meeting this PM. you would have saved me from the folly of trying to be heard." for I had intended to get him to excuse me.— "My dear woman" said he—"You <u>were</u> heard—your voice was loud enough—but your audience were determined <u>not</u> to hear."

I went home with Mrs Davis & her son,[130] without any further conversation.

Back in Boston, Dall participated in a women's rights meeting organized by herself and Caroline Severance.

BOSTON MASS.
FRIDAY MAY 27. 1859.

Wrote & thought all the morning, but fearing something might be wrong at Mercantile Hall, went down there an hour & a half before the convention began.* Found the floor unswept & the door untended. Sent Nicholas for some flowers for the desk, made him sweep the floor, & then tended the door until Mr Nell[131] came, a part of the work I did not mean to do! Had a great deal of trouble from women who wished to invade the platform to speak of temperance, spiritualism, & the like. Was therefore quite worn out when I rose to speak. I introduced Mrs Severance who read a brief address—& a poem, sent in by Mrs Nowell.[132] Then Harriot K. Hunt made a pithy and sensible speech, wisely confining herself to about ten minutes. Then followed—Jas. F Clarke— then myself†—then Sargent, Ames, and Phillips.[133] We might have had more

---

*This women's rights meeting was being held in conjunction with the Anniversary celebrations in Boston. *The Liberator* (June 10, 1859, p. 92) gives an account of the day's activities, and a number of the speeches (including Dall's) were published in a pamphlet, *Report of the Woman's Rights Meeting at Mercantile Hall, May 27th, 1859* (Boston, 1859).

†Dall spoke on the "Progress of Woman" (Register of Public Addresses, Dall Papers, Bryn Mawr). *The Liberator* singled out her address as giving "evidence of elaborate and careful preparation" (September 30, 1859, p. 154).

good speakers but would not risk too much and we have had a meeting that we may be grateful for forever. It was such a complete success as we never looked for— We moved as Wendell said in "silver slippers."

The hall passages, lobbies &c—were thronged—at least 800 people went away, unable to get standing room. There was no noise no restlessness, in spite of the extreme heat. The audience seemed to stand on tiptoe & hold their breath. Mr Philips made the best speech he has made this week.

As Abby Folsom,[134] began to raise her voice after I had dismissed the audience, I went down into the crowd, & asked it to disperse. It yielded instantly. I stood quietly by the door, guiding the curious—& my hand was almost tearfully grasped by hundreds whom I never saw—thanking me for the pleasure of the occasion. Many blessed me audibly—women of wealth & position never in such a throng before—and all seemed excited beyond anything I ever saw. I seemed in a dream—came home & dressed for a party Mr Sargent gave us, where I had as nice a time as a worn out body could—but I was interrupted while dressing by two or three congratulatory calls—and three bunches of flowers—roses—violets & lilies of the valley. . . .

BOSTON SATURDAY
MAY 28. 1859.

More congratulatory calls. I was to have gone to Lynn this morning—since we have a committee meeting on Sunday, I am not willing to leave.

So went to Board meeting. Paid Mrs Nowell for her poem $3.00. Paid young reportees for labor $8.00—& cleared every thing completely with a residue of $16 for future expenses. Went to Anti Slavery Office & had a talk with Gen.—Tubman,* known on the Plantations as Moses—a most interesting person, who came from the Eastern Shore & has freed fifty slaves, since she became a fugitive going back into the slave states—eight times in ten years. I came home & tried to lie down but there was a great deal to do.

---

*Harriet Tubman (1820?–1913), fugitive slave and rescuer of slaves, was born into slavery in Maryland. In 1849 she escaped to Philadelphia and before the Civil War is believed to have made some nineteen trips into Maryland to escort slaves (estimates of the number range from sixty to three hundred) to freedom. For much of this time she lived in St. Catharine's, Ontario, then moved to a farm near Auburn, New York. During the war she served as a spy, scout, and nurse. After the war she began the Harriet Tubman Home for Indigent Aged Negroes. Illiterate herself, she promoted the establishment of freedmen's schools in the South and was a supporter of women's suffrage. After her long struggle for compensation for her wartime services, in 1897 Congress finally awarded her a pension of twenty dollars per month (*NAW*).

Was writing up a fresh lecture list having discovered several omissions in the old one, when the Whipples[135] came with flowers & congratulations.

I never saw anything so active as the sympathy we roused yesterday.

BOSTON. SUNDAY—

MAY 29. 1859.

Was gladdened by the sight of Sarah Clarke's[136] face at church. She congratulated me so warmly—said, had she known we were to have a meeting she would have come from Newport to attend. Margaret Foley[137] could not contain her delight. "Your day is coming" said she. "You outdid yourself and the music Hall will be thronged to hear you."

I have had a great deal of this personal compliment, but I do not care for it, the warm pressure of Mr Clarke's* hand when I turned round upon the platform—was worth more than the words of a nation—but God be praised I do care for the general glow of feeling there is about the meeting. It has acted like a great sponge—and cleared our books of that terrible New York "subtraction" . . .

In the next entry, written months later, Dall is vacationing in western Massachusetts.

CONWAY MASS—

TUESDAY. AUG 2. 1859.

I spent the whole morning—that is till 2 P.M in correcting, & making notes for, the first copy of my lectures, from which I intend to print. I did not mean to do this, but to seek rest, if I could get it till I returned to town, but I found that rest would not come—my mind was busy with the subject & I could not put it off. True rest I find only in the steady but not <u>hurried</u> pursuit of my vocation. Two things remain to be done, to write my preface, & a letter to Mr. Clarke—

The dedication is to Mrs Jameson[138]— I should have liked to dedicate it to John Patton, in some such form as this—

To John Patton Esq

of Montreal,

to whose valuable library

---

*James Freeman Clarke.

        & generous farseeing sympathy I
           owe whatever progress I
             have made in social
               Science,
       these lectures are gratefully
              dedicated.

Had he been a married man, so it would have stood, but[139] I thought it might embarrass him, & I would not give him a worthless gift. If I gain anything of popularity by these lectures, I will dedicate to him the whole volume, but it is hardly likely, that I shall be permitted that comfort....

Here, Dall is again back in Boston.

MONDAY. OCT. 24. 1859.

Sewed all the morning— In the afternoon carried all my advertisements, and made several calls. Had a letter from Mr Dall in which he tries to comfort me, for my failure in New York last May— There was a better comprehension of me, in this letter, than in all he has said or done since we were married—yet it made me sigh—for kind as he meant it should be, he did not comprehend all.

TUESDAY. NOV. 1. 1859.

Sick—felt compelled in spite of no cook to go & see how mother was. Had a most distressing scene with her. Meeting the Sewalls[140] went to hear Thoreau on John Brown.* Many of the sharpest things he said were in very bad taste— but it was on the whole a grand tribute to the truest American who has lived since George Washington. I was surprised for I had thought Mr. Thoreau, <u>only</u> a philosopher.

---

*Thoreau was lecturing at the Tremont Temple in the Fraternity lecture series, as a substitute for Frederick Douglass, who had gone to Canada following allegations of his involvement in the Harper's Ferry scheme. Militant abolitionist John Brown (1800–1859) had led a raid on the federal arsenal at Harper's Ferry on October 16; he was captured and would soon be tried, convicted, and executed. Thoreau's lecture, "A Plea for Captain John Brown," had been delivered in Concord on October 30 and would be repeated later in Worcester. *The Liberator* noted that the "exciting theme" of John Brown "seemed to have awakened the 'hermit of Concord' from his usual state of philosophic indifference, and he spoke with real enthusiasm for an hour and a half ... bestowing hearty praise upon the enterprise at Harper's Ferry, and as hearty dispraise upon the apathy and reserve shown in regard to it by those portions of the periodic press which did not take the equally shameful ground of direct censure. Mr Thoreau took special pains to include the *Liberator* in the censure" (November 4, 1859, p. 174).

Dall began her new series of lectures, "Woman's Right to Labor," on November 7, 1859. The first lecture was entitled "Low Wages and Hard Work."

MONDAY.

NOV. 7. 1859.

Mr Severance called this morning, to say Mrs Severance had been ill for a week with neuralgia, and would not be able to go to my lectures at all, much less, attend me, as she always has.

I felt a little prepared for some such thing. On the whole, this is such a day, as I hope I may never have to chronicle again— The new servant just engaged is so wilful & troublesome, that I have already given her notice. Mary[141] was crazy with pain, & just as I wished to dress for lecture, I was obliged to have the Dr to open her felon*— Then some one sent to see if I were ill, as there was no advertisement in the Transcript.†

I cannot explain the heart-sinking I felt at this announcement. I would not believe it was malicious, as some one suggested, but I saw at once, that my opportunity was gone— I kept up as well as I could—but there was no calmness in my last hour at home. As soon as I found Mrs Severance could not come, I sent for another friend and found she had left town. Then for another—for with my near-sighted eyes, I never like to dress for public occasions alone,— and Mary with her felon, could not put in a pin. Just as I was depending on this person, she sent me word that people had come to tea & I must excuse her. To crown all, a new pair of Alexander's gloves did not fit, although of the right number. In an attempt to find an old pair, the lid of my heavy packing trunk fell upon my left hand cutting the knuckle to the bone. As a last resort, I borrowed of Aunt S. and went down alone.

As I had expected, the audience was small, Mr May[142] rose & said the clock was fast, but I explained the difficulty and went on. The attention was of the deepest. Sarah Clarke came to me, afterward—and spoke tender loving words, and from Barbara and Louise,[143] I had of course, warm encouragement. Still I came home sad, with the feeling—I am not worthy—I am not worthy—knelling through my heart.

---

*An infection at the end of a finger or toe.

†The lecture series had been advertised earlier in the *Transcript* under the heading "Woman's Right to Labor/Mercantile Hall Course of lectures on Female Labor" (*Transcript,* October 25, 1859, p. 2). The advertisement for this evening's lecture appeared a day late on November 8 (p. 2). The lecture is briefly reviewed in the *Advertiser* for November 14 (p. 2).

"Thou hidest them in the secret of thy presence from the pride of man; thou shelterest them in thy pavilion from the strife of tongues—"[144] Was it so? I will trust in Him.

It is not often that I chronicle small troubles, but this is for my children to read— If they can remember moments when their mother was too abrupt & positive to seem kind, they will find in this page one excuse—

TUESDAY. NOV. 8. 1859.

I sent a letter to the Transcript this morning by Mr May—[145] It was perfectly calm & moderate. Of course, I could not sleep last night. This afternoon, the Sewalls & Mays,[146] expressed themselves warmly, & I was, quite surprised when I went down to mother's to find that father, liked the lecture, & was not troubled by the smallness of the numbers. I was surprised that he was there, and expected he would be mortified. The pleasure of finding myself mistaken is very great. This evening I heard Emerson on "Courage."[147]

On November 20, 1859, Dall heard an extraordinary sermon by a young minister who was to be a central figure in her life for the next few years.

BOSTON. SUNDAY. NOV 20. 1859.

A [sermon] from a Mr [Towne]* which was the most [extraordinary] thing I ever heard. I think he must be nearly [insane].[148] Only Mrs J. F. Clarke[149] & myself felt so very much distressed, & she went into the pulpit, at once, and told him, he must never preach the sermon again. I dined at mother's & then father took me to drive— The wind was very cold, and our conversation cheerless enough—for it was about mother and what could be done to put a stop to the present condition of things, a topic on which I dare not dwell. . . .

*Edward Cornelius Towne (1834–1911), a member of the Yale class of 1856, studied theology in New York and (until December 1859) at the Yale Theological Seminary. Probably shortly before Dall first heard him, Towne began to incline away from Orthodoxy toward Unitarianism and was ordained at a new Free Church in South Braintree, Massachusetts, in July 1860. In the spring of 1861, he began a seven-year pastorate at the First Parish (Unitarian) Church in Medford; during part of this time, he boarded with Caroline Dall. He was active in the Radical Club in Boston. After leaving Medford, he entered upon a peripatetic period in which he did literary and journalistic work, as well as some preaching, in numerous locations. He died "of paranoia" in a Brooklyn hospital on June 20, 1911 (*Bulletin of Yale University: Obituary Record of Yale Graduates 1910–1911* [7th series, No. 9, July 1911]: 192–194).

In December, Dall lectured at the Concord Lyceum before a distinguished audience.

WEDNESDAY— CONCORD. MASS.

DEC. 14. 1859.

I took the Omnibus a little before 7 AM. & rode to the Fitchburg depot. At the Concord dépôt Mr Brown & his wife & Mr Surette[150] met me. Mrs Brown kindly carried me to Mrs Alcott's where I passed a pleasant morning, talking to her and the girls,[151] and deciding which lecture I would read.* After a vegetable dinner, I went back to Mrs Brown's in her sleigh. The sewing circle took tea there, and having done the agreeable as well as I could, I dressed and was taken down to the Town Hall where I was to speak. A heavy snow storm had increased since morning to a drifting gale. The driving cold was so painful on my cheeks, that I was faint & dizzy with the reaction. Mr Brown, said, You need not expect anybody tonight—but there were about four hundred persons.

Mr Reynolds[152] who introduced me, Mr Alcott, Thoreau Frank Sanborn,[153] Mrs Emerson & others, paid me compliments with that dignified reserve that such persons do.[154] But Edith Emerson,[155] said a few words to Mrs Brown, worth them all. "I cannot often keep awake," she said, "during the best lectures, but I heard every word of this, she was so <u>earnest</u>."

CONCORD MASS-

THURSDAY. DEC 15. 1859.

Early this morning I drove down with Mr Brown[156] to Frank Sanborn's— where he showed me his pretty parlor & dining room, and then I went with him to his school, where I heard the first recitations staying more than an hour.

Mrs Brown then appeared and took me to Mrs Alcott's & Mrs Horace Mann's[157]—where I had a most interesting call. Mrs Mann seemed very much interested in my work, & told me that she thought Miss Lydia Mann[158] & Mrs Alcott—were both women, prepared & ready to work in responsible posts—

As Confessor—to women committed to trial—or as Confessor to the

---

*Dall apparently decided on the third of her series "Woman's Claim to Education," using the lives of Mary Wollstonecraft and Margaret Fuller as illustrations, called here "Lives of Noted Women." See "Caroline Dall in Concord," *The Thoreau Society Bulletin* 62 (Winter, 1958): 1–2, and Register of Public Addresses, Dall Papers, Bryn Mawr.

States' Prison, Mrs Alcott would do admirably—& the thought gave me new courage.

She read me an article she wrote about it in 1855— Mr Alcott spoke to me about my lectures, in tones it was very pleasant to hear. He had felt a sadness all through, which I do not <u>know</u> anything about, & confessed a fear that I sheathed far too often & too long—a legitimate weapon <u>satire</u>. He asked me if I had not to use a great deal of self control—in that respect. I told him that I began so early to do so, that I had nearly ceased to feel it. We then called at Mrs Emerson's where the Philosopher appeared in a dressing gown of royal purple, faced with velvet, and I entered for the first time the room where "Nature" was written. He lent me Vishnu Sarma,[159] and then we parted—I promising to return to tea.

I then dined with Frank, his sister,[160] and Miss Waterman, one of his teachers, and had a very pleasant time.

Mr Alcott joined me, just as I walked over to the Hoars— I found all the family were dining with the Pritchards and went in there, to see Lizzy.[161] They all seemed to have been much disappointed by the bad weather, which had kept them in, last night. I then went to Thoreau's where Mr Alcott left me. Much to my surprise I was glad to learn from Sophia[162] that he had liked my lecture.

She said he could seldom endure to listen, but that she saw by his eyes as soon as he came home, that he had been pleased. When she asked him; "Yes," he answered "it was good" "I liked her—because she did not look in the least like Mrs Smith!!" * We had much pleasant talk—I saw Ellery Channing's[163] house—& his last Poem, dedicated to Thoreau,[164] & all the store of Orient literature, Mr Cholmondeley[165] had lately sent him.

Soon Frank's hack came to carry me to Emerson's where I was delighted to see Mrs Frank Brown, a daughter of Mrs C. K. Whipple.[166] Then came Alcott Thoreau, & Frank. It was a genial pleasant circle sat down to tea, but my time was so short—I grudged every moment to food.

I heard a good deal I wanted to know. I teased Mr. Alcott for deserting me— and he replied with emphasis that he had been with Mr Reynolds & that Mr Reynolds <u>believed</u> in <u>Mrs. Dall</u>! which of course I was glad to hear.

Frank went with me to the Depot—& took me <u>to the minute</u>. On my way I

---

*After Elizabeth Oakes Smith lectured in Concord on December 31, 1851, Thoreau wrote in his journal that "she was a woman in the too common sense after all." Smith asked him to carry her lecture to the hall, and the result was that his pocket smelled like cologne. See Walter Harding, *The Days of Henry Thoreau* (New York: Dover Publications, 1982), 304–305.

read the last third of Sir Rohan's Ghost—which I did not much like after all—Higginson's praise—[167] It is one of his wilful caprices to which the world, will refuse to yield.

BOSTON. MASS.
FRIDAY. FEB. 3. 1860 . . .

Home to read Conway's Dial,* and some letters &c—

I was much touched by Conway's notice of "Labor" which I had not seen before.

How unfit I am to be named with Margaret, I know very well, but it was pleasant to find one person, inclined to throw <u>her</u> mantle over me—and it brought a tear of strong resolve to my cheek—

Dall's work on behalf of women drew her to the attention of Edward Towne, whose sermon had so startled her, and of English feminists. At home in Boston, she received a cash award from the Hovey Fund to support her work.

BOSTON. MASS.
TUESDAY. FEB. 7. 1860.

I shall certainly remember the month of Feby. 1860— What with the remarkable expression of sympathy[168] from E.C.T.† and the two events of today, my cup seems to overflow—

First, a letter from England, announcing that my lecture on the formation of public opinion is really in press—and is to be freely distributed throughout the liberal party—and this after I had given up all hopes! Miss Parkes writes that she shall make "<u>mild</u>" extracts for the Journal.[169]

Second, a call from C.K. Whipple Esq. on the part of the Trustees of the Hovey fund.‡ They have decided to give me from $150 to $200—and Mr

---

*Moncure D. Conway (1832–1907), disciple of Emerson, Unitarian minister in Cincinnati, had begun a new periodical, its title *(The Dial)* reflecting his Transcendentalist associations. His review in the January 1860 issue of Dall's *"Woman's Right to Labor"* said that the book caused him to "feel that Margaret Fuller's mantle did not pass into heaven with her."

†Edward Towne.

‡The Hovey Fund, a bequest of $40,000 established upon the recent death of Boston merchant and abolitionist Charles F. Hovey, was intended to support reform causes. Charles King Whipple (1808–1900) was an active abolitionist and nonresistant, assisting in editing the *Liberator* and the *Non-Resistant* and serving as treasurer of the New England Anti-Slavery Society. The Hovey Committee trustees (who included, besides Whipple, Stephen S. Foster, Abby Kelley Foster, William Lloyd Garrison, Francis Jackson,

Whipple came to request a pecuniary statement on my side, which should lead them to determine which.

I thank God for these first two public recognitions—and at this moment—, when I would so gladly, I cannot tell John—he would take no pleasure in hearing.

John Patton, troubled by family responsibilities and his own financial situation, was visiting Dall. Apparently there was some sort of crisis in their relationship.

BOSTON—

THURSDAY. MAR 15. 1860.

I was sorry to find John had not slept, but he seemed calmer than yesterday. I was obliged to leave him for a time to go to enquire the character of a girl, and do some household errands. . . . While he was gone, I wept a long while—it seemed to draw the bitterness out of my pain; I took E.C.T.'s note out of my pocket, and tried to comprehend the past and the present—tried to see what God would have me do, but my eyes were very dim— I can and will give up every hope—if I could only keep the lives of others free from pain it shall be enough, no matter for my own.

God grant it be not too late.

I asked myself—why I was left alone, without the present affection—I so much need, and I seemed to understand the answer better than before. If God has really any work for me to do for women I suppose I must do it alone—for human affection takes such strong hold on me, that I cannot give myself to its ties half-way.

It is so easy, so blessed to give up my own work and find it, in fulfilling that of another—! I would so much rather minister than be ministered unto. And, if I needed any, I might have found a new proof of this weakness of mine, in the experience of this last trying sickness—*How everything, shrank into re-

---

Wendell Phillips, Parker Pillsbury, and Henry C. Wright) administered the fund, dispensing $8,000 a year for five years. See Walter M. Merrill and Louis Ruchames, eds., *Letters of William Lloyd Garrison*, 6 vols. (Cambridge, Massachusetts: Belknap Press, 1971–1981), 5:23, 31; and Newburyport VR.

*Dall had recently nursed through the measles not only her children but also Edward Towne, who had caught the disease from them. He stayed in the Dall household for the several weeks of his recovery.

motest perspective, in the light of the sick room—There were hours, when I might have written, if my will had been strong enough—might have continued even the preparation of my lectures— When Willie was first taken, I did so, but soon, it all changed to watching & waiting—to preparing for or giving rest to the beloved ones. There are those, who would wonder to find me blaming myself—for that, and would think it only fit and womanly. But I know, that my nursing might have been quite as faithful, without my throwing my whole life into it as I did, and as I always do, when circumstances open a channel for my pent-up—nature.

God sees that I am wilful—full of unrest—and he cannot cheer me—with the love I need, till I am more humble—faithful & patient.

I was sewing when John returned—with such a headache— We talked for two or three hours, after the children went to bed—and John was generous— He acknowledged that I was right in all I did, and that I had borne with him too long. I am afraid I pained him unnecessarily, but I could not at the moment help it. My head was bursting— He saw that I could not bear it, and drew near, "Let me put my hands upon it as if I were your brother," but I shook from head to foot with a wild shudder of pain.

He asked me to pray for him & with him, and I did & grew calmer.

If I did not believe in God what should I do?

BOSTON. MASS.
TUESDAY. MAR 20. 1860.

A day of great suffering— John was ill all night, if I had known it, I should have gone to him, but of course, he was too proud to call me. He looked like death when he came down, I pitied him, yet felt that the deepest & tenderest pity, would say very little. The carriage came for him at 7 o'clock—but we rose early—& I had an hour of most distressing talk. He asked me for Spiridion, and I wrote his name in it, and gave it to him—he offered to return the little token of affection which I gave him, when I left Toronto five years ago—but of course I would not take it. I shall always feel for him a tender [two illegible words erased] regard, such as that token expressed—only I shall never again depend upon him for sympathy or comfort— I shall not ask more. [approximately five illegible words erased]. I told him at the last, that I thought he was ungenerous, that he had made me suffer more than was necessary recklessly— I might have added that it was both indelicate and inexcusable to offer me gifts on this visit, whatever he gave the children, but I spared him, for I know that in his heart, he was innocent in doing it.

God forgive me, if I added one feather's weight to his full cup— I cannot be happy, till I know that he has reached home safely.

I sewed all the morning to calm myself—not daring to try to write. After dinner I read the Athenaeum, & to get back into a natural state went to Marie's lecture on the Uterus.[170] It was very sensible and well delivered, but my heart would not stop aching.[171] I went over to see Uncle Wm. who improves, and then took a cup of cocoa & tried to read some of E.C.T's book—but I could not keep it up—and after a long cry on the sofa—truly <u>alone</u>—for I felt deserted of God, even, I went to bed.

Dall and Caroline Severance were the chief organizers of another women's rights meeting that took place in Boston in June 1860.

BOSTON MASS—
FRIDAY. JUNE 1. 1860.

. . . I sent Mr Town down to the Melodeon, to secure the windows and look after the doorkeepers. I went with Katy later—. There was the usual inefficiency about the preparations, C.M.S.* came late, and after the hour for the meeting arrived, insisted on waiting for her husband to arrange our flowers— However, at last, when patience was no virtue, and the hour had come, I sent Miss Southwick[172] to hire some vases, and did the needful myself.

Will it be believed that John T. Sargent did not come—<u>because</u> his name was not in our <u>first</u> advertisement, and because if he espoused an unpopular cause—he thought he ought to have all the credit that attached to it![173] Angels & ministers of grace defend us. Now that the meetings are over—and I thank God on my knees for a splendid success, I can afford to forget the irritations which were heaped into today, only one must be recorded, it was so remarkable in kind and quality.

. . . I then proceeded to speak from my minutes as far as the subject of Labor—carried me.† I never had so hearty a welcome.

I was followed by the Rev. S. J. May, who referred in the most graceful man-

---

*Caroline Severance.

†Dall recorded this talk as "Woman's Labor" (Register of Public Addresses, Dall Papers, Bryn Mawr).

ner to me, several times while he was speaking, in a way, which could hardly fail to inspire a certain respect in the audience.

As I sat down—a note from W. T. Clark[174] informing me that he was too ill to speak was put into my hands— Mrs Cheney[175]—saw the embarrassment in which I was placed, and went in search of General Tubman[176] to relieve me— As I turned to thank her—I saw Higginson & went immediately to urge him to speak. His look struck me in a moment—inflamed & irate, he looked like the "red and angry" visage, which hung over Jane Eyre's bed, the night before her wedding. "I am glad to see you," I said, "as you did not come to the Committee meeting yesterday, I supposed you were not coming. Now for your speech." "No!" said he, in the most excited and angry manner, "no, I will never speak on a platform, where less than half of the speakers are women! It is useless. Such a meeting as you are holding here today does more harm than good. Women must speak for themselves."

"Where shall we get the women," I asked.

"Plenty of them, plenty in this audience," he continued—

"We should be glad to see them," I replied "but Mr Higginson, while we women argue for men—we expect such men as you—to argue for our women, we cannot expect women to tread these boards, till men like you show, that they consider it respectable."

"It's no use to speak of it" replied he determinately, "my mind is made up, on that subject— I shan't speak under such circumstances, and Mrs Dall—" speaking with an emphasis, & anger which drew the attention of the audience, "Mrs Dall you made two misstatements in your address—it is ruinous, you must be careful—"

"Indeed," said I—after a moment's pause, thunderstruck by a manner to which no words can do justice— "Indeed, I am not in the habit—"

"You are in the habit, the constant habit" he reiterated in a tone, which quieted me, at once, for I saw I was speaking to an insane man— "You must change it—"

"What particular mistake have I made today?" I inquired.

"You said General Tubman—had been back into slavery, 13 times—she has been but eight—and that story of Miss Mitchell[177] which I told you, was greatly altered— She never said—that no man had ever thought to do what she had done &c &c—"

I am quite sure, that H's intention in this matter was to break up my composure, and prevent matters going on triumphantly. The malicious desire shone out of his eye—but of course—it is a thing not to be proved.

Hinton[178] had been speaking in a dull way about Kansas law, while this was going on, as soon as he closed—I led our dark friend Moses,[179] forward, and as soon as the storm of applause, which succeeded had broken, I said,

"My friends—I am told that in the address which I have just made, I have made two mistakes. Now you know that I believe in faithful work—see also, that I believe in faithful confession— I <u>heard</u> that Harriet Tubman had been back into slavery, 13 times. Before I rose to speak this afternoon, my friend Mrs Cheney confirmed the impression, but it seems, she has only been back 8 times—

I am also told that I made a mistake in the anecdote I related of Miss Mitchell. As I do not know what it was, I cannot retract it, but when you hear the story again, make the allowance for me. We had once in this neighborhood a professor of Chemistry, quite famous—for breaking retorts, and spilling his mixtures— When his last drop of acid, had been spilled, he would turn round to his class, and say "Gentlemen, the experiment fails, but the fact—remains the same." So I to you—if the illustration fails—the argument remains the same."

This brought down the house and also Mr Higginson—for he left the stand soon after.

Now—what was the matter? God knows— Perhaps—he was vexed, that he was not on the new Committee—which he would have been, had he thought it proper to attend the meeting— Perhaps, he wanted the anecdote of Maria Mitchell for his own speech— I certainly should not have used it, had I known he was in the house. Perhaps he was vexed, to find us less dependent on his patronage than Lucy Stone.

Perhaps—he wanted to make the best speech—& didn't see his way—

Shall we meet this sort of people in Heaven, I wonder, and if so, shall I be angelic enough to be pleased with their society?

Our friend Moses, saved the audience & me, from the perplexities into which so many withdrawals had thrown us—.

She was followed by Garrison who made a very good speech, except that he travelled off of the platform once, into the Union—and I would have called him to order, only I thought he would think I was avenging poor Edward Town's wrongs—so I left him & he soon righted himself.

Mrs Severance was too weak to manage the platform[180]—so I[181] adjourned the meeting—

In opening the meeting I had told them, how much they owed to her efforts, and how our work had been done the last two years—

When I rose—I said:

"Two ladies have called this meeting, the speakers are their guests, and this platform is their drawing room—. It is not sufficiently understood that this is not a free platform in the control of the audience—*It is hoped that however you may desire to hear women, you will be silent when the friends, & the best friends of women speak. We expect Mr Phillips to make our closing speech this evening—but we do not expect to have him called for."

This was aimed at the gallery, & made the evening meeting perfect in order— I was overwhelmed with congratulations as soon as I hurried through the crowd, for the interval was very short. Lucy Goddard,[182] says, "Every body says it was the best speech—you ever made in your life" &c &c— What touched me most was a little Bloomer,† who said she wanted to speak—but saw me so evidently anxious and troubled, that she would do nothing to perplex me.

A great many people insisted on shaking hands with me, and Mrs Tolman[183] stopped to say, "It was the best thing you ever did & everybody else thinks so—" It seemed as if they thought the meeting lived & died with me— so I had to run to escape.

At home, for a short hour, I would gladly have wept away the pain of Higginson's treatment—but I knew red eyes would not do, so I spent most of the time in walking rapidly back & forth—and so kept down my restlessness.

We had again a full house, though it rained hard—though the Fraternity held a meeting to commemorate Mr Parker's loss,‡ and there was a crush at the Bell & Everett meeting.[184]

To my amaze—Mr & Mrs Josiah Quincy[185] came to ours.

---

*Attempting to avoid the chaos of such meetings as the one in New York in May 1859, and controversial topics such as free love and marriage, the organizers (principally Severance and Dall) confined the speakers to the three topics of the education, vocation, and civil position of woman. The *Liberator* noted that the Boston meetings were not "conventions for free discussion, but anniversary meetings for the delivery of addresses, by speakers previously engaged" (July 6, 1860, p. 106).

†A follower of Amelia Bloomer's clothing reforms.

‡Theodore Parker had died of tuberculosis in Italy on May 10. For the Fraternity, see note 190.

I opened the meeting with the subjects of Law—Literature and Losses—
... I closed with a tribute to Mr Parker—which I could have made much richer
—had I dared in speaking to a popular audience. I reread—the Resolution—
and the audience rose in a mass, to do honor to his memory. As they stood,
moved to tears and reverence, I longed to break into a prayer, but I dared
not trust the sympathies of a popular audience, and I said with all the emotion
I felt—

"He is not so far from us, but he knows what we are doing. Let us honor
him, not merely by this solemn posture—and reverent silence but by perme-
ating our Lives as he did, with the sacred fires of Love & Truth."

There was nothing—hurried, nothing theatrical in all this, and as after a
pause, I turned from the desk the audience resumed their seats. ...

... As I turned back from the platform, God knows a sweet peace fell upon
my soul. The meetings were over, and had been a success!

It is not egotism which leads me to preserve my own words—in conduct-
ing the meetings. The time may come when my motive will be apparent— I
have not tried to preserve the "best speech I ever made."

I came out more slowly than in the morning, but amid general unmeaning
congratulation, two pleasant things happened.

Two young colored girls sought me, and took my hand—and with tears in
their eyes tried to pour out admiration & gratitude.

Then I encountered the Chapman party,[186] all radiant— I thanked them
for coming—after the fatigues of the week. "Why" said Mary—"I haven't spent
such a delightful afternoon & evening for an age." Deborah Weston, said "Mrs
Dall, I must tell you, you are my favorite speaker!! I went to the New York meeting but it was not equal to this— Mrs Stanton cannot compare with you."

Mrs Chapman, put her arms round me, and kissed me, "Well," said she
"the desire of our eyes is at last fulfilled. Nothing could be finer than this. You
have not a thing to regret." I walked home. Oh how, I thanked God—for rest
at last.

At noon, I did not think Mr Town satisfied, so I asked him no questions,
thinking beside, that, his own fatigue & worry, at seeing the crowds that got in
without pay, might have unfitted him to judge. Tonight he came home radiant— He said the meeting was as pure as a marble statue, & repeated many absurd things he had heard others say. A little sleep tonight.

... I gave the day, to setting to rights. Had I wished I could have been very un-happy—for Sallie[187] came home from a call she made at a leading reformer's full of the talk that I was conceited—presuming—thought I knew more than any body else—&c &c—& above all, that my dress was too short. This last im-portant fact, I discovered for myself—and not a little did it add to the mental wear of yesterday—. I must either stay at home, or wear the dress I had, & I knew it showed nothing but the edge of clean white skirts[188] The platform was so much higher than any we ever had, that it seemed as if we were half way up a flight of stairs.

As to the rest, I never anchored my peace on any man's opinion. <u>This</u> I did think as I reflected on the account Sallie brought—that—perhaps I had mis-taken my calling—if there was not in me, eloquence enough to charm people out of such thoughts. I was glad to find on enquiry, how few of my near friends had been troubled about my <u>dress</u>, raised by my <u>thought</u>—and it does seem to me, no one ought to speak in public who cannot lift the audience, <u>above</u> the speaker....

On October 23, 1860, Dall was lecturing before the Parker Fraternity at the Tremont Temple, perhaps the largest audience of her career. Her topic was "The Progress of the Woman's Cause." Despite inclement weather, the lecture hall was "almost filled" for the hour-and-a-half lecture.[189]

Father came up to bring the brooch I was to wear tonight. Beside that, I saw no one; recited my lecture, and sewed quietly on Sarah's dresses. Finished the last work I had cut out. Was a little worried by Mrs Severance's not coming to tea in time. Every thing went well—with my own dress—and with my lecture. I spoilt some of my best sentences, by trying to get along without notes, but no one knew it but myself, & probably no one cared. The children rode down with me & they & Mr Town filled the carriage on my return. Their sympathy was very precious. I believe every one was satisfied & it was a decided success. The audience was a crowd in spite of the worst night of the season. One re-mark I overheard amused me—

"How did you like it?", asked a young lady of a young gentleman—

"Very much indeed! How animated she was! I asked some one this morning what sort of a lecture it would be—& they said "not much," but wasn't she splendid? I guess they were prejudiced."

Mr Slack[190] said, "Mrs Dall you have surpassed my fondest anticipations." I was too excited to sleep after it—but not in the least discomposed before.

BOSTON. SUNDAY.
DEC 16. 1860.

I heard Mr Clarke this morning, I wished very much to hear Phillips at the Music Hall,* but did not feel able.

I dined with father, where every thing was glum & stiff, as if I were the living embodiment of secession, though not a word was said. . . .

It is very extraordinary that there should be such a resurrection of the mob spirit— I could not help hovering round the crowd, till I knew Phillips was safe at home.

With the lecture on January 23, 1861, on "U.S. Law, and the Secret of Success," the third of her series "Woman's Rights Under the Law," Dall completed the long-range plan that she had begun in February 1858: the delivery of four series of three lectures each, on the woman question.

BOSTON WEDNESDAY.
JAN 23D. 1861.

This afternoon I gave my last lecture on Law, and so closed my last public course—self proposed.† Thank God! it is over—& I can never have another duty so hard— After the lecture, I gave a little synopsis of what I had done in my four years. I spoke gently of the duty the women had not done, & I bade that audience farewell.

It is certainly a success, to have given four courses, without any loss— and some small gain pecuniarily considered—& what gain women hereafter make, will be due, in no small measure—to the labor on my part for those four years. . . .

*Wendell Phillips was delivering the Sunday sermon, "Mobs and Education," before the Twenty-eighth Congregational Society at the Music Hall (*Transcript,* December 15, 1860, p. 2).

†The lecture was delivered at the Young Men's Christian Union (*Transcript,* January 22, 1861, p. 3). Dall later remembered "A large audience" (Register of Public Addresses, Dall Papers, Bryn Mawr).

The next day Dall attended a meeting of The Massachusetts Anti-Slavery Society at the Tremont Temple that was disrupted by organized opposition.

BOSTON THURSDAY.
JAN 24. 1861.

... After taking a light dinner at Parker's,[191] I went down to the Temple & found a crowd there watching for Phillips and saw at once that the meeting had adjourned. I then went to the Chapmans,[192] where I sat talking while they dined, and saw Edmund Quincy.

Charles Follen[193] & Phoebe Garnaut[194] joined us, and we went together to the Hall. Though we entered through a great crowd, after trying in vain, every private entrance, we received no personal insult, only were obliged constantly to hear, that the "Lord never made niggers for nothing but slaves &c &c" The scene of the afternoon is sufficiently reported in the newspapers— There is no need that I should dwell upon it. One of the newspapers said, that some of the ladies were frightened, and looked in vain for a way of escape. That was not true, not even of the remotest audience. One country—woman, in the middle of the gallery, sat knitting through every thing. The stronger men crowded the front of the platform, so that we were nearly pressed to death— but every one was calm & self-possessed. . . . Under all—I felt so sad. Those poor Irishmen! As the missiles flew about, I felt that some of them came from my father's hand—and it seemed as if the thought would choke me— If I died from a chance blow—it might save his soul, & God knows I was more than willing—but there was no real danger only the appearance of it.

Nothing could be more absurd than Mayor Wightman.* Decent men sometimes lie, but they don't often lie like fools.— Had I known that he would close the doors—I should not have left the hall—at all. As it was, I did not think

---

*Joseph M. Wightman (1812–1885), Democratic mayor of Boston who had been inaugurated on January 7. The son of an immigrant tailor, Wightman had risen from his apprenticeship to a machinist to successful entrepreneurship and the presidency of the Massachusetts Charitable Mechanics Association (Melvin G. Holli and Peter d'A. Jones, *Biographical Dictionary of American Mayors, 1820–1980: Big City Mayors* [Westport, Connecticut: Greenwood Press, 1981]). During this meeting of the Massachusetts Anti-Slavery Society, Wightman appeared and announced that he was dissolving the meeting by orders of the trustees of the building. But the trustees, being present, denied this, and forced him to read their letter, which showed that they had requested him to protect the assembly. He now partially succeeded in doing so, and promised fifty policemen to protect the evening session. Instead, however, he finally prohibited the evening meeting, using police to guard the doors. See Thomas Wentworth Higginson, *Cheerful Yesterdays* (Boston: Houghton, Mifflin and Company, 1898), 243–245.

it safe, to leave Ellen Town[195] sick & excitable in ignorance of my fate, & I left the Hall about five minutes before the Police, cleared the platform.

It snowed so severely that I could not wisely return, so I did not join the consultation at Mr Phillips house.

I rode home—with ten of the rioters, & found that all they knew was, that they had turned "Gov. Andrew[196] out of his own hall" & that the Mayor, "wasn't the man to stand insult."

BOSTON

FEB. 10. 1861.

...I went into Garrison's, ... and William, the son who is in the bank at Lynn[197]—told me that a most villainous assault had been made upon my personal character by Parsons Cooke in the Puritan Recorder—under cover of a review of my Lynn lecture.* Mr Cooke did not hear the lecture himself, but took the report of his daughter, and does not seem to understand the meaning of the word representative any better than the Lynn Reporter.[198] ...

BOSTON

MONDAY. FEB. 11. 1861.

... The abominable scandal of Parsons Cooke—has travelled out to West Roxbury & made all manner of trouble. Kate[199] was greatly excited. She wanted a late letter of Mr Dall's to prove we had never been separated—a volume of Channing to show that somebody beside myself thought well of Mary Wollstonecraft—my lecture to read to the Committee & show that I had not been advocating free-love. Poor Kate.

She brought the paper to show me—& it was so much worse than I expected that it made me sick & faint....

---

*Parsons Cooke (1800–1864), a religious editor and longtime Congregational clergyman at Lynn, was a noted controversialist (Oscar Fay Adams, *Dictionary of American Authors* [Boston, 1905]; Rossiter Johnson, *Twentieth Century Dictionary of Notable Americans* [Boston, 1904]). His article in the *Boston Recorder* (its name had recently been changed from the *Puritan Recorder*), an Orthodox newspaper, was indeed vicious. It referred to the phenomenon of women lecturing as "hen-crowing," associated Dall's lecture with "infidel abolitionists," particularly Theodore Parker, and accused her of "corrupting the youth" by trying to annihilate marriage. "We believe in free speech," the article went on, "But even the freedom of speech has its limits. When obscenities constitute the material of a lecture, it is time for the police to interfere." No doubt most disturbing to Dall, the writer insinuated a kinship of spirit between Dall ("who is, and has been for years, separated from her husband by the breadth of the globe, he being a Unitarian missionary in Calcutta, and she being a missionary of another kind in America") and Mary Wollstonecraft, one of the subjects of her lecture, whom the writer denounced as "the most debauched and shameless of women" (*Boston Recorder,* February 7, 1861, p. 2).

BOSTON. MONDAY.

FEB. 18. 1861.

. . . I found Kate Payson quite composed when I got out to West Roxbury. No one seemed to have expected that I should give up the lecture. The Hall was crowded—before beginning—I expressed my regret, that I had not chosen instead of the Fraternity Lecture, one upon "four Representative Women" which I had lately delivered in Lynn & other places. I added that if at the close of this lecture, there was either sufficient curiosity concerning the subject or sufficient confidence, in me, to lead them to desire it—I would give them that lecture gratuitously. This was received with immense applause. The lecture was as perfect a success as a human being could have. I kept them near an hour & a half, but they seemed reluctant to go— After we got home Mr York[200] said in his foreign way, "I do think no one was hurt tonight."

BOSTON. TUESDAY.

FEB. 19. 1861.

I found on examining the envelope handed me last night, that the money came two dollars short—so I left it behind me, with a note for Mr Woodbury.[201]

Arrived at the station, I saw this gentleman, who was so prejudiced against female speakers, that he was hardly willing to bring me the invitation to lecture. He now approached me with compliments, said I might consider that I have conquered W. Roxbury, that the gentlemen met directly after the lecture, & subscribed enough to pay for the other lecture, as they were not willing that I should give it gratuitously. He regretted the mistake about the money, was as civil as Punch—and carried my basket to Washington St. like a tractable mastiff.

I found plenty of work—but was sick & faint all day.

May this roll like a sweet morsel under Parsons Cooke's tongue.

CHAPTER TWELVE

Wars, Public and Private

April 14, 1861–September 9, 1865

"*S*titch, stitch, stitch," is Caroline Dall's description of how she spent countless hours during the Civil War, sewing for the soldiers. Besides this effect on her everyday activities, the war was a significant force in her life in several other respects. First of all, she believed strongly in the Union cause and was vitally interested in the war's conduct and outcome as a means of achieving emancipation. Remarkably, she shows us, the once-despised abolitionists were suddenly being lionized, William Lloyd Garrison and Wendell Phillips honored at Harvard. But this feeling was not unanimous, even at Harvard, as Dall's journal demonstrates, giving us a firsthand report of the raging debate on the war's goals, reflected in the high feelings exposed shortly after the war's beginning at a meeting of Harvard alumni. She herself argued, to disheartened Boston citizens who were at a low ebb following a major defeat, "the moral end of the war." Early optimism in the North soon faded, and Dall's journal presents a memorable vignette of Boston's reception of the news of the Union defeat at the Second Battle of Bull Run. Dall witnessed the maneuvers of the first black regiment, the Massachusetts Fifty-fourth, led by Robert Gould Shaw, and describes her reaction: "I think I never was so thrilled with patriotic feeling in my life, . . . the men with the shambling gait of fugitives looked so thoroughly in earnest, so sad yet so resolved." The last days of the war produced what she called "the most exciting news of my life-time," but this was closely followed by the devastating report of Lincoln's assassination, news that affected Dall profoundly. "Oh God!" she wrote, "do let me wake from this night mare & find it all a dream."

The war effectively put a temporary end to Dall's women's rights work.

Even so, she engaged in an exchange with Elizabeth Cady Stanton in *The Liberator* and the *National Anti-Slavery Standard* concerning women's political participation. Stanton had written Dall urging her to help mobilize women to defeat Lincoln in his race for a second term, and Dall responded in print that women should not become involved in partisan politics—a position that Stanton tore to shreds in her published reply. Dall's own stance seems a curious one for a woman's rights woman to take, and it can be understood only in terms of her great admiration for and trust in Lincoln, which she articulated in this piece. Dall also created something of a local sensation by her article in a Boston paper attacking American manufacturers for profiteering during the war. These articles brought her to the attention of members of Congress, and Congressman William D. Kelley in turn drew her defense of Lincoln in *The Liberator* to the attention of the president. Lincoln then wrote directly to Dall. (Exasperatingly, she does not reveal the content of the letter, which apparently does not survive.)

On the personal front, Dall faced traumatic situations involving both her husband and the young clergyman Edward C. Towne. Charles Dall's first attempted visit home was aborted when the ship on which he was traveling from England sustained severe storm damage and was forced to turn back. Charles decided to return to India without seeing his family, from whom he had then been separated for six and a half years. A year later he tried again, this time completing the journey, but as far as Caroline was concerned, his visit proved disastrous. Apparently little real communication occurred between Charles and Caroline, she writing, "It seems to me, that we, & all we do are like the shadows on a magic lantern to him, & nothing real but the Mission." They had disputes over money matters, over Edward Towne's prerogatives in the household, and most of all over their son, Willie, whom Charles wished to take back to India with him. For months it was presumed that Willie would go, and Caroline outfitted him for the trip, but at the last moment these plans fell through, Willie unwilling to agree to his father's conditions. Charles returned to India with "not one tender word" to his wife in farewell.

Dall's acquaintance with Edward Towne had developed into a close relationship. She had recognized his talents, though eccentric, from the first time she heard him preach, and had devoted herself to furthering his career. He had been attracted to her by her pamphlet *"Woman's Right to Labor."* When, with Dall's help, he became the Unitarian minister in Medford, outside Boston, she rented a house there, before long, and took him as boarder. Dall continued to come into Boston for Sunday services at the Church of the Disciples, where she acted as Sunday school superintendent, but she participated in the social life of the Medford parish as well. Her relationship with Towne quickly deteriorated with the stress of everyday interaction; he was moody, and she was no doubt controlling. He moved out in a huff, owing Dall, by her accounting, significant money. More seriously, though, he mutilated her papers, taking back his original admiring letters to her and cutting out passages in her journal relating to him. Her response was to write out at length in her journal the entire history of their relationship. When the debacle was over, she prayed, "God bless and keep him forever, & oh my father, send me some hard work to do—something that will employ every faculty & tax every muscle—and so press down my pain,—for it will not die." She moved back into Boston at Easter 1864 and asked God to "help me to a resurrection of my life—forgive me the weakness & presumption which made me undertake a friendly task too heavy for me, and give me courage to live down the misunderstanding that is no easier to bear, because it is in part deserved."

The sad spectacle of the end of this connection raises the question of why Dall went about collecting, as it were, relationships like this one that were doomed to failure. In some ways Edward Towne was a variant of Charles Dall, both of them unable to function for long in regular ministerial positions. Perhaps, since Towne was twelve years Caroline's junior, and the indecisive Charles Dall, though older than she, was described by acquaintances as "child-like," both of them activated the mothering instinct that seems to have been an important part of her personality. But differences in her respective relationships with these two men existed from the beginning. Caroline did not seek out Charles Dall, nor was she attracted to him; rather, he happened along at exactly her most vulnerable moment. In contrast, there was something electric in her initial revulsion and eventual attraction to Edward Towne. She was gratified by his early appreciation of her women's rights work, and she clearly found great fulfillment in supplying his needs—physical (nursing him through a severe case of the measles), financial (engineering his freedom from debt), domestic (becoming his housekeeper), and professional (providing him with books, promoting his career among her Unitarian friends). Although they were not lovers, he was the emotional focus of her life for several years. No doubt Edward Towne had reason to resent Dall's attempts to manage his life, but he was also probably grateful for her devotion and generosity. However,

Towne was not a balanced man (he married and divorced one of his Medford parishioners, left the ministry, led a peripatetic lifestyle, and died in a hospital "of paranoia"), and their estrangement was inevitable. During several years after the end of their relationship, Towne was Dall's great enemy, doing his best to discredit her and to shut her out from the radical religious circle to which they both belonged. His behavior to Dall was so vindictive that she suffered a double blow: not only was she losing the man who was at the center of her life, but she was forced to admit how flawed her judgment of him had been. In retrospect, she was horrified at her own folly.

John Patton, the other man in Dall's life at this time, was, like Towne, younger than she and an ardent admirer of her intellect. The journals of the Toronto years make clear that there was a mutual physical attraction between him and Caroline. For many years after she left Toronto, he continued to be devoted to her and her children. But his financial crises, family troubles, fatal illness (he would die of tuberculosis in 1870 at about age forty-three), and, toward the end of his life, depression and cynicism, took their toll on his relationship with Dall. In March 1860, in one of the great errors of her life, Dall deliberately chose to transfer her emotional focus from John Patton to Edward Towne. She and John later had a rapprochement, but the damage could not be entirely undone, and besides, John soon was in the physical decline leading to his death.

It almost seems as if some such figure was a necessity in her life: a man in whom she was emotionally invested, to the point that she lived and breathed his successes and failures. After Charles Dall's departure, Edward Towne's defection, and John Patton's death, Dall sustained, for several years each, similar sorts of relationships with three other men, all much younger than she. Caroline's one atypical relationship with a man was her early involvement with Samuel Haven, old enough almost to be her father. But Haven withdrew, of course, before the long-term viability of their relationship could be tested.

Dall's strong personality created problems for other sorts of relationships as well. Throughout her life she regularly unwittingly offended others, thanks in large part to her outspokenness and insensitivity to the feelings of others. During the closing years of this volume, for example, she badly damaged her relationship with the Alcott family: Although she was midwife to the publication of Louisa's first published novel, *Moods,* helped her sister May to market her artwork in Boston, and attempted to find work and arrange conversations for Bronson, Dall then published a review that was critical of the very novel that she had helped to get published. She could not comprehend the basis of the family's obvious coolness in response, writing in exasperation, "Well—I was to blame somewhere—perhaps in time, God will show me where." This penchant for frank speaking, apparent even when she was a teenager, helped to earn her a widespread reputation for egotism. The problems it was to cause in her life were only beginning.

In April 1863, Dall returned for the first time to Canada, a homecoming that was a salve to her sore heart. The Beattys, the Wilsons, Mrs. Copland, the Browns, and other old friends welcomed her warmly. "It seems as if the people here remembered every word I spoke while I was here," she marveled. "No where in the United States, after an entire cessation of intercourse for nine years, could I find such a welcome, as I have received here." Dall also took great comfort in renewing her relationship with John Patton, who agreed to become the custodian of her papers in the place of Towne, and who listened to her troubles without comment or judgment.

It was also in the mid-1860s that Dall made the acquaintance of the remarkable James family, including Henry Sr., his wife Mary, and their children, William, the future psychologist and philosopher; Henry Jr., the future novelist; and Alice, the diarist. After dining with them, Dall wrote in her journal what, for her, would not have been an offhand remark: "I like his family." And she herself was apparently a figure of considerable interest to that family, for she learned later that the character of her mind had been a subject of discussion among them: Was it masculine, or was it feminine? Henry Sr., in particular, seems to have become her great admirer; when Dall complimented the mind of Eliza Clapp, a mutual acquaintance, James rejoined, "Why speak of her intellect beside your own. . . . She's a mere baby—beside you."

An overriding concern of Dall's in the first half of the 1860s was the future of her son Willie. Having finished high school, he did not wish to take a regular college course, although he spent a short time studying privately with Harvard's famous naturalist, Louis Agassiz. He attempted and failed to get an appointment to Annapolis. Barely seventeen in August 1862, he tried to enlist in the Union army, but was ultimately dissuaded by those to whom his mother sent him for advice, perhaps most persuasively their minister, James Freeman Clarke, who advised "that boys so young gave invalids not soldiers to their country." His father returning home soon thereafter, Willie at first planned to go to India with him, but was finally forced to reconsider. He had canceled the trip, so he told his relatives, out of " 'distrust of his father's motives & stead-

fastness.' 'It is hard to write it of my father,' he said, 'but it is true.'" Some
months later Dall's worst anxieties were realized when she saw "Willie entering the gate with a soldier's blouse on—I was cutting away the fading roses
from the porch, having just finished my mending. I never shall forget the sinking at my heart. Where are you going Willie? I said. 'Over to Watertown with
Captn Currier, to defend the arsenal' he answered, & asked for half a dozen
things in a breath." The occasion was the unrest associated with violent draft
riots that had taken place in Boston the day before. Buoyed by the support and
advice of John Patton, who happened to be visiting, Dall didn't attempt to dis-
suade Willie. And for some days he stood guard. But once this crisis was past,
he was still at loose ends, clerking in various firms in Boston. Finally, Willie
went West to seek his fortune, Mark Healey having arranged a clerkship for his
grandson with the Illinois Central Railroad in Chicago. His mother "broke
down utterly" as she saw him off.

But Willie Dall was rapidly becoming his own man. Once in Chicago he
joined a scientific expedition to Russian Alaska, a part of Western Union Telegraph Company's exploration of a possible overland route for its cable to Europe. Caroline was worried and dismayed by this news. When she received,
months later, a letter from his superior praising Willie's behavior in "a great
many difficult & awkward positions" and predicting a bright future for him, it
was somehow an almost unhoped-for relief. Her marriage had violated a law
of God, she seemed to feel, and she had apparently feared that "the girlish vanity which made me marry his father" would be punished by the failure of their
son. Now she could look upon this letter as "God's mercy, after my weary waiting these twenty years." An era of her life seemed complete; she now had faith
that Willie would prosper.

---

*The Union surrender of Fort Sumter in South Carolina, on April 13, 1861,
marked the beginning of the Civil War.*

BOSTON SUNDAY.
APRIL 14, 1861.

The first news of the surrender of Fort Sumter—which any one has seemed
willing to believe. That the North has lost seems impossible to bear—and yet,

how much more we deserve. If I do not often write now, of political matters—it is only because my strength is so much less than my interest—I cannot bear the strain. Mr Clarke[1] must have sat up all night to write his sermon, which was full of interest. . . .

TUESDAY. JULY 16. 1861.

The Visitation of the Divinity School.

A sleep of eleven hours, gave me courage to start for Cambridge. I rode out to Mrs Austin's[2] & went with her to the Chapel. . . .

. . . The rest of the Journal for the two following days—is filed here in the shape of a letter to my sister Fannie.[3] I was too tired to sleep this night.

THURSDAY. JULY 18.

1861

Dear Fannie, . . . I had no thought of going to Cambridge, until Tuesday morning—but Monday night I slept eleven hours, right straight through, and it refreshed me very much. Then Dr Clarke[4] said to have my mind diverted, & get <u>quiet nights</u> would do more than anything, & I felt sure of both at Cambridge. The position of the country was the true excuse for going. You know Harvard College has always held a very important position in relation to the politics of the country. In the Revolution, a Commencement dinner was as important as a meeting held in Queen St. I could not bear not to be there. . . . After the services,[5] all the alumni—old & young, go to Harvard Hall to dinner, & here took place a debate which will be remembered as long as any of them live. My dear friend, William H. Channing has just returned from England—and they called upon him to explain the position of England to this country. Mr Channing showed how different the feeling of the people was from that of the Times—but urged all the while, that we could never have the hearty sympathy of any European nation, unless we made this a war for freedom. Dr Osgood of New York[6] replied insisting that it should be no such thing—that good faith to our own people required that the old compromise should be restored. He was spiteful and bitter against the Abolitionists, and declaimed like a fool against the mother country. This brought Dr Hedge to his feet, who declared that if this did not prove a war of emancipation, we should be eternally disgraced in the eyes of the world. That every inch the sword cleared should be cleared for freedom, that he would not raise a dollar for the soldier if he did not believe it &c &c. He was highly excited & made a terrific appeal. Then up sprang Geo.

Ellis,[7] all his face deformed with rage. He hoped there were no reporters present, to report the extremely injudicious words of his learned brother. Like a parched pea—sprang Dr Hedge to <u>his</u> feet.

"God willing there may be any number here; what I have said now, I will say forever & in the face of the whole world—" & so it went on—till near an hour late the Alumni went in to the Appleton Chapel—to hear Mr Clarke's discourse.[8] It was upon Christ & Anti-Christ—a fine noble exposition of present political duty—but all the ministers in heat & fury, were silently fuming in memory of the debate they had had, & instead of going to tea, the moment they left the Chapel they surged back to the dinner Hall. There Dr Stebbens of Woburn,[9] who had found it hard work to keep still till Clarke had done— roared out all he had to say—like a lion. He said he told the troops that went from Woburn, not to leave a slave on any soil they touched & not to serve under any man, who talked about returning a fugitive. If he thought the war would create no change, he would begin to preach treason, tomorrow. Some of the smaller fry followed in a discussion not worth reporting. I went to Dr Francis'[10] where I found half a dozen ladies beside myself ready to help the ministers to a bountiful tea— The long windows opened on to a beautiful, cool, garden overlooked by a broad piazza, strewed with chairs. The two rooms were crowded. Good tea & coffee—then bread & butter, cake & raspberries, were abundant & well served. The ministers poured in at last in hot haste. Ellis was too angry to come at all— The grace of God struggled harder than usual with the grace of Samuel Osgood. He would hardly speak three words to me, or indeed to any body—(though I am sure it was a condescension to notice him.) wondered if I hadn't a sister in Springfield but couldn't remember her name, but sat in a lonely chair on the piazza, twirling his watch key & swelling like a big turkey cock. Then I seized Dr Hedge and just under Osgood's ears told him, how glad & grateful I felt. He was in a great flutter— how had I heard it all—? but I wouldn't tell. When I entreated him to say openly before the world all that he had said—he exclaimed; "You see what my <u>impulses</u> are!" I begged him to make them principles. Then I talked with Channing for an hour— He told me about Stebbens,[11] which I had not known till then, & lighted up like an arch-angel, so as I ran up stairs to go away, I said, "It's shabby of <u>you</u>, Dr Hedge, to shut us out of Harvard Hall,[12] I <u>hope</u> there was a Reporter there." "Indeed," said he, "<u>I</u> don't shut <u>you</u> out, I would far rather <u>you</u> were there." Perhaps I may tell you, dear Fanny, that there was a very marked attention shown me at this party, and one gentleman just from abroad, told me that every where in England, France, Belgium Germany, & Italy—he found my book on Labor[13] on everybody's table. I think it may be true as I have heard, that there is a cheap foreign reprint of it.

Charles has just written a letter (received today) conveying an invitation from the English Ladies through Miss Carpenter[14] for me to attend the meeting of the Association of Social Science, at Dublin, in September—and offering me half a year's salary to use. Of course, I shall not go—but it is pleasant that they thought of me....

... Will you believe me, when I add that an official invitation was extended to Wm. Lloyd Garrison to attend the college dinner! They could have done no more to a crowned head. Some day they will make him LLD. McDaniels & Alden[15] had good patriotic orations, but I could not attend to them. A singular scene occurred, when the degrees were conferred. John A—Andrew & Winfield Scott,[16] were made Doctors of Law. The Governor was applauded, till he had to rise & bow, but in Latin of unusual excellence & sonorous beauty, Felton[17] turned from summing up his excellencies, to rehearsing those of General Scott. He had to pause, every body rose— Every boy & man tossed his hat—every girl waved her handkerchief for a three times three, till the old roof rung with the hurra's— Governor Andrew—caught the thrill, while it quivered on the air—and sent it from his pencil's end to the Telegraph Office. There has not been such a Commencement <u>Dinner</u> within the memory of man— President Quincy, at 90[18]—spoke with the freshness of youth, Everett[19] with the padlock off, Andrew with the steam <u>on</u>, Phillips & Garrison present!! John L. Motley[20] magnificent & modest in reply to an overwhelming reception....

yrs—Carrie.

BOSTON. THURSDAY. FAST DAY.
SEPT 26. 1861....

Still depressed & expectant about Mr Dall.* As letters have been forwarded from Liverpool, addressed to him, here, & the great Eastern† was to sail on

---

*Charles Dall had come as far as England, on his way home for the first time since his departure in February 1855.

†The *Great Eastern* steamship, designed by Isambard Kingdom Brunel and J. Scott Russell, is considered the prototype of the modern ocean liner. At the time of its launching in 1858, it was the largest ship in the world. On this voyage from Liverpool it was badly damaged in a storm and had to return to port. The ship was financially unsuccessful as a passenger liner; it was later used to lay the transatlantic cable.

the 9th, the day after his last advertised preaching there, I think he must have been in the Great Eastern—. The Persia passed it putting back for repairs. God help me. . . .

After weeks of anxiety in which she was unsure of Charles's fate, Caroline Dall learned that he had indeed been on the Great Eastern, *was unharmed, had returned to Liverpool, and would presumably catch the next steamer for the United States.*

BOSTON OCT. 14. 1861.

On Friday Oct. 11. Uncle Wm. received from Mr Dall a letter, which so disappointed & distressed me—that I have hardly any memory of what has occurred since then.

He reported that the result of his attempt to come home in the great Eastern had been such—that it did not seem probable that his constitution would bear the three consecutive voyages, that would be necessary, if he were to return to this country before going to India, so he proposes to go back without seeing us at all, & asks my consent & uncle Wm's—to his doing so.

The argument as he states it seems very specious, but it does not deceive me. The more unwell he is, the more it is his duty to come home & see his children; the shorter his life is likely to be, the more imperative the necessity that they should meet once more. Most of the time since then, I have spent in bitter weeping—it is of no use, to record here, all the need I had that Mr Dall should come home—my prayer that he might come and seal with his public approbation my public career—my hope that he would once in strong terms, tell his children what he owed to their mother—would express his satisfaction in what I had done for them, and in the pecuniary success of my life. Were he able to give it, I very much needed that he should give his advice about Willie's future—and I wanted also to obtain his express sanctions—to my plans about my own papers.

There are many persons who might object to my disposal of these, if I had not his express consent, I cannot get it in writing so as to be satisfactory. Oh, that I were worthy to go home, that God would take me to himself—life is such a bare & bitter struggle.

For myself—I had many private reasons to greatly desire this return.

I have not slept since the news came, & in spite of every effort to the contrary, have wept most of the time. . . .

... As I read over Mr Dall's Journal, I feel that I ought not to regret so bitterly his continued absence. I am amazed to see how little his family life satisfied him, & how the care he was obliged to take of the house & children in our days of poverty & suffering, wore on his strength & spirits. ...

One remark amused me—<u>& pained</u>, pained because it showed how little he ever understood me.

One day, when I had been cooking all day in a hot kitchen to provide for a large meeting of the Association, he writes—"I am amused to see how determined Carrie is, not to be excelled as a housekeeper by any one she knows."

No such determination ever entered my head. I did my cooking, as from a child I had always done everything,—as well as I possibly could, and I positively did not know or care how others did theirs, unless the failure was outrageous.

A lonely dull day—stitch, stitch, stitch.* ... In the afternoon, Marie[†] came to see me, to propose the establishment of an "American Woman's Journal—" of which she wishes me to edit the Reformatory portion. Mary Booth[21] is to be the Literary Editor. Mr Phillips[22] promises the funds for the first issue in October next. As far as I understand it—I heartily approve the plan, and do not refuse to work.[‡]

Marie amused me—by her earnestness— "I have told them all," she said "that I will not work without you. You have given your life to this cause. You are the <u>most talented</u> woman in America, especially in New England. The place is yours by right. They do not understand you as I wish—they think you are hard to work with— So you ought to be."

No Marie—I am not talented— I have only a little common sense, and a great deal of perseverance—,.

While Marie was here, there came also, Mr Slack[23] who wanted me to speak in the Music Hall on Sunday. I flushed a little as I reminded him,

---

*During the war Dall spent much time sewing for the soldiers.

†The physician Marie Zakrzewska.

‡This journal never materialized.

that I had always told him, that for this service, I must have proper notice I cannot be sought as a "pis aller,"[24] without being allowed time for decent preparation—...

BOSTON. SUNDAY.

APRIL 20. 1862.

Went down to the Music Hall to hear Miss Dickinson.* This is indeed a girl of 19 to be proud of.

If I had spoken, I should desire no better than to speak as she spoke—

Her pronunciation shows Southern training; the timidity of youth—now & then shows itself, but she has logic, historical acuteness clear argument—and a masterly treatment. All these great gifts lifted & swept on—by a stream of as pure patriotic feeling as ever flowed through a woman's breast.

Her voice—as good as to loudness as could be wished, is not so flexible—& thrilled by feeling as I hoped—but it must be as she grows older—.

God grant I am not mistaken in this woman—at all events I give thanks for her today. Can she often do so well as she did today? I do not know—the question—of a continuous power remains to be settled—but this first experiment is thoroughly satisfactory. She is capable of study—which neither Lucy Stone nor Antoinette Brown were. I went up to her and kissed her proudly, and bade her God speed. Then I introduced many others to her. She promised to come & see me this evening—saying it had been one of the great pleasures she promised herself in Boston.[25]

... Mr Garrison & Miss Dickinson, came in the evening. I enjoyed her visit very much, but promise myself a better talk with her alone tomorrow.

---

*Anna Dickinson (1842–1932), lecturer, was born in Philadelphia into a Quaker family. When she was not quite nineteen, she attracted much attention with her successful lecture at the Concert Hall in Philadelphia on "The Rights and Wrongs of Women." The lecture that Dall attended, arranged by Garrison, was followed by appearances elsewhere in New England. Dickinson's message was an emotional plea that the war be turned into a crusade for emancipation. In 1863 she turned her talents on the platform to campaigning for Republican candidates. In January 1864 she spoke in the U.S. House of Representatives before a distinguished audience that included President Lincoln. After the war she was for some years a star on the lyceum circuit, earning as much as $20,000 a year. Her lectures demanded the emancipation of women, socially and economically as well as politically, but she remained detached from the organized suffrage movement. After her popularity waned in the 1870s, she turned to the theater, writing plays and acting. She returned to the platform in 1888 to lecture against Grover Cleveland and was so vehement that her sanity was questioned, and she was forced to stop lecturing. She was briefly committed to an asylum. Her last forty years were spent in New York City and Goshen, New York, in the household of friends *(NAW)*.

BOSTON MASS.

MONDAY. APRIL 21. 1862.

This has been a bitter, bitter day, only redeemed by my pleasant talk with Miss Dickinson. I had planned to go out early with her, and so was to have an early dinner, when Mr Towne came in,* and a good deal excited, by a proposition of Mr Brooks's[26] that he should go to board with Eunice Hall,[27] and by some talk that had gone on between Miss Lucy[28] & Mrs Tebbets,[29] as to my un-popularity, and my "having made, Mr Dall so much trouble in Toronto."

Eight years gone—and my silence has not quieted the slander! I thought it dead of starvation years ago—not the prejudice that grew out of it, but the dis-tinct charge now repeated. May God have mercy! Must my children suffer, till they die, from this miserable report? I wept long & bitterly till my head ached so, that I hardly dared go to meet Miss D. I took her down town while I bought Sadie's trunk & then preferring my society to any diversion, this child of nineteen, came home to talk with me. She has had no more sympathy from reformers than I—no help at home—&c &c— Her mother seems the "counterfeit" of mine. . . .

She seemed to have looked to me, as her salvation, asked all manner of questions about study &c—& I showed her all my methods.

God bless her. When she went I was too ill to sit up longer.

In late May Dall and her children moved to a rented house in Medford, and Ed-ward Towne became her boarder.

MEDFORD TUESDAY.

AUG 26. 1862.

. . . Came home to the great distress of finding that Willie had been trying to enlist, after failing to secure the Cadetship†—and was so set on it, that the manifest impropriety of doing any-thing with his father so near him, yet not present did not seem to strike him in the least. In tears & pain—I gave him money & sent him to his grandfather uncle & J.F.C.[30]—to get other counsel. He had been advised in favor of it, by Father Cleveland[31] & Mr. Pren-tiss.[32] . . .

---

*Edward Towne, for the past year minister at the Unitarian Church in Medford, was about to make new living arrangements. Dall herself was considering moving to Medford and taking him as a boarder.

†Willie Dall had tried to get an appointment to the Naval Academy at Annapolis.

... I worked very hard up stairs all day, & E.* most kindly supplied Sadie's place more than once— He felt for my suspense & anxiety about Willie & tried to relieve it. About noon Willie came home. He was in the depths of Sadness. I did not need to question to know that he had found no one on his side. Mr. Clarke said that boys so young gave invalids not soldiers to their country; Father—that he could advise nothing with Mr. Dall so near arriving— Uncle William flew into a passion & refused to listen. Poor boy! he bore it very well— ...

Dall went into Boston from Medford on Sunday, August 31, to act in her capacity as superintendent of the Sunday school at the Church of the Disciples. She was expecting the arrival of Charles Dall, traveling on the Panther.

... The first thing I heard when I reached town was, that the Panther was in the bay. I heard Mr. Clarke preach, yet hardly heard him, for I longed for the service to be over, that I might hurry home to help prepare lint & bandages.† ...

No one who was in Boston today—will ever forget it. No one but will be proud to own it as a birth place. The car which I took from Dover St. to Court —was crowded to a crush with women & bundles. Most of them were weeping. "Give way," said rough men to each other, "those bundles are sacred." When we got to the Tremont House—a dense crowd had pressed between it & the Hall. All were eagerly gaping for rumors. About the Tremont Temple a semi-circular rope was stretched enclosing several hundreds of cubic feet. At Three Tables—placed in the center & at each end, men took down subscriptions for the freight fund. Within, on the side walk immense boxes were being packed. In the building 1800 women sewed all day. Through each of the three passages stretched lines of men standing 6 ft apart— When we drew near, women with bundles were crowding all the avenues and the streets as far as one could see. Delicate women in Sunday attire, followed by one two or three

*Edward Towne.

†Boston had received the sobering news of the Union defeat at the Second Battle of Bull Run on August 30, with approximately fifteen thousand casualties, leaving Virginia virtually free of Union troops.

servants carrying bundles as large as themselves pressed among the ruder sort. The bundles were passed over the barrier, tossed from hand to hand along the lines, till they reached the inner work-room— I got out, & going up to the Clerks got all the information I needed for Medford. The impression seemed to be, that Pope[33] reinforced, was fighting again.

In the car that went to Medford every body was bitterly depressed. The women thought—that if we conquered in the end, the life of the Camp would ruin our young men, that they would come home coarse, licentious cruel. I could not stand this, and the end was, that I appealed aloud to the women, in a plea lasting—partly in a conversational way, nearly the whole time we were coming out, as to the moral end of the war. How moved the whole population were we can judge from the fact, that one could hear a pin drop in that rattling car—& there was not a smile at me on man's or woman's face.

Across the square, as we came in to Medford, a perfect crowd were hurrying with bundles. The Town Hall, and the <u>Towne</u> vestry were full & I divided myself between one & the other, until I saw Mr. Towne & delivered my news. The Selectmen sent round in Medford & stopt all the services, ordering the citizens & such relief as they could spare to the town Hall. Together Mr. Towne & I went to see Mrs Lincoln[34]—and Miss Mary[35] who would suffer most in the excitement. Nat. Hall was with his sister. I saw the fine view from the rear of our House for the first time today.

Willie came out at dusk to tell me, that his father would not get up till tomorrow.[36] I was surprised to find that in the general distress, I had forgotten my private pain, not having thought of the Panther, after thinking of nothing else for months, since I heard she was in the bay. An evening of quiet rest.

MEDFORD MASS.
MONDAY. SEPT. 1. 1862.

... I staid at home to meet Mr. Dall, who came at 10—and I bore the meeting more quietly, & with less result physically than I expected. He is very calm, but sadly changed. We spent most of the day in talking. ...

MEDFORD MASS.
TUESDAY. SEPT 9. 1862—

Rose as usual at 4½ A.M. to a very busy day. Made a kind of study for Mr Dall in the little room—off the ell, at his request where he could have air & sun &

flies! Was very weary & hoped he would express some gratification but he did not. It seems to me, that we, & all we do are like the shadows on a magic lantern to him, & nothing real but the Mission. . . .

MEDFORD—MASS.

THURSDAY. SEPT. 11. 1862. . . .

Etta Page[37] brought some flowers. I had a little conversation with her about the pic-nic, which evidently displeased Mr. Towne. He thought I was taking too much on myself. I wish I could meet all his moods, but my only refuge is to go on—steadily doing what seems most forbearing, thoughtful & kind to me.

No absolute external rule, would meet the necessities of my position two days in succession. . . . Mr. Dall wonders how I can sacrifice myself to my present position—he remembers how much John used to do for me—& wonders how I can get along without the care—the tender providence to which for those four years I was accustomed.

MEDFORD. MASS.

SATURDAY. SEPT. 13. 1862.

A very busy morning. I don't think Mr. Towne felt well, he was perplexed about his sermon and came up stairs for a recess & to have his hair combed. I found him when I came back from an errand at Miss Mary's[38] reading my Journal. He declares that I once gave him permission to that effect.[39] Well, I am not sorry—but I will keep the book out of sight—for the future. He was very sweet the rest of the day. I sewed in the study, after I came back from my French Class, and in the evening read Trollope's Book on America for a notice of my own books in which I am inclined to thank him.* . . .

---

*Following his visit to the United States in 1861, English novelist Anthony Trollope (1815–1882) published *North America* (New York, 1862), in which he treated Dall as the spokesperson of the American women's movement. In his chapter "The Rights of Women" Trollope took issue with Dall's *"Woman's Right to Labor,"* concluding his long rejoinder, "The question has all been settled . . . by a higher power. [Women] are the nursing mothers of mankind, and in that law their fate is written with all its joys and all its privileges. . . . The best right a woman has is the right to a husband, and that is the right to which I would recommend every young woman here and in the States to turn her best attention" (262).

MEDFORD. MASS.

MAR. 25. 1863. WEDNESDAY.

In yesterday's letter Mr Dall claims $250 from me, in repayment of money
given me for business not <u>private</u> purposes—last September. At the time I told
him I would take it as a loan, & repay it as fast as I could. He said "If I take
Willie to India with me, & have to pay for his outfit & my own and both passages—I may need it in April."

"In that case," I said "you will have no difficulty, for two quarters' salary
will be due you from the A.U.A. but if you should, at any sacrifice I will make
it up."

Now he raises double the money required for his own passage & Willie's,
& $50 over, merely to gratify his own selfish love of ease,—breaks his word to
his child, & after wasting 6 months of Willie's time—& of my strength &
money in preparing him for India—turns upon me, & requests me to furnish
this money—to help out the overland passage!

So help me God I will not do it.

I went up to see Miss Mary & she advises me not. . . .

MEDFORD. MASS.

MONDAY. APRIL 6. 1863.

. . . It was dinner time before Mr Dall came. I did not go to table. He talked with
Willie all the afternoon, with no result except impugning my veracity. It has
come to the worst Toronto state—a question of truth between us two, with my
children in this case, for umpires. And I forget so—if I could only have remembered how it used to be—I might perhaps have spared myself something.
God knows. Still, I did not meddle in the matter— I kept apart—only when
Willie came to me, I told him—if need were—I would mortify myself to any
extent to prove to him that I had spoken the simple truth. A little cross ques-
tioning of his father, however, showed that he could not hold to his own statements & settled that matter.

After tea, Willie told me the question of his going or not going was settled,
& in this wise. His father put him the question—Are you willing to go to India and act for two years wholly under my advice, whether <u>in</u> or <u>out</u> of the Mission School? and Willie said at once "Decidedly not." I had a good deal of
reproach to bear as having upheld him in his decision— Oh Mr Clarke,[40] I
wish you knew all. . . .

MEDFORD. MASS.

SUNDAY. APRIL 12. 1863.

... A very painful talk with Mr Dall before he went to church. ...

He was showing a statement of Willie's reasons for not going to Calcutta, which he declared Willie had seen & approved. I knew it could not be so, & on speaking to W. of it, he showed great indignation saying that he had distinctly—told his father, that he did not assent to one word of it. He then wrote notes to the various members of the family, stating his true reason—in a manly way—namely "distrust of his father's motives & steadfastness." "It is hard to write it of my father," he said, "but it is true." ...

MEDFORD MASS.

FRIDAY. APRIL 24. 1863.

Rose very early—& had breakfast half an hour before the usual time, to be in readiness for Mr Dall. ... Such a farewell—an hour of hurried packing—and not one tender word. God forgive him. ...

In April 1863 Dall returned to Toronto for a visit, the first time since leaving in October 1854.

TUESDAY MORNING—

APRIL 28. 1863. ...

... We reached Toronto at 11.45 AM— and I found a carriage waiting to take me to Dr Beatty's. There I had the warm welcome I expected .... Dr. & Mrs Beatty go to Philadelphia next week & Dr Wilson expects to sail for Scotland with Janie next week. ... I hoped an entire bath & change of clothes—would wake me up & while I was in the midst of it, Dr & Mrs Wilson were announced. I need have no doubt about <u>their</u> love, it was good to have Maggie's arms round me again, & to have her pleading—pleading that if I must be home by the 8th. I would not go to Montreal, but stay with her to the last minute. Dr Wilson took my hand & pressed it to his lips— "Good God!" he said holding it up—as if he would look through it—"you are a mere shadow of a ghost." I promised to go to them tomorrow. They lunched with us, and as soon as they were gone Dr Wilson having as he said six hours work for every <u>one</u> left him, I went out—with Mrs Beatty, to make calls. ... On King St. I was amazed to see several young girls run up to me, express their delight & beg me to go home with them. They proved to be children, who had outgrown my memory of them.... Mrs Copland looked the perfect lady that she always was—one whom no years can spoil, no surroundings sully. Her pure widow's cap—is just as spotless in the old Brewery as it could be at Windsor.

She folded me again and again, in her arms from time to time, one of the tearless sobs—of those who have grown old— "Oh!" said she, "I had given it up. I thought I never was to see you again, in this world—and every day—every day—I have prayed for it." She was very much moved, I laid my head down on her shoulder—to be comforted—my own mother never loved me as she does.

... What I am to do here—I cannot see—every body says—"Have you seen so & so—" & every body adds—"You cannot go till I have had you for a week." ...

TORONTO. CANADA—
WEDNESDAY. APRIL 29. 1863.

It was very touching yesterday to see how every body remembered the children, and told me many an anecdote I had forgotten. Emily & Martha[41] showed me the book mark Willie worked when he was six years old. It seems as if the people here remembered every word I spoke while I was here. No where in the United States, after an entire cessation of intercourse for nine years, could I find such a welcome, as I have received here, find people so precisely as I left them. I wish Mr Towne were here, no words of mine, could show him, what was true, as their actions would. Once through the cold <u>surface</u> of the English heart and we come to something very real & sincere....

After breakfast—the family* would have gone up to Yorkville with me but I felt it best to go alone. I have so much to think of & to feel, that I do not greatly care for the presence of any but near friends.

I went up by the church—which I half built—but never entered, & stood leaning on the fence, the tears—flowing fast—when I heard Dr Workman's voice, and narrowly escaped obstructing his path, as he came out & got into the chaise. The workmen are finishing off the basement—the very basement that John & the architect, spent so many hours over, with me, ten years ago. Strange that I should come back for the first time just as the debt is paid off— and my own plans—being at last carried out—even to the second vestry. The walk proved longer than I expected, but the greeting from all the Wilsons,[42]

*Dall was staying with the Beattys.

was so precious to me. Mary Ainslie[43] whom I had never seen till now, told me yesterday, that I could never seem like a stranger to her, the Wilsons had told her so much about me. Even the servants in Mrs Beatty's house, remember me—and Henrietta said this morning— "I would like you had come—<u>after</u> the house cleaning." Mrs. Wilson took me into her own chamber, and would have the truth about Mr Dall— At last, I told her I could talk no more, it made me so ill, and I have so few pleasant thoughts to trust to for recovery. Then she reproached herself, & touched my hands & cheeks so sadly. Indeed, I don't know whether I have done well to come here, for they all make so much of my illness,—not ostentatiously but with quiet pain showing what they think. That they are so sincere about it—makes it worse, but it ought not—for no one can know as I do, how far this emaciation has gone.*

... In spite of all his hurry—Dr W. has devoted himself to me, like a brother today....

TORONTO & MONTREAL.

MONDAY. MAY 4. 1863....

We reached Montreal at 11—& walked the length of the dépôt without seeing anyone though I felt sure John was looking for me. At last some one touched my hand. "If you had not had an escort" said he "I might have found you before." I did not need to look at his face twice to know that I had not lost <u>his</u> respect—and that whatever passing pain, disturbed him three years ago, was gone forever. Nor do I think I should lose it—if I could tell him all my weakness despair & folly— I would trust him to forgive what he cannot understand. Nor do I feel like a hypocrite before him— He trusts & respects me, because he really knows me. If the time ever comes when the secrets of all hearts are revealed—perhaps some others whom I have served[44] better, may do the same. It is weary waiting though. We were both a good deal moved —& drove silently up to Mrs Brown's[45] who welcomed me warmly. She lives in quite a palace. Champion is at Quebec on Parliamentary business and Arthur[46] is quite sick of intermittent fever. I saw that John would have given a good deal for a few words of my affairs then & there, for he lingered as long as he dared—but I was too exhausted & as soon as possible made a movement towards my chamber.

---

*Dall's health and appearance had been affected by her distress resulting from conflicts with her husband, worry about Willie, and the growing distance between her and Edward Towne.

MONTREAL. CANADA—
TUESDAY. MAY. 5. 1863.

I could not sleep last night—my thoughts wandered <u>home</u>—& I dreaded very much the coming talk with John. Not that I doubted him—but my suffering is so sharp—& my wounds so recent, that I feared they might bleed in his sight. As soon as it was morning I got up to write up my Journal. After breakfast, John sent half a dozen bottles of ale. It seemed strange to have anybody caring for me again in such ways— He seemed to know I should miss the Toronto stimulants. He came up early, and after delivering several Toronto messages to him from the Wilsons & others, I went down to the store with him & looked through the stock, as I used to do in old times. Then we went to Dawsons[47] in search of Mr Towne's books, & then looked in vain for a pen wiper I wanted. John was very unwilling I should walk & seemed to grudge every step. I wished more than once, that he was my brother, that I [might][48] have told him all. In the afternoon, I had after his dining here, at Mrs B[rown]'s request, 4 hours of close talk. He was very much shocked & surprised, but he said he was partially prepared by a very incoherent letter from Mr Dall to himself & another to Mrs Brown. We made little talk—but he said he thought I had got through the worst, & the stand I had taken would prevent any thing so bad from ever coming again. God knows, but this I know, that I shall not be here to meet it— Oh God! have I not earned my rest? May I not come to thee, before anybody can ever pain me more! John was very glad to take my trust, but spoke of his life as a very uncertain thing— When he comes to Boston, he will help me to pack my papers. There is great comfort in talking to him about business matters because he makes no needless question or trouble— Many an executor would have been jealous of the superior power conferred on Mr Towne at first, but when I was about to give an explanation of it, he interrupted me generously— "You cannot help it—you must make an actual transfer and could only do it to a person in the same house. If you are satisfied I shall be— only I hope [approximately five illegible words][49]—. . . ."

A few days later, Dall returned to Medford, where relations were strained with Edward Towne.

MEDFORD. MASS.
THURSDAY. MAY. 14. 1863.

Prepared for Mr Towne's reception, & held one of the most distressing interviews I ever held in my life. . . .

When Mr Towne's health made it desirable to stop Sadie's Latin lessons, she had a beautiful silver paper cutter made, which with the following note, she left on his table the morning I went to Canada— It was marked in allusion to an old jest—between them—

E.C.T. from the "said" S.K.D.

Dear Towsy,

I was very sorry, when mamma told me, my Latin lessons must stop. I am afraid I have been a great deal of trouble to you, but I don't feel very well, & I never have been well taught before. I thought I should like to give you something all myself to show you how grateful I am. Mamma thought you would like this little paper cutter because it will never break & you can carry it in your pocket. Will you take it, with a kiss from the

said S.K.D.

This morning note & paper cutter were both returned to me, Mr T. saying he could not accept them. He said Sadie had not done as well as she could & knew it— That the note was nothing but a piece of conceit—beside she had no business to use money for such purposes. I said "Mr Towne, I think that was a matter for me to settle." "No," he said "I don't like her character & I won't encourage these airs." I told him, he certainly should not discourage them, for the child should never hear from me—how her gift had been received. I could not think without tears of the weary days she spent in ordering this folder & getting it well marked. I foresee that it will not be long, before Mr Towne leaves me, and for that reason, I put on paper, one of the few instances I can preserve of the moods, which will lead to the separation. Let this suffice —my children will remember. . . .

MEDFORD THURSDAY—MAY 28. 1863.

On my way to the cars, got a letter from the Post, which almost compelled me to keep my bed for the day. It was from John—most undeserved rebuke and bitter to bear.* There are mischief makers in Montreal. I was going in to Mr Hallowell's[50] Office to see the black regiment pass—but I could not see— I wrote—till a spasm of agony came on, so sharp that I dared not add a line and gave my letter to Mr Hallowell to mail. I went with Wendell Garrison[51] and Mrs Captn Appleton,[52] within the lines, after I was somewhat recovered.

I could not help forgetting my private pain a little, in the enthusiasm of

---

*This letter does not survive, and the journal does not suggest what provoked it.

seeing Robt Shaw[53] in command, and congratulating the Governor* on this great success. I think I never was so thrilled with patriotic feeling in my life, and the men with the shambling gait of fugitives looked so thoroughly in earnest, so sad yet so resolved. . . .

MEDFORD. MASS.

TUESDAY JUNE 2. 1863.

. . . Finished reading my Canada Journal to Aunt Mary.[54] Mr Towne came in from the woods while I sat there. Came home to make up calling Journal† for him. At dinner he told me in a very rude way, that he did not want me to write any in the new book I had provided. He would take the book (as a gift from me!) but nothing more. "Very well," I said "I do not wish to do so much labor unless it be to save you trouble."

This did not please him, and calling me to his study, he gave me to understand that he should leave me, by the end of this month. That some of his friends (seeing his <u>discomfort</u>!) on Sunday while I was in Boston—undertook to provide for him, &c &c. I told him that I wished nothing but his comfort— but I felt that he ought to remain here till the fall, and leave me with apparent courtesy & good-will. I thought the services I had rendered him, would require that—for his own sake. I besought him to use common prudence and not speak <u>of</u> me, as he spoke to me. "Let me be the worst woman in the world" I said—"no one will justify <u>you</u>, in speaking ill of me— I am not a stranger in Massachusetts." I begged him to put his leaving me, on the ground of the uncertain tenure of the house, since Tim Swan's death,[55] and his own desire of economy. He insisted that he would make what complaints he chose, raved as he has done before, about the high price I charged him for the whole use of the house—tried to persuade me, that I had not a sincere friend in the world &c &c.— I left him with a heavy heart—as I remembered the long sickness through which I nursed him, & afterward his sister Ellen—entirely uncompensated by money—my thoughtful provision for her comfort, the providing of clothing & books to the amount of a hundred dollars—three years—ago— the paying of his debts to the amount of 15 hundred dollars, & the steps—taken which brought him to Medford—it seemed to me, he must be thoroughly in-

---

*John A. Andrew, who had pressured the Lincoln administration to allow blacks to fight in the Union army.

†That is, a list of calls made and received by Towne.

sane, to talk to me, about <u>money</u>. I told him that his going would subject me to great pecuniary loss—& I felt that he ought to keep his books here till fall, and pay me the usual half-board. He said he should do no such thing—

As I left the room, my tearful eyes lighted on the many expensive books which my hands—had placed, from my private earnings on his shelves—on the new gold pen, & case—I gave him from my desk, a few weeks ago, on the books so painfully brought from Toronto to his order—to the silk umbrella—the travelling bag, the writing & dressing cases—the shawl &c &c—which at various times the last three years, had marked my sense of his needs—. I am not apt to count up my own—gifts—but I could not help it tonight. . . .

MEDFORD MASS.

WEDNESDAY. JUNE 24. 1863.

This morning I helped Mr Towne to pack clothing & books, and they were all in Miss Lucy's[56] house by ten o'clock. Then I went over to Miss Lucy's and helped to arrange the new rooms. . . . When all was over, & done—& I had no excuse for loitering, I shook hands with him. "Edward," I said "words are of no use between us. I shall never again defend myself to you. I shall leave my faithfulness in small things to prove my truth in large."

I was sick at heart and came home—meaning to go to bed, but I had a little errand at Miss Mary's & went up to attend to it, when I came out—I met Mr Towne half way up the lane. "Do you want anything of me," I asked, my aching heart, a good deal surprised, "Yes," he said hesitating "I was coming to ask you to give me a glass of ale." I was only too glad. I got some ice—gave him what he wanted, and thanked him for asking. He staid a little and spoke more pleasantly than for a long while.

At night, I wished to look at the letters he wrote me—when "Woman's Right to Labor" was published. I took up my Letter book or file of letters for 1859— I could not help feeling that my active ministry to Mr Towne's life, ended with today. I was moved in the fullness of a pained womanly heart to turn back to the beginning of it. I searched in vain, and was astonished to find they had all been cut out—. It will be remembered by my children that when I was ill in the winter, and my friend Mr Patton, not near enough to be spoken with, I put all my papers into Mr Towne's hands, under a deed of gift, to be finally transferred to Mr Patton, & to save them from being unfairly dealt with. The end shows how little we know when, where, & whom to trust. Mr Dall himself would have injured my papers less. Mr Towne's sensitiveness made him cut away from my journal all my early criticisms, criticisms valuable, in proportion as they were severe, since they showed that I had no prejudice in his favor, and had to <u>learn</u> his value. Doubtless, his taste is now offended at the impulsive openness of his first letters—& he has taken a liberty, he had no right to take till after my death, & destroyed all that I had in his handwriting—to justify my warm—true interest, expressed when no one else believed in him.

    With this at my heart I went to bed this night.

THURSDAY JUNE 25. 1863.

Early this morning, I took the church records—and some copies of the Commonwealth, round to Mr Towne— I did not discover till I had been to his room twice, that he had gone to Boston. I then took a piece of waste paper from the outside of his desk, & wrote these words, or nearly—"I find the three letters written to me, when 'Woman's Right to Labor' was published, have been withdrawn from my care. What they were to me, personally, you know—so precious that two of them I could repeat by heart, what they are to you, <u>prudentially</u> perhaps you do not know. If you wish, you may speak to me, about them, if they are already destroyed, I must do the best I can to repair the loss."

    I left this lying in the Record—went up to Mrs Lincoln's to see Agnes[57] lying ill of scarlet fever, and to show her a few photographs. Then I came home. I went to put away some papers in my India desk, when I heard some one coming down from my study. I looked up & saw Mr Towne looking extremely excited & ill, with a paper in his hand. "I have a note here," said he, "which I will let you read if you will promise to give it back to me." I promised & took it. It was a note addressed to me, which he had written in my study, not finding me at home.

    He began by complaining of my intrusion into his study & my writing a note there; would prevent it by an open rupture, by instructions to Miss Lucy, by refusing to recognise me if I met him in the company of others. He regretted he had come to ask me for the ale yesterday, would never do it again—threatened me in various ways if I presumed to restore his letters from memory &c— In fact, the note was wholly insane—and could only be endured by one who could trace it as I did to physical causes. It seemed useless to talk so I did not tell him, that these threats towards one to whom he was known to be under such heavy obligations, would only harm himself—that they could not frighten me, but in tender & soothing words, I tried to persuade him that it was necessary for his own good, that those letters should be preserved. I did not dwell on my own loss, on the great violation of my confidence, I merely told him, that they furnished the only justifiable beginning of our intercourse. He said he had destroyed all but the first, and that he would not restore. I begged him to keep it. If, said I—you die obscure, it is of no consequence, if you become a distinguished person—it is of a great deal. I tried to make him feel, that it was due to me, that the letter should be preserved, showing as it did a sympathy in my peculiar work which could not fail to rouse me.

I suffered dreadfully in talking. At times he was violent, at times he wept. I cannot tell to this moment, whether I talked to a sane or insane person. I tried to soothe him. I showed him the friendliest intentions but it was all in vain. I got him some ice water—and left him. In five minutes he had quitted the house....

I am very sorry to make this plain record here. What has induced Mr Towne to distrust me, to mutilate my Journal—take back, not only my letters— but the Memorial of Mr Tebbets[58] in which he had written such kind words— I cannot tell—but I beseech those who read this Journal, to make no use of this record, unless imperative reasons require. All who love me, will for my sake love him, & shelter his memory, if it should ever be proved that they cannot truly honor it. I could cast off my own child as easily as Edwd Towne.

And having read thus far—my warm impulsive Willie, my thoughtful indignant Sadie, my kind friends, Dr Bartol and Mr Clarke, don't say—"It is outrageous mother should be treated so, after all she's done—" "He ought to be thrashed for doubting mother's word,"— "This is what comes of helping young men overmuch." "This is just what we expected."

—No, don't let these things be said— I am not sorry for all I have done— So far as he will permit, I shall do yet more— I am only sorry—it was not done before it was too late, for often now I fear, that his magnificent powers will permanently lose their balance, and can never be set wholly right....

My pecuniary anxieties press. I called on the Farleys[59] & offered to take the Episcopal minister to board.

MEDFORD MASS.

WEDNESDAY. JULY 8. 1863.

A quiet morning. A delightful enjoyment of my book & the summer calm, such as I have not had for three years. I did not know how heavy a burden I carried for E.C.T. till I dropt it last Saturday—with my respect, for his integrity.

I have thought about him, a little—& whether I ought to be ashamed of having loved him so well—& been so blind to his weakness. I think not. I loved him with a "pure heart fervently" and as God loves & forbears—tried to love & forbear. . . .

John Patton came for a visit in Medford in July 1863. Serious draft riots were occurring in New York, and would soon spread to Boston.

MEDFORD. MASS.

MONDAY. JULY 13. 1863. . . .

The children went into the woods & picked some strawberries for Uncle John's[60] dinner. Louisa Hall who came out to spend the day, went up to Miss Mary's for a little. John slept most of the afternoon, and we were prevented from walking by fast falling rain. We got the first terrible news of the riot in New York.* Nothing tries my patience like such things. It seems as if 500 peaceable citizens with arms in their hands might have quelled this riot. I read the Reviews in the evening. Gummed all John's linen, which I am to mark tomorrow.

MEDFORD. MASS.

TUESDAY. JULY 14. 1863.

Two letters from Mother in London. Marked John's linen—mended stockings—& suffered, oh, I cannot tell how much—from the horrible accounts from N. York— Told John part of E.C.T.'s story, while I bound the bottom of my brown checked silk dress. He makes no comments, for which I am thankful. I wish to tell the facts, but I could not bear to hear him criticized. . . . Mrs Hallowell[61] made a call, and told us about the riot in Boston,† and of course we passed an excited night.

---

*Riots against the draft occurred in New York City July 13–16 and spread to Troy, New York, and Boston. In New York a mob of fifty thousand, made up mostly of Irish working men, burned a black church and orphanage, attacked the office of the New York *Tribune,* vandalized the home of the provost marshal, and terrorized large parts of the city. The result was $1,500,000 in property damage, more than a dozen people killed, and hundreds injured. See Mark Mayo Boatner, *The Civil War Dictionary,* revised ed. (New York: McKay, 1988).

†The draft riots in Boston were mild compared to those in New York. A mob gathered, began stoning the troops, and dispersed after the soldiers fired on and killed several of the rioters (Boatner, *The Civil War Dictionary*).

MEDFORD MASS.

WEDNESDAY. JULY 15. 1863.

Willie went in town, to get his Uncle John's coat, & returned at 10, having visited the scene of the riot, bringing sad accounts. We went in an hour later, & saw everywhere the traces of serious preparation. . . . Just as John was going to Brookline it rained so hard that he gave it up, & I was very glad;—the rumors of disturbance were so many. Mrs Frederick Tudor[62] met me, & asked me to make a representation from her to the Committee, as to the riotous—preparations for tonight. She had been in to the rooms* but no one knew her. I did so, but found them fully prepared for the burning of Phillips & Garrison's houses —&c. &c— Brought John out with me, gave Jeanie[63] a French lesson, & after I came home—saw Willie entering the gate with a soldier's blouse on— I was cutting away the fading roses from the porch, having just finished my mending. I never shall forget the sinking at my heart. Where are you going Willie? I said. "Over to Watertown with Captn Currier,[64] to defend the arsenal" he answered, & asked for half a dozen things in a breath. John said I must not stay him, & indeed I felt he was quite fit for this service & ought to go, but oh! the trial!

It will seem very trivial to mothers who have sent their children to the field, but better battle—than the ruthless mob.

After tea, we went down & stayed with Mrs Hallowell, whose husband remains with the 44th for the night.[65] She was feeling the excitement and we staid and chatted about photographs and news for—an hour. . . .

MEDFORD. FRIDAY.

JULY 17. 1863.

. . . drove to the arsenal, carrying Willie clean clothes and some food. But he would take neither, because the other men could not have them. He looked very tired having been on guard at the bridge for two nights. He asked for a comb—which I drove to the village to buy. It made my heart ache to leave him. The rain overtook us, just before we got home I think I was never so knocked up by a drive.

---

*The offices of the Anti-Slavery Society, where preparations were under way to defend their members against the attacks of rioters.

After John Patton left, Dall visited her family in Lynn, where the guest minister for the day was Edward Towne.

LYNN. MASS.

SUNDAY. AUG 16. 1863.

I went to church, and heard the sermon I so well remember, "a very present help in time of trouble." My tears would fall, but thank—Heaven I sat where the minister could not see me. I shook hands with him after church, and asked if he went back tomorrow morning but I did not once see his face clearly— I cannot tell whether he is any better or not—but the tones of his voice were softened & clear. God bless and keep him forever, & oh my father, send me some hard work to do—something that will employ every faculty & tax every muscle—and so press down my pain,—for it will not die. I am weak & sick. Every morning when I get up, it seems too hard work to dress myself, and as if nothing would ever compensate for the effort.

I miss John very much. How shall I ever bear it when I get back to Medford. . . .

THURSDAY. SEPT 17. 1863. . . .

Whoever turns back to the month of January 1860—will find that the record from Jan. 9th to Jan 26—has been strangely cut away. Whoever is familiar with my letter files, will miss from those files following the letter of Andrew Peabody,[66] Nov. 1859—three letters which I have often shown written by Edwd C. Towne. This record & these letters were cut away without my knowledge & consent, by Mr Towne himself. How & why God knows better than I, and the only explanation I can give of the matter is a brief synoptic sketch of my acquaintance with him, which must follow here.

On Nov. 20. 1859. Mr Towne preached for Mr Clarke a sermon full of extraordinary matter which he has since destroyed,—from Deut. 32.11. "As an eagle stirreth up her nest." This sermon was entirely wanting in mental perspective & fit proportion, but it probably contained more proofs of genius, than any he has preached since. The impression it gave was of an insane person—or one truly possessed of a demon—it frightened my little boy so that I sent him out of church. Mrs Clarke[67] was so shocked by some things in it that she went up into the pulpit and told him, that he ought not to preach that sermon as he was engaged to do, for Dr Bartol in the afternoon.

I never expected to see this person again—and I did express plainly—to a degree that caused some ridicule, the suffering the services had occasioned. Of the man—I only thought that he was extremely ill in health, and unbalanced in mind, and never expected to see him again. But on Dec 25. I received a warm impulsive letter beginning "Dear Lady" and written without any knowledge of my being married or unmarried—expressing the strongest sympathy in the views set forth in "Woman's Right to Labor." There was nothing improper in this note but it was written with a peculiar freedom, and had it been the result of judgment, instead of a mere freak of impulse I should have said it—was a lasting honor to him to have written it. It could not but interest me powerfully. I answered it, explaining that I was married, that I had heard him preach, and had shared Mrs Clarke's feeling with regard to the sermon—that I was grateful for his sympathy, and should be glad to lend or give him books to read, as he requested, & to direct some studies of the position and duties of women. I cannot remember now—his exact words of praise, but I <u>do</u> remember, that when Mrs Putnam's "Record of an Obscure Man" was published,[68] he said "This book gives me in relation to its subject, the same impression of rare culture, wise moderation and steady common sense, that "Woman's Right to Labor" did." Having despatched my letter I showed his to Mr Clarke, who gave me in return, the letters <u>he</u> had received from Towne—(now gone at his request to Braintree) and an account of the conversation he had about him with Dr Hedge. Dr Hedge said he couldn't tell whether Towne was only insane or—very much in earnest.

"In earnest, take my word for it," I said to Mr Clarke and soon there came a letter in reply to mine, which threatened to force me to take back my words— "Shared Mrs Clarke's feeling in regard to your sermon!!!" it began quoting from mine "Had I known it you are the last person on earth whom I would have addressed—" & it went on pouring out the bitter pain of a sensitive spirit in a way, that made my tears start while my lips jested.

I wrote again, but more than one letter was necessary before on January 9. 1860, Mr Towne came to see me, and I supplied him freely with reform books. My acquaintance with him was formed between Jan 9, and Jan 27, and though I saw much to attract and delight me, I saw also much to occasion doubt and misgiving. I recorded my impressions freely, as I had every right to do—for he was a stranger seeking me of his own accord. He told me a sad story of privation starvation, illness unbefriended and love unreturned....

Mr Towne was frequently my guest after this—and in February fell ill at my house of a terrible disease[69] contracted from my little boy. He was ill four weeks. He came there of his own accord, when he first felt ill because as he said at the time, he wholly trusted my friendship. I nursed him, <u>with</u> my two sick children, to my own great loss of strength. I thought it a privilege <u>then</u>, I think it so <u>now</u>, after all these months of pain, but the nervous irritation was so great, that only extraordinary care could have saved his life. His illness was a heavy expense, and during it, in his delirium—I became aware of his debts and of other troubles hitherto concealed. I did what a good mother must have done, I promised the debts should be paid, and he believed me.[70]

When he recovered, Dr Bartol informed by me of his circumstances, gave him $50 with which he went to South Pass in Illinois, to see the mother[71] from whom he had been parted by poverty for 5 years. What I did for Mr Towne entailed some painful sacrifices on my children, but I asked their permission for what I did, and they gave a cheerful consent to parting with luxuries, which they missed long after he had ceased to remember the care which restored his stomach to healthy action. I endeavored to make the Braintree people, do something for him, but they would not, & I clothed him at my own expense, and afterward got the sum made up by private contributions.

After Mr Towne had gone West I stirred about the matter of his debts. . . . I think the whole amount paid out for his needs—journey, clothing, books —& debts amounted to 1350 dollars. It was on the 20th of June 1860 that Thomas Gaffield[72] gave him the check to pay his New Haven debts, and on the evening of the 21st. he brought me back the receipted bills. The recollection of the emotion he showed, will be grateful to me, on my dying day. I had worked without any selfish motive—for nearly four months to set him free— and now of the check Thomas gave him, $500 was a loan, for which I privately had offered security. So little was he accustomed to the use of money, that at this time I gave him $50 for his purse at Braintree, where he found his salary—inadequate to his first wants. I afterward took up the first note due to Gaffield—I think for $250— I obtained $100 from Oct. Frothingham[73] in August—& so went on.

The fact of the debt to Thomas kept me in intimate relations with Mr Towne, for he saw he must have a larger salary, and I wished to help him to obtain one.

From the beginning of our acquaintance there were painful seasons, when I tried to make Mr Towne feel that he ought to go without what he could not pay for. That he might not think this proceeded from selfish motives, I <u>gave</u> him of books & articles of convenience, to the very [best] of my ability while

I <u>urged</u> his own economy. In Nov. 1860. after a long & intimate correspondence with his mother, his sister Ellen came to me—& resided four months in my family— She was severely ill for two. I had expected to educate her, in return for certain services rendered, but my experience developed such traits of selfishness & deception, that I thought it fortunate that . . . the Dr imperatively ordered her return to the milder climate of Illinois. Her brother thought so too at that time, as I have letters in his own handwriting to prove. She was involved in a clandestine engagement which gave us both great trouble. Mr Towne gave me on Christmas 1860, the only expensive gift I ever received from him, a copy of the Forest Hymn[74] in which he wrote a beautiful testimony to his feelings of gratitude & affection. I let him see that I did not approve the expenditure.

In March—or February—Ellen left for home—by my aid and that of friends, thoroughly clothed & provided for— In April 1861—Mr Towne was settled in Medford. I had taken steps the previous August, to have him preach there as a candidate, and though it is unfit that I should enter into ways & means, these resulted in his settlement.

During the following year, I had much care of him in seasons of sickness, for he always came to me, if he was slightly ill, or I went to him, if he was more so—and I had much anxiety on account of the purchase of a horse for $150 which I did not approve—and which ultimately turned out disastrous. In all this time, I kept Mr Towne's counsel in delicate matters. I never spoke of Ellen beyond the few, who necessarily knew her, and who often cautioned [me] to beware of the development of certain family traits in Mr Towne himself. He used my house, my books, &c. with the same ease as if they belonged to himself— I did not wonder, but I sometimes wished for his sake that the freedom were a little less. When in April 1862 it became necessary for him to leave Mrs Page,[75] it did not seem strange to me, that knowing my desire to move out of town, he wished me to come to Medford & keep house for him.

It was after long and painful consultation with my friends that I consented to do so, but I had no dread <u>then</u>, of misunderstandings with him. I feared it might make trouble in the congregation; but we never can foresee from <u>whence</u> our troubles will come. I risk nothing in saying that I have wholly satisfied the Medford people, that they have been uniformly kind and generous to me, and <u>that</u>, in spite of all the painful complications occasioned by Mr Dall's return. . . . The only unkind remark I ever knew of, was Miss Lucy Osgood's. I wish a more ignorant person had made it.

But if Mr Towne were asked he would perhaps say—that

1. He had suffered under my "hard judgment & rule"
2. That I had charged him money not my due.
3. That I had interfered by being present at his receptions.

To this I reply, that having made myself sponsor to those who aided him, for Mr Towne—I did gently—tenderly—& sometimes with tears, advise against the constant purchase of expensive books—against the delay of necessary parish calls—against a growing indifference to Sunday School duties &c—and still farther against a selfishness which led him to put off what was disagreeable, and to visit chiefly to please himself.

I know that the persistency of my character and the strength of my language, will make it easy for many to believe that I may have urged my views improperly. I know—& Mr Towne, knows, that he had taught me many sharp lessons before I came here— I <u>was</u> forbearing—my children & friends said far too much so. While I besought him not to <u>buy</u> books—I procured for him the use of a share in the Athenaeum. I gave him whatever my literary position gave me the chance of picking up, & bought for him to the extent of my ability— trusting that some one else would some day do as much for my Willie, did he need it. I copied long extracts for him, when the effort was too great [for him], & tempted him to extensive purchases. I pleaded against his writing on the margins of his books, premature theological criticisms—I protected these criticisms from the eyes of strangers, read them carefully before I judged, and felt—friend of Parker & lover of Emerson—as I am—that he was deficient in the power to appreciate Christ, in true religious humility— I never hoped to open his eyes by argument—but I did trust that my own personal self denial would show what I thought & felt of Christian living.

I kept a Parish record for him, (that for 1862 is, by accident—still in my possession) and once a fortnight gave him a list of the calls most needing to be made— I tried to make it easy for him, and did my utmost by making my house pleasant to the Parish to bring about a cordial entente between him & his people.

When I found the people complaining that his interest in the Sunday School was wearing off, I tried by sympathy to revive it— . . . I undertook to teach him French— My lessons were given the last thing before retiring. No matter how weary or sick, I always sat up till he came home, that he should not miss the opportunity.

[76]As to <u>money matters</u>, my bitterest grief has been, that words should be possible between Mr Towne & me, about them. If he is not insane—he has

shown a degree of meanness—of which I could not have conceived him capable in dealing with an utter stranger. I append here his own record of the agreement between us when I came to Medford.[77] For all the privileges he claimed, I asked him $6.00 a week, the common price in the square, for one room & board <u>without</u> fire or lights.

For this $6.00. I furnished both. When the war occasioned the price of coal to rise to $12.50 a ton—I could not continue this, and with his consent raised the price to $8.00. But when he paid the first quarterly bill, April 1st. he complained bitterly—and I bore it in silence. I charged the same price up to July 1st—for he gave me no <u>proper</u> notice of leaving, and left me to pay all those expenses alone, which <u>incurred on his account</u>, it was understood we should divide. This bill, he repudiated and left me with $67 of it unpaid. . . .

May God forgive him, no one <u>but</u> himself can ever know—how true it is, that I am the last person whom he should ever defraud of a dollar. Poor friend!

3. My coming into his room on reception evening—was not at first intended, but grew into a habit because the people liked me, & asked for me—& because Mr Towne himself was thereby relieved of much tedious work. He did not complain of it, till he was going from me and even then, I left him alone, whenever I could do it, without seeming rude to personal friends. His request for my absence would have been enough, at any time <u>before</u> the trouble began.

I have answered all his charges but one, made to me in moments of bitter irritation—namely that I had deceived him, from the first as to the authority which Mr Dall claimed over my arrangements, and therefore all agreements made with me were void.

I cannot reply to this except by saying that Mr Towne knows if any one on earth—does—that I am truthful & sincere, and his own observation, ought to have convinced him, young & inexperienced as he is, that the attitude Mr Dall took towards me last winter, was something wholly new & by me utterly unexpected.

And now, what ground of complaint have I against my friend.

1. Instead of being pleased at my success with his people as I thought he would be, he was jealous of it, & this increased to such a pitch, that the sound of my voice in happy conversation became irritating to him. He called the formation of my reading class, an attempt to make a <u>party</u> for myself in the Parish!!

2. He took dishonorable liberties with my private papers. Last winter, near to death, and in great perplexity, I wished my private papers to be put into safe custody. For more than two years it had been understood that in the

event of my death he was to edit my reform papers, & in conformity with this idea I made Mar 28. 1863 a deed of gift—and actually put the papers into his possession—adding to them on account of my emergency, my journals, letters, &c.

I supposed that he understood that they were not to be touched until after my death, and my trust in his honor was so entire that I never thought of saying to him, as I put them into his private drawers, "don't open them." ... It was by degrees—that I ascertained my loss, I never missed the letters written me about Woman's Right to Labor till June 26—or thereabouts—but I believe my Journals & files were mutilated that day.[78] From this time forward, he did his utmost to take away, every expression of his regard for me— ...

In one way, I have done Mr Towne lasting service, I have prevented his publicly taking rash & absurd positions more than—once— At the outset but for me he would have refused to administer the Communion—but for me he would have printed autobiographical matter that was better burned—but for me—he would have got into more than one personal quarrel. ...

I have written this in haste, as a security for the future with no memoranda—there may be errors in dates or dollars—named but there is none in the statement otherwise.

MEDFORD. MASS.
SATURDAY. OCT. 10. 1863.

When Willie came home last night, he brought me a letter from Charles. It was a wise, kind, thoughtful letter, the first I can truly say I have had from him for eight years. If he had always written in this wise, I should have been a happy woman. I took it in to father this morning, and he was as much pleased as I was, and responded kindly promising to look at the W. Canton St. house— &c &c—*...

Dall left Medford and moved back to Boston, to a rented house in the South End.

BOSTON. SUNDAY. MAR 27. 1864
Easter.

I slept last night in this house No 70 Warren Avenue for the first time. I rose on this lovely Easter morning grateful to God for many things. When I left

*Dall had asked her father's help in seeking a house to rent in Boston.

Medford yesterday morning—after having passed three nights at the Lincolns[79]—& three days unpacking in town, I left a note for Miss Osgood[80] with a bunch of flowers for her—& a closed box—for Mr Towne. . . . To Miss Lucy, I wrote a few words of kind farewell, & remembering—the doubt I had had of the Medford people,—before I went there, I took occasion to express my gratitude to the "kind Medford people," who had lightened my trials this winter. . . . May God help me to a resurrection of my life—forgive me the weakness & presumption which made me undertake a friendly task too heavy for me, and give me courage to live down the misunderstanding that is no easier to bear, because it is in part deserved.

BOSTON. TUESDAY.

MAR. 29. 1864.

After two days hard work the house looks like home. I had a bitter grief tonight, in the shape of a cool note from Miss Osgood, utterly surprising & unprovoked, in return for my flowers— I answered it—copy in my letter book—.* I can scarce sleep tonight for the pain. . . .

BOSTON. SUNDAY.

APRIL 17. 1864.

Perplexed about the sale of various matters in the Medford House. Sadie came home from there last night, also with Willie's going to Chicago—† He starts on Tuesday.

---

*Lucy Osgood's note, dated March 26, 1864, very formally written in the third person, thanked Dall for the flowers but noted that "knowing herself not to have been of the number of those 'generous Medford friends,' whose aid & sympathy have cheered Mrs Dall during her residence here, she cannot rejoice in the reception of civilities to which she is not entitled." A copy of Dall's reply is now filed with her correspondence (Dall Papers, MHS). In it she expressed her grief at the reception of Miss Lucy's note, claiming ignorance of how she might have wounded her. She continued, "In what I have suffered this last year, from the estrangement of a friend [apparently Edward Towne] who had tested my weaknesses for years, & ought for my kindness sake to have had patience with them, I have sought no sympathy & made no explanation." She finally pled, "Miss Lucy, do not form a judgment in a case which has only come fairly before God. I shall never vindicate myself, unless my children are made to suffer for my sake. If they are, the means which are in my hands I shall use, at whatever cost to myself." She concluded the letter, "With sorrow that you have not read me better but with sincere respect for yourself, even if you cannot respect me."

†Eighteen-year-old Willie Dall, who despite his mother's efforts could not find suitable employment in the Boston area, was going to Chicago at the invitation of her friend, Unitarian minister Robert Collyer (1823–1912). Collyer also had been actively and thus far unsuccessfully seeking a position for Willie. On April 18 he wrote to Caroline Dall, "Send Willie right to us, we will keep him a month anyhow and by that time he will see what can be done. It shall be no expense to him not only for his fathers sake little woman but for your sake too" (Dall Papers, MHS).

... Willie received a letter from his grandfather ordering him to be employed on the Illinois Central.* It was a strange† letter—but will give him some chance.

BOSTON WEDNESDAY.

APRIL 20. 1864.

Went with Willie to the dépôt. Broke down utterly last night & this morning. It may be best to have him go. God may bring great & unforeseen good out of it—but I can never forget that the cruelty of his own kin, drives him away. If among his <u>wealthy male</u> friends—there was one—who cared for my sickness & loneliness, I need not have given him up.

BOSTON MASS.

FRIDAY. JUNE 3. 1864.

A very busy morning. Another note from Mr Walker[81]—about "ego-ism." This charge has been made against every reformer since the world began—& it seems strange to me, that a person of Mr Walker's refinement does not see that it is inevitable, & that it does not really touch me. The egotist is not a magnanimous person—but irritable, selfish—reluctant. No one would ever feel able to come & tell me to reduce my egotism, if I were really an egotist. No one would have told Hawthorne or Margaret Fuller. . . .

BOSTON. SUNDAY.

JUNE 5. 1864.

... I find on looking back that I have said nothing about Mrs Stanton's letter addressed to me in last week's Liberator.‡ It is too absurd to notice at all, & I

---

*That is, Mark Healey has arranged a job for Willie in Chicago with the Illinois Central Railroad.

†An asterisk was added later at this point, and the following note was interlined: "*It contained a condition that if he was not satisfied with his clerkship, that he should ask no farther help."

‡Elizabeth Cady Stanton's letter was in response to Dall's letter published in *The Liberator* of May 6, 1864, which in turn was Dall's negative response to a private undated letter from Stanton that urged women to become politically active in the presidential campaign in order to "overthrow . . . the present dynasty"— that is, the Lincoln administration. Dall's article advised that women not become involved in partisan politics, aligning themselves with a particular candidate. In response, Stanton called Dall's letter a "paradoxical letter of fragmentary thoughts, thrown together without logic or arrangement" and argued forcefully for the necessity of woman's influence even in the nitty-gritty of presidential politics. Whereas Dall's letter had praised Lincoln, Stanton blamed him for continuing to support slavery and denying suffrage to free blacks (*Liberator*, June 3, 1864, p. 89). Stanton's letter also appeared in the *National Anti-Slavery Standard* of June 11, 1864.

am sorry for the Editors who have to publish it. When Garrison told me, she had written me a very <u>severe</u> letter, I supposed there was at least a shadow of reason & truth in it, which might give me trouble, but there is none— I could not vindicate myself nor answer her, except by printing her first unwomanly letter—& that I would not do without her consent. . . .

BOSTON. MASS.

MONDAY. JUNE 13. 1864.

. . . The Members of Congress seem to think I need instruction in regard to finances—for they have begun to send me their speeches— Mr Kelley* also sends two this morning in regard to the <u>Condition of the Freedman</u>. His first response I suppose to my letter to him.† . . .

TUESDAY. JUNE 14. 1864.

Went over to Aunt S's to enquire about Uncle, whose cataract was removed last night. Found a letter from Judge Kelley‡—& one from Sydney Gay[82]—on my return. Charming both of them. . . .

---

*William Darrah Kelley (1814–1890), formerly a Philadelphia judge, was now a congressman (he would serve fifteen terms). Strongly opposed to slavery, Kelley had abandoned the Democrats to become one of the founders of the Republican Party and was considered the best Republican orator in the House.

†Dall had written to Kelley on June 6 because she had earlier received a letter from Sarah Pugh, an antislavery acquaintance in Philadelphia. Pugh told Dall that Kelley had been a recent visitor to their home and that "The Standard was in my hand in which I had just been looking over, with much interest, your letter to the 'Women's loyal League,'—whose present position did not please me,— I read to him the part of your letter relating to Mr Lincoln—beginning 'What would I have, you ask me.' 'Most excellent words! I have not seen so much wisdom written on the subject. Had I time I would write to Mrs Dall. Do you know her? Will you not write & thank her for me, her words are very sound—tell her that the President moves as fast as he thinks the people will sustain him' " (letter of May 13, 1864, Dall Papers, MHS).

‡Congressman William D. Kelley's letter of June 12 was in response to Dall's to him of June 6. He told her that he had called on Lincoln at the White House on the evening of June 9 and given her letter to the President, who asked him to thank her for "your tender confidence and tender consideration." Kelley had since sent Lincoln the *Liberator* with Dall's letter marked (presumably her letter "To the Women of the Loyal League" in the *Liberator* of May 6, 1864, in which Dall vigorously defended Lincoln). Kelley went on to agree with Dall that no "backward step" must be taken regarding emancipation, and to assure her that Lincoln was also firm. Finally, he commented on the question of "clothes reform" among women, urging Dall to "do nothing to discourage it" (Dall Papers, MHS). Perhaps his advice had an influence on Dall, for though she began by opposing the movement, later (though she did not agree with all its goals) she supported the effort to buy goods of American manufacture (Ms. Journals, May 19, 1864 and January 18, 1865).

SATURDAY

JULY 2ND. 1864.

. . . Sometime this week I have had an autograph letter from President Lincoln but it was private.

BOSTON—MONDAY. SEPT 12. 1864.

A long pause to be filled by no very important record. We went to Concord—& staid till Tuesday afternoon—not longer because we remained with the Alcotts,* and on account of sickness in the families, did not go to Gov. Brown's[83] nor to Elizabeth Prichard's[84] at Lincoln. I saw all my old friends. At the Alcotts' I had a truly delightful time. I heard Mr Alcott tell the story of his early life & was so captivated by it, that when he talked to me about conversations for the winter I insisted they should be on his Autobiography & under conditions he yielded. I came home promising to see Mrs Howe[85] & make some arrangements. I am also to read Louisa's novel of "Moods" † & try to find a publisher for it— I am to get May some pebbles to paint—& if possible get an appointment for Mr A. but this last will be difficult. I wrote to Miller McKim at once.[86] . . .

BOSTON. FRIDAY.

DEC. 9. 1864.

Went down early [to Lynn] . . . to try to persuade father to loan me the money to get my furs. I shall earn enough this winter to do it, but cannot get my money in season. He said I had no <u>right</u> to them—so I did not press it—I do not want them for mere show— They act favorably on <u>my</u> throat though this is not the common experience. Last winter those given me in Toronto, were so shabby—that I tried to do without them—but suffered till I put the old things on. <u>This</u> winter I <u>cannot</u> wear them—& I am grieved not to have, what I need—solely for want of my father's sympathy. I want to buy good ones, that they may last me my life time. When father came up, mother was crying. I asked what was the matter. He said every time I came—there was a fuss—that Marion would

---

*Dall and her daughter Sadie were staying with the Bronson and Abby Alcott family.

†Louisa May Alcott wrote *Moods,* which turned out to be her first published novel, in the winter of 1860 at Orchard House in Concord. Bronson Alcott, her father, had been trying unsuccessfully for years to find a publisher for it. Dall took it home with her, read it, corresponded with Louisa about its merits and defects, found a publisher, and read the proofs. The novel was in print by the end of this year.

not enter the room, while I was—there. I asked him what I had <u>done</u> to Marion— "I was a Woman's Rights Woman!" "Well," I said "Do you wish me to
stay away from the house?" "He was not prepared to order that."

I might have said that I came only for my mother's sake, but I refrained.

If I were my father—Marion Healey should treat her sister decently....

BOSTON. MONDAY. JAN 9. 1865.

Beside various literary jobs—wrote up Madame Clarke* &c all the morning—
and in the afternoon—, made a call on Helen Parsons[87] & dined with Henry
James.† I like his family. Wrote for Mrs Clarke all the evening.

BOSTON. FRIDAY. JAN. 13. 1865.

...In the midst of [writing a letter], came Henry James—partly to bring me
Miss Clapp's letter[88]—or rather his letter to Miss Clapp, she having recalled
her own, & partly to decide a question—so absurd (when brought to me) that
no one would credit me—if I had not his own hand in proof. He and his boys—
he said—had been pleased with my visit, & had been discussing my character— The boys said my mind was masculine— He with riper age & quicker
insight declared it feminine—& wanted my <u>own judgment</u> on the subject!!

"Fussy & futile distinction of sex—" he once said of "Absolute Science"[89]
— Humph! thought I—quite fussy & futile here, but I laughed & told him
what I thought.

Lizzie Meriam[90] came in while he was here, to get some copying to do for
me—which I wished to send to England. I began in a joke—to tell her what Mr
James had come for. "Oh, don't speak! let me guess! may I?" she exclaimed,
clasping her hands— "Feminine, <u>strongest</u> feminine!" she added. "We had a
dispute about you in the vestry the other day—& I could not see what people
meant, by calling you ultra & masculine!" It was very strange that neither she

---

*That is, she recorded the reminiscences of Rebecca Hull Clarke (1790–1865), James Freeman
Clarke's mother. After the death of her husband Samuel C. Clarke left her penniless, Rebecca Clarke man-
aged in the last thirty-five years of her life to become a successful businesswoman. See Arthur S. Bolster,
Jr., *James Freeman Clarke* (Boston: Beacon Press, 1954), 4, 60, 286.

†Henry James Sr. (1811–1882), lecturer and writer on religious, social, and literary subjects, strongly
influenced by Fourier and Swedenborg, was living in Cambridge. In addition to his wife, Mary Walsh
Robertson James (1810–1882), the family at home at this time consisted of sons William (1842–1910), the
future psychologist and philosopher, and Henry (1843–1916), the future novelist; and daughter Alice
(1850–1892), the diarist.

nor H. J. seemed to see the least impropriety in talking to me, in this way, about myself. Do they think I am human? Mr James in support of his own view, told me what he had said to his wife, after first meeting me, at Mrs Clarke's.

"I have had a curious experience," said he "we had a little talk. I think she was on her guard—" I know I was. "She said little, did not assert herself, but I felt her predominance, wanted her approval, found myself growing diplomatic in order to obtain it. I was conscious of a sort of dread, which I never feel for a man,—so I am now." continued he quite innocently—Something was said about Eliza Clapp's intellect. "Why speak of her intellect beside your own" said he, "She's a mere baby—beside you."

It was the funniest thing I ever knew. It never seemed to me for a moment that he was talking about me—& when I told Ames[91] tonight, he fairly rolled on the floor—in convulsions of laughter. . . .

BOSTON. JAN 19. 1865.

. . . I had letters from Willie excessively painful in their defiant spirit.[92] Went to Mrs Bartol to see Mrs Adams[93]—to Dr Bryant's[94] to enquire about the Behring's Sts. Expedition*. . . . Sewed at mother's—till it was time to hear Henry James on Carlyle[95]—the finest lecture I ever heard. Was complimented by Sara Clarke—Mr Calthrop,[96] Jas. R. Lowell,[97] Wendell Phillips, & Henry James &c &c—about Habits of trade.† For the first time since last May, Mrs Josiah Quincy[98] bowed.

Wrote to Willie with a very heavy heart. His letters show no proper respect for me—

*Dall refers to the Western Union–sponsored Russian American Telegraph Expedition that was about to get under way. The purpose of the expedition was to find a route for a telegraph line that would connect the United States with Europe, running through British Columbia, the Yukon Territory, Russian America (Alaska), and Siberia. The expedition, which left later in the year, included a Scientific Corps among whose members was Dall's twenty-year-old son, William Healey Dall. This was the beginning of his distinguished career as a naturalist.

†Dall's article by this title appeared in the *Boston Daily Advertiser* on January 18. Subtitled "A Review of the Reports of the Economic Leagues in New York and Boston," it expressed Dall's sympathy with the leagues' goal of curtailing luxurious dress for the duration of the war, but dwelt upon her outrage at the "coolness, the moral indifference" shown by American manufacturers and retailers as they admitted (under pressure of the economic leagues) their practices of putting foreign labels on American goods and making exorbitant profits. Her own conclusion was that it was ladies' duty "to buy, not *American* goods, but *well-made* goods, wherever they can be found, giving the preference to American when of good quality and openly sold as such."

BOSTON. SATURDAY.

FEB. 4. 1865.

Sewed till eleven and then attended to errands, until it was time for my class. Am grieved to have no news of Willie. I feel sad & troubled about him. He seems—to me, to be just now wilful & selfish. Wilful my son, might be—but selfish? God help me to bear the great disappointment. . . .

SUNDAY. FEB. 19. 1865.

I often wonder what my lot would have been like, if I had been beautiful, and as attractive to men as I am to the young women of my reading class. Then, I suppose I should have belonged to the Atlantic Club, and have been able to get an article into the N. American without manoeuvering or waiting. But God does not carry great reforms, by wrapping them in jelly. They get no hold on men, till they are swallowed like genuine medicine, with full knowledge of their quality & full faith in their power.

Still—I am glad for her sake, that my daughter is to be pretty & graceful. . . .

FRIDAY. MAR. 10. 1865.

The time unrecorded[99] has passed in illness—in strivings to replace an ungrateful servant—in perfecting arrangements for teaching Mrs Henry Whitney[100]—in bearing the sad news that Willie is to go to Behring's Straits and in preparing for his comfort. On Sunday last—Mar. 5—I went with Mrs Tolman[101] to hear Mr Alcott,* it was a stupid affair. . . .

SUNDAY APRIL 9. 1865. . . .

Since I wrote last—we have had the most exciting news of my life-time. When I read last Sunday afternoon that the rebel lines were broken in eight places— I knew that the end must come soon. I could not be glad— I was oppressed —awed— Dark over me fell the responsibility of closing with the wretched leaders—of pursuing the rebel rout, of trying to appease all the irritations that must come with peace.

Then came Monday, with the sudden & unexpected news of the evac-

---

*Bronson Alcott was lecturing at the Melodeon under the auspices of the Parker Fraternity on "Religious Views and Issues of Our Time" (*Transcript,* March 4, 1864, p. 2).

Caroline's daughter, Sarah ("Sadie") Keen Dall, circa 1857–1861, when she was between eight and twelve years old. Caroline's son, William ("Willie") Healey Dall, age nineteen, at about the time he left on the Western Union Telegraph expedition to Alaska. (Courtesy of Massachusetts Historical Society)

uation of Richmond & Petersburg,* Tuesday with its glorious meeting at Faneuil Hall,† & lovely fairy-like show of fireworks in Chester Park. Then Wednesday & Thursday with all the sympathy & excitement of Lincoln's presence in Richmond.‡ Today—we look for the last news. God grant Lee[102] may escape out of our hands.

WRITING APRIL 22.

BOSTON MASS.

MONDAY APRIL 10. 1865.

Came the news of what?

So terrible has been the excitement of the last two weeks, that dates names, places have faded from memory—and I dare not trust myself. It must be more than a week since that terrible assassination!

---

*Jefferson Davis and his cabinet (except for the secretary of war) left Richmond on the evening of April 2, and the Confederate army's evacuation of Richmond and Petersburg, Virginia, was completed in the early morning hours of April 3.

†This was a "Jubilee Meeting" in honor of the fall of Richmond. *The Liberator* (April 14, 1865, p. 57) carries an account of the event.

‡President Lincoln arrived in Richmond on April 4 and spent the night there.

On Sunday April 9—I talked to my S.S. Scholars about the ides of April. Did I dream that they were to be crowned & made historic like the ides of March.[103] I told them that before Thursday—we should doubtless have tidings that would change our fast into a thanksgiving—the tidings of Lee's surrender. It came—what a glorious sermon Mr Clarke preached—and on good Friday April 14—how happy we all were! It was our last happy day! . . .

On Saturday morning—April 15. the sun rose with the lovely warm blush of summer—Sadie & I were dressing with light hearts— Suddenly the milkman pressed into the vestibule and shouted, "Tell Mrs Dall that Lincoln & Seward[104] are both assassinated." "Nonsense," I said, after a moment's pause of horror. "Nonsense Seward is sick in bed." I thought it was a canard— Sadie said—"What stories they <u>do</u> tell!" We went down to breakfast stopping to pick up the Advertiser on the way. Sadie lifted it—turned white as a sheet— & shouted "Mamma!" I had no need to ask— At exactly 15 min—past seven— while the last breath was quivering from his lips, we were weeping bitterly, over the horrid tale.

At last—Sadie said, "What will you do, mamma?" "I will go out" I said "I <u>should</u> stifle here." I walked all the way down town starting just as the bells began to toll. I shall never forget that walk nor the serious grief—on every face. I saw two men who looked indifferent, perhaps exultant—. I could have killed them. Twice up & down State St. I walked. Such grief even to tears—on every face! "He has died for the people—" they said. I heard of the mass-meeting of merchants, at the Tremont Temple and went there.[105] Franklin W. Smith whom the President had so lately pardoned presided.[106] I never saw him before— but I don't like his face. It was a noble meeting—yet not one of our first Speakers—took part in it,—if I except Judge Russell.[107] It was a moment to feel the popular pulse & remember its throbs forever. I went then to my own reading class. I expected no one. About 20 ladies came— We read from the Bible & also from—"Julius Caesar—" and talked of all the bearings of the matter.

I took tea at father's—and saw Mrs Clark—& Mr James[108]—came home— put black on my bonnet—and hung black streamers to my door bell.

BOSTON WEDNESDAY. APRIL 19. 1865.

This was the day of the President's funeral. I could not think or work— I left the people busy about the floor and went to church—. . . . Oh God! do let me wake from this night mare & find it all a dream. I never can get energy or strength to work again till I can shake it off.

SATURDAY. APRIL 22. 1865.

I go through all my duties like a ghost—Greek class & French yesterday—History today—but no interest in either. I cannot—cannot think. God knows if I shall master it.

BOSTON. MASS.

FRIDAY. MAY 26. 1865.

... It is rather vexatious that Louisa Alcott should pretend to be surprised at my notice of "Moods" after all the correspondence that passed between us,* & my speaking my mind more than balances, it appears—the reading of the proof—& the getting of the publisher.

BOSTON.

FRIDAY. JUNE 23. 1865.

Class Day.

Very unexpectedly to myself, I was able to go to Cambridge. . . .

I had compliments & good cheer from Dr Hill & Dr Sparks,[109] Dr Hill gave me a good talk. He feels as I do, that this is really the first time in which it has ever been worth while to live. He told me two things to be remembered.

1. He was at the funeral services [for Lincoln] in Washington & was of course, profoundly impressed but there was he said <u>one</u> moment more eloquent than any speech. President Johnson[110]—walked up to the bier and looked steadily at the face of his friend. A perceptible thrill passed through the assembly. No words moved them like that.

2. When the news came of the surrender of Lee, Dr Hill went in to morning prayers, prepared to give the boys a holiday. He made a very short speech

---

*Dall had reviewed Alcott's *Moods* in the *Commonwealth* (January 28, 1865, p. 1), praising some aspects of it, but strongly objecting to other features, especially to the dilemma of the heroine, who marries a man of sterling qualities whom she greatly admires but cannot love, and is therefore miserable. Dall observed that "Marriage is necessarily imperfect," and declared that "if a woman can conceal her aversion to any man sufficiently to marry him, then her duty requires her to conceal it for the rest of her life, and *duties* are, in God's mercy, always *possible*." An unhappy match "is, of course, the sharpest of all trials, but it admits of alleviation, and a woman may, in spite of it, make home happy and herself useful." And she suggested that it is "a little presumptuous for women who have not experienced the Divine power of marriage itself, to decide exactly how far that power can save and help." Dall is correct in stating that she had raised these issues earlier with Alcott. Alcott's lengthy letter of September 13, 1864, to Dall (in the Dall Papers, MHS) responds to these criticisms.

telling them what the day was historically, and then announced the holiday. He expected applause for the pupils were wholly unprepared—but they walked quietly out— As he followed them, he heard one voice—"<u>Fellows!</u>" When he got into the air, they had clustered at the W. End of the Chapel—& were singing "Old Hundred!" Later in the day it was "Coronation" & "John Brown."

CHARLESTOWN N.H.

TUESDAY. AUG. 1. 1865.

A very rude note from Mrs Alcott informing me that Louisa has sailed with plenty of credentials.*

This in reply to a kind note from me—offering letters, whether it should be Louisa or May—for I really could see no motive for <u>Louisa</u>'s going abroad.

A somewhat strange return for all the trouble I took in selling paper cutters for May, & correcting proofs for Louisa—last winter. This is the only note I have had from her since I wrote the criticism on "Moods" & that I presume is the only cause of offence. Yet I distinctly told Louisa, that while I thought the publication of "Moods" would help her pecuniarily—and was therefore to be allowed, yet if I found a publisher for it & reviewed it, I should say exactly what I thought. Mr Loring[111] knew of this agreement & said that fault-finding helped a book, far more than praise.

Well—I was to blame somewhere—perhaps in time, God will show me where. . . .

If I would permit myself, I <u>could</u> be perfectly miserable, about my India affairs.†

I wish I knew where to turn, for advice. Perhaps I have only to be quiet & still—perhaps I ought to write and recall my husband knowing as I do, that he is not fit—for responsibility—perhaps—but I do not dare— Sarah could not bear the reality, as well as I can the torment of suspense.

---

*This note from Abigail May Alcott is in the Dall Papers. Dall has annotated it as follows: "A curious proof of how real services may be forgotten when slight offence is taken. That I sold pictures for May—got a publisher & corrected proofs for Louisa is here resented because I did not approve of 'Moods' <u>morally</u>!" Louisa May Alcott had sailed for Europe, and Dall had written the family offering letters of introduction to acquaintances there.

†On July 21 Dall wrote in her journal that she had received letters from Charles and was "afraid [his] memory is entirely gone. I can rely on no pecuniary statements."

SATURDAY. SEPT 9. 1865.

This morning while I was writing an article on Theism & Christianity,[112] Sadie came home from Lynn, and began setting the house in order, child-fashion.

Presently, she came up from the front parlor, with a bit of twisted paper in her hand— "Mamma!" said she, "what do you leave your letters from Mr Kennicott* lying round for?"

"I never had a letter from Mr Kennicott" said I "Here it is," she answered & produced the following.

Victoria. Vancouver's Island July 22. 1865

Madame, I take the liberty of addressing you to say that I think Mr Dall's prospects are most excellent. Many circumstances connected with the Expedition have been most disagreeable to us all, and it has been a great comfort to me, to have such a companion as Mr Dall with me, while now, I consider it a matter of no small importance to science, that I can leave almost the entire scientific operations of the Expedition under his charge, I being obliged to go into the interior. You have reason to be proud of such a son. Among <u>intelligent</u> men he is universally admired. He would have willingly undertaken the somewhat dangerous Expedition up the Yukon River;— but consented to take charge of the scientific operations for me, upon my representations that there was no one but him to whom I could trust that important duty. I believe he will greatly benefit by his experiences on this Expedition though he may gain nothing pecuniarily. I have seen him placed in a great many difficult & awkward positions, but never saw anything on his part, that did not make <u>me</u> proud to think him my friend. And I repeat,—<u>you</u> may well be proud of such a son.

Respectfully R. Kennicott.

*Robert Kennicott (1835–1866), naturalist and explorer, at age twenty-one had helped found the Chicago Academy of Sciences, of which he was later curator and then director. He had previously made a comprehensive natural history survey of southern Illinois in 1855 and had conducted an expedition to British and Arctic America in 1859. In 1865, he took part in the Western Union Telegraph Company-sponsored expedition to northwestern America for the purpose of surveying a route for an overland telegraph line to the Old World. Kennicott was leader of the party, which included Dall's son Willie, that was surveying Alaska and the Yukon River. Part of the expedition's responsibility was the gathering of specimens of the natural history of the region, to be divided between the Chicago Academy of the Sciences and the Smithsonian. While on this expedition Kennicott died of heart disease at Fort Nulato, Alaska, in May of the following year, and Willie took over his position *(DAB)*.

If I had lost that letter—! these words which are God's great mercy, after my weary waiting these twenty years! And I have so often feared that the girlish vanity which made me marry his father—would be punished by Willie's balked experience!! . . .

What a pure joy I should have missed! . . .

Epilogue

$\mathcal{I}$n the next decade Dall turned much of her attention to working for the American Social Science Association, an organization that addressed all sorts of societal problems from a scientific perspective. As one of the organization's founders, she wrote its first constitution, served as a long-term officer, and participated in hard-fought battles over the place of women in its hierarchy. In the late 1860s and 1870s, she took on a more public role in the Unitarian Church, filling pulpits occasionally (although she was never ordained), participating in a ministerial association, and publishing copiously in the denomination's periodicals. Dall was also a sort of freelance journalist, publishing widely in newspapers and other publications. Although she generally worked fairly effectively within the largely male power structure of the church and the Social Science Association, Dall found herself increasingly at odds with the leadership of the women's movement in both New York and Boston. Her exclusion from the New England Women's Club in 1868 was one of the great blows of her life, and helped her determine to leave her native city. Additionally, with the death of both her parents, no family ties held her in Boston, for she was also alienated from her sisters.

In 1878 Dall moved to Washington, D.C., to live near her son, and during most of her remaining thirty-four years she continued to live an active and fascinating life, deserving of a volume in its own right. Her daughter married and moved to Buffalo, and Dall spent significant time there each year, as well as several weeks in Boston each summer. In 1880 she made a solo journey west to California by rail and the next year published *My First Holiday,* her only work of travel literature, which included her horrified description of Leadville, a Colorado mining town. The unexpected death of her husband in 1886 in India proved to be a surprisingly hard blow.

Caroline Dall made a big splash in Washington. She became the friend of political and scientific luminaries, including such figures as George Frisbie Hoar, Massachusetts senator; John Wesley Powell, explorer of the Grand Canyon; ethnographer Alice Cunningham Fletcher, the first woman to hold an academic position at Harvard; and Spencer Fullerton Baird, secretary of the Smithsonian. For years she was active in Washington society, making regular calls at the homes of cabinet members and other distinguished Washingtonians. Her own reception days attracted a distinguished list of callers—partly on account of her interesting collection of objets d'art, ranging from American art pottery to Japanese artifacts, but probably even more on account of the renowned hostess herself. She was the intimate of First Lady Frances Cleveland and the leader of a reading group for young women.

While in Washington, Dall continued to write for newspapers in New England and elsewhere, and in her seventies she published several works on the Boston Unitarian-Transcendentalist culture in which she had grown up. In 1895 she delivered a lecture in Washington that was published two years later as *Transcendentalism in New England: A Lecture*. While her audience probably expected a rehearsal of anecdotes from her youthful acquaintance with the now-venerated Transcendentalists, what she gave them was an unabashedly feminist interpretation of the movement, asserting that it began (through Anne Hutchinson) and ended (through Margaret Fuller) with a woman. Known as "Madam Dall" in her later years in Washington, she was an institution; a publication on her son after his death recalled her as "a scholarly woman, strictly puritanical and frankly outspoken, whose critical and incisive remarks, verbal as well as written, were rather dreaded by the less stable members of Washington society."[1]

Caroline Healey Dall died on December 17, 1912. Her ashes are buried in the Healey family plot at Mount Auburn Cemetery, in Cambridge, Massachusetts.

Acknowledgments

$\mathscr{O}$ver the many years during which this project has been under way, I have accumulated many debts. Scholars all over this country and abroad have generously shared their expertise and advice with me, among them Bernard Bailyn, David Boocker, Patricia Cline Cohen, Karen Dandurand, Thomas Doughton, Roy E. Finkenbine, Richard Wightman Fox, the late William Gilmore, Ann Gordon, Dean Grodzins, Mark Hamilton, Janet Headley, Charles Hobson, Alan Hodder, Melissa Homestead, Elizabeth Hulse, Lucia Knoles, Megan Marshall, Loren McClanahan, Colin McCoy, Julian Mason, Richard P. Morgan, Ralph H. Orth, Beverly Palmer, Stephen D. Pratt, Robert Richardson, Richard Ryerson, Jennifer Shea, David Silverman, Clare Taylor, Fredrika Teute, Albert von Frank, Merv Walsh, and Michael Winship. I am grateful to them.

The contributions of two venerable institutions—at both of which Caroline Dall herself did research—have been essential to this project. I am grateful to the Massachusetts Historical Society for permission to publish these selected journals from the Caroline Wells Healey Dall Papers, 1811–1917. It was at the invitation of the Society's editor of publications, Conrad E. Wright, that I first agreed to edit Dall's journals for the Society, and he has steadfastly supported that project through many delays. The careful work of Ondine Le Blanc, editor of the scholarly edition of Dall's journals to be published by the MHS, has left its imprint on this edition as well. Donald Yacovone and Ed Hanson, other members of the editorial staff, have also given invaluable advice and assistance. I am greatly indebted to the MHS library staff: librarian Peter Drummey has been a cheerful provider of whatever I have needed and an incredible source of information on all things Bostonian; and reference librarians Virginia Smith, Jennifer Tolpa, Nicholas Graham, and Kimberly Nusco have given truly professional service. Other MHS staff members, including Anne Bentley, Brenda Lawson, Mary Fabiszewski, Paul Tsimahides, Nancy Heywood, and Chris Steele, have contributed significantly to the project in various ways, as have directors Louis L. Tucker and William M. Fowler, Jr. To the American Antiquarian Society, where I spent a year in residence, I express my profoundest gratitude. Marie Lamoureux, Thomas Knoles, Caroline Sloat, John Hench, Laura Wasowicz, Dennis Laurie, Philip Lampi, Georgia Barnhill, Nancy Burkett, Joanne Chaison, S. J. Wolfe, and volunteer Jane Dewey have been extraordinarily helpful, and in a real sense, every staff member at AAS was a collaborator on the project. The year's residence at AAS, as well as occasional return visits, enabled me to profit from the remarkable cohort of scholars who assemble there at any given time and regularly act as sounding boards for each other. I am grateful to the AAS and to the Mellon Foundation for the opportunity to benefit from this wonderfully collegial experience.

Numerous other institutions and their staffs, including the Bryn Mawr College Library, the Schlesinger Library, the First Unitarian Congregation of Toronto, the Unitarian Church of Montreal, the Cobourg (Ontario) Public Library, the University of Toronto Archives, the Boston Athenaeum, David Fahie at the Toronto Necropolis, Ken Lister at the Royal Ontario Museum, Frances O'Donnell at the Andover-Harvard Theological Library, and Sally Hinkle and Emily Novak at Historic New England, have graciously supplied me with information, and I thank them. I am grateful for a Radcliffe Research Support Grant that provided my first opportunity to conduct research on Caroline Dall, and for a Massachusetts Historical Society Research Fellowship. I wish to thank my former home institution, Tennessee Technological University, for its support of my work through faculty research grants and a noninstructional assignment, and especially Deans Joseph Lerner and Robert Briggs and English Department chairpersons Stephen Tabachnick, Karen Ray, and Robert Bode.

In a project that has required scores of trips to New England, I have repeatedly enjoyed the hospitality of Liz and Lin Parsons, Virginia Smith, Peter Drummey and Celeste Walker, and Betsy Homsher. Their generosity has made my work not only more feasible but infinitely more enjoyable.

Several friends and colleagues have read significant portions of the manuscript and provided useful feedback and encouragement: Guy R. Woodall, Gary Collison, Donald Ratcliffe, Jay Fliegelman, Harry Orth, Betsy Homsher, Peter S. Field, Alma Dolen Roberts, Jane Bingham, Grayce Scholt, and Philip Shimola. I am especially indebted to Phyllis Cole for her detailed critique of much of this manuscript. Betsy Homsher helped me verify the journals text. Joel Myerson has provided crucial encouragement for many years. Guy Woodall, my former colleague and earliest mentor, is largely responsible for my scholarly concentration on the Transcendentalists. Over several decades he has generously shared his own expertise and provided encouragement and inspiration. Whitney Dall, Caroline Dall's great-great-grandson, obligingly answered my questions about family memory and artifacts, and he and his wife, Barbara K. Dall, then generously gave additional family papers and portraits to the MHS, where scholars may have access to them. I am particularly grateful to Megan Marshall for connecting me with Beacon Press. All the professionals at Beacon have been wonderful to work with, and I especially thank Joanne Wyckoff, my editor, for her guidance and enthusiasm for this project. More than a century ago Caroline Dall published a book with Beacon Press, and I am certain that she would have approved of this choice of publisher for her journals.

No words are adequate to thank my husband, Pat, who throughout the long process of this project has provided his unqualified moral and logistical support. In the last few years he has taken on the role of patron as well, making possible my full-time devotion to the project.

Notes

ABBREVIATIONS AND SHORT TITLES

ANB   *American National Biography,* John A. Garraty and Mark C. Carnes, eds., 24 vols. (New York: Oxford U. Press, 1999)

DAB   *Dictionary of American Biography,* 22 vols. (New York: Charles Scribner's Sons, 1928–1958)

DCB   *Dictionary of Canadian Biography* (University of Toronto Press, 1966)

DFN   Caroline Healey Dall's Dead Friends Notebook (Dall's listing of the dates of the deaths of acquaintances, usually with their age, the cause of death, and the nature of her relationship with them), Dall Papers, Massachusetts Historical Society

DNB   *Dictionary of National Biography,* Leslie Stephen and Sidney Lee, eds., 22 vols. (New York: Oxford University Press, 1908–1909)

Heralds *Heralds of a Liberal Faith,* Samuel A. Eliot, ed., 4 vols. (Boston: Beacon Press, 1952)

MHS   Massachusetts Historical Society, Boston, Massachusetts

Ms. Journals Caroline Healey Dall's journals in manuscript, Dall Papers, MHS

NatCAB *National Cyclopaedia of American Biography,* 63 vols. (New York: J. T. White, 1898)

NAW   Edward T. James et al., *Notable American Women, 1607–1950,* 3 vols. (Cambridge, Massachusetts: Belknap Press of Harvard University Press, 1971)

n.d.   No date of publication given

NEHGR *New England Historical and Genealogical Register,* publication of the New England Historic Genealogical Society

NEHGS New England Historic Genealogical Society

NEQ   *New England Quarterly*

n.p.   No place of publication given

n.s.   New series

SAR   *Studies in the American Renaissance,* ed. Joel Myerson, 20 vols. (Charlottesville: University Press of Virginia)

Transcript *Boston Daily Evening Transcript*

VR   Vital Records (Official records of births, marriages, and deaths, kept by towns, cities and states. Most town and city vital records before 1850 have been published and are widely available; state vital records are generally available in repositories on microfilm.)

INTRODUCTION

1. Gunther Stuhlmann, ed., *The Journals of Anaïs Nin* (London: Owen, 1966), 1:vii.
2. Thomas Mallon, *A Book of One's Own: People and Their Diaries* (St. Paul, Minnesota: Ruminator Books, 1995), xvii.
3. Arthur Ponsonby, *English Diaries: A Review of English Diaries from the Sixteenth to the Twentieth Century with an Introduction on Diary Reading* (New York: George H. Doran, 1923), 5.

CHAPTER ONE

1. Several Italian editions of the works of Silvio Pellico (1789–1854), Italian Romantic writer, appeared in the 1830s. *Cartas marruecas,* an epistolary novel, satirical and didactic, by the Spanish writer José Cadalso (1741–1782), was first published in 1789.
2. François-René, vicomte de Chateaubriand (1768–1848), French Romantic writer; his "Gaul" was included in his *Oeuvres Romantiques* (Paris: Les Marchands de Nouveautés, 1831).
3. Scottish poet James MacPherson (1736–1824) claimed that poems he published in the 1760s were translations of medieval works in Gaelic by a poet named Ossian. These poems have come to be regarded as forgeries.
4. Hannah H. R. Gibbs Wild (1803?–1882), mother of Healey's friend Catherine (Caty) H. Wild (1823?–1892) (DFN).
5. Two years younger than Healey, Ednah Dow Littlehale (1824–1904) was a student at Joseph Hale Abbot's school, which Healey had recently left. The daughter of Ednah Parker Dow Littlehale (d. 1876) ("Mrs Littlehale") and Boston merchant Sargent S. Littlehale (1787–1851), she later married the artist Seth Wells Cheney. She was an active reformer, one of the founders of the New England Women's Club, and the author of *Louisa May Alcott: Her Life, Letters and Journals* (1888). See Frederick H. Littlehale, *A Complete History and Genealogy of the Littlehale Family in America* (Rutland, Vermont: A.W. & F.H. Littlehale, 1889), 27, 39.
6. Anna Meriam Renouf (1821–1842), daughter of Edward and Eliza M. Renouf, one of Healey's closest friends, fatally ill with tuberculosis (Mt. Auburn Cemetery Records, Cambridge, Massachusetts).
7. Probably Richard Haughton, editor of the Whig paper the *Boston Atlas.*
8. At the Boston Athenaeum. In May 1838, the Athenaeum had bought several pictures from the collection of Count Celestini. These included works by Poussin, Rembrandt, Van Dyke, and others. See *Catalogue of the Twelfth Exhibition of Paintings in the Athenaeum Gallery* (Boston: John H. Eastburn, 1838) and Josiah Quincy, *History of the Boston Athenaeum* (Cambridge, Massachusetts: Metcalf and Co., 1851), 143.
9. See Luke 18:10–14.
10. See Revelation 6:16; Luke 23:30.
11. *Elements of General History, Ancient and Modern,* by Scottish historian Alexander Fraser Tytler (1747–1813). The work was first published in Edinburgh in 1801, by W. Creech, and had been through many American editions.

12. According to Herodotus, Xerxes, King of Persia, allowed himself to be tricked into attacking the Greek fleet under unfavorable conditions, and the resulting Battle of Salamis (480 B.C.) was disastrous for the Persians. In attacking, he ignored the advice of Artemisa I, princess of Caria. More than twenty years later, Caroline Healey Dall the feminist would use Artemisa as an exemplar of a woman of independence and wisdom. See Dall's *Historical Pictures Retouched; A Volume of Miscellanies* (Boston: Walker, Wise and Company, 1860), 142–144.

13. Caroline Dall later added in pencil a marginal note: "No such questions would have arisen if there had not been plenty of servants to do the work—"

14. Caroline Dall's reminiscence *"Alongside": Being Notes Suggested by "A New England Boyhood" of Doctor Edward Everett Hale* (Boston: Thomas Todd, 1900) gives an extended account of her coming-out party; she says there that the table was decorated with an extravagant "five hundred camellias mixed with myrtle" (51).

15. Apparently a would-be suitor whom Dall identified in her Dead Friends Notebook as Wilson Jarvis Welch (1818?–1885). Upon his death she wrote, "This young man—made my first ball for me, & wished me to open it with him. I refused because he had taken too much wine, which required much courage in those days. He sent me valuable gifts but I returned the parcels unopened. He was the first person who ever wished to marry me—but never <u>asked</u> me. I gave him no chance. He was saved by an excellent wife." See DFN; Harvard University, *Quinquennial Catalogue of the Officers and Graduates* (Cambridge, Massachusetts: Harvard University Press, 1925); Harvard Class of 1839, *Class Album. 1839.1879* (Cambridge, Massachusetts: Harvard University, 1879).

16. Philip Dormer Stanhope, Lord Chesterfield (1694–1773), English statesman and author, famous for letters of advice to his son.

17. Sixty years later, Caroline Dall gave a somewhat different version of what is apparently the same incident: in *"Alongside"* she said that she refused to dance the opening dance at her own ball because she was asked by a young man "whom I did not respect, and with whom I would not take the first step toward intimacy. Having refused him, of course I could take no other partner" (52).

18. James Walker (1794–1874), prominent Unitarian clergyman and professor of natural religion, moral philosophy, and civil polity at Harvard, later became president of the college.

19. George Gordon, Lord Byron (1788–1824), whose memoirs were destroyed by his publisher, lest they embarrass his family.

20. Francis C. Gray (1790–1856) was educated as a lawyer but never practiced; he was a wealthy benefactor of Harvard College and America's first great print connoisseur and collector. This was the first of three lectures that he delivered before the Boston Society for the Diffusion of Useful Knowledge on the subject of "Lectures." See Marjorie B. Cohn, *Francis Calley Gray and Art Collecting for America* (Cambridge, Massachusetts: Harvard University Art Museums, 1986) and Helen R. Deese and Guy R. Woodall, "A Calendar of Lectures Presented by the Boston Society for the Diffusion of Useful Knowledge," *SAR 1986* (Charlottesville: University Press of Virginia), 50.

21. William Adam (1796–1881), Scottish-born Baptist missionary to India, who converted to Unitarianism. He came to the United States in 1838 and lectured, taught, preached, and was briefly a professor at Harvard. He delivered three lectures this season on "India" before the Boston Society for the Diffusion of Useful Knowledge. He was later associated with a Utopian community at Northampton, Massachusetts, then held brief pastorates at Toronto and Chicago. By 1855 he had returned to England. See *Dictionary of Unitarian & Universalist Biography,* www.uua.org/uuhs/duub (accessed September 29, 2004); Spencer Lavan, *Unitarians and India* (Chicago: Exploration Press, 1991), 41–55; Deese and Woodall, "A Calendar of Lectures Presented by the Boston Society for the Diffusion of Useful Knowledge," 50.

22. Hypatia (d. 415) was learned in math, astronomy, and philosophy; because she taught Neoplatonist

philosophy in Alexandria, she was torn to pieces by a mob of Christians. Healey, perhaps meeting her here for the first time, takes to heart the warning of the dire results stemming from an intellectual woman's stepping outside her sphere. Yet she clearly identifies with this "first lecturess" and in 1853 would publish her own version of Hypatia, who thus became one of her "retouched" pictures, a woman rescued from the negative judgment of history. See "Hypatia," *The Una* 1 (May 2, 1853): 51, reprinted in Dall's *Historical Pictures Retouched* (1860).

23. In Roman mythology, the immortal spirits of the dead.

24. English poet and critic John Dryden (1631–1700) famously satirized the mediocre playwright Thomas Shadwell (1640–1692) in the poem "MacFlecknoe," but I have not located the specific comment Healey refers to.

25. Caroline C. Choate (b. 1822), daughter of the late John Choate (1792–1823) and Sarah Gardner Fairfield Choate (1797–1856). Caroline Choate later married Francis D. Darling (1818–1893). Mrs. Choate and her daughters Caroline and Martha had recently moved to Boston and were becoming close friends of Caroline Healey. See E. O. Jameson, *The Choates in America, 1643–1896* (Boston: A Mudge & Son, 1896), 213, 321; DFN.

26. Probably daughters of Oliver and Hannah Smalley Eldredge, who included Emelyn (1820–1894), who married the artist William Wetmore Story; Hannah Wells (b. 1822), who married Nathaniel Greene; and Harriet Maria (b. 1823), who married John H. B. McLellan (Cambridge VR; *NEHGR* 92:354, 93:120).

27. Probably Augustus R. Pope (1819–1858), Harvard Divinity student, who was, like Healey, a Sunday school teacher. She took a keen interest in his education and development as a Bible teacher, and was perhaps infatuated with him.

28. Josiah Quincy (1772–1864), president of Harvard from 1829 to 1845.

CHAPTER TWO

1. Newly constructed in 1840 and bounded by Beach, Lincoln, and Kingston Streets, this hotel was the largest in the country. See Justin Winsor, ed., *Memorial History of Boston* (Boston: J.R. Osgood and Co., 1881), 4:40.

2. Elizabeth Palmer Peabody (1804–1894) had just opened this store at 13 West Street, which for the next ten years was a center for Boston intellectuals and particularly the Transcendentalists. Peabody had earlier served as A. Bronson Alcott's assistant at the Temple School and was attending meetings of the Transcendental Club; she was to continue to have a varied career, as writer, publisher, educator (she established the first English-speaking kindergarten in America), and reformer.

3. Edward William Lane's translation, *The Thousand and One Nights, Commonly Called, in England, The Arabian Nights' Entertainments*, 3 vols. (London: C. Knight, 1839–1841). This work, the first listed on Peabody's broadside announcing the new store (August 1840), is described as "splendidly bound and illustrated" and is priced at sixteen dollars.

4. Dante Alighieri (1265–1321), Petrarca (or Petrarch; 1304–1374), and Ariosto (1474–1533) were all Italian poets.

5. Peabody had published this series of three articles in the *Christian Examiner*, vol. 16 (May 1834): 174–202, (July 1834): 305–320, and vol. 17 (September 1834): 78–92. The articles examine some of the crucial events of Genesis and the spiritual insights and lessons to be derived from them in a historical perspective, in light of the relatively primitive culture that produced them.

6. In the third of the published articles, "Public Worship: Social Crime, and Its Retribution," Peabody

suggested that the lesson to be learned by the response of Noah's sons to his drunken behavior after the flood was "that a veil is to be drawn by kindred over the weaknesses of their kindred; or at least by children over the degradation of their parents." *Christian Examiner* 17 (September 1834): 88.

7. Caroline Healey had been writing and publishing moral sketches since she was thirteen. They had appeared in Boston's *American Daily Traveler* and the Unitarian *Christian Register*.

8. In a later revision, Dall canceled "transcendentalist" and substituted "Fourierite" in different ink.

9. Frederic Henry Hedge (1805–1890), German scholar, Unitarian minister, future Harvard professor, and member of the Transcendentalist group. He had been preaching in Bangor, Maine, since 1835 but returned to Boston occasionally, such visits often precipitating meetings of the Transcendental Club. This was the first of Hedge's six lectures, all of them entitled "The Philosophy of Literature," delivered before the Society for the Diffusion of Useful Knowledge.

10. The German writer Jean Paul Richter (1763–1825) and the British authors Henry Fielding (1707–1754), Robert Burns (1759–1796), and Edmund Spenser (1552–1599) all experienced poverty at some point in their careers. "Schonner" probably is a reference to Johann Schoner (1477–1547), German mathematician and geographer.

11. Dall has later, in pencil, revised "my pen" to "these pages."

12. Sophia Ripley participated in the Transcendental Club and various conversation groups, contributed three articles to *The Dial*, and acted for a time as a kind of editorial assistant for the journal.

13. Dall has later inserted "her" in pencil.

14. *Essays* (Boston: J. Munroe and Co., 1841), by Ralph Waldo Emerson, which contained several of his most famous essays, including "Self-Reliance," "The Over-Soul," and "Circles."

15. James Freeman Clarke, a graduate of the Harvard Divinity School and distant cousin of Margaret Fuller, had recently returned from Louisville, Kentucky, where he preached and helped edit the *Western Messenger*. In Boston he founded the Church of the Disciples, for which he preached, except for a three-year break, for the rest of his life.

16. Charles Stearns Wheeler (1816–1843), instructor in history at Harvard. Wheeler was a part of the Transcendental circle and was thought to show great promise (he had already been responsible for bringing out American editions of Carlyle, Macaulay, and Tennyson), but he died two years later while traveling in Germany.

17. William Wetmore Story, son of U.S. Supreme Court justice Joseph Story, practiced law in Boston at this time.

18. Theodore Parker (1810–1860), Unitarian minister at West Roxbury, was beginning to make his reputation as a leading radical within the church. He was filling in for George Ripley, who had preached his farewell sermon at the Purchase Street congregation the preceding Sunday. The sermon that Parker preached on this date was "A Sermon of Idolatry." See Dean Grodzins and Joel Myerson, "The Preaching Record of Theodore Parker," *SAR 1994*, 80.

19. Washington Allston (1779–1843), American artist and author, who had worked in Italy and in England, then returned to Boston. His *Lorenzo and Jessica* was completed in 1832.

20. Thomas Crawford (1813/1814–1857), American sculptor in Italy; his *Orpheus* was bought in 1840 by the Boston Athenaeum.

21. Emerson's gift was in appreciation for Sophia Peabody's "labor of love" in making a medallion of his deceased brother Charles. It included copies of works by Michaelangelo, Raphael, Leonardo, and Correggio that he and Elizabeth Hoar had commissioned a friend to buy in Italy. See letters to William Emerson, June 30, 1840, and April 21, 1841, in *The Letters of Ralph Waldo Emerson*, ed. Ralph L. Rusk (New York: Columbia University Press, 1939), 2:307, 393.

22. Eliza Rotch Farrar, author of *The Young Lady's Friend*.

23. The room that Healey describes was located in the house at 6 Hancock Street, on Beacon Hill, where the family had lived since September 1836.

24. Psyche was, in classical mythology, a princess of great beauty who inspired the jealousy of Venus and the love of Cupid. Eventually Jupiter made her immortal and gave her in marriage to Cupid. St. Cecilia (fl. 3rd century), one of the most famous Roman martyrs of the early church, is the patron of music, and Thalia is one of the nine Muses, the patron of comedy and idyllic poetry.

25. Domenichino (1581–1641), Bolognese painter.

26. Marco Bozzaris (1788–1823), Greek patriot.

27. Dall wrote later that she had purchased this bouquet at the cost of "much time & money." She knew that she had annoyed Fuller by what Fuller took to be her self-conceit, and she "wished her to understand by my flowers, that I had not done so intentionally." Fuller apparently did not receive the flowers in this spirit, for Elizabeth Peabody told her the next day that she should not have sent them. See Dall, "Conversations upon the *Mythology of the Greeks*," in Joel Myerson, "Caroline Dall's Reminiscences of Margaret Fuller," *Harvard Library Bulletin* 22 (October 1974): 419. The original is in the Dall Papers, Schlesinger Library.

28. From Fuller's poem on Orpheus, later included in Fuller's *Woman in the Nineteenth Century*.

29. Martha Choate.

30. Martha Hubbard Fairfield (b. 1772), wife of Boston merchant John Fairfield (b. 1772) and grandmother of Healey's friends Martha and Caroline Choate (1850 U.S. Census; E. O. Jameson, *The Choates in America*, 213).

31. James Walker.

32. Harvard professor (and later president) Cornelius C. Felton (1807–1862) and his wife, Mary Whitney Felton (1815–1862). See Frederick Clifton Pierce, *Whitney: The Descendants of John Whitney* (Chicago: W.B. Conkey, 1895), 245–246.

33. Probably David Reed (1790–1870), editor, publisher, and founder of the *Christian Register*, and his wife Mary Ann Williams Reed (b. 1805?) (*DAB; Ancestry.com*, accessed December 6, 2004).

34. The family of Elizabeth Williams Whitney (1805–1849) and her husband Benjamin D. Whitney (1807–1892), brother of Mary Felton and a business associate of Healey's father. Their daughter Mary Williams Whitney (1832–1864) later married Dr. Jeffries Wyman (Pierce, *Whitney: The Descendants of John Whitney*, 245–246, 426).

35. Francis Bowen (1811–1890), Harvard tutor in intellectual philosophy and political economy; he was later editor of the *North American Review* and Alvord Professor of Natural Religion, Moral Philosophy, and Civil Polity at Harvard *(DAB)*.

36. Jones Very (1813–1880), poet and preacher, presented a phenomenon of great interest to the Transcendentalist circle at this time. As a result of religious excitement, temporary mental derangement, or (as he claimed) divine inspiration, he astonished friends and enemies (the Harvard and Unitarian establishments) alike with his bizarre pronouncements. He had been dismissed in 1839 from his position as Greek tutor at Harvard and had spent a month in an asylum because of what was viewed as his fanatical religiosity.

37. Perhaps the Dr. Jeffries Wyman (1814–1874) who became a leading American anatomist and professor of anatomy at Harvard; or Dr. Morrill Wyman (1812–1903), a Cambridge physician; or Dr. Rufus Wyman (1778–1842), their father, early American psychiatrist *(DAB)*.

38. William Gustavus Babcock (1820–1911). He would graduate from the Divinity School three years later and become a Unitarian minister. See *General Catalogue of the Divinity School of Harvard University* (Cambridge, Massachusetts: Harvard University Press, 1901).

39. Charles Lowell and Cyrus Bartol, senior and junior ministers of the West Church. Charles Lowell

(1782–1861), father of poet James Russell Lowell, was minister there from 1806 until his death. During his ministry it was "the largest congregation in Boston . . . the home of three or four hundred of the leading families of the community" (*Heralds* 1:47), including the Healeys. He was a father figure to Caroline Healey Dall, who in 1860 published a tribute to him in her *Historical Pictures Retouched,* then in her old age reprinted the article separately as *Reverend Charles Lowell, D.D. . . .* (Boston: T. Todd, 1907). In 1837 Cyrus Augustus Bartol (1813–1900) joined Dr. Lowell as associate minister, gradually taking over most of the duties, and remaining as pastor of the society until its dissolution in 1889. Bartol was associated with the Transcendentalists and, later, the Free Religious Association. His wife, Elizabeth Howard Bartol (1803–1883), mentioned below, was formerly Caroline Healey's childhood Sunday school teacher and was now an important mentor to her. Upon Elizabeth Bartol's death, Caroline Dall wrote of her in her Dead Friends Notebook, "A unique woman—a mother to me for a whole half century."

40. Probably Charlotte Billings Hastings (1821–1907), daughter of Eliza Bullard and Cyrus Hastings; in 1847 she married popular lecturer E. P. Whipple. See Samuel Bradlee Doggett, *Seth Bullard of Walpole, Massachusetts* (Norwood, Massachusetts: Plimpton Press, 1930), Sheet C, and *NEHGR* 93:115.

41. Probably James Tucker Fisher (1817–1864). See Philip A. Fisher, *Fisher Genealogy* (Everett, Massachusetts: Massachusetts Publishing Co., 1898), 321.

42. Luke 24:27.

43. Henry James Hudson (1821–1901), member of the Harvard class of 1843 and a Divinity School graduate in 1847. He was to hold various pastorates in Connecticut, Massachusetts, and New York.

44. Horatia Sewall Ware (1815–1893), daughter of Horatio G. Ware and Keziah Goodenow Ware, and a member of the West Church. See Emma Forbes Ware, *Ware Genealogy* (Boston: Charles H. Pope, 1901), 133.

45. Sarah Stone Balch (1821–1848), a friend of Healey's from Newburyport, who later married Frederick Beck. See Galusha B. Balch, *Genealogy of the Balch Families in America* (Salem, Massachusetts: E. Putnam, 1897), 302–303.

46. The allusion is to Matthew 18:7: "Woe unto the world because of offenses! for it must needs be that offenses come; but woe unto that man by whom the offense cometh!"

CHAPTER THREE

1. Samuel Foster Haven (1806–1881), librarian at the American Antiquarian Society, was a distant relative of Caroline and her aunt Maria.

2. The State Lunatic Hospital at Worcester had first received patients in 1833.

3. The American Antiquarian Society in Worcester was incorporated in 1812 as an organization "to encourage the collection and preservation of the Antiquities of our country, and of curious and valuable productions in Art and Nature [that] have a tendency to enlarge the sphere of human knowledge." See Nancy H. Burkett and John B. Hench, *Under Its Generous Dome: The Collections and Programs of the American Antiquarian Society,* 2nd ed. (Worcester, Massachusetts: Oak Knoll Press, 1992), 19.

4. The American Antiquarian Society has no record of ever having had the desk of Cotton Mather, although it does hold the Mather library.

5. Probably Isaiah Thomas (1749–1831), patriot, printer, publisher, and founder of the American Antiquarian Society. A portrait of Thomas by Ethan Allen Greenwood was willed to the Society at his death.

6. At this time, for a very brief period, Healey was taking piano lessons.

7. Lucretia Chandler Bancroft (1765–1839) was the wife of Aaron Bancroft, one of the founders and the first president of the American Unitarian Association; George Bancroft the historian was their son. The Society still has some of Lucretia Bancroft's letters in its George Bancroft Papers. "Mrs Jo' Willard" is probably Emma Hart (Mrs. John) Willard (1787–1870), educator and champion of higher education for women in New England and New York.

8. William Lincoln (1802–1843), Worcester lawyer and historian, had served as Librarian of the American Antiquarian Society. The library referred to is the Revolutionary papers that the Massachusetts legislature authorized Lincoln to collect, in 1837. Christopher Columbus Baldwin (1800–1835), lawyer, newspaper editor, and antiquarian, was the first librarian of the American Antiquarian Society.

9. Healey's abstracts of lectures she had heard in Boston, probably those delivered by James Walker the previous winter.

10. John Quincy Adams (1767–1848), former president, now a member of Congress.

11. Thomas Kinnicutt of Worcester (1799–1858), Speaker of the Massachusetts House of Representatives and member of the American Antiquarian Society (*Proceedings of the American Antiquarian Society,* April 1854).

12. The elder Richard H. Dana (1787–1879), poet and man of letters. His son and namesake was the author of *Two Years before the Mast.*

13. John Davis (1787–1854), a Worcester native, was governor of Massachusetts at the time. He was married to Eliza Bancroft, daughter of Aaron and Lucretia Bancroft and sister of historian George Bancroft. Lucretia Bancroft (1803–1887) was the sister of Eliza Bancroft Davis and George Bancroft. See George Chandler, *The Chandler Family: The Descendants of William and Annis Chandler* (Worcester, Massachusetts: Press of Charles Hamilton, 1883), 471.

14. "Loco foco" was a term applied earlier to the liberal faction of the Democratic Party; by 1841 it was generally synonymous with "Democrat."

15. This letter, dated December 3, is in the Dall Papers, MHS; it is partially printed in John Weiss, *Life and Correspondence of Theodore Parker* (New York: D. Appleton & Company, 1864), 1:175. Healey had written Parker a long letter on November 29, beginning a lengthy correspondence and friendship. This letter too is in the Dall Papers, MHS.

16. Probably Claudius Buchanan Farnsworth (1814–1897), a recent Harvard graduate who would become a lawyer.

17. Anna Renouf.

18. Dr. John C. Warren (1778–1856), the Healey family physician, was a prominent Boston physician and surgeon, and a professor at the Harvard Medical School.

19. This lecture, the second in Emerson's series on "The Times" delivered at the Masonic Temple, was printed as "The Conservative" in *The Dial* 3 (1842): 181–197.

20. Probably Ann (or Anne) Kuhn (1795–1880), the aunt of Austin Kuhn. She was Caroline Healey's early Sunday school teacher at the West Church (*NEHGR* 51:444–445).

21. Marcia Porter Foster (1768–1846), stepmother of Caroline Wells Healey's mother. Her first name is variously given as Marcy, Mercy, and Marcia; Caroline Dall reports that she changed her name from "Mercy" to "Marcia" after reading Roman history. See Frederick Clifton Pierce, *Foster Genealogy* (Chicago: F.C. Pierce, 1899), 284, and "Family History of William H. Dall," 1:204, Dall-Healey Papers, MHS.

22. On November 24 Healey had attended a ball at Faneuil Hall honoring the visiting Prince de Joinville (1818–1900), French naval officer and third son of Louis-Philippe.

23. Emerson's fifth lecture in his series "The Times."

24. James Walker delivered twelve lectures on "Natural Religion" in Boston beginning in January 1842.

Healey's manuscript "abstracts" of these lectures comprise more than ninety densely written pages. The intended audience seems to have included her aunt Maria Foster, Samuel F. Haven, and possibly other friends in Worcester.

25. Englishman John Locke (1632–1704), whose empiricist philosophy the Transcendentalists rejected.

26. This is one of the first indications in Healey's journal of her father's impending financial collapse, a fact which she has not yet grasped.

27. Probably Charlotte Hastings.

28. Probably Judith Peirce Kendall (b. 1821?), daughter of Sewall and Sarah Kendall and a member of the West Church (*NEHGR* 93:124, 94:160; 1850 U.S. Census).

29. Horatia Ware.

30. Alvan Clark (1804–1887) was a successful portrait painter in Boston for thirty years. At age forty he took up the study of optics and later founded Clark & Sons, producing the world's largest telescopes for major observatories. In testing the telescopes, Clark discovered a number of double stars.

31. Abigail Leonard Cunningham (1797?–1879) and her husband, Andrew Cunningham (b. 1790?), Boston merchant and shipowner (Harvard University Archives, under Horace Cunningham; 1850 U.S. Census; DFN), and Daniel P. Parker (1781–1850), Boston merchant, and his wife, Mary W. Parker (1783–1863). See Robert D. Weeks, *Geo. Weekes: Genealogy of the Family of George Weekes* (Newark, New Jersey: Press of L.J. Hardham, 1885), 199.

32. Frances Burney (later D'Arblay) (1752–1840), English novelist, began keeping a diary at age sixteen, portions of which were published by her niece, Charlotte Barrett, 1842–1846.

33. Frances Burney was friends with Hester Thrale (later Piozzi) and her circle, which included English lexicographer, writer, and critic Dr. Samuel Johnson (1709–1784).

34. Edwin Howland (1810–1864), member of the West Church and a business associate of Mark Healey (*NEHGR* 92:249). See also Franklyn Howland, *A Brief Genealogical and Biographical History of Arthur, Henry, and John Howland* (New Bedford, Massachusetts: F. Howland, 1885), 181–182.

35. Sophia Peabody had bought the furniture from the proceeds of her work as an artist and had decorated it with outline drawings.

36. Wife of Odysseus, prototype of marital fidelity.

37. Presumably Healey's misspelling of Aeneas, Trojan warrior and hero of Vergil's *Aeneid*.

38. Perhaps a copy of the famous *Phoebus and the Hours Preceded by Aurora,* by Bolognese artist Guido Reni.

39. "Thank God that" canceled later by Dall.

40. "it saved . . . the sheet" canceled later by Dall.

41. Lawyer Charles Greeley Loring (1794–1867), a fellow member with the Healeys of the West Church. In 1851 he defended the fugitive slave Thomas Sims.

42. Joseph Sargent (1842–1845), son of Healey's Worcester friends Joseph and Emily Whitney Sargent (1817–1897), was born on October 17. See Frederick Clifton Pierce, *Whitney: The Descendants of John Whitney* (Chicago: F.C. Pierce, 1895), 245–246.

43. Presumably one of the recipients of Healey's charitable "visits."

44. Charles William Foster (b. 1805), her mother's brother (Frederick Clifton Pierce, *Foster Genealogy,* 284).

45. Healey's draft of this letter is in her letterbook (Dall Papers, MHS). In it she rebukes her father for the lack of confidence in his wife and children that has prevented him from informing them earlier of his financial woes. For herself, she feels "neither despair nor dismay," and urges him not to think that his many years of hard work have produced no fruit: "Have you not given me, at least—a fine education, many literary advantages—many means of getting a livelihood—an acquaintance with the best—and a

passport into, <u>any</u> society, I may desire? Is not your name—known far and wide, as that of an honest man—?" She pledges "to sacrifice my time, my talents, and my strength if need be, to retain for my sisters, the advantages of Mrs Lowell's tuition," and asks, "Do you not think that I can work and starve for your comfort?"

46. Mary Ann ("Mannie") Smith (1820?–1906), teacher, and sister of Caroline's art teacher, Dorcas Smith (later Murdoch). Mannie later married William Channing Appleton (1816?–1892). The Appletons and Murdochs were lifelong friends of Caroline Dall (DFN).

47. Miriam Clarke Mason Sears (b. 1788), wife of David Sears (1787–1871), wealthy Boston philanthropist, Harvard overseer, and vice president of the Massachusetts Historical Society. The Searses had ten children. See Samuel P. May, *The Descendants of Richard Sares (Sears) of Yarmouth, Mass.* (Albany, New York: Munsell's Sons, 1890), 260–263, and *Ancestry.com* (accessed October 2, 2004).

48. Probably Abby Russell Pope Ritchie (b. 1820?), wife of Boston hardware dealer Edward Samuel Ritchie (1814–1895) (*NEHGR* 68:118; *Ancestry.com*, accessed October 2, 2004).

49. John Elliott Thayer (1803–1857), a Boston broker (*Ancestry.com*, accessed October 2, 2004; *Boston Directory* 1842).

50. Augustus Pope.

51. Probably Samuel F. Coolidge (1789?–1858) of the firm of Coolidge and Haskell, auctioneers (*Boston Directory* 1843; Boston VR).

52. Ellen W. Healey, Caroline's sister.

53. Haven's letter, dated June 20, is in the Dall Papers, MHS. In attempting to comfort her by minimizing the significance of her father's current financial crisis, he speaks of Healey's "exaggeration of the supposed calamity" and continues, "[W]hile I admire your resolute plans of personal exertion I do not imagine that there will be the least necessity for carrying them into effect." He notes that having "gone the rounds of experience" and having "personal knowledge of every kind of suffering," he finds his own character improved. He believes she would "profit still more from equal discipline," but he does not believe that she is "yet to be subjected to it." Healey seems to take exception to both his playing down the gravity of her troubles and his assumption that she is inexperienced with suffering.

54. Samuel Gould carried Healey's mail to Worcester.

55. The somewhat paternalistic tone of this letter, which Healey objects to, and which clearly departs from the subdued romantic strain of earlier letters, is intensified in a letter Haven writes a few days later (July 8–9, 1842), in which he minimizes the seriousness of her situation: "I do not see why my cousin Carrie should sacrifice her health or her tranquility because her father has met with a commercial misfortune" (Dall Papers, MHS).

56. Ezra Stiles Gannett (1801–1871), a graduate of Harvard (1820) and the Harvard Divinity School (1823), was from his ordination in 1824 until his death minister to the Federal Street Church in Boston, for many years as colleague to Dr. William Ellery Channing. The first secretary of the American Unitarian Association, at this time he edited the Unitarian *Monthly Miscellany of Religion and Letters*, where he intended to make use of Healey's translations. Gannett was a leader of the conservative Unitarian party and later edited the *Christian Examiner* (1844–1849) (*Dictionary of Unitarian and Universalist Biography,* www.uua.org/uuhs/duub, accessed October 2, 2004).

57. Robert Cassie Waterston (1812–1893), graduate of the Harvard Divinity School, was a minister-at-large in Boston. He superintended the Pitts Street Chapel Sunday School, where Caroline Healey taught (*Heralds* 2:112–113).

58. "For as the rain cometh down, and the snow from heaven, and returneth not thither, but watereth the earth, and maketh it bring forth and bud, that it may give seed to the sower, and bread to the eater: So

shall my word be that goeth forth out of my mouth: it shall not return unto me void, but shall accomplish that which I please, and it shall prosper in the thing whereto I sent it. For ye shall go out with joy, and be led forth with peace: the mountains and the hills shall break forth before you into singing, and all the trees of the field shall clap their hands. Instead of the thorn shall come up the fir tree, and instead of the brier shall come up the myrtle tree: and it shall be to the Lord for a name, for an everlasting sign that shall not be cut off."

59. George Cheyne Shattuck (1783–1854), Boston physician and founder of the Shattuck School in Faribault, Minnesota (*NatCAB* 12:197).

60. William Batchelder Greene (1819–1878) had resigned his army commission (second lieutenant) in 1841 and settled near Boston, joining Brook Farm for a time. He became one of Elizabeth Peabody's many discoveries; she enthusiastically introduced him to the other Transcendentalists. Greene studied divinity at Harvard, graduating in 1845, and preached for several years at Brookfield, Massachusetts. He married Anna Blake Shaw (1817–1901), sister of Healey's childhood friends Elizabeth and Joseph Coolidge Shaw. After residing in Paris from 1849 to 1861, Greene commanded the Fourteenth Massachusetts Infantry (later the First Massachusetts Heavy Artillery), 1861–1862. Returning to Boston, he was a mathematician and scholar of Hebrew literature and Hebrew and Roman antiquities. Greene died in England. See Wesley T. Mott, ed., *Biographical Dictionary of Transcendentalism* (Westport, Connecticut: Greenwood Press, 1996); Elihu Rich, ed., *Appleton's Cyclopedia of Biography* (New York: Appleton, 1856); Russell Duncan, *Blue-Eyed Child of Fortune: The Civil War Letters of Colonel Robert Gould Shaw* (Athens: University of Georgia Press, 1992), 106, 109, 301; Joel Myerson, *The New England Transcendentalists and the Dial* (Rutherford, New Jersey: Fairleigh Dickinson University Press, 1980), 155–56, 267; and DFN.

61. Parker's letter of July 20 is in the Dall Papers, MHS. He tells Healey that he is certain that she will be able to turn her current adversity to profit, as she had done her previous prosperity. He has been looking (unsuccessfully thus far) for an appropriate position for her.

62. The identity of this clergyman is unknown.

63. Alonzo Hill (1810–1871) was for almost forty-four years minister to the Unitarian Second Parish in Worcester (*Heralds* 3:168–170). The position mentioned in the letter of August 12 was an instructorship of girls from ten to fourteen, "thoughtless rude unmanageable." It paid $286 a year (Dall Papers, MHS). "Temptation" refers to the fact that Samuel F. Haven lived in Worcester.

64. Mary W. Parker, wife of Daniel P. Parker, and mother of Henry Tuke Parker (1824–1890), just graduating from Harvard. Henry Parker graduated from the Harvard Law School three years later (*NEHGR* 93:59; *Quinquennial Catalogue of Harvard University*).

65. Mrs. Gurney's boardinghouse was on Appian Way in Cambridge (*Cambridge Directory*, 1848).

66. Harrison Gray (1795?–1846) of Hilliard, Gray & Co., Boston publishers and booksellers.

67. Hope Savage Shaw (1793–1879) was the wife of Lemuel Shaw (1781–1861), for thirty years chief justice of the Massachusetts Supreme Judicial Court (*NEHGR* 67:326–327).

68. Abbott Lawrence (1792–1855) was a leading Boston merchant, manufacturer, diplomat, Congressman, and philanthropist. He was married to Katherine Bigelow Lawrence (1793–1860). The reference is to what became known as the Webster-Ashburton Treaty with Great Britain, ratified on August 20 by a large majority in the Senate. Lawrence was a commissioner charged with settling the northeastern boundary dispute between Canada and the United States, an issue on which the treaty achieved a compromise *(DAB)*. See also Patricia Bigelow, *Bigelow Family Genealogy* (Flint, Michigan: The Bigelow Society, 1986), 1:175.

69. Lydia S. English (1800?–1865), who operated a prestigious school for young women in Georgetown. Founded in 1831, the school was for many years located at the corner of 30th and N Streets. See Wil-

helmus Bogart Bryan, *A History of the National Capital from Its Foundation through the Period of the Adoption of the Organic Act* (New York: Macmillan, 1916), 2:208.

70. Sarah Choate, mother of Martha.

71. Healey's maternal grandfather, Samuel Henry Foster (1771–1847) (Frederick Clifton Pierce, *Foster Genealogy*, 200, 284).

CHAPTER FOUR

1. Manuscript Journals, May 26, 1880, Dall Papers, MHS. Samuel Haven was actually only sixteen years older than she and was seventy-five in 1880, but the identity of the suitor is unmistakable.

2. "to pass . . . him" canceled later by Dall.

3. Wilhelm M. L. de Wette (1780–1849), a German theologian who was becoming known in America through recent English translations. De Wette was a mediating liberal theologian who sympathized with the radical Higher Critics but did not go so far as David Strauss and others in rejecting the literal interpretation of the Bible. Three volumes of de Wette were a going-away gift to Healey from West Church minister Cyrus Bartol.

4. The lyrics of this song were by popular English poet Felicia Hemans and the music "by Her Sister."

5. Probably one of the other teachers.

6. A slave or servant at the school.

7. Ephesians 6:5–9; Philippians 2:7.

8. Dall later inserted "it" in pencil.

9. John Abercrombie (1780–1844), Scottish physician and metaphysician, wrote two popular works: *Inquiries Concerning the Intellectual Powers and the Investigation of Truth* (1830) and *The Philosophy of the Moral Feelings* (1833). Both went through many editions, and apparently Miss English's school used one or both *(DNB)*.

10. One of Healey's students, Katherine Richenda Barnard (1823–1895), was the daughter of English natives Robert Barnard (1786–1852), secretary-treasurer of the Chesapeake and Ohio Canal, and his wife, Sophia Cropley Barnard (1796–1872). Healey was to visit them several times at their Georgetown home, "Normanstone," and resumed friendship with Katie after she herself moved to Georgetown in 1878 *(Ancestry.com,* accessed May 5, 2003; DFN).

11. Charles Lowell, senior pastor at the West Church in Boston.

12. Sarah Josepha Hale (1820–1863), known as Josepha, was, like Healey, a beginning teacher at Miss English's. She was the daughter of author and editor Sarah Josepha Hale and the late David H. Hale. In the late 1850s Josepha ran a successful young ladies' school in Philadelphia *(NAW)*.

13. The Cranches, Healey's surrogate family in Washington, included Judge William Cranch (1769–1855), his wife, Anna ("Nancy") Greenleaf Cranch (1772–1843), and their youngest child, Margaret ("Margy" or "Margie") Dawes Cranch (1819–1895), who became Healey's best friend during her stay in Georgetown. See James Edward Greenleaf, *Genealogy of the Greenleaf Family* (Boston: F. Wood, 1896), 223, and *ANB*.

14. On December 31, 1841, Samuel Haven had sent Healey a volume that he called "Specimens of American Literature," which the accompanying letter described as "a mnemonic of my regard and remembrance at the beginning of a new year" (Dall Papers, MHS). Probably the book was *The Boston Book: Being Specimens of Metropolitan Literature* (Boston: G.W. Light, 1841), a gift book edited by George S. Hillard.

15. George J. Abbot (1812–1879) and his wife, Annie Taylor Gilman Emery Abbot (1815–1861), became two

of Healey's best friends in Washington. They were Unitarians, and George Abbot, like Healey's father's family, came from Hampton Falls, New Hampshire. Abbot had finished in the Harvard class of 1835 and served as principal of the Western Academy for Boys in Washington, 1837–1850. Then he entered the State Department under Webster and his successors, serving as Webster's private secretary, then as head of the Consular Bureau, and in consular posts in England and Canada. From 1871 to 1876 he was a professor at the Meadville (Pennsylvania) Theological School. See Lemuel Abijah Abbott, *Descendants of George Abbott, of Rowley, Mass.* (Boston: T.R. Marvin & Son, 1906), 2:679–680.

16. Harriet L. G. Strother Stringfellow (1807–1847), the wife of Horace Stringfellow, rector of Trinity Church in Washington (*Ancestry.com,* accessed November 6, 2003).

17. Caroline Phelps (1814–1904) married Stephen Greenleaf Bulfinch in December of this year. See Oliver Seymour Phelps and Andrew T. Servin, *The Phelps Family of America* (Pittsfield, Massachusetts: Eagle Publishing Co., 1899), 1:507–508, and DFN. Caroline Phelps had been living with the Josiah Quincy family, as teacher and companion (Letter of Caroline Phelps to Healey, August 5, 1842, Dall Papers, MHS). Healey originally wrote "of Quincy," and later corrected it in pencil to "of the Quincies."

18. William Greenleaf Eliot (1781–1853) was a merchant and postal official in New Bedford before moving to Washington after the War of 1812 *(ANB)*.

19. Charles Henry Appleton Dall (1816–1886), Healey's future husband, was born in Baltimore but had lived from the age of seven with an aunt and uncle in Boston. He had graduated from Harvard in 1837 and from the Divinity School in 1840, served for a year in a ministry-at-large in St. Louis (where he was associated with the son-in-law of the Cranches, William G. Eliot), preached briefly in Mobile, Alabama, and then traveled to Europe. He had returned very recently and assumed the ministry to the poor in his native city. See Caroline Healey Dall, ed., *Memorial to Charles Henry Appleton Dall* (Boston: Beacon Press, 1902), 8–10.

20. Ann French Brown (1808–1898), originally of Chester, New Hampshire. Her husband was Simon Brown (1802–1873), of Newburyport, Massachusetts, librarian of the House of Representatives. The Browns later moved to Concord, Massachusetts, where he became an agricultural editor and then lieutenant governor. See Social Circle in Concord, *Memoirs of Members of the Social Circle in Concord*, 3rd ser. (Cambridge, Massachusetts: The Riverside Press, 1907), 76–84; DFN.

21. John Purdy (b. 1805?), Washington merchant. Healey later described him as "a house painter—but very wealthy" and "most zealous in behalf of our church" (1850 U.S. Census; Ms. Journals, December 30, 1842).

22. Benjamin Brown French (1800–1870) and Elizabeth Richardson French (1805–1861), from New Hampshire. Benjamin French, the half-brother of Ann French Brown, was chief clerk in the House of Representatives, and, following Polk's election, was promoted to Clerk of the House. Still later he was commissioner of public buildings. Selections from French's journal have been published as *Witness to the Young Republic: A Yankee's Journal, 1828–1870,* ed. Donald B. Cole and John J. McDonough (Hanover, New Hampshire: University Press of New England, 1989).

23. Mary Smith, a slave.

24. "pocket unread . . . and loved" canceled later by Dall, and the new page following "and loved" is cut out. The text resumes, on the same date, with "tonight."

25. William Brent (1774–1848) was for many years clerk of the court for the District of Columbia; he had also been a temporary secretary to President Jefferson. His second wife was Elizabeth Neale Brent (1799/1800–1863). See David M. French, *The Brent Family; The Carroll Families of Colonial Maryland* (Alexandria, Virginia: D. M. French, 1981), 63, and Chester Horton Brent, *The Descendants of Col. Giles Brent, Capt George Brent and Robert Brent, Gent* (Rutland, Vermont: Tuttle Publishing Co., 1946), 137–138.

26. As President Tyler's first wife, Letitia, had died September 10, 1842, Priscilla Cooper Tyler (1816–1889), the wife of his son Robert (1816–1877), was the official White House hostess. The daughter of actor Thomas A. Cooper (who was the adopted son of William Godwin, English social reformer), she had been a professional actress before her marriage. See Robert Seager II, *And Tyler Too: A Biography of John and Julia Gardner Tyler* (New York: McGraw-Hill, 1963), 71, 123–125, 517, 637.

27. Caleb Cushing (1800–1879), Massachusetts politician, was at this time a Whig member of the House of Representatives.

28. Baron Alexander de Bodisco (1784?–1854), Russian envoy to the United States, had at age fifty-six married Harriet Williams, the sixteen-year-old daughter of a government clerk in Washington. Harriet Williams had been a student at Miss English's school. See *NEHGR* 8:196 and Benjamin Brown French, *Witness to the Young Republic,* ed. Donald B. Cole and John J. McDonough (Hanover, New Hampshire: University Press of New England, 1989), 243.

29. Probably William Greenleaf Cranch (1796–1872), son of the judge.

30. Jane Brent Sweeny (d. 1847), niece of William Brent and owner of a tavern on A Street, near New Jersey Avenue (Chester Horton Brent, *The Descendants of Col. Giles Brent, Capt George Brent and Robert Brent, Gent,* 136–138; *Washington Directory* 1843).

31. William McKendree Gwin (1805–1885), congressman from Mississippi. Healey's relationship with him was problematic; he made what she felt were inappropriate revelations about his marriage in letters to her (Ms. Journals, February 25, 26, 28, March 1, 1843). Gwin had a checkered public career but much later was elected U.S. senator from California.

32. John C. Calhoun (1782–1850), United States senator from South Carolina.

33. A draft of this letter is in Healey's letterbook (Dall Papers, MHS). In it she confessed to having, for the last year, "felt an interest in one—who neither felt nor sought to inspire, any interest in me." She had hoped in coming to Washington to find "forgetfulness," but "I have not yet done so." Her interest in Dall, she wrote, "is very deep, but I feel that it respects your cause, quite as much as yourself." She noted that he wanted help in that cause, and wanted it "<u>now</u>"; this she could not promise, since it might be "many months . . . before I could think of any other duty than that I owe to my family." She left it to him to "remember or forget what you last wrote."

34. Dall later underlined "seeks in me . . . his work" and added: "Here was the mistake! 1895—"

35. Sarah Balch, engaged to Frederick Beck.

36. Psalms 4:7.

37. William Bullock (fl. 1808–1828), English traveler, naturalist, and antiquarian, published in 1824 *Six Months' Residence and Travels in Mexico (DNB)*.

38. Caroline Dall later in pencil added an asterisk at this point and a note at the end of the entry: "Never done—"

CHAPTER FIVE

1. Catherine Wild and Martha Choate.

2. Seth Wells (1811–1850), a West Church friend of Healey's, was the posthumous son of Seth Wells (1768–1810), merchant, and Hannah Doane Wells (1777–1841). See Alfred Alder Doane, *Doane Family* (Boston, 1902), 253, and Watertown VR.

3. Anna Sargent Parker (1782–1873), wife of the wealthy Boston merchant John Parker (1783–1844). See Emma Worcester Sargent and Charles Sprague Sargent, *Epes Sargent of Gloucester and His Descendants* (Boston: Houghton, Mifflin and Company, 1923), 24.

4. Xenophon (c. 435–354), disciple of Socrates, was a Greek military commander, essayist, and historian.

Dall was reading *The Cyropaedia; or Institution of Cyrus,* probably in the version translated by Maurice Ashly Cooper (New York: Harper, 1843).

5. Abigail Leonard Cunningham, a family friend and neighbor.

6. John T. Sargent (1808–1877), a graduate of the Harvard Divinity School in 1830, formerly minister-at-large at the Suffolk Street Chapel in Boston. This work was administered by the Benevolent Fraternity of Churches, organized in 1834 to sustain work among the poor in Boston. In November 1844 Sargent lost this position as a result of exchanging pulpits with Theodore Parker (*Heralds* 2:105, 108–109; 3:284).

7. Dall later added a note in the margin: "The exercise which every body tried to prevent my taking—actually saved my life Aug 21st—by the strength it gave to my muscles taxed by 3 days of labor."

8. Janet(te) Alexander, midwife who attended Dall (1840 U.S. Census; *Boston Directory* 1845).

9. *Narrative of the United States Exploring Expedition* by Charles Wilkes (1798–1877), who had commanded an expedition exploring the Antarctic continent, Pacific islands, and coast of the American Northwest (1838–1842). His five-volume *Narrative* appeared in 1844 (*DAB*).

10. On December 26, 1844, Theodore Parker had delivered the "Thursday lecture" at the First Church in Boston. His sermon—"The Relation of Jesus to His Age and to the Ages"—was offensive to members of the Boston Association of Ministers, and in response the First Church withdrew its outstanding invitations to future lecturers and took complete control of the selection of speakers. Parker then published his *Letter to the Boston Association of Congregational Ministers Touching Certain Matters of their Religion* (Boston: Charles C. Little and James Brown, 1845), in which he asked the ministers "to inform me what is Orthodoxy according to the Boston Association" and to answer twenty-four theological questions. See Henry Steele Commager, *Theodore Parker* (Boston: Little, Brown and Co., 1936), 98–100.

11. Austin Dall (1819–1899), Charles Dall's brother, visiting from Baltimore. See John William Linzee, *History of Peter Parker and Sarah Ruggles* (Boston: S. Usher, 1913), 132.

12. Robert C. Waterston.

13. Mark Healey was one of the five Boston men who invited Parker to form a new congregation in Boston and guaranteed his salary; William Dall was the congregation's treasurer.

14. Charles Briggs (1791–1873), secretary of the American Unitarian Association (1835–1847) (*General Catalogue of the Divinity School of Harvard University*). "Mr. Briggs's" probably refers to the offices of the AUA.

15. Mary Jane Ware (b. 1811), the older sister of Dall's friend Horatia Ware. See Emma Forbes Ware, *Ware Genealogy* (Boston: Charles H. Pope, 1901), 133; Bigelow Society, *Bigelow Family Genealogy* (Flint, Michigan: The Bigelow Society, 1986), 1:368.

16. Louisa Simes (1811?–1889), an unmarried woman who became a long-term friend of the Dalls (*NEHGR* 84:33; DFN).

17. Josiah Moore (1800–1881) was a minister in Duxbury from 1833 until his death (*Heralds* 3:209). One of his theories was that a woman could learn the "Science of Universals" by cooking fish (Theodore Parker to Dall, August 4, 1846, Dall Papers, MHS). Partially printed in John Weiss, *Life and Correspondence of Theodore Parker* (New York: D. Appleton, 1864), 1:340–341.

18. Susan Pickering Lyman Haven Kittredge (1813–1881), the widow of William Haven, was now married to Portsmouth physician Rufus Kittredge (1789–1854). See Lyman Coleman, *Genealogy of the Lyman Family in Great Britain and America* (Albany, New York: J. Munsell, 1872, 389, and Mabel T. Kittredge, *Kittredge Family in America* (Rutland, Vermont: Tuttle, 1936), 68–69. Mary Rantoul Peabody Lyman (1813–1887) was the wife of John Pickering Lyman (1807–1874), a leading Portsmouth businessman active in the Unitarian church, and the sister of Unitarian minister Andrew P. Peabody. The "Mrs. Kittredge" just mentioned was John P. Lyman's sister. See Selim Hobart Peabody, *Peabody (Pay-*

body, Pabody, Pabodie) Genealogy (Boston: C.H. Pope, 1909), 106; *Federal Fire Society of Portsmouth, N.H.* (Portsmouth, New Hampshire: The Society, 1905), 56; *NEHGR* 83:184, 307; 113:263. Susan Pickering Parker (d. 1858) was the widow of Nathan Parker (1782–1833), pastor of the South Parish, Portsmouth, from 1808 until his death. Dr. Parker led the parish into the Unitarian fellowship (Lyman Coleman, *Genealogy of the Lyman Family*, 389; *Heralds* 2:159–163).

19. François Marie Charles Fourier (1792–1837), French Utopian socialist thinker, and Parke Godwin (1816–1904), lawyer, writer, editor, translator, and supporter of Brook Farm. Godwin edited the community's Fourierist periodical *The Harbinger* and was later long associated with William Cullen Bryant, his father-in-law, on the *New-York Evening Post*. Dall was reading his *A Popular View of the Doctrines of Charles Fourier* (New York: J.S. Redfield, 1844) *(DAB)*.

20. Emanuel Swedenborg (1688–1772), Swedish scientist, theologian, and mystic, whose thought exerted a significant influence on many of the Transcendentalists, especially Emerson.

21. *Vestiges of the Natural History of Creation* was published anonymously in 1844 by the Scottish editor and publisher Robert Chambers (1802–1871). It presented a kind of proto-evolutionary theory of development that was seen by many readers as an attack on the orthodox view of Creation.

22. Sarah Phillips Beck (1816–1902), the daughter of Sarah H. B. Beck (1799–1865), widow of Frederick Beck. Sarah P. Beck was visiting the Dalls from Boston (1850 U.S. Census; DFN; *Boston Directory* 1843).

23. Margaret Fuller's *Papers on Literature and Art* (New York: Wiley and Putnam, 1846) was just out.

24. Germaine de Staël (1766–1817), French woman of letters, political writer, and conversationalist, kept a salon in Paris for leading intellectuals.

25. Sarah Hussey Southwick (1821–1896), daughter of Joseph and Thankful Hussey Southwick. She served as treasurer and then secretary of the Boston Female Anti-Slavery Society; her mother had previously been its president. See Walter M. Merrill and Louis Ruchames, eds., *Letters of William Lloyd Garrison*, 6 vols. (Cambridge, Massachusetts: Belknap Press, 1971–1981), 5:272; *Liberator*, October 31, 1845, p. 1.

26. Marianne Haliburton was the daughter of Andrew Haliburton (1771–1846), Portsmouth bank president, and Sarah A. Haliburton (b. 1800?). See William Rutherford and Ann Clay (Zimmerman) Rutherford, *General History of the Halliburton Family* (n.p., 1972), 1:42; 1850 U.S. Census.

27. Ambrose Wellington (1819–1895) was master of the Smith School on Belknap Street, which had in the preceding year enrolled 116 boys and 64 girls. See *Boston Directory* 1847–1848; Lemuel Stattuck, *Report to the Committee of the City Council Appointed to Obtain the Census of Boston for the Year 1845 . . .* (Boston: J.H. Eastburn, 1846), 28.

28. Except for the first sentence, Dall later canceled this entire entry.

29. Elizabeth Oliver Shores (1797?–1863) was the wife of James F. Shores (1792?–1871), Portsmouth bank cashier (*Portsmouth Directory* 1851; *NEHGR* 82:424, 83:309).

30. Charles Augustus Cheever (1793–1852), longtime Portsmouth physician. See *Extracts from the Writings of Charles A. Cheever, M.D. with a Memoir by A. P. Peabody* (Boston: John Wilson & Son, 1854).

CHAPTER SIX

1. Francis F. Stedman (b. 1824?), son of William and Miriam Stedman (1850, 1860 U.S. Census).

2. Probably Elizabeth Lewis Porter (1823–1876), the wealthy daughter of War of 1812 hero and statesman Peter Buell Porter (*Ancestry.com*, accessed October 11, 2004).

3. George Washington Warren (1813–1883) and Georgiana Thompson Warren (b. 1822?), fellow travelers. George Warren, a lawyer, had served in the Massachusetts legislature and had been defeated as

a Whig candidate for Congress in 1846. He was at this time the first mayor of the city of Charlestown, Massachusetts (1847–1851), and became a state senator (1853–1854). See Thomas C. Amory, *Class Memoir of George Washington Warren* (Boston: Rockwell & Churchill, 1886), 128–144; *NatCAB* 5:90.

4. Probably John Hale Wait (b. 1806) (*Ancestry.com*, accessed October 11, 2004).

5. The article appeared in the August 27 issue of *The Liberator*. See journal entry for August 26.

6. Thomas Carlyle (1795–1881), British romantic author. His *German Romance: Specimens of Its Chief Authors; with Biographical and Critical Notices* (Boston: J. Munroe, 1841) included translations of works by Hoffman, Richter, and Tieck, among others.

7. William Ritchie Jr. was the son of the former minister at Needham, William Ritchie (d. 1842). See Needham VR and George Kuhn Clarke, *History of Needham Massachusetts, 1711–1911* (Cambridge, Massachusetts: Harvard University Press, 1912), 239–240.

8. Experience Stow Newton Hersey (b. 1789), whose husband Elijah had died on August 25 (*Ancestry.com*, accessed October 8, 2004).

9. This sermon, delivered at the Melodeon on March 5, 1848, following the former president's death on February 23, was published as *A Discourse Occasioned by the Death of John Quincy Adams*. See Dean Grodzins and Joel Myerson, "The Preaching Record of Theodore Parker," *SAR 1994*, 98.

10. A sweetened and flavored dessert made from gelatinous or starchy ingredients and milk.

11. Dr. Josiah Noyes (1801–1871), who had studied medicine at Dartmouth, was Needham's first licensed physician (Clarke, *History of Needham Massachusetts*, 573–575).

12. Mary C. Smith Revere (1800–1869), wife of Needham merchant George Revere (*NEHGR* 145:307–308).

13. Mary Rowe, a widow from Boston, whom Dall had contracted to act as nurse.

14. Dr. John C. Warren, the family physician of Dall's childhood.

15. William M. Stedman (b. 1795?) one of Charles Dall's parishioners (1850 U.S. Census).

16. Dall's story "Annie Gray" appeared in the 1848 antislavery annual the *Liberty Bell*, 184–207.

17. A second edition of Thomas Carlyle's *Life of Schiller* (first published in book form in 1825) had come out in 1845. Friedrich Schiller (1759–1805) was a German romantic poet and playwright.

18. Their Portsmouth friend Elizabeth P. Spalding (1803–1878) was visiting with the Dalls. *The Rhine* by Victor Hugo (1802–1885), first published in 1842, had appeared in English translation in several editions.

19. Dr. Samuel Johnson authored the periodical *The Rambler*, consisting mainly of moralizing essays.

20. *Winter Evenings, or Lucubrations on Life and Letters*, by the English miscellaneous writer Vicesimus Knox (1752–1821).

21. Dall must mean the American Institute of Instruction, founded in Boston in 1830, which conducted annual lectures on education. See Carl Bode, *The American Lyceum* (New York: Oxford University Press, 1956), 116–117.

22. Probably Ann Greene Chapman (d. 1837), Maria Weston Chapman's sister-in-law (*Liberator*, April 7, 1837).

23. On May 4, 1842, Healey, while visiting friends in Greenfield, Massachusetts, heard a lecture by Nantucket abolitionist George Bradburn (1806–1880).

24. Dall is probably referring to two works in the Boston Museum collection, identified only as Apollo Belvidere and Venus. See *Catalogue of the Paintings, Portraits, Marble and Plaster Statuary, Engravings and Water Color Drawings, in the Collection of the Boston Museum . . .* (Boston: William Marden, 1849).

25. Probably Sarah Gray Hawes (b. 1791?), wife of Boston merchant Prince Hawes (1790–1859) (1850 U.S. Census; Suffolk Probate Records; *Ancestry.com*, accessed October 10, 2004).

26. Allen Dodge (1804–1878), Webster supporter, was active in the Essex Agricultural Society. See Charles

M. Wiltse and Harold D. Moser, eds., *The Papers of Daniel Webster: Correspondence 1844–1849* (Hanover, New Hampshire: University Press of New England, 1984), 6:69.

27. Richard Sullivan Fay (b. 1806), wealthy Lynn resident (*Ancestry.com,* accessed October 10, 2004; 1850, 1860 U.S. Census).

28. Charles Wainwright March (1815–1864), Harvard class of 1837, newspaper writer and associate of Webster, published in 1850 *Reminiscences of Congress,* which he renamed in its fourth edition (1852) *Daniel Webster and His Contemporaries.* He became U.S. vice consul at Cairo and died in Egypt. See William D. Mountain, *March Family* (n.p., 1985–1993), 7:144. March's sister, Susan Sparhawk March (b. 1821?), was a member of the South Parish Church where Dall attended in Portsmouth (*NEHGR* 82:422).

29. Dall later canceled "condescension" in pencil and inserted "courtesy."

30. Rufus Choate (1799–1859) was a prominent Massachusetts lawyer and politician; he had served out the remainder of Webster's term in the Senate when the latter was appointed William Henry Harrison's secretary of state. Daniel Putnam King (1801–1850) of Danvers served in the House of Representatives from 1843 until his death in 1850.

31. George Revere (1795–1870), wealthy Needham merchant, grandson of patriot Paul Revere (*NEHGR* 145:307–308; 1850 U.S. Census).

32. Charles C. Shackford (1815–1891) and his second wife, Martha Bartlett Shackford (1826?–1903). It was at Shackford's ordination at the Hawes Place Church in South Boston that Theodore Parker had preached his *Transient and Permanent* sermon in 1841. From 1846 to 1865 Shackford was minister to the Second Congregational Society at Lynn. He then opened a school for young girls in Boston, and still later was professor of rhetoric and general literature at Cornell University (*NEHGR* 11:151; Harvard University Archives; DFN).

33. Thomas Wentworth Higginson (1823–1911), currently minister to the Free Religious Society at Newburyport, and later to the Free Church in Worcester. He was associated with the Transcendentalists, the Free Religious Association, and numerous reform movements, led a black regiment in the Civil War, was mentor to Emily Dickinson, and had a successful literary career. He and Caroline Dall were to have a long association in reform activities, particularly in the area of women's rights.

34. 2 Thessalonians 3:13.

35. Acts 3:6.

36. *Elementary Geology* by Edward Hitchcock (1793–1864), which appeared in numerous editions.

37. The English historian George Grote (1794–1871) published his four-volume *A History of Greece, from the Earliest Period to the Close of the Generation Contemporary with Alexander the Great* in New York, 1846–1849. Solon was an Athenian statesman and poet of the sixth century B.C.

38. James Freeman Clarke.

39. Wendell Phillips (1811–1884), a member of Boston's society elite, associated himself in the 1830s with the less than popular abolitionists, defending William Lloyd Garrison from a mob in 1835, and was now the movement's leading orator. In 1865 he became president of the American Anti-Slavery Society (see *ANB*). Stephen Symonds Foster (1809–1881) and Abigail Kelley Foster (1810–1887), husband and wife, were abolitionist lecturers, sometimes distinguished by their extreme rhetoric and anticlericalism; at this time they were living near Worcester. Abby, as she was known, was one of those who pushed for the public participation of women in the movement, thus precipitating a split in 1840 between the Garrisonians, with whom she was allied, and the more conservative faction. Both the Fosters were women's rights advocates. Frederick Douglass (1818–1895), the escaped slave turned abolitionist lecturer, writer, and editor, had since 1847 been living in Rochester, New York, where he founded his own paper, the *North Star*. Charles Lenox Remond (1810–1873), a free black who grew up in Salem,

had become in 1838 an agent of the Massachusetts Anti-Slavery Society, lecturing in England and in New England *(DAB)*.

40. Charles C. Burleigh (1810–1878) was a prominent abolitionist, anti-Sabbatarian, and opponent of the death penalty. As an agent and lecturer for the Middlesex Anti-Slavery Society, he was with Garrison when the latter was mobbed in Boston in 1835. He frequently contributed to the *Liberator* and was for a time the editor of the *Pennsylvania Freeman (DAB)*.

41. George P. A. Healy (1813–1894), native Bostonian, was a popular and prolific portrait painter. He became best known for his work *Webster Replying to Hayne,* hanging in Faneuil Hall *(DAB)*.

42. Probably Richard S. Fay.

43. *A Week on the Concord and Merrimack Rivers* was Thoreau's first book, published in the spring of 1849. Dall was reading one of only a few over two hundred copies of the book that were sold.

44. Dall later inserted in pencil "(to paint him.)." Healy was at Andrew Jackson's home, the Hermitage, near Nashville, shortly before Jackson's death on June 8, 1845. His portrait of Jackson, completed in 1861 and based on the original study made in 1845, is now at the Corcoran Gallery.

45. Joseph Blanco White (1775–1841) was a theological writer born into an Irish family in Spain. As a Catholic priest who gave up Christianity, he feared the Inquisition. Escaping to England, he took up Anglican, then Unitarian, Christianity. He had many publications; possibly Dall read *The Life of the Rev. Joseph Blanco White, written by himself with portions of his correspondence,* ed. John Hamilton Thom (London: John Chapman, 1845).

46. Charles William Orne (b. 1827), son of Edward F. and Mary Williams Orne; and William Henry Orne (1827–1882), son of Richard Elvin Orne (b. 1795) and Ann Fisk Allen Orne, were first cousins (*Ancestry.com,* accessed October 11, 2004).

47. Pontotoc is in northern Mississippi; Richard E. Orne was a land agent there (1850 U.S. Census).

48. The family had been reading in the evenings British essayist and historian Thomas Babington Macaulay (1800–1859), probably his *History of England: From the Accession of James the Second* (Boston: Phillips, Sampson and Company, 1849).

49. Elizabeth Hunt Noyes (1815–1902), wife of Josiah Noyes (Clarke, *History of Needham Massachusetts, 1711–1911,* 573–575).

50. William Frederick Teulon (1803–1884), an English-born physician, served only briefly as Universalist minister (*Ancestry.com,* accessed October 11, 2004; see also S. F. Smith, *History of Newton, Massachusetts* (Boston: American Logotype Co., 1880), 466.

51. The Mortons were neighbors to the Dalls. The family included Otis Morton (b. 1784?), carpenter, his wife Persia Morton (1792?–1855), and their fourteen-year-old daughter, Mary E. Morton (Needham VR; 1850 U.S. Census).

52. Theodore Parker and William Lloyd Garrison.

53. Elisha Lyon (1778–1862), hat manufacturer and church and community leader, was deacon of the church from 1826 to 1849. By 1858 he was involved in the establishment of a new Orthodox church in Needham. See Clarke, *History of Needham, Massachusetts, 1711–1911,* 226, 284, and A. B. Lyon(s) and G. W. A. Lyon, *Lyon Memorial: Massachusetts Families* (Detroit: Graham Printing Co., 1905), 349.

54. Thomas Kingsbury (1795–1859), Needham farmer, was also a deacon (*Ancestry.com,* accessed October 11, 2004; 1850 U.S. Census).

55. Edgar Kimball Whitaker (1806–1883), Boston merchant, prominent Needham citizen, representative in the General Court, and in 1851 a member of the Governor's Council; an active member of Charles Dall's church. See Ephraim Seward Whitaker, *The Whitaker Chart,* typescript at New England Historic Genealogical Society (Boston), 1900, 645–648, and Samuel May et al., *Descendants of John May of Roxbury, Mass., 1640,* 2nd ed. (Baltimore: Gateway Press, 1978), 47–48.

56. *A Harmony of the Gospels, on the Plan Proposed by Lant Carpenter, LL.D.,* ed. J. G. Palfrey (Boston: Gray and Bowen, 1831).

57. Miss Harris was probably Harriet (Hatty) Harris (later Hicks) (1825?–1908), daughter of John and Eliza Harris (1850 U.S. Census; DFN). The newborn Mary N. Prentiss must have been orphaned; when the census was taken on August 16, 1850, she appeared, aged ten months, in the household of Dall's friends Thomas and Miranda Kingsbury of Needham (1850 U.S. Census). The Misses Parker were probably Elisa (b. 1802?) and Sarah (b. 1804?) Parker of Needham (1850 U.S. Census). Mrs. Baury was Mary Catherine Henshaw Baury (1798–1873), wife of Alfred Louis Baury, Episcopal rector, Newton Lower Falls; see "Tombstone Records at Newton, Mass.," DAR typescript (NEHGS, 94). William Shimmin (1777–1856) was a prominent Boston merchant (*NEHGR* 11:188). Sarah G. Sawyer (1818?–1850) was the orphaned daughter of Lucy Thacher Sawyer (1792–1820) and Abner Sawyer, and an old friend of Dall's. She was fatally ill with consumption (Roxbury VR; *Ancestry.com,* accessed February 26, 2005). Mary Clark Shannon (1813–1887) was a leading citizen of Newton who used her wealth in philanthropic causes. Notable among these was the Rebecca Pomroy Newton Home for Orphan Girls that she helped establish in 1872. See George E. Hodgdon, *Shannon Genealogy* (Rochester, New York: The Genesee Press, 1905), 208–212. John Harris (b. 1780?), employed at the Boston Custom House, and his wife, Eliza Harris (1790–1874), were Charles Dall's parishioners; Harriet (Hatty) Harris was their daughter (1850 U.S. Census; Ms. Journals, March 27, 1874). Betsey Sumner Kingsbury (b. 1828), daughter of Needham farmer Thomas Kingsbury and his first wife, Clarissa, was a staunch friend of the Dalls (1850 U.S. Census; Massachusetts VR).

58. Martha Fisher MacIntosh (b. 1808?), wife of Nathan MacIntosh (b. 1805?), Needham shoemaker (Needham VR; 1850 U.S. Census).

59. The household of Elizabeth K. Cheney Mills (b. 1810) and Davis Collins Mills (b. 1800), a prosperous butcher (Needham VR; 1850 U.S. Census).

60. Probably Dall refers to *Report of a Special Committee of the Grammar School Board, Presented August 29, 1849, on the Petition of Sundry Colored Persons Praying for the Abolition of the Smith School* (Boston: J.H. Eastburn, 1849). The committee recommended against the black community's request for the desegregation of Boston schools. A minority report by Charles T. Russell agreed with the petitioners' position.

61. A collection of poems published in 1842 by English poet Robert Browning (1812–1889).

62. Probably Edwin Martin Stone (1805–1883), minister-at-large in Providence, Rhode Island, who formerly preached in Beverly and was a member of the Massachusetts legislature. See J. Gardner Bartlett, *Gregory Stone Genealogy* (Boston: The Stone Family Association, 1918), 555.

63. The *Boston Directory* for 1850–1851 lists Henry V. Degan (b. 1815?) as chaplain of the reformatory (1860 U.S. Census).

64. The family of Dall's friend and correspondent Olivia Dabney (1815–1888), who was baptized in the West Church in Boston; as the daughter of the late American consul to Fayal, John Bass Dabney (1767–1826), Olivia spent most of her life on that island, in the Azores. Olivia Dabney's nephew John Pomeroy Dabney was married to Sarah H. Webster, the daughter of accused murderer Dr. John W. Webster. See Rose Dabney Forbes, *Fayal Dabneys* (n.p., 1931), 8, 23, 75, 139–140; Roxana Lewis Dabney, *Annals of the Dabney Family in Fayal* (Boston, n.d.), 1:67, 2:529; DFN.

65. Throughout the trial and after he was found guilty, Webster steadfastly proclaimed his innocence. Not long before the execution date, however, he confessed to the killing but maintained that it was not premeditated *(DAB).*

66. Mary Sumner Fairbanks (1786–1870), widow of Gerry Fairbanks. She kept a boardinghouse on Highland Street. See Lorenzo Sayles Fairbanks, *Genealogy of the Fairbanks Family in America, 1633–1897* (Boston: American Printing and Engraving Company, 1897), 294; *Roxbury Directory* 1848.

67. The Town and Country Club.

68. Probably Elizabeth L. Tucker (b. 1818), daughter of Needham farmer Enos H. Tucker (b. 1784) (*Ancestry.com,* accessed October 11, 2004; 1850 U.S. Census).

69. *The Seven Lamps of Architecture,* published in 1849 by British art critic John Ruskin (1819–1900).

70. Henry Wadsworth Longfellow's *The Seaside and the Fireside* was just off the press. Dall later altered the lowercase initial "s" in "seaside" to uppercase, in pencil.

71. Washington Irving (1783–1859) collected a number of his tales set in the Hudson River valley into this volume (New York: G.P. Putnam, 1849).

CHAPTER SEVEN

1. Lucia Gardner Fairfield Wells (1804–1876), widow of George Wadsworth Wells, and her niece, Dall's old friend Martha Choate (now Spelman) (*Ancestry.com,* accessed October 13, 2004).

2. Sir Austen Henry Layard (1817–1894), excavator of Nineveh, published *Nineveh and Its Remains* in 1849; an American edition appeared in 1850 *(DNB).* *The Caxtons,* by English novelist Edward Bulwer-Lytton (1803–1873), was serialized in *Blackwood's,* then published in its complete form in 1849. *The Wilmingtons* was a recent novel by Anne Marsh-Caldwell (1791–1874), one of the most popular of English novelists at this time *(DNB).* A. Welby Pugin (1812–1852) published *The True Principles of Pointed or Christian Architecture* (London: J. Weale, 1841). *Valpy's National Gallery of Painting and Sculpture; Illustrated with Forty-Six Beautiful Engravings on Steel, from the Old Masters . . .* by Abraham John Valpy (1787–1854) was published in London (1833?). The second volume of *The History of Ancient Art* by Johann Joachim Winckelmann (1717–1786), translated by G. Henry Lodge, appeared in Boston in 1849. Hawthorne's *The Scarlet Letter* had just been published.

3. George S. Appleton (1821–1878), Philadelphia (and later New York) publisher and bookseller (*NatCAB* 2:510).

4. Lydia Howe Champney (1784–1866), widow of John Champney, had a house on Parker Street, corner of Washington (*Roxbury Directory* 1850; *Ancestry.com,* accessed October 13, 2004).

5. *Jane Eyre,* published pseudonymously in 1847 by English novelist Charlotte Brontë (1816–1859), was Dall's favorite novel.

6. Parker preached "Of Woman" at the Melodeon. See Dean Grodzins and Joel Myerson, "The Preaching Record of Theodore Parker," *SAR 1994,* 103.

7. Mary W. Parker was the widow of Dall's old friend and benefactor Daniel P. Parker, who had died a few weeks earlier. Mary Elizabeth Hubbard Fairfield Wadsworth (1808?–1881) was the second wife of Alexander Wadsworth (1806–1898), a deacon of the West Church, of whom Dall herself published a memorial. Mary Wadsworth was also the aunt of Dall's friend Martha Choate Spelman. See Horace Andrew Wadsworth, *Two Hundred and Fifty Years of the Wadsworth Family in America* (Lawrence, Massachusetts, 1883), 151, 163; Caroline H. Dall, *In Memoriam Alexander Wadsworth* (n.p., n.d.), 8; DFN).

8. William Henry Channing (1810–1884), Unitarian minister and reformer. A graduate of Harvard (1829) and the Divinity School (1833), he had preached in New York City and Cincinnati and edited the *Western Messenger* from 1839 until its demise in 1841. In 1843–1844 he had edited *The Present,* a Fourierist publication, to be followed in 1849–1850 by *Spirit of the Age.* Channing published in 1848 a three-volume memoir of his uncle William Ellery Channing, and he was, with Emerson and James Freeman Clarke, one of the editors of *Memoirs of Margaret Fuller Ossoli* (1852). He headed the Religious Union of Associationists, a Christian socialist group originally associated with Brook Farm. Since the closing of that venture, the Associationists (sometimes called the First Church of Humanity) had been meet-

ing in Boston, generally holding an afternoon and an evening service on Sundays. The sermons that Dall heard over the next few weeks were apparently a public thrust by the group; generally the evening services were restricted to the members. Channing became, for a time, an important model to Dall, who admired particularly his nonconfrontational style, but their contact was limited after they both left Boston in the early 1850s, he for Rochester and later England. See Wesley T. Mott, ed., *Biographical Dictionary of Transcendentalism* (Westport, Connecticut: Greenwood Press, 1996) and Charles Crowe, "Christian Socialism and the First Church of Humanity," *Church History* 35 (1866): 93–106.

9. William H. Channing.

10. Probably William W. Clapp (1826–1891), editor of the Boston *Saturday Evening Gazette (DAB)*.

11. Probably Rebecca Davis Parker (1810–1894), the widow of Ebenezer Grosvenor Parker. She would later marry George S. Tolman, and was a longtime friend of Dall's. See William T. Davis, *Genealogical Register of Plymouth Families* (Baltimore: Genealogical Publishing Co., 1985), 83; Massachusetts VR.

12. Anna Q. T. Parsons (1812?–1906) was active in the Religious Union of Associationists and other reform circles in Boston. Her home in Pinckney Street was a cooperative house run to some extent on "Brook Farm principles." See Helen Dwight Orvis, "A Note on Anna Q. T. Parsons," in Marianne Dwight, *Letters from Brook Farm, 1844–1847* (Poughkeepsie, New York: Vassar College, 1928), xiii–xv. William Francis Channing (1820–1901), physician and inventor, was the son of the Reverend William Ellery Channing. His current wife was the former Susan Elizabeth Burdick (1823–1894). The Blackwells were a large reform-minded family, the children of Samuel (1790–1838) and Hannah Lane (1798–1870) Blackwell from Ohio. Perhaps the likeliest members of the family to have been at Faneuil Hall were the Cincinnati abolitionists Samuel C. Blackwell (1824–1901), who later married the minister Antoinette Brown, and his brother Henry Brown Blackwell (1825–1909), who later married Lucy Stone, the antislavery and women's rights activist. See DFN; *Blackwell Newsletter* 2 (1980): 4; *DAB; NAW*.

13. Francis Jackson (1789–1861), prominent citizen of Boston, was president of the Anti-Slavery Society for a number of years. He and two others guaranteed Garrison's support when the *Liberator* was in financial difficulty (*NatCAB* 2:318).

14. Edmund Quincy's wife was the former Lucilla Pinckney Parker (1810–1860), daughter of Dall's old friend Daniel P. Parker. See *NEHGR* 11:73, 92:250; H. Hobart Holly, *Descendants of Edmund Quincy* (Quincy, Massachusetts: Quincy Historical Society, 1977), 23.

15. Lemuel Shaw, chief justice of the Massachusetts Supreme Judicial Court.

16. The Ladies' Physiological Institute, founded in Boston in 1848, sponsored lectures on health-related topics. According to its constitution, its objects were "to promote among Women a knowledge of the HUMAN SYSTEM, the LAWS OF LIFE AND HEALTH, and the means of relieving sickness and suffering." Dall herself became an active member in 1856. The organization proved enduring; its papers through 1966 are at the Schlesinger Library. See Martha H. Verbrugge, *Able-Bodied Womanhood* (New York: Oxford University Press, 1988), 51, 65.

17. Samuel K. Lothrop (1804–1886), Unitarian minister; George Barrell Emerson (1797–1881), prominent Boston educator.

18. Sarah Holland Adams (1823–1916), daughter of Sarah M. and Zabdiel B. Adams and sister of Annie Adams Fields (wife of the publisher James T. Fields). She later lived for nearly twenty years in Weimar, Germany, and gained a reputation as the first English translator of Hermann Grimm's *Life of Goethe*. See Samuel May et al., *Descendants of John May of Roxbury, Mass.,* 2d ed. (Baltimore: Gateway Press, 1978), 46–47; Andrew Adams, *A Genealogical History of Henry Adams* (Rutland, Vermont: Tuttle Company, 1898), 460; Judith A. Roman, *Annie Adams Fields* (Bloomington: Indiana University Press, 1990), 99.

19. Parker Pillsbury (1809–1898) was lecture agent for the New Hampshire, Massachusetts, and American

Anti-Slavery societies. He was also involved in other reform movements, including the women's rights movement. The fact that he came from humble beginnings (his father was a blacksmith and a farmer) perhaps explains what seems to be Dall's class-conscious comment *(DAB)*.

20. Members of the Littlehale family in Boston included Ednah D. and Sargent S. Littlehale and their children, Mary Frank (1820–1904), Eliza D. (b. 1822), Ednah Dow (later Cheney; 1824–1904), and Helen P. (1833–1878). See Frederick H. Littlehale, *A Complete History and Genealogy of the Littlehale Family in America* (Rutland, Vermont: A.W. & F.H. Littlehale, 1889), 39; DFN.

21. Charlotte Hastings Whipple, a friend of Dall's from her West Church days, and her husband, Edwin Percy Whipple (1819–1886), a self-educated man who was rapidly becoming one of the most highly respected literary critics in America and, after Emerson, the most popular lecturer. See *DAB* and Denham Sutcliffe, " 'Our Young American Macaulay,' Edwin Percy Whipple, 1819–1886," *NEQ* 19 (1946): 3–18.

22. Charles F. Hovey (1807–1859), wealthy Boston dry goods merchant and abolitionist. See Walter M. Merrill and Louis Ruchames, eds., *Letters of William Lloyd Garrison*, 6 vols. (Cambridge, Massachusetts: Belknap Press, 1971–1981), 4:8–9.

23. Frederick Cabot (1822–1888) was a former resident of Brook Farm, where he acted as accountant for the community. An abolitionist, he was now a life insurance agent in Boston. See L. Vernon Briggs, *History and Genealogy of the Cabot Family, 1475–1927* (Boston: C.E. Goodspeed & Co., 1927) 2:650–651; 1850 U.S. Census.

24. Either Benjamin A. Gould (1787–1859), former head of the Boston Latin School, now prominent merchant, or his son Benjamin A. Gould (1824–1896), the astronomer *(DAB)*.

25. Rebecca Davis Parker.

26. Charles List (1817?–1856), counselor. Probably the conversation took place at his office at 46 Washington Street. He was a boarder with the Joseph Southwick family at 4 High Street (*Boston Directory* 1850–1851; Merrill and Ruchames, *Letters of William Lloyd Garrison* 5:272).

27. Woodbury M. Fernald (1813–1873), Swedenborgian minister, published *Compendium of the Theological and Spiritual Writings of Emanuel Swedenborg* (Boston: Crosby and Nichols, 1854), and other Swedenborgian materials (1850 U.S. Census).

28. Lidian Jackson Emerson (1802–1892).

29. Ednah Littlehale (later Cheney).

30. Thomas Wentworth Higginson.

31. Harriot Kezia Hunt (1805–1875) was apparently the first successful woman physician in the United States, practicing from 1835 to 1875. She had studied medicine with English practitioners and in 1853 would receive an honorary degree from the Female Medical College of Philadelphia. Hunt believed that ignorance of physiological laws was a major cause of poor health among married women, and she had a leading role in organizing the Ladies' Physiological Institute in 1843. She was also an advocate of women's rights, antislavery, temperance, and the admission of women to medical schools. See *NAW* and Martin Kaufman et al., eds., *Dictionary of American Medical Biography* (Westport, Connecticut: Greenwood Press, 1984).

32. Such a picture is unknown today. Either Dall was mistaken about when it was taken, or it has been lost.

33. Abigail May Alcott (1800–1877), member of a family of reformers (her brother was abolitionist Samuel Joseph May), and the wife of Bronson Alcott. She was at one time an early social worker in Boston. See Cynthia H. Barton, *Transcendental Wife: The Life of Abigail May Alcott* (Lanham, Maryland: University Press of America, 1996).

34. French essayist Michel de Montaigne (1533–1592).

35. German romantic author Johann Wolfgang von Goethe (1749–1832).

36. Hermes Trismegistus, sometimes identified with the Egyptian god Thoth, was the supposed author of a collection of first- to third-century treatises on occult, theological, and philosophical subjects. Pythagoras (sixth century B.C.) was a Greek philosopher and mathematician.

37. Plutarch was the author of *Morals*.

38. George Lunt (1803–1885), Newburyport native, a lawyer who published poetry and local color novels, had been appointed U.S. attorney for the district of Massachusetts by President Taylor. A conservative Democrat after the collapse of the Whig party, he edited the *Boston Daily Courier* from the mid-1850s through the Civil War and was a proslavery apologist *(ANB)*.

39. John Gore Torrey (1791–1863), president of the Columbian Bank in Boston. See John William Linzee, *The Linzee Family of Great Britain and the United States of America* (Boston: Fort Hill Press, 1917), 2:803.

40. William G. Ridgely (b. 1788?), chief clerk in the Navy Department, owned four slaves in 1850, an adult woman and three children (*Washington and Georgetown Directory* 1850; 1850 U.S. Census).

41. Dall had known Clement Moore Butler (1810–1890) when she lived in Georgetown, 1842–43, and he was rector there. He now ministered to Trinity Church, Washington. See David Moore Hall, *Six Centuries of the Moores of Fawley, Berkshire, England, and Their Descendants* (Richmond: O.E. Flanhart, 1904), 50; *NatCAB* 10:34.

42. Both of Butler's letters are in the Dall Papers, MHS.

43. Ira Gould was a prominent American-born mill owner on the Lachine Canal, and with John Young he owned the St. Gabriel Hydraulic Company, which controlled water rights at the St. Gabriel lock on the canal (*DCB* 9:367). His letter of April 12, 1851, is in the Dall Papers, MHS.

44. After her move to Toronto in May, Dall was kept informed on Williams's situation by her family. On July 20 her mother wrote that Williams had returned and that he had $200 and was trying to raise the remainder of the $500 that his owner was demanding. "[H]e is thin but seemed in good spirits. . . . He can have work enough but he is very particular where he goes." On October 12 she writes again that "Williams got all his money but $30 and R.C. Winthrop has promised to settle with his owner; and I am thankful for the poor creature, and when you think of it $500 is a great deal for a man to raise." The Boston Vigilance Committee in the meantime had been providing support for Williams's family. But his life seems to have taken an unforeseen turn. In 1852 Williams, then a waiter in Montreal, was listed as the father of a son born to an Irish mother, Margaret Maguin. He seems to have stayed in Montreal after all; the 1871 census lists him and Maguin as having several children. The fate of his former wife and child is unknown. See Gary Collison, *Shadrach Minkins: From Fugitive Slave to Citizen* (Cambridge, Massachusetts: Harvard University Press, 1997), 189–190.

CHAPTER EIGHT

1. Threadneedle Street is in the heart of the old City of London.

2. Probably the wife of Jacob Latham, an original member of the Toronto society (First Unitarian Congregation of Toronto archives).

3. Caroline Sewers Copland (or Copeland) (1795?–1886), wife of William Copland Sr. (d. 1862), Toronto brewer, who was an original member of the Toronto Unitarian Church and a subscriber to the support of Charles Dall (*Toronto Directory* 1850–51; DFN; letter of Caroline Copland to Dall, May 12, 1862; Dall Papers, MHS; First Unitarian Congregation of Toronto archives).

4. Probably Alexander Hunter (b. 1806?), carter, an original member of the Toronto Unitarian church (1871 Canadian Census; First Unitarian Congregation of Toronto archives).

5. John Patton (1827?–1870), born in the small town of Clomis in northern Ireland, was a Toronto china, glass, and earthenware importer, a wholesale supplier to the backcountry, and a major subscriber to Charles Dall's support. Patton became the Dalls' boarder and held the highest place in Caroline's affections for the next decade. In 1857 he moved to Montreal, leaving the Toronto firm to his father, and ran John Patton and Co., specializing in the same business. He died in Montreal of consumption, having never married. Patton's birth date is uncertain; records of the Necropolis, the Toronto cemetery where he is buried, list his age at his death as thirty, thus placing his birth date in 1840, but that date, which would make him only eleven at this point, is clearly impossible. The Unitarian Church in Montreal, of which Patton was a member when he died, lists his age at the time of his death as forty-four; when Dall herself visited his grave more than four years after his death and discovered the error in the cemetery's records, she wrote that he was actually forty-three, which would have made him five years younger than she. Some of Patton's letters to Dall and to her daughter Sarah (at this time called Lily), of whom he was especially fond, survive at the Schlesinger Library and at the MHS, but Dall destroyed many others (*Toronto Directory* 1856; First Unitarian Congregation of Toronto archives; Necropolis Cemetery, Toronto; Montreal *Gazette,* December 27, 1870, p. 2, and April 6, 1871, p. 3; Ms. Journals, May 30, 1875).

6. George Washington Hosmer (1803–1881) was the Unitarian minister in Buffalo (1836–1866) and was then president of Antioch College (1866–1873) (*Heralds* 3:174–179).

7. Dall was reading Charles Fourier's *Passions of the Human Soul,* translated by Hugh Doherty (London and New York, 1851).

8. Samuel May Jr. (1810–1899), Unitarian clergyman (Harvard Divinity School, 1833) and abolitionist, cousin of Samuel Joseph May. He was general agent of the Massachusetts Anti-Slavery Society. See Walter M. Merrill and Louis Ruchames, eds., *Letters of William Lloyd Garrison,* 6 vols. (Cambridge, Massachusetts: Belknap Press, 1971–1981), 4:7–8. May's letter of January 24, 1852, is in the Dall Papers, MHS.

9. Thomas Henning (1822?–1888) was the first secretary of the Canadian Anti-Slavery Society and a member of the editorial staff of the Toronto *Globe,* the area's most important newspaper. Isabella Brown Henning (1823–1888), his wife, was also the sister of George Brown, editor of the *Globe.* See Robin Winks, *The Blacks in Canada* (Montreal: McGill-Queen's University Press, 1971), 253; 1871 Canadian Census; Toronto *Globe,* December 29, 1888, p. 1; and J. M. S. Careless, *Brown of the Globe* (Toronto: Macmillan, 1959), 1:4.

10. Cf. James Freeman Clarke, Ralph Waldo Emerson, and William H. Channing, eds., *Memoirs of Margaret Fuller Ossoli* (Boston: Phillips, Sampson and Co., 1852), 1:16.

11. A small disc of dried paste that when moistened was used to seal a letter.

12. Cf. *Memoirs of Margaret Fuller Ossoli,* 2:48–49.

13. Probably the daughter of Boston businessman Francis Wilby and his wife Sally Robins. The Wilby family lived on Green Street next door to the Healeys during part of Caroline Healey's childhood (Boston VR; *Boston Directory* 1825; 1820 U.S. Census).

14. Cf. Margaret Fuller's "first friend," described in *Memoirs of Margaret Fuller Ossoli,* 1:32–42.

15. Probably an episode in *The Doctor,* by English Romantic writer Robert Southey (1774–1843), which Dall had read in 1846.

16. Dall probably refers to the statement by one of Fuller's brothers that "I had always viewed her as a being of different nature from myself, to whose altitudes of intellectual life I had no thought of ascending" (*Memoirs of Margaret Fuller Ossoli,* 2:124).

17. "I think, therefore I am," the basic tenet of the philosophy of Descartes.

18. John 9:39; 2 Timothy 4:1.

19. The wife of William Hedge, former treasurer of the Toronto Unitarian Church and one of the original subscribers for Charles Dall's salary (First Unitarian Congregation of Toronto archives). William Hedge was the brother of Frederic Henry Hedge, Unitarian minister and lecturer. The Toronto Hedges shortly moved to Quebec. Dall corresponded for some time with Mrs. Hedge, counseling her concerning her unhappy marriage.

20. Probably Gábor Naphegyi (1824–1884), author of *Hungary: From Her Rise to the Present Time* (New York, 1849).

21. *Memoirs of Margaret Fuller Ossoli*, 1:83.

22. *Memoirs of Margaret Fuller Ossoli*, 1:96.

23. *Memoirs of Margaret Fuller Ossoli*, 1:107.

24. *Memoirs of Margaret Fuller Ossoli*, 1:119–120.

25. *Memoirs of Margaret Fuller Ossoli*, 1:211.

26. *Memoirs of Margaret Fuller Ossoli*, 1:229.

27. Emerson in the *Memoirs* (1:236) wrote of "the presence of a rather mountainous ME" in Fuller.

28. *Memoirs of Margaret Fuller Ossoli*, 2:22.

29. *Memoirs of Margaret Fuller Ossoli*, 2:90.

30. *Memoirs of Margaret Fuller Ossoli*, 2:93.

31. *Memoirs of Margaret Fuller Ossoli*, 2:111.

32. "I was . . . to that?" canceled later.

33. Cf. *Memoirs of Margaret Fuller Ossoli*, 2:122–123.

34. *Memoirs of Margaret Fuller Ossoli*, 2:129.

35. Cf. *Memoirs of Margaret Fuller Ossoli*, 2:144–150, 159–160.

36. Cf. *Memoirs of Margaret Fuller Ossoli*, 2:273–277, 311, 316–317.

37. *Memoirs of Margaret Fuller Ossoli*, 2:277.

38. Psalms 105:18.

39. Cf. Luke 7:47.

40. The unsigned article took the form of a review of the new complete edition of Milton's works. *North British Review* 16 (1852): 295–335.

41. Dall's phraseology plays upon the first line of Elizabeth Barrett Browning's sonnet "To George Sand: A Desire": "Thou large-brained woman and large-hearted man." George Sand (1804–1876), French novelist, was controversial both for her writings and her personal life, which included affairs with Frédéric Chopin, Prosper Mérimée, and Alfred de Musset.

42. To the public exercises at Harvard.

43. Mary Harris Colman, originally from Charlestown, was the widow of Henry Colman (1785–1849). He graduated from Dartmouth (1805), preached at Hingham, ran an academy at Brookline, preached at the First Independent Church in Salem, and finally became a farmer at Greenfield, publishing on agricultural topics. See George T. Chapman, *Sketches of the Alumni of Dartmouth College* (Cambridge, Massachusetts: Riverside Press, 1867), 122–123.

44. Sophia Dana Ripley, Margaret Fuller, and probably Cornelia Romana Hall Park Sumner (b. 1807), friend of the Peabody family, and a medium. She was one of three non-family members who were guests at the wedding of Sophia Peabody and Nathaniel Hawthorne. Cornelia Hall married Thomas B. Park in 1830; he lost his fortune and went West, and they eventually divorced. In 1847 she became the wife of Henry Sumner (1814–1852), and still later of Alfred E. Ford. See David B. Hall, *Halls of New England* (Albany, New York: J. Munsell's Sons, 1883), 324, and William Sumner Appleton, *Record of the Descendants of William Sumner* (Boston: D. Clapp & Son, 1879), 176.

45. "but we cannot . . . love" canceled later by Dall.

46. Galen Orr (b. 1816) was a hinge maker (*Ancestry.com,* accessed October 15, 2004; 1850 U.S. Census).

47. The House of Industry housed the poor and persons sentenced for relatively minor offenses; the associated House of Reformation held juvenile offenders, and William Dall was one of its directors. The House of Correction housed more serious offenders. The Lunatic Hospital and the Perkins Institution and Massachusetts Asylum for the Blind were also located in South Boston. See Justin Winsor, ed., *Memorial History of Boston* (Boston: Osgood, 1881), 4:648–649; *Boston Directory* 1852.

48. A public grammar school for boys and girls on Fort Hill (*Boston Directory* 1852).

49. Louisa Workman (later Baker), a relative (perhaps a niece) of Dr. Joseph Workman, head of the insane asylum in Toronto and prominent in the Toronto Unitarian Church. She had traveled with Caroline and Willie Dall from Toronto to Boston.

50. Perhaps Dall has in mind William H. Channing's description of Fuller's Jamaica Plain conversational style: "Her opening was deliberate, like the progress of some massive force gaining its momentum" (*Memoirs of Margaret Fuller Ossoli,* 2:20).

51. Elizabeth Shannon March (b. 1831) was the niece of Dall's friend Mary Shannon of Newton. In 1861 she married Boston veterinarian Josiah Henry Stickney (1826–1901). See George E. Hodgson, *Shannon Genealogy* (Rochester, New York, 1905), 294.

52. Oliver Noble Shannon (1811–1869) of Newton, brother of Mary C. Shannon (George E. Hodgson, *Shannon Genealogy,* 301–302).

53. That is, John Patton.

54. A river in Quebec known for its wild and picturesque scenery.

55. Mary C. Shannon's nieces, Mary Shannon (1836–1901), daughter of Oliver and Harriet Burlin Shannon, and Elizabeth March. The younger Mary Shannon, eventually heir to her aunt, carried on her aunt's charitable and reform agenda (George E. Hodgson, *Shannon Genealogy,* 302–306).

56. Dall later in pencil corrected "it" to "he."

57. Lydia Dodge Cabot (1785–1863), the wife of John Cabot (1772–1855) and a resident of Newton. She was the mother-in-law of Theodore Parker. See L. Vernon Briggs, *History and Genealogy of the Cabot Family* (Boston: C.E. Goodspeed & Co., 1927), 1:267–268; 2:643.

58. Mary C. Shannon.

59. *A Wonder-Book for Girls and Boys* (London, 1851; Boston, 1852).

60. John Strickland Moodie (1838–1844), third of the Moodies' seven children, died before he was six. See Carl Ballstadt, Elizabeth Hopkins, and Michael Peterman, eds., *Susanna Moodie: Letters of a Lifetime* (Toronto: University of Toronto Press, 1985), 361.

61. Dall's *Essays and Sketches,* which she must have sent to Moodie.

62. The last three words were canceled later and replaced by "many writers beside."

63. Dall later canceled "save . . . vol."

64. Webster had died on October 24, 1852.

65. Dall later inserted here in pencil "well."

66. Cf. Proverbs 4:23.

67. *Elegy without Fiction: Sermon, Oct. 31, Suggested by the Deaths of Webster and Rantoul* (Worcester, 1852) by Thomas Wentworth Higginson, antislavery activist and minister at the Free Church in Worcester.

68. *A Discourse Occasioned by the Death of Daniel Webster: Preached at the Melodeon, October 31, 1852* (Boston: B.B. Mussey & Co., 1853).

69. Dall was doing this needlework for the church sewing circle.

70. Thomas Whitridge, Charles Dall's brother-in-law.

71. Elsewhere in her journal, Dall described what she was reading from Goethe as his "Letters from Italy."

She probably referred to a section of volume two of the two-volume *Auto-Biography of Goethe* (London, 1848–1849): "Letters from Switzerland and Travels in Italy."

72. Caroline Dall's mother-in-law, Henrietta Dall; and her sister-in-law, Maria Louisa Dall (later Atkinson) (1830–1874), known as "Louisa."

73. A Toronto resident, probably the daughter of William Hedge.

CHAPTER NINE

1. There was no volume of the antislavery annual the *Liberty Bell* published in this year or the next, and at Dall's direction, the article "The Plymouth Festival; or, 'Two Sides to Every Story' " was sent on to the *National Anti-Slavery Standard,* where it appeared in the issue of March 11, 1854, p. 168 (Samuel May Jr. to Dall, February 2, 1854, Dall Papers, MHS). In the article Dall gave an account of the Pilgrim Festival that she attended in Plymouth the preceding August, then bemoaned the fact that the country, in its accommodation to slavery, had not lived up to the ideals of the Pilgrims.

2. Lucy Maria Simpson Brown (1826–1908) of Ashfield, Massachusetts, and her husband, Champion Brown (1822–1892) of Whately, Massachusetts, were parishioners and good friends of the Dalls. Champion Brown was a Toronto merchant and an original and major subscriber to Charles Dall's support. See J. H. Temple, *History of Whately, Mass.* (Boston: T.R. Marvin & Son, 1872), 211–212; James M. Crafts, *History of the Town of Whately, Mass.* (Orange, Massachusetts: D.L. Crandall, 1899), 407–408; First Unitarian Congregation of Toronto archives; Ashfield VR; Dead Friends Notebook.

3. Daniel Wilson's influential *The Archaeology and Prehistoric Annals of Scotland* (Edinburgh: Sutherland and Knox, 1851).

4. Wilson's family, a wife and two daughters, remained in Edinburgh and joined him in May of the following year.

5. Ezekiel Francis Whittemore (1818–1859), prominent Toronto businessman and politician *(DCB)*.

6. Dall's later note at the beginning of this entry reads: "Money sent us, had all been contributed under the distinct understanding that there was to be no debt. The work must now be done all over again."

7. An inventory of Paul Kane's books at the Royal Ontario Museum lists the probable source of this entertainment: Camille Bonnard, *Costumi dei secoli XIII, XIV e XV, ricavati dai piu autentici monumenti di pittura e di scultura . . .* , 2 vols. (Milan: R. Fanfani, 1832–1835).

8. John Bentley was a Toronto druggist and stationer. John Henderson was probably a boot- and shoemaker, a subscriber of five pounds for Charles Dall's salary (*Toronto Directory* 1850–1851; First Unitarian Congregation of Toronto archives). James Manning was an insurance agent who had subscribed five pounds to Charles Dall's support (*Toronto Directory* 1850–1851; First Unitarian Congregation of Toronto archives). John O'Malley, dry goods dealer, was an original member of the Toronto church who had subscribed one pound to Charles Dall's salary (*Toronto Directory* 1856; First Unitarian Congregation of Toronto archives). Samuel Walton (b. 1825?) was an agricultural implement maker; his wife was Mary Walton (1831?–1900) (*Toronto Directory* 1856; 1871 Canadian census; Ms. Journals, October 8, 1900).

9. Dall later added the following note at the beginning of this entry: "This want of frank action was really the first sign of the failure of my husband's powers."

10. Probably this exchange included three letters that survive in the Toronto Unitarian Church archives. The first, from Charles Dall to Joseph Workman (December 17, 1853), proposes instituting a night school for boys, and says Dall "will go to the house of God with a lighter heart for having striven to be reconciled with my brother." A reply from Workman to Dall (December 20, 1853) says that the differ-

ences between them are in his view not personal ones. He refuses any further elaboration of his opinions, and encloses five pounds for the school. On December 22 Dall replies, saying he is "entirely disappointed in your letter," and refusing the five pounds.

11. Several recent illustrated editions of *Elegy Written in a Country Church-Yard,* by English poet Thomas Gray (1716–1771), had been published.

12. Probably the two-volume edition of *The History of the Christian Religion and Church, During the First Three Centuries,* by German church historian Johann August Wilhelm Neander (1789–1850), published in New York in 1853.

13. *The English Humorists of the Eighteenth Century,* by English novelist William Makepeace Thackeray (1811–1863), appeared in London in 1853.

14. Sir Robert Peel (1788–1850) was a British statesman and former prime minister.

15. Probably Mira (or Myra) Simpson Rowe (1810–1897) from Massachusetts, visiting her sister L. Maria Brown (*Ancestry.com,* accessed November 10, 2004).

16. Dall's sister Ellen Healey was traveling in Europe.

17. R. A. Goodenough was a Toronto produce merchant and secretary of the Corn Exchange and Millers' Association (*Toronto Directory* 1856).

18. Mary Agnes Fitzgibbon (1851–1915), Susanna Moodie's two-year-old granddaughter, was the oldest child of Charles Thomas Fitzgibbon (d. 1865), barrister, and Agnes Dunbar Moodie Fitzgibbon (1833–1913). Mary Fitzgibbon became an author among whose publications was one that played upon the title of her grandmother's famous book: *A Trip to Manitoba, or Roughing It on the Line* (Toronto: Rose-Belford Publishing Co., 1880). See Carl Ballstadt, Elizabeth Hopkins, and Michael Peterman, eds., *Susanna Moodie: Letters of a Lifetime* (Toronto: University of Toronto Press, 1985), 114, 172, 360.

19. On the preceding day, Charles Dall had written what Caroline described as "a kind note" to Joseph Workman, "asking an interview" (Ms. Journals, December 28, 1853, MHS).

20. Agnes Moodie Fitzgibbon.

21. Paul Kane's studio on King Street.

22. Philips Wouwerman (1619–1668), Dutch painter of horses, landscape, battle, and hunting scenes. See Walther Bernt, *The Netherlandish Painters of the Seventeenth Century* (London: Phaidon, 1970), 3:140–142.

23. Probably John Major, commission broker (*Toronto Directory* 1856).

24. Zebediah Sisson (b. 1794?), who ran a planing machine, an original member of the Toronto Unitarian Church and a subscriber to Charles Dall's support (1871 Canadian Census; *Toronto Directory* 1850–1851; First Unitarian Congregation of Toronto archives).

25. Probably "G. Briggs," subscriber in 1850 for Charles Dall's salary (First Unitarian Church of Toronto Archives).

26. George W. Hosmer had come from Buffalo to preach for Charles Dall. In the ensuing months, he played a role as arbitrator during the troubles in the Toronto church.

27. Dall later added an "X" here and the following note perpendicularly in the margin: "ˣNo, we could not—as it proved."

28. A medicine used to alleviate cough and pain, consisting of equal parts of opium, ipecac, licorice, saltpeter, and tartar vitroleus. It is named for its inventor, English physician and privateer Thomas Dover (1660–1742). See John Walton et al., eds., *The Oxford Medical Companion* (Oxford: Oxford University Press, 1994).

29. Dall later added this note at the end of the entry: "Here the Doctors gave Mr Dall up, he would not take brandy—but John and myself—followed up the treatment for three days and nights—of crumbs soaked in brandy & given every 10 minutes—"

30. Annie Simpson (d. 1854), daughter of Annie Elizabeth Adriance Simpson (b. 1827) and Francis Henry Simpson (1821–1893), physician and brother of L. Maria Brown.

31. Caroline Cocks Whitridge (1801–1894), wife of John Whitridge (1793–1879), who was the brother-in-law of Charles Dall's sister Henrietta Dall Whitridge (*Ancestry.com,* accessed October 17, 2004).

32. John Hall, a subscriber of five pounds for Charles Dall's support, and partner with his more prominent brother-in-law, John George Bowes (1812?–1864), several times mayor of Toronto, in the wholesale dry goods importing business (*Toronto Directory* 1850–1851; *DCB* 9:76).

33. This first half of this entry, up to the sentence that begins "To know this," was written later by Dall on an inserted sheet, to replace the excised original portion of this entry.

34. Paul Kane and Daniel Wilson became close friends, Wilson relying heavily on Kane's expertise about Plains and Pacific Coast Indians in his major work, *Prehistoric Man (DCB).*

35. George W. Hosmer, Unitarian minister at Buffalo.

36. Dorothea Dix, in Washington at this time, seems to have been in contact with Charles Dall's family in the Baltimore area. Here resumes the regular journal page. Dall added "To know . . . has been" in different ink at the top of the page.

37. William H. Channing.

38. Probably Dall's most recent letter from Charles was one dated April 10, written from his family home near Baltimore, in which he reported that he had "gained a little—but <u>very</u> little" since leaving Toronto. He continued, "If I <u>read</u> anything interesting my head soon begins to swim. If I <u>listen</u> to reading—tis all the same.—If I <u>talk</u>, at all freely, my head hums painfully. If I refuse to take any part in conversation yet over hear it, I have a similar experience—If I shut myself up in silence or take to my pillow . . . still I find 'thoughts chasing thoughts like hare & hounds'"(Dall Papers, Bryn Mawr).

39. Dall's letterbook records letters to Dix on April 13, 18, and 27 (Dall Papers, MHS).

40. Catherine Mary ("Katie") Moodie (1832–1904), oldest child of Susanna and John W. D. Moodie, became a favorite of Dall's. In 1855 she married John Joseph Vickers (1818–1896), a successful Toronto businessman, and they had ten children (*Susanna Moodie: Letters of a Lifetime,* 115, 360; DFN).

41. The Wilsons' new living quarters, which Dall had helped prepare, were in Yorkville, immediately north of Toronto proper, at Abbotsford Place on Bloor Street.

42. That is, from William Dall, Charles Dall, and Austin Dall.

43. Champion Brown had recently resigned as a church trustee.

44. Zebediah Sisson, his wife, Mary Graham Sisson (b. 1799?), and their niece Charlotte Lilias Sisson (1831–1912) (1871 Canada Census; *Ancestry.com,* accessed October 17, 2004).

45. Probably [*name unavailable*] Standen Sisley (d. 1854), the wife of John R. Sisley, proprietor of Transit Co. & Express and of a British and French warehouse. He was an original member of the Toronto church (*Toronto Directory* 1850–1851; *Toronto Globe,* November 13, 1851; First Unitarian Congregation of Toronto archives; Ms. Journals, March 2, 1854).

46. Donald Moodie (1836–1893), Susanna Moodie's son.

47. Bithia Hincks (1823?–1894) and Fannie Hincks (later Tower; b. 1831) were daughters of William Hincks (1794–1871) and his first wife, the late Maria Ann Yandel (*Ancestry.com,* accessed May 22, 2003; 1860 U.S. Census).

48. Joseph Bem (1794–1850), an exiled Polish general, had developed a series of charts to aid in the teaching of history. These charts consisted of grids in which each square represented a year. Color-coded symbols were placed in the squares to represent historically significant events. Elizabeth Peabody toured the Northeast to promote these charts; she also published a guide to the system, *The Polish-American System of Chronology* (Boston: G.P. Putnam, 1850) and later her own textbook, *Chronological History of the United States* (New York: Sheldon, Blakeman & Company, 1856), which included

colored charts based on Bem's work. See Bruce A. Ronda, ed., *Letters of Elizabeth Palmer Peabody, American Renaissance Woman* (Middletown, Connecticut: Wesleyan University Press, 1984), 274–275.

49. Egerton Ryerson (1803–1882) was the superintendent of education for Upper Canada. He was also a professor of divinity and later chancellor of Victoria College. See *Toronto Directory* 1850–51, 1856, and Jesse Edgar Middleton's *The Municipality of Toronto: A History* (Toronto: Dominion Publishing Company, 1923), 2:857.

50. Paul Kane's studio on King Street.

51. Raritan Bay, founded in 1853 and located at Eagleswood, New Jersey, was a Fourierist cooperative society that was an offshoot of the North American Phalanx. At the invitation of its founders, Marcus and Rebecca Spring, the abolitionist Theodore Dwight Weld established a school there. Peabody was his assistant and lived there with her father. The society ceased to exist about 1858. See Robert S. Fogerty, *Dictionary of American Communal and Utopian History*, reprint edition (Westport, Connecticut: Greenwood Press, 1980); Ronda, ed., *Letters of Elizabeth Palmer Peabody*, 276.

52. Perhaps John Crookshanks King (1806–1882), Boston sculptor, who did busts of Emerson, Webster, and John Quincy Adams. See Mantle Fielding, *Dictionary of American Painters, Sculptors, and Engravers* (New York: J.F. Carr, 1965).

53. Annie Elizabeth Adriance Simpson.

54. Sarah Patton (1794–1857), John Patton's mother, and her daughters Sarah Jane Patton (later Reynolds; 1834–1887) and Mary Patton. See the records of the Toronto Necropolis.

55. Dall later added in pencil "N.J."

56. Francis Simpson.

57. Ezra Stiles Gannett, minister at Boston's Federal Street Church.

58. That is, she left the boat from Toronto when it docked at Lewiston, New York, and boarded a coach for Niagara Falls, intending to go from there to Buffalo.

59. Elizabeth Hunter DeLaporte (1826–1916) and Antoine (or Anthony) Valentine DeLaporte (1819–1909), clerk, an original member of the Toronto church and subscriber to Charles Dall's support, later an elder, were parents of Rose Mary DeLaporte (later Hobson; 1852–1941). See *Toronto Directory* 1856; First Unitarian Church of Toronto Archives; Annual Report (January 1881) of First Unitarian Church, in Diary of Joseph Workman, University of Toronto Archives; Toronto Necropolis; *Ancestry.com*, accessed September 1, 2003.

60. Annie Simpson.

61. Dall inserted here in different ink "in his talk."

62. Dall later added in pencil: "At 8 yrs old"

63. Dall later in different ink canceled "he" and inserted "Mr Dall."

64. James Patton (1796–1872), born in Ireland, was in the china, glass, and earthenware importing business with his son (*Toronto Directory* 1856; Ontario VR).

65. The four volumes of *The Baronial and Ecclesiastical Antiquities of Scotland* by Robert William Billings (1813–1874) were published by W. Blackwood and Sons in 1845–1852.

66. Joseph Adams (b. 1825?), homeopathic physician (*Toronto Directory* 1856; 1871 Canadian Census).

67. James Patton, the father of John.

68. William Thomas Aikins (1827–1897), physician and medical educator, later this year became dean of the Toronto School of Medicine, and beginning in 1862 was its president. He contributed greatly to the professionalization of medicine in Ontario (*DCB*).

69. The letter was not published in the *Christian Register*.

70. Paul Kane.

71. Dall spent the night in Cobourg at "The Chestnuts," home of Harriet Kane's family, including her

parents, Eliza Clarke Cory Clench (1801–1888) and Freeman Schermerhorn Clench (1795–1877), a noted cabinetmaker. Her brothers included Thomas Barton Clench (1821–1877), Eliakim Cory Clench (1825–1891), William Carrell Clench (b. 1827), and Freeman Schermerhorn Clench (1829–1904) (Letter of Jessie J. Lowe in National Archives of Canada; copy in Cobourg Public Library).

72. Thomas Cheesman (1760–1835?), English engraver and draftsman, was a cousin of the Stricklands. Susanna stayed in his London home for several months in 1826 as a companion to his niece, Eliza. Three decades later she published a reminiscence of Cheesman: "My Cousin Tom: A Sketch from Life," *British American Magazine* (May 1863) (Carl Ballstadt, Elizabeth Hopkins, and Michael Peterman, eds., *Susanna Moodie: Letters of a Lifetime,* 6).

73. Apparently an in-law of Agnes Moodie Fitzgibbon.

74. Maria Margaret Breakenridge Murney (1817–1875), wife of the Hon. Edmund Fuller Murney (1811–1861); their two oldest daughters were Catharine Mary Murney (later Ridley; 1836–1900) and Isabelle Maria Murney (1839–1902) (*Ancestry.com,* accessed September 11, 2003; *DCB* 9).

75. This letter is not in the Dall papers.

76. The Stanwix House was the most popular hotel of the day in Albany, New York. See Cuyler Reynolds, *Albany Chronicles* (Albany, New York: J.B. Lyon Co., 1906), 504, 556.

77. Grace Greenwood was the pen name of Sarah Jane Clarke (1823–1904), whose poems and magazine pieces had made a reputation for her, and who later became a successful lecturer. In 1853 she married Leander K. Lippincott (b. 1831?) of Philadelphia. The marriage was not a happy one, and in 1876 Lippincott was involved in a scandal regarding fraudulent Indian land claims. He fled abroad and was not heard from again (*NAW;* 1850 U.S. Census).

78. Annie Simpson.

79. Sarah and Mary, John Patton's sisters.

80. Paul Kane.

81. John Murray (1822–1886), who temporarily supplied Charles Dall's pulpit, graduated from the Meadville Theological School in this year. He later held pastorates at Rockford, Illinois; Houlton, Maine; and Ilminster, England. See *General Catalogue of the Meadville Theological School 1844–1944* (Chicago, 1945).

82. Francis S. Primrose, M.D., who was certified to practice in 1834 by the Upper Canada Medical Board. See *Toronto Directory* 1850–1851 and William Canniff, *The Medical Profession in Upper Canada 1783–1850* (Toronto: W. Briggs, 1894), 78.

83. Annie Simpson.

84. Ida Brown (b. 1851), daughter of Champion and Maria Brown.

85. Eunice Tucker Simpson (1784–1870), Maria Brown's mother. See Frederick G. Howes, *History of the Town of Ashfield* (Ashfield, Massachusetts: Published by the town, 1910), 275; *Ancestry.com,* accessed May 1, 2003.

86. Annie Cora Brown was born on June 28, 1854. See James M. Crafts, *History of Whately, Mass.* (Orange, Massachusetts, 1899), 407–408.

87. The Sisley children's mother had died of cholera on July 25.

88. Dall later canceled "homeopathic" in pencil.

89. Probably Mrs. Brown's brother, Francis Simpson.

90. William Henry Hurlbert (formerly Hurlbut) (1827–1895) was the anonymous author of *Gan-Eden; or, Pictures of Cuba.* A graduate of Harvard (1847) and the Divinity School (1849), then a student in the Harvard Law School (1852), he spent several years in the Unitarian ministry before becoming a journalist and eventually editor-in-chief of the *New York World* (Harvard Archives). The other book that Dall was reading was probably John Ruskin's *Stones of Venice*; volumes 2 and 3 had appeared in 1853.

91. Penetanguishene was a town on an inlet of Lake Huron, thirty-two miles northwest of Barrie.

92. John Jacob Astor (1763–1848), wealthy American capitalist.

93. From Henry Wadsworth Longfellow's poem "Flowers." The word "aster" comes from the for "star."

94. Character in Dickens' *Bleak House,* the senile wife of Joshua Smallwood.

95. "Mrs" altered later to "Mr".

96. A bay formed where the Matchadash River discharges into Sturgeon Bay, which is itself a part of the larger Georgian Bay.

97. A river that runs north from the south end of Georgian Bay, a part of Lake Huron.

98. Cf. Genesis 3:8–9.

99. Probably Charles Thompson of Toronto, stage and steamboat owner (*Toronto Directory* 1850–1851).

100. John Woods Brooks (1819–1881), engineer and railroad executive from Massachusetts, was the super-intendent under Boston investor John Murray Forbes (who had the title of president) of the Michigan Central Railroad. It was Forbes who described Brooks in his role as chief of construction for the Sault Ste. Marie Canal as "a perfect Napoleon in his way … With 1500 men of the roughest sort in the wilderness, nobody to lean on, the cholera raging around him, and the work of two years to be driven through in six months" he reached the goal "by dint of *will*." The following year Brooks became president of the company and was also a central figure in other Forbes ventures in Illinois, Iowa, and elsewhere. See Thomas Childs Cochran, *Railroad Leaders 1845–1890* (Cambridge, Massachusetts: Harvard University Press, 1953), 37–38, 266–282.

101. An island in Lake Huron off the eastern tip of Michigan's Upper Peninsula.

102. Lime Island in the St. Mary's River was a source for limestone for forts on the eastern shore of Michigan's Upper Peninsula.

103. Thomas James Mumford (1826–1877) was the Unitarian minister in Detroit. He was later (1864–1872) minister in Dorchester, and then editor of the *Christian Register*. His wife was the former Sarah Yeates Shippen (1830–1855) (*Heralds* 3:263–265; *Ancestry.com,* accessed April 30, 2003).

104. A ceramic ware resembling unglazed porcelain.

105. The Patton family. Dall, her daughter, Sarah, and John Patton had been staying with his family for the past few days while making final preparations for the Dalls' move.

106. This sentence canceled later by Dall.

107. The children's nurse, whose services Dall had terminated in March 1853.

CHAPTER TEN

1. M. Louisa Hall (1826?–1884) was the daughter of broker Adin Hall (1795–1856) and Eunice Davis Hall. She was a long-time friend of the Healey family, and the families were later neighbors in Pemberton Square, Boston (1850 U.S. Census; Massachusetts VR). See David B. Hall, *The Halls of New England* (Albany: New York: J. Munsell's Sons, 1883), 308; DFN.

2. John Ayres (1807–1888) and Elizabeth P. Ayres (b. 1813?), West Newton neighbors. John Ayres, a clerk in Boston, was a close friend of Theodore Parker. See Massachusetts VR; 1850 U.S. Census; Walter M. Merrill and Louis Ruchames, eds., *Letters of William Lloyd Garrison,* 6 vols. (Cambridge, Massachusetts: Belknap Press, 1971–1981), 4:291.

3. Anna Lewis Thacher Savage (1797–1884) and her husband, Charles Tyler Savage (1797–1879), a former ship's captain and now a Boston broker, old friends of Dall's who lived in West Newton. Charles Savage was one of the founders of the Unitarian Society there and the first treasurer of the Newton Athenaeum. See Lawrence Park, *Major Thomas Savage of Boston and His Descendants* (Boston: D. Clapp & Son, 1914), 53–54.

4. Henry Ward Beecher (1813–1887), Congregational clergyman, was the best-known American preacher of the nineteenth century. Lyman Beecher (1775–1863), his father, was himself a renowned preacher and former president (1832–1850) of Lane Theological Seminary in Cincinnati.

5. Simon Crosby Hewitt (b. 1816), publisher of *The Una* and a spiritualist, conducted business at 15 Franklin Street, Boston *(Ancestry.com,* accessed October 24, 2004; 1860 U.S. Census; *Boston Directory* 1855). He was the author of *Messages from the Superior State* (Boston: B. Marsh, 1852), a work that purported to report the messages communicated by a deceased reforming clergyman, John Murray, through a medium, John M. Spear. His letter of January 10, 1855 (erroneously dated 1854), asking permission to include Dall's name as one of the editors, is in the Dall Papers, MHS.

6. Bela Marsh (1797–1869) was a publisher and bookseller, also located at 15 Franklin Street (*Boston Directory* 1855). He and Hewitt may have been partners; he was the publisher of Hewitt's book cited above.

7. "about John" canceled later in pencil by Dall.

8. Charles Lowell, Dall's beloved minister at the West Church for more than twenty years, had just published two volumes: *Sermons: Chiefly Occasional,* and *Sermons: Chiefly Practical* (Boston: Ticknor and Fields, 1855). Dall's review was published in the *Monthly Religious Magazine* 15 (January 1856): 43–49, then reprinted in *Historical Pictures Retouched,* and still later as *Reverend Charles Lowell, D.D., Pastor from January 1, 1806, to January 20, 1861, of the West Church, Boston, Massachusetts* (Boston: T. Todd, 1907). She took the occasion "to pay the tribute demanded by love and honor to his pastoral care, rather than the cold duty of a critic to [the] literary merits" of the sermons (*Historical Pictures Retouched,* 389).

9. Dall's Toronto friends Professor Daniel and Margaret Wilson.

10. This editorial appeared in the next issue of *The Una,* volume 3 (February 1855), on pages 25–57. Dall acknowledged taking a role in the editorship, but said that she would primarily still be "ransacking the records of the past, and supplying biographical matter to these pages."

11. Dall has apparently confused the date. According to the *Transcript* (February 27, 1855, p. 3), the ship was cleared on February 27.

12. Elizabeth Howard Bartol (1842–1907), the thirteen-year-old daughter of Cyrus and Elizabeth H. Bartol. She later became an artist, a notable pupil of William Morris Hunt at the Boston School of Design; see Peter Hastings Falk et al., eds., *Who Was Who in American Art* (Madison, Connecticut: Sound View Press, 1999). *The Rose and the Ring, or the History of Prince Giglio and Prince Bulbo: A Fireside Pantomime for Great and Small Children,* written and illustrated by the English novelist William Makepeace Thackeray, had appeared in December 1854.

13. William H. Channing's semiautobiographical fragment that appeared in two installments in the first two numbers of the *Dial* 1 (July, Oct. 1840):48–58, 233–242.

14. Caroline L. Floyd Champney (1821–1865), the wife of Edward Walter Champney (1810–1886), Woburn dry goods merchant and brother of the artist Benjamin Champney (1817–1907). She was born in Brooklyn, New York, where her father, John Floyd, superintended the building of government ships. At the age of seventeen, after the death of both of her parents in Maine, she moved to Boston to support herself. There in 1845 she married, and four years later the Champneys moved to Woburn, where they lived at this time. See 1860 U.S. Census; Julius B. Champney, *History of the Champney Family* (Chicago: P.L. Hanscom & Co., 1867), 53–54; *Ancestry.com* (accessed August 21, 2004); *In Memoriam: Mrs. Caroline L. Champney* (n.p., 1865?), 5–6, 24–26.

15. Caroline Dresser (b. 1826), teacher, daughter of John and Eleanor Brown Macomber Dresser of Castine, Maine *(Ancestry.com,* accessed November 6, 2004; 1860 U.S. Census).

16. Two years later the Champneys adopted her orphaned niece and nephew (*In Memoriam: Mrs. Caroline L. Champney,* 18, 28).

17. John Campbell Cluer (1800–1886), a Scottish emigrant who was a temperance advocate, abolitionist, and street preacher. He had been arrested but not convicted for attempting the rescue of fugitive slave Anthony Burns. About 1869 he became a special officer in the prison in Boston and then held a position now known as probation officer (*Transcript,* September 10, 1886, pp. 4–5; *Liberator,* February 7, 1851, p. 24; Merrill and Ruchames, eds., *Letters of William Lloyd Garrison* 3:315–316).

18. Louisa Hall.

19. Caroline C. Toppan, at 20 Bulfinch Street (*Boston Directory* 1855).

20. George Sennott (d. 1879), a Vermont native, was a former teacher, classical scholar, and at this time a Boston lawyer. In 1859 he was sent by the abolitionists to Virginia to help defend John Brown and the other Harper's Ferry raiders. Frank Sanborn described him as "an educated man, a lawyer, and rather celebrated for his defence of criminals. He was a low type, and much given to liquor." On this occasion, according to the account in the *Liberator* (September 28, 1855, p. 156), Sennott observed that the established doctrine of legal nonentity of women occasionally resulted in the husband's being punished for the crimes of the wife. He also urged "individual effort" among women to enter the legal profession. Dall in response urged individual effort among members of the legal profession in accepting women into their profession. See the *Daily Advertiser,* July 10, 1879, p. 1, and Edward J. Renehan Jr., *The Secret Six* (New York: Crown Publishers, 1995), 210.

21. Sarah Moore Grimké (1792–1873), Sallie Holley (1818–1893), and Caroline Putnam (c. 1825–1917). Sarah Grimké left her native South Carolina for Philadelphia in 1821, partly in protest against the system of slavery. Her sister Angelina (1805–1879) joined her in 1829, and in the mid-1830s they became active in antislavery work and moved to New York. In response to criticism of their public speaking, the sisters became pioneer defenders of the rights of women to vote and to make laws. Sarah published in 1838 the pamphlet *Letters on the Equality of the Sexes, and the Condition of Woman.* In that same year, they gave a lecture series in Boston, and Angelina married Theodore Weld, himself an abolitionist. At this time the three of them were associated with the Raritan Bay Union, a socialist community in New Jersey (*NAW*). Sallie Holley, abolitionist lecturer and future educator of freed Southern slaves, was born in Canandaigua, New York, the daughter of Erie Canal promoter and abolitionist Myron Holley and Sally House Holley. After graduating from Oberlin College, she became an agent for the American Anti-Slavery Society. After 1870 she worked in the Holley School for freedmen in Virginia. See *NAW*; John White Chadwick, *A Life for Liberty: The Anti-Slavery and Other Letters of Sallie Holley* (New York: G.P. Putnam's Sons, 1899), 18–20; Eugene Chapin, *By-Gone Days* (Boston, 1898), 25–26. Caroline F. Putnam (1826–1917), a native of western New York, was the longtime companion and coworker of Sallie Holley from their college days at Oberlin (*NAW*; Merrill and Ruchames, eds., *Letters of William Lloyd Garrison* 5:123).

22. On September 24, Sallie Holley wrote to a friend: "Of all the women who spoke, Mrs. Dall most thrilled and interested me. Everything she said indicated culture and genius; with noble thought and solemn consecration. She reminded me of Margaret Fuller" (John White Chadwick, *A Life for Liberty,* 149).

23. Wendell Phillips.

24. A later note in the left margin of this entry reads, "I do not think any of my lectures, unless the Fraternity ever equalled the success of this day. Debate suits me in public. Sept 1861."

25. William Lloyd Garrison, Theodore Parker, David A. Wasson, Charles Hodges, and Samuel Johnson; all except Garrison were clergymen. David Wasson (1824–1887), dismissed from his ministry to an Orthodox church in Groveland because of his liberal views, had founded an independent society. He later took over the pulpit at Theodore Parker's Twenty-Eighth Congregational Society for a year, and eventually turned to literary work (*Heralds* 3:373–376). Charles E. Hodges (1824–1870) had finished at the Divinity School in 1850. For one year (October 1854–October 1855), he conducted services for the small Unitarian congregation in Newton in the afternoons and preached at Watertown in the morn-

ings. See Biographical Folders, Harvard University Archives, and Lawrence Shaw Mayo, *The First Unitarian Society in Newton 1848–1923* (n.p., 1923), 33.

26. Antoinette Brown (later Blackwell; 1825–1921) is believed to be "the first ordained woman minister of a recognized denomination" in the country. She graduated from Oberlin College in 1847 and then met resistance in her determination to take a theological degree there. She was allowed to attend classes but was not allowed to graduate when she completed the course in 1850. For two years she lectured on women's rights, antislavery, and temperance issues, and preached occasionally in the pulpits of liberal ministers, including Theodore Parker and T. W. Higginson. In 1853 she was ordained at a Congregational church, but in 1854 became a Unitarian. She was involved in a number of reform movements and in 1856 married Samuel, a member of the reform-minded Blackwell family *(NAW)*.

27. Susan B. Anthony (1820–1906), the great women's rights advocate, was from 1856 to 1861 the principal New York agent for the American Anti-Slavery Society. Born in rural Massachusetts and raised in rural New York, she had taught in local schools and a female academy and had managed the family farm. In 1850 she met Elizabeth Cady Stanton and formed with her a lifelong alliance to fight for women's rights. She was the force behind a number of women's rights conventions in New York before the war. During the Civil War she and Stanton organized the Women's Loyal National League, a political action group that urged Negro emancipation. She supported Frémont and opposed Lincoln's reelection in 1864, and after the war fought against the Fourteenth and Fifteenth Amendments because they excluded women from the franchise. For a time she and Stanton were associated with George Francis Train, a wealthy Democrat and apparent racist who financed their weekly paper *Revolution*. In 1869 she and Stanton formed the National Woman Suffrage Association. For most of the remainder of her life, she traveled throughout the country, speaking and writing on behalf of woman suffrage *(NAW)*.

28. "Mrs. Fagan of Philadelphia" appealed to women to enter the medical profession (*Liberator,* September 28, 1855, p. 156). This was probably Fanny D. Fagan (d. 1878), who published children's poems and Sunday school hymns for the Unitarian Church in Philadelphia in the 1860s.

29. John Patton and Eliza Beatty.

30. Caroline Toppan.

31. The revised resolution read: "Resolved, that under a republican government, we consider the ballot woman's sword and shield; the means of achieving and protecting all other civil rights; her college, to open to her all the advantages of high culture; her indisputable right; and its attainment the basis of all other rights; and we urge it upon the National Convention, soon to assemble in Cincinnati, to devote their chief attention to this object" (*Liberator,* September. 28, 1855, p. 156).

32. Charles F. Hovey, Boston merchant and reformer.

33. Elizabeth Oakes Smith (1806–1893), author, lecturer, reformer, was married to writer Seba Smith. Her unconventional dress at the second National Woman's Rights Convention in Worcester had caused Susan B. Anthony to deny her the presidency of the convention. A contributor to *The Una,* she was one of the first women to lecture on the lyceum circuit. In 1854 she published a women's rights novel, *Bertha and Lily (NAW)*.

34. Wendell Phillips.

35. Emilie Kossuth (1817?–1860), formerly Madame Zulawski, the exiled sister of Hungarian patriot Lajos Kossuth. She was divorced from her husband, who took her children and earnings. See Franklin Benjamin Hough, *American Biographical Notes* (Albany, New York: J. Munsell, 1875), and letter of Mary Mann to Dr. Nathaniel Peabody, February 19, 1854, Olive Kettering Library, Antioch College.

36. Paulina Wright Davis.

37. Louisa Hall's letter expressed her appreciation of the work of the convention in showing woman her

potential "usefulness and happiness, would she but have faith and courage." Of Dall herself she wrote, "There seemed a peculiar propriety that in a Convention held in Boston, you, born and educated here, should take so active a part, and I do hope that if, when the next W.R. Convention is to be held in Boston, the President's chair should be offered you, you will accept a position which seems yours by right as a Bostonian. For all the true, brave, tender, Christian words you uttered from that platform, I who perhaps better than any other, of your auditors know at what personal sacrifice and anguish they were uttered, thank you from my heart—They will not, they cannot have failed of reception in many an earnest mind, and they will bring forth fruit in due season. To me, they have been words of cheer and strength" (letter of September 23, 1855, Dall Papers, MHS).

38. Letter of October 7, 1855, Emerson Papers, 280 (734), Houghton Library, Harvard University.

39. Florence Nightingale (1820–1910), English reformer who professionalized nursing. She was currently supervising nursing services to the British army in the Crimea *(DNB)*. In fact, at the recent Woman's Rights Convention, Dall had remarked that Nightingale would have been better qualified for her nursing work in the Crimean War if she had had "the medical education women are deprived of by the laws of institutions, and the tyranny of public opinion." *Liberator* 25 (September 28, 1855), 156.

40. Ellen Maria Tarr (1830–1913), daughter of Benjamin Tarr and Maria Dyer Tarr of Androscoggin, Maine. A former member of the Boston Union of Associationists, she and her sister Mary Jane Tarr were Newton neighbors of the Dalls. In 1856 Ellen married William Douglas O'Connor (1832–1889) and during their long residence in Washington became a famous hostess. O'Connor at this time was a journalist at the Pennsylvania *Saturday Evening Post,* a position which would be terminated in 1859 because of his sympathetic treatment of John Brown. Thereafter he became a civil servant in Washington, D.C., and the friend and defender (*The Good Gray Poet,* 1866) of Walt Whitman. Following O'Connor's death, Ellen married in 1892 Albert L. Calder of Providence (*ANB;* Rhode Island VR; *Ancestry.com,* accessed April 4, 2003). See also Sterling Delano, "A Calendar of the 'Boston Religious Union of Associationists,' 1847–1850," in *SAR 1985,* 258.

41. The West Newton English and Classical School, whose proprietor was Nathaniel T. Allen (1823–1903). Allen, formerly the principal of the "Model School" for the state Normal School for Young Ladies in West Newton, in 1854 established this new private school for boys and girls, which achieved a national reputation (*NatCAB* 20: 212–213). See also Frank Allen Hutchinson, *Genealogical and Historical Sketches of the Allen Family of Dedham and Medfield, Mass.: 1637–1890* (Lowell, Massachusetts: privately printed, 1896), 55, and Henry K. Rowe, *Tercentenary History of Newton 1630–1930* (Newton, 1930), 140–141.

42. Probably a part of Dall's presentation at the women's convention on September 19 and 20 on the legal status of women in the New England states. These reports were being printed.

43. Elizabeth P. Ayres.

44. Lucy Stone and Antoinette Brown.

45. Caroline Coddington Thayer (1805–1891), philanthropic Bostonian, was the daughter of Nathaniel and Susan Soper Thayer. A semi-invalid, she was a close friend of Theodore Parker and a supporter of the antislavery and women's rights causes (Massachusetts VR; Merrill and Ruchames, eds., *Letters of William Lloyd Garrison* 4:96–97).

46. Paulina Wright Davis's letter of October 1 proposed making *The Una* a weekly, run by "an association of editors." She asked if Dall would consider being the "resident editor" for a salary of $600 annually. This plan would be financed by a "wealthy friend," probably Davis's husband Thomas Davis (1806–1895) (Dall Papers, MHS).

47. Bela Marsh, publisher and bookseller at 15 Franklin Street.

48. Probably Dall refers to a letter from Davis dated October 28, in which she objected to *The Una*'s be-

ing "entirely diverted from its original purpose," stated that "as you are well aware I did not know that you were going to be the Editor," and withdrew her name from all connection with the paper (Dall Papers, MHS).

49. Elizabeth Peabody, having taken a great interest in Emilie Kossuth, the exiled sister of Hungarian patriot Lajos Kossuth, wrote and published a pamphlet eulogizing another sister, Susanne (1820–1854). *Memorial of Mad. Susanne Kossuth Meszlenyi* (Boston, 1856) was intended to stimulate interest in the cause of Emilie Kossuth. See Bruce A. Ronda, ed., *Letters of Elizabeth Palmer Peabody, American Renaissance Woman* (Middletown, Connecticut: Wesleyan University Press, 1984), 280.

50. Eliza Thayer Clapp (1811–1888), adopted daughter of Eliza and Isaac Clapp of Dorchester, was the author of *Words in a Sunday School* (Boston, 1842) and *Studies in Religion* (New York: C. Shepard, 1845). According to her obituary, she was "a lady of superior abilities and attainments. Her knowledge of English and of German Literature was extensive and discriminating." See Ebenezer Clapp, *Clapp Memorial: Record of the Clapp Family in America* (Boston: D. Clapp, 1876), 264; *Transcript*, February 29, 1888, p. 1.

51. The first edition of the revolutionary *Leaves of Grass* by New York poet Walt Whitman (1819–1892) was just out.

52. Paraphrase of *In Memoriam*, Conclusion, lines 122–124, by English poet Alfred, Lord Tennyson (1809–1892): "And, star and system rolling past, / A soul shall draw from out the vast / And strike his being into bounds."

53. Sarah Turner Brooks (1800?–1862), widow of Alexander Scammell Brooks (*NEHGR* 19:193; 1860 U.S. Census; Ms. Journals, June 23, 1862, Dall Papers, MHS).

54. Mary E. Webb (c. 1829–1859) was the daughter of a Virginia slave mother and a Spanish gentleman; her mother ran away to New Bedford, Massachusetts, before Mary's birth, and the two of them later settled in Philadelphia, where Mary met and married Frank J. Webb. She was giving dramatic readings throughout the Northeast and Midwest in 1855–1856. In 1856 she and her husband would travel to England (their journey was marred by being denied passage on a Cunard steamer), where she performed to acclaim at Stafford House, the residence of the Duchess of Sutherland, met the Duchess of Argyll, Lady Hatherton, and Lady Byron, and appeared before Parliament. She and her husband settled in Jamaica in 1858 in an attempt to cure her tuberculosis, but she died there the following year (letter of Roy E. Finkenbine to Helen R. Deese, March 22, 1996; *Liberator*, August 15, 1856, p. 131). Mary Webb was performing in the "Lectures on Slavery" series at the Tremont Temple. Harriet Beecher Stowe herself had adapted *Uncle Tom's Cabin* for the readings (*Transcript*, December 5, 1855, p. 2).

55. Evangeline St. Clair, "Little Eva" of *Uncle Tom's Cabin*.

56. Lydia Maria Child, Eliza Follen, Louisa Gilman Loring, Mary B. Dwight, William F. and Susan Channing, and Mary Jane ("Jeannie") Tarr. Lydia Maria Child (1802–1880), was an abolitionist, author of popular novels, and former editor of a children's magazine. From 1841 to 1849, she edited the *National Anti-Slavery Standard* in New York; in 1852 she and her husband retired to a small farm in Weymouth, Massachusetts *(DAB)*. Eliza Lee Cabot Follen (1787–1860) was the widow of German émigré, Harvard foreign language professor, antislavery activist, and minister Charles T. C. Follen (1796–1840). She was herself an editor and writer, chiefly of children's books and magazines and antislavery tracts. Louisa Gilman Loring (1797–1868) was the daughter of Frederick and Abigail Gilman of Gloucester and the wife of Boston lawyer and ardent abolitionist Ellis Gray Loring; see Charles Henry Pope, *Loring Genealogy* (Cambridge, Massachusetts: Murray and Emery, 1917), 255–256. Mary Bullard Dwight (d. 1860) was the wife of John Sullivan Dwight (1813–1893), former Unitarian minister, music and literary critic, editor of the *Harbinger,* associate of the Transcendentalists, and formerly a Brook Farmer; see Benjamin W. Dwight, *The History of the Descendants of John Dwight, of Dedham, Mass.* (New York: J.F. Trow & Son, 1874), 2:1013; *DAB*. Mary Jane ("Jeannie" or "Jennie") Tarr (1828–1897), Ellen Tarr's

sister, like Ellen, had graduated from the State Normal School at West Newton in 1850. In 1859 Jeannie Tarr married William F. Channing, who had divorced his wife Susan; see *Ancestry.com* (accessed April 4, 2003) and *Catalogue of Graduates of the State Normal School at Framingham, Mass.* (Boston, 1889).

57. Bridget Naven (b. 1810?), longtime domestic servant of William and Sarah Dall (1850 U.S. Census).

58. Passage beginning with illegible words through "either" heavily canceled later.

59. Susan Willey (b. 1814). She and her sister Clarissa (b. 1819), unmarried daughters of the late Isaac and Susan Ryan Willey, were neighbors of the Dalls. See Henry Willey, *Isaac Willey, of New London, Conn., and His Descendants* (New Bedford, Massachusetts: E. Anthony & Sons, 1888), 71–72.

60. Christiana Duncan Dudley (1822?–1874), wife of Boston attorney Elbridge G. Dudley. The Dudleys were active in antislavery activities and were friends of Theodore Parker, to whose conversation Christiana Dudley took Dall. See Dean Dudley, *History of the Dudley Family* (Montrose, Massachusetts, 1894), 1:445, 480–482; 1850 U.S. Census.

61. Harriet Stevens was an old friend from Portsmouth.

62. William F. Channing.

63. Susan Willey.

64. Charles F. Hovey.

65. Mary Caroline Hinckley, from Hallowell, Maine. She later became a radical women's rights and free love advocate, living with the eccentric spiritualist and reformer John Murray Spear at Kiantone, a utopian nudist community in New York State. After she bore his child, he divorced his wife and married her in 1863. She graduated from Pennsylvania Medical University (an "alternative" medical school in Philadelphia) and then served on its faculty. In 1870 she and Spear moved to California, where she helped to organize the first women's suffrage organization in the state. See Bruce A. Ronda, *Elizabeth Palmer Peabody* (Cambridge, Massachusetts: Harvard University Press, 1999), 238–239; John Patrick Deveney, *Paschal Beverly Randolph* (Albany: State University of New York Press, 1997), 18–19, 21; and Ann Braude, *Radical Spirits: Spiritualism and Women's Rights in Nineteenth-Century America,* 2nd ed. (Bloomington: Indiana University Press, 2001), 150.

66. Emmanuel Vitalis Scherb, a German-speaking Swiss emigrant, supported himself by lecturing, teaching, and preaching. See Andrew Hilen, ed., *The Letters of Henry Wadsworth Longfellow* (Cambridge, Massachusetts: Harvard University Press, 1966–1982), 3:331.

67. Wendell Phillips and Stephen Foster.

68. Ephraim Nute (1819–1897), 1845 graduate of the Harvard Divinity School, had been sent in 1855 by the American Unitarian Association as a missionary to Lawrence, Kansas, where he was one of the leaders of the Free State settlers (*Heralds* 3:275–276).

69. John Cordner (1816–1894), Irish-born minister, became in 1843 the first minister of the Unitarian Society of Montreal, which was the first Unitarian congregation in the Canadas. His was a significant voice in the city on matters of reform, religion, and politics for the more than thirty-five years that he pastored the congregation. In 1879 he retired to Boston, the home of his wife, Caroline Parkman Cordner *(DCB)*.

70. Theodore Parker.

71. Lewis Glover Pray (1793–1882) was Sunday school superintendent at the Twelfth Congregational Society in Boston and would later (1863) publish a history of that church. His *Boston Sunday School Hymn Book,* first published in 1833, had gone through numerous editions.

72. Reinhold Solger (1817–1866), Prussian-born scholar and revolutionary, had settled in Roxbury in 1853 and supported himself by writing and by public lecturing on history and modern German philosophy. In 1857 and 1859 he delivered twelve lectures at the Lowell Institute in Boston *(DAB)*.

73. Samuel G. Goodrich (1793–1860), author and publisher, published a number of Hawthorne's tales as

editor of the giftbook *The Token,* in the 1830s. Goodrich created the extremely successful "Peter Parley" series of children's books; Hawthorne is believed to be the author of at least one of these *(DAB).*

74. The Harris family were friends from the Dalls' years in Needham. William (b. 1826?) was a civil engineer; his mother was Eliza (1860 U. S. Census).

75. Moses Winch (b. 1801?), Needham farmer (1850 U. S. Census).

76. Apparently the midwife who attended the birth of Sadie, identified then as "Mrs. Gardiner" (see entry for October 16, 1849).

77. Stephen Pearl Andrews (1812–1886), reformer and eccentric philosopher. Among his proposals were the purchase of slaves by a loan from Great Britain, spelling reform, an international language (which he invented), and a radical, semianarchistic social and political system *(DAB).*

78. The actress Fanny Kemble (Butler) (1809–1893).

79. Oliver H. Wellington, M.D., ran the New York City Water-Cure. See Harry B. Weiss and Howard R. Kemble, *The Great American Water-Cure Craze* (Trenton, New Jersey: Past Times Press, 1967), 69, 142.

80. Julia Ward Howe, A. Bronson Alcott, Emmanuel V. Scherb, Ralph Waldo Emerson, probably John W. Browne, E. P. Whipple, Samuel Sewall, Thomas R. Gould, Ednah D. Cheney, and William F. Channing. Julia Ward Howe (1819–1910), poet, biographer, and reformer, was married to Dr. Samuel Gridley Howe, who opposed his wife's entering public life. She nevertheless persisted with her writing, gaining renown for the "Battle Hymn of the Republic" in 1862, then later helping to found the New England Women's Club, founding and editing the *Woman's Journal* in 1870, taking an active role in the suffrage movement, and preaching and lecturing *(NAW).* John W. Browne (1810–1860), Boston lawyer and abolitionist, college friend of Charles Sumner, played a variety of prominent roles in the antislavery movement before his accidental death in a fall from a train in 1860; see Irving H. Bartlett, "Abolitionists, Fugitives, and Imposters in Boston, 1846–1847," *NEQ* 55 (March 1982): 97–110, and Merrill and Ruchames, eds., *Letters of William Lloyd Garrison* 3:547. Samuel E. Sewall (1799–1888), lawyer and reformer, was one of the founders of the New England Anti-Slavery Society in 1831. He was elected in 1851 to the state Senate as a Free-Soiler and drafted the bill giving married women the right to hold property, which later became law. He became a long-term friend of Dall *(NatCAB* 10:466–467). Thomas R. Gould (1818–1881) was a sculptor; Dall had known him since her Sunday school work with the West Church as a young woman.

81. Low characters in, respectively, *Henry IV,* Parts 1 and 2; *The Tempest;* and *A Midsummer Night's Dream.*

82. David A. Wasson.

83. Entire entry, following the date and up to this point, canceled later.

CHAPTER ELEVEN

1. Dall's servant.

2. Hugh Johnson Anderson (1801–1881) was governor of Maine, 1844–1847, and had since held bureaucratic appointments from Presidents Pierce and Buchanan. See Robert Sobel and John Raimo, eds., *Biographical Directory of the Governors of the United States, 1789–1978* (Westport, Connecticut: Meckler Books, 1978).

3. Catharine M. Anderson (b. 1846?), daughter of Moses and Lucy A. Anderson (1850, 1860 U.S. Census).

4. Joseph W. Strange (b. 1811?), machinist (1860 U.S. Census).

5. Franklin Muzzy (1806–1873), prominent Bangor businessman, had risen from artisan to successful businessman, operating an iron foundry and machine shop in the city. He had served in the state legislature and state senate, and was president of the latter in 1855. His wife was Caroline North McComber (b. 1810) (*Ancestry.com,* accessed June 3, 2002). See Caroline Toner, "Franklin Muzzy: Artisan Entrepreneur in Nineteenth-Century Bangor," *Maine Historical Quarterly* 30 (1990):70–91.

6. The Muzzys' daughter, Elizabeth Little Muzzy (b. 1839?), married in 1859 William Drew Washburn, who became a prominent Minneapolis businessman and politician, serving as U.S. congressman and senator. See *NEHGR* 13:273; 1850 U.S. Census; and *Biographical Directory of the American Congress, 1774–1949* (Washington, D.C.: U.S. Government Printing Office, 1950).

7. Norombega Hall, designed by William G. Morse, was built in 1854–1855 and destroyed by fire in 1911. The second-story hall where Dall spoke was 117 by 56 feet, with a 39-foot ceiling. It seated 1,500 on the floor and another 500 in the galleries and on the raised platform. See Deborah Thompson, *Bangor, Maine, 1769–1914: An Architectural History* (Orono: University of Maine Press, 1988), 359–360.

8. John Edwards Godfrey (1809–1884), lawyer, probate judge, and prominent citizen of Bangor. For a time he edited the antislavery and temperance newspaper, the *Bangor Gazette.* His wife, mentioned below, was Elizabeth Angela Stackpole Godfrey (d. 1868). See John Edwards Godfrey, *The Journals of John Edwards Godfrey* (Rockland, Maine: Courier-Gazette, 1979), 9–13.

9. George Healey, her brother.

10. John Childe (1802–1858) of Springfield (brother to David Lee Child, husband of Lydia Maria Child), a West Point graduate and a financially successful civil engineer, had as a widower married Dall's sister Ellen in 1856. Now he was mortally ill.

11. Dall's friend Anne Catharine Payson (1817–1895), originally of Peterborough, New Hampshire, daughter of Thomas and Sarah Hennessey Payson. See Albert Smith, *History of the Town of Peterborough* (Boston: G.H. Ellis, 1876), 221–223, and DFN.

12. Eliza Jones Hersey Andrew (1826–1898), wife of John A. Andrew, future governor of Massachusetts (Massachusetts VR).

13. E. P. and Charlotte Whipple.

14. Clarke, pastor of the Church of the Disciples, of which Dall was a member, was one of several friends whom Dall had asked to read her lectures.

15. William de Rohan (1819–1891), American soldier of fortune, was born "Dahlgren" but took his mother's name after a quarrel with his brother John, admiral of the U.S. Navy. He fought in Turkey, the Argentine Republic (where he commanded the naval forces), Chile (as admiral of the navy), and Italy (as Garibaldi's chief of staff); he was a naval commander in England (*NatCAB* 5:24).

16. John Milton Earle (1794–1874) was a Worcester journalist and legislator. An early supporter of the antislavery cause, from 1823 to 1858 he managed and edited the Worcester *Spy.* Earle served in both houses of the Massachusetts legislature in the 1840s and 1850s; at this time, he was a member of the upper house. See Pliny Earle, *The Earle Family* (Worcester, Massachusetts: C. Hamilton, 1888), 205–209.

17. Stephen A. Chase (1796–1876) was a longtime member of the state house of representatives. See *NEHGR* 88:28; *Poole's Annual Register of the Executive and Legislative Departments of the Government of Massachusetts,* 1858 (Boston: Dutton and Wentworth, 1858); and *Boston Daily Advertiser,* July 28, 1876.

18. John Wells Foster (1815–1873), a native of Petersham, had graduated from Wesleyan University in 1832, then studied and practiced law in Ohio. He had since turned his energies to geology and politics, having participated in a geological survey of the Lake Superior region. In 1852 he returned to Massachusetts and became an organizer of the Native American party; in 1855, he withdrew and helped found the Republican party in that state, but was defeated in a race for Congress. He served only one term in

the Massachusetts legislature, for he soon moved to Chicago, working first for the Illinois Central Railroad, and then devoting himself to his scientific studies and becoming president of the American Association for the Advancement of Science (*NatCAB* 10:169).

19. Dall has later, in pencil, canceled "Miles Standish" and substituted "Reginald Foster."

20. James M. Usher (1814–1892), of Medford, served in both houses of the state legislature; at this time, he was in the senate. He was also a Universalist minister, Boston bookstore owner, and publisher of *The Nation,* a weekly temperance newspaper. See Edward Preston Usher, *A Memorial Sketch of Roland Greene Usher* (Boston: Nathan Sawyer & Son, 1895), 116–119.

21. The *Transcript* reported the appearance of Dall and Higginson before the legislative committee, noting that Dall "based her argument for female voting on the humanity of the sex, and because we should never have a humane government till the feminine element was recognized, in all its completeness." Higginson "regarded women as better qualified to vote than the hordes of foreigners" who could vote and argued against taxation without representation. The *Transcript* commented, "It partakes decidedly of the ludicrous to see a grave legislative committee nominally debating upon a subject like this of female rights, which they approach with preconceived opinions that they would not relinquish under any amount of persuasive eloquence" (February 12, 1858, p. 2).

22. Dall's later penciled note inserted at this point reads: "It was on this occasion that T.W.H. stole from me, the title of his tract, 'Why should we teach women the alphabet.'" Dall refers to Higginson's article "Ought Women to Learn the Alphabet" in the *Atlantic Monthly* 3 (February 1859): 137–150.

23. Harriet Winslow Sewall (1819–1889) and her husband, abolitionist attorney Samuel E. Sewall. See Nina Moore Tiffany, *Samuel E. Sewall: A Memoir* (Boston: Houghton, Mifflin and Company, 1898), 31, 90, 119; and Walter M. Merrill and Louis Ruchames, eds., *Letters of William Lloyd Garrison,* 6 vols. (Cambridge, Massachusetts: Belknap Press, 1971–1981), 5:272.

24. Samuel Gridley Howe (1801–1876), educator of the handicapped and social reformer, was director of the Perkins Institution for the Blind in Boston; he was married to Julia Ward Howe *(ANB)*.

25. Mary Patten (1837–1861) must have seemed to Dall the embodiment of Fuller's injunction in *Woman in the Nineteenth Century,* "Let them [women] be sea-captains if they will!" Patten had recently achieved fame when, at age nineteen, she took command of the ship of which her husband, incapacitated by illness, was the captain. Dall later wrote of the dramatic incident when Patten, "with two little children clinging to her skirts," a husband "bereft of reason," and a "mutinous mate," successfully sailed the clipper *Neptune's Car* around Cape Horn and eventually into port. See David Cordingly, *Women Sailors and Sailors' Women* (New York: Random House, 2001), 109–115, and Dall, *The College, the Market, and the Court* (Boston: Lee and Shepard, 1867), 47, 123.

26. George H. Kuhn (1795–1879), Boston businessman and West Church member, father of Dall's late friend Austin Kuhn, and a lifelong friend of hers (*NEHGR* 51 [1897]:444–446); James T. Fisher; Edwin P. Whipple; probably Mary Frank Littlehale; and William F. Channing.

27. Joseph Hale Abbot (1802–1873), educator. After graduating from Bowdoin in 1822 and serving briefly there as tutor in modern languages and librarian, he taught for several years at Philips Academy, Exeter, New Hampshire, then for many years conducted a private school for girls in Boston (as he would later do in Beverly). Caroline Healey attended his school in the 1830s (*NEHGR* 77:lxxxv).

28. The editor has in her possession what is probably a duplicate of this pitcher. Made in 1847 by the English manufacturer Samuel Alcock, it is a piece of Parian ware depicting the Old Testament figures Naomi and her two daughters-in-law.

29. "and it became . . . things [illegible words]" canceled later.

30. Charlotte R. Holman (1818?–1859), wife of Boston merchant Oliver Holman. The Holmans resided in Medford (1855 Massachusetts Census; *Transcript,* November 29, 1859, p. 2).

31. Edward Everett Hale (1822–1909), longtime pastor of the South Congregational Church (Unitarian),

Boston, and a successful author and editor. Hale was acting as literary advisor to Dall, and had tried to help her find a publisher for *Spiridion*. Decades later, Hale's reminiscence of his youth, *A New England Boyhood* (New York: Cassell, 1893), was answered by Dall's *"Alongside": Being Notes Suggested by "A New England Boyhood" of Doctor Edward Everett Hale* (Boston: Thomas Todd, 1900).

32. Caroline Champney.

33. Samuel Sewall.

34. James M. Usher, chairman of the legislative committee before which Dall spoke on February 12.

35. George Healey.

36. James Dall (1781–1863) was her father-in-law.

37. Stone to Dall, March 18, 1858, Dall Papers, MHS.

38. William Lloyd Garrison; Samuel May Jr.; Henry C. Wright; Francis Jackson; William C. Nell (1816–1874), Boston black abolitionist journalist, author, and organizer; and Charles L. Remond.

39. Anna Attmore Robinson Chase (1801–1876), wife of state legislator Stephen A. Chase (*Ancestry.com*, accessed November 6, 2004).

40. Lucy Stone later wrote to Dall "to exonerate [her]self from seeming neglect," saying that she had understood that Susan B. Anthony had arranged private accommodations for Dall and that she had so written Dall. The convention voted to pay Dall's expenses despite her absence. Stone hoped that "another year will find arrangements more perfect" (Stone to Dall, May 18, 1858, Dall Papers, MHS).

41. Louisa Serena Kip Austin (1802–1859) lived at 61 East 17th Street. She was the widow of John Phelps Austin (1791–1842), a New York City merchant, and the aunt by marriage of Charles Dall (his mother's brother's wife). See William Allen Day, *The Descendants of Richard Austin of Charlestown, Massachusetts* (St. Petersburg, n.d.), 55–56, 123–124; *New York City Directory* 1857.

42. Elizabeth Lemon Glover Felt (1802–1880) and her husband, Willard Felt (1796–1862), were natives of Massachusetts, Willard Felt having been a stationer in Boston before moving the business to New York. Dall was sometimes their houseguest in New York. See John E. Morris, *The Felt Genealogy* (Hartford, Connecticut: Case, Lockwood & Brainard Co., 1893), 156, 318–319.

43. Maria Louisa Austin Felt (b. 1835), the daughter of Louisa Austin and John P. Austin, and thus Charles Dall's first cousin, had married in 1854 Willard L. Felt, the son of Dall's friends Willard and Elizabeth L. Felt (William Allen Day, *Descendants of Richard Austin* [n.p., n.d.], 123–124).

44. Probably Mary Hedge (1803–1865), the sister of Frederic Henry Hedge. See Robert N. Hudspeth, ed., *Letters of Margaret Fuller*, 6 vols. (Ithaca, New York: Cornell University Press, 1983–1994), 1:190.

45. Mary E. Rowe (b. 1843?), daughter of William D. Rowe (b. 1810?) and Mira Simpson Rowe, who was the sister of Dall's Toronto friend L. Maria Brown. John Patton was apparently boarding with the Rowes (*Ancestry.com*, accessed November 10, 2004; 1850, 1860 U.S. Census).

46. Charles F. Hovey.

47. Isaac R. Butts (1796–1882) was a printer and publisher whose business was on School Street (*Boston Directory* 1858; Massachusetts VR).

48. Dall's sister Frances Healey.

49. Samuel H. Winkley (1819–1911), Unitarian clergyman and Healey family friend. Winkley was for fifty years minister-at-large for the Benevolent Fraternity of Churches in Boston, having charge of the Pitts Street (later Bulfinch Place) Chapel. See *General Catalogue of the Divinity School of Harvard University* (Cambridge, Massachusetts: Harvard University Press, 1901), 45.

50. Later note inserted: "I did pay the whole. Sept/61."

51. Rebecca Davis Parker Tolman.

52. Perhaps Dall has in mind a passage from Emerson's *American Scholar*: "Wherever Macdonald sits, there is the head of the table."

53. Caroline Putnam.

54. *Transcript,* November 1, 1858, p. 2.

55. Manuscript Journals, November 8, 1858.

56. The widowed Rebecca Turner Livingston (b. 1805?) lived with her cousins William and Sarah Dall (1850 U. S. Census).

57. Louisa Simes, a friend of the Dalls since their residence in Portsmouth.

58. Theodoric Severance.

59. Elizabeth Cady Stanton (1815–1902) was a driving force behind the 1848 Seneca Falls Convention and the author of its "Declaration of Sentiments." After 1851 she was associated with Susan B. Anthony, and became a preeminent advocate for women's rights, serving as president of both the National Woman Suffrage Association and (after its merger with the American Woman Suffrage Association) the National American Woman Suffrage Association.

60. That is, Caroline Severance was to replace Elizabeth Cady Stanton as the speaker for the Parker Fraternity at the Tremont Temple.

61. Probably Louisa Hall.

62. Arthur B. Fuller (1822–1863), the brother of Margaret Fuller, was the Unitarian minister at Boston's North Church.

63. Elbridge Gerry Dudley (1811–1867) was a Boston lawyer active in the antislavery movement. He was friends with Theodore Parker, Emerson, Wendell Phillips, and William Lloyd Garrison. See Dean Dudley, *History of the Dudley Family* (Montrose, Massachusetts, 1894), 1:480–482.

64. This sentence canceled later.

65. James Freeman Clarke.

66. Probably John W. Browne.

67. Worcester *Spy,* February 15, 1859, p. 3.

68. Maria Louisa Russell Firth (1822–1860), wife of reformer Abraham Firth (Dall, "A Memorial," unidentified newspaper clipping on the death of Maria Firth, Scrapbook 1, Dall Papers, MHS).

69. Louisa Gladding Brown (1800?–1888) and her husband, William Brown (1797–1869), a merchant tailor, lived at 17 Pearl Street. Both William and his brother Theophilus were friends and admirers of Henry Thoreau. See Mildred McClary Tymeson, *Rural Retrospect: A Parallel History of Worcester and Its Rural Cemetery* (Worcester, Massachusetts: Albert W. Rice, 1956), 182, 183; *Worcester Directory* 1859).

70. Theophilus (1811–1879) and Sarah Ann Knowlton (1825–1907) Brown. See *Rural Retrospect,* 183; Worcester VR; Federal Writers Project, *Index of Birth, Marriage and Death Records of the First Unitarian Church of Worcester* (1936, typescript at *NEHGR*), 11. Theo Brown, a tailor like his brother William, was an admirer and friend of Henry Thoreau.

71. Samuel F. Haven.

72. T. W. Higginson.

73. Oramel Martin (1810–1892), Worcester physician (Tymeson, *Rural Retrospect,* 222).

74. Dall identified Alice Holliday (d. 1868) as an Englishwoman who went to Egypt in 1836, under the auspices of the Society for the Promotion of Female Education in the East. By her own account, Holliday enjoyed great success during ten years of providing education for young women, including those in the royal harem. See Dall's *The College, the Market, and the Court* (Boston: Lee and Shepard, 1867), 31–37.

75. Harriet P. F. Burnside (1827?–1903) and Elizabeth Dwight Burnside (1829–1899) were the daughters of the late Samuel M. Burnside, Worcester lawyer, and his wealthy widow, Sophia D. F. Burnside (1860 U.S. Census; *Rural Retrospect,* 14, 184).

76. Sallie Holley.

77. Sarah Elizabeth Coffin Hall (1816–1901), wife of Nathaniel Hall (1805–1875), Unitarian minister at Dorchester (Gertrude T. Jacobs, *What the Child Saw* [n.p., n.d.], [15]). Dall was their houseguest.

78. Probably one of the brothers of Sarah Coffin Hall.

79. Dall delivered the second in her series of lectures on "Woman's Claim to Education" (Register of Public Addresses, Dall Papers, Bryn Mawr).

80. James Walker, president of Harvard, 1853–1860.

81. Worcester *Spy,* February 21, 1859, p. 2.

82. Elizabeth A. Daley was Dall's source for leeches.

83. Pickering Dodge (d. 1863), member of the Harvard class of 1823, was a Worcester manufacturer (*Worcester Directory* 1861; Harvard Archives).

84. Lucy A. Chase (1822–1909) was the daughter of a prominent Quaker abolitionist family in Worcester. She and her sister Sarah were later to teach freedmen in the South during and after the Civil War. See Worcester VR; William Lincoln, *History of Worcester, Massachusetts* (Worcester: Charles Herse, 1862), 370; Tymeson, *Rural Retrospect,* 186; Henry L. Swint, *Dear Ones at Home: Letters from Contraband Camps* (Nashville: Vanderbilt University Press, 1966), 4–7.

85. Harrison Gray Otis Blake (1816–1898) taught school and did private tutoring in Worcester. He was among that city's group of admirers and friends of Henry David Thoreau (1817–1862) and later edited and published selections from Thoreau's journals, bequeathed him by Sophia Thoreau (Harvard Class Book, Class of 1835 [Boston, 1886], 49–50). This was apparently Thoreau's first delivery of this lecture. He submitted it to the *Atlantic Monthly* and corrected the proofs on his deathbed; it was published in October 1862, a few months after his death. Many years later Dall published in the *Buffalo Daily Courier* (April 14, 1881) a brief appreciative account of it: "Never since [hearing this lecture] have I been in the country at that season when his description of the royal ranks of the purple poke berries and the steady beaming of the yellow hank weed on the hillside has not risen to my mind. He fascinated every one of us, and yet he had been so hard to persuade!" See Walter Harding, *A Thoreau Handbook* (New York: New York University Press, 1959), 71; Joseph Slater, "Caroline Dall in Concord," *The Thoreau Society Bulletin* 62 (Winter, 1958): 1–2.

86. Caroline Putnam.

87. Bithia and Fannie Hincks.

88. Sarah E. Hall.

89. Isaac Clapp (1784–1861), Boston merchant who lived in Dorchester, father of Eliza.

90. Samuel May Jr.

91. Edward Jarvis (1803–1884), Dorchester physician who treated the insane. In 1854 he was a member of a commission to study the condition of the insane in Massachusetts; his report resulted in a new state hospital for the insane. Jarvis became interested in vital statistics and was an important consultant for the federal censuses of 1850 and 1860. He wrote extensively on physiology, vital statistics, sanitation, education, and insanity. Years later he and Dall would be associates in the American Social Science Association *(DAB).*

92. Probably Evelina Sylvester Smith (b. 1800), wife of Dorchester schoolteacher Increase S. Smith (*Ancestry.com,* accessed November 7, 2004; 1860 U.S. Census).

93. Julia Child Bradford Quincy (1817–1881), wife of Thomas Dennie Quincy, an early friend of Dall's (*NEHGR* 20:270–271, 35:287, 83:203–204; *Transcript,* March 19, 1881, p. 12; DFN).

94. The house of Dr. William Palmer Wesselhoeft (1835–1909), 22 Bedford, was near Peabody's brother Nathaniel's apothecary shop at 20½ Bedford (*Boston Directory* 1859; *NEHGR* 64:102).

95. Caroline M. Severance.

96. Penciled note added later reads: "The allusion was copied from Cousin—her long hard ride had soaked her saddle in <u>blood</u>—not menstrual!" Dall refers to Victor Cousin's *Secret History of the French Court Under Richelieu and Mazarin; or, Life and Time of Madame de Chevreuse,* probably the English translation by Mary L. Booth (New York: Delisser and Procter, 1859).

97. The Worcester *Spy* (February 24, 1859, p. 2) praised the lecture, noting that Dall spoke "plainly and

fearlessly" and "kept the undivided attention of her audience to the last." The brief notice by "W." in the *Christian Inquirer* of Dall's sermon and lecture at Haverhill the preceding Sunday observed that "She conducted the services in a very beautiful and impressive manner, and delivered a discourse of great interest, compact with thought, expressed in choice and elegant language. . . . Both her sermon and lecture were listened to by large congregations, and but one sentiment respecting them found utterance, viz.: that they were deeply interesting, and profitable, and calculated to do good" (February 26, 1859, p. 3).

98. Frank Russell Firth (1847–1872) was the eleven-year-old son of Dall's Worcester friends Maria and Abraham Firth, with whom she was staying. He became an engineer, graduating from the Massachusetts Institute of Technology in 1868, and worked on railroad construction in the West. He was killed in the collapse of a railroad bridge in Kansas at the age of twenty-five. See *Memoir of Frank Russell Firth* (Boston: Lee and Shepard, 1873).

99. Samuel F. Haven.

100. Abby Kelley Foster. She and her husband Stephen lived on a farm at Tatnuck, outside Worcester, long known as Liberty Farm. See Zelotes W. Coombs, "Stephen Symonds and Abby Kelley Foster," *Worcester Historical Society Publications* n.s. 1 (April 1934): 382.

101. Paulina ("Alla") Wright Foster (1847–1925) had been undergoing treatment for a spinal curvature, probably scoliosis, and Abby Foster had devoted herself to nursing her. See Dorothy Sterling, *Ahead of Her Time: Abby Kelley and the Politics of Anti-Slavery* (New York: W.W. Norton, 1991), 316–317.

102. May Louisa Firth (b. 1851?), daughter of Abraham and Maria Louisa Russell, later married a Dr. Sheldon. See Abraham Firth, *J. F. R. F.: A Memory* (Boston: University Press, 1885).

103. Sarah E. Chase (1836–1915), sister of Lucy Chase, daughter of Anthony and Lydia Earle Chase. During the war both sisters taught freedmen at Port Royal and continued to work in the South for some time after the war (*Rural Retrospect,* 186). Their letters home are included in Henry L. Swint, ed., *Dear Ones at Home: Letters from Contraband Camps.*

104. Anne H. Earle Southwick (1822–1912) of Worcester was the daughter of John Milton and Sarah H. Earle, and the wife of Edward Southwick (1812–1867) (Pliny Earle, *The Earle Family,* 205–209; Worcester VR; WPA *Index to Births, Marriages and Deaths,* 61).

105. Elizabeth Clapp (b. 1820?) (1860 U.S. Census).

106. Eleanor Buffum (b. 1820), the daughter of David and Susan Ann Barker Buffum, was the sister of Worcester resident Ann Buffum Earle, wife of Edward Earle. She later married Joseph Cottle, or Cattell, of Damascus, Ohio. See Owen A. Perkins, *Buffum Family* (Ft. Worth, Texas: Miran Publishers, 1983), 2:146, 241.

107. Isabel Rogers, four-year-old daughter of Seth Rogers, practitioner of hydropathy who established the Worcester Water Cure (or Hydropathic Institute) in 1850, and Hannah Mitchell Rogers. See Lincoln, *History of Worcester*, 355; Harry B. Weiss and Howard R. Kemble, *The Great American Water-Cure Craze* (Trenton, New Jersey: Past Times Press, 1967), 129–130; 1860 U. S. Census.

108. Alonzo Hill, T. W. Higginson, and H. G. O. Blake and his second wife, Nancy Pope Howe Conant Blake (1829?–1872). See *Harvard Class Book,* Class of 1835 (Boston, 1886), 49–50.

109. Macready's performance at Washburn Hall was to include her recitation of the entire play without the aid of book or prompter (Worcester *Daily Spy,* March 9, 1859, p. 3).

110. Eliza Clapp's letter expressed her objections to Dall's negative approach to the woman question, that is, to her pointing out the wrongs done her by men: "How much a woman gifted like yourself can do to advance or retard the elevation & developement of women. Why not devote your fine powers to this—& leave vulgar errors to become obsolete—and above all why not avoid all approach to attack or reproach upon the other unfortunate half of creation? . . . Meanwhile let no woman's hand take from

woman's brow the crown that has ever to the discerning eye marked her as queen—the power & priv-ilege of self-sacrifice.—" Elizabeth Peabody enclosed Clapp's letter with her own to Dall, stating that it expressed her own views better than she could herself. Peabody went on to urge Dall again to leave out the Madame de Chevreuse incident "since persons as decent as I am—<u>thought</u> of what is not im-proper for a woman to think of but only to speak of." She also passed along the information that the Reverend Nathaniel Hall thought it was "dreadful to speak of an eunuch—<u>explaining his peculiarity</u> even as you did" (both of these letters are undated and are located at the end of the correspondence for 1859 in the Dall Papers, MHS).

111. Nathaniel Hall.
112. Dall's egotism is not broached in either of the letters she has just mentioned, but in one from Peabody received later this day (see below).
113. Ezra S. Gannett, Robert C. Waterston, and Samuel H. Winkley.
114. Nathaniel Hall's letter of March 15 and Sarah Hall's of March 16 both express strong support for Dall's work, even when their judgment differs with hers on particulars. Nathaniel Hall concludes by declar-ing "how truly and deeply I honor you for the sacrifices you have made and are making for your con-viction's sake" (Dall Papers, MHS).
115. Susan B. Anthony.
116. See entry for March 17, 1859.
117. Dall had heard Emerson lecture the preceding night on "The Law of Success."
118. This was the third lecture of Emerson's current private series taking place at the Freeman Place Chapel (*Transcript,* April 6, 1859, p. 2).
119. The *Times* estimated the audience at 1,700. Its account was favorable to the women and sharply criti-cal of the unruly crowd. It described "Caroline H. Doll" as "a brief little woman, of a thin face, and rather a thin voice" and gives a brief summary of what she says of "Mary Wolstencraft [*sic*], the daugh-ter [*sic*] of Godwin." The only fault that could be found with her remarks was that she "justified the marriage of her heroine to one, to whom she refused to be united according to the marriage ceremony." Dall was continually interrupted by "cries of 'Louder, 'Louder,' 'Sit down,' 'Go on,' &c." and finally sat down. The *Tribune* (May 13, 1859, p. 5) unflatteringly described Dall as "a lady of about thirty-five years or upward, of far from prepossessing appearance." Her speech "was exceedingly tame, and consisted mainly of extracts from the writings of [Wollstonecraft and Fuller], with comments upon the same, and a biographical sketch." In the *Herald* Dall was represented as "a sharp specimen of womanhood, who hardly comes within Byron's description of the 'Ripe and real,' with a profusion of gold chains and seals, and a woful absence of hoops"; she left the stage, according to the reporter, "somewhat ungra-ciously, amid a storm of noise." The accounts of all three papers confirm Dall's version of the rowdi-ness of the audience not only during her talk but also throughout the speeches of the other women and of Wendell Phillips.
120. Daniel Edgar Sickles (1825–1914), an attorney and New York state legislator, had in 1853 married Theresa Bagioli, the seventeen-year-old daughter of an Italian music teacher. Sickles's career blos-somed, as he became secretary of the U.S. legation in London, a member of the state senate, and then a U.S. congressman (1857–1861). On February 27, 1859, he shot and killed Philip Barton Key, the son of Francis Scott Key, whom he believed to be involved with his wife. In a celebrated trial, for the first time a plea of temporary aberration of mind was entered, and won Sickles an acquittal. He and his wife reconciled, and he went on to become a major-general in the Civil War and then minister to Spain. Afterwards he was successful in his attempts to obtain the land for Central Park for New York City *(DAB).*
121. Elizabeth Johns Neall Gay (1819–1907), who had been one of the delegates to the 1840 London anti-

slavery convention that refused to seat women, was married to Sydney Gay, abolitionist editor, and lived on Staten Island (Merrill and Ruchames, eds., *Letters of William Lloyd Garrison* 2:662).

122. Joseph Avery Howland (1820?–1889) was a Worcester businessman, active in local politics and the antislavery and women's rights causes (Merrill and Ruchames, eds., *Letters of William Lloyd Garrison* 4:457, 5:113).

123. Dall had for months been plagued with carbuncles, painful staphylococcal infections, around her face, neck, and shoulders. The swelling resulting from one of these abscesses was severely affecting her hearing.

124. Lucretia Mott (1793–1880), Quaker minister, abolitionist, and pioneer women's rights advocate, one of the organizers of the Seneca Falls convention.

125. The Smithsonian House was at 606 Broadway.

126. Ernestine Potowski Rose (1810–1892), Polish-born feminist, reformer, and freethinker. In England she became acquainted with reformers, and after her marriage in 1836 came with her husband to New York City. She had cooperated with Paulina Wright (later Davis) and Susan B. Anthony as early as 1840 in an attempt to get a married women's property bill passed by the New York legislature. A friend of Robert Owen, she had participated with him in 1845 in a Convention of the Infidels of the United States, in New York City *(NAW)*.

127. Stephen Pearl Andrews.

128. Stephen Pearl Andrews and Henry C. Wright had presented radical proposals about marriage at the 1858 convention. See Dall's journal for May 17, 1858.

129. Each speaker was allotted thirty minutes.

130. Mary Fenn Robinson Davis (1824–1886) was a spiritualist lecturer and reformer, the subject of a scandal because of her Indiana divorce and remarriage to Andrew Jackson Davis. In the following decades she lectured on temperance and women's rights, wrote poetry, and was a member of the women's club Sorosis. The son mentioned here was Charles G. Love, her son by her first marriage *(NAW)*.

131. Probably black abolitionist William C. Nell.

132. Sarah Allen Nowell (b. 1804?) had published *Poems* (Boston: A. Tompkins, 1850), and would soon publish *The Shadow on the Pillow; and Other Stories* (Boston: A. Tompkins, 1860). Her poem on this occasion eulogized Florence Nightingale, Rosa Bonheur, and Harriet Hosmer and asserted "the equality of man and woman in the creation." See 1860 U.S. Census; and Elizabeth Cady Stanton, Susan B. Anthony, and Matilda Joslyn Gage, *History of Woman Suffrage* (New York: Fowler & Wells, 1881), 1:263.

133. John T. Sargent, Charles Gordon Ames, and Wendell Phillips. Ames (1828–1912), early a Baptist minister, later gave up the ministry, becoming an editor, temperance and antislavery reformer, and lecturer. He converted to Unitarianism, in 1859 becoming a member, as was Dall, of James Freeman Clarke's Church of the Disciples. Soon thereafter he became a Unitarian preacher, holding pastorates in Bloomington, Illinois, Cincinnati, and Albany, and on the West Coast. He edited the *Christian Register*, 1875–1880, and at age sixty succeeded Clarke as minister of the Church of the Disciples, remaining there until his death *(DAB)*.

134. Abby Folsom (1792?–1867), born in England, came to the United States in 1837 and became an active abolitionist. She was notorious as "a harmless fanatic on the subject of free speech, and was frequently removed from meetings and conventions on account of her determined desire to speak" *(NatCAB* 2:394).

135. E. P. and Charlotte Whipple.

136. Sarah Ann Clarke (1808–1896), sister of James Freeman Clarke and close friend of Margaret Fuller, was a landscape painter who studied with Washington Allston and exhibited at the Boston Athenaeum and

the American Art Union. She became one of Caroline Dall's most faithful long-term friends. After the Civil War, Sarah Clarke moved to Marietta, Georgia, where she established and ran a library for freed slaves. See George C. Croce and David H. Wallace, eds., *The New-York Historical Society's Dictionary of Artists in America, 1564–1860* (New Haven, Connecticut: Yale University Press, 1957).

137. Margaret Foley (1820–1877) was a sculptor in marble, wood, and terra cotta. Born in Vermont, she had moved to Boston and supported herself by cameo carvings of portraits and ideal heads, then by teaching at Westford, Massachusetts. In 1855 she moved to Rome and joined the circle of expatriate American artists that included William Wetmore Story and Harriet Hosmer. She created the large fountain for the Philadelphia Centennial, now located in Fairmount Park. See *NatCAB* 9:121; Chris Petteys et al., *Dictionary of Women Artists* (Boston: G.K. Hall, 1985).

138. Anna Brownell Jameson (1794–1860), British author and reformer. She had just published a new edition of her lectures, *Sisters of Charity and the Communion of Labor,* prefaced by a fifty-page letter to Lord John Russell, president of the National Association for the Promotion of Social Science, on the condition and requirements of the women of England. The dedication of the printed version of Dall's lectures, *"Woman's Right to Labor;" or, Low Wages and Hard Work: In Three Lectures, Delivered in Boston, November, 1859* (Boston: Walker, Wise, 1860) reads, "In Grateful Commemoration of Her Letter to Lord John Russell."

139. Insertion added later at this point: "considering the subject of the book."

140. The Samuel Sewall family.

141. Dall's servant.

142. Samuel May Jr.

143. Barbara Channing and Louisa Hall. Barbara Higginson Channing (1816–1880) was the daughter of Dr. Walter and the late Barbara Higginson Perkins Channing, and the sister of William Ellery Channing the younger.

144. Psalms 31:20.

145. Samuel May Jr.

146. The families of Samuel Sewell and Samuel May Jr.

147. Emerson was lecturing before the Parker Fraternity at the Tremont Temple (*Transcript,* November 8, 1859, p. 2).

148. The bracketed words in these two sentences replace in different ink Dall's original words, which she erased. It seems likely that she erased these words after she developed a close relationship with Towne, then restored them after their estrangement. Dall's note added later in the margin reads: "As I read this (Sept 1861—) & have the light of a long & intimate acquaintance thrown on that first sermon, I feel how near—the 'divine earnestness' is to insanity in the eyes of all the world."

149. Anna Huidekoper Clarke (1814–1897), wife of James Freeman Clarke, whose pulpit Towne was supplying.

150. Simon and Ann Brown, friends of Dall's from her year in Washington and Georgetown; Louis Surette (1819–1897), Concord merchant (Massachusetts VR).

151. Abigail May Alcott, the future "Marmee" of *Little Women,* and her daughters, Anna Bronson (1831–1893), Louisa May (1832–1888), and Abby May (1840–1879). Elizabeth Sewell (b. 1835) had died in 1858. See Richard L. Herrnstadt, *The Letters of A. Bronson Alcott* (Ames: Iowa State University Press, 1969), vii–ix. See also Chapter 7, note 36.

152. Grindall Reynolds (1822–1894) was minister to the Unitarian Church in Concord, 1858–1894 (pastor emeritus after 1881) and secretary of the American Unitarian Association, 1881–1894 (*Heralds* 3:323–329).

153. Franklin Benjamin Sanborn (1831–1917), second-generation Transcendentalist and Concord teacher

who would become an author, journalist, and reformer. His life and work were to intersect often in the following years with Dall's. See Wesley T. Mott, *Biographical Dictionary of Transcendentalism* (Westport, Connecticut: Greenwood Press, 1996).

154. Alcott reported in his own diary, "Hear Mrs. Dall's lecture. She gave us accounts of the principal incidents in the lives of Mary Wollstonecraft, Harriet Martineau, Lady Morgan, Mrs. Jameson, Margaret Fuller & others. It was a well considered performance, and gave pleasure to our people generally" ("Diary for 1859," December 14, 1859, Amos Bronson Alcott Papers, Houghton Library, Harvard University).

155. Edith Emerson (1841–1929), daughter of Lidian Jackson Emerson and Ralph Waldo Emerson, married in 1865 William H. Forbes (*NEHGR* 84:220).

156. Simon Brown.

157. Mary Peabody Mann.

158. Lydia B. Mann (1798–1888), sister of Horace Mann, was a teacher for half a century. See George S. Mann, *Genealogy of the Descendants of Richard Man of Scituate, Mass.* (Boston: David Clapp & Son, 1884), 26.

159. *The Heetopades of Veeshnoo Sarma, in a Series of Connected Fables, Interspersed with Moral, Prudential, and Political Maxims,* translated by Charles Wilkins (Bath: R. Cruttwell, 1787). In 1842 Emerson included excerpts of this work in the third volume of *The Dial.*

160. Sarah Elizabeth Sanborn (b. 1823) was her brother's assistant for several years in the private school that he conducted in Concord. From 1863 to 1889 she was the confidential secretary of the Massachusetts Board of State Charities. In 1891 she retired to the family homestead at Hampton Falls, New Hampshire. See V. C. Sanborn, *Genealogy of the Family Samborne or Sanborn in England and America* (Concord, New Hampshire: Rumford Press, 1899), 296.

161. "The Hoars" refers to the family of the late prominent Concordian "Squire" Samuel Hoar (1778–1856), including his wife, Sarah Sherman Hoar (1783–1866); daughter Elizabeth Hoar (once engaged to Charles Emerson); son Edward Sherman Hoar (1823–1893), friend and traveling companion of Thoreau; and son Ebenezer Rockwood Hoar (1816–1895), Concord lawyer and later U.S. attorney general, and his family. "The Pritchards" were the Moses (b. 1789?) and Jane T. (b. 1791?) Prichard family. A daughter, Elizabeth Hallet Prichard ("Lizzie") (1822–1917), had been friends with the Dalls during the early months of their marriage in Baltimore; she was now married to Edward Sherman Hoar. See *Ancestry.com,* accessed November 8, 2004; Elizabeth Maxfield-Miller, "Elizabeth of Concord: Selected Letters of Elizabeth Sherman Hoar to the Emersons, Family, and the Emerson Circle, Part 1," *SAR 1984,* 229–298; Mott, ed., *Biographical Dictionary of Transcendentalism.*

162. Sophia Thoreau (1819–1876), Henry's sister.

163. William Ellery Channing the Younger (1817–1901), known as Ellery, Transcendentalist poet, friend of Thoreau, and widower of Margaret Fuller's sister Ellen.

164. Ellery Channing's *Near Home* (Boston, 1858) consisted of a long poem of that title, prefaced by an opening dedicatory poem entitled "To Henry."

165. The English aristocrat Thomas Cholmondeley (1823–1863), who met Thoreau on a visit to Concord in 1854, boarded with his family, and became his friend and correspondent, sent him in 1855 the generous gift of a forty-four-volume collection of Oriental books (Mott, ed., *Biographical Dictionary of Transcendentalism,* 44–46).

166. Lizzie Goodwin Brown was the wife of Lidian Emerson's nephew Frank Brown; Charles K. Whipple was the second husband of Emmeline C. Goodwin (b. 1813?). See *Selected Letters of Lidian Jackson Emerson,* ed. Delores Bird Carpenter (Columbia: University of Missouri Press, 1987), 158, and the 1860 U.S. Census.

167. This anonymous novel was by the young Harriet Elizabeth Prescott (later Spofford) (1835–1921) of Newburyport, a protégée of T. W. Higginson. Spofford became a popular and prolific writer *(NAW)*.

168. Later note added in margin reads: "The letter expressing this sympathy for the first time Dec 23.1859. is now (June 1863) in Mr Towne's own keeping—It ought to be claimed by any biographer of mine."

169. Bessie Rayner Parkes (later Belloc; 1829–1925), along with Matilda Hays, edited the *English Woman's Journal.* In 1854 she published anonymously *Remarks on the Education of Girls,* objecting to the restrictions on female education. She had earlier (November 4, 1859) written to Dall, asking her to be Boston agent for the *English Woman's Journal.* The public opinion lecture had already, apparently without Dall's knowledge, appeared as *A Lecture on the Existing Public Opinion in Regard to Women* (London, 1858). Bessie Rayner Parkes's letter also commissioned Dall to collect for American subscriptions to the *English Woman's Journal* and to take a percentage of her collections. Parkes went on to answer Dall's queries about William Godwin's family and about George Eliot's "elopement" (letter of January 20, 1860, Dall Papers, MHS). See also Virginia Blain, Patricia Clements, and Isobel Grundy, eds., *The Feminist Companion to Literature in English: Women Writers from the Middle Ages to the Present* (New Haven, Connecticut: Yale University Press, 1990).

170. Marie Elizabeth Zakrzewska (1829–1902), pioneering female physician, was born in Berlin, and received the M.D. degree at Western Reserve University in Cleveland in 1856. In 1857 she and Elizabeth Blackwell established the New York Infirmary for Women and Children, staffed by women, and for two years Zakrzewska was its resident physician and general manager. In 1859 she became associated with the short-lived New England Female Medical College of Boston, then in 1862 she founded the New England Hospital for Women and Children. Marie Zakrzewska is perhaps more than any other person responsible for the success of American women in medicine in the nineteenth century *(NAW)*. Dall edited her story, *A Practical Illustration of "Woman's Right to Labor;" or, A Letter from Marie E. Zakrzewska, M.D. Late of Berlin, Prussia,* published in December of this year in Boston. On this occasion she was probably lecturing to the Ladies' Physiological Institute.

171. "but...aching" canceled later.

172. Sarah H. Southwick.

173. Sargent's letter to Dall of June 7, 1860, confirms that he was offended to have been included in the phrase "and others" in the newspaper advertisement announcing speakers (Dall Papers, MHS).

174. William Travis Clarke (1828–1883), Unitarian minister at Haverhill.

175. Ednah D. Cheney.

176. Harriet Tubman.

177. Maria Mitchell (1818–1889), astronomer, a native of Nantucket, had already discovered a new comet (1847) and been the first woman elected to both the American Academy of Arts and Sciences and the American Association for Advancement of Science. In 1857–1858 she traveled abroad meeting famous European scientists, and upon her return, a group of women headed by Elizabeth Peabody presented her with a five-inch Alvan Clark telescope. Mitchell became one of the original professors at Vassar College when it was opened in 1865, and founded in 1873 the Association for the Advancement of Women *(NAW)*.

178. London-born Richard J. Hinton (1830–1901), instrumental in the formation of the Republican party, was an abolitionist newspaperman in Kansas and had been a close associate of John Brown. He was an officer during the Civil War, recruiting and commanding black troops. In 1865 he was named inspector general of the Freedmen's Bureau (Merrill and Ruchames, eds., *Letters of William Lloyd Garrison* 5:63).

179. That is, Harriet Tubman.

180. Note inserted later reads: "could not speak so as to be heard,"

181. This word is underlined in different ink, the same as that of the inserted note.
182. Lucy Goddard (1804?–1897) was, like Dall, a member of the Church of the Disciples. Dall described her as "exceedingly beautiful but haughty" in her youth and wrote that James Freeman Clarke "made a philanthropist of her, after the days of coquetry had ended." Goddard later became president of the New England Hospital for Women and Children (Dead Friends Notebook, Dall Papers, MHS; *Fair at the Hotel Vendome for the Benefit of the New England Hospital for Women and Children* [Boston, 1899], 48).
183. Rebecca Tolman.
184. John Bell (1797–1869) of Tennessee, a moderate on slavery and a strong supporter of the Union, and Edward Everett (1794–1865) of Massachusetts, former Unitarian minister, professor and president at Harvard, congressman, governor of Massachusetts, and ambassador, had been nominated for president and vice president respectively by the recently formed Constitutional Union Party. This Faneuil Hall meeting of the "friends of the National Union Party" was to ratify the recent nomination of Bell and Everett in Baltimore (*DAB*; *Transcript*, June 1, 1860, p. 2).
185. Josiah Quincy (1802–1882), former mayor of Boston, and Mary Jane Miller Quincy (1806–1874). See H. Hobart Holly, *Descendants of Edmund Quincy* (Quincy, Massachusetts: Quincy Historical Society, 1977), 29–30.
186. This group included Maria Weston Chapman (1806–1885) ("Mrs Chapman" mentioned below), prominent Boston abolitionist, formerly editor of the annual the *Liberty Bell;* her sister-in-law Mary Gray Chapman (c. 1798–1874); and Maria's sister Deborah Weston (1814–1889) (Merrill and Ruchames, eds., *Letters of William Lloyd Garrison* 4:354, 383).
187. Sallie Holley.
188. Later insertion at this point: "; as the crowd looked up from the pit."
189. *Transcript*, October 23, 1860, p. 2. The Boston *Daily Atlas and Bee* gave a full account of the lecture (October 24, 1860), and it was published in the *Liberator* (October 26, 1860).
190. Charles W. Slack (1825–1885), abolitionist, temperance advocate, editor, and member of the state legislature, was active in the "Fraternity" of the Twenty-eighth Congregational Society (Theodore Parker's church), sponsor of this lecture series. In 1862 he became editor and publisher of the Boston *Commonwealth* (*NEHGR* 39:400; *Transcript*, April 11, 1885, p. 1; Merrill and Ruchames, eds., *Letters of William Lloyd Garrison* 4:228).
191. The Parker House hotel.
192. The home of Maria Weston Chapman.
193. Charles C. Follen (1830–1872) was the only child of Charles and Eliza Lee Cabot Follen. Graduating from Harvard in 1849, he became an active abolitionist and later fought in the Civil War (Merrill and Ruchames, eds., *Letters of William Lloyd Garrison* 4:529).
194. Phoebe Garnaut (b. 1837?), adopted daughter of Wendell and Ann Phillips, was born the daughter of Eliza Garnaut, a Welsh immigrant, and her French husband, who died before his daughter's birth. Eliza Garnaut served as a nurse in the Wendell Phillips household, and when she died of cholera, the Phillipses adopted the eleven-year-old daughter. On December 25, 1862, she married lawyer and journalist George W. Smalley. See the 1850 U.S. Census; Oscar Sherwin, *Prophet of Liberty: The Life and Times of Wendell Phillips* (New York: Bookman Associates, 1958), 305; James Brewer Stewart, *Wendell Phillips: Liberty's Hero* (Baton Rouge: Louisiana State University Press, 1986), 91; and *DAB*.
195. Edward Towne's sister, Ellen Elizabeth Towne (b. 1845), who was living with Dall as a sort of housekeeper (*Ancestry.com*, accessed November 9, 2004).
196. John Albion Andrew (1818–1867), governor of Massachusetts (1861–1866). He was, like Dall, a member of James Freeman Clarke's Church of the Disciples.
197. William Lloyd Garrison Jr. (1838–1909) had a successful career in business, beginning as a bank cashier

and becoming by 1865 a wool broker (Merrill and Ruchames, eds., *Letters of William Lloyd Garrison* 5:9).

198. A clipping labeled by Dall "Lynn Reporter Feb. 1861." argued that the four women whom Dall treated in her lecture (Mary Wollstonecraft, Lady Morgan, Charlotte Brontë, and Margaret Fuller) "should not be held up as 'representative women.'" The concluding sentence summed up the writer's defense of the domestic role as woman's true sphere: "There is a higher and far nobler type of womanhood, and while we may respect the genius, wit and talent which adorns the illustrious names [of Dall's representative women], we may reserve our love and honor for the thousand noble, loving, faithful wives and sisters and mothers, who, though they may never have shone upon the page of philosophy, history or fiction, are yet real, true, whole-hearted 'representative women'" (Scrapbook 1 [Dall's own collection of clippings and the like], Dall Papers, MHS).

199. Kate Payson, who was on the committee for another lecture Dall was to give in West Roxbury.

200. John York (b. 1817?), teacher; though an American citizen, he was born in Greece. Dall seems to have been hosted by him and his wife Julia E. York (b. 1824?), also later a teacher (1860, 1870, 1890 U.S. Census).

201. Probably Joseph Page Woodbury (1816–1875), who operated planing machines in Boston and lived in West Roxbury (*Boston Directory* 1861; *Ancestry.com,* accessed June 5, 2002).

CHAPTER TWELVE

1. James Freeman Clarke, minister of the Church of the Disciples.
2. Susan Austin.
3. This letter is pasted onto the pages of Dall's journal.
4. Dall's physician, Dr. Edward H. Clarke (1820–1877).
5. The services of the annual visitation of the Harvard Divinity School.
6. Samuel Osgood (1812–1880), who had early in his career been associated with the Transcendentalists, and had been since 1859 minister of the Church of the Messiah in New York City. In 1870 he became a minister in the Episcopal Church (*General Catalogue of the Divinity School of Harvard University* [Cambridge: Harvard University Press, 1901]).
7. George E. Ellis (1814–1894), pastor of the Harvard Church, Charlestown, and later president of the Massachusetts Historical Society (*Heralds* 3:99–102).
8. The *Christian Register* (July 20, 1861, p. 114) printed an extensive summary of James Freeman Clarke's discourse on "the coming of Christ and of his *Anti*-Christ."
9. Rufus P. Stebbins (1810–1885), associated with the temperance, peace, and antislavery causes, was the first president of Meadville Theological School (1844–1856). From 1856 to 1862 he preached at the First Unitarian Society of Woburn, and in 1862 was elected president of the American Unitarian Association (*Heralds* 3:353–357).
10. The home of Convers Francis, near Harvard Yard. Francis (1795–1863), a member of the Transcendentalist circle, was Professor of Pulpit Eloquence and Pastoral Care at Harvard.
11. That is, apparently, the story she has just related about what Stebbins told the troops.
12. A collation took place at Harvard Hall at two o'clock between the program of the Visitation of the Divinity School and the meeting of the alumni.
13. *"Woman's Right to Labor,"* published the previous year.
14. Mary Carpenter (1807–1879), English reformer, was the daughter of the Unitarian clergyman Lant Carpenter (1780–1840) and Anna Penn Carpenter (d. 1856). She had been responsible for the establishment of schools in slums, of reformatories, and of industrial schools in England. A visit to England

by Charles Dall's protégé Jogut Chunder Gangooly in 1860 had excited her interest in India, and she subsequently made three extended visits there, giving advice on education and prison discipline and serving as the superintendent of a female normal school in Bombay. She was active in the social science congresses in Britain, frequently presenting papers based on her work *(DNB)*.

15. Joseph Hetherington McDaniels (1840–1938) graduated first in his class this year and went on to teach at Lowell High School and then to be a longtime professor of Greek at Hobart College in New York (1868–1912). He was a frequent contributor to *The Nation*. See *Fifth Report: Harvard College Class of 1861* (New York, 1892), 74; *Who Was Who in America*, vol. 1. Leonard Case Alden (1839–1863) spoke on "National Character Elevated by National Affliction." In May 1863 he joined the Massachusetts Fifty-fifth as Second Lieutenant; because of ill health he resigned several months later and died on October 5, while on his way home, in a hospital at Hilton Head *(Fifth Report: Harvard College Class of 1861*, 1–3).

16. Winfield Scott (1786–1866), since 1841 general-in-chief of the U.S. Army, had distinguished himself in the War of 1812 and the Mexican War. A Southerner, he remained loyal to the Union upon the outbreak of the Civil War, but his age and lack of success early in the war forced his resignation on November 1, 1861.

17. Cornelius C. Felton, president of Harvard 1860–1862.

18. Josiah Quincy (1772–1864), president of Harvard 1829–1845.

19. Edward Everett, president of Harvard 1846–1849.

20. Boston historian John Lothrop Motley (1814–1877), author of the popular *The Rise of the Dutch Republic: A History*, 3 vols. (New York: Harper & Brothers, 1856).

21. Mary Louise Booth (1831–1889), New York journalist, author, translator, women's rights advocate, and magazine editor.

22. Wendell Phillips.

23. Charles Slack.

24. A last resort.

25. Marginal note added later reads: "It was through my influence that Annie D got her <u>first</u> opportunity to speak for the Fraternity—"

26. Charles Brooks (1795–1872), Medford native, preached at Hingham, 1821–1839, then was professor of natural history at the University of the City of New York, 1838–1844. He retired to Medford, publishing in 1855 *History of the Town of Medford* (*General Catalogue of the Divinity School of Harvard University*).

27. Eunice B. Hall (1805?–1892) lived alone except for a domestic servant (1865 Massachusetts Census; Middlesex County, Massachusetts, Probate Records).

28. Lucy Osgood (1791–1873), daughter of David Osgood, longtime minister at Medford, and his wife, Hannah Breed Osgood; Dall depicts her as a brilliant woman and the *grand dame* of Medford. See Ira Osgood, *A Genealogy of the Descendants of John, Christopher and William Osgood* (Salem, Massachusetts: Salem Press, 1894), 64–65, and Ms. Journal, June 20, 1873, Dall Papers, MHS.

29. Ellen Sever Tebbets (1835–1904), wife of Theodore Tebbets (1831–1863), former minister of the First Parish in Medford, who had recently resigned because of ill health, and whom Edward Towne replaced. See *General Catalogue of the Divinity School of Harvard University*; Charles Brooks and James M. Usher, *History of the Town of Medford* (Boston: Rand, Avery, 1886), 259–261; and *NEHGR* 26:318, 97:386.

30. James Freeman Clarke.

31. The Rev. Charles Cleveland (1772–1872), almost ninety years old, was the longtime city missionary to the poor of Boston. See Edmund James Cleveland and Horace Gillette Cleveland, *The Genealogy of the Cleveland and Cleaveland Families* (Hartford: Case, Lockwood & Brainard, 1899), 1:505–506.

32. George Washington Prentiss (b. 1808), Boston coal dealer and, like Dall, member of the Church of the Disciples. See C. J. F. Binney, *History and Genealogy of the Prentice or Prentiss Family* (Boston, 1852), 89–90.

33. General John Pope (1822–1892), in command of the Union forces. Pope was relieved of his command following this defeat.

34. Abigail Bigelow Stone Lincoln (1820–1879), wife of Algernon Sydney Lincoln (1812–1887), Boston bank teller and active member of the Unitarian Church in Medford. See J. Gardner Bartlett, *Simon Stone Genealogy* (Boston: Stone Family Association, 1926), 385–387.

35. Mary Brooks Hall (1796–1869), sister of Medford farmer Peter Chardon Hall and also of Unitarian ministers Nathaniel Hall and Edward Brooks Hall. She became Dall's closest friend in Medford. See David B. Hall, *The Halls of New England* (Albany, New York: J. Munsell's Sons, 1883), 308, 318.

36. That is, Charles Dall would not come to Medford until the next day.

37. Henrietta Page (b. 1844) was the oldest of the three children of Henry and Eliza Page, with whom Edward Towne had boarded when he first came to Medford. See Bigelow Society, *Bigelow Family Genealogy* (Flint, Michigan: Bigelow Society, 1986–1993), 2:259.

38. Mary B. Hall.

39. Added later at this point: "!! As if I ever could! I must have stopped writing it—if I had!"

40. James Freeman Clarke.

41. Sisters Martha (c. 1805–1885) and Emily (b. 1821?) Thompson had kept a school in Toronto that Willie Dall attended (DFN; Dall Journals, June 9, 1892).

42. The Daniel Wilson family.

43. Mary Ansley (b. 1839?), daughter of Barzillai and Mary Ann Ansley of New Brunswick, was Eliza Beatty's niece. She later married the prominent broker Gordon Monges of Philadelphia (1880 U.S. Census; *Ancestry.com,* accessed December 6, 2004; *NatCAB* 17:245).

44. "served" is written over an erased illegible word.

45. L. Maria Brown. Like John Patton, she and her husband, Champion Brown, and their family had moved to Montreal since Dall left Toronto.

46. Arthur Moulton Brown, the two-year-old son of Champion and Maria Brown. See James M. Crafts, *History of Whately, Mass.* (Orange, Massachusetts, 1899); *Ancestry.com,* accessed November 18, 2004).

47. Dawson Brothers, Montreal publishers and booksellers.

48. Dall's journal reads, "that I made have told him all."

49. "only I hope [approx. 5 illegible words]" canceled later by Dall.

50. Richard Price Hallowell (1835–1904), a Boston merchant who lived in West Medford. He recruited for the black Massachusetts regiments (the Fifty-fourth and Fifty-fifth) and was at times a member of a bodyguard for William Lloyd Garrison and Wendell Phillips at public meetings. After the war he worked for freed slaves, establishing schools in the South, and was a manager of the Home for Aged Colored Women in Boston. See *DAB*; Walter M. Merrill and Louis Ruchames, eds., *Letters of William Lloyd Garrison,* 6 vols. (Cambridge, Massachusetts: Belknap Press, 1971–1981), 5:418.

51. Wendell Phillips Garrison (1840–1907), the third son of William Lloyd and Helen Garrison, became an author and editor, being best known as a founder (1865), longtime literary editor, and eventually editor of *The Nation.* With his brother Francis Jackson Garrison he published the *Life of William Lloyd Garrison* in four volumes (1885–1889) (Merrill and Ruchames, eds., *Letters of William Lloyd Garrison* 6:14–15; *NatCAB* 1:197).

52. Mary Rice Marsh Appleton (b. 1839?), wife of John W. M. Appleton, recruiting officer for the Fifty-fourth Massachusetts black regiment (1870 U.S. Census; *Ancestry.com,* accessed July 15, 2003).

53. Robert Gould Shaw (1837–1863), son of Dall's acquaintances Francis George and Sarah Blake Sturgis Shaw, had been chosen to command the Massachusetts Fifth-fourth.

54. Mary B. Hall.

55. Timothy Swan (1829–1863), son of Joseph and Ann Rose Swan, died at Medford on May 10 (Medford VR; *Transcript,* May 12, 1863, p. 2). Dall was renting the house from the Swans.

56. Lucy Osgood.

57. Agnes Wyman Lincoln (1856–1921), young daughter of Algernon and Abigail Lincoln. Much later she became curator and librarian (1900–1919), then vice president (1920–21) of the Medford Historical Society. See J. Gardner Bartlett, *Simon Stone Genealogy* (Boston: Stone Family Association, 1926), 385–387.

58. That is, Towne's own sermon *A Memorial of Rev. Theodore Tebbets* . . . published earlier that year.

59. Robert Farley (b. 1801?), Medford lawyer, and his wife Ann (b. 1810?) (1855 Massachusetts Census).

60. John Patton, called "Uncle John" by the Dall children.

61. Anna Coffin Davis Hallowell (1838–1913), granddaughter of Lucretia and James Mott and the wife of Richard P. Hallowell.

62. Euphemia Fenno Tudor (1814?–1884) was married to Frederic Tudor (1783–1864), known as the "Ice King" for his success in building the business of shipping ice from Boston to the American South and as far away as Calcutta (*DAB; Transcript,* March 11, 1884).

63. Jane Webb ("Jeanie") Hall (1851–1871), the oldest child of Peter Chardon Hall and the late Ann Rose Swan Hall, and the niece of Mary B. Hall (David B. Hall, *The Halls of New England,* 318; Ms. Journal, November 28, 1871).

64. Charles Currier (b. 1826?), Medford grocer, served as a captain in the Fifth Regiment of the Massachusetts Volunteer Militia from September 15, 1862, until July 2, 1863, just a few days earlier. When the regiment was called up again from July to September 1864, he served as quartermaster. See *Massachusetts Soldiers, Sailors, and Marines in the Civil War* (Norwood, Massachusetts: Norwood Press, 1931), 1:318, 337.

65. That is, Dall and John Patton went to the home of her Medford neighbor Anna Hallowell, whose husband Richard was staying overnight with the Massachusetts Fifty-fourth (not the Forty-fourth) Infantry.

66. Andrew Preston Peabody (1811–1893), Plummer Professor of Christian Morals at Harvard and editor of the influential *North American Review* (1854–1863) (*Heralds* 3:288–296; *ANB*).

67. Anna H. Clarke.

68. Mary Traill Spence Lowell Putnam (1810–1898), writer, was the daughter of Dr. Charles Lowell. Her work on slavery, *Record of an Obscure Man,* was published in Boston in 1861 (*Roxbury Directory* 1850; *NEHGR* 16:364, 92:251).

69. The disease was measles.

70. Asterisk added later at this point, and the following note in the left margin: "*This promise undoubtedly saved his life. He believed me like a child & went to sleep."

71. Sophia A. Hawkes Town or Towne (1813–1874), wife of Ebenezer Towne (1802–1892). See Anne Sabo Warner, *A Bicentennial History, Goshen, Massachusetts, 1781–1981* (Goshen: Goshen Historical Commission, 1980), 216, 346; *Ancestry.com,* accessed November 9, 2004.

72. Thomas Gaffield (1825–1900), long associated with the West Church and active in the Sunday School, was a partner in the firm of C. G. Loring & Co., window glass. In 1869 he retired from business and was involved in a number of philanthropic endeavors (*Transcript,* December 7, 1900, p. 9; DFN).

73. Octavius Brooks Frothingham (1822–1895), minister for the Third Congregational Unitarian Church in New York City, later called the Independent Liberal Church. He was later president of the Free Religious Association, a biographer of Parker, George Ripley, and William H. Channing, and a historian of the Transcendentalist movement. See David Robinson, *The Unitarians and the Universalists* (Westport, Connecticut: Greenwood Press, 1985), 262; *Heralds* 3:120–127.

74. By the poet William Cullen Bryant (1794–1878).

75. Eliza Wales Bigelow Page (b. 1815), the wife of Medford merchant Henry A. Page, with whom Towne first boarded in Medford (Bigelow Society, *Bigelow Family Genealogy*, 2:259).

76. Dall later added here the numeral 2, indicating that she is responding to the second of Towne's presumed objections to her treatment of him.

77. Dall has pasted into her journal a statement from Edward Towne dated April 14, 1863, in which he declared that Dall had leased the house in her own name but on his behalf, with the understanding that he would pay "not less than the rent of the house, whatever that rent might be, & to further pay of the expenses of the house such part as might be due to my having the entire control & use of the establishment." This statement was prepared because of a dispute with Charles Dall at that time concerning Towne's prerogatives in the house.

78. On April 8, 1863, while she was in Boston.

79. Abigail and Algernon Lincoln.

80. Lucy Osgood.

81. James P. Walker (1829–1868) of the publishing firm Walker and Wise, associated with the American Unitarian Association (Madeleine B. Stern, "James P. Walker and Horace B. Fuller: Transcendental Publishers," *The Boston Public Library Quarterly* 6 [July 1954]: 123–140). The firm published a number of Dall's works including, in October of this year, *Sunshine: A New Name for a Popular Lecture on Health*.

82. Sydney Gay (1814–1888) was the editor of the *National Anti-Slavery Standard*; Dall had stayed with him and his family in Staten Island in the summer of 1863. Gay's letter, in the Dall Papers, MHS, thanks Dall for her account of a day spent with his mother, Mary Allyne Otis Gay (d. 1866) of Hingham, widow of lawyer Ebenezer Gay (1771–1842) (*NEHGR* 33:52; Ancestry.com, accessed August 14, 2002).

83. Dall's old friend Simon Brown had been lieutenant governor of Massachusetts, 1855–1856.

84. That is, Elizabeth Prichard Hoar, wife of Edward S. Hoar.

85. Julia Ward Howe.

86. J. Miller McKim (1810–1874), abolitionist, was an official of the Pennsylvania Freedmen's Relief Association. Judging from his reply to her, Dall asked him to help get a position for Alcott as "general superintendent for Washington." McKim responded that he knew of Alcott and "of course thinks very highly of him," but he did not believe that an appointment would be made to this position soon (*DAB*; McKim to Dall, September 10, 1864, Dall Papers, MHS).

87. Helen M. Parsons (1821?–1901), the sister of her friend Anna Q. T. Parsons (1850 U.S. Census; DFN).

88. Eliza Clapp; the letter is unidentified.

89. Dall may refer to the recently published *Philosophy as Absolute Science* (Boston, 1864) by Ephraim L. Frothingham and Arthur L. Frothingham.

90. Eliza F. Meriam (b. 1841?) was the daughter of Eliza Francis Jackson Eddy and her first husband, Charles D. Meriam, and the granddaughter of abolitionist Francis Jackson and his wife, Eliza Copeland Jackson (1850 U.S. Census; Ancestry.com, accessed November 18, 2003).

91. Charles G. Ames.

92. "I had . . . defiant spirit." canceled later.

93. Probably Olive Scott Howe Adams (1802–1892), wife of Paul Adams (1797–1891), president of the Boston Five Cent Savings Bank (*Boston Directory* 1865; 1860 U.S. Census; Mt. Auburn Cemetery Records, Cambridge, Massachusetts).

94. Henry Bryant (1820–1867), Boston physician (Harvard class of 1840; Harvard Medical School 1843). He was active in the Boston Natural History Society. See Thomas Francis Harrington, *The Harvard Medical School* (New York, 1905), 3:1473.

95. James's lecture at Chickering's Hall was for the benefit of the New England Freedmen's Aid Society (*Transcript,* January 18, 1865, p. 3).

96. Samuel R. Calthrop (1829–1917), a native of England educated at Cambridge University, came to the United States in 1853 and was ordained a Unitarian minister. Calthrop had a particular interest in science and was something of an inventor. See *Heralds* 3:247; *Who Was Who in America*; Elihu Rich, ed., *Appleton's Cyclopedia of Biography* (New York: Appleton, 1856).

97. James Russell Lowell (1819–1891), poet, critic, editor, and the son of Dr. Charles Lowell, Dall's old minister at the West Church.

98. Helen Fanny Huntington Quincy (1831–1903), daughter of former Massachusetts Supreme Court Judge Charles P. Huntington and Helen Sophia Hunt Huntington, and wife of author and reformer Josiah Phillips Quincy (1829–1910). See Huntington Family Association, *The Huntington Family in America* (Hartford: Huntington Family Association, 1915), 726–727.

99. There had been no journal entries since February 28.

100. Fanny Lawrence Whitney (1828–1883) was the daughter of William Lawrence and Susan Ruggles Bordman Lawrence, and the wife of prominent Boston merchant Henry Austin Whitney (1826–1889). Dall was giving her French lessons (*MHS Proceedings,* 2nd Series, 5:424–429).

101. Rebecca Parker Tolman.

102. Robert E. Lee (1807–1870), commander of Confederate forces.

103. In the ancient Roman calendar the "ides" was the fifteenth day of March, May, July, or October, or the thirteenth day of any other month. The term was also used broadly to refer to this day and the seven days preceding it. The murder of Julius Caesar on the ides of March made the date infamous.

104. William H. Seward (1801–1872), Lincoln's secretary of state.

105. This open meeting at noon was reportedly attended by an "immense" crowd (*Transcript,* April 15, 1865, p. 2).

106. Franklin W. Smith (b. 1815?) and his brother Benjamin G. Smith were arrested in 1864 and charged with fraudulent delivery to the Navy. They were tried and convicted, but on March 18, 1865, Lincoln annulled the sentences (1860 U.S. Census; Abraham Lincoln Papers, Reel 93, Library of Congress).

107. Thomas Russell (1825–1887) was first justice of the superior court of Massachusetts.

108. Probably Rebecca Clarke, and Henry James Sr.

109. Thomas Hill (1818–1891), whom Dall had heard speak at Class Day in 1841 when he was a student, was now president of Harvard; Jared Sparks (1789–1866), a former history professor and president of the college, was a pioneering documentary editor and historian.

110. Andrew Johnson (1808–1875).

111. Aaron Kimball Loring (1826–1911), the book's publisher. Dall had successfully brokered the deal between him and Louisa Alcott.

112. This article, signed "A Theist who desires to be a Christian," appeared in the *Christian Register* of September 16, 1865, p. 150. It is a response to an article by the same title in the *Christian Examiner* by Francis Ellingwood Abbot. Dall approved much of what Abbot said, but was concerned that the ablest men of the new free religious movement were losing public sympathy "by pure want of temper."

EPILOGUE

1. Paul Bartach et al., *A Bibliographical Sketch of William H. Dall,* Smithsonian Miscellaneous Collections, vol. 104, no. 15 (Washington, D.C., 1946), 2.

Index

Credits